THE

Last

New

Land

The Last New Land

STORIES OF ALASKA PAST AND PRESENT

EDITED BY WAYNE MERGLER

FOREWORD BY JOHN HAINES

ALASKA NORTHWEST BOOKS™
Anchorage • Portland

To my children, Joanna, Heather, and Seth,
and
To their children, Wade, Maile, and Noah,
Alaskans all.
Here is your legacy.

Third printing 2002

Library of Congress Cataloging in Publication Data
The last new land : stories of Alaska, past and present / edited by
Wayne Mergler.
p. cm.   Includes index.
ISBN 0-88240-481-4 (hb). — ISBN 0-88240-483-0 (sb)
1. Short stories, American—Alaska. 2. Alaska—Social life and customs—Fiction.
3. Alaska—History—Fiction.   I. Mergler, Wayne, 1944–   .
PS571.A4L37   1996
810.8'032798—dc 20   96-30733

ORIGINATING EDITOR   Marlene Blessing
EDITOR   Ellen Harkins Wheat
DESIGNER   Carol Haralson
COMPOSITION   Fay L. Bartels

All artworks reproduced in this book are by Bill C. Ray, Alaskan painter. Cover painting:
Unimak (1995), oil on canvas, 151 x 111 cm. Drawings: p. i, *The Cove* (1996); p. iii, *Verdon*
(1995); p. iv, *Amaknak* (1995); p. xiii, *By Tenakee* (1994); p. xvii, *By Haines* (1995); p. 1,
From Jane's (1995); p. 41, *Unalaska* (1994); p. 135, *Northsound* (1995); p. 325, *Eaglecrest*
(1995); p. 465, *The Horn* (1995); p. 549, *Megaptera* (1995); p. 655, *The Music* (1994);
all drawings are graphite on paper, approx. 12 x 15 cm. All artworks are reproduced
here by permission of the artist.

ALASKA NORTHWEST BOOKS®
An imprint of Graphic Arts Center Publishing Company
P.O. Box 10306, Portland, OR 97296-0306
503-226-2402; www.gacpc.com

Printed in the United States of America

Contents

VI

THE ANIMAL PEOPLE   549

VII

INTO THE NOW   655

ACKNOWLEDGMENTS

No book this ambitious can ever be compiled without the generous assistance of others. I am extremely grateful to all who gave their support to this undertaking. Special thanks to all the writers and/or publishers who generously allowed their works to be included in this anthology. A nod to Bud Helmericks and his coinage of *The Last New Land*.

To the people of Alaska Northwest Books, I owe much, notably: Sara Juday, whose friendship and support made the book happen; Marlene Blessing, who believed in the project and gave me confidence in the process; Ellen Wheat, editor extraordinaire, who kept me on track; Ann Chandonnet, for her work beyond the call of duty and for lending her knowledgeable support; Geri Faris, whose gracious assistance always lifted my spirits; Kris Fulsaas for her hard work; and Carolyn Smith, for conscientious editorial work on the manuscript.

Heartfelt appreciation to the following people: Fay Bartels, for her amazing keyboarding and formatting; Senator Johnny Ellis and staff for their support of my work; Lynn and Ron Dixon, of Cook Inlet Book Company in Anchorage; Jerry and Sandy Harper, of Cyrano's Bookstore in Anchorage; Bruce Merrell, Nancy Lesh, and Dan Fleming, three extraordinary research librarians who helped me so much; Jenny Zimmerman, my first fan, who was supportive of the book when it was an idea; Lou Mayer, Senior and Junior, for use of a printer which saved the project; and Mike Dunham, for a friendly favor.

And my special gratitude goes to my wife, Maureen O. Mergler, for years of love and support, always appreciated.

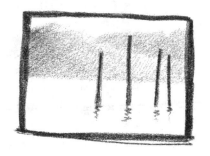

Foreword

J O H N   H A I N E S

couple of years ago, a woman acquaintance, a doctor in Fairbanks, remarked when I told her I might be moving to Anchorage: "For me, Anchorage is *not* Alaska!" I knew what she meant by this; it was an expression I had heard from others in reference to the drastic imposition of a modern urban profile—of expressways and office high-rises, of a bustling legal and commercial center—on a landscape still fundamentally new and uncultivated. Yet I replied to her: "But Anchorage *is* Alaska," a comment that caused her to reflect and say, "Well, you're right about that."

It is this divided response that characterizes the typical American attitude toward Alaska—a place physically remote to the majority of people yet immediate in its emotional appeal and dreamlike significance. No matter how familiar that repeated phrase, "the last frontier," it remains true of Alaska in many ways, and represents a theme that requires continual evaluation as this century nears its end and the global state of mind now asserts itself, whether we mean by that the corporate exploitation of remaining resources or the more considerate response we know as environmental protection—the extremes within which the fate of lands and nations seems destined to be decided in our time.

There are, it seems to me, two latent and opposing forces at work in the settlement of a new land—opposing motives and consequences that, once set in motion, must play themselves out. Accordingly, the European colonization of North America has left in its wake much irresolution, and the arguments are still with us. To the thoughtful reader a collection of writings such as this presents these conflicting views: on the one hand, discovery and exploration, adventure and romance, and on the other, displacement and theft—all at one time accepted as "manifest destiny."

We may otherwise think of this anthology as a guide: from an earlier intuitive and spiritual connection of land and people, in which an essential and precarious balance is maintained between the two, to the intrusion of an alien, competitive culture determined to seize both land and resources and wring from them the utmost in material profit. At this point in history, and despite the painted images and stirring written accounts, it is difficult to see anything admirable, for example, in the Russian encounter with the Natives of southcoastal Alaska; and when the first flush of adventure is dispensed with, not much better can be said for the later incursions of American missionaries, gold-seekers, and fur-traders. In nearly all instances the effect on Native cultures was catastrophic.

In responding to what we read in this anthology, we may be excited, even enlightened, by the adventures, the romance and the poetry, and at times the deeper reflection that emerges. But we should also be awake to the instruction that is here for us, in that repeated encounter of people with other peoples, aware now as we must be of the risks and abuses, the thoughtlessness and ruthlessness, of so many early encounters.

I write as one who, at an early age, felt that urge toward adventure in a new land, and who, rather than daydream about it, went to Alaska and lived out the potential in that dream. Having done that, it remained for me to think my experience through and write about it so that others might know something of what I had learned.

It is reasonable to ask, in view of our present diminished world, what is a young person today to dream on? What farther field of adventure, what new land or new people? What Africa, what Greenland or Alaska? On this planet we are running out of adventures in the old-fashioned sense, losing those remote, mysterious places where something essential to our depleted modern sensibilities is still intact. Alaska is one of those places, though the attraction now would seem in part to be an illusion.

There have been moments when I wished we could leave some things and places alone. Once the grand features of Alaska, the high and noble peaks and remote hinterlands, were places of contemplation and veneration, the abode of the gods and the earth spirits, and beyond trespass. Our modern response is all too often the recreational equivalent of that will to dominate, to possess and exploit, every known resource and feature of the earth. And when those open, mysterious places can no longer be found, we may face a real and profound crisis; how we deal with this may be part of the true drama of the next century.

There is, then, a difference between earlier writing to be found here, when a certain innocence prevailed, and later writing that reflects a time when that innocence is no longer possible. There is what we know as factual truth—of names, dates, and verifiable events: it is called history. And there is the truth of poetry, of myth and legend, which is in some ways more real than the truth of history, going deeper into the heart and meaning of things and events.

It is fitting, therefore, that the opening sections of this anthology begin with Native legends and stories: in their essential poetry we are as close to the origin of things as we may get. The singularity of these stories is due to their grounding in myth and legend—in the suppositional text of nature from which all mystery and poetry ultimately derive. The factual reporting of events that is characteristic of our time can rarely compete with this. Myth and legend, converted to history, may again be reconciled in poetry, a way of speech and thought, of imagination, that can grasp the facts and return them to legend.

The range of material collected here is impressive. We find many of the familiar classics of the North, and numerous additions from more recent writing. It is especially rewarding to read the contributions of contemporaries like Tom Sexton, Linda Schandelmeier, Nick Jans, and Sheila Nickerson, among others. It is good also to enjoy once again a poem by Hamlin Garland, a nearly forgotten figure from an earlier day when poetry was still read and listened to by the general public. We may wonder what additional undiscovered material is out there by writers of Alaska few have heard of. What of the unpublished journals and letters that may survive the camps, the trails, and the temporary settlements? Some day an anthology might be made of these.

And another book could be collected of work by contemporary writers who focus with clarity and passion on the social and political implications of our frontier exploitation of lands and peoples—the relentless efforts toward "development" that will not cease until the last resource is taken, the last fish caught, the last tree cut. The American rallying cry, as voiced by Carl Sandberg, "Where to? What next?" will not be sufficient now.

So let us turn to this anthology and to the several versions of Alaska that live in the contemporary imagination. Among the dominant themes are those influenced by history and mythology, by geology and anthropology, and by a popular inclination to romance and poetry. All of these in some way refer back to the manifold history of this continent, a history that is, in many human respects, still to be realized. The reader will find here something of all of these, an imperfect and continuing record, as we near the end of the century. And something more: a celebration, of a land and its impact on the people who have come to live here, or who have ventured, if only for a brief time, into its hidden places.

Introduction: Voices of the North

WAYNE MERGLER

When I first read Jack London's *White Fang,* I was in the fifth grade in Cleveland, Ohio. That story fired my imagination and those of most of the other kids in Miss Ganas's class. For weeks, the boys played "wolves," roaming in noisy packs across the playground, snarling and snapping at any enemies—usually girls—who dared approach us. The wolf play ended eventually, but the fascination with *White Fang* and Jack London and with the literature of Alaska lingered. For our next assigned book report, I recall reading *The Call of the Wild,* and I was one of several giving a report on that novel. I remember at that age, we all faithfully watched a popular TV program about Sergeant Preston of the Yukon, a Canadian Mountie, who, with his brave husky King, tracked down bad guys and had thrilling adventures, all against a backdrop of magnificent wilderness. That show contributed to my vision of Alaska as a remote frontier, much like the Old West, but with colder weather, lots of snow, and dogteams instead of horses. I was hooked on this newfound interest in all things Northern.

By the time I reached junior high school, I had discovered the novels of Rex Beach, notably *The Spoilers* and *The Silver Horde,* which only supported this image of rugged Alaska as an eternal gold-rush world of gunfighters, claim-jumpers, and dance-hall beauties with hearts of gold. For a long time, the works of Jack London and Rex Beach, along with the gold-rush poetry of Robert Service and Joaquin Miller, defined Alaska's literature for me. And for many of today's readers, they still do. It was certainly this vision of Alaska that my grandfather, a devoted reader of London, Beach, and Service, had all his life. When, in 1968, I announced that I was heading for Alaska, he shook his head and said, "You won't be able to survive in Alaska, boy. Life's rough there. You'll have to build your own log cabin and hunt for your food and chop your own firewood for cooking. I don't think you're tough enough."

I came to Alaska for many reasons, but one idea that persistently tickled at the back of my mind was that Alaska was an almost untapped source for a writer. Except for the few years in Cleveland, I had lived most of my life in the South. I was well aware of that region's literary heritage, of the novels of William Faulkner, Eudora Welty, Robert Penn Warren, and Carson McCullers, the stories of Flannery O'Connor, the dramas of Tennessee Williams. The South, it seemed to me, had been explored widely by brilliant writers. I wanted to go somewhere new, someplace unprobed by literature. I didn't know many writers of Alaska but I presumed that region had not yet produced a William Faulkner, a writer who could bring Alaska to life as Faulkner had vivified the South. In my youthful dreams, I hoped that I might be that writer.

In the almost thirty years I have lived in Alaska, I have not realized my dream of becoming the Faulkner of the North. But I quickly came to realize that Alaska has a rich and complex literary tradition. This literature has early roots in the oral storytelling of the original Alaska Natives. And the tradition grows, as more Alaska writings are published, creating an impressive body of literature, often referred to affectionately as Alaskana. Among these writings are such nonfiction classics as *Two in the Far North* by Margaret Murie, *The Stars, The Snow, The Fire* by John Haines, *The Last Light Breaking* by Nick Jans, and *Two Old Women* by Velma Wallis.

It is my goal in *The Last New Land: Stories of Alaska, Past and Present* to offer a representative selection of the distinctive literature of Alaska. I have gathered writings of fiction, nonfiction, and poetry which tell good stories and offer a broad sampling of Alaskan themes and experiences. This anthology is a collection of pieces *about* Alaska, written by both residents and nonresidents. These writers share a common bond—each has been creatively stirred by the uniqueness of this place called Alaska, "the last new land." Some are writers who have lived their entire lives in Alaska and whose ancestors were among the first Alaskans (such as Emily Ivanoff Brown, Velma Wallis, Mary TallMountain, and Sidney Huntington). Some came to Alaska to live and to work (John Haines, Tom Sexton, Frank Dufresne, Ruben Gaines). Some lived here only briefly, but left their mark (Jack London, Rex Beach, Hamlin Garland). Some simply visited Alaska and were inspired by it (Edna Ferber, Ernie Pyle). Others never came to Alaska at all, but were still captured by its myth (Rudyard Kipling). This collection also is a mixture of well-known writers (Jack London, James Michener, Margaret Murie, Barry Lopez) and some of Alaska's new voices (Carolyn Kremers, Seth Kantner, Tom Linklater).

The Last New Land is divided into seven parts that identify characteristic themes of Alaska's literature. Within each part, the pieces are arranged in a loose chronological sequence, giving the reader a sense of the history of Alaska through its literature.

Part I, In the Distant Time, presents old stories from the oral tradition of local Native cultures, as well as some work by contemporary writers who have set their works in the remote past. These pieces all tell of life in that period before contact with the white man which many Natives refer to as the Distant Time. The earliest tales in the anthology, Eskimo and Tlingit legends, explore creation and how things came to be in a world not yet inhabited by man. James Michener, in an excerpt from his novel *Alaska,* writes of the first Alaskans coming across the Bering land bridge from Siberia, pursuing the elusive woolly mammoth. Sue Harrison's *Mother Earth Father Sky* and Elyse Guttenberg's *Summer Light* are interpretations of prehistoric Alaskan life. And Nick Jans's essay "The Old Man's Winter" from *The Last Light Breaking* tells of an Inupiat Eskimo mystic who predicted the coming of the white man.

Part II, Arrivals, offers stories of how different individuals got to Alaska. The lure of the Northland has always been magnetic: some people were drawn by the promise of adventure, while others sought wealth in the form of furs, gold, or oil. Some came to escape lives of unhappiness and failure. And they are still coming. In fact, any Alaskan can tell you that one of the most often asked questions when one resident meets another is: "So, what brought you to Alaska?" In this section the stories are of people following furs (E. P. Roesch's *Ashana*), gold (Rex Beach's *The Spoilers*), and the railroad (Rex Beach, *The Iron Trail*). Children tell of being brought here by parents seeking new lives (Margaret Murie's *Two in the Far North*); young men head

North after the devastation of World War I, looking for peace and adventure (Frank Dufresne's *My Way Was North*). A young girl in the 1920s comes to teach school in the wilderness (Robert Specht's *Tisha*). A young man named Tom Linklater, like so many others, had *Only Come to Visit* and stays on. Whatever their reasons for coming, most were caught up in the magic of the North and found a home there.

Part III, Of Land, Sea, and Air, gathers stories about the land itself, about the splendid beauty of the place, about the restless seas that beat upon its rocky shores, about the skies overhead in which eagles soar alongside airplanes. In the literature of Alaska, a prevalent theme is the challenge of the environment—how people struggle and cope with the region's vastness and the power of the land. The writings in this section are of Alaskans taking on that challenge, whether on land, sea, or in the air: from Betty John's *Libby*, whose heroine confronts human emotions and wild walruses in the windswept Pribilof Islands, to Charlie Brower's *Fifty Years Below Zero*, which describes adjusting to a new life in the arctic village of Barrow, to Bill Sherwonit's pioneering mountain climbers of "The Sourdough Expedition of 1910" in *To the Top of Denali*, to Chuck Keim's challenged homesteaders in *Change*, to Spike Walker's breathtaking account of life aboard a crab boat in *Working on the Edge*. These stories, besides describing human relationships with the natural environment, also offer insights into the modes of transportation that have contributed so much to Alaska's modern development: sailing ships, steamships, fishing boats (Joe Upton's *Alaska Blues*), the railroad, the airplane (Rudy Billberg/Jim Rearden's *In the Shadow of Eagles*), and the dogteam (Klondy Nelson's *Daughter of the Gold Rush*).

Part IV, The Hunt, presents stories of hunting and fishing, archetypical activities for Alaskans. Alaska remains one of the few places left on earth where people still hunt and fish to survive, and in the literature of Alaska, a hunting story often transcends a recounting of the pursuit of game. The earliest Native tales tell of the great hunt and man's hunting prowess. Today, in Native villages, subsistence hunters still seek game for their families and their neighbors. While among non-Natives, hunting and fishing may often be sporting rather than subsistence activities, here too the mettle of man or woman is often measured by hunting and fishing skills. And these activities yield some of the most thrilling Alaskan stories ever told. In this section, the hunters are both Native (in Richard Nelson's *Shadow of the Hunter* and Sidney Huntington/Jim Rearden's *Shadows on the Koyukuk*) and non-Native

(W. Douglas Burden, *Look to the Wilderness*), subsistence hunters (*Island Between* by Margaret Murie), sport hunters (Pam Houston's "Dall" from *Cowboys Are My Weakness*) and hunters in self-defense (Wayne Short's *The Cheechakoes*.) They are also trappers and fishermen, as in works by John Haines (*The Stars, The Snow, The Fire*) and Nick Jans (*The Last Light Breaking*). Here are hunters in pursuit of the woolly mammoth, polar bear (including the legendary ten-footed one), whale, grizzly, giant Kenai moose, Dall sheep, seal, wolverine, lynx, and salmon—as well as those hunting photographs (Nick Jans's *A Place Beyond*).

Stories of enduring in a harsh land make up Part V, Survival. In the literature of Alaska, survival takes many forms. The severe winter climate of the North, the harshness of the vast wilderness, the abundance of often dangerous wild animals, the sheer challenge of being alone on the land—all of these issues of physical survival are compelling material for writers of life in Alaska. The struggle to survive, as the ultimate equalizer in the Northern wilderness, is the subject in Velma Wallis's *Two Old Women*, as well as in Jack London's classic story *To Build a Fire*, about a man who is helpless against unrelenting nature. Included in this part of the book are tales of those who survive and those who don't, of individuals who struggle with the severe elements of nature or who find themselves having to adapt to challenging circumstances (for example, Jim Greiner's dramatic story of bush pilot Don Sheldon from *Wager with the Wind*). Also included are stories about emotional survival, as described in Mary TallMountain's poignant poem *Brother Wolverine*. A harrowing, true-life mountaineering survival tale is told by Art Davidson in *Minus 148°*. And the popular humorous ballad by Robert Service, "The Cremation of Sam McGee," is one of the most bizarre pieces of literature of the North Country.

Part VI, The Animal People, encompasses a theme suggested by the Natives' traditional reverence for animals which includes the belief that animals are people in their own right, fully the equals of human beings. Native tales often make reference to the wolf people or the bear people, the salmon people, the otter people. When a Native takes an animal's life for food or clothing, the Animal People must be thanked and honored for their generosity. Alaskans have traditionally depended on using the meat of animals for food, the fur for clothing and warmth, the skins for shelter and clothing, and the bones, tusks, and teeth for weapons, tools, and ornaments. Until very recently, dogs were used for transportation by nearly everyone in the North. Alaska literature is full of stories about animals and wild-life, so abundant and so necessary in Alaska. In this section we meet some fascinating animals, including loons (Sally Carrighar's *Icebound Summer*), salmon (the Tlingit legend *The Prince and the Salmon People*), wolves (James Greiner's *The Red Snow,* and the poetry of John Haines and Tom Sexton), caribou (the Eskimo legend *The Man Who Became a Caribou* and John Haines's poem *The Field of the Caribou*), seals (Rudyard Kipling's *The White Seal*), bears (Walt Morey's *Gentle Ben* and Frank Dufresne's *No Room for Bears*), and the story of a naturalist and his dog (John Muir's *Stickeen*).

The final section, Part VII, Into the Now, focuses on a rapidly changing modern Alaska. As man seeks to develop the North Country, the new and the old encroach on each other. Alaska's cities—Anchorage, Fairbanks, Juneau—are a world apart from the archetypical Northern wilderness. And it is in urban centers that Alaska's most poignant contemporary theme, the clash of cultures—Native and non-Native—is so often played out (Frances Lackey Paul's story of *Kahtahah,* a Tlingit girl caught between two worlds). Included are stories that set the city in disjunctive contrast to the beauty of the surrounding natural world (John Straley's *The Woman Who Married a Bear* and Dana Stabenow's *A Cold-Blooded Business*), stories of cities burst-ing with vitality (Kim Rich's *Johnny's Girl*), and tales of gritty towns that operate on frontier ethics (Ronald Johnson's *Out of the North*).

As Alaska is settled and developed, continuing conflicts of progress and preservation are played out. Included is a tale of life in Prudhoe Bay during the oil boom (Ed McGrath's *Inside the Alaskan Pipeline*). Art Davidson, in an excerpt from *In the Wake of the* EXXON VALDEZ, writes of the devastation of the 1989 *Exxon Valdez* oil spill on a Native community. Richard Leo, in *Edges of the Earth,* flees urban America, seeking something primal and heal-ing in the Northern wilderness. Seth Kantner, in *Burying the Tongue Bone,* describes the daily experiences of a non-Native boy growing up in a remote Native village, and Nick Jans's "Beat the Qaaviks" from *The Last Light Breaking* explores the powerful influence of the sport of basketball on Native schoolchildren in today's Alaska.

This collection of writings is intended to reveal the spirit and the flavor of the special place that is Alaska—the last new land—and to give the reader an engaged understanding of the individuals who have shared its wonders.

I
...

In the
Distant Time

The Creation Legend

TLINGIT LEGEND

This version of a Tlingit creation story is retold by Alaskan writer John Smelcer. As an infant, Smelcer was adopted into an Ahtna Athabascan family. A poet, publisher, and lecturer, Smelcer has taught at the University of Alaska Anchorage. His books include THE RAVEN AND THE TOTEM *(1992),* CHANGING SEASONS *(1995), and* A CYCLE OF MYTHS *(1993). With D. L. Birchfield he co-edited the anthology* DURABLE BREATH: CONTEMPORARY NATIVE AMERICAN POETRY *(1994). "The Creation Legend" is reprinted from* THE RAVEN AND THE TOTEM.

very long time ago, Raven was flying over the big waters and saw a beautiful fish woman swimming below. Raven fell in love with her and flew down to ask her to marry him. The fish woman was happy to see him, but before she would marry him she made him agree to one condition.

"I will marry you, Raven," she said, "if you will make some land so that I don't have to swim all of the time and I can dry my hair on the beach."

Raven agreed to her request and flew away to make land. He wanted someone to help him so he went to find help.

He flew around until he found a seal swimming in the warm waters.

"Seal," said Raven, "I need some sand from the bottom of the sea. Will you dive down and bring up some for me?"

Raven was very clever and did not tell the seal what he wanted the sand for.

Seal replied, "I will have to ask Frog for the sand."

Raven thought for a moment and said, "If you will ask Frog to get the sand for me, I will grant you both a favor."

"Oh," said Seal, "I'd like to have a shiny, warm coat of fur to keep me warm instead of these slimy scales. Then I could swim in the colder waters and keep warm."

Raven promised Seal the fur coat if he'd get the sand for him. At once

Seal dived to the bottom of the sea where he found Frog. He told him of Raven's request and promise to grant them both a favor.

Frog told Seal, "Tell Raven that if he wants my sand he will have to make me Keeper-of-the-Earth's-Treasures, once and for all."

Seal was amazed at such a request but told it to Raven who was also amazed.

"That's asking for a lot," Raven said, "but tell Frog that if he gives me the sand I will grant his request."

With that, Seal again dived down deep to speak with Frog, all the while wishing that he had asked for more than just a fur coat.

When he told Frog that Raven agreed, Frog filled an old frogskin with sand and gave it to Seal.

As soon as Raven had the sand, he flew high into the air where the wind was blowing the strongest. Then, he opened the frogskin and cast the sand into the wind where it was scattered to all four corners of the world. Every place that a grain of sand landed, an island was formed. Some islands were bigger than others because the sand grain it was made from must have been bigger than others.

Once the land was made, the fish woman walked on the beach and dried her hair for the first time in her life. She agreed to marry Raven, and from their marriage came the great Raven clan.

For their help, Seal received a warm fur coat and Frog became the guardian of the earth's treasures.

How Raven Brought Light

ESKIMO LEGEND

*The figure of trickster Raven appears in traditional legends of the northern
Native peoples. "How Raven Brought Light" is an Eskimo version of one of
the most familiar of Raven tales, interpreted here by teacher and author
Ethel Ross Oliver from her book* FAVORITE ESKIMO TALES RETOLD *(1992).*

In one village far to the north lived an orphan boy. He lived in the
igloo of his grandmother but he used to go each day to the kazhga to
hear the hunters talk. He always sat over the entrance, which was the
least wanted place. No one paid much attention to him as he sat
there. After the light disappeared the chief called all the medicine men
together and asked them to use their magic powers to bring back the light.
The shamans came to the kazhga to work their magic. They tried everything
in their power, but nothing worked. Day after day the orphan boy watched
from his place over the entrance. Suddenly one day he scoffed at their
unsuccessful attempts. He shouted, "Ha, I could do better!"

Angry, the shamans drove the boy from the kazhga, saying, "Go! Do not
come back until you bring back the light." The orphan, frightened and tearful, ran to his grandmother's igloo.

"Why do you cry?" asked the old woman.

"The shamans drove me from the kazhga and told me I must bring back
the light before I enter it again. I do not know where the light has gone,"
the boy answered.

"Dry your eyes and put on this black parka." The grandmother held up
a fine black parka such as the boy had never seen.

The boy took the garment and examined it carefully by the flickering
light of the seal oil lamp. Turning to his grandmother the boy said, "Tell me

how to find the light. Surely you must know where it is for you had to have it to sew this parka so well."

The old woman only smiled at the boy. Then she said again, "Put it on. Take your snowshoes and this bit of muktuk to eat. Walk until you come to a place. You will know when you find it. I can tell you no more."

The orphan slipped the parka over his head and his grandmother said, "Pull the hood over your face."

The boy did and immediately he became a raven. The old woman removed the gut window pane, and as the raven flew out into the darkness she called, "You've no need for snowshoes now."

The raven traveled for a long time and the darkness remained the same. Overhead the stars circled about in the sky but no day ever came. At long last far, far away against the bulk of a mountain a tiny pinpoint of light appeared. Then it was gone. As he puzzled about its disappearance it suddenly reappeared. He flew steadily toward it, watching it come and go.

After flying a very long time, the raven finally reached the mountain. One side lay in total darkness while the other side was bathed in light. The light was so bright the raven had to shield his eyes. Squinting, he saw that the light came from a bright ball lying beside an igloo. Before the igloo was a giant who was shoveling snow. As the giant threw the snow over his shoulder he shut out the light. This, then, was what had caused the light to appear and disappear.

Raven alighted on the dark side of the mountain and by pushing up his beak became a boy again. He walked across the snow to the giant's igloo. There he stood waiting for the giant to speak to him. Finally the giant stopped throwing snow and looked up. The boy saw then that his shovel was made of the shoulder blade of a whale.

"Who are you and where did you come from?" bellowed the giant.

"I am an orphan and I have come from the north to live with you." The boy looked up directly at the huge man.

"All the time?" asked the giant. "Why?"

"It is dark up north in all the villages and I do not like to live in darkness."

"If you live here with me you must shovel snow as I do," said the giant.

"I have no shovel," replied the orphan. He glanced toward the ball of light as he spoke, wondering how he was to get it and carry it away. He thought if the giant went to get a shovel for him he could steal the light.

However, the giant just stretched out his long arm and took up a shovel that was leaning against the igloo. The boy was certain that it had not been there a moment before.

He took the shovel and looked at it. Unlike the giant's shovel, which was made of the shoulder blade of a whale, this one was made of the shoulder blade of a walrus and was much smaller. The boy started shoveling snow, all the time thinking, "What can I do to get him to go into the igloo so I can steal the light?"

At last he said to the giant, "My hands are cold. I have no mittens."

The giant took off his mitts, each of which was made of the entire skin of a polar bear. They were so large that the boy could have crawled into one and been completely hidden. "Put these on," said the giant as he handed them to the orphan. The boy reached for them and immediately they became small enough to fit him.

For a while longer they worked and no further ideas came to the boy. Then the giant put down his huge shovel and turning to the orphan said, "I am hungry. Come, let us go into the igloo and eat meat."

The big man stooped and entered the underground passage to the igloo. He pushed aside the bearskin curtain over the doorway and let it fall behind him, for he thought the boy had followed him into the igloo. The orphan boy, however, saw his chance as the giant entered the passage. He dropped his shovel, snatched up the ball of light and thrust it under his parka. Instantly the world was plunged into darkness. The stars sprang out. From the igloo came the bellow of the giant and the orphan heard him scrambling about, trying to find the entrance.

Quickly the boy pulled his parka hood over his face and at once became a raven again. Off he flew to the north with the ball of light. It was so dark that Raven could not tell where he was going, so after a time he broke off a piece of light and threw it from him. For a while it was bright as day. Raven looked back. He could see the giant on monstrous snow-shoes racing along below him, so when the light faded he flew again in darkness trying to lose the big man who was following him. Soon he began to fear that he might be off his course, so he broke another piece from the ball of light and cast it from him. Again the world about him was flooded with light. He looked down. Although the giant appeared to be slowing down, he still followed. The giant looked up and shook his fist at Raven. Raven saw him cup his hands around his mouth and shout something but the wind in Raven's feathers prevented him from hearing the angry giant. Raven flew on.

Time after time Raven was forced to break off bits of light so he could see to find his way back to the village. Each time he looked down he saw that the giant had fallen farther behind, until at last he had disappeared.

Finally, off to the north, Raven saw the igloos of his village. The ball of light was now much smaller so he decided not to break off any more of it before he reached the village. It was dark, therefore, when he arrived. He pushed up his beak and once more became the orphan boy. He entered the kazhga and handed the chief what was left of the ball of light.

"Here is your light," he said. The chief took it out and threw it up into the sky where it belonged. The boy watched as the world became light again. Then he went to his grandmother's igloo. His grandmother welcomed him home, saying, "I see you have had a good journey."

The boy took off the black parka and thereafter wore it only when he wanted to exercise its magic powers. He became the greatest shaman of all and sat with the chief in the most desirable place in the kazhga.

Legend of the Aurora Borealis

ESKIMO LEGEND

"The Legend of the Aurora Borealis" is an Eskimo story retold by Emily Ivanoff Brown (1904–1982), also known by her Eskimo name "Ticasuk." Born in the village of Shaktoolik, she became driven late in life by the need to record her knowledge of Eskimo culture. Brown attended the University of Alaska Fairbanks to become a writer; among the professors who encouraged her were Charles Keim and Jimmy Bedford. Brown is the author of TALES OF TICASUK *(1987),* THE ROOTS OF TICASUK *(1981), and* THE LONGEST STORY EVER TOLD *(1981). This tale about the aurora borealis (kiguruyat) is reprinted from* TALES OF TICASUK.

L ate one evening, a boy invited his younger brother to watch the kiguruyat play football. He led his brother farther away from their igloo and they both sat down in the shadow of a willow. "You must not whistle or talk loudly, Tusuk. If you do, they'll come down to us very quickly and they might lift us upward," he warned his brother.

"OK, now tell me the story," Tusuk answered impatiently.

This is the story he told:

One wintry night, many years ago, while two boys were playing outdoors late at night, they heard hissing sounds above their heads. Suddenly they saw a flash of many colors which blinded their eyes. Kiguruyat approached them unexpectedly. The older brother felt responsible for the safety of his brother so he gave him hurried directions, "Cover your face with your hood quickly! Now, lie flat on the snow like this."

He showed him how by pressing his hooded face against the soft snow, and the boys huddled side by side until the kiguruyat's assault had vanished. They sat up very slowly and crawled to a nearby willow which had been covered partially by a snowdrift. They noticed then that the kiguruyat had moved further away in the sky. The younger brother asked, "What kind of ball are they kicking around up there? And why doesn't it fall to the ground?"

"They are using a child's head, the head of a once disobedient boy who had wandered off, possibly to watch the kiguruyat play football. The reason the ball doesn't fall down to us is because the spirits have powerful magic streets they walk on. The last wanderer was so attracted by the beautiful colors that he forgot to go home."

"And what happened to him?" asked his brother.

"The leaders of the team may have directed one of his men to grab the onlooker. The spirit came down noiselessly, bit the boy's hood, and lifted him bodily by his teeth and brought him up to his group."

"Poor boy, did he cry?" the younger brother asked.

"No! He did not have time to cry because the leader of the team chewed his head off with his sharp fangs. And you know as well as I do, a boy's neck is as frail as this twig," he said at the same moment he broke a twig in two.

"Do you think the kiguruyat are using his head for a football?"

"Yes," answered Qweexoxok.

"We should go home now, Qweexoxok, before they snatch us away, too," suggested his younger brother with fear.

"Let's wait until the kiguruyat run farther away. Here, hold my hand tightly." His brother extended his right hand and gave his final directions, "Hang on to my hand while we run for safety."

Both watched for a chance to escape.

"Now! Run! Cover your mouth and breathe into your parka under your chin."

Just as they reached the skin-covered umiak which was turned upside down on tripods, the kiguruyat came flying overhead. Fortunately the boys hid under the overturned boat.

They squatted down, huddled together. After the hissing sounds had subsided somewhat, the boys ran as fast as they could to their igloo entrance to escape from another attack of the kiguruyat.

"Qweexoxok, if you were not with me the kiguruyat would have taken me away. I will protect my baby brother from now on. I am glad I have a big brother to take care of me."

How Mosquitoes Came to Be

TLINGIT LEGEND

"How Mosquitoes Came to Be" is a Tlingit legend, retold here by Richard Erdoes, who discovered the tale in an English-language source published in 1783. Erdoes, a resident of New Mexico, is the author of several books, including AMERICAN INDIAN MYTHS AND LEGENDS *(1984) and* TALES FROM THE AMERICAN FRONTIER *(1991). "How Mosquitoes Came to Be" is taken from* AMERICAN INDIAN MYTHS AND LEGENDS.

Long ago there was a giant who loved to kill humans, eat their flesh, and drink their blood. He was especially fond of human hearts. "Unless we can get rid of this giant," people said, "none of us will be left," and they called a council to discuss ways and means. One man said, "I think I know how to kill the monster," and he went to the place where the giant had last been seen. There he lay down and pretended to be dead.

Soon the giant came along. Seeing the man lying there, he said: "These humans are making it easy for me. Now I don't even have to catch and kill them; they die right on my trail, probably from fear of me!"

The giant touched the body. "Ah, good," he said, "this one is still warm and fresh. What a tasty meal he'll make; I can't wait to roast his heart."

The giant flung the man over his shoulder, and the man let his head hang down as if he were dead. Carrying the man home, the giant dropped him in the middle of the floor right near the fireplace. Then he saw that there was no firewood and went to get some.

As soon as the monster had left, the man got up and grabbed the giant's huge skinning knife. Just then the giant's son came in, bending low to enter. He was still small as giants go, and the man held the big knife to his throat. "Quick, tell me, where's your father's heart? Tell me or I'll slit your throat!"

The giant's son was scared. He said: "My father's heart is in his left heel."

Just then the giant's left foot appeared in the entrance, and the man swiftly plunged the knife into the heel. The monster screamed and fell down dead.

Yet the giant still spoke. "Though I'm dead, though you killed me, I'm going to keep on eating you and all the other humans in the world forever!"

"That's what you think!" said the man. "I'm about to make sure that you never eat anyone again." He cut the giant's body into pieces and burned each one in the fire. Then he took the ashes and threw them into the air for the winds to scatter.

Instantly each of the particles turned into a mosquito. The cloud of ashes became a cloud of mosquitoes, and from their midst the man heard the giant's voice laughing, saying: "Yes, I'll eat you people until the end of time."

And as the monster spoke, the man felt a sting, and a mosquito started sucking his blood, and then many mosquitoes stung him, and he began to scratch himself.

People of the North

FROM *Alaska*

J A M E S   A .   M I C H E N E R

*Pulitzer Prize–winning novelist James A. Michener is the author of many
popular works of historical fiction of place, including* SAYONARA *(1954),* HAWAII
(1959), CENTENNIAL *(1974),* POLAND *(1983),* TEXAS *(1986), and* ALASKA *(1988).
This excerpt from* ALASKA *portrays the arrival of Alaska's first people, who,
anthropologists theorize, crossed the Bering Land Bridge from Asia to
North America at least 12,000 years ago in pursuit of game, in this case
the woolly mammoth.*

By the end of their first day, it was apparent to all the travelers
except the very young that this journey was going to be extremely
difficult, for in the course of that entire day they saw not a single
living thing except low grasses which were permanently bent by
the ceaseless wind. No birds flew; no animals watched the untidy
procession; no streams flowed, with small fish huddled along their banks.
Compared to the relatively rich land they had known before the hunger
time struck, this was bleak and forbidding, and when they pitched their
sleds against the wind that night, the runners worn from having no snow to
glide upon, they could not avoid realizing what a perilous trip they were
attempting.

The second day was no worse but the impact was, because the travelers
could not know that they had at the most only five days of this before they
reached the slightly improved terrain of Alaska; they were wandering into
the unknown, and so it remained for the next two days. In all that time they
came upon nothing they could eat, and the meager stores they had been
able to bring with them were nearly depleted.

"Tomorrow," Varnak said, as they huddled in the bare lee of their sleds
on the third night, "we shall eat none of our stores. Because I feel certain
that on the next day we shall come to better land."

"If the land is to be better," one of the men asked, "why not trust that we shall find food there?" and Varnak reasoned: "If the food is there, we shall have to be strong enough to run it down, and fight it when we overtake it, and dare much. And to do all that, we must have food in our bellies."

So on the fourth day no one ate anything, and mothers held their hungry children and tried to comfort them. In the warmth of the growing spring they all survived that trying day, and on the late afternoon of the fifth day, after Varnak and another had run ahead, drawing upon their courage and the spare fat from other days, they returned with the exciting news that yes, in another's day march there was better land. And that night, before the sun went down, Varnak distributed the last of the food. Everyone ate slowly, chewing until teeth met on almost nothingness, then savoring each morsel as it vanished down the throat. During the next days they must find animals, or perish.

In midafternoon of the sixth day, a river appeared, with reassuring shrubs along its banks, and on the spur of the moment Varnak announced: "We camp here," for he knew that if they could not find something to eat in such a favorable location, they had no hope. So the sleds were brought into position and over them the hunters raised a kind of low tent, informing the women and children that this was to be their home for the present. And to firm their decision to wander no farther until they found food, they started a small fire to keep away the insistent mosquitoes.

In the early evening of this day the youngest of the grown men spotted a family of mammoths feeding along the riverbanks: a matriarch with a broken right tusk, two younger females and three much younger animals. They remained motionless, well to the east, and even when Varnak and five other Chukchis ran out to watch, the animals merely stood and stared, then turned back to their grazing.

In the growing darkness Varnak assumed control: "Tonight we must surround the beasts, one man in each direction. When dawn breaks we shall be in position to cut one of the younger animals off from the rest. That one we will run to earth." The others agreed, and Varnak, as the most experienced, said: "I will run to the east, to head off the mammoths if they try to return to some homeland pasturage," but he did not move in a direct line, for that would have carried him too close to the animals. Instead, he plunged into the river, swam across, and went well inland before heading east. As he ran he kept the six huge beasts in sight, and with an expense of effort that might have exhausted a lesser man fortified with ample food, this starving little hunter, running breathlessly in the moonlight, gained the commanding position he sought. Swimming back across the river, he took his stance beside some trees, and now if the mammoths sought to flee eastward, they would have to run over him.

As night ended, the four Chukchis were in position, each man with two weapons, a stout club and a long spear tipped at the end and along the sides with sharp bits of flint. To kill one of the mammoths, they knew that each man must sink his spear close to some vital spot and then beat the wounded animal to death as it staggered about. From long experience, they knew that the initial chase, the culminating fight and the tracking of the wounded animal to its death might take three days, but they were prepared, because they either completed their task or starved.

It was a mild March day when they closed in upon the mammoths, and Varnak warned them: "Do not try to spear the old matriarch. She'll be too wise. We'll try for one of the younger ones."

Just as the sun appeared, the mammoths sighted them, and began to move eastward, as Varnak had anticipated, but they did not get far, because when they approached him, he daringly ran at them, brandishing his club in one hand, his spear in the other, and this so confused the old matriarch that she turned back, seeking to lead her troop westward, but now two other Chukchi men dashed at her, until, in despair, she headed due north, ignoring spears and clubs and taking her companions with her.

The mammoths had broken free, but all that day as they ran in one direction or another, the determined hunters kept on their trail, and by nightfall it was apparent to both animals and men that the latter could keep in contact, no matter how cleverly the former dodged and ran.

At night Varnak directed his men to light another fire to keep away the mosquitoes, and he suspected correctly that this would command the attention of the exhausted mammoths, who would remain in the vicinity, and at sunrise on the next day they were still visible, but the camp where the Chukchi women and children waited was far in the distance.

All that second day the tiring mammoths tried to escape, but Varnak anticipated every move they attempted. No matter where they turned, he was waiting with that dreadful spear and club, and toward the end of the day he would have succeeded in isolating a young female had not the old matriarch anticipated *his* move and rushed at him with her broken tusk.

Forgetting his target, he leaped aside just as the fearful tusk ripped by him, and with the old matriarch safely out of the way, he moved in, brandished his spear, and drove the young mammoth to where the other men waited.

Deftly, in accordance with plans perfected centuries before, the hunters surrounded the isolated animal and began to torment her so adroitly that she could not protect herself. But she could trumpet, and when her screams of terror reached the old matriarch, the latter doubled back, driving directly at the menacing hunters and scattering them as if they were leaves fallen from an aspen tree.

At this moment it looked as if the wise old mammoth had defeated the men, but Varnak could not allow this to happen. Knowing that his life and that of his entire group depended on what he did next, he dove headfirst, throwing himself directly under the feet of the young mammoth. He knew that one step of one powerful foot would crush him, but he had no alternative, and with a terrible upward thrust of his spear he jabbed deep into her entrails and rolled clear of her. He did not kill her, nor did he even wound her fatally, but he did damage her so seriously that she began to stagger, and by the time he rose from the ground, the other hunters were screaming with joy and starting to chase their prey. Unable to retrieve his spear, which dangled from the belly of the mammoth, he nevertheless ran after her, brandishing his club and shouting with the others.

Night fell and once again the Chukchis built a fire, hoping that the mammoths would remain within range, and the great beasts were so fatigued that they were unable to move far. At dawn the chase resumed, and guided by a trail of blood, and encouraged by the fact that it grew wider as the long day progressed, the Chukchis kept running, and finally Varnak said: "We're getting close. Each man to his duty." And when they saw the massive beasts huddling within a stand of birch trees, he grabbed the spear of the youngest Chukchi and led his men toward the kill.

It now became his duty to neutralize the matriarch, who was stomping the earth and trumpeting her determination to fight to the end. Bracing himself, he walked precariously toward her, he alone against this great beast, and for just a moment she hesitated while the other men crashed their clubs and spears against the exposed body of the wounded mammoth.

When the old grandmother saw this, she lowered her head and drove right at Varnak. He was in mortal danger and knew it, but he also knew that once he allowed that fierce old creature to rampage among his men, she could destroy them all and rescue her young charge. This must not be allowed to happen, so Varnak, showing a courage few men could have exhibited, leaped in front of the charging mammoth and jabbed at her with his spear. Confused, she fell back, giving the other men breathing space in which to finish off their prey.

When the wounded mammoth stumbled to her knees, blood streaming from many wounds, the three Chukchis leaped upon her with their spears and clubs and beat her to death. When she expired, they acted in obedience to procedures observed through thousands of years: they slit open her innards, sought for the stomach loaded with partly digested greens, and hungrily consumed both the solids and the liquids, for their ancestors had learned that this material contained life-giving nutrients which human beings required. Then, their vigor restored after the days of starvation, they butchered the mammoth, producing cuts of meat big enough to sustain their families into the summer.

Varnak played no role in the actual killing; he had given the mammoth the first wound and had driven off the old matriarch when the latter might have disrupted the hunt. Now, exhausted, deprived of food for so many days, and depleted of what little strength he had by the arduous chase, he leaned against a low tree, panting like a spent dog, too tired to partake of the meat already steaming on the new fire. But he did go to the immense carcass, make a cup with his hands, and drink the blood he had provided his people.

Summer Light

E L Y S E   G U T T E N B E R G

Novelist Elyse Guttenberg lives in Fairbanks. She has worked with the literature review panel of the Alaska State Council on the Arts and co-edited, with Fairbanks writer Jean Anderson, INROADS, *an anthology of Alaskan fellowship writers. Her novels include* SUNDER, ECLIPSE, AND SEED *(1992) and* SUMMER LIGHT *(1995).* SUMMER LIGHT, *from which this selection is excerpted, is a fictionalized account of prehistoric Alaska based on the author's anthropological research.*

T here was a place along the beach where the wind had bent a row of seagrass into hoops and a trail of flecked white boulders pointed out a line between the tundra and the sea. It was down below the bluff where the sod roofed houses of the Bent Point village stood, but farther east than Elik usually walked for wood, and close against the water's edge.

She marked it carefully that morning when she woke to find the autumn fog had finally lifted and her mother sent her out for a load of the weathered driftwood that always blew in with a storm.

The air was sharp though the wind had settled and it was early—the sun had not yet warmed enough to melt the morning frost, but Elik tugged her boots off just the same. She started in to wade along the curving line of foam—not far, she told herself and only for a moment. But she stopped because she heard the sound of voices call her name.

Elik turned, wondering if another of the young women had also woken early and thought to gather seagrass or search for razor clams but no one was there.

To one side lay the endless sea, dark water, white tipped waves showing where the fog had rolled itself away. Away from the point, the way she'd come, lay clumps of beach grass, taller drying racks beside the dugout houses and only in the distant haze, a rise of round-topped hills to break the view.

Seabirds fighting to catch the wind. A glaze of frost on the pebbled beach; no ice—though winter would not be far. Nowhere, as far as she could see, was anyone else out walking.

Curious now, she stepped back, turned and stood so the wind no longer whistled in her ear.

There were sounds—yes. Almost like voices. She could hear them in between the hum of wind and breaking waves, the ravens who had come up now, teasing at her back. This time the sound was layered, distant and then near. Part of the sound was a mournful, high pitched cry, part a rhythmic breath. Was that her name she heard? Had someone called her name?

Elik squinted back toward the sloping roofs, searched among the wavering lines of morning fires till she picked out the large roof of the *kasgi,* the village ceremonial house. It was possible one of the men had taken up a drum and was beating out a verse. But no—a drum's sound would have been deeper and more regular and most of the men had been gone these last two days, following after caribou.

It wouldn't be Naiya—her sister seldom woke so early when their father and older brother weren't waiting for their food. And not her grandmother; Alu's profile beneath her caribou blankets had been quiet as a string of hills when Elik left to gather wood. And besides—these sounds were not from the village—they were from the sea.

Elik turned. She heard it again: a run of words she almost understood, deep now, and laughing. Maybe a woman's voice, but maybe not a person after all.

Half in excitement, half in fear Elik stood there listening. A white beluga whale could make that sound, like a whistle or a high pitched keening. Clicking with its tongue. Not breaching—that would have been different, with the slap of a tail and the wake moving out. If it was a whale and if it blew, she might yet spot a cloud of moisture or the color of its back as it sliced the waves. But larger whales seldom came so near their shore and the season was wrong. Not enough of an ice pack for walrus. A seal could easily be nearby, tucked in between the waves, watching her as it bobbed for air. But seals had different voices, not given to sounds like these.

And then she saw it. A loon, a huge and beautiful loon, not yet faded to its winter brown. White spots on black, striped necklace around its throat. Had it lost its mate? She'd seen no others along the shore.

It was floating through the waves now, directly toward her, laughing in that way loons had, like no other sound she knew, so close the thought of it made her dizzy.

The loon slowed, dipped its pointed bill, its entire head beneath the water. A moment later it was up again, the smallest silver-blue herring clutched inside its bill. The fish wiggled. The loon tilted back its head. Below its neck, hidden in the downy feathers of its chest she saw the face, the loon's inner spirit smiling as it floated in toward shore.

Only at the last moment, just as it would have reached dry ground, the loon held still. There in the shallows—something more was happening. The wings, the great long ruffling wings drew back.

Elik's heart beat wildly. There was a man inside. A man was stepping out. As simply as if he'd turned his feathers to a coat. Dark and tall, his face was smooth, nose sharp, his cheekbones high. He opened his mouth. He was going to speak. He was going to tell her something but he coughed instead and she couldn't understand. He coughed and shook his head and could not speak and his arms—his arms changed into wings again. Wings beating the air with a sound as if the wind were coughing.

And then he was gone. The sounds all faded.

Elik stood absolutely still.

What had it been? The loon's spirit soul? Its *inua*? Was it possible? A loon's spirit had noticed her, one young girl—no, not just a girl, not a child but a person who was a woman now. Daughter of Chevak and Gull. Daughter of the Real People living in the Bent Point village, the place where the land reaches into the sea?

With a feeling of awe, Elik looked farther out to where the thin line of clouds chased and caught each other in their morning game. But then another thought, a different question made her stomach go suddenly light and quickly, she lowered her gaze and stepped back from the breaking waves.

Tundra Song

TIM MCNULTY

Conservationist, poet, and nature writer Tim McNulty lives in the foothills of the Olympic Mountains in Washington state. He has written many books of poetry and natural history, including an award-winning series of books on national parks with photographer Pat O'Hara. His poems have been published widely in the United States and Canada, and his nature writings have been translated into German and Japanese. His articles on conservation issues and natural history have appeared in numerous magazines and journals. "Tundra Song" is taken from his collection IN BLUE MOUNTAIN DUSK *(1992).*

The cairn people
range wide
over this low ebbing land

from hummock top to distant
hummock,
tracing the wind's shiftless way,
they

are the sole inhabitants
among drifters & birds;
they plant their stone feet
deep in it

—coarse, dry fleck of lichen,
tundra rose
adrift in matted heather—

briefly, between the snows,
they make one feel
at home, almost,
alone

in the wide & quiet emptiness
of the days.

Mother Earth Father Sky

SUE HARRISON

Fiction writer Sue Harrison is the author of Mother Earth Father Sky
(1990) and its sequels, My Sister the Moon *(1992) and* Brother Wind
*(1994). This well-researched trilogy is set about 9,000 years ago in the
Aleutian Islands. The following excerpt, from* Mother Earth Father Sky,
*tells a part of the story of Chagak, an Aleut woman, who has been rescued
from her murderous husband, Man-who-kills, by Shuganan, a carver.*

The baby was under Chagak's suk, bound to her chest with a leather
sling. Chagak's breasts had grown heavier and fuller each day during
her pregnancy but seemed to lose some of their tenderness as the
baby sucked. He was a strong, fat baby, his head covered with dark
hair. He does not look like his father, Chagak told herself. Had she
not heard the sea otter whisper that he looked like her brother Pup or even
her own father? Maybe he carried their spirits or the spirit of one of the men
of her village.

But perhaps he carried the spirit of Man-who-kills. Who could say?

Even if he did not, it was the duty of a son to avenge his father. To kill
those who had killed the father. How would a man feel if he had to kill his
mother to honor his father?

Chagak tried to make her fingers work on the basket she was weaving, a
fine, tightly woven basket with split willow for the warp and rye grass for
the weft, but she could not keep her thoughts from her son. Shuganan sat
near an oil lamp on the other side of the ulaq, smoothing an ivory carving
with sandstone.

He had not said much to Chagak in the three days since the birth, though
once Chagak had asked him if he thought she should take the child back to
Aka, to let his spirit go to her village's mountain. He had given her no true
answer, only saying that she must decide herself. It was her child, not his.

Chagak looked at the old man. He had never truly recovered from Man-who-kills' beatings. Although Shuganan never complained of the pain, he held himself carefully, favoring his left side, and his limp was more pronounced. But it seemed that, in exchange for one thing, the spirits had given another. Shuganan's carvings were better, more intricate, so detailed that Chagak could make out the individual feathers of a soapstone suk, the thin ivory hairs on an old man's head.

"Shuganan," Chagak said, trying to speak softly, but in the quiet of the ulaq her words sounded loud, and even the baby jumped when she spoke.

Shuganan looked up at her and paused in his work, but Chagak could think of nothing to say. How could she tell the old man that she just wanted him to talk, wanted words in the ulaq to pull her from her thoughts?

Finally she said, "Do you think, if the child lives, he will have to kill us to avenge his father's death?"

Shuganan's eyes rounded, and for a long time he studied Chagak's face. "No one can know what the spirits will tell a man to do," he said, his words coming slowly, as if as he spoke he were thinking of other things. "But do not forget, a man who avenges father must also avenge grandfather. Who killed your family?"

"If he kills you for his father's spirit, who will he kill for his grandfather's spirit? Perhaps the only one he should kill would be me. But I am old. I will probably die before the child is old enough to have his own ikyak."

"You have decided to let him live then?"

"I have made no decision. I do not know what to do. I do not know enough about the ways of the spirits to choose."

Shuganan held her eyes with his. "Do you hate him?" he asked.

The question surprised Chagak. "What has he done to me that I should hate him?" she asked. "But I hated his father."

"You loved his grandmother and grandfather. His aunts and uncles."

"Yes."

Shuganan bent over his work, did not look up at Chagak. "I think he should live."

Chagak sucked in her breath. Something inside wanted to scream out that the child should die, that his spirit would surely carry the taint of his father's cruelty. But instead she put away her weaving and then took the baby from his carrying strap. She removed the tanned hide that was tucked between his legs and dusted his buttocks with fine white ash she had collected from cooking fires and kept in a small basket.

Then she wrapped him again and picked him up.

"I need to know what kind of man he will be," Chagak said. "His father's people are so evil. What chance does he have to be good?"

Shuganan studied Chagak's face. It was time he told her, but still he held the deep dread of losing her. Once she knew, perhaps she would leave.

But he had been alone many years, and he still had to make the journey to warn the Whale Hunters. Who could say whether he would survive that? But the thought that Chagak might leave was something horrible to him, and he realized how much he had missed people, how much he needed to talk and laugh.

But if he told her the truth, then perhaps she would decide to keep the baby, to let the child live, and then the plans he had been making might be possible, and Chagak would have her true revenge.

So he said: "There is much you do not know about me. Now is the time for me to tell you. Listen, and if you decide you cannot stay with me, I will help you and your son find another place to live, and I will stay here and tell Sees-far that you and Man-who-kills both died. He will believe me. He will see the death ulaq."

Chagak pulled the baby close to her and, when he began to cry, slipped him under her suk and into the carrying strap. She was squatting on her haunches, elbows on her upraised knees, her chin resting on her hands, and Shuganan smiled, a sadness pulling at him. She looked like a child prepared for the storyteller.

He cleared his throat and said, "I know Man-who-kills' language and his ways because those things were no secret to me even as a child." He paused, trying to see if Chagak understood, if there was any fear or hating in her eyes. But she was sitting very still and gave no sign of her thoughts.

"I was born in their tribe, of their village. My mother was a slave captured from the Walrus People; my father, or the one who claimed to be my father, was the chief of the village.

"He was not a terrible man, not cruel, but since my mother was a slave, we had little, and since I was tall, thinner and weaker than the other boys, I was not allowed to own an ikyak, nor was I instructed in hunting or using weapons. But I made my own weapons, first only pointed sticks with tips hardened in fire, but then, by watching the weapon-makers in the camp, I learned to make harpoon heads of bone and ivory and to knap flint and obsidian.

"Usually I worked in secret, for I did not know if my father would approve. But as the other boys became hunters, I decided I did not want to be called a boy forever, to never have the joys and responsibilities of being a man, so I began to make a harpoon. I worked carefully, calling on spirits of animals to help me. I spent all of a summer working on it, carving the barbed head. I carved seals and sea lions on the wooden shaft, then smoothed it until it was as soft as down.

"One day, when the sea was too rough for hunting and my father was sitting at the top of his ulaq, I gave him the harpoon, and though he said nothing, I saw the wonder in his eyes, and later that day and the next I saw him showing the weapon to other men.

"Three, perhaps four days later he began an ikyak frame and told my mother to sew a cover for it. That summer he taught me to hunt and he gave me a harpoon that had belonged to his father.

"For the first time I felt as though my father's people were my people, and I worked hard to please them. I learned to hunt and I continued to carve. My father filled our ulaq with pelts and fine weapons—things other hunters gave in exchange for my carvings.

"I had fourteen summers when I went on my first raid." Shuganan stopped, then said quickly, "I did not kill anyone. We raided, but usually only to get weapons, perhaps capture a woman for a bride, and most women came willingly.

"I brought back nothing, but there was an excitement, something I cannot even yet explain, a power in capturing what belongs to others.

"But sometime during that summer a shaman came to our village. He and my father became friends. The shaman claimed to be the son of a powerful spirit and he did signs with fire, making flames come from sand and from water. He knew chants that made men sick and medicine that made them well again. Soon everyone believed what he told them, and since his beliefs were similar to ours, it was not difficult to follow him.

" 'If a hunter gains the power of the animals he kills,' the shaman told us, 'then will he not gain the power of the men he kills?' "

Shuganan heard Chagak suck in her breath, but he continued, "It was something that even I believed for a time."

He stopped, but Chagak remained still. Her head was lowered so Shuganan could not see her eyes.

"Our raids became killing raids," Shuganan said, his voice soft. "But I found, though it was easy to knock a man down and take his weapon or his ikyak, it was a terrible thing to kill him. And each raid was worse for me, and not only for me but others as well.

"By then I was old enough to take a wife and have a ulaq of my own, and there were a number of us who decided to find wives and leave our village—to start a new life without the killing.

"We were told we could go, but we would not be given wives. Some then decided to stay, others left, but as I was packing my ikyak, the men of the village came to me. The shaman told me I could not go. That, though I did not have to raid, I must stay with our people, and if I did not, he would make chants that would kill my mother and all the men who had been allowed to leave.

"I stayed alone in a ulaq, someone guarding, someone bringing food. My earlobe was clipped as my mother's once was. A sign that I was slave, not hunter. Each day I was told what to carve, for the shaman saw great power in my carvings. He said that a man who owned the carving of an animal would draw a small portion of the living animal's spirit and carry the power of that spirit with him always.

"It was a horrible time for me, Chagak," Shuganan said, his voice low. "I spent two years doing nothing but carving. I had always loved the feel of ivory or wood, but I grew to hate it. I wanted to escape, but if I left, who could say what the shaman would do? But one day, when my mother brought food, I saw that my pain was also her pain, and it was her grief that gave me power to do what I did.

"The shaman often came into the ulaq and watched me, though neither he nor I spoke, but one day as he was watching I showed him a whale's tooth my brother had brought me and told the shaman I had dreamed a design for it and that it would be a gift for him.

"I carved many animals over the surface of the tooth. Around the animals I carved tiny people, images of each man we had killed during our raids. And for some reason as the shaman watched me do all this, he began to trust me. He gave me more freedom in the camp, once even let me go with others seal hunting, but what he did not know was, in the night, when I was in my sleeping place, I also carved.

"I made a place in the center of the tooth for an obsidian knife I had been given in exchange for a carving. I made a plug of ivory to cover the hole and

I never let the shaman hold the tooth. Finally, when I had finished, I told him I would make a ceremony of giving.

"He did as I asked and came to the edge of the beach in early morning, when no one was yet awake except a few of the women.

"I had told the shaman to bring his weapons and make a hunting chant. He brought many weapons: harpoons, spears, bolas, and spear throwers. When he began the chant, I placed the carved tooth in his hands and told him to close his eyes. Then I pulled out the knife and pushed it into his heart. He did not even call out, just opened his eyes and died.

"I stole his weapons and an ikyak and traveled many days until I found this beach, then made a ulaq and lived alone. I took seal and sea lion and learned to sew my own clothes." Shuganan rubbed his hands over his forehead and cleared his throat. "I traded with the Whale Hunters, and after three years of living alone I traded for a wife." He paused, then said, "We were happy."

Chagak looked up at him. "So you lived here alone, the two of you," she said. "And you hunted and carved."

"No, for a long time I did not carve," Shuganan said. He shook his head. "It seemed to be something evil. But there was a part of me that was crying, as if I mourned a death. And mornings when I woke, my hands were numb and aching.

"Then my wife had a dream. A woman she did not know spoke to her, told her that I should carve, that my carving could be something good. A joy to the eyes and help to the spirit. I think the woman was my mother, and I think her spirit came to us on its journey to the Dancing Lights.

"I mourned her death, but I began to carve again, and the emptiness I had felt for so many years was replaced with peace. Then I knew my carving was something good."

Shuganan stopped talking and moved closer to Chagak. "Now you know that I was part of Man-who-kills' tribe," he said. "Do you hate me?"

For a long time she said nothing, but she did not move her eyes from his face. Shuganan felt that even his heart was still, waiting for her reply. Finally she answered, "No. I do not hate you. You are like a grandfather to me."

"You can love a grandfather but not a son?" Shuganan asked quietly.

Chagak began to rock. She crossed her arms over the child within her suk, felt the warmth of his skin next to hers. The hopelessness she had carried since she had first known she was pregnant slipped away and in its place joy grew, hard and strong and shining. "He will live," Chagak whispered.

The Old Man's Winter

FROM *The Last Light Breaking*

NICK JANS

Nick Jans came to Alaska in 1979 in search of adventure and stayed. He has been a big-game guide, managed a trading post, and traveled over 50,000 miles of arctic wilderness. A contributing editor to Alaska *magazine, Jans lives in Ambler, Alaska, an Inupiat Eskimo village, where he teaches and writes. His book* THE LAST LIGHT BREAKING: LIVING AMONG ALASKA'S INUPIAT ESKIMOS *(1993) is a collection of personal essays, from which "The Old Man's Winter" is taken.*

Mark Cleveland sits on his porch steps in Ambler, remembering the first airplane he ever saw. "Up at Kobuk, around 1930s. It was springtime, maybe April. We hear it from long ways off, some kind of motor all right, but we don't know what it is. Then we see it, coming in low. Two wings, like this—" his hands become a biplane. "It landed on the ice in front of town. First time we see that kind. We sure look!" Mark laughs, his white hair haloed in the sun.

He stares off across the river. "Maniilaq knew it would happen like that," he nods, and looks straight into my eyes, as if challenging me to disbelieve. "White men coming from the east, riding up in the sky. That old man always knew everything."

That old man. People often refer to him without using his name, Maniilaq, which, roughly translated, means "rocky cliffs." There is a mountain called that above Kobuk village, not far from the place where he was born. That dark, ragged heap of basalt rises over dozens of lesser peaks, looking as though it fell from the moon. I'm not sure whether the mountain lent its name to the man or vice versa, but either way it's a fitting monument to a figure who loomed over the human landscape of his time. Maniilaq—a wandering holy man who saw The People's future and led them toward it, risking death and ignoring ridicule. Some say he was the voice of God.

After years of hearing snatches of tales, unsure what to believe myself, I set out in search of Maniilaq and his real story. But the further I dug, the more I found myself caught up in a world beyond facts.

This much is certain: Maniilaq was once flesh and blood. Perhaps a third of the upper Kobuk people can trace their family trees back to him; elders like Clara Lee can recite dozens of names, starting with Maniilaq's mother and working forward to the present through a maze of uncles, cousins, and siblings:

> [Maniilaq's] mother was Qupilguuraq. [Maniilaq] was the eldest. His younger sisters were Imgusriq, Qapuluk and Sinaana. As far as I know, Itluun was the name of his son. He also had a daughter. . . . As for Imgusriq, her children were Qapqauraq, Qaksri and Paniyaq. . . .

A surprising amount is known of Maniilaq's life, thanks to an oral tradition that, for centuries, took the place of a written language. Now television, radio, and books are the storytellers, and most of those who remember the old ways are gone. But some of their heritage was rescued over the last four decades, partly by the 1978 NANA Region Elders Conference dedicated to Maniilaq. The accounts recorded there form a remarkable document—a web of memories stretched across time, bearing witness to a man whose vision of the future continues to unfold as he predicted.

Charlie Aqpaliq Sheldon admonishes, "We are attempting to speak about something of importance, something that our descendants will experience. Although what we say today will seem new to us, it will become as a legend in the future. . . . Whatever we experienced yesterday has become history. . . . Our meeting now will be history tomorrow."

Susie Anigniq Stocking, frail and ancient, struggling to remember, apologizes to everyone: "You see, I do not know everything. It seems that I am merely an ordinary person."

The elegance and restraint of these voices reverberate, their poignancy magnified by the fact that most of those who spoke at the conference are now dead. It doesn't matter what you believe; these accounts, transcribed word for word in the elevated style of formal Inupiaq, come from the heart of The People. Maniilaq's story is their own, one that reminds them of who they are.

Maniilaq was born in the early 1800s near a place called Qala, not far from the present village of Kobuk. He and three younger sisters were raised by their mother, Qupilguuraq. As the eldest child in a fatherless household, responsibility came early to Maniilaq. He helped to build their winter sod house and became adept at snaring rabbits and ptarmigan, often going out alone. As he rested in the woods one day, a small bird spoke to him. "*Taatagiik, taatagiik,*" it called—"Father and son, father and son." Mesmerized, the young Maniilaq returned to the place many times, and sometimes sat all day, listening, filled with a strange, radiant calm. Soon the message became "*Taatagiik, taatagiik. Isrummiqsuqti, isrummiqsuqti*"—"Father and son, father and son, the source of intelligence, the source of thought." When he finally told his mother about the bird, she worried that he was becoming an *anjatkut,* a shaman, one who moved between the worlds of spirits and men. He reassured her, and went on listening.

As Maniilaq grew into a young man, his "source of intelligence" guided his thoughts. He found he could catch any animal he wished, and he obeyed when his inner voice chose a wife for him. For a time, he and his family lived peacefully. But, although he kept to himself, others began to notice what Beatrice Mouse calls "the brilliant light within him." Inevitably, the *anjatkut* sought him out, demanding he show them his powers.

The Inupiat of the northwest arctic had no true religion, no deities or rituals of worship. Yet they had a profound belief in the supernatural which verged on dread. The land swarmed with spirits *(tuungak)* and ghosts *(piinjilak),* all potentially hostile. Even normal actions, performed improperly, could bring illness or death to an entire camp. Any bad fortune—from poor hunting to difficulty bearing children—had its roots in *spiritus mundi.* To protect themselves, The People observed an elaborate system of taboos. An upper Kobuk man named Kahkik told anthropologist Louis Giddings, "Those people think if they cut a piece of caribou skin during fishing season and tan it, they will die. . . . When the moon gets dark those people, if they forget and leave food out in the cache, they have to throw it away."

In such a world, the *anjatkut* reigned supreme. Only they had the power to intercede with the spirits, warn of invisible dangers, and offer protection to ordinary people. With the help of *kila* (familiars) and the *tuungak* (spirits) themselves, *anjatkut* could travel by astral projection into the world beyond and set things right. The most powerful among them flew to the moon and waged fierce, sometimes fatal battles with other shamans. Some *anjatkut* were evil, and killed people; others were healers. The services of either were available for a price. Payment might be in furs, meat, the favors of a daughter, or obedience to a special taboo.

Disobeying or showing disrespect to an *anjatkut* was unthinkable; when a group of these men challenged Maniilaq, he should have been terrified. Beatrice Mouse, 87 years old herself in 1978, remembers what her mother told her as a child:

> The people of Qala and Suluppuaugaqatuuq gathered together at Paa. . . . [They] had heard, with apparent disbelief, about Maniilaq referring to his "source of intelligence." When they had gathered, Maniilaq appeared calm as he rested in a prone position and told the *anjatkut* to go ahead and summon their spirits. He did not become uncomfortable as the *anjatkut* chanted their incantations and performed their rituals. . . . They sang all night long, offering oil and food into a fire. . . . In the meantime, Maniilaq remained calm and undisturbed.
>
> When they were done, they turned to him and sarcastically asked him, "What is the matter? Are you too frightened to speak? Are you afraid now? Why don't you talk about the one you are always referring to as your source of intelligence?" There were many who taunted him and ridiculed him.
>
> Finally, he stood up and began to pace in a circle. *"Hi, hiii! Yaiy!"* he exclaimed, adding, "My dear source of intelligence, you have blessed me with another day. . . ." Mother was among those sitting on the floor who saw and heard him as he paced in a circle and spoke in front of the audience. Once again he exclaimed, *"Hi hii,* you all will come to know and understand my source of intelligence. However, it does not matter what I say now. You will not comprehend my meaning." That is what he said to them, adding, "When the necessities of life become easier to obtain and survival becomes easier, then you will understand. . . . Even the practice itself of being an *anjatkut* shall disappear."

Enraged at this impertinence, the *anjatkut* stalked off into the darkness. The watchers soon followed, certain that Maniilaq would be dead by morning. But he and his family went home to bed as if nothing had happened.

The elders tell how, later that night, the *anjatkut* returned, traveling in their astral forms, intent on "swallowing" Maniilaq's soul. They searched for it, but they found themselves blinded by an intense glow that surrounded his home. They groped about all night, murder in their hearts, searching for an opening to squeeze through. All the while, Maniilaq and his family slept peacefully behind their shield of light.

This was the first of dozens of attempts that the *anjatkut* made on Maniilaq's life. His lack of fear was insulting, his defiance unsettling. Singly and in groups they tried to "swallow" him, but the elders say that even the most powerful, Ayaunigruaq and Tuuyuq, could not penetrate his brilliant aura. In a celebrated confrontation near present-day Kotzebue, Maniilaq told these *anjatkut* he could "swallow" *them* if he wished, and still no harm came to him. As this news spread, people began to nod when Maniilaq's name was mentioned.

Now he traveled up and down the Kobuk like an Old Testament prophet, covering huge distances by foot, kayak, and dogsled, defying local shamans, making bold predictions. Often he'd pull into a camp, settle in, and deliberately break whatever deadly taboo presented itself—scraping animal hides during the summer, or mixing beluga *muqtuq* (blubber) with berries in the same meal. People watched incredulously and sometimes fled in panic, sure that he and his children, who often accompanied him, would be struck dead. When he'd appear again, the next day, healthy and unharmed, they feared him all the more. It was as if they'd seen someone fall from a great height and simply walk away.

The elders insist that Maniilaq was doing far more than quashing empty superstitions. Both Charlie Sheldon and Kahlik are careful to point out that people *did* die from taboo violations before Maniilaq interceded. Mark Cleveland makes the same point when I ask him if he thinks Maniilaq changed what happened or just what the people believed. "What happened," Mark says emphatically. "Before, someone would die. Maniilaq changed that. But even now, I never work with skins in summertime. Not many people here will. After fishing is done, it's okay again, we start sewing."

"But if Maniilaq made it all right, why follow a superstition?"

Mark pauses, then grins like an elf. "Just making sure."

Some of the harshest taboos were directed toward women, who were considered inferior from birth. When a girl reached puberty, she was forced to live alone for a year in a hut built by her parents. Forbidden to look upon men, she had to hide her face even from her mother. Beatrice Mouse remembers:

> When traveling up the river to a camp where a girl was in isolation, it was difficult to stay away, especially if she happened to be your best friend. On one such occasion, I brought some seal oil and berries to my friend, who

was in isolation, and she burst into tears. What a pity it was when these girls were sometimes kept hungry.

Women were also shunned during their periods, and widows were declared carriers of contagion. The most stringent taboo of all, though, was directed at pregnant women. Even in the depths of winter, a woman in labor was expected to stagger into the woods and give birth alone; no one could help her without fear of contamination. Friends might build a fire for her and lay down a caribou hide, but that was all. After she'd had her child, she crawled to a snow shelter that had already been prepared, where she would stay for ten days, and then move to yet another hut before she could return home. If her infant was a girl, it might be cast out and left to die.

Maniilaq attacked these dictums hardest of all. He said that women were more precious than men and deserved tender care rather than cruelty, that such barbarism would be unthinkable in the future. And though these taboos outlasted Maniilaq by a generation, they slowly faded out.

Although Maniilaq's reputation was spreading, many people still ridiculed him. Others kept their distance, and with good reason: his actions as well as his words marked him as a madman. Not only did he bathe regularly and sleep on willow branches; everywhere he went he carried a long pole which he would raise when he made camp. At regular intervals (some claim every seventh day) he would tie something—elders disagree what it was—to his pole as a signal for people to gather. On these days he would refuse to travel or hunt; instead, he'd beat his skin drum, sing, and make his predictions to anyone who would listen.

The *iivaqsaat* (literally, those who travel around bends in waterways) were coming. These pale-skinned strangers, Maniilaq said, would ride out of the east, traveling in swift boats and fire-powered chairs in the sky. They'd bring many wonders to The People: thin birch bark on which to write, a way to contain fire inside houses, and the ability to speak across great distances. A large city would grow at the mouth of the Ambler River, where the *iivaqsaat* would seek something of great value in the earth. Mark Cleveland insists that one day the village will become a city stretching all the way to the Jade Mountains, eight miles away.

And, Maniilaq said, "Light will come in the form of the word"—one of many obvious references to Christianity, which arrived with Friends Church missionaries just before the turn of the century. He spoke, too, of a "grandfather" whose glorious power would soon be seen. Hearing of Maniilaq, the missionaries were quick to adopt him (posthumously, of course) as a prophet of God—a move that no doubt hastened their acceptance, even as it confirmed Maniilaq's stature.

As I read through the accounts of the dead, as I look into Mark Cleveland's earnest face, I want to share the belief that I find there. But I can't help insisting, deep down, on a logical explanation for Maniilaq and his visions. He certainly was a man of intelligence and courage, and I don't begrudge him a certain prescience—one born of rational thought. Defying the shamans and their taboos wasn't magic, I tell myself, just a triumph of common sense. It's likely he'd heard of white men and their God through travelers from the south. The Russians were trading on the Yukon River a century before Maniilaq was born, and Otto von Kotzebue, a Russian naval officer who explored the northwest arctic coast in 1816, saw iron knives among the Inupiat, showing that contact already existed with the outside world. Yet I can't explain how a nineteenth-century Eskimo envisioned outboard motors, aircraft, and telephones decades before their invention, or how he saw Ambler a century before its founding. When I offer elders my logical version, they only shake their heads. How can a *naluaqmiu* understand?

Not all of Maniilaq's predictions have come to pass. Elders speak of an equal number awaiting fulfillment, and many of these are tinged with darkness. There will be two consecutive winters, they say, when the snow will reach the treetops and a great famine will occur. A whale will surface on the upper Kobuk, and finally a day will come that appears to be split in half. When asked what lay beyond that day, Maniilaq is reported to have said, "All the people—I don't know what they are going to do, all the people."

While the old people offer little speculation on these last prophecies, they all agree with Susie Stocking:

> Now, we can see that Maniilaq's predictions have been fulfilled. We, ourselves, have lived through the changes and have seen his words come true . . . the rest will come. It will not fail to be fulfilled. The one who told about the future of the world has already predicted it.

Nothing, it seems, can surprise these people more than what they have already witnessed. "Just like the Bible," one tells me. "That old man can't miss."
Somewhere before the turn of the century, perhaps a decade before the

missionaries, miners, and traders poured into the Kobuk valley, Maniilaq disappeared. He was last seen at the mouth of a slough called Tunnuuraq, where Ambler stands today. They say he headed north, an old man traveling alone through the mountains, across Anaktuvuk Pass to Barrow, then east-ward toward Canada, dragging his pole and beating his drum for whoever would listen. Some say he died on the trail; Maniilaq claimed his body would not be found on earth, and that his pole would mark his place of departure. Neither a pole nor a body has ever been found; it's as if he rode his sled off the edge of the earth.

Maniilaq is gone, but his children remain. I teach them in school, trade jokes with them at the post office, and ride with them through the sky. I suppose I'm one of Maniilaq's children, too—one of the *iivaqsaat* who arrived one day, holding out the future. Now together we bear its weight. Somehow it's easiest for the elders, who watched it all happen. There is a serenity about them as they sit in church, nodding together. They lived hard, good lives, rooted in the traditions of Inupiaq; this strange new world bemuses them, but they're still sure of who they are.

But what about the young men who call city league basketball a career, or the dozens of young mothers living on welfare? In a very real sense, the struggle between Maniilaq and the shamans hasn't stopped. Now the new *anjatkut* of alcohol, television, and consumer goods exact their price of obe-dience. Doing figurative battle against them is the Maniilaq Association, a branch of NANA usually known simply as Maniilaq: a bureaucracy offering free health care, food stamps, counseling programs, and myriad other ser-vices—infant nutrition, cultural awareness, summer jobs, housing, even help with vegetable gardens. Beneath layers of irony lies a question: are these *naluaqmiut*-sponsored services the embodiment of the "easy" future the original Maniilaq predicted or the source of his despair?

Fourteen years ago, on that first canoe trip, Peter and I searched for Qala. We didn't know it was Maniilaq's birthplace, or even who Maniilaq was. We just saw the spot marked on our maps, indicating an abandoned Eskimo settlement. But there was nothing there to see. All we found were clouds of mosquitoes, brush, moose tracks, and a few depressions that could have been old house pits.

I often pass by the spot where Maniilaq camped, just below the mouth of Tunnuuraq. It's the lower end of Alex Sheldon's dog yard now; the slope is littered with rusted cans, caribou bones, and plastic bags. Just uphill is a tiny shack—one of Ambler's sewage pumping stations, often in poor repair. At times the stench can be overpowering. Few people know that this was the place where perhaps the greatest of The People was last seen in the Kobuk valley. When I ask my junior high students what they know about Maniilaq, most smile and shrug.

Spring is late this year. Mark Cleveland has just died, and now, in late May, when the willows should be sprouting and the river rushing by, snow lies three feet deep behind my cabin. I stand with old Shield Downey, looking out over the frozen Kobuk, which shows no sign of wakening. "When do you think it will break up?" I ask. "I don't know," he says. "Maybe this is the big winter that old man talked about."

The Circle of Totems

PEGGY SHUMAKER

Poet Peggy Shumaker lives in a log house near Ester, Alaska, and is a professor in the MFA program in creative writing at the University of Alaska Fairbanks. She was born in California and grew up in Tucson, Arizona, where she received her education in creative writing at the University of Arizona. Her first book of poems, ESPERANZA'S HAIR, *was published in 1985. She was awarded a Poetry Fellowship from the National Endowment for the Arts in 1989. Her poem "The Circle of Totems" was first published in* BLACK WARRIOR REVIEW, *and then appeared in her poetry collection of the same name,* THE CIRCLE OF TOTEMS *(1988). Shumaker's most recent poetry collection is* WINGS MOIST FROM THE OTHER WORLD *(1994).*

At Saxman, the totems slash down
through the mist, anchor themselves
deep in the Ketchikan muskeg
with one massive stomp
of each flat foot.
The ground, the people,
shiver, and look up.
            The totems have chosen
this place, where alder and hemlock
crowd so thick a horse can't pass through
so tight the thick-skinned she-bear
swiping at salmonberries
must shove her cubs with the backside
of one blunt-clawed paw.
            The totems have chosen
this rock, where chum and sockeye
whip upstream in a creek crammed full—
more fish than water—a creek where
eagles and ravens squawk, both clans
gorging themselves against the lean times,
freshening mouths lately filled

by unread entrails
from the canneries' pilings.
                              The lowest mouth
on one tall pole clamps down on the wrist
of an anguished boy. He heads out on a morning
that's spitting at him, a fine drizzle
beading his eyelashes. Weaves down
at the lowest tide to hunt devilfish,
feeling already the slick circles against his tongue.
Chewy arms for seconds
coil in the cast iron stewpot.
He can tell from the sky
this will be a good day
for devilfish.

From the surface, bayside,
his eyes show him only himself,
wavering, squinting, hanging out
on a snag at the water's edge.
One branch cracks loose, so he
pokes around, jabbing into the mouths of stone
even this low tide covers. The branch
sings a thuck and scraping song,
hard bark against hard rock,
till the boy's arms grow heavy.
His stomach sings too now, an empty song,
and he sees in his mind the hand
of his mother, patting his shoulder,
loving him even when he brings her
nothing. He wades knee-high.

At first, it's the same story—
wood against stone under a loosening sky—
but on the third try, something
throws back his stick, a soft spitting out
of its splintering. Devilfish!
He reaches right down to grab its arm,

reaches back and down so he's bent
breathing hard, reaches far in,
fingers stretched and tickling—

    Then the whole world
                    bites down!

For a moment he thinks this red-black cloud
is ink, squirted across his face
by the struggling one.

Only later does he claim it as pain,
his arm stuck in the frozen-hinged maw
of this stone-beast his fist and feet can't hurt.
He yanks and jimmies, tries relaxing
but feels only the distant spreading of his bones
traveling through his opening flesh.

    When he remembers to breathe,
he takes the deepest breath he can remember.
As soon as it's in, it wants out,
forces itself as a rippling long scream
up the hillside, through rocks and thickets,
past the work sheds where two Tlingit carpenters
are jacking up the roof of the carver's barn.
That scream clears the fog and brings the people,
his whole village, down.
                  The strongest men
try with iron bars to break the face
of the great rock oyster.
But the water's coming home, as it does.
Up to his hips, his waist,
the boy knows this is his day,
straightens himself as much as he can.
He looks at his people,
at the eagle,
the raven,

the beaver-tail clan.
The water around his chest
lifts him a little, and he sings
his own song, a song of red and black,
of salmon shimmering in their buttons,
a song of fur buried under a stake
at the beach, so sand and water
can scrub it white, white fur
his mother will sew at the edges
of new moccasins,
the ones he will wear a long time
without any holes wearing through.

His people remember the song,
though it passed through the air
only once. They sing it
for the master carver who sharpens
his chisels and sets to work,
freeing the boy's spirit
from a five-ton trunk of cedar.
The carver's tools chant—

      Remember, remember, remember.
      Prepare. Prepare. Prepare.

II

Arrivals

The Sea Gull

ESKIMO LEGEND

A teacher and an amateur anthropologist, Ethel Ross Oliver came to Alaska in 1921. She taught school in the Aleutian Islands and married Aleut author Simeon Oliver. She is the author of JOURNAL OF AN ALEUTIAN YEAR *(1992) and* FAVORITE ESKIMO TALES RETOLD *(1992). "The Sea Gull" is excerpted from* FAVORITE ESKIMO TALES RETOLD.

Long and long ago animals and birds lived like humans. They hunted and fished and talked like ordinary people. An animal or bird could change into human form merely by pushing its nose or beak up on its forehead where it remained like a cap. Then its fur or feathers became its parka. When it wanted to change back to its original form the nose or beak was simply pulled back down into place.

Once, long ago, when animals still had this power a sea gull flew along the beach of Tigara. All about him was ice and snow. Looking down he saw a young girl walking a little distance from the village. As he flew over she looked up and saw him. She smiled happily. "First sea gull! Soon ice and snow will go. I am hungry to see sunny land."

Sea Gull remembered the beautiful land he had flown over a short time before. He decided he would take the girl back to see it. He flew on a little farther and landed behind a rock. He pushed up his beak and immediately became a fine looking young man in a feather parka. He wandered back down the beach until he met the girl.

"Come with me and I will show you a land without ice and snow," Sea Gull said to her invitingly.

"Oh, no, I cannot go. I would be afraid to go to a strange land. Besides," she added, "you have no dogs and sled or even a kayak. How does one travel to this land you speak of?"

"We do not need a sled or dogs or a skin boat. If you will come with me I will bring you safely home again," Sea Gull promised.

Curious to see the land the young man spoke of and curious to know how they would travel without dogs and sled or skin boat, the girl said, "I will go with you, but you must bring me back before nightfall."

"Get behind me and put your arms around my neck. Now close your eyes tightly. You must not open them until I tell you or something bad will happen," Sea Gull warned.

The girl did as she was told. Suddenly she felt the ground fall away beneath her feet. They rose into the air. Wind rushed by her ears. The girl was frightened; she cried out, "Turn back, turn back!" But they flew on. Her head rested on the feathered shoulder of the young man and she decided to take one little peek so she opened one eye a tiny bit. She was flying through the air on the back of a great bird! Quickly she shut her eye again.

At last they landed and the girl slid to the ground. She opened her eyes and looked about her. It was as the young man said. The ice and snow had disappeared here. In their place flowers bloomed on the tundra. Many birds hovered over it and sang. A soft wind blew and at her feet moss berries were ripe for picking. The girl was happy to see this fine land.

"Rest yourself here and eat berries," said the gull-man. "I must go over yonder and see what lies beyond." He walked away across the tundra and the girl started to pick moss berries. She did not see him pull his beak down over his forehead and turn again into a sea gull as he reached the top of a small hill. She did look up as the large white gull soared over her and wondered at its great size.

Hours passed and the young man did not return. Now she knew he had indeed been a gull. Day after day went by and still the gull-man did not come back for her. She grew sad and lonely. She was sure he would never return so she sang a song of great sorrow:

> The sea gull has left me
> Alone in a strange country.
> I shall never see my home again.
> I am all alone.
> This is her song of loneliness and sorrow.

The Tragedy of Anna Petrovna

FROM *Russian America*

HECTOR CHEVIGNY

*Hector Chevigny (1904–1965), born in Montana, had a lifelong fascination
with Alaska. He wrote three authoritative histories of the period (1799–1867)
when Alaska was Russian territory:* LOST EMPIRE, LORD OF ALASKA, *and*
RUSSIAN AMERICA. *The* promyshlenniki *about which Chevigny writes are the
rugged Russian fur trappers and traders, early independent adventurers
comparable to the Old West's mountain men. "The Tragedy of Anna Petrovna"
is excerpted from* RUSSIAN AMERICA *(1965), a history of the Russian
colonization of Alaska.*

The exploring expedition which set out from New Archangel in the
fall of 1808 for the purpose of locating a site for a fort in the
Columbia River region was under the command of a naval officer
by the name of Nikolai Bulygin. With him was his young and
attractive wife. Anna Petrovna Bulygina was to have the distinction
of being the first white woman to set foot on New Albion, the name, borrowed from the English, by which the Russians denoted the vast stretch of
coast between California and Russian America.

The leader of the promyshlenniki assigned to the expedition was Timofei
Tarakanov, one of Baranov's most experienced men. Tarakanov was probably born in eastern Siberia, a descendant of the old promyshlenniki, and
had been in the colony at least ten years. He was with the garrison of the
first fort built at Sitka in 1799 and was one of the few not killed on the spot
at the massacre in 1802. Captured, taken to a Tlingit village, he witnessed
the death by torture of two of his comrades. He was the last man to be rescued by Captains Ebbets and Barber.

Unfazed by the experience, he made himself one of the colony's foremost
dealers with the Tlingits, whose speech he learned. He had an ear for the
speech of all the natives, who generally respected him highly, the Aleuts in
particular. When the practice of poaching otter along California was insti-
tuted, he went on a number of the voyages as foreman of the Aleut crews,

having the respect and liking also of the American skippers. He was inventive and resourceful, having great skill with his hands. Though classed as a hunter, he could have qualified as a carpenter or metal-worker. He could also, as he had demonstrated, center a target with a Moscow musket at two hundred feet. He went with the Columbia River expedition in the capacity of supercargo. He would have charge of activities such as trading and other dealings with the Indians.

The expedition departed New Archangel at virtually the same time that Kuskov and his men set out for the purpose of reconnoitering the region just north of California. Neither party was to build a fort. They were both to return and report before final action would be taken. The Columbia-bound vessel, commanded by Nikolai Bulygin, was the *Saint Nicholas,* a fine little brig acquired from the Yankees. Aboard were twenty people: seventeen men, four of them Aleuts, and three women, Aleuts with the exception of Anna Petrovna, whom Bulygin "loved more than himself," in the words of Tarakanov, who was to give a first-person account of what occurred. His narrative was preserved for publication, thanks to the interest in history taken by a ranking naval officer.

Bulygin, who had been in the colony about two years, was better liked than most of the naval men. He had proved himself able and was considerate of others. The indications all are that he and Anna Petrovna had not been married long. She was popular, was probably about eighteen, and plainly had a zest for adventure. What Tarakanov may have thought of having her on such an expedition, his narrative does not say. He had no words of criticism for superiors. In the event of shipwreck a young white woman was likely to create special problems. Much of the coast they were to survey was rocky; all of it was wild, beset by fog and rain and peopled by savages known to take slaves. But Bulygin obviously had entire confidence in his skill as a navigator. Besides, the *Saint Nicholas* was taut and strong, and they had Vancouver's excellent charts. And, should some accident befall them, according to plan they would make for Gray's Harbor and await Kuskov, who was scheduled to meet them there with his party in December.

They traded as they went, at the Queen Charlotte Islands and down Vancouver Island. Every Company operation, including exploring, was expected to pay for itself. As of old, the men were on shares; what they made depended on the year's take of furs. They lay to and fired a gun when totem poles showing above the dark, wet forest indicated a village. As many as a hundred canoes at a time would put out from shore, bringing otter. Since the Americans often visited these parts, the natives had guns. Tarakanov would allow only three of them aboard at a time.

Their progress was further delayed by storms alternating with periods of no winds at all. They were becalmed for four days off the Strait of Juan de Fuca, which they did not try to enter, repelled, no doubt, by the dense fog forever shrouding the entrance. Few vessels ventured in, despite Vancouver's clear indication of the passage. On a night late in October they anchored near Destruction Island, so named as a memento of the experiences of previous mariners with the Indians of the adjacent mainland, the Olympic Peninsula of the present State of Washington.

Disaster struck with dumfounding suddenness. Everything went wrong at once. Bulygin had thrown out three anchors to hold the *Saint Nicholas* against a strong sea current, but a stiff southeaster came up, adding so much pull on the cables that they snapped, one after the other, cut by sharp submerged rocks. A foreyard broke, ending hope of maneuvering the brig against the wind. On the morning of November 1 she was on the mainland rocks. So precarious was her situation that Bulygin ordered her evacuated and camp made on the beach, despite the rain, which at that season at that place comes in off the ocean in torrents, drawn inland by the high, cold Olympic Mountains.

Guns were issued as the tents went up, Tarakanov telling everyone to keep a sharp lookout for Indians. Enslavement at their hands was to him a fate "a hundredfold worse than death itself." Indians were not long in coming out of the thick forest fringing the beach, "a multitude" of them suddenly appearing, half naked and barefoot. To Tarakanov's relief they had no guns, only spears, which showed how seldom this section of the coast was visited by traders. These were Quillayute Indians, unrelated to the Tlingits and more primitive, but speaking a language sufficiently close to those known to Tarakanov for him to understand it.

They were merely curious, not hostile. They had a village nearby, as Tarakanov learned from the chief, who was affable. On learning that whites were in the vicinity, they had come running over to have a look. Their curiosity was unbounded. They were all over the camp, examining everything, fingering whatever attracted them. They tried to make off with some objects, provoking tussles. "Bear with them," Tarakanov advised. "Get them out of here peacefully." But someone lost his temper, perhaps hitting one of the Indians. They backed off, offended, throwing spears and stones, felling Tarakanov and drawing blood from Bulygin. Guns began going off. Three of the Indians were killed before the others withdrew into the forest.

The rest of the day passed in futile attempts to salvage the *Saint Nicholas.* In the morning Bulygin announced that without further delay they would start walking to Gray's Harbor, which lay less than seventy miles to the south. They should be there in plenty of time to meet Kuskov in December. The warmest parkas and the best sealskin mukluks were issued. Every man was given two muskets to carry and a pistol. Slings were made, in which to carry kegs of powder, bags of shot, axes and other tools of the kind, provisions, trade goods, and the most valued of their personal belongings. Because the Quillayutes were likely to loot the brig, everything which might serve them as a weapon was thrown into the water. Then they set out, at their heels the dog who was the pet of the expedition. One who no doubt relished this as adventure as Filipp Kotelnikov, a youthful student who had come on the voyage.

As events were to show, the Quillayutes had been holding angry council at their village, debating how to avenge the three deaths and the wounds inflicted on them. They had not failed to notice how the whites protected that woman of theirs who had blue eyes and yellow hair. She would fetch a fine price from some wealthy tribe. When the sentinels appointed to watch the movements of the whites ran in with word they were on the march, fifty warriors ran after them to see where they were going and to harry them with spears and stones. The word went out all over the peninsula: Indians came running from miles around. In view of the direction the whites were taking, they would presently come to the Hoh River, which they would find too deep to wade. It was decided to set a trap for them there.

The heaviness of the constant rain gave Tarakanov and his companions one of their greatest problems as they slogged on, hugging the shoreline and avoiding, as much as they could, the forest with its hidden throwers of spears and stones. Loaded down as they were, it was difficult to see that the firing mechanisms of their muskets were kept dry at all times. The rain was coming down in sheets when, on November 7, they reached the Hoh River, which they soon saw would take boats to cross.

On the opposite shore stood a village made up of a number of large huts with dugout canoes moored nearby. Also there, watching intently, were some two hundred Indians. Only later was Tarakanov to realize that a quarter of them had been his party's pursuers. After a parley he conducted through cupped hands, two of the canoes were brought over, one large enough to carry nine in addition to the paddlers, and a smaller, for four passengers. Several trips would have to be made to get everyone and all the baggage across, but that was as well. They should not all be on the water at the same time.

Bulygin was giving the orders. He and Tarakanov would be among the last to cross. The ladies would go first, Anna and the two Aleut women. They, the student Filipp Kotelnikov, and the Indian paddler shoved off in the small canoe. The nine men who followed in the larger had their muskets at the ready to give protection when the women reached the opposite shore. But in midstream their paddlers unplugged holes that had been cut in the bottom and jumped overboard, leaving them to a hail of spears and arrows from the Indians ashore. Their muskets were too drenched to shoot back. They could use them only as paddles in a frantic effort to get back to safety, at the same time stopping the upwelling water with their feet. Meanwhile Anna and those with her were paddled across and whisked out of sight.

Bulygin could only rave and curse. In the sluicing rain he had allowed his musket to get too wet to spark shots, and so had all the men on his side of the river, including Tarakanov. They could give no cover to the men trying to paddle clear of the spears and arrows. When their canoe was pulled in, not one of them was unwounded. The Indians, having heard no shots, concluded that they could wipe out the whites and moved upstream to cross over for the purpose. By the time the attackers were on them, Tarakanov and the others had their arms dried and cleaned. Even so it took an hour to drive back the Indians, two of whom had guns. Manifestly this exposed position on the riverbank had to be abandoned. Carrying the seriously wounded in their arms, leaving behind much of their equipment, including the tools for repairing guns, they set out for higher ground.

When they had gone only a little way, one of the wounded begged simply to be set down in the brush. He could not endure the pain, said Khariton Sobachnikov, who was dying of the arrowhead in his belly. It had to be as he asked. All wept as they laid him down in a secluded place, bade him farewell, and prayed God to have mercy on his soul.

For nearly a week they plunged on through the forest in increasingly disorganized fashion, finding no campsite that offered an adequate food supply. They had used up their provisions; they lived on the few mushrooms they could find and on tree fungi. Finally they were constrained to kill and eat the dog. Meanwhile another of the wounded had died. Bulygin was no fit leader in a situation such as this. He was so unacquainted with woodcraft he did not know how to use an ax or shoot down a bird. And the thought of what might be happening to his wife had him in such a state that "it was impossible to look on him without compassionate tears." At length he asked Tarakanov to take command, confessing that he knew not how to get them out of their desperate situation.

Tarakanov asked to have the request in writing and, scrupulously following promyshlennik practice, had the men vote on it. He was unanimously elected leader. Taking the necessary risk of exposing the fact they were still in the vicinity, he led a raid on a small Indian village for its dried fish. The harrying they received after that decided Tarakanov to abandon the coast region. They would, he told the men, go up the Hoh River and into the mountains. There they would winter and think out what to do next. It was too late even to think of resuming the attempt to make Gray's Harbor. Kuskov could not now be met in time.

They had not gone far up the Hoh when two chiefs caught up with them. Presenting a mass of whale blubber for sale, they asked also how much would be paid for the white woman. Bulygin, when this question was translated to him, "was beside himself with joy." He contributed even his epaulets to the pile of trade goods and the personal valuables given up by all the men, the Aleuts included. But the chiefs were unsatisfied. They also wanted four guns. Tarakanov's reply to that was that they had to see Anna first. The chiefs had to concede it was only reasonable to prove they would not be selling a dead body.

Anna was brought from the opposite shore of the river in a canoe, but only about halfway. Bulygin had to talk to her across several yards of water. They "were drowned in tears and could hardly speak. She tried to comfort him, saying she had been well treated and had met with no harm." Her words were no doubt belied by her appearance. Those who had been captives of the Quillayutes for any length of time were usually gaunt, exhausted, and filthy. The chiefs now resumed negotiations, repeating their demand for four guns. When Tarakanov conceded no more than one broken musket, they ordered Anna taken away and they departed.

Bulygin, when he understood what had been said, was beside himself with anger. Ignoring the fact he had given up the leadership, he ordered the men to pay the price. Tarakanov tried to reason with him, pointing out that that meant giving up a quarter of their usable guns. Owing to their lack of tools for the making of repairs, they were now all down to one good musket apiece, and more were bound to go out of commission. Besides, any guns given away would be used against them. Bulygin only repeated his orders, adding a tearful plea. Tarakanov then sharply told the men that any who complied need no longer consider him their comrade. He prevailed. In bitter silence the march up river was resumed.

Some ten weeks later, in February of 1809, they came back down the Hoh in a crude boat with a friendly Indian as their pilot. Tarakanov, who had pulled them through the winter with no further casualties, had proposed they build the boat in the hope of making it out to sea. They should be able to reach Destruction Island, where passing ships could be signaled, or they might even attain the Columbia, which was being visited by the Americans. They would see how things 'went when they reached salt water.

Bulygin was again in command. When the proposal to build the boat was made he came out of the stupor that had possessed him and asked to be reinstated. Tarakanov had been agreeable. They would need his skill as a navigator. Bulygin seemed wholeheartedly of the opinion they should now all devote themselves to getting back to civilization, until they neared the village on the lower river where they had been tricked. He then announced he intended making an effort to find out what had become of his wife.

The men were angry. This was foolhardy. No longer did they have enough guns or ammunition to risk battle. But Tarakanov persuaded them to obey, and luck seemed with them for a change. Two Indians were easily captured and held on the boat in wait for their people to make the next move. One of the two was a woman whose husband proved to be of tribal importance. Very concerned about his wife, he begged for four days' time, during which he would try to bring back the white woman, who had, he said, been given in tribute to a chief of the Makahs, a tribe living on the Strait of Juan de Fuca.

Bulygin decided to do his waiting where his two hostages would not be easily taken from him. Leaving the boat pulled up on the riverbank, he made camp on a cliff a mile distant. There, together with the men and the captives, he waited eight days. Word then came that a delegation of Makahs had arrived and were at the river, waiting to parley. To ascertain the truth of this, Bulygin sent Tarakanov, who went well armed with several men. It was all as reported. The Makahs were there, waiting, fifteen of them, headed by an obviously wealthy old chief named Utra-Makah, who wore a European shirt, trousers, and a fur cap. All of them seemed prosperous and above most of the natives thereabouts. And with them, "to our joy," was Anna Petrovna.

She was not the woebegone girl they had last seen the previous fall. Indeed her appearance was a great surprise. She looked healthy; she was clean; she was warmly garbed in good fur clothing and moccasins. And she had a different air. She was a person of power and influence among the Makahs. Though Tarakanov did not later say so in as many words, clearly she had become a favorite wife of the chief who had acquired her. What she had to say, when the greetings and expressions of surprise were over, "struck us all like thunder. . . . We listened with horror and bitterness. . . ."

Speaking "decisively and firmly," she refused to leave her present situation only to go wandering again in search of escape with no certainty of finding it, enduring more privations and dangers. What they should do, she told Tarakanov, was join her, voluntarily give themselves over to the Makahs, a kindly people who would treat them as well as she was treated. She could give assurance on the point; she had made the arrangement. They would be at villages on Juan de Fuca Strait, where two ships had of late put in, she had heard. When another appeared they would not be hindered from asking the captain to take them home. Tarakanov told her he would have to go talk to Bulygin.

It took Bulygin some time to believe the story and when he did "he was like a madman. He seized a gun and rushed away with the intention of shooting his wife." But he could not go through with it. He halted, burst into tears, asked Tarakanov to go talk again to Anna, who was to be told how close she had come to getting shot.

Her comment was sharp. "Tell my husband I have only contempt for his threat." Death did not frighten her, she said. What did was the risk of enslavement "by an evil and barbarous people." Having offered an arrangement by which they would all be safe and perhaps soon find their way home, she had no more to say.

Again Tarakanov hiked the mile back to the cliff and reported to Bulygin, who listened closely, stood a moment in thought, then collapsed. He was put to bed, crying helplessly and saying he wanted to die. The men wanted to get back to the boat, be on their way. Only Tarakanov gave thought to Anna's proposal. It was eminently worth considering, in view of her information that ships were now visiting the strait. As for the treatment they would be accorded, Anna should know what she was talking about. All things considered, joining her seemed a safer gamble than trusting themselves to that boat they had built. That evening he told the assembled company that he for one wished to surrender himself to the Makahs.

A rancorous discussion ensued, some charging Anna with the intention of betraying them, for love of her chief, apparently. In vain they were reminded that, after all, she was a Russian. The majority, from Ivan Bolotov to Savva Zuev and Kasian Zyrianov, voted to continue on with the boat. Only four sided with Tarakanov: his close friend Kozma Ovchinnikov, two of the Aleuts, and Bulygin, who was evidently letting his thinking be done for him. It was agreed that the party should split, though not in enmity. They would all pray for the safety of one another. Next day Tarakanov took the two Indian captives back to their people and conferred with the trousered Makah chief, who assured him that everything would be as Anna had promised.

When she and those who had chosen to go with her had departed for the strait, the others relaunched the boat, their destination Destruction Island. They came to grief at once, the boat striking a rock and sinking when barely past the river's mouth. They all made it back to shore but had lost all their arms and ammunition. They were quickly captured by the Quillayutes, who sold two of them, an Aleut and a Russian, as far away as the Columbia. The Makahs bought some of the others, who thus rejoined their former companions.

The Makahs lived in wooden communal dwellings which provided no privacy and forever smelled of stale smoke and rancid fish oil, but by comparison to their neighbors to the south they lived richly, and their hospitality was at first all that Anna had said it would be. Tarakanov and Bulygin were made the property of the kindly Utra-Makah, who treated them entirely as guests, not slaves. His village, to Tarakanov's gratification, had a clear view of the strait to the fog-shrouded entrance. Vessels venturing in would immediately be seen. Anna was at another village until her owner obligingly bought Bulygin, whereupon they were together again, in a manner of speaking. The captives scattered through the various villages included one John Williams, though who he was and how he got there, Tarakanov's narrative does not say.

Spring wore into summer; no ships appeared. The Indians, whose mood could change quickly, tired of maintaining so many captives in what, to them, was luxury, and put them increasingly to work. They also began to "pass us from hand to hand," by sale or as gifts to friends and relatives. Even Anna found herself sold to someone else at another village. Again she and her husband were apart. Presently the captives were nothing but slaves, made to work interminably in all weather and given the worst of the food, usually revoltingly unfresh fish. Only Tarakanov appears to have been retained by his first owner. He managed it by making himself too useful and interesting to Utra-Makah to be got rid of. With tools he made himself, he fashioned dishes of wood and toys for the children and invented a device with which to signal in time of war.

In August Anna Petrovna died, apparently a suicide. Tarakanov, who details how others met death, in this case was laconic, stating only the fact and the month. She had reason to despair. August was the last month when a ship could reasonably be expected that year. None knew better than she how hideous was the situation into which she had led her husband and compatriots. Her last owner "was such a barbarian he would not permit her body to be buried and had it simply thrown into the forest." Bulygin gave up trying to live after that. He "went into a decline," succumbed to an infection of some sort, and died in February. Dead too was Tarakanov's close friend Ovchinnikov. They might all be dead if no ship came this year either.

The season was approaching when the ships sailing to New Archangel would be passing not many miles out from that cursed fog hugging the entrance to the strait. Tarakanov put his inventive mind on the problem of signaling those ships. A kite! A kite would rise well above that fog and be judged the work of only a European. He made one of some thin material stretched over a wood frame. His string was twisted gut. The Indians marveled, saying that he had found a way to reach the sun. There was even talk of making him a chief.

Tarakanov, a pious man, surely dropped to his knees when, in May of that year of 1810, a vessel materialized out of the fog. And she was one he knew, the Boston brig *Lydia,* commanded by Captain J. Brown. And when Tarakanov was aboard, who should clasp him in his arms but Afanasii Valgusov, whom the Quillayutes had sold to the natives on the

Columbia, where Brown had ransomed him. As for the Aleut sold down the Columbia, he had been rescued the previous year by Captain George Ayers of the *Mercury*.

After some haggling, Brown offered the Makahs for each of their captives, including John Williams, five blankets, twelve yards of cloth, a saw, a mirror, two knives, five bags of powder, and five of shot. Word of the price went out over the Olympic Peninsula so quickly that in four days the gaunt survivors were being brought in from as far away as the Quinault River. Some owners of captives tried to hold out for more than the standard price, but Brown put a stop to that by seizing one of them and putting him in the *Lydia*'s brig. Counting Williams, Brown rescued thirteen souls, including the two Aleut women, all who had survived the expedition, with the exception of the young student Kotelnikov, who was known to be alive but was at some place too distant for the Indians to trouble to find him. Seven were dead of the twenty who had sailed with the *Saint Nicholas*.

The rescued saw New Archangel again on June 9, 1810. They had been away twenty-one months, fifteen of them in captivity. To the clerk assigned to him for the purpose, for he was illiterate, Tarakanov began dictating the report telling of the fate of the first white woman to set foot on the shores of the Pacific Northwest.

Ashana

E. P. ROESCH

*E. P. Roesch is the pen name of writing team Ethel and Paul Roesch of
Washington state. They are the authors of* ASHANA *(1990), a novel of Russian
Alaska, which tells the story of a true-life Dena'ina Athabascan princess who
was the reluctant mistress of Alexander Baranov, the Russian "Lord of
Alaska." In the following excerpt, the Russians, led by Alexander Baranov,
invade Yaghenen (the Kenai Peninsula) and take the chief's daughter,
Ashana, hostage.*

Hostages! I demand hostages! Young people from your village,
Chief Ni'i. From every Yaghenen village." The words of the alien
slashed into me as I cringed beside my mother, Sem, [and] heard
her whisper, "Stand still, Ashana, stand still."

"No. No hostages from my village." Ni'i, my father, hurled
the words back at him.

Ni'i, the leader, the qeshqa, of several Kahtnuht'ana villages beside the
coves and along the rivers of Yaghenen, had been arguing with Aleksandr
Andreevich Baranov, the leader of the band of invaders. "Russians," they
called themselves, but in our tongue we said *Tahtna*.

Our men knew what the aliens wanted: They came to steal our furs, as
they had already been doing for a long time across the length of the Ułchena
Island chain in the waters of western Aláyeksa. Now they came to seize our
men for the sea hunts, just as they had enslaved the Ułchena seagoing
hunters, leaving their bereft families to starve. The Tahtna could not reach
many of our people as yet, but winter was coming and our summer camps
high in the mountains would soon be snowed in. Our people always moved
back to the villages along the shores of Yaghenen when the cranes began to
fly south.

The cords in my father's neck tightened. He jammed his raven-headed
speaking staff into the ground as if to draw strength from it. The women

around me shrank back against the wall of our house, their children huddled behind them. The leaders of the clan pressed close to Ni'i.

I pushed myself hard against my mother, and there was fear in her voice as she murmured, "Quiet, Qanilch'ey, Ashana. Do not call his attention to you." Her hand clutched mine, and her fingers dug into my skin.

Throughout my fifteen years, my mother's strength had comforted me whenever I was frightened, but during those days the evil facing us seemed stronger than she was. The alien leaders of the band of *promyshlenniki*, the fur hunters from the Siberian *taiga,* first matched wits, then broke into open argument with my father; this lasted until late on the third day, when the fog drifting into our village began to dim the waning light, making the aliens seem grotesque and menacing.

Baranov bragged again, his demands growing harsher. "Vitus Bering discovered Aláyeksa for my country more than fifty years ago. He sailed here in 1741, as my people count time. And now Tzarina Catherine the Great, Empress of all the Russias, has ordered me to take possession of your land for her glory."

"Discovered our land? How can you say *discovered*?" My father's voice was filled with scorn. He added proudly, "Yaghenen is our home here on the shores of Tikahtnu, the great ocean river. You call our land *Kenai*. That is not its right name. I remind you: Its name is Yaghenen. We Kahtnuht'ana Athabaskans have lived in Aláyeksa for many generations; we go back into the dim past of all human beings, and we know what our land is named."

"Ni'i, you don't understand. Listen. Always, after Russians discover a country, we give our protection to the new people. And I will give you good Russian names. Chief Ni'i, I will call you Raskashikov. My Tzarina has granted me authority over this land. I give you proof of her benevolence." Baranov motioned to one of his men, who rummaged in a pack and drew out a copper plate. The alien leader handed the shiny metal object to my father. "See the imperial mark of Tzarina Catherine the Great. It is the emblem of power, respected by people everywhere." He pointed to the grooves on the metal surface.

My father traced the incised lines with his finger, then silently passed the piece to our shaman.

While our leaders handled the metal plate, Baranov pressed on. "Keep my gift as a bond of friendship between us. Display it. The entire world will know that the Tzarina has claimed your people for her subjects."

Ni'i, tall, muscular, proud in the rich tradition of our forefathers, towered above the intruder; Baranov, paunchy, alien in his baggy dress, hair the color of the mottled seaweed along our shores, gripped his whip as he stared at my father: two bull caribou, each the leader of his herd, their horns locked in struggle.

Through the minds of us Kahtnuht'ana people, voices echoed from across Aláyeksa: cries born of suffering, cries that recalled how the Tahtna had first tramped from boats many times larger than ours onto the shores of the Ułchena island of Attu far to the west, and had then stayed to steal furs, to plunder land and people, sweeping eastward along the Ułchena chain, coming unbidden to Kadyak Island and then to Yaghenen. I knew those voices echoed heavily in the words our leaders and my father exchanged that evening.

Mothers belonging to the clans on the Ułchena Islands to our west qui-etened their children with threats of the Tahtna: *Hush, my child, Ivan Soloviev will get you.* They told how Ułchena hunters had been roped and bound back to front, twelve deep, on the shores of their island home; how the fur hunter Ivan Soloviev fired straight into the line of men to show off the power of his gun. A single shot tore through the bodies of eight hunters.

Be good, or the men from Siberia will steal you away.

Ułchena homes had been stripped of their men; daughters and wives had been raped and left for dead or dragged off as hostages.

Ssssh, my little one.

In 1784, only eight years before Baranov threatened Yaghenen, Grigorii Shelekhov had settled his Siberian trading company on Kadyak Island, striking terror as far as his hands reached. He levied Ułchena men for his sea hunts, but some deserted the alien camps and returned home for the hunting and fishing season, so that their families would be fed. As a warn-ing to those who did remain with Shelekhov, his hunters forced the escaped Ułchenas at gunpoint from their villages and marched them far into the tundra, where they were beaten and speared, then booted into heaps and left to die.

My father and the other qeshqa of our clans knew it was that same Grigorii Shelekhov who had sent Aleksandr Baranov to our shores to man-age his fur trade. That long-ago day Baranov must have sensed resistance building among us, for he changed the direction of his argument.

"Let us not talk of injustice." His eyes were fixed on my father, his voice remained cold. "As I told you, I bring you the protection of Russia. And Tzarina Catherine will show you how to be civilized."

A murmuring stirred my people. There was much shuffling of feet as the elders pressed around my father, urging him to send the aliens away.

More words. Like the tides of Tikahtnu that lap the shores of Yaghenen, the parley between Baranov and my father pushed out, pulled back. Each leader, crafty in language, wary in the way he expressed himself, spurned concessions and covered up any signs of weakness. The tension in Ni'i's face and neck told me of his rising stubbornness, but the flicker in his eyes disclosed a fear I had not seen before.

"I have told you, Baranov, we have never needed your protection in the past. I repeat, we do not need it now." My father handed back the metal plate, the mark of Imperial Russia.

"You dare spurn Tzarina Catherine the Great and my country?"

I have no clear memory of what happened next. Movement . . . shouts . . . the loud noise of guns. Three of our hunters lay dead, and throughout our village people stood as if rooted to the ground, their only sounds the low moans of despair. There was no time to learn what had happened; I heard steps racing away behind me and turned to see two of our boys dash up the ladder toward the openings on the roof of the house. Again the sound of gunfire stabbed in my ears, a violent crack like that made when the limb of a tree, whipped by winter winds, is torn loose from its trunk. One of the boys, Shila, halted as the blast rang out, poised a moment in midair, then half turned and fell backward with a shriek that haunts me to this day. Blood gushed from his back.

My senses warned me to flee, but I could not move; my mother held me firmly by the hand. The cries of the fallen boy dwindled to low moans, and then there was silence.

Wailing filled the air of Yaghenen. Baranov's voice cut through the cries: "Ni'i, we shot those men because they threatened us with their bows. I warn you, tell your fighters there must be no more of that." He spoke quickly in his alien tongue, and the strangers again pointed their guns at us. My mother pushed me behind her, and I sank to the ground. I thought we were all going to be killed, but the guns fired over our heads. The smoke and thunder stilled the wailing. Unable to hold herself rigid any longer, Shila's mother threw herself onto his lifeless body, her grief pouring out as her son's blood had done. But the women whose husbands lay dead stood silent, motionless.

As the Ułchena had learned before us, so we Kahtnuht'ana learned that day the truth of the Russians in Aláyeksa.

My father shook his raven-headed staff at Aleksandr Baranov. "Murderer! You lie! You do not come in peace!"

As if nothing had happened, Baranov said, "The time for talk has passed. I *will* take hostages to Pavlovsk on Kadyak, Aláyeksan hunters *will* do work for my company. And you Kahtnuht'ana *will* provide meat and fish for my camps. If the men I levy fail to do their work, hostages will be killed. You leave me no choice, Raskashikov. Your people must obey me." He snapped his whip.

Women threw themselves onto the earth. Men gripped their bows, and a rumble as of distant thunder rolled through them. I stared into the holes of the aliens' guns. Our shaman alone dared a gesture of defiance; arms arched skyward, his silent lips implored the help of spirits greater than the leaders of our clans.

Again, Baranov commanded, "Order your men to lay all their bows and spears on the ground. Over here."

Voice low, eyes down, the Ułchena interpreter passed on the demand. When my father hesitated, Baranov ordered his men to prepare to fire. As Ni'i repeated the command, some of our men began to protest, but more shots fired low overhead forced them to stack their spears, arrows, and bows under Baranov's watchful eye. A few men hung back, clustered, and tried to hide weapons behind them. More alien shots. My father's stern voice spoke again, and the last of our men stamped furiously to the pile, glaring first at Ni'i, then at Baranov. Anger seethed within every Kahtnuht'ana as he shed his arms, most of them crafted by the owner himself.

Shifting his stance, Aleksandr Baranov turned toward me; his eyes bore into mine, cold as the blue ice of Aláyeksa's glaciers. "From your house, Chief Raskashikov, I demand your daughter. Her royal rank shall serve me."

"No! I pledged Ashana to Jabila, a man from a clan north of this village." My father's words sounded strong, then his voice broke. "He has paid the bride price. She is his wife."

"Your bride prices mean nothing. Such couplings do not have the blessing of the Holy Russian Church. Only priests may unite a man and a woman in marriage."

I thought of my husband, Shani Jabila, named for the summer rainbow. Jabila! Safe on the hunt far from the evil men. Jabila with the strength of a bounding caribou, the heavy grace of a wary grizzly, the eyes of the eagle. But most of all the quick mind, the spirit, of tiqun, the wolf, an intelligence that had sustained Jabila's clan from that ancient time when the tiqun first changed from animals to people. *Jabila, hear me now! Stay far away from these men.*

Our clan elders pressed close around my father, trying to piece together a way to resist. Several hunters knelt to pick up the bodies of the murdered men and the boy and to bear them to a ceremonial place deep in the forest. My friend Shila, lightning, killed by the lightning of alien guns; his life ended in storm as it had begun in storm. Shila was well named, for Kahtnuht'ana custom directs that the baby be called by the first image the mother sees after its birth.

"Stop! None of you will leave. Pledge me the hostages." Baranov's words chilled like the winds that howl across our land in the time of cold.

Qil'i, evil, settled a blanket of silence over everyone. As I huddled on the ground, I asked the secret animal being within me, my joncha, to bear me away to join Jabila. I struggled to blot out the murders, the word "hostage." In the face of guns he could not best, my father conceded to the intruders young men of our villages as hostages, and an ongoing supply of fish and game.

We had lost control.

"Qanilch'ey Ashana." My father motioned to the shaman to help me to my feet. "Windflower." His staff tilted downward, no longer borne high with a leader's pride.

"Ashana, this day chulyin, bird of our clan, turns the evil side of his spirit upon us and takes back the Light. The man Baranov demands that you go"—Ni'i's face turned from me and his voice fell—"as hostage from my house. I would say no, and die. But if I refuse, many in this village will be killed . . . the men and the boy . . ." He choked as he pointed to the dead bodies in the dirt, the hunters still kneeling around them.

I thought of a fragrant flower picked in the morning, torn from its meadow with drops of dew still clinging to its petals, that by afternoon wilts and loses its delicate freshness.

"I cannot. I will not go. I belong to Jabila!" Agony shook me, and my cry mingled with the wails of our women.

"My daughter, I offer to go in your place, but he refuses me. He demands you for his woman." My father's spirit crumbled as if a pestilence fevered his body and sapped his will.

"No! No! No! Jabila, Jabila!" But he was hunting far from home and could not hear me.

Sitka

LOUIS L'AMOUR

Louis L'Amour (1908–1988) remains a best-selling storyteller with eighty-four books and more than four hundred short stories to his credit. Among his popular novels of the American West are HONDO, THE COMSTOCK LODE, BENDIGO SHAFTER, *and* THE CHEROKEE TRAIL. *More than thirty of his novels and stories have been adapted for films and television. A native of North Dakota, L'Amour traveled extensively across America to research his frontier stories. He produced only one work about Alaska,* SITKA *(1957), a swashbuckling adventure set in the days of old Russian Alaska. In the following excerpt, American adventurer Jean La Barge has just arrived in Sitka on the cargo ship* Susquehanna *from San Francisco.*

On the morning of the eleventh day the *Susquehanna* was skimming along through a bright blue sea with the sun just above the horizon when Jean came on deck. Barney Kohl came down the port side to meet him. "Cape Burunof is just astern, and that's Long Island over there."

Jean took the glass and studied the horizon astern, but there were no sails in sight. Evidently they were arriving well ahead of the Russian ship.

"Barney, we'll have to work fast and smart. I'll go ashore and see Governor Rudakof and try to get things moving." He studied the islands ahead. "As soon as I'm in the boat, start getting that wheat up. I'll try to have a lighter alongside before noon."

"They won't move that fast," Kohl advised. "We'll be lucky if we start discharging cargo before tomorrow afternoon." A glance at LaBarge's jaw line made him qualify the remark. "Unless you think of a way to start them moving."

"I will . . . I've got to. But in the meantime I want a man on deck with a rifle at all times. Nobody is to come aboard without written authorization from me, and I mean nobody. The crew is to stand by at all times—we may have to get out of here at a moment's notice."

"Suppose they try to keep you here?"

"They couldn't unless they arrested me on some charge, and we haven't done anything wrong yet."

"Suppose they arrest you anyway?"

"It could happen . . . then you head for Kootznahoo Inlet and I'll join you there."

"If not . . . what?"

Jean chuckled. "If I'm not there in two weeks, come back and break me out. I'll be ready to leave."

For a man who had never sailed these waters LaBarge knew a lot about them. Kootznahoo was a likely spot. A ship could lie there for weeks and never be observed. Of course, LaBarge had said he did know this coast better than anyone; it might not be just a boast.

Ordinarily American ships had no trouble in Sitka. The government's friendship varied according to its needs, for the diet in Sitka, even on Baranof Hill, was often restricted, and famine a risk. Rudakof had been friendly on the surface, and now, with grain purchased by Rotcheff, they should be welcome.

The *Susquehanna* dropped her hook in nine fathoms off Channel Rock. At this distance from the port LaBarge knew he would at least have a running start for open water.

The sunlight was bright on the snow-covered beauty of Mount Edgecumbe, and it shimmered over The Sisters, and to the east, over Mount Verstovia. Moving down the channel, LaBarge could see the roof of Baranof Castle, built in 1837, and the third structure on the site. The Baranov era had been a fantastic one, for the little man with the tied-on wig had ruled some of the world's toughest men with a rod of iron, and had just barely failed to capture the Hawaiian Islands.

Jean wore a smoke-gray suit with a black, Spanish-style hat. His boots were hand-cobbled from the best leather, and he looked far more the California rancher and businessman than a ship's master and fur trader. And he chose to look so.

With him in the boat were Ben Turk and Shin Boyar, aside from the boat crew. "You're to get around," he said to the Pole, "listen, and if it seems advisable, ask questions. I want to know the gossip around town, patrol ship activity, what ships have called here, conditions in town. Then return to the boat."

Boyar nodded solemnly. "It is a beautiful place. I who have suffered here, I say it." He gestured toward Mount Edgecumbe. "It is as lovely as Fujiyama."

A dozen loafers watched the boat come to the landing, their manner neither friendly nor hostile. Boyar disappeared into the crowd, and with Turk at his side, LaBarge started for the Castle. Leaving the old hulk that served for a landing, they walked down the dim passage through the center of the log warehouse and emerged on the street leading to the Hill. Along the way were booths where Tlingit Indians gathered to sell their wares, baskets of spruce roots, hand-carved whistles of rock crystal, beaded moccasins and a few articles of clothing. Jean stopped at one stand to buy a walrus-tusk knife for a letter opener. He would send it to Rob Walker when he had a chance: a souvenir of Sitka.

As they walked, people turned to stare. Jean's hat was unusual, and his dress elaborate for the place and time, although many illustrious visitors had come to the Castle.

On the terrace before the Castle, Jean paused to look back. The town itself was little and shabby, but the setting was superb! Tree-clad islands dotted the channels that approached the town, their fine shores rising picturesquely from the sea. All this . . . and behind them Alaska, the Great Land.

A stalwart Russian with close-cropped blond hair admitted them and they waited in an inner room while the servant took their names to the governor. The waiting room was, for this place at the world's end, fantastic. Here were statues and paintings worthy of the finest museum.

The Russian appeared in the door, holding it open. "If you please," he said in a husky voice, "this way."

Rudakof was a stocky, corpulent man with a round face and sideburns. He got up, thrusting out a hand, but his smile was somewhat nervous. "Captain LaBarge? I am mos' happy to see you." He paused, obviously anything but happy. "What can I do for you?"

Jean placed his papers on his desk. "I am delivering, as of this moment, a cargo of wheat, ordered for delivery here by His Excellency, Count Alexander Rotcheff, emissary of His Imperial Majesty, the Czar."

Rudakof's eyes bulged a little. The roll of titles had their effect but he was afraid of Baron Zinnovy, who had told him definitely that intercourse of any sort with foreign ships or merchants was to cease. Yet the wheat had been ordered by Count Rotcheff, and Rudakof was also afraid of him. Still, of the two he was most afraid of Zinnovy.

Jean guessed the sort of man he confronted. "There was a crop failure in Canada where wheat was previously purchased, and so the Count acted without delay."

A crop failure in Canada? Rudakof had heard nothing of this, but then what did he ever hear? Nobody told him anything. If there was a crop failure it could mean a serious food shortage in Sitka . . . perhaps famine.

He mopped his brow. "Well, uh, there has been no message, Captain, no authorization. You will have to wait until—"

"I can't wait. The money is on deposit in a San Francisco bank, but if you aren't prepared to receive this cargo I'll have to dispose of it elsewhere. I imagine there are businessmen in the town who would jump at a chance to buy."

Rudakof's face grew crimson. "Oh, come now!" he protested. "It is not so serious, no?" He struggled to find any excuse to delay the decision. "You will have dinner with me? There is much to do. I must think . . . plan."

"I'd be honored to stay for dinner. But in the meantime you will order the lighters for us?"

"Wait, wait!" Rudakof brushed a hand as if to drive away an annoying fly. "You Americans are so impetuous. The lighters are busy, and must be requisitioned. They must—"

"Of course." LaBarge was firm. "But you are the director; the authority is yours. You can order them out."

Rudakof became stubborn. "Dinner first, then we will talk."

Realizing further argument at this point would be useless, Jean shrugged. "As you like . . . but we plan to be out of the harbor by tomorrow."

"Tomorrow?" Rudakof was immediately suspicious. "You are in a hurry." He rustled some papers on his desk. "You talked to Count Rotcheff in San Francisco. Did you also see Baron Zinnovy?"

LaBarge frowned as if making an effort to recall. "Do you mean that peculiar young officer? The one in the pretty little white suit?"

Rudakof blanched with horror at the description. "The man you speak of"—he struggled with emotion—"is Baron Paul Zinnovy, of the Imperial Navy!"

"I believe he did say something of the sort. But wasn't he the one who was in some kind of trouble in St. Petersburg? Such a young man, too!"

Rudakof refused to meet his eyes. He was more worried than ever. This infernal American knew too much. He, Rudakof, had heard whispers about Zinnovy, but he did not like to think of them. Even a disgraced nobleman could have friends in high places, and if there was any shake-up here, trust the Baron to emerge on top, with those who served him.

Yet Rudakof did not wish to be held accountable for refusing a cargo of wheat that might save Sitka from famine. The colony was too dependent, and some of the citizens, like that merchant Busch, had friends who were influential also.

Promising to return for dinner, LaBarge left the Castle. "Stalled," he told Turk, who had waited for him, "but I think we can get it done by tomorrow night."

"You might even have a week," Turk suggested, without much hope. "A lot could happen in Frisco."

LaBarge wasn't so sure. Without doubt Zinnovy would have left for Sitka soon after the *Susquehanna* cleared, and some time had been lost on the Columbia River, picking up the wheat.

Count Rotcheff might delay because he did not relish putting himself in the hands of his enemies, yet he was not a man to shirk his duty, and sooner or later they must come to Sitka.

Sending Turk to the dock with a message for Kohl, he strolled through the few streets of the town. The dark-skinned Tlingit women, picturesque in their native costumes, gathered along the street, each with some trifle to sell, and each walking with a pride of bearing that belied the menial position into which they were placed by the Russians. The Tlingits had been a warlike people, an intelligent people, physically of great strength, who were in no way awe-struck or frightened by Russian weapons. They had wiped out the first colony at Sitka in 1802, and given the right opportunity, believed they could do it again.

Pausing before the clubhouse built by Etolin as a home for employees of the company, Jean watched two husky *promyshleniki* stagger by, drunk and hunting trouble. Shin Boyar was across the street, but he waited until the *promyshleniki* were gone before he crossed.

He stopped near LaBarge and without looking at him, said quietly, "You kicked up a fuss, Cap'n. Feller from the Castle hustled to the waterfront, jumped into a boat and took off for that new patrol ship, the *Lena*."

Rudakof was acting with more intelligence that he had given him credit for possessing. He must have come upon a plan that would place him in a better bargaining position before they met at dinner."

"Found a man I know," Boyar continued, "told me Zinnovy threw a scare into Rudakof. Officially, the director outranks him, but Zinnovy has frightened Rudakof with his influence in St. Petersburg."

"Go back to the boat and tell the boys I want a close watch. At the first sign of that Russian square-rigger I want to be notified, no matter where I am or what I'm doing."

They could leave now, but payment depended on delivery of the wheat, and moreover, he needed the cargo space. The schooner was small and lightly built, and without that space he could do nothing.

He walked to the knoll and seated himself at a table in one of the tea-rooms. A girl came to his table, smiling in a friendly way, and he ordered honey cakes and tea. Sitting over the tea he tried to surmise what Rudakof was planning. Obviously, he wanted neither to lose the wheat nor see the schooner leave before Zinnovy returned.

The waitress was a pretty blonde with braids wrapped around her head and dark blue eyes that laughed when her lips smiled. Her mouth was wide and friendly, and as she refilled his cup, her eyes caught his. "You are Boston man?"

"Yes."

"You have beautiful ship." She spoke carefully and chose her words hesitantly. "When I was small girl a Boston man gave me a doll from China. He said he had a little girl like me."

"I'll bet," Jean smiled at her, "he'd like a big girl like you."

"Maybe. I think so." Her eyes danced. "Most Boston men like to have girl." She wrinkled her nose at him. "Even Eskimo girl."

An idea came to him suddenly. How much pressure could Rudakof stand? Suppose a little pressure could be generated?

He spoke casually. "Count Rotcheff ordered a cargo of wheat for delivery here on my ship, and now Rudakof won't accept it."

"He is a fool!" She spoke sharply. Then what he had said registered. "You have *wheat*? Oh, but we need it! You must not take it away!"

"I'd like to unload tonight or tomorrow," he said, "but I doubt if I can get a permit."

"You wait!" She turned quickly and went into the kitchen, and listening, he heard excited talk. A few minutes later a stocky, hard-faced Russian emerged from the kitchen and stalked angrily out the door.

LaBarge sat back in the chair. The tea was good and the honey cakes like nothing aboard ship. He had a feeling something had been started that not even Rudakof could stop. Sitka was a small town. In the several hours before he was to meet Rudakof at dinner everyone in town would know he had a cargo of wheat, and if a wheat shortage existed, the director should begin to feel the protests.

When he had finished his tea he placed a gold coin on the table. When she handed him his change, he brushed it aside. "You did not tell me your name?"

"Dounia." She blushed. "And you?"

"Jean LaBarge."

"It is too much. I cannot take the money."

He accepted the change, then returned half of it. With a quick glance to see if anyone saw, she pocketed it. "You might," he suggested, "whisper something to the man who just left."

"My father."

"You might whisper that if Rudakof does not unload the cargo promptly, I shall be forced to leave. Unless . . . and this you must whisper very softly, unless someone came at night to unload it, someone who could sign for it, someone reliable, whose name Count Rotcheff would accept."

The Killing

FROM *The Spoilers*

REX BEACH

Rex Beach (1877–1949) was a popular turn-of-the-century novelist. He grew up in Chicago, and persuaded his brother to grubstake his 1898 trip to the Klondike during the gold rush. From his experiences in the Far North, he produced several best-selling romances, most notably THE SPOILERS *(1900),* THE SILVER HORDE *(1909), and* THE IRON TRAIL *(1912). In "The Killing," excerpted from* THE SPOILERS, *a naive young woman has stowed away on a steamer bearing stampeders to Nome.*

For four days the *Santa Maria* felt blindly through the white fields, drifting north with the spring tide that sets through Behring Strait, till, on the morning of the fifth, open water showed to the east. Creeping through, she broke out into the last stage of the long race, amid the cheers of her weary passengers; and the dull jar of her engines made welcome music to the girl in the deck state-room.

Soon they picked up a mountainous coast which rose steadily into majestic, barren ranges, still white with the melting snows; and at ten in the evening under a golden sunset, amid screaming whistles, they anchored in the roadstead of Nome. Before the rumble of her chains had ceased or the echo from the fleet's salute had died from the shoreward hills, the ship was surrounded by a swarm of tiny craft clamoring about her iron sides, while an officer in cap and gilt climbed the bridge and greeted Captain Stephens. Tugs with trailing lighters circled discreetly about, awaiting the completion of certain formalities. These over, the uniformed gentleman dropped back into his skiff and rowed away.

"A clean bill of health, captain," he shouted, saluting the commander.

"Thank ye, sir," roared the sailor, and with that the row-boats swarmed inward pirate-like, boarding the steamer from all quarters.

As the master turned, he looked down from his bridge to the deck below, full into the face of Dextry, who had been an intent witness of the meeting.

With unbending dignity, Captain Stephens let his left eyelid droop slowly, while a boyish grin spread widely over his face. Simultaneously, orders rang sharp and fast from the bridge, the crew broke into feverish life, the creak of booms and the clank of donkey-hoists arose.

"We're here, Miss Stowaway," said Glenister, entering the girl's cabin. "The inspector passed us and it's time for you to see the magic city. Come, it's a wonderful sight."

This was the first time they had been alone since the scene on the after-deck, for, besides ignoring Glenister, she had managed that he should not even see her except in Dextry's presence. Although he had ever since been courteous and considerate, she felt the leaping emotions that were hidden within him and longed to leave the ship, to fly from the spell of his person-ality. Thoughts of him made her writhe, and yet when he was near she could not hate him as she willed—he overpowered her, he would not be hated, he paid no heed to her slights. This very quality reminded her how willingly and unquestioningly he had fought off the sailors from the *Ohio* at a word from her. She knew he would do so again, and more, and it is hard to be bitter to one who would lay down his life for you, even though he has offended—particularly when he has the magnetism that sweeps you away from your moorings.

"There's no danger of being seen," he continued. "The crowd's crazy, and, besides, we'll go ashore right away. You must be mad with the con-finement—it's on my nerves, too."

As they stepped outside, the door of an adjacent cabin opened, framing an angular, sharp-featured woman, who, catching sight of the girl emerging from Glenister's state-room, paused with shrewdly narrowed eyes, flashing quick, malicious glances from one to the other. They came later to remem-ber with regret this chance encounter, for it was fraught with grave results for them both.

"Good-evening, Mr. Glenister," the lady said with acid cordiality.

"Howdy, Mrs. Champian." He moved away.

She followed a step, staring at Helen.

"Are you going ashore to-night or wait for morning?"

"Don't know yet, I'm sure." Then aside to the girl he muttered, "Shake her, she's spying on us."

"Who is she?" asked Miss Chester, a moment later.

"Her husband manages one of the big companies. She's an old cat."

Gaining her first view of the land, the girl cried out, sharply. They rode on an oily sea, tinted like burnished copper, while on all sides, amid the faint rattle and rumble of machinery, scores of ships were belching cargoes out upon living swarms of scows, tugs, stern-wheelers, and dories. Here and there Eskimo oomiaks, fat, walrus-hide boats, slid about like huge, many-legged water-bugs. An endless, ant-like stream of tenders, piled high with freight, plied to and from the shore. A mile distant lay the city, stretched like a white ribbon between the gold of the ocean sand and the dun of the moss-covered tundra. It was like no other in the world. At first glance it seemed all made of new white canvas. In a week its population had swelled from three to thirty thousand. It now wandered in a slender, sinuous line along the coast for miles, because only the beach afforded dry camping ground. Mounting to the bank behind, one sank knee-deep in moss and water, and, treading twice in the same tracks, found a bog of oozing, icy mud. There-fore, as the town doubled daily in size, it grew endwise like a string of domi-noes, till the shore from Cape Nome to Penny River was a long reach of white, glinting in the low rays of the arctic sunset like foamy breakers on a tropic island.

"That's Anvil Creek up yonder," said Glenister. "There's where the Midas lies. See!" He indicated a gap in the buttress of mountains rolling back from the coast. "It's the greatest creek in the world. You'll see gold by the mule-load, and hillocks of nuggets. Oh, I'm glad to get back. *This* is life. That stretch of beach is full of gold. These hills are seamed with quartz. The bed-rock of that creek is yellow. There's gold, gold, gold, everywhere—more than ever was in old Solomon's mines—and there's mystery and peril and things unknown."

"Let us make haste," said the girl. "I have something I must do to-night. After that, I can learn to know these things."

Securing a small boat, they were rowed ashore, the partners plying their ferryman with eager questions. Having arrived five days before, he was exploding with information and volunteered the fruits of his ripe experience till Dextry stated that they were "sourdoughs" themselves, and owned the Midas, whereupon Miss Chester marvelled at the awe which sat upon the man and the wondering stare with which he devoured the partners, to her own utter exclusion.

"Sufferin' cats! Look at the freight!" ejaculated Dextry. "If a storm come up it would bust the community!"

The beach they neared was walled and crowded to the high-tide mark with ramparts of merchandise, while every incoming craft deposited its quota upon whatever vacant foot was close at hand, till bales, boxes, boilers, and baggage of all kinds were confusedly intermixed in the narrow space. Singing longshoremen trundled burdens from the lighters and piled them on the heap, while yelling, cursing crowds fought over it all, selecting, sorting, loading.

There was no room for more, yet hourly they added to the mass. Teams splashed through the lapping surf or stuck in the deep sand between hillocks of goods. All was noise, profanity, congestion, and feverish hurry. This burning haste rang in the voice of the multitude, showed in its violence of gesture and redness of face, permeated the atmosphere with a magnetic, electrifying energy.

"It's somethin' fierce ashore," said the oarsman. "I been up fer three days an' nights steady—there ain't no room, nor time, nor darkness to sleep in. Ham an' eggs is a dollar an' a half, an' whiskey's four bits a throw." He wailed the last, sadly, as a complaint unspeakable.

"Any trouble doin'?" inquired the old man.

"You *know* it!" the other cried, colloquially. "There was a massacree in the Northern last night."

"Gamblin' row?"

"Yep. Tin-horn called 'Missou' done it."

"Sho!" said Dextry. "I know him. He's a bad actor." All three men nodded sagely, and the girl wished for further light, but they volunteered no explanation.

Leaving the skiff, they plunged into turmoil. Dodging through the tangle, they came out into fenced lots where tents stood wall to wall and every inch was occupied. Here and there was a vacant spot guarded jealously by its owner, who gazed sourly upon all men with the forbidding eye of suspicion. Finding an eddy in the confusion, the men stopped.

"Where do you want to go?" they asked Miss Chester.

There was no longer in Glenister's glance that freedom with which he had come to regard the women of the North. He had come to realize dully that here was a girl driven by some strong purpose into a position repellent to her. In a man of his type, her independence awoke only admiration and her coldness served but to inflame him the more. Delicacy, in Glenister, was lost in a remarkable singleness of purpose. He could laugh at her loathing, smile under her abuse, and remain utterly ignorant that anything more than his action in seizing her that night lay at the bottom of her dislike. He did not dream that he possessed characteristics abhorrent to her; and he felt a keen reluctance at parting.

She extended both hands.

"I can never thank you enough for what you have done—you two; but I shall try. Good-bye!"

Dextry gazed doubtfully at his own hand, rough and gnarly, then taking hers as he would have handled a robin's egg, waggled it limply.

"We ain't goin' to turn you adrift this-a-way. Whatever your destination is, we'll see you to it."

"I can find my friends," she assured him.

"This is the wrong latitude in which to dispute a lady, but knowin' this camp from soup to nuts, as I do, I su'gests a male escort."

"Very well! I wish to find Mr. Struve, of Dunham & Struve, lawyers."

"I'll take you to their offices," said Glenister. "You see to the baggage, Dex. Meet me at the Second Class in half an hour and we'll run out to the Midas." They pushed through the tangle of tents, past piles of lumber, and emerged upon the main thoroughfare, which ran parallel to the shore.

Nome consisted of one narrow street, twisted between solid rows of canvas and half-erected frame buildings, its every other door that of a saloon. There were fair-looking blocks which aspired to the dizzy height of three stories, some sheathed in corrugated iron, others gleaming and galvanized. Lawyers' signs, doctors', surveyors', were in the upper windows. The street was thronged with men from every land—Helen Chester heard more dialects than she could count. Laplanders in quaint, three-cornered, padded caps idled past. Men with the tan of the tropics rubbed elbows with yellow-haired Norsemen, and near her a carefully groomed Frenchman with riding-breeches and monocle was in pantomime with a skin-clad Eskimo. To her left was the sparkling sea, alive with ships of every class. To her right towered timberless mountains, unpeopled, unexplored, forbidding, and desolate—their hollows inlaid with snow. On one hand were the life and the world she knew; on the other, silence, mystery, possible adventure.

The roadway where she stood was a crush of sundry vehicles from bicycles to dog-hauled water-carts, and on all sides men were laboring busily, the echo of hammers mingling with the cries of teamsters and the tinkle of music within the saloons.

"And this is midnight!" exclaimed Helen, breathlessly. "Do they ever rest?"

"There isn't time—this is a gold stampede. You haven't caught the spirit of it yet."

They climbed the stairs in a huge, iron-sheeted building to the office of Dunham & Struve, and in answer to their knock, a red-faced, white-haired, tousled man, in shirt-sleeves and stocking-feet, opened the door.

"What d'ye wan'?" he bawled, his legs wavering uncertainly. His eyes were heavy and bloodshot, his lips loose, and his whole person exhaled alcoholic fumes like a gust from a still-house. Hanging to the knob, he strove vainly to solve the mystery of his suspenders—hiccoughing intermittently.

"Humph! Been drunk ever since I left?" questioned Glenister.

"Somebody mus' have tol' you," the lawyer replied. There was neither curiosity, recognition, nor resentment in his voice. In fact, his head drooped so that he paid no attention to the girl, who had shrunk back at sight of him. He was a young man, with marks of brilliancy showing through the dissipation betrayed by his silvery hair and coarsened features.

"Oh, I don't know what to do," lamented the girl.

"Anybody else here besides you?" asked her escort of the lawyer.

"No. I'm runnin' the law business unassisted. Don't need any help. Dunham's in Wash'n'ton, D.C., the lan' of the home, the free of the brave. What can I do for you?"

He made to cross the threshold hospitably, but tripped, plunged forward, and would have rolled down the stairs had not Glenister gathered him up and borne him back into the office, where he tossed him upon a bed in a rear room.

"Now what, Miss Chester?" asked the young man, returning.

"Isn't that dreadful?" she shuddered. "Oh, and I must see him to-night!" She stamped impatiently. "I must see him alone."

"No, you mustn't," said Glenister, with equal decision. "In the first place, he wouldn't know what you were talking about, and in the second place—I know Struve. He's too drunk to talk business and too sober to—well, to see you alone."

"But I *must* see him," she insisted. "It's what brought me here. You don't understand."

"I understand more than he could. He's in no condition to act on any important matter. You come around to-morrow when he's sober."

"It means so much," breathed the girl. "The beast!"

Glenister noted that she had not wrung her hands nor even hinted at tears, though plainly her disappointment and anxiety were consuming her.

"Well, I suppose I'll have to wait, but I don't know where to go—some hotel, I suppose."

"There aren't any. They're building two, but to-night you couldn't hire a room in Nome for money. I was about to say 'love or money.' Have you no other friends here—no women? Then you must let me find a place for you. I have a friend whose wife will take you in."

She rebelled at this. Was she never to have done with this man's favors? She thought of returning to the ship, but dismissed that. She undertook to decline his aid, but he was half-way down the stairs and paid no attention to her beginning—so she followed him.

It was then that Helen Chester witnessed her first tragedy of the frontier, and through it came to know better the man whom she disliked and with whom she had been thrown so fatefully. Already she had thrilled at the spell of this country, but she had not learned that strength and license carry blood and violence as corollaries.

Emerging from the doorway at the foot of the stairs, they drifted slowly along the walk, watching the crowd. Besides the universal tension, there were laughter and hope and exhilaration in the faces. The enthusiasm of this boyish multitude warmed one. The girl wished to get into this spirit—to be one of them. Then suddenly from the babble at their elbows came a discordant note, not long nor loud, only a few words, penetrating and harsh with the metallic quality lent by passion.

Helen glanced over her shoulder to find that the smiles of the throng were gone and that its eyes were bent on some scene in the street, with an eager interest she had never seen mirrored before. Simultaneously Glenister spoke:

"Come away from here."

With the quickened eye of experience he foresaw trouble and tried to drag her on, but she shook off his grasp impatiently, and, turning, gazed absorbed at the spectacle which unfolded itself before her. Although not comprehending the play of events, she felt vaguely the quick approach of some crisis, yet was unprepared for the swiftness with which it came.

Her eyes had leaped to the figures of two men in the street from whom the rest had separated like oil from water. One was slim and well dressed;

the other bulky, mackinawed, and lowering of feature. It was the smaller who spoke, and for a moment she misjudged his bloodshot eyes and swaying carriage to be the result of alcohol, until she saw that he was racked with fury.

"Make good, I tell you, quick! Give me that bill of sale, you ———."

The unkempt man swung on his heel with a growl and walked away, his course leading him towards Glenister and the girl. With two strides he was abreast of them; then, detecting the flashing movement of the other, he whirled like a wild animal. His voice had the snarl of a beast in it.

"Ye had to have it, didn't ye? Well, there!"

The actions of both men were quick as light, yet to the girl's taut senses they seemed theatrical and deliberate. Into her mind was seared forever the memory of that second, as though the shutter of a camera had snapped, impressing upon her brain the scene, sharp, clear-cut, and vivid. The shaggy back of the large man almost brushing her, the rage-drunken, white-shirted man in the derby hat, the crowd sweeping backward like rushes before a blast, men with arms flexed and feet raised in flight, the glaring yellow sign of the "Gold Belt Dance Hall" across the way—these were stamped upon her retina, and then she was jerked violently backward, two strong arms crushed her down upon her knees against the wall, and she was smothered in the arms of Roy Glenister.

"My God! Don't move! We're in line!"

He crouched over her, his cheek against her hair, his weight forcing her down into the smallest compass, his arms about her, his body forming a living shield against the flying bullets. Over them the big man stood, and the sustained roar of his gun was deafening. In an instant they heard the thud and felt the jar of lead in the thin boards against which they huddled. Again the report echoed above their heads, and they saw the slender man in the street drop his weapon and spin half round as though hit with some heavy hand. He uttered a cry and, stooping for his gun, plunged forward, burying his face in the sand.

The man by Glenister's side shouted curses thickly, and walked towards his prostrate enemy, firing at every step. The wounded man rolled to his side, and, raising himself on his elbow, shot twice, so rapidly that the reports blended—but without checking his antagonist's approach. Four more times the relentless assailant fired deliberately, his last missile sent as he stood over the body which twitched and shuddered at his feet, its garments muddy and smeared. Then he turned and retraced his steps. Back within arm's-length of the two who pressed against the building he came, and as he went by they saw his coarse and sullen features drawn and working pallidly, while the breath whistled through his teeth. He held his course to the door they had just quitted, then as he turned he coughed bestially, spitting out a mouthful of blood. His knees wavered. He vanished within the portals and, in the sickly silence that fell, they heard his hob-nailed boots clumping slowly up the stairs.

Noise awoke and rioted down the thoroughfare. Men rushed forth from every quarter, and the ghastly object in the dirt was hidden by a seething mass of miners.

Glenister raised the girl, but her head rolled limply, and she would have slipped to her knees again had he not placed his arm about her waist. Her eyes were staring and horror-filled.

"Don't be frightened," said he, smiling at her reassuringly; but his own lips shook and the sweat stood out like dew on him; for they had both been close to death. There came a surge and swirl through the crowd, and Dextry swooped upon them like a hawk.

"Be ye hurt? Holy Mackinaw! When I see 'em blaze away I yells at ye fit to bust my throat. I shore thought you was gone. Although I can't say but this killin' was a sight for sore eyes—so neat an' genteel—still, as a rule, in these street brawls it's the innocuous bystander that has flowers sent around to his house afterwards."

"Look at this," said Glenister. Breast-high in the wall against which they had crouched, not three feet apart, were bullet holes.

"Them's the first two he unhitched," Dextry remarked, jerking his head towards the object in the street. "Must have been a new gun an' pulled hard—throwed him to the right. See!"

Even to the girl it was patent that, had she not been snatched as she was, the bullet would have found her.

"Come away quick," she panted, and they led her into a near-by store, where she sank upon a seat and trembled until Dextry brought her a glass of whiskey.

"Here, Miss," he said. "Pretty tough go for a 'cheechako.' I'm afraid you ain't gettin' enamoured of this here country a whole lot."

For half an hour he talked to her, in his whimsical way, of foreign things, till she was quieted. Then the partners arose to go. Although Glenister had arranged for her to stop with the wife of the merchant for the rest of the night, she would not.

"I can't go to bed. Please don't leave me! I'm too nervous. I'll go *mad* if you do. The strain of the last week has been too much for me. If I sleep I'll see the faces of those men again."

Dextry talked with his companion, then made a purchase which he laid at the lady's feet.

"Here's a pair of half-grown gum boots. You put 'em on an' come with us. We'll take your mind off of things complete. An' as fer sweet dreams, when you get back you'll make the slumbers of the just seem as restless as a riot, or the antics of a mountain-goat which nimbly leaps from crag to crag, and—well, that's restless enough. Come on!"

As the sun slanted up out of Behring Sea, they marched back towards the hills, their feet ankle-deep in the soft fresh moss, while the air tasted like a cool draught and a myriad of earthy odors rose up and encircled them. Snipe and reed birds were noisy in the hollows and from the misty tundra lakes came the honking of brant. After their weary weeks on shipboard, the dewy freshness livened them magically, cleansing from their memories the recent tragedy, so that the girl became herself again.

"Where are we going?" she asked, at the end of an hour, pausing for breath.

"Why, to the Midas, of course," they said; and one of them vowed recklessly, as he drank in the beauty of her clear eyes and the grace of her slender, panting form, that he would gladly give his share of all its riches to undo what he had done one night on the *Santa Maria*.

A New Crisis

FROM *The Iron Trail*

REX BEACH

Rex Beach (1877–1949), like Jack London, Robert Service, and Joaquin Miller, actually spent time in Alaska before writing about it. Beach stayed through a winter, earning his keep by cutting wood for steamers on the Yukon River. "A New Crisis" is excerpted from THE IRON TRAIL *(1912), a romantic novel based on an early failed effort to build a railroad across Alaska. Beach's fictitious town of Cortez, Alaska, is a thinly disguised Valdez, an important ice-free shipping port now better known as the terminus of the trans-Alaska pipeline.*

With the completion of the railroad to the glacier crossing there came to it a certain amount of travel, consisting mainly of prospectors bound to and from the interior. The Cortez winter trail was open, and over it passed most of the traffic from the northward mining-camps, but now and then a frost-rimed stranger emerged from the cañon above O'Neil's terminus with tales of the gold country, or a venturesome sledge party snow-shoed its way inland from the end of the track. Murray made a point of hauling these trailers on his construction-trains and of feeding them in his camps as freely as he did his own men. In time the wavering line of sled-tracks became fairly well broken, and scarcely a week passed without bringing several "mushers."

One day, as O'Neil was picking his way through the outskirts of the camp, he encountered one of his night foremen, and was surprised to see that the fellow was leading a trail-dog by a chain. Now these malamutes are as much a part of the northland as the winter snows, and they are a common sight in every community; but the man's patent embarrassment challenged Murray's attention: he acted as if he had been detected in a theft or a breach of duty.

"Hello, Walsh. Been buying some live stock?" O'Neil inquired.

"Yes, sir. I picked up this dog cheap."

"Harness too, eh?" Murray noted that Walsh's arms were full of gear—enough, indeed, for a full team. Knowing that the foreman owned no dogs, he asked, half banteringly:

"You're not getting ready for a trip, I hope?"

"No, sir. Not exactly, sir. The dog was cheap, so I—I just bought him."

As a matter of fact, dogs were not cheap, and Walsh should have been in bed at this hour. Murray walked on wondering what the fellow could be up to.

Later he came upon a laborer dickering with a Kyak Indian over the price of a fur robe, and in front of a bunk-house he found other members of the night crew talking earnestly with two lately arrived strangers. They fell silent as he approached, and responded to his greeting with a peculiar nervous eagerness, staring after him curiously as he passed on.

He expected Dr. Gray out from Omar, but as he neared the track he met Mellen. The bridge superintendent engaged him briefly upon some detail, then said:

"I don't know what's the matter with the men this morning. They're loafing."

"Loafing? Nonsense! You expect too much."

Mellen shook his head. "The minute my back is turned they begin to gossip. I've had to call them down."

"Perhaps they want a holiday."

"They're not that kind. There's something in the air."

While they were speaking the morning train pulled in, and O'Neil was surprised to see at least a dozen townspeople descending from it. They were loafers, saloon-frequenters, for the most part, and, oddly enough, they had with them dogs and sleds and all the equipment for travel. He was prevented from making inquiry, however, by a shout from Dr. Gray, who cried:

"Hey, Chief! Look who's here!"

O'Neil hastened forward with a greeting upon his lips, for Stanley was helping Eliza and Natalie down from the caboose which served as a passenger-coach.

The young women, becomingly clad in their warm winter furs, made a picture good to look upon. Natalie had ripened wonderfully since her marriage, and added to her rich dark beauty there was now an elusive sweetness, a warmth and womanliness which had been lacking before. As for Eliza, she had never appeared more sparkling, more freshly wholesome and saucy than on this morning.

"We came to take pictures," she announced. "We want to see if the bridge suits us."

"Don't you believe her, Mr. O'Neil," said Natalie. "Dan told us you were working too hard, so Eliza insisted on taking you in hand. I'm here merely in the office of chaperon and common scold. You *have* been overdoing. You're positively haggard."

Gray nodded. "He won't mind me. I hope you'll abuse him well. Go at him hammer and tongs."

Ignoring Murray's smiling assertion that he was the only man in camp who really suffered from idleness, the girls pulled him about and examined him critically, then fell to discussing him as if he were not present.

"He's worn to the bone," said Eliza.

"Did you ever see anything like his wrinkles? He looks like a dried apple," Natalie declared.

"Dan says he doesn't eat."

"Probably he's too busy to chew his food. We'll make him Fletcherize—"

"And eat soup. Then we'll mend his underclothes. I'll warrant he doesn't dress properly."

"How much sleep does he get?" Natalie queried of the physician.

"About half as much as he needs."

"Leave him to us," said Eliza, grimly. "Now where does he live? We'll start in there."

O'Neil protested faintly. "Please don't! I hate soup, and I can't allow anybody to pry into my wardrobe. It won't stand inspection."

Miss Appleton pointed to his feet and asked, crisply:

"How many pairs of socks do you wear?"

"One."

"Any holes?"

"Sometimes."

Natalie was shocked. "One pair of socks in this cold! It's time we took a hand. Now lead us to this rabbit-hole where you live."

Reluctantly, yet with an unaccustomed warmth about his heart, O'Neil escorted them to his headquarters. It was a sharp, clear morning; the sky was as empty and bright as an upturned saucepan; against it the soaring mountain peaks stood out as if carved from new ivory. The glaciers to right and left were mute and motionless in the grip of that force which alone had power to check them; the turbulent river was hidden beneath a case-hardened armor; the lake, with its weird flotilla of revolving bergs, was matted with a broad expanse of white, across which meandered dim sled and snow-shoe trails. Underfoot the paths gave out a crisp complaint, the sunlight slanting up the valley held no warmth whatever, and their breath hung about their heads like vapor, crystallizing upon the fur of their caps and hoods.

ONeil's living-quarters consisted of a good-sized room adjoining the office-building. Pausing at the door, he told his visitors:

"I'm sorry to disappoint you, but your zeal is utterly misplaced. I live like a pasha, in the midst of debilitating luxuries, as you will see for yourselves." He waved them proudly inside.

The room was bare, damp, and chill; it was furnished plentifully, but it was in characteristically masculine disorder. The bed was tumbled, the stove was half filled with cold ashes, the water pitcher on the washstand had frozen. In one corner was a heap of damp clothing, now stiff with frost.

"Of course, it's a little upset," he apologized. "I wasn't expecting callers, you know."

"When was it made up last?" Eliza inquired, a little weakly.

"Yesterday, of course."

"Are you sure?"

"Now, see here," he said, firmly; "I haven't time to make beds, and everybody else is busier than I am. I'm not in here enough to make it worth while—I go to bed late, and I tumble out before dawn."

The girls exchanged meaning glances. Eliza began to lay off her furs.

"Not bad, is it?" he said, hopefully.

Natalie picked up the discarded clothing, which crackled stiffly under her touch and parted from the bare boards with a tearing sound.

"Frozen! The idea!" said she.

Eliza poked among the other garments which hung against the wall and found them also rigid. The nail-heads behind them were coated with ice. Turning to the table, with its litter of papers and the various unclassified accumulation of a bachelor's house, she said:

"I suppose we'll have to leave this as it is."

"Just leave everything. I'll get a man to clean up while you take pictures of the bridge." As Natalie began preparing for action he queried, in surprise, "Don't you like my little home?"

"It's awful," the bride answered, feelingly.

"A perfect bear's den," Eliza agreed. "It will take us all day."

"It's just the way I like it," he told them; but they resolutely banished him and locked the door in his face.

"Hey! I don't want my things all mussed up," he called, pounding for readmittance; "I know right where everything is, and—" The door opened, out came an armful of papers, a shower of burnt matches, and a litter of trash from his work-table. He groaned. Eliza showed her countenance for a moment to say:

"Now, run away, little boy. You're going to have your face washed, no matter how you cry. When we've finished in here we'll attend to you." The door slammed once more, and he went away shaking his head.

At lunch-time they grudgingly admitted him, and, although they protested that they were not half through, he was naively astonished at the change they had brought to pass. For the first time in many days the place was thoroughly warm and dry; it likewise displayed an orderliness and comfort to which it had been a stranger. From some obscure source the girls had gathered pictures for the bare walls; they had hung figured curtains at the windows; there were fresh white covers for bed, bureau, and washstand. His clothes had been rearranged, and posted in conspicuous places were written directions telling him of their whereabouts. One of the cards bore these words: "Your soup! Take one in cup of hot brandy and water before retiring." Beneath were a bottle and a box of bouillon tablets. A shining tea-kettle was humming on the stove.

"This is splendid," he agreed, when they had completed a tour of inspection. "But where are my blue-prints?"

"In the drafting-room, where they belong. This room is for rest and sleep. We want to see it in this condition when we come back."

"Where did you find the fur rug?" He indicated a thick bearskin beside the bed.

"We stole it from Mr. Parker," they confessed, shamelessly. "He had two."

Eliza continued complacently: "We nearly came to blows with the chef when we kidnapped his best boy. We've ordered him to keep this place warm and look after your clothes and clean up every morning. He's to be your valet and take care of you."

"But—we're dreadfully short-handed in the mess-house," O'Neil protested.

"We've given the chef your bill of fare, and your man Ben will see that you eat it."

"I won't stand for soup. It—"

"Hush! Do you want us to come again?" Natalie demanded.

"Yes! Again and again!" He nodded vigorously. "I dare say I was getting careless. I pay more attention to the men's quarters than to my own. Do you know—this is the first hint of home I've had since I was a boy? And—it's mighty agreeable." He stared wistfully at the feminine touches on all sides.

The bride settled herself with needle and thread, saying:

"Now take Eliza to the bridge while the light is good; she wants to snap-shoot it. I'm going to sew on buttons and enjoy myself."

O'Neil read agreement in Eliza's eyes, and obeyed. As they neared the river-bank the girl exclaimed in surprise; for up out of the frozen Salmon two giant towers of concrete thrust themselves, on each bank were massive abutments, and connecting them were the beginnings of a complicated "false-work" structure by means of which the steel was to be laid in place. It consisted of rows upon rows of piling, laced together with an intricate pattern of squared timbers. Tracks were being laid upon it, and along the rails ran a towering movable crane, or "traveler," somewhat like a tremendous cradle. This too was nearing completion. Pile-drivers were piercing the ice with long slender needles of spruce; across the whole river was weaving a gigantic fretwork of wood which appeared to be geometrically regular in design. The air was noisy with the cries of men, and a rhythmic thudding, through which came the rattle of winches and the hiss of steam. Over the whole vast structure swarmed an army of human ants, feeble pygmy figures that crept slowly here and there, regardless of their dizzy height.

"Isn't it beautiful?" said the builder, gazing at the scene with kindling eyes. "We're breaking records every day in spite of the weather. Those fellows are heroes. I feel guilty and mean when I see them risking life and limb while I just walk about and look on."

"Will it—really stand the break-up?" asked the girl. "When that ice goes out it will be as if the solid earth were sliding down the channel. It frightens me to think of it."

"We've built solid rock; in fact, those piers are stronger than rock, for they're laced with veins of steel and anchored beneath the river-bed."

But Eliza doubted. "I've seen rivers break, and it's frightful; but of course I've never seen anything to compare with the Salmon. Suppose—just suppose there should be some weak spot—"

O'Neil settled his shoulders a little under his coat. "It would nearly kill Mellen—and Parker, too, for that matter."

"And you?"

He hesitated. "It means a great deal to me. Sometimes I think I could pull myself together and begin again, but—I'm getting old, and I'm not sure I'd care to try." After a pause he added a little stiffly, as if not quite sure of the effect of his words: "That's the penalty of being alone in life, I suppose. We men are grand-stand players: we need an audience, some one person who really cares whether we succeed or fail. Your brother, for instance, has won more in the building of the S. R. & N. than I can ever hope to win."

Eliza felt a trifle conscious, too, and she did not look at him when she said: "Poor, lonely old Omar Khayyam! You deserve all Dan has. I think I understand why you haven't been to see us."

"I've been too busy; this thing has kept me here every hour. It's my child, and one can't neglect his own child, you know—even if it isn't a real one." He laughed apologetically. "See! there's where we took the skiff that day we ran Jackson Glacier. He's harmless enough now. You annoyed me dreadfully that morning, Eliza, and—I've never quite understood why you were so reckless."

"I wanted the sensation. Writers have to live before they can write. I've worked the experience into my novel."

"Indeed? What is your book about?"

"Well—it's the story of a railroad-builder, of a fellow who risked everything he had on his own judgment. It's—you!"

"Why, my dear!" cried O'Neil, turning upon her a look of almost comic surprise. "I'm flattered, of course, but there's nothing romantic or uncommon about me."

"You don't mind?"

"Of course not. But there ought to be a hero, and love, and—such things—in a novel. You must have a tremendous imagination."

"Perhaps. I'm not writing a biography, you know. However, you needn't be alarmed; it will never be accepted."

"It should be, for you write well. Your magazine articles are bully."

Eliza smiled. "If the novel would only go as well as those stories I'd be happy. They put Gordon on the defensive."

"I knew they would."

"Yes. I built a nice fire under him, and now he's squirming. I think I helped you a little bit, too."

"Indeed you did—a great deal! When you came to Omar I never thought you'd turn out to be my champion. I—" He turned as Dr. Gray came hurrying toward them, panting in his haste.

The doctor began abruptly:

"I've been looking for you, Murray. The men are all quitting."

O'Neil started. "All quitting? What are you talking about?"

"There's a stampede—a gold stampede!"

Murray stared at the speaker as if doubting his own senses.

"There's no gold around here," he said, at last.

"Two men came in last night. They've been prospecting over in the White River and report rich quartz. They've got samples with 'em and say there are placer indications everywhere. They were on their way to Omar to tell their friends, and telephoned in from here. Somebody overheard and—it leaked. The whole camp is up in the air. That's what brought out that gang from town this morning."

The significance of the incidents which had troubled him earlier in the day flashed upon O'Neil; it was plain enough now why his men had been gossiping and buying dogs and fur robes. He understood only too well what a general stampede would mean to his plans, for it would take months to replace these skilled iron-workers.

"Who are these prospectors?" he inquired, curtly.

"Nobody seems to know. Their names are Thorn and Baker. That gang from Omar has gone on, and our people will follow in the morning. Those who can't scrape up an outfit here are going into town to equip. We won't have fifty men on the job by to-morrow night."

"What made Baker and Thorn stop here?"

Gray shrugged. "Tired out, perhaps. We've got to do something quick, Murray. Thank God, we don't have to sell 'em grub or haul 'em to Omar. That will check things for a day or two. If they ever start for the interior we're lost, but the cataract isn't frozen over, and there's only one sled trail past it. We don't need more than six good men to do the trick."

"We can't stop a stampede that way."

Dr. Gray's face fell into harsh lines. "I'll bend a Winchester over the first man who tries to pass. Appleton held the place last summer; I'll guarantee to do it now."

"No. The men have a right to quit, Stanley. We can't force them to work. We can't build this bridge with a chain-gang."

"Humph! I can beat up these two prospectors and ship 'em in to the hospital until things cool down."

"That won't do, either. I'll talk with them, and if their story is right— well, I'll throw open the commissary and outfit every one."

Eliza gasped; Gray stammered.

"You're crazy!" exclaimed the doctor.

"If it's a real stampede they'll go anyhow, so we may as well take our medicine with a good grace. The loss of even a hundred men would cripple us."

"The camp is seething. It's all Mellen can do to keep the day shift at work. If you talk to 'em maybe they'll listen to you."

"Argument won't sway them. This isn't a strike; it's a gold rush." He turned toward the town.

Eliza was speechless with dismay as she hurried along beside him; Gray was scowling darkly and muttering anathemas; O'Neil himself was lost in thought. The gravity of this final catastrophe left nothing to be said.

Stanley lost little time in bringing the two miners to the office, and there, for a half-hour, Murray talked with them. When they perceived that he was disposed to treat them courteously they told their story in detail and answered his questions with apparent honesty. They willingly showed him their quartz samples and retailed the hardships they had suffered.

Gray listened impatiently and once or twice undertook to interpolate some question, but at a glance from his chief he desisted. Nevertheless, his long fingers itched to lay hold of the strangers and put an end to this tale which threatened ruin. His anger grew when Murray dismissed them with every evidence of a full belief in their words.

"Now that the news is out and my men are determined to quit, I want everybody to have an equal chance," O'Neil announced, as they rose to go. "There's bound to be a great rush and a lot of suffering—maybe some deaths—so I'm going to call the boys together and have you talk to them."

Thorn and Baker agreed and departed. As the door closed behind them Gray exploded, but Murray checked him quickly, saying with an abrupt change of manner: "Wait! Those fellows are lying!"

Seizing the telephone, he rang up Dan Appleton and swiftly made known the situation. Stanley could hear the engineer's startled exclamation.

"Get the cable to Cortez as quickly as you can," O'Neil was saying. "You have friends there, haven't you? Good! He's just the man, for he'll have Gordon's pay-roll. Find out if Joe Thorn and Henry Baker are known, and, if so, who they are and what they've been doing lately. Get it quick, understand? Then 'phone me." He slammed the receiver upon its hook. "That's not Alaskan quartz," he said, shortly; "it came from Nevada, or I'm greatly mistaken. Every hard-rock miner carries specimens like those in his kit."

"You think Gordon—"

"I don't know. But we've got rock-men on this job who'll recognize ore out of any mine they ever worked in. Go find them, then come back here and hold the line open for Dan."

"Suppose he can't locate these fellows in Cortez?"

"Then—Let's not think about that."

Do You Fear the Wind?

HAMLIN GARLAND

Hamlin Garlin (1860–1940) was a Wisconsin-born poet, short-story writer, and novelist known for his gritty portraits of Midwestern farm life. He is best remembered for two of his eight autobiographical works, A SON OF THE MIDDLE BORDER *and* A DAUGHTER OF THE MIDDLE BORDER *(1921), which won a Pulitzer Prize. Garland's poem "Do You Fear the Wind?" was inspired by his adventures in the Klondike during the gold rush of 1898. Here the poet challenges young men to join the great adventure.*

Do you fear the force of the wind,
The slash of the rain?
Go face them and fight them,
Be savage again.
Go hungry and cold like the wolf.
    Go wade like the crane:
The palms of your hands will thicken,
The skin of your cheek will tan,
You'll grow ragged and weary and swarthy
    But you'll walk like a man.

Two in the Far North

MARGARET E. MURIE

Margaret E. Murie came to Alaska as a child of nine in 1911 and became the first woman to graduate from the University of Alaska Fairbanks. For decades, she has been a respected writer and environmentalist, widely appreciated for her essays of her travels throughout Alaska with her husband, biologist and illustrator Olaus Murie, and for her work as one of the founders of the Wilderness Society. Margaret Murie's many books include the classic memoir TWO IN THE FAR NORTH *(1978) and the novel* ISLAND BETWEEN *(1977). The following excerpt presents the first two chapters of* TWO IN THE FAR NORTH.

A nine-year-old girl can see and hear a lot. Too old to hold the center of any group with the charm of babyhood, too young to be considered a hazard to conversation, sturdy, round-eyed, my dark hair in a Mary Jane bob with a big butterfly bow on top, I could be quietly everywhere at once. I saw and heard.

So the Alaska most vivid in my memory is the one I saw first as a nine-year-old, traveling from Seattle to Fairbanks with Mother, in September, on the last trip before "freeze-up."

Daddy, my loved and loving stepfather, was already up there, at work on his new job as Assistant U.S. Attorney. One morning as I came downstairs to breakfast I saw a Western Union messenger boy standing with Mother in the front hall of our Seattle home. The telegram said: "Can you catch Str. *Jefferson* September 15th? Last steamer to connect with last boat down the Yukon. Will meet you in Dawson."

I remember running the several blocks to the dressmaker's. "We're going to Alaska in three days and Mother wants to know can you get her a traveling dress made." In those days you didn't just go downtown and buy a dress; it was a project.

Three days. My stepfather had faith in the calm efficiency of that sweet brown-eyed woman. The dressmaker friend came and went to work in the midst of trunks and boxes. My grandmother came and flipped from room to room amid a torrent of words. "I just don't see how Millette can *expect* you to catch that boat!" And: "Minnie, do you think you should *try* to do this—in your condition?" Even while she feverishly stowed linens and clothing and dishes in the big round-topped trunks.

"In your condition"—that was a queer-sounding phrase. What condition? But then I was sent running on another errand. And finally, on the afternoon of the third day, there was Grandmother, still in a torrent of words, and between tears and laughter, sitting atop the largest round-topped trunk so the dressmaker's son could get it closed, while the dressmaker sewed on the last of the black jet buttons down the back of the brown wool "traveling dress" with garnet velvet piping around the neck and sleeves. I remember how soft to the touch that brown wool cloth was.

The boats for Alaska always sailed at nine in the evening, and it was like going to the theater—a real social occasion for the Seattle folks—going to the pier to see the steamer off to the North. Down through the great cavern of the dock warehouse, brightly lighted for sailing time, smelling of salt sea and tar and hemp and adventure. A great crowd of people, and stevedores with handcarts pushing their way through, yelling: "Gangway! Gangway!" A great wave of noise compounded of the churning of engines and the hissing of steam, and voices in every key, shouts, laughter. At last to the long opening in the side wall, and there was the ship's white side and the red-and-white gangplank.

I was dressed in my new black-and-white "shepherd check" dress with brass buttons down the front and a red collar and red cuffs, and my new red coat with black silk "frogs," and a red hat with shirred satin ribbon around the crown (and I knew the red Mary Jane hairbow would be crushed by it), and shiny black boots with patent-leather cuffs at the top and a red silk tassel. My stomach was tied in a knot of breathless, almost-not-to-be-borne sensation, and I was clutching all my going-away presents—coloring books, paper-doll books, crayons, a new volume of *Black Beauty*. Mother stood in the midst of a cluster of friends, looking so pretty in her new dress and her coat with the green velvet collar, and she too had her arms full of gifts— boxes of candy, books, the newest *Ladies' Home Journal*. All around us people were carrying or receiving packages. Going to see someone off for Alaska always meant bringing a parting gift. The first moments of letdown after the ship was under way would be brightened by the opening of packages.

For a nine-year-old, no sorrow, only excitement—being hugged all around, and nearly jumping out of my skin when the deep-throated, echoing five-minute whistle blew and set off a crescendo of squeals and shouts and admonitions from the crowd.

"Here you go!" A perkily blue-and-gold uniform sets me up onto the first cleat of the gangplank—really, really going somewhere! Step down onto the deck, find a spot at the rail. Every passenger is at the rail—why doesn't the ship roll over? Hang on to the packages. What if one should fall? From some mysterious realm above come heavy voices of authority; bells clang far down inside; down slides the gangplank to be rolled away onto the pier. That was the last tie being cut. Now it is really happening. Looking down over the ship's side, I see water, and it widens and widens, and faces are looking up, handkerchiefs waving, voices and faces fading away. "See you next June." "Don't take any wooden nickels." "Tell Joe to write." "Hope Queen Charlotte won't be too rough!"

The faces of Grandmother and all our friends are only white blurs now. We are out in the cool black windy bay and the ship is heading out and all the passengers are moving now—moving into their new little world, the Str. *Jefferson,* Gus Nord, Master.

To a nine-year-old, a ship's stateroom was a wonder of a place, such fun—the berths with their railings, the washbowl that pulled down into place, the locker seat with its red plush cushions. Our room opened into the "saloon," and that was another wonder—red plush-covered soft divans and big chairs, soft carpet underfoot, a broad stairway with a shining brass railing that curved down into the dining saloon.

There were other children aboard, and here on the carpeted floor at our mothers' feet we played our games while the women sat with their "fancy work," all of us in a cozy yet adventurous little world of our own. We children cut out paper dolls, and played Parcheesi, and colored pictures, and the women discovered one another, old Alaskans telling new ones all they knew, while fingers flew. Mother was crocheting a long black-and-white wool shawl; the huge amber crochet hook fascinated me.

A lovely routine that was over too quickly. Then, as ever, the days of ship life flew by too fast. Meals, and naps, and always the falling asleep and waking again to the sweet pulse and throb of the ship's engines and the muted hiss of water along her sides. Then racing about on deck, and hide-and-seek on the forward deck, and quiet hours in the lounge, and "dressing for dinner"—which meant, for me, being scrubbed, and having my hair brushed till it shone, and a different bow tied and fluffed into a butterfly, and either the pink challis or the shirred white China silk dress, and the "best" shoes, black patent leather with high tops of brown-calf buttoned straps. Then stepping out to wait for the musical dinner gong and to see what the three other little girls had on this time!

After four days of this delightful life there was talk of about what hour the *Jefferson* would dock at Skagway. I remember it was daytime, and we had been sliding for hours up a long channel of glass-smooth water edged on either side by the ever-present dark green forest that lay below shining white mountains.

Skagway nestled into the delta fan at the mouth of a canyon, embraced on three sides by steep wooded slopes. In front, the very blue waters of the Lynn Canal, which is not really a canal but a long fiord. A long pier extended out to deep water. The little town seemed to sparkle in the September sun. Many of the buildings were of white-painted lumber; some were half-log structures. Back toward the canyon, in a grove of cottonwood trees and spruces, stood Pullen House.

In a frontier town, the feature least frontierish is likely to be the most famous and admired. So Pullen House, looking like a southern manor, with lawns, flower beds, a pergola, a little stream flowing through the lawn and spanned by a rustic bridge. Inside, no homemade frontier furnishings, but heavy Victorian walnut and mahogany and plush, walls crowded with pictures, bric-a-brac, and souvenirs. For here was the whole history of Skagway. Pullen House was the tangible dream of a woman who had come there in the gold rush only fourteen years before, a widow with a daughter and three little sons. She had lived in a tent shack and made dried apple pies and sold them to the hordes of pie-hungry, home-hungry, adventure-hungry men of the days of '98. Thus her grubstake, and Pullen House.

Harriet Pullen, once met, could never be forgotten. She welcomed Mother as a beloved daughter come home, for she remembered Daddy from the days when the District Judge from Juneau came up to Skagway twice a year with his retinue, including his young court reporter, and held court. They always stayed, of course, at Pullen House. "Ma" Pullen, tall, red-haired, statuesque, with suffering and strength and humor in every feature—even a nine-year-old sensed this.

We slept in a room full of overpowering furniture, in a great ark of a bed with headboard reaching toward the ceiling. But this was the special room, the room many important people had occupied when traveling north. The commode had the most gorgeous basin, and a pitcher, blooming with red roses, so heavy I could not lift it.

In the morning, Mrs. Pullen ushered us out into the long pantry behind the immense kitchen. "My favorite boarders always get to skim their own cream. Mr. Gillette always loved to when he stayed here," she said.

Here was the other unfrontierish feature of Skagway. Ma Pullen's great pride was a Jersey cow, the only cow in that part of the world, and in the pantry stood the blue-enameled milk pans. The guest was given a bowl and a spoon and allowed to skim off cream for his porridge and coffee. Skimming your own cream at Pullen House in the land of no cream was a ritual talked of all over the North in those days.

Being on a train for the first time provided more excitement. I had to examine every detail of the red plush-covered seats and curlicue-brass-trimmed arms, and jump from one side of the aisle to the other, trying to see everything, yet my only clear recollection from that day is looking down into Lake Bennett near the summit—such turquoise water, such golden birch trees all round it. I think all other impressions were drowned in my rapt absorption in the gorgeous uniforms of the two Northwest Mounted Policemen who came aboard to check us through at the border of the Yukon Territory.

This same impression dominates my memory of the three days traveling downriver from Whitehorse to Dawson. There was one of these gorgeous creatures aboard, and he suffered the company of an adoring small round-eyed girl. I remember sitting with him on the stern deck. I don't remember any of the conversation.

It was dusk at five o'clock, for it was late September in the Land of the Midnight Sun. The passengers on the sternwheel steamer *Casca* were all crowded at the rail on one side while the *Casca* huffed and puffed in the great surge of the Yukon and was maneuvered with uncanny skill toward the dock at Dawson. Her stern wheel chuff-chuffed rapidly in reverse, bells clanged, and with a great swoosh of water the wheel chuff-chuffed forward again. Her high-pitched, exciting whistle blew three times—a greeting to the "Queen of the Klondike" and the crowd of her citizens standing all expectant on the dock.

The *Casca*'s passengers pressed closer to the rail, straining to look, straining to recognize loved, feared, or dreaded faces. Squeezed against the white-painted iron mesh below the rail, new red hat pushed askew, heart beating fast, I stood, determined to see everything.

Mother stood quietly beside me, but I could feel her excitement too. We were both looking for the big tan Stetson hat that would tell us Daddy had managed to catch that last upriver steamer and was here to meet us.

The Yukon begins to widen at Dawson; the hills are farther apart and seem bigger and higher, and certainly more bare. Here we were sensing a quite different world, the world of "the interior." The hill behind Dawson seemed to be sitting high above the town, with arms spread about the sprawling clot of man's hurriedly built, haphazard structures. Even then, in 1911, the gold towns had electricity, and now at dusk lights were beginning to show here and there all over the delta shape of the settlement.

The *Casca,* having chuffed upstream above the dock, was now sliding down closer in, closer in, a young Indian poised to jump with the bowline. There arose cries of "I see Jim!" "There's Mary!" And shouts from the crowd on the dock: "Hey Doc, you old so-and-so, I *knew* you'd be back!"

A bell clanged once somewhere inside the *Casca,* the engines stopped, the Indian boy jumped, for a few seconds more the great wheel turned— over and over—and then how quiet it was! Everyone seemed impressed by the silence for a moment. That is the kind of moment which lives on for- ever after, when you are nine and in an utterly new and so different world. Then Mother cried out: "There he is!" And there he was, indeed, right at the front, where a crew of Indian boys waited to hoist the big gangplank.

There was moose steak for dinner that night, in Dawson's famed Arcade Café. Under the white glare of the many bulbs, amid the great babble of a happy crowd, everyone talking to everyone and calling back and forth among the tables—I remember most keenly that huge thick slab of meat with a heap of fried potatoes beside it. We had arrived in the North. What the steak cost, I do not know. But that was the Yukon, that was Alaska. I think my gentle mother began to learn about the north country that night. All was costly, everything was done on a lavish scale, life was exciting and each day a story in itself, and nothing was worth worrying about. The finest things that could be hauled into this country from Outside were none too good for these pioneers who were braving the climate and the terrain of this untamable land. If all might be lost in a season in the diggings, then they would have the best while they could.

The hotel rooms reflected this spirit. The wallpaper was likely to be a

Greek amphora design in gold, all fluffy with curlicues, on a deep-red ground. There might be a flowered pink Brussels carpet on the floor, a white bedstead with more curly designs and brass knobs on each of the four posts; chairs with more fancy designs and turned legs. There was one with a lion's head carved in its back. At the windows, lace curtains which scratched your nose and neck if you wanted to part them to look down into the street.

The street. The next morning I stood looking down at it. It was full of big-hatted men, fur-capped men, men in Derby hats, men with beards, men in breeches and bright shirts and high laced boots, men in long city overcoats, men in denim parkas. Some were hurrying along, boots clattering on the boardwalk; others were standing about in small groups. There seemed to be a lot of talk and gesturing and much laughter, a feeling of excitement and of things happening. A team of big gray horses came down the dusty street to the dock drawing a load of luggage. Behind them came a team of Huskies pulling a long narrow cart on wheels, also piled with luggage. "See? They use dogs when there is no snow, too," Daddy said.

The three of us were at the window now. Across the street the carts were disappearing into the dock warehouse. The autumn stream of old-timers leaving for Outside for the winter, and of others moving in, was at its peak. One more boat from downriver was due in. It would really be the last one upriver for this season; and on it we would be going downstream, to Tanana, and from Tanana up the Tanana River to Fairbanks. "The *Sarah* should be in any time now," Daddy said. "Look downriver."

I already knew what direction that was, and over the roofs of the row of docks and warehouses, the broad brown river was there, filling our view, the brown hills beyond seeming far away. Downstream, around a sand-colored bluff, a puff of white wood smoke, then a beautiful three-toned whistle, sad and sweet and lonely. "There she is! Only she and her three sisters have that voice!" exclaimed Daddy.

In 1911 the river steamer was queen. There was a great fleet then, nearly all with feminine names, churning and chuffing their stern wheels up the rivers and sliding briskly down them. When the great two-stacker Mississippi-style steamer came in to any dock, she came like a confident southern beauty making a graceful curtsy at a ball. There were four of these on the Yukon—the *Susie,* the *Sarah,* the *Hannah,* and the *Louise*—and they lived their lives between St. Michael at the mouth of the river and Dawson, 1,600 miles upstream. That part of the Yukon is very wide all the way, with plenty of water, a great river. There was another of the big boats, bearing a masculine name, *Herman,* but "he" seemed a bit dirty and a little slower.

Now in the street below there was shouting and calling, and all the town emptied in a rush toward the dock, where the beautiful huge white *Sarah* was sliding in to make a landing.

We left Dawson early the next evening. There was still some daylight, and it seemed that all of Dawson was on the dock to see us off. Back in those times "the last trip of the year" was no meaningless phrase. It meant that all the supplies for the community, enough to last until "the first boat in the spring" came, had to be already delivered and safely stored away in the warehouses and stores—and everyone hoped he hadn't forgotten to order something important. It meant that everyone who felt he could not stand another soul-testing northern winter had better be leaving on this boat. It meant that all those who had been Outside all summer and felt they couldn't stand any more of the tinsel and heartless life of the cities Outside were there, on their way back downriver, or on beyond to Fairbanks, or to wherever they felt they belonged and could try it again. These were aboard the *Sarah.* They were mostly single men, but there were a few families, like us, going into the country to make a home, to follow a career.

How vivid that scene! Again squeezed up against, and almost under, the rail, among all those grownups, I tried hard to see and hear everything.

"Sure you got all your suitcases aboard?"

"Hope that winter dump's a good one."

"Say hello to Charlie."

"Oh, we'll winter through all right."

"See you in the spring!"

Everyone was smiling, tossing jokes back and forth. That was the way of the North always, but even a nine-year-old could sense the sad things too. Maybe we won't see you in the spring; maybe that winter dump won't be so good; maybe this country is too tough for us. Maybe . . .

There is one thing gone forever from our world—the irrevocability of those departures, before the age of the airplane. This was the last boat, and Nature would take over from now until the middle of June. Freeze-up was coming. There would be no chance of seeing any of these faces until another year had rolled away. The *Sarah*'s stern wheel, so huge I was afraid to look at it, began to turn. The swirl and push of water, shouted commands from up above us. The young freight clerk in his navy-and-gold uniform came hurrying up the gangplank, papers in hand, always the last one aboard. A voice from up above shouted down to him: "Sure you got everything? All right, cast off!"

The big cable fell into the river with a splash that must have sent a shiver of finality down many a spine. Up came the gangplank, and the two gorgeous Mounties stood alone and calm down where its lower end had rested. The *Sarah* slid rapidly into the current, and there was a great hissing and churning as bells rang and she slowed, and turned, and straightened out into midstream. Then the three beautiful blended tones, long-drawn-out and echoing from the domed hill behind the town, and from the dock an answering chorus of shouts, and big hats waving.

The *Sarah* was even more exciting than the *Jefferson*. From all the adult conversation I listened to, I gathered that we were lucky to catch her on this last trip, that she was the queen of the fleet, that her captain "knew the river," that she "had the best food." She was, it seemed to me, enormous, both long and broad, and with a great space up front on the main deck, under the upper deck, where everyone gathered when there was anything interesting outdoors, and inside, a large "saloon" all done up in green plush and white paneling and gold trimming, like a drawing room in a fairy-tale palace. Besides this there was a card room, where the men gathered, and a ladies' lounge, where the women sat with their needlework and their talk.

To me, and to the two little boys about my own age who were the only other children on board, the card room and the big deck were the more interesting places. And here we first came in touch with the early Alaskans' attitude toward all children. Children were rare; they were a symbol of everything that many of these men had given up in heeding the call of gold and adventure; they were precious individuals. Out on the deck there were always two or three men eager to play hide-and-seek with us, with shouts and merry antics, swinging themselves about the steel poles which held up the upper deck above us. And inside we were allowed to sit beside someone at the Solo table, and play with the chips while the game went on, and because Daddy knew these men and their big hearts, we children were not forbidden any of these joys.

Life was almost more interesting than one could bear. Every day there were stops at wood camps when the *Sarah* had to take on the many cords of birch and spruce that kept her huge boiler going. Daddy took me and the little boys ashore to walk about a bit, among the long stacks of wood cut in four-foot lengths; to watch the Indian deckhands so cheerfully going up and down the wide plank into the boiler room of the *Sarah* with their trucks loaded, racing down with a shout and a laugh with an empty truck, straining up the slant with a full one, still smiling. Life seemed a big happy game for everybody in that land. We saw red squirrels in the thick woods behind these wood piles, and sometimes had time to pick a handful of bright red low-bush cranberries before the *Sarah* sounded a short blast which meant her appetite was satisfied for now.

There were Indian villages. A row of tiny log cabins in a straggly line atop a cut bank, backed by the forest, and down below the bank, usually, on the little strip of beach, all the village dogs, chained to stakes, howling their loudest at the approach of the steamer, for it meant food thrown out from the galley for them to fight over.

Sometimes the *Sarah* pulled in to these villages to let off some prospector or trapper going into the far back country for the winter. One of these I remember well. He was called Red Rodgers, a tall, lusty, loud-voiced extrovert with flaming red hair and a long beard. His few boxes of provisions had been quickly wheeled down the plank and onto the shore, but he himself carried his gold pan and pick and shovel and with a great shout leaped from the gangplank onto the beach, and turned to shout a few last lusty, cheery words to friends aboard as the *Sarah* slipped out into the current. Behind him, black spruces stood out against a gold sunset which somehow looked cold. Even then, in my child's mind, I wondered: Did he feel a bit sad, too, as the big white ship slid away downstream?

Everybody went ashore at the towns—Eagle, with the beautiful hills nearby; Circle, atop a high bank, a cluster of log buildings where not long before had been a tent city of ten thousand. We were there in the evening in a misty rain; the wide freight plank and the warehouse of the Northern Commercial Company were hung with kerosene lanterns so the freight could be unloaded. We were in the United States now, and the Law was not a beautiful red-and-blue uniform and a strong impassive face, but a jovial round face, a hearty voice, heavy brown woolen trousers, a bright plaid shirt—the U.S. Deputy Marshal. He and his pretty wife came to take us to their bright log-cabin home, and she laughed at Mother's city toe-rubbers: "Those are cheechako rubbers—they won't help you much up here!"

The two little boys and I would have gone happily on and on into the future aboard the *Sarah*; it was a perpetual birthday party. Shining white tablecloths, gleaming silver, white-coated waiters urging all kinds of goodies onto our plates. We all must have had stomachs of iron. We were even allowed to stay up sometimes for the "midnight lunch," which was served at ten in the evening. And at every town, our sourdough friends were eager to buy candy or anything else at the trading posts. My coat pocket bulged with lemon drops.

But one day in warm yet crisp September sunshine, the *Sarah* reached Tanana, where the river of that name poured a wide flood into the Yukon. From here on down to the sea the Yukon would truly be a great river, and the *Sarah* could push five barges of freight ahead of her if need be. Here those who were traveling on downriver to St. Michael and Nome and the Outside must say good-by to the rest of us, and we must say good-by to wonderful *Sarah* and go aboard the *Schwatka,* which was not really so tiny, but looked like a midget beside *Sarah.*

But the *Schwatka* had pleasure for a child which made up for her small size. It was cozy; there was only one small "saloon," and everyone gathered there. Though I had sadly waved good-by to the two little boys, who were staying in Tanana, where their father was employed at the army fort there, Fort Gibbon, some of the good sourdough friends were still aboard and always ready to play games and tell me stories (and how I wish I remembered the stories!). I was invited by the captain up into that mystical place, the pilothouse, from which I could watch the whole river at once, and the deckhands working, and the Huskies tied on the bow, and the man taking the soundings, hour after hour. For now we were in a different river world— a river swift and swirling and carrying a great load of silt and now in its autumn low-water stage, with long sand bars nearly all the way, on one side or the other.

Here river navigation was a fine and definite art. There was a certain expert sweep of the sounding pole, a certain drone to the voice: "Five" and a pause—"Five" and a pause—"and a half four"—getting more shallow— "Four" and a pause—"and a half three." And here the face would be lifted to the pilothouse. What was next? A bell, and a slowing of the engines, and the pilot leaning out the window, looking. And sometimes an awful shuddering thump. We were on the bar! Always at this point Daddy took me down out of the pilothouse. I realize now it must have been to allow the officers free rein in their language as they wrestled with the river. Sometimes they could reverse and slide off. Sometimes they sent a crew in a small boat to the other side, or to some point on the bank, to sink a great timber called a deadman; a cable was attached to the timber, and the freight winch would begin to whine, and slowly, so slowly, the *Schwatka* would be pulled off into deeper water and we could go on again for a spell.

Slow travel, in the Alaska of 1911, provided plenty of time for books and games and paper dolls, for dressing and undressing the brown teddy bear, for visiting the galley and watching the baker rolling out pies and cookies; for peering down into the engine room to watch the play of the long shaft attached to the paddle wheel, sliding forward, knuckling back, terrifying, fascinating—but so long as we heard the chuff and whoosh of that wheel, we knew all was fine, and I know, to this day, of no more soothing, competent, all-is-well sound.

To Mother, arriving in Fairbanks must have been fraught with all kinds of wondering and half fears; she must have been feeling very far away from all she had known. To me, it was just more excitement and more new faces, and new conversation to listen to, often quite interesting.

As it was the fall of the year, there wasn't enough water for the *Schwatka* in the Chena Slough, the small tributary of the Tanana on which Fairbanks had been built. So at the little village of Chena, twelve miles below the town, passengers and freight had to be loaded onto the intrepid Tanana Valley Railroad. Yes, a real train, a real engine, two cars full of people now old friends, reaching the end of a three-week journey together. Even when the train came to the end of its twelve-mile journey, we were not yet at the end of ours, for the main town was across the slough, and horse-drawn carts were at the station to meet the train. So was "Dad" Shaw, owner of the very respectable hotel of the town, the Shaw House, where Daddy had been living and where we were now welcomed as part of the family. There was a big lobby, full of men who all knew Daddy; there were some friendly women too, for on Sunday nights it was a custom with many families to take dinner at the spotless and cheerful Shaw House dining room. Some of the sourdoughs of the journey were staying here too.

Yet when Mother tucked me into a single bed in Daddy's high-ceilinged room, I felt a bit strange. What were the captain and the cook and all the rest on the *Schwatka* doing now? And how empty and quiet the little lounge must be. And where, by now, was the *Sarah?*

....

Such a final sound—"the last boat," "the freeze-up." But in Fairbanks that year it was an unusually late, mild, sunny autumn. Daddy knew everyone, it seemed, and there were even some picnics with his friends who had horses and buggies, driving out through the golden birch woods and the green spruce forest which extended thick and untouched behind the town, out to the Tanana River, four miles south, a marvelous place of sand and stones and bleached logs to sit on and serve lunch on and clamber over.

After a few days of this exciting life (and without school too!) Daddy found one vacant house—one way out on the edge of town, eight blocks from the river, the last house on the last street of the Fairbanks of that year. It was log of course, and sturdy, but with only four rooms: a living-dining room about sixteen by twenty; behind it a bedroom and a kitchen; and off at one side, a lean-to bedroom built of slab wood. This cabin was home for ten years.

The back door opened into a woodshed-storage place. All such places were called caches, and off one corner of this was what in those days sufficed for sanitary convenience. That was one of the first phenomena of the northern towns. Late in the night on certain nights we might be awakened by a clatter out there. The most heroic soul on the frontier was emptying the can. Lying curled down warm in the middle of my bed in the lean-to bedroom, I would hear the stamping and clatter, the jingle of harness, the low "giddap" to the horses, the creaking of sled runners on the snow, out there in the cold dark.

Added to this was the problem of water. I know Mother really wondered about this life sometimes! Oh, there was a well, and a hand pump in the kitchen sink (the sink drained into a slop bucket which had to be carried outdoors). But the water was so terrifically red and rusty and hard and smelling of iron that Mother could not use it. So we had a big whiskey barrel, with a cover, just inside the kitchen door, and "Fred the Waterman" came every day with his tank wagon or sleigh. First he look at the kitchen window, to see if the square blue card said two or four, then filled the buckets hanging at the back of his tank—five gallon oil cans fitted with handles of thick copper wire; after this he quickly hooked them onto the hooks of his wooden yoke and came stamping in. "Cold today, yah, yah." Fred's last name was Musjgherd—nobody ever tried to pronounce it. Nobody knew his nationality or how he had come to this far place. But he owned a well which poured forth clear, sweet water, and this directed his life. He was our friend, Fred the Waterman, and his black horses the fattest, sleekest, best-cared-for in town.

So that was the water situation. As for the rest, Mother by some magic touch made it home—colorful and warm and somehow, with everything we owned in those four rooms, still uncluttered.

Neighbors told Mother of how the living room had looked before. The house had belonged to a Mrs. Jackson, a nervous woman with a background of luxurious city life, who had brought her city furnishings along. True, she didn't belong on the Alaska frontier, and now was gone, but she had not taken it all with her. Even Mother was dismayed about the wallpaper in the living room. As in all the cabins of those days, over the log walls was tacked "house lining"—unbleached muslin cloth—which was also stretched across from eave to eave, making a low ceiling, called a "balloon ceiling." Then the whole was covered with wallpaper. In this case Mrs. Jackson had consented to have *some* light, and the ceiling was white with a "watered silk" silvery overlay, very popular then for ceilings. But the walls jumped at you. They were of a deep red paper with a sort of coat-of-arms figure about a foot high—in gold! The tall front window and the little square ones on each side were curtained in what was called scrim, in a very fancy pattern in red, blue, and tan. On the floor was a Brussels carpet, all roses on a tan background; in one corner was a wide couch "cozy corner" affair, the mattress covered with red rep; in another corner a tall corner cupboard, the bottom part hung with red-and-white-striped material. Mrs. Jackson, the neighbors said, had had this filled with hand-painted china—altogether a lively room. As soon as possible, Mother had the walls covered with light-tan burlap.

I think my mother felt the unspeakable isolation more than she would ever say. She kept it locked away inside, while she went serenely about the task that was hers—adapting her very civilized self to creating a home and bringing up a family on this far frontier, with the man she loved. I realize now that I felt this in her, even while not feeling it myself at all. To an eager, curious child, everything was interesting here.

One thing I remember is that Mother could hardly stand the howling of the dogs. Not too far from our house, across the fields and beyond a slough and some spruce woods, was the dog pound, down on the river. Alaska was a dog country then; there were always plenty of strays, or whole teams being "boarded out" there, so whenever that famous six-o'clock whistle blew there was a chorus not to be ignored—it was too close to our little log house—

and Mother thought they "sounded so mournful." To me it was just an interesting noise. The trouble was that the "six-o'clock whistle" blew at six A.M. and seven A.M. and at noon and one P.M. and finally at six P.M., and the chorus was just as great each time, to say nothing of the frenzied tune when that awful fire siren stopped us all in our tracks. That one was enough to make any dog howl; it made all of us want to, besides stabbing us with cold fear each time. Perhaps to the dogs those whistles signified the ancestor of all wolves howling to them. They had to respond. Anyway, I am sure that later, when we moved down close in to town, Mother was glad to have put some distance between herself and that opera.

She had enough to do, that first winter, to adjust to this new life. I can see clearly now that things that were of no thought and little trouble to me, a child, were a daily series of battles for her, gentle and sweet and straight from the city and expecting my first half sister in the spring, and with Daddy gone through Christmas and far into January, traveling by dog team on the Yukon from village to village, for he was the field man for the U.S. Attorney, and the Law had but recently come to this part of the wild North.

Temperatures, and stoves. On one side of the living room stood the indispensable stove of the North, a Cole Airtight Heater. This took in big heavy chunks of spruce wood. In the kitchen, close to the back window, we had the big wood range. This took endless feeding with split spruce. When the thermometer went down to minus 20, and 30, and 50, and sometimes stayed there for weeks, the pattern of life was set—feeding the stoves. But, since the houses were small and low-ceilinged, and had storm windows and "bankings" of earth about three feet high all around the outside walls (where a riot of sweet peas grew in the summer), we were warm. But Mother's feet were always cold. She would go busily about her housework for a half hour, then open the oven door and sit with her feet in the oven for a few minutes, then back to work. Thank heaven for the nine cords of good spruce wood all neatly ricked up in the back yard. And for the cellar under the kitchen, where all the supplies were stored—vegetables and canned goods, jams and jellies. And out in the cache, in a special cupboard, we had cuts of moose and caribou, all wrapped and frozen oh so solid, and bundles of frozen whitefish. We were fairly self-contained, in a little bastion against the 50-below-zero world outside.

We did have some helpful things: electric lights, so Mother could use her new electric iron, and a telephone, so that during those very cold spells she could talk to her friends—and there were fine friends, but most of them lived on the other side of town.

The house nearest us was vacant that first year. (Later our wonderful friends Jess and Clara Rust moved into it.) Across the street there was only one house, and after Daddy left for his long winter journey that house became a source of worry to Mother. One day we saw six enormous mustachioed, fur-coated, fur-capped men moving their gear into that house—six of them! They were what Fairbanks called "Bohunks"—Slavic men of some kind—tremendous in stature and strength. They worked in the mines in the summer. I don't think Mother had ever seen such huge men before. For weeks the only sound from them was the terrific noise they made late each night, coming home from an evening in town, stamping the snow from their boots at their front door, which sounded as though they were stamping on *our* front doorstep and coming right on in. Then one day there was a gentle knock at our back door. I opened it and there stood one of these giants. He looked at me solemnly and said one word: "Ax!"

I flew in terror to Mother, but when she came, the giant made her understand by a few gestures that he would like to cut some wood for us. And he did. After that the stomping and the singing in Russian, or something, meant only that *our friends* were home from a convivial evening on Front Street.

Uncle Charley

FROM *My Way Was North*

FRANK DUFRESNE

*Frank Dufresne (1895–1966), for many years the director of the Alaska Game
Commission, was also a writer, editor, and naturalist. In 1920, a young
Dufresne, "trying to find [himself] after two lost years in the muddy shell-holes
of France," boarded a steamer in Seattle for Nome. What followed was an
intriguing life of high adventure chronicled in his autobiography,* MY WAY
WAS NORTH *(1966), from which "Uncle Charley" is excerpted.*

Nome in 1920 was a fading gold camp. From a noisy tent city
strung helter-skelter along the beach sands where thousands of
stampeders had washed out quick fortunes, it had shrunk to a
few hundred diehards. False-fronted saloons, once staffed with
gamblers and painted ladies tolling newly-rich prospectors in off
the street, now stood empty and forlorn. Battered by twenty winters of
shrieking blizzards off Bering Sea, the jerry-built structures sagged badly
out of plumb, propped up with two by fours like tired old men leaning on
their canes. Boardwalks resting on the soggy tundra squirted water up
through cracks and broken boards at my every step. On my way through
town a pack of loose sled dogs bounding down the narrow road spattered
dirty water on my Sunday pants.

During the few days the *Victoria* would be anchored off Nome Beach
"lightering" freight through the shallow breakers, we round-trippers were
free to meander through the famous old gold camp. I had a special mission.
I'd promised to make inquiries about a lost uncle who in 1897 had up and
quit his steady job as a Boston shoe clerk to join the Klondike Stampede.
There'd been reports that Uncle Charles had later left Dawson to float down
the Yukon River for the big strike at Nome, and then there was no more
word. Nobody had heard from him in several years, and the members of the
family weren't sure he was alive. Other passengers were likewise ferreting
around for vanished kinfolks, but I hit paydirt first.

A stubble-faced Goliath in Stetson hat and rubber boots bellied out through the sagging doors of a place called the Board of Trade and came clumping down the sidewalk. He looked like one of those shaggy characters from "The Shooting of Dan McGrew"; one who had tramped across many a far place. When we met head on, I asked him if in all his travels he'd ever run into a man named Charles Rice. The tipsy giant rolled back on his heels as if I'd kicked him in the shins, and roared loud enough to halt all foot traffic in Nome.

"CHARLEY RICE!" He started to shove me off the boardwalk, then stopped to peer suspiciously. "Ya' tryin' t' get smart with me, sonny?" Lumbering off down the spurting sidewalk, he bellowed a final remark over his shoulder. "HELL, CHARLEY'S MAYOR OF THE TOWN!"

So, I quickly found the lost uncle, and that night I stayed ashore to bunk on his spare cot. He told me he'd several times struck enough gold to return home and buy his own bootery, as he'd planned, but in the process he'd lost all interest in selling shoes, or ever seeing Boston again. "This is the land, boy," he said. "Right here around Nome. Gold all over. Only the cream has been skimmed. You'll make your stake in no time, young fellow."

I told him I'd have to make it pretty quick, because I was due to sail south again as soon as the steamer finished unloading. Uncle Charley was speechless for a moment, staring at me as though he suspected all the weak-minded blood in the family had settled in this one nephew. In his probing blue eyes, his bulging muscles, his out-thrust black-bearded chin, I saw a man who would never again be content to bow and scrape and polish his hands before lady shoe customers. Something very drastic had happened to him. He'd changed to fit the new country, and I liked what I saw.

He took me for a stroll down Front Street which ran within a few feet of the thundering surf, past all the half-collapsed wooden buildings. They'd looked dismal when I first saw them. Now, under Uncle Charley's reminiscing, the ramshackle places seemed to straighten up on their old foundations and come alive with history.

On our left, the lettering "Northern" still could be made out through the flaking paint. Here, said Uncle Charley, his friend Tex Rickard used to run a square gambling hall and pour whiskey fit for a man to drink. "We served on Nome's first city council together," remembered Uncle Charley. "Good man for the country. Maybe he'll come back some day after he gets through promoting all those prize fights down in the States."

A great barn of a place, heaved out of shape by the frost, held special memories for Uncle Charley. It marked Nome's once famous Eagle Hall where musicians and actors from as far away as New York came to entertain with concerts and stage shows. It was also the center of local talent perfor mances. "Before he wrote that book about the Spoilers, a young fellow named Rex Beach used to put on blackface skits in there," said Uncle Charley. "I like to died laughing at him. The town lost its best end man in the minstrel shows when Rex took up writing for a living."

I could hear pool balls clicking when we passed the swinging doors of a place called the Nevada. Tourists stood watching a couple of halfbreed Eskimo boys idly knocking the balls around. To Uncle Charley it was noth ing now. But take it a few years back. . . . "Bartender in there was a man who used to be marshal somewhere in the southwest, name of Wyatt Earp. Guess he was the only real gun man in camp. You'd see him walking along the beach flinging empty whiskey bottles in the air and smashing them with his six-shooters. Didn't stay in Nome but a short time; went back to Nevada or California or somewhere."

Uncle Charley had seen an endless parade of important people pass through Nome. He'd met Jack London, already a famous author when he boated down the Yukon to catch a steamer to San Francisco. There'd been Frank Gotch, the wrestling champion, meeting all comers and pinning their shoulders to the mat with the greatest of ease. Prizefighter Jack Twin Sullivan, fighting under assumed names, had barnstormed the gold camps, knocking local hopefuls stiff. Roald Amundsen, Norwegian South Pole dis coverer, was a familiar figure around Nome with his big eagle-beak nose, his Homburg hat and tight-fitting gray suit, and courtly manners. Through the years, Uncle Charley had greeted big name globetrotters; dukes and counts, potentates and grand poobahs from all over the world coming to look at a real gold camp.

Go back to the smug obscurity of a New England bootery? Not Uncle Charley! Not while Nome needed him (though he didn't get a penny for serving as mayor); not while there was gold hiding right under the grass roots waiting to be found! Why, all you had to do was strap a pick and gold pan on a packboard, go out there on the tundra, and look for it!

That's what he had me doing next day, and in style. In the days of the Spoilers a narrow-gage railroad led for miles across the flat tundra to the foothills and up through the bare mountains. Like Nome itself, the flimsy affair had fallen to ruin, its light-weight rails warped into fantastic curves. Snowslides had carried away entire sections, while across the swaybacked trestles the rails dangled perilously.

To negotiate this roller-coaster horror, Uncle Charley had contrived a railroad buggy of sorts from the wheels and axles of abandoned equipment, and used it to exercise his sled dogs during the short Arctic summer. After we'd loaded a prospecting outfit aboard, and with the mayor's guiding hand on the brake, the dogs took us on a wild ride to the hills, careening, twisting, jumping the rails, splashing through bogholes in clouds of spray. Uncle Charley kept pointing with his free hand at old gravel piles overgrown with weeds where some early day prospector had hit it rich. Right over there Joe Brown made his fortune in a single summer. On the other side of the tracks a character named Snakehead Dooley had taken out a cool million and headed back to Ireland with it to kiss the Blarney rock again. Nobody had missed; they'd all hit it big.

But I had a hard time paying proper attention to all these success stories. What took my eye were the chattering "sic-sic" spotted squirrels scooting tails-up ahead of the racing dogs and scuttling into their burrows just in time. Little birds called longspurs, fluttered aloft like skylarks, singing their heads off as they slowly parachuted back to earth. Flocks of sandpipers, hook-billed curlews and robin-breasted dowitchers whipped around our heads, whistling their shrill alarms. Between knee-high tussocks grew carpets of salmonberry vines loaded with luscious soft berries that looked like clusters of salmon eggs. Brilliantly colored wildflowers were everywhere; patches of cotton-tipped sedges and masses of bright blue forget-me-nots. Never had I seen the likes of the wild mushrooms—acres of scarlet capped russulas, boletas, and giant puffballs! Every pool had its pair or two of ducks with broods of half-grown young flapping into the weeds.

At the base of Anvil Mountain we passed an active mining operation; streams of water from giant hydraulic nozzles cutting away a hundred feet of overlying frozen muck to lay bare an ancient shore of Bering Sea. Uncle Charley said that gangs of "shovel-stiffs" had in earlier years heaved enough pay dirt into old-style sluice boxes to make a dozen millionaires. Now, mining syndicates were getting ready to ship some big dredges up from California to rework this same third beach line. They'd take out more and more millions, he admitted, but it wouldn't be like finding new gold. That was the real challenge! Prospectors like him were still looking for the source of all this wealth; some place back in the mountains from which the nuggets had been flushed by floods in ages past; some place richer than anything yet uncovered in the Nome country; a mother lode just waiting for the lucky man to find it!

Uncle Charley was thinking of this hidden pot of gold, not the scenery, when he halted the pupmobile on a high dome, staked the sled dogs in a patch of scrub willows alongside an alpine rill, and tossed them each their daily ration of one dried salmon. "They'll be all right until tomorrow night," he said, as he busied himself stowing paraphernalia into a couple of packsacks.

I turned to look back over the way we had come, and the sight was enough to make a man's breath catch in his throat. An immense, colorful panorama of tundra stretched for more miles than I could see across a tree-less expanse, dotted with hundreds—no, thousands of potholes winking in the afternoon sun. Creeks and rivers looped in endless convolutions across the boggy muskeg to the turbid sea, and Bering Sea itself curved away past the coast of Siberia, lurking in the haze, and on into infinity across the top of the world. In this grandeur of unpeopled space, Nome was but a dot of coal-smoke smudging out on its once golden sands, fading away in the past. From our far distance, all the rest—the deserted, wind-torn miners' shacks and puny gravel heaps—looked to be all but reclaimed by the wilderness, so that it looked like it was in the beginning. It was profoundly moving. Before I weighed my words, I blurted out to Uncle Charley, "No wonder you never came home from the Gold Rush!"

Uncle Charley didn't seem to hear me. His mind was on the present. "Hold still a minute," he ordered. I stood like a horse while he flung a loaded packsack across my withers, cinched up on the surcingle, and made motions like putting a bit between my teeth. He finished draping the load with assorted items like picks, shovels, gold pans, skillet and gun, then gave me a final slap on the rump. "Giddup, Dobbin!" he said. "We got a few miles to go before making camp."

He shouldered a somewhat bigger pack and led the way around the mountain to where a sizable flow of water came thundering down a rocky chute to plunge into a deep pool before leveling off across the tundra. Melt-ing summer snow and every rainstorm sluiced fresh deposits of sand and gravel out of the high country. Uncle Charley said that some day he hoped to find this river hole loaded with "color." That would be the day to trace the upstream source, testing with samples of dirt in his gold pan until he found where it came out of the ground.

We shucked our packs, and I watched the pioneer prospector kneel at the water's edge, expertly dipping and twirling until the lighter material was carried away over the lip of the shallow pan. I leaned close to see what remained. A couple of pin-point yellowish flecks glinted in the bottom. Uncle Charley tilted the gold pan into the current and let them wash away. "We'll try it again," he said.

It wasn't any use—not this time, anyway. Colors, yes, but definitely not the big find. He sampled several other places along the shoreline with similar results. There would be no baring of the adenoids and shouts of "Eureka!" on this trip. Uncle Charley was only mildly let down. He'd panned thousands of creeks without finding a sign of gold. It was all part of being a prospector. This one was, temporarily, just another blank.

But not to me! Never had I seen a better fishing hole. A run of bright blue salmon had moved in from Bering Sea until they were blocked from further upstream migration by the falls, and now the air was full of them trying to leap the obstruction. Among the milling salmon were schools of red-spotted trout, and a fish called a grayling with fan-shaped dorsal fins, color-speckled like miniature peacock tails. There wasn't the slightest sign of a fisherman's boot heel, and the thought of it nearly drove me out of my mind, because in all our back-packed gear there wasn't a scrap of angling material.

Uncle Charley took care of that in his own way. He waded out into the shallow end of the pool, and when a salmon swam past he swung a shovel and bashed it on the head.

I helped him pitch the begrimed, spark-holed tent he'd carried on many a stampede, then spread sleeping bags on a natural mattress of gray reindeer moss inside. We rigged the sheet-iron stove and Uncle Charley crumbled dry willow twigs, and lit the fire with an old-fashioned sulphur match torn off a thin, wooden comb. While he was mixing a batch of biscuits from his sourdough starter, he had me gathering a bowl of sugar-sweet blueberries to stir in the batter. By the time they were browned, the coffee pot was boiling over, and the red slabs of salmon were smoking in the skillet with a tantalizing aroma.

Afterward, we lay in our sleeping bags looking out the open tent flap while the sun dipped down like a great blob of molten copper into the pale green Bering Sea. In its dying rays of magenta and deep purple, we watched an enormous migration of sandhill cranes float down from the sky like five thousand open umbrellas and settle with noisy clamor on the hills around us. I told Uncle Charley that this was the feature of his Alaska that stirred me deepest; not the gold, but the primitive land itself with its exciting plenitude of wild things; that if I stayed, this was what would hold me.

Tisha

ROBERT SPECHT

Robert Specht is a California-based writer and editor. TISHA: THE STORY OF
A YOUNG TEACHER IN THE ALASKA WILDERNESS *(1976) is based on a true
story. "Tisha," the Athabascan students' way of pronouncing "teacher," is
Anne Hobbs, who arrived in Alaska in 1927 at the age of nineteen to teach
school in the wilderness gold-rush community of Chicken. In this excerpt,
Anne Hobbs stubbornly confronts relentless winter cold, frontier provinciality,
and racial prejudice.*

If there's one thing that fires up a class for the day's work, I'd found,
it's some good rousing singing the first thing in the morning. And this
class was no exception. Right after we went through *Yankee Doodle*
and a few other songs, I started my two beginners out with some
busywork, then gave reading-comprehension tests to a few of the
older kids. While they were busy I worked with Isabelle and Elvira on long
division.

In the middle of it Willard got bored with what he was doing and started
scaring little Joan by telling her a bear was going to get her next time she
went to the outhouse, so I had to separate them temporarily.

About mid-morning Merton Atwood showed up. He was even quieter
than Uncle Arthur, glancing down shyly every time I happened to look his
way. He watched Elvira do a long-division example at the board, then
Isabelle, but when my oldest boy, Robert, did an example I saw him raise
his hand.

"Mr. Atwood?"

"Mert." He shifted uncomfortably.

"Mert."

"How come that didn't come out even?" he asked me, pointing to the
board.

"That's long division with a remainder," I said. "You come out with a
fraction."

He stayed until lunchtime. The example was still on the board and he went up and stared at it. "That easy to learn?" he asked me.

"Long division? Easy as pie."

"Alwuz been in'risted in learnin' that. Alwuz wan-ned to, but never did."

"Come by after school some time and I'll show you."

"I might do that," he said. "I just might."

"You could do me a favor too."

"What's that?"

"Could you draw me a simple map of Chicken here on the board with a dot to show where everybody in the class lives?"

He did it for me. He drew in Chicken Creek and then drew lines for the two other creeks that Joan Simpson and Robert Merriweather lived on. After lunch I told the class about the project I had in mind. "It's something we can all work on together," I said. "We're going to make a map of Chicken, something like this one, but bigger. We're going to use one whole wall for it. Everybody can draw a little picture of their own cabin and we'll put it up in the right place."

They liked that idea, of having the place they lived in and their name right up where everybody could see them. "But that's only part of the project," I said. "What we'll do is find out all about Chicken—its history and geography, what grows here, what's produced here, everything. After that we'll find out about other places."

"But there's nothing to know about this place," Jimmy said. "There's nothing here."

"Oh, I can think of a dozen things I'd like to know about it. Just one, for instance—does anybody know how Chicken got its name?"

Nobody did, so I asked Robert Merriweather if he'd ask around and write a report on it. He said he would. Then we decided that the next day we'd go on our first field trip to collect leaves and rocks and any other interesting things we could find.

After school, as the children went out the door, there was a roly-poly Indian woman waiting on the porch. She was bundled up in a light blue flannel coat that was made out of a blanket, and she had a little girl with her. "How you do, Tisha," she said. "My name Rebekah Harrin'ton. I come see you."

"I'm glad to meet you," I said. "Come on in."

"This my kid," she said when we were in my quarters. "Lily. Lily, you say how you do."

Lily peered up at me from under a peaked hat of wolf fur. I could barely see her eyes under it. "How you do," she said. She was charming.

Mrs. Harrington put a paper sack down on the table. She took out a few pounds of dried salmon. "F'you. Present."

"Thank you. I was just about to have some tea. Would you like some?"

"I like. Yes." I took her coat. She sat down and made herself comfortable, hitching her skirt up a little. She had on a couple of other skirts underneath it. "You got nice place," she said.

"Thanks to Fred Purdy."

"Ah, Fred he good boy, you make bet on that. Whole Purdy family got good people. Everybody like."

It took her a few minutes to get around to why she'd come, and it was just what I was hoping for. She wanted to enroll Lily in school. "You not got too much lotsa kids now?"

"Not at all. I don't have enough. How old is Lily?"

"Fo'. He be fi' soon—Janawary."

When she said "he" I looked at Lily again to make sure she was a little girl. She was. "She's a little young," I said, "but I think it'll be all right."

"Oh, he be one smart kid my Lily," she assured me. "Learn like hell. Already he write A, B, F, P—many alphabets. My husbin Jake he teach." All of a sudden she became sad. "Only one bad thing, Tisha. Lily he scare come school all alone heself. Need Momma."

"You can sit with her till she gets used to it."

"You mean it?"

"Of course." With all the old-timers who'd been coming in I couldn't see any harm being done.

Her grin was as big as sunshine. "You one helluva good joe, Tisha. I come with Lily tomorrow."

The next morning they were almost the first ones to arrive. After the Pledge of Allegiance I told the class that Lily was going to be their new classmate. "She's a little shy," I said, "so I'd like you to be especially nice to her."

"How about *her*?" Jimmy Carew said, pointing to Rebekah. "She comin' too?"

"Until Lily gets used to school and can come on her own."

There were some snickers.

"Is anything wrong?" I asked. But nobody said anything.

I didn't think anything more about it, and once we got down to work the class didn't either, but the next day Evelyn Vaughn told me that her father said the school board wanted to have a meeting right after school.

The three of them came into my quarters looking solemn—Maggie Carew, Angela Barrett and Mr. Vaughn. I was surprised to see Angela on the board since she didn't have any children. I asked them if they'd like some coffee or tea, but they said no. The four of us sat around the table and Mr. Vaughn rapped his knuckles on it. "The meeting will come to order," he said.

They asked me a couple of questions about what I'd been doing, and I told them about the project. They didn't seem too impressed. Mr. Vaughn got right to it. "How come you're letting that Indian woman come to school?" he said.

"Mrs. Harrington? She's just sitting with Lily."

"Is that what she told you?"

"Yes. She said that Lily was a little scared to come by herself, so I said it would be all right if she sat with her until Lily was used to it."

"Well, we don't like it," Angela said.

"She's not bothering the class at all," I said. "She's quiet as a mouse."

"We want 'er kicked out," Angela said sharply.

"And the kid along with her," Mr. Vaughn added.

I was stunned. "Lily? But why?"

"She's under age. A kid has to be over five and under sixteen to go to this school. You know that."

"I know, but does it matter that much?"

"It matters to us," Mr. Vaughn said. "You have enough to do to teach our own kids properly without wasting time on some little siwash that doesn't belong here."

"I don't think it's doing any harm to let her come," I said to Maggie Carew. She hadn't said anything up to now and I had the feeling she'd be more receptive than the other two. "She's a bright little girl, and besides that we don't even have a full enrollment. We're supposed to have ten and all we have is eight."

"The law is that this school is for kids from five to sixteen," Mr. Vaughn said before Maggie could answer, "and the law's the law. Let's take a vote on it. I vote that Lily Harrington, being too young to attend this school, be expelled. How do you two vote?"

"I vote the same way," Angela said.

"Maggie?"

"You got a majority already," Maggie said. "You don't need mine."

"We'd like to make it unanimous."

"I'm all for throwin' Rebekah out," she said, "but I don't care about the kid one way or the other."

"You abstain?"

"Yeah." She didn't seem too happy about the whole thing.

"You've got your orders," Mr. Vaughn said to me. "See that you carry them out."

After they left I sat thinking about it. I couldn't believe it—that people could act that way. Just because someone was an Indian. I was ashamed of them. And I was ashamed of myself too. If I'd had any guts I'd have told them off, let them know what I thought of them. But I didn't. I'd let them buffalo me because I was new and I'd been scared of them. Now I had to tell Mrs. Harrington her little girl couldn't come to school.

I asked her to stay after school the next day, then I told her. The look on her face made me wish I was a thousand miles away. She knew as well as I did why the school board didn't want Lily, but all she said was, "He sure like go school my Lily."

"I know. I'm going to write to the commissioner about it, Mrs. Harrington. I'm going to ask him if he can make an exception in Lily's case. I'm sure he will. In the meantime, if you want to, you could bring Lily over here after school a couple of times a week and I could tutor her."

"What tooda, Tisha?"

"Teach. I could teach her here in my quarters a couple of times every week."

"You do that?"

"I'll be glad to. Let's make it every Monday and Thursday right after school. You can learn at the same time."

She smiled. "Tisha, you make me too much happy. You bet we come!" She went out beaming.

That wasn't the end of it, though, because the next morning, right after we finished singing, Rebekah and Lily showed up again. With them was a big man, Rebekah's husband Jake, and all I needed was one look at him to know there was going to be a storm. He was as nice as could be to me, though. He took off his Stetson and said he was pleased to meet me. Then he asked me what swivel-eyed jackass said his little girl couldn't come to school.

I took him into my quarters and explained the whole thing to him.

"The school board, eh. . . . Well, little lady, I gather *you* don't have any objections to my little girl gettin' educated."

"None at all."

"You sit tight then, while I have a little talk with the school board."

He slammed out of my quarters and went right next door to Mr. Vaughn. We could hear everything that happened from the schoolroom. He pounded on Mr. Vaughn's door and what followed after that was probably the finest and most eloquent cussing I'd heard since I was a little girl in Blazing Rag. It started off with him calling Mr. Vaughn a mangy, misbegotten, worm-eaten egg-sucker and went on improving with every sentence. Not one of us in that classroom said a word the whole time. All we could do was marvel at it. There were a couple of silences in between the cussing, but it went on gathering steam for about five minutes without one word being repeated. "Now you potbellied, yelping, walleyed sonofabitch," Mr. Harrington finished off, "is my little girl goin' to school or ain't she?"

We couldn't hear what Mr. Vaughn said, but not ten seconds later Mr. Harrington strode back in as red as the smoked salmon Rebekah had brought me. "Little lady," he said, "Mr. Vaughn said that if it's all right with you, the school board would be pleased to have Lily attend your class." He even remembered to take off his hat.

"I'd be delighted, Mr. Harrington."

"How about you?" He asked Rebekah. "You want to give me a hand takin' out the sluice box or park here for a while?"

"I come help you, Jake," Rebekah said proudly.

"Well then let's go, woman. There's work to do."

I'd have kicked my heels together and jumped up and down if I'd been alone. The whole thing couldn't have worked out better if I'd planned it. Lily was in school, Mr. Vaughn got what was coming to him, and I was off the spot with the school board.

For the next few days everything went fine. The class really took to the idea of the map of Chicken. It started us talking about all the different kinds of maps there were, treasure maps and world maps, weather maps, and produce maps. We decided that since we had a whole wall to use we ought to show not only where everybody lived, but some of the things we'd found on our field trip. We'd come back loaded with treasures—birch and cottonwood leaves, samples of willow and alder, and rocks galore. Elvira Vaughn had even found a piece of black silicon with a shell fossil in it. After some discussion we decided to put some of them up on the map. The rest we'd make up books about—leaf books and fur-sample books, animal-picture books and food books. The project began to take on shape. When it was finished, we decided, we'd invite everybody in Chicken to come and see what we'd done. The class was so enthusiastic about it that I had trouble bringing them back to their regular lessons.

Robert Merriweather's report turned out to be excellent and I tacked it on the wall.

HOW CHICKEN GOT ITS NAME

Chicken got its name from the first prospectors who came here. There was a lot of Ptarmigans here and they thanked God for it because they were hungry. They were so grateful they wanted to name this place Ptarmigan, but they couldn't spell it. They named it good old American Chicken instead. This is what Uncle Arthur said.

Mert Atwood says this isn't true. Chicken got it's name because they found gold nuggets as big as chicken corn here.

No one can ever know the real truth, I guess.

Inside of a few days the schoolroom began to feel like one, with pictures and lesson papers all over the walls, our rock collection on one of the shelves, and a little herb garden sitting in tin cans on one of the window sills. Not that we didn't have our troubles. With everybody doing different things in one room there were bound to be arguments. When my three beginners were restless they'd get in everybody's hair. Willard would bother the older children or start scaring Joan and Lily by telling them about a wolf coming into their cabin some night to eat them up. They'd begin to cry, disturbing the others, so I'd have to find coloring work or something else for them all to do, or let Willard go home for a little while.

Aside from that the only other problem was interruptions. Everybody in and around the settlement seemed to feel the school was the one place open to the public any time. Mr. Strong had told everybody I had the key to his store, so every so often someone would come in wanting to buy something. A few times it was people like Angela, who lived in the settlement, and I was able to tell them to come back after school, but a couple of other times it was people who lived some distance away, like Joe, and I had to leave the class. I finally posted a notice on the school door saying no goods could be purchased at the store during school hours.

On Friday still a third old-timer wandered in. His name was Ben Norvall, a wrinkled old basset hound of a man with drooping moustaches. He was just about the most well-spoken individual I'd met here so far. He could quote Shakespeare by the yard and he offered to lend us his whole set of Shakespeare's works if we promised to take care of it. The only bad thing about him was that he looked and smelled something awful. I mentioned him to Maggie Carew and she told me not to let him in again.

"If you do," she said, "you're ruinin' it for the rest of us. No one's lettin' him in until he burns those clothes he's got on and takes a bath. As long as he's got a place to go he won't do it."

By the time the first week was over I felt pretty good. As far as I could tell the class was really interested in what they were doing and they liked coming to school. The only trouble I could see I might have was teaching Robert arithmetic. He was pretty good, and I'd have to do some studying to keep ahead of him. Aside from that I was pretty optimistic.

I shouldn't have been though, because on Monday I was in trouble with the school board again. This time it was over Chuck. He showed up Monday morning about fifteen minutes before school. Robert had already started the fire in the schoolroom stove, and I was inside my quarters making my bed. Outside, Jimmy Carew was tossing a ball against the porch base and talking with the Vaughn girls. All of a sudden he stopped and there was silence, until Jimmy said, "Where'd *you* come from?"

"From Louse Town," Evelyn Vaughn said.

"Who is he?" Jimmy asked her.

"Mary Angus' kid."

"You talk English?" Jimmy asked him.

"Yiss," Chuck said.

"Whattaya want here?"

"Come school."

"Like hell you are," Evelyn said. "This is a white school."

"I come here."

"Who says so?"

"Tisha, she say I come."

" 'Tisha'? Who the hell's Tisha?"

"He means Teacher."

"I know what he means."

I went outside. "Good morning, everybody," I said. "Hello, Chuck—nice to see you here finally. How are you feeling?"

He looked down at the ground and mumbled, "Good."

He looked anything but good, though. He was thinner than ever and his lips were all chapped. His clothes didn't help any. His mackinaw was so small his wrists stuck out and his pants were so big the bottoms were ragged from scraping the ground.

We had the Pledge of Allegiance inside because it was so cold out that ice bridges were forming all along the edges of the creek. After we sang I introduced Chuck, gave him a seat and started everybody working. When they were all busy I took him over in a corner and gave him a second-grade reader to read from for me. He didn't do well with it, but he did fine when I tried him with a first-grade reader. His arithmetic wasn't bad either.

The class was restless that morning, too many of them preoccupied with giving each other looks about him. A couple of times he got hit by a spit-ball, but I couldn't see who did it.

During recess the older kids wanted to play dodge ball. After we showed Chuck how to play I took my three young ones on the side to play with them. After just a few minutes had gone by, the dodge ball game got out of hand. I didn't see it until it was too late. By the time I stepped in Chuck's nose was bleeding, and he was crying. They'd made him "it." I took him into my quarters, and after the bleeding stopped and he was cleaned up, I called everybody back inside. "Who started the rough stuff?" I asked Robert.

"Nobody," he said. "We all just did it."

"I'm surprised at you. You should have stopped it."

"It wasn't my fault. They don't want him."

"Who's 'they'?"

He didn't answer.

"Well let me tell you something—all of you. Whoever 'they' are, if 'they' do anything like this again, 'they' are going to be in trouble."

During vocabulary with the older children I gave Evelyn Vaughn the word "intelligent" to put into a sentence.

"Siwashes aren't very intelligent," she recited. A few of the older kids giggled.

"Can you tell me what the word siwash means?" I asked her.

"Sure. It's a dirty low-down black Injun."

More giggles. I felt like throttling her. "There are certain words," I said, "which I don't want to hear in this class room. One of them is siwash."

"What's wrong with it, Teacher?" Jimmy asked. "Everybody says it."

"It's a mean word—like hunkie or nigger or kike. Now," I asked Eleanor, "do you think you can find another sentence for me?"

"How about if I said *Indians* aren't very intelligent?"

"Do you really think that's true?"

"I sure do," she answered.

"All Indians?"

She nodded.

"How about people who are only part Indian?"

"You mean like half-breeds? I guess so," she said.

"I should tell you," I said, "that my own grandmother was an Indian. That makes me part Indian too. Do you think there's anything wrong with my intelligence?"

Eleanor shifted uncomfortably. "No."

"Is that really true, Teacher?" Jimmy said.

"Yes, it is."

"What kind of an Indian was she?" Elvira Vaughn said.

"Kentuck."

"I never heard of that kind."

"They're like any other kind—Comanche or Sioux, any kind of Indian."

"Oh, well," Jimmy said. "They're *American* Indians. They're different from the ones we got here."

"Why?"

"They just are."

"If they are it's not very much. Indians are Indians, and there are all kinds."

"Was your grandmother like these Indians?"

"I'll tell you the truth," I said. "If you saw her in the Indian village you'd think she was one of them."

"How come you don't look Indian then?"

"I guess I take after my grandfather. He was white."

"*That's* why you're smart enough to be a teacher."

"Not necessarily. My grandmother was a pretty smart woman. A lot of people said she was smarter than my grandfather."

Robert Merriweather hadn't said anything up to then. He raised his hand. "If your grandmother was an Indian," he said logically, "then your father was a half-breed."

"I guess that's right. But you know something? Where I come from nobody cared about it. As a matter of fact whenever anybody found out I was part Indian they thought that was a pretty interesting thing to be. . . . Now we've got work to do, but just remember, what people are doesn't matter, whether they're Indian or Irish or Negro or anything else—they're just people."

When school was over for the day, Chuck hung around for a few minutes. "You tell truth, Tisha?" he asked me. "You Indian?"

"I'm part Indian, yes."

"You make moccasin?"

"No. I don't know how to do that."

"Cut fish?"

"Not too well."

"Trap?"

"I'm afraid not."

He thought it all over. "Funny Indian," he murmured.

Elvira Vaughn knocked at my door right after supper that night. She was all embarrassed. "My father said to tell you that me and my sisters won't be coming to school tomorrow," she said.

"How come?"

"My father said you'd know why."

I didn't sleep too well that night, and the next morning I was up at five. I did some washing just to keep busy, then I brought some wood in. By 8:30, when Robert arrived to start the fire, I was in the schoolroom putting some work on the board and listening for anybody who'd be coming. At a quarter to nine Isabelle Purdy and Joan Simpson arrived just as I went out to ring the hand bell for the first time. A few minutes later Rebekah brought Lily in, and right after that Chuck arrived. The Vaughn girls didn't show up at all. And neither did Willard and Jimmy. At nine I went out and rang the bell for late call, but there was nobody in sight. The settlement was quiet.

During recess I saw Willard and Jimmy playing up by the roadhouse. I decided to go over and talk to them, but as soon as I headed in their direction they ran indoors.

I tried to go on as if it was just a normal day, but every time I'd look at those five empty chairs I felt miserable. After school I must have sat for an hour drinking tea and trying to think what to do. Finally I threw on a sweater and went next door to the Vaughn cabin.

Mr. Vaughn opened the door.

"I wonder if I could talk with you for a few minutes?" I asked him.

"What about?"

"About the girls not being in school today."

"What about it?"

"Well, I know they're not sick. I wondered why they were absent."

"I kept them home."

"Will they be in school tomorrow?"

"We'll see," he said. Then he closed the door.

I stood there looking at the closed door, feeling like a little girl who'd done something awful. I started over to the roadhouse, then I changed my mind. I just didn't have the guts to stare into another face that might look at me as if I was a stone. So I went back to my quarters and stared at the walls for another hour.

I hadn't done anything wrong, but I still felt guilty. They were the ones who were wrong—Maggie and Angela and Mr. Vaughn. They were all wrong. They had no right to keep Chuck or Lily or any other little kid out of the school just because they thought they were dirt. There were plenty of people who'd thought I was dirt when I was a kid. I could even remember one teacher who used to favor the kids who came to school dressed in nice clothes. She was always calling on them and smiling at them, while she looked at the ones like me as if we were trash. She'd even made me wear a sign one day when she found lice in my head during health inspection. I'd gotten them from playing with two kids next door and I'd never had them before, but she made me sit in the corner all day wearing a cardboard sign with "Dirty" printed on it. As long as I lived I'd never forget that. Or her. I'd hated her from then on.

I tried to think what I'd do if I was Miss Ivy, but it didn't help at all. She just wasn't the kind of person you fooled around with. She'd have gone right up to Mr. Vaughn and Maggie Carew and told them she expected to see their children in school the next day and no nonsense about it, and that would have been that. By suppertime I couldn't even think about eating. I decided that I'd wait till after supper, then I'd go over and talk to Maggie. The idea of going through another day, and maybe more, with less than half a class was unbearable.

Maggie saved me the trouble, though. Just before six Jimmy knocked at the door. "My mother says is it all right if the school board comes over after supper?"

"Sure. You can tell her 7:30 would be fine."

Before 7:30 came I went through a half a dozen conversations with them, and if I was able to say half the things I'd thought of I'd get a speech prize. I gave them quotes from the Declaration of Independence, the Bill of Rights and the Ten Commandments and ended with some beautiful phrases about how education was the birthright of all Americans. As soon as they trooped in, right on the dot, though, I felt just as tongue-tied as I'd been on the first day of school. They were grim. They turned me down when I offered them tea.

I had the stove going really hot so they'd be comfortable. Angela Barrett took off her sweater right away and my eyes nearly popped out. Her arms had so many tattoos they looked like an art gallery.

"I prepared the minutes of the last meeting," Mr. Vaughn said, opening a composition book. "I'll read them."

"We can do without that," Maggie said.

"We're supposed to read the minutes," Mr. Vaughn said.

"What for?" Maggie said. "We know what we said."

"Are you making a motion that we waive them?"

"Wave 'em, fry 'em or boil 'em, I don't care. Let's get to what we come for."

Mr. Vaughn cleared his throat. "We'd like to know on what grounds you've taken Joe Temple's half-breed into the school."

"The same grounds on which I'd take any pupil in, Mr. Vaughn."

"He doesn't belong here. If you weren't a cheechako you'd know that. He belongs in the Indian village school."

"But he's not *in* the Indian village now."

"That has nothing to do with it. He shouldn't be in the same school with our children."

"I don't want to argue with you, but I don't see on what grounds you want to keep him out."

"According to the law," Mr. Vaughn said, "this school is open to, and I quote, 'white children and children of mixed blood who lead a civilized life.' You are aware of the law, I take it."

"Oh yes," I lied.

"Then there's your ground—'children of mixed blood *who lead a civilized life.*' That kid isn't civilized. None of those Indians from that village are."

Now that it came right down to it, faced with the three of them I wasn't feeling as brave as I thought I would.

"Well?" Mr. Vaughn said.

"Isn't that your interpretation, Mr. Vaughn? Chuck can read, he can write, as far as I can see he's like any other little boy who—"

Maggie cut me off. "My kid says he can't even talk civilized." This time she was in agreement with them.

"Besides that he's a bastard," Angela said.

"I hadn't even thought about that," Mr. Vaughn said.

"I don't see how I can do what you're asking," I said.

"Oh, you don't," Mr. Vaughn said.

"No. I just can't tell that little boy to get out of class for no good reason." And you wouldn't make me tell him either, I thought, if Chuck had a father who'd knock your block off.

"You've been given the reason. We're telling you the reason. We're not running a school for uncivilized siwashes and the law will back us up. Now are you going to tell him or do I have to do it myself?"

"I can't."

"Then I'll do it for you. We'd better take a vote on it to show we're doing it lawfully. I make a motion that the half-breed child known as Charles Temple be excluded from the school on the grounds that he does not lead a civilized life. How do you two vote?"

Maggie and Angela said aye.

"That settles it," Mr. Vaughn said.

Maybe it settled it for them, but it didn't for me. I was so mad I could have thrown the stove at them.

"We don't want you to have any hard feelin's, Annie," Maggie said. "We're just tryin'a show you what's best. You're still new here, ya know."

"I know."

"I'll take that tea if you're still offerin'."

I served her and Angela some. Mr. Vaughn didn't want any.

"Want you to know my kids think you're a good teacher, too." Maggie said, taking a sip.

"If there's no further business," Mr. Vaughn said, "we can close this meeting."

Not as far as I was concerned. Without my even having to think about it I heard myself say, "It's too bad I had to come all the way out here for nothing."

"How's that?" Mr. Vaughn said.

"I'm going to have to close the school."

About to take another sip, Maggie made a sound into her cup and put it down quickly. "You what?"

"I'll have to close the school," I repeated.

Mr. Vaughn's eyes narrowed. "What are you talking about?"

"I don't have enough of an enrollment," I said. I had to hold my hands tight in my lap, they were shaking so much.

"You got plenty enrollment," Maggie said.

"No I haven't," I said, trying to keep my voice even. It sounded to me as if I was squeaking. "Under the law there has to be ten pupils."

"You got my two boys, his three girls, the Merriweather kid, Simpson's little girl, and Isabelle and Lily."

"That only makes nine."

"I hear Nancy Prentiss is coming out. That'll make ten."

"*If* she comes out. Right now there's only nine."

"Well, so what?" Maggie said. "That's just a technicality. Plenty of schools don't make the enrollment." She snorted. "If you hadda rely on a full enrollment all the time there'd never be a school in the bush."

"I don't know anything about that," I said, "but this is my first teaching job in Alaska and I don't want to start out by breaking the law." My hands were sweating and my heart was pounding so loud I thought they could all hear it.

Maggie stared at me for a long moment as the point got home to her. Mad and disgusted, she pulled in one side of her mouth. "You telling us you'd pack up and git?"

"That's what I'd have to do, Mrs. Carew."

"You're bluffing," Mr. Vaughn said.

"No I'm not. You told me yourself—the law is the law."

He was so mad I was afraid he might smack me or something. "You dirty little snotnose," he snarled. "How dare you give us an ultimatum!"

"Simmer down, Arnold," Maggie said.

"Like hell I will." Even the veins on his goiter were standing out. "I never heard of anything like this in my life!"

"Will somebody please tell me what's going on?" Angela yelled.

"We're being blackmailed, that's what's going on," Mr. Vaughn said. "We've got a second Catherine Winters here—another Indian lover. I heard you're part siwash," he said to me, "now I believe it. For my part you can just pack up and get the hell out of here right now. As far as I'm concerned this meeting is adjourned." He walked out without saying another word.

Angela had her arms crossed in front of her. She didn't say anything, but her expression spoke worlds. It was pure hate.

"Angela, you go on back to the roadhouse," Maggie said. "I'll be there in a few minutes."

When she was gone Maggie said, "You're expectin' to teach in Eagle next year I take it."

"Yes."

"If I was you I wouldn't—not if you keep that little half-breed in the class. They got a school board there too. If they don't want you they don't have to take you. They're not gonna like it when they hear about this."

"There's not much I can do about that."

She got up. "You got gall, I'll say that much for ya—more gall than a Government mule. You're a good kid and I like ya, but I'm gonna tell ya something and I'll tell ya right to your face—don't go too far or you won't be teachin' in Eagle or anywhere else in Alaska next year. People are goin' to be writin' to the Commissioner about this, more people than you think. You're a little too interested in siwashes for your own good."

"I don't want any trouble, Mrs. Carew, but that little boy is entitled to—"

"Never mind what he's entitled to. Maybe you don't want trouble, but you got a peck of it right now."

"I didn't ask for it."

She buttoned up her coat. "You got it nevertheless. I'd advise you to watch your step. I'm willin' to look the other way on this. Other folks won't. You'll find that out."

She walked out without saying good-bye.

Only Come to Visit

TOM LINKLATER

Tom Linklater is a poet, fiction writer, and dramatist who lives in Juneau.
"Only Come to Visit" is his first published work.

I first got here in August, heard somethin', and asked a local:
"Eagle," she said, "flappin' its forty-foot wings once."
"Oh," I said.
Her parents had huge tomatas and a car up under a tarp
used only for smoochin' and smokin' fish, not drivin'.
Couple minutes later I saw another eagle swoop down
and eat take-out.
Then there was a bear in the other lane requestin' exact change.
Her parents said moose lived next door.
I asked: "What do you mean it's not gonna get dark tonight?"
Then I was a banker and a welder and a doctor.
A whale big as my uncle's farm jumped out of the water
in front of the municipal buildin', right downtown.
A porcupine slow danced with a broom in my kitchen.
Mountain goats wrote memos on my roof.
I started a radio station, built a sauna, and became Governor.
A bear ate my bicycle seat.
Two mosquitoes stole my car and rammed a tourist camper
out at the end of the road.
I found gold under my house, got frostbite, went drinkin' with wolves.
Finally, at the end of the week, I wrote to the folks back home
and said: "Whoo-eee, you gotta see! This here ain't Kansas."

Looking Back I Remember

J O A N N E   T O W N S E N D

Poet Joanne Townsend lives, writes, and teaches in Anchorage. Her poems have appeared in Harpoon, The Fireweed Journal, Interim, *and* Poetalk. *She was appointed Alaska's eighth poet laureate in 1988, and has been the recipient of an Alaska State Council on the Arts Individual Artist's Fellowship. "Looking Back I Remember" first appeared in* IN A DREAM (FOUR POETS) *(1991).*

How afraid I was, our first year here,
to walk on the frozen lake. I watched
the fishholes being cut, the snowmachines
whiz across, but couldn't trust.
"It's solid lady, down to ten, twelve feet,"
the oldtimer said. Easter Sunday we
drove to Portage. Families hiked
along the ice to the glacier, pilgrims,
blue sparks against that cold sun. I dreamed
forsythia, places where daffodils pushed
through warm loam. The pussy willows
brought false hope. It snowed in May.
Before the mirror I examined white
sprouts in my hair and pulled them,
root by stubborn root.

Radovin

TIM McNULTY

Tim McNulty is a poet and nature writer who lives with his family on Washington state's Olympic Peninsula. His poetry, which comes out of the natural landscape of the northwestern United States, is known for its simple, unaffected expression. The poem "Radovin," about the memories evoked in an old Alaska miner's cabin, was included in his 1992 poetry collection, IN BLUE MOUNTAIN DUSK.

Dying embers, Chitistone wind,
waiting out the weather
in an old miner's shack:
autumn mountain rain.

Across the creek,
long switchback up the cliffside,
packing it all on your back; bit
and powder charge, spring to fall,
every day a little deeper
into the glinting memories of earth.

By candlelight,
the rough-hewn walls and thin
plank shelves are still littered
with bank notices, forms
from the Bureau of Mines—tattered
and mouse-nibbled: Glacier Creek
via Cordova, 1964.

Stew simmers in your old pot,
the blackened iron stove.
I almost expect you to duck in
out of the rain,
Radovin,
park your lonely ghostly bones down
on a bench,
spit against the stove.

One by one
the empty bucket loads
roll past on the washed-out road.

Rainy mornings, cross-legged,
deeper into the bottomless mind—

No strike, no hidden vein,
just you and me, ghost, and the rain
over the slant tarpaper roof.
Was it
somewhere in the pick and shovel-bending
work of it
came the prize?

Or late afternoon at the tunnel-mouth,
shadows playing against high canyon walls,
an eagle
dropping from the snowy light.

III

Of Land, Sea, and Air

The Little Old Lady
Who Lived Alone

A T H A B A S C A N   L E G E N D

"The Little Old Lady Who Lived Alone" is an Athabascan legend, transcribed by linguist James Kari as retold by John W. Chapman. The transcription first appeared in Athabaskan Stories From Anvik *(1981), published by the Alaska Native Language Center at the University of Alaska Fairbanks, edited by James Kari and Jane McGary. The Alaska Native Language Center, founded in 1972, is devoted to the research and documentation of the state's Indian, Eskimo, and Aleut languages. James Kari has devoted more than twenty years to finding, transcribing, translating, and publishing oral Athabascan literature.*

T here was a little old lady who lived alone. She always worked by herself. In summer she set a net and caught a lot of fish. She cut them and hung them up and dried them, and then she put them in her grass cache. She was happy, since she had plenty of food. When winter came, she cooked, but she cooked only bones, even though she had plenty of food. "Late winter I will run short," she thought. Sometimes she just made Indian ice cream—snow and oil mixed up—and ate that.

Every evening at dusk she opened the curtain. She made a fire and put on a pot and cooked, and dished up her food. "That's enough," she thought. "I'll close the curtain and go to bed." So then she put dirt over her fire, went out, climbed up on the roof, and closed the curtain. She went back in the doorway. She stood there, as if listening. She listened really hard. She stuck her fingers in her ears and twirled them around. Then she heard something—someone singing. She ran inside. She grabbed the washbasin out from under the shelf and poured water in it and washed her face. She combed her hair. When she was done, she reached down and got out her workbag and took out clothing, and put on her fishskin parka.

Then she went out again. In a little while, someone began to sing. Then she went back in. She got up on the shelf. She stayed there, spinning sinew. After a short time, she went out again and listened. There was someone singing. The old lady thought, "I wonder if it's a man." She went down below the house and looked around the shore. And there she saw a little fish, singing as it swam. She picked up a stick and struck the water with it. Then she went back home. She went inside. After she had sat a little while, she went back out. It was quiet. "It must have been a man," she thought. She got lonely, and began to cry. Then she went off crying into the woods.

That is the end of the story.

Eggs

FROM *Once Upon an Eskimo Time*

EDNA WILDER

Writer and artist Edna Tucker Wilder was born in Bluff, Alaska, a small mining community on the Bering Sea. She is the daughter of an Eskimo woman and an English gold rush stampeder. A resident of Fairbanks, she has written two books, SECRETS OF ESKIMO SKIN SEWING *(1976) and* ONCE UPON AN ESKIMO TIME *(1987), now in its sixth printing.* ONCE UPON AN ESKIMO TIME, *from which "Eggs" is excerpted, describes a year in the life of her mother, Nedercook—a story told to Wilder in 1967–68, when Nedercook was 109 years old.*

Each day Nedercook would check to see whether the murres (black and white diving birds) had started to lay eggs. This she could do by looking just over the cliffs at a section where the birds roosted on the cliffs. These sea birds did not bother to build a nest but rather laid their eggs on the bare ledges, or any place on the cliff where the bird could sit. If the mother was not careful and flew off suddenly, the egg would roll off and break as it fell, unless it was over water. On calm days when the water was clear, her father would often go in his kayak and, using a long pole with a little skin basket fastened to the end, scoop the eggs from the bottom of the sea. Sometimes he would even manage to scoop up a crab.

Inerluk thought he was too old to climb the cliffs like his two sons and other young men of the village. Sometimes the young men would use a long piece of rawhide; they would pound a stake into the ground, tie the rawhide to it, and then follow the rawhide over the cliff. They would fasten their parkas securely at the waist and then as they reached the eggs they would slip them in through the neck openings of the parka until it was full. They would then climb back up and unload, going back if there were still more eggs within easy reach. Some of the older men took a break while doing this and cracked an egg or two while still on the cliff, and drank the contents. Usually other able-bodied young men went egg gathering with Nedercook's brothers. And depending upon how far up the coast they were going, some women and children followed along—the women picking the wild sorrel and onions. Egg hunters preferred to go over the cliffs on calm days or during the cool of evening. The days were now so long that the nights never became dark. The sun seemed to barely dip below the horizon before it was coming up again. At this time all the little tundra birds would start their singing, even before the sun was showing.

When the egg hunters returned to the village the older people often drank the uncooked eggs from the shell, but the young preferred to have them boiled.

Nedercook and her mother had a spot a little way up along the cliff where they often went. Kiachook had a pole with many pieces joined to make it long, with a little basket on the end. They would drag this with them. Kiachook would stand at the cliff's edge, balancing against the breeze from the sea, slip her long pole over the edge of the cliff, and scoop up the eggs that were within reach. The murres raised but one young. If they lost an egg at the beginning of the season they would lay another in a day or two; if that one was taken they could continue laying eggs until about the middle of July.

On one of the egg-gathering trips, Kiachook, knowing how young Nedercook liked to participate in the gathering of food, said that she saw a puffin come from a hole not too far from the top of the cliff, and that farther down there might be a gull's nest. Nedercook was excited and wanted to go after the egg, but her mother said, "Next time. We need rope." On these trips they usually picked a bag of sorrel before returning home.

Nedercook could hardly wait for the next trip, but on the scheduled day it was stormy and windy. Her mother said, "No good, we wait." Nedercook knew how treacherous the wind at the cliff's edge could be. It would blow you back away from the edge, just when you got braced against it, then suddenly it would whip around, blowing you toward the edge. Either way was bad, and the wind did both, as if wanting you to fall over the edge.

Starting out the next day, Nedercook made sure that the piece of rawhide was in her packsack. Her heart was light as she pulled and dragged Kiachook's long pole over the uneven tundra. Impatiently she sat back a few feet from the cliff's edge, where her mother always made her sit. She watched her mother advance confidently to the edge of the cliff. Getting her feet in a secure position, she would begin sliding the long pole slowly down over the edge until it reached the first egg. She turned and twisted the pole so the egg would roll into the little basket without rolling off the cliff. Slowly, hand over hand, she would bring the pole back and while holding the pole with one hand, remove the egg with the other. She placed it on the ground or in the dried sealskin hunting sack she brought especially for this. Kiachook would repeat this until there were no more eggs within reach of her pole. When her mother started to drag the pole back up away from the cliff, Nedercook could relax and move because her mother was out of danger.

Nedercook took the rawhide rope out of her packsack and her mother tied it around her small waist. Then her mother sat down a few feet from the edge, holding the rope between her hands. Nedercook's spirits were high, she was going to get one or maybe two puffin eggs, and her mother had said that there might be a gull's nest a little father down. Eagerly and happily she went over the cliff, down a few feet to a narrow ledge which continued at a 45-degree angle slanting down the face of the cliff. The ledge narrowed a few feet farther down, where the cliff above seemed to bulge outward above it. Still farther down it narrowed and crumbled to nothing. Nedercook was too anxious to find the eggs to be cautious. Without hesitation, as soon as her feet touched the ledge, she went down on all fours. In her eagerness she paid no attention to the fact that her head was much lower than her hind end. She proceeded happily to crawl down. Soon finding two whitish puffin eggs, she placed them in her parka. Continuing down she looked for the gull nest, but there was no nest and there were no more eggs. Then she noticed that the ledge had turned and petered out to nothing.

"I'd better go back," she thought as a flicker of panic touched her heart. Then, and only then, did Nedercook realize the mistake she had made. Her knees, hips and feet were higher than her head, and behind her, in the direction she wished to go. She tried to turn so she could look back, but the ledge was too narrow for any such move and the incline too steep. In this very dangerous, awkward and uncomfortable position, her body seemed to freeze. In front the ledge ran out and the cliff fell away, 300 feet down, down to where the breakers, still angry from yesterday's storm, crashed against the rocks. A cold fear started to fill Nedercook's heart, a fear such as she had never felt before. She looked at the moving water far below. In between was the constant movement of hundreds of flying birds: murres, puffins, gulls and cormorants. It was enough to make one dizzy, to say nothing of being in this awful position.

What can I do, she thought, as she called faintly "Mama" in her native tongue. But her mother was too far away to hear her above all the sounds from birds, the breeze and waves. For long minutes she remained in position, feeling very uncomfortable and unsafe. What can I do? kept running through her head. To try to turn would be to fall off the cliff, because she had crawled down under the rocks that bulged outward above her, making her position even more insecure. After a time she thought, maybe I should just jump out and turn around as I do. But then she remembered that there was no peg of wood to hold her, only her mother's hands; with the unexpected weight the rawhide would either slip through them or she would pull them both to their death, crashing on the rocks and waters below. She shuddered and was glad that she had not done this on impulse. No, that would not do, but what? what, she thought, should I do?

She put her head down to her hands as if trying to shut out the sight before her eyes. For several minutes she crouched in this position, her body pressed against the cliff. A calm seemed to fill her mind; her body gained strength and courage. No matter how hard it is, her being seemed to say, you came down this way—now you must go back up.

Slowly, very cautiously, she raised her right knee and foot, since they were the ones nearer the cliff. She kept her leg pressed to the cliff as she inched it up and back. Then ever so carefully she inched the other knee and foot back. Her hands followed. As she did this she noticed that the rawhide tightened ever so gently. Up over the uneven rocks she slowly made her backward way, inch by inch, until she reached the wider ledge. When she neared the top, the ledge was wide enough for her to get her knees in position, and she turned around, facing the ledge. The rest was easy.

Kiachook looked much relieved as Nedercook climbed back from the cliff's edge. "You all right? I worried, you long time."

When Nedercook removed only two parrot eggs her mother remarked. "Two eggs, too long, don't go down again." Nedercook was not planning another trip anyway—not down there.

Around the evening meal praise was high for her and for the good flavor of the two special eggs Nedercook had given to her parents. Nedercook was more quiet than usual. She had learned a big lesson this day and, although she did not say anything to her family, her mind brought the experience back to her many times. She was thankful that she had not acted in panic, but had waited for other thoughts to enter her mind. She shuddered at the remembrance that, had she jumped, she and her mother would not be sitting here enjoying the evening meal.

Nedercook often watched the raven during the month of July, at least the first half of the month, when the murres' eggs lay on the cliffs. The raven would fly up from the cliff, where it had stolen an egg, carrying the egg in its beak. He would fly to a spot on the tundra, hop around, then bury the egg, hop around some more, and then fly off to get another. He would bury or hide each one in a different place—sometimes near the cliff's edge, and the next time possibly one-quarter to a half-mile inland. Nedercook tried to locate the eggs a couple of times, but they were too well hidden.

July 13th

FROM *Libby*

....

BETTY JOHN

Betty John's book LIBBY: THE SKETCHES, LETTERS, AND JOURNAL OF LIBBY
BEAMAN, RECORDED IN THE PRIBILOF ISLANDS 1879–1880 *is the fictionalized
account of her grandmother's brief sojourn as the first white woman to live in
the Pribilof Islands of the Bering Sea.* LIBBY, *from which "July 13th" is
excerpted, is a spirited rendering of a Victorian lady's artistic, marital, and
domestic sensibilities during her stay in a strange, wild place.*

I am afraid to write, yet I must write, what happened today. I write
with the hope that perhaps the whole episode will become clear. I try
to understand why it happened, why I let it happen. But some things
are beyond human calculation, beyond human control. I know these
are difficult days. The killing season should be ended, but because we
have had extremely bad weather at times, it has been prolonged. Fortunately
it has been cool enough to keep the pelts from rotting, which they usually
begin to do about now. The men are tired and excitable, and so are the animals, especially the bulls at the height of their mating season. They fight
constantly and viciously over the matkas, and one of the favorite pastimes
of the natives is to stand at the edge of the harems and bet on the fights just
as men at home might bet on a cockfight or a wrestling match. Aleuts will
bet on anything that presents a challenge. So they pick their favorite bulls
and spur them on from the sidelines.

I've stayed away from the rookeries because I do not like the noise and
heat of battle. Yet now that the baby seals are being born, I've wanted to
watch them closely so I can write fully about them, which means, of course,
that I have to spend some time close enough for careful observation.

Walking is not easy on this island. There are no well-worn paths anywhere except to the spring, where we get our drinking water, about a mile
and a half away from here. I am tired of always walking in that direction,

which is inland, because no seals are to be seen along the way. The longer walks I had once anticipated taking so far have proved to be short excursions only. Some obstacle—such as slippery rocks, deep ravines, sudden fissures, or bogs—always stands in the way of going on to the farther rookeries.

Today started out to be such a beautiful day, the clearest we've had so far. Since I couldn't stand the din from the killing grounds and knew that the men had just finished driving the seals in from Polavina across the island, I decided I would take advantage of the path the animals wore down. Mr. Elliott told me that Polavina is the most beautiful sight on the island and an interesting rookery. I wanted to see it before the rains washed away the seals' path and while the weather still permitted sketching.

John did not, as was his custom, ask what I would be doing all day. If he had, and if I had told him, he would have forbidden me to go. Instead, and with a certain amount of resentment in his voice, he announced that he had been ordered—"*Ordered,* Libby"—to supervise the killings at Novastoshnah.

"You knew you would be sent. The log records that the assistant agent always supervises the operation at Novastoshnah."

"But it means that I must leave you alone here, alone and unprotected."

"I can manage. Do not worry." I had assumed he'd be gone for just the day, so I made my plans accordingly.

Past Kamminista's volcanic peak I climbed, seeing dead and dying seals along my path, rejected seals that had been left to find their way back to the sea or perish in this high, unfamiliar region so unlike their natural habitat. Flesh flies swarmed thick upon them, and white foxes lurked among the rocks, shy of me, but waiting to scavenge as soon as I had passed. I have no fear of the white foxes. They will not harm a living, moving creature. They are the island's sanitation corps.

I've had no real fear of meeting any Aleut. I know them all by name. They've all been friendly to me even when they've had kvas. We mumble a greeting—possibly *spasibo* for an answer—and go our separate ways. I've come upon children hunting birds' eggs. They are less silent, less secretive. I hear their laughter before I come upon them. Their elders sometimes give me quite a start. But I've known no real fear of anything so far up here on the islands. That is why I could not understand why John was so fearful for me.

But later, when I began to reconstruct the horrible day, I could understand. Three times I thought I saw a slight motion out of the corner of my eye. Something, or someone, kept disappearing behind a rock like a wraith. None of the natives would act that way. Then I suddenly remembered that Mr. Morgan had brought up a few stranger Aleuts from Attu whom the natives did not like. I dismissed the thought of them because they were all employed. I'm not sure whether I'd really have been frightened if I had met a strange Aleut face to face in that high rugged place. I breathed more freely when I came onto the open dunes. No further thought of danger crossed my mind.

How still the air was on the high dunes, away from the din and stench of the killing grounds! Then as I approached, I could hear the noise of the bachelor parade ground below me, and even that seemed wholesome. The wheeling, screaming birds had a hypnotic effect. They calmed me. I followed the recent driving trail over the last tumbled rocks, down to a broad plateau above a seacoast shelf. This plateau extends about a half mile inland from the edge of a sheer cliff, which drops directly down several hundred feet into the sea. This bachelor parade ground teemed with hundreds and hundreds of holluschickie that had escaped the killings for another year. The herd seemed scarcely decimated, and the bachelors appeared particularly happy on their pink sand and highly polished basalt playing field.

I passed between Polavina Sopka, a high conical peak, and a lovely little lake with a margin of jagged rocks on one side and great grass-covered dunes on the other. Vivid flowers dotted the grass like confetti—giant nasturtiums and great patches of deep blue gentians, early brilliant phlox such as I've never seen before, pulse with its delicate odor (when the wind was not from the rookery), and other flowers I must learn.

I sat on a ledge at the very edge of the cliff, at this point a highly polished red rock that goes straight down to steely blue-black ledges far below, where bull seals exercise full rein over their harems. Below them the surf boomed tremendously against the rock, polishing it to even greater smoothness. At first I could not figure out how the seals could get back and forth to the ledges, or how the holluschickie could get way up on the high parade grounds. Every other rookery I had seen had a slow and gradual rise for approach; this one had a forbidding perpendicular wall.

Then I saw them coming up the face of the wall using little ledge-like outjuttings for stairs. These small steps seemed to present no problem to the seals in spite of their clumsy gait, which is an inching movement. They seemed to have established some order of precedence for those going up or down. Here and there, where a few had forgotten the rules, they just climbed over each other or turned and went in the same direction. I saw not one tumble off those narrow ledges.

The cliff gentles off far to the south and as soon as I had made a rough sketch, I clambered in that direction to get nearer to the baby seals, which I wanted to sketch accurately and from close up. I came to a place where many newborn pups nursed contentedly. I decided that they are about the most adorable baby animals anyone could wish to watch.

I sat on a rock close to and slightly above a small harem, a good vantage point for working. Fortunately the wind came from behind me and blew the stench out to sea. I sat for a long time just watching, fascinated by the ways of the pups with their soulful human eyes and their bleatings like little sheep when their mothers pulled away from nursing them and left them. After a while I began to sketch.

Naturally all around me, I could hear the barking and hissing, the spitting and coughing of the bulls, some challenging others for invading the boundaries of their harems or fighting over their wayward wives. But the problems of the adult seals were remote from the objects of my concern—the little pups. I could not help noticing how beautiful the young matkas looked, sleek and docile except for a slight whimper now and then when one gave birth to a kotickie or was bumped into by a clumsy bull ten times her size. The screaming birds and the *baroom* [sound of the surf] of the sea added to the din. But in spite of the commotion, I managed a few fair sketches of several pups.

"Seal mating is no sight a lady should have to witness," is what one of the men at mess probably wanted to say to me the night before. Instead he had again warned me, "Don't go near the rookeries during the mating season, Mrs. Beaman. The bulls are somethin' fierce then and mought do ye some harm. They have no use for anyone who interferes. They'll charge ye and tear yer ta bits."

"Aye," said another. But I caught the glance between them and knew they were trying to spare me the sight of actual mating.

Well, this day so much of it had been going on around me that I had little curiosity about it. I wanted to do my sketches of the little kotickie. But suddenly the bull right below me challenged the bull of the next harem over a sleek little matka that was escaping his domain for the other's. I had to stop and watch; the drama was such a human one and so close that I felt personally involved and ready to root for the bull of the little cow's choice. The hissing and spitting and swaying of the two battling monsters became so vicious that I stepped to higher ground. I should have continued sketching the babies, but the fight was too fascinating not to watch to the bitter end. Those two bulls were out to kill each other, and they set about using their powerful shoulders and teeth in such a way that neither could come out of it whole, no matter who won.

But in the middle of the row, my attention was diverted to a third bull who had taken advantage of the fight to carry off the little seal the other two were fighting over. I hadn't realized that I was sitting on the edge of this new seacatch's harem until he brought the trim little matka to my feet and plopped her down on the very ledge I had so hastily vacated. There he gave her a most ungentle trouncing, thumping and scolding her, while I retreated to still higher ground, now more curious than ever about what the other two would do when they discovered their prize gone. But the scene so close to my feet was even more intriguing.

The matka's new lord and master, after several more thudding blows that sent her yelping against the rocks, began to caress her by rubbing his long neck along her sleek body. Immediately she wriggled and snuggled up to him, as if to acknowledge his overlordship. They nosed each other all over, especially about the face, and she did not struggle to get away or to go back to the two suitors still warring over her. Instead she slithered up and down beside him. They fondled each other more and more excitedly. The expressions in their eyes were all too human expressions of passion and desire. I could not help myself. I had to watch, with not even a scientist's impersonal interest or an artist's justification, but with frank curiosity and a sense of personal involvement.

Suddenly the little matka flattened out on the pinkish sand and let the great bull cover her. Their mating lasted a long time with frequent convulsive movements that set their whole bodies to quivering. I grew limp with my own intense absorption in the scene, my sketchbook and crayon forgotten in my hands. Slowly I began to realize the enormity of what I had stopped to watch and was ashamed of myself for succumbing to such an unladlylike experience, so contrary to my careful upbringing and even my own convictions. I wanted to run from my shame. I stood up, bent on going back to the dunes and away from this mass of mating, fighting seals.

I turned to face the Senior Agent standing silent, just behind me!

"Interesting, isn't it, Elizabeth?" he asked with a thin smile on his lips and mockery in his eyes. I wanted to faint into nothingness, to disappear beneath the sand and tufa, to be anywhere but there on that spot. A blush of embarrassment and confusion spread from the roots of my hair down to my toes. I tossed my head and ran past him up the rise toward the parade ground and the little lake. But the earth was so uneven and my eyes so blinded by tears of anger and shame that I stumbled often and could not run from him with the dignity I wished to show. I lost my sketch pad and crayons clambering over a particularly difficult rock in my path. He, following more easily, picked them up and handed them to me.

"Thank you," I said coldly and turned away from him toward home, wondering if he would follow me all the five miles back just to mock me. But a sudden storm, such as come quickly and go quickly, struck violently, making of the seals' driving trail a river of mud through which I floundered. Lightning on these islands is always terrifying. The Pribilofs are noted for the most harrowing electrical storms in the world, and this morning's was the worst since I've been up here, more so because I was out in it and unprepared for it. The sheet lightning spread steely blue over us with a hiss that ended in deep thunderous rolls out over the Bering. The direct lightning hit in great, vivid darts against rocks and crevices as though intent on blasting the island into bits. Thunder cracked instantaneously with the darts. It has deafened many natives and company men in the past, and I was afraid for my own hearing with each deafening crack.

There was nowhere to take shelter on the dunes of the open plateau, nowhere until I reached Boga Slov, "Word of God," with its great boulders and ledges. But Boga Slov got its name because it attracted the lightning more than any other spot in the Arctic, and this morning was no exception. Lightning illuminated the peak, which looked like a finger of God pointing a warning to all those who would break the rules.

I kept straight on toward home, floundering in the awful mud, stumbling over the jagged basalt, drenched to the skin without my oilskin, and, most of all, angry with myself for now being vulnerable to the Senior Agent's scorn.

As I came past the mountain and onto the road that forks to the spring,

I think I would have fallen but for the firm grasp he took on my arm to help me over the little flash flood between us and the final stretch of the road. He had been following me all the way! And in silence he now followed me the rest of the way. How can I ever hold up my head again or look the man in the eye?

But—he had called me Elizabeth, my first name!

Fifty Years Below Zero

CHARLES D. BROWER

Charles D. Brower (1863–1945) grew up in New York, and came to Alaska at age twenty to investigate coal-mining possibilities near Cape Lisburne. Like many others enticed by the Far North, Brower never left, settling in the small isolated Eskimo whaling community of Barrow. He was variously a whaler, miner, trapper, and tradepost keeper. In this excerpt from his autobiography, FIFTY YEARS BELOW ZERO *(1942), Brower, his Inuit wife, Toctoo, and acquaintances face shifting pack ice and grim frontier justice in the Arctic.*

W hat's that? Listen!"

Toctoo and I were mushing back to the coast after returning to Takpuc's peaceful camp for a few more weeks' fishing. Overtaken by inky blackness at the end of a short December day's travel, we had hastily thrown up a snow shelter in the dark and crawled inside.

There it came again above the howl of the west wind—a deep, ominous rumbling that seemed to shake the frozen universe.

"What is it?" I repeated.

In those days my ignorance brought many a teasing laugh from Toctoo. But now her voice sounded quite solemn as she explained that it was the ice crushing offshore.

It was my turn to laugh. We were many miles from the coast.

But Toctoo was right. On reaching Utkiavie a couple of days later the first thing we saw was a great ridge of ice piled up all along the shore, with what was left of the old "Ino" smashed and twisted and buried beneath the crush. If we hadn't built our house on a hill . . . !

Even the fifty-foot bluff on which the village stood couldn't always be depended on for safety, according to Mungie. A few years before I came among them, a strong west wind, coupled with just the right current, had forced heavy ice almost to the beach; and this in turn pushed the thinner inshore ice onto the very top of the bluff—right into the village. Several houses near the edge were crushed with everyone inside. It had all happened in the middle of the night.

Mungie scanned the Arctic horizon a moment, thoughtfully, as if recalling the vivid details. Then he added that his father had been among those killed.

Conscience got the better of me in the spring of 1890, and for once I attended to repairs and outfitting instead of going off hunting. In a way, it might have been a lot better had I spent my time hunting and so added a little more meat to the small number of caribou being killed by the natives. Few even took the trouble to try. It was more fun staying home and making hooch.

Con finally got them to sell us four carcasses, but all they would accept in pay was more flour and molasses for replenishing their stills.

Whaling went no better. The ice was terrible. Although Woolfe had fitted out two whaleboats and had Portuguese Joe and our former shipmate, Charlie Ice, with him, his crews were mostly inland Eskimos who knew little about whaling. He had even shipped a good-for-nothing native woman who had run away from her last husband in Nubook and was now living with Joe.

Between hooch, inland natives and dangerous ice conditions, it was left to Pat and Fred to take the only whale killed that year.

Their boat lay on a ridge of ice which started to move, leaving holes along the edge. Suddenly, a whale broke water and lay spouting right in front of them. Pat was asleep in the bow. When shaken by Fred, he grabbed his second bomb-gun without harpoon or line and, still half asleep, darted it out as far as he could. The gun hit the water and slid along until the end of the rod touched the whale's side. Next instant the exploding bomb turned the animal belly-up.

This happened in the middle of May. Towards the end of the month the season closed on a note somberly attuned to that wretched season. It concerned Joe's woman.

She had been telling Joe for some time that soon she would have to go back to her other man at Nubook. And Joe had been urging her to. I don't think he ever cared much for her in the first place. But with a job in hand, she refused to leave until the whaling ended and Woolfe paid her off.

That was the situation at the end of May when she and Joe started to walk ashore from the boat.

Halfway in, they sat down to rest on a sled that someone had left in the ice roadway. They were sitting there talking, according to the woman, when the Eskimo came along with whom she had lived at Nubook before meeting Joe. But instead of showing anger at finding them together, he acted friendly enough, and at Joe's invitation sat down on the sled with them to talk things over.

"Sure, take her," Joe told him, "only you'd better wait 'til all the boats are in. Then she'll have a payday and you two can go back and start over again."

This seemed to suit the Eskimo fine. So pretty soon Joe got up and started for home, leaving the pair seated there together.

The woman said he hadn't gone more than fifty feet when suddenly her man hauled his rifle out of its sack and shot Joe through the small of the back. He must have died instantly. To make sure, though, the native walked up close and shot him again, this time through the head.

Leaving the body sprawled out in a pool of crimson slush, the man and woman walked on into the village where she told some of the Eskimos what had happened. Apparently, nobody laid a hand on the man. He just took his sled and two dogs and headed inland.

Our party knew nothing of all this until Mungie sent a young man out on the ice to tell us. Con then sledded the body ashore, and before long every white man in the place was making for the station.

What we had long dreaded but never discussed had come at last—an Eskimo killing a white man. Had it been Eskimo against Eskimo we could have left it to the natives to settle. This was far more serious. Nobody knew whether the Eskimos would back us up in punishing the murderer, or stand together against us.

After we had thrashed it out a while, getting nowhere fast, the need for a prompt decision of some sort was brought home to me by a glance through the window. Half of Utkiavie, it appeared, was milling around outside waiting to see what the white men would do.

"Way I look at it," I said, getting the floor at last, "this is the time for a firm hand. I don't know how they're going to take it, but I do know what they're going to think of us if we let this murderer get away with it."

There were nods all around. Woolfe summed it up:

"Aye, the man must be punished proper."

We called in Mungie and the other headman, Angaroo, and announced that we were going to arrest the Eskimo, and if he were guilty, as the woman said, he must be executed.

They showed no surprise. At the same time they refused to help, pointing out that the dead man wasn't one of their kind.

The murderer had been gone a couple of hours by now, but one of the old women said that no man could travel fast in the soft snow with only two dogs. She even hinted that he might be found not far from the village, waiting to see what would happen.

It fell to Con, Pat and me to go out for him. The trail led three miles beyond the village. And there, as the woman had said, we found our man waiting. He was standing behind his sled in a gully, rifle over arm.

At sight of us, he threw a cartridge in the chamber. When we kept on walking steadily nearer he took to covering first one then another, unable to make up his mind which of us to shoot first.

Nobody spoke. Those last twenty-five feet were the most unpleasant I ever walked.

With his rifle pointing straight at the pit of my stomach, the man made just one mistake. He waited an instant too long before shifting it to Pat who was closest to the sled. For in that split-second, Pat vaulted over, knocked the gun in the air and grabbed his man.

Con and I soon had him down and, lashing his hands behind him, we headed back to the station where the rest of our crowd were watching anxiously. Every Eskimo had left.

Believing that all the natives should be on hand for the trial, we sent word to the village. Only Mungie and Angaroo and a few of the older men showed up. However, they brought the woman along as witness and listened stolidly while she repeated what had happened on the road coming in.

She said that after the shooting she had gone with the man because he would have killed her if she hadn't. Beyond readily agreeing with everything she said, the prisoner had nothing to add except that if we let him go he would never kill another white man.

We found him guilty. The sentence was death.

It was not a popular verdict among the Eskimos, their point being that there would have been no killing except for the woman.

But at last Angaroo reminded them that had the victim been an Eskimo some other Eskimo would certainly kill the murderer and maybe his whole family. Therefore, it was right for him to die. He did think, however, that since the woman had caused it all, she also should be shot. This last, of course, we wouldn't consider.

Although all of us were hoping that the natives would at least agree to carry out the actual execution, they absolutely refused. So that, too, was left for us.

Old John loaded four rifles with ball cartridges, the others with blanks. Nobody knew which was which. Then we took the native half a mile inland and shot him. One official touch remained for Mungie. As headman, he made the woman wrap the body in deerskin and leave it where it lay.

We buried Portuguese Joe over the hill not far from the station—the first white man I ever helped bury at Point Barrow. Later that summer the woman went away in one of the whalers and we didn't see her again.

When the *Bear* arrived, Woolfe handed Captain Healy a written report setting forth all the circumstances of the murder. It was a meticulous, long-worked-over document which we hoped would enable the authorities to justify our action as clearly as we did ourselves. The result was somewhat different from what we had expected.

Said Healy, severely: "I don't want your damn report, Woolfe."

"But, Captain—it explains—"

"You men had a perfect right to shoot that fellow on sight."

And tearing up the report, Captain Healy tossed the pieces overboard.

Alaska

JOAQUIN MILLER

Joaquin Miller was the pen name of Cincinnatus Hiner Miller (1837–1913), a popular and colorful American poet, novelist, and dramatist. As a young man Miller joined the California gold rush, rode for the Pony Express, and lived among Native Americans. He took the name "Joaquin" from the notorious California bandit Joaquin Murietta. In 1898, at the age of sixty-one, Miller persuaded a California newspaper to let him cover the Klondike gold rush. He hiked the grueling Chilkoot Trail and made his way to Dawson. His books include Pacific Poems *(1870) and* Songs of the Sierras *(1871). "Alaska" is his tribute to that great Northern adventure.*

Ice built, ice bound, and ice bounded,
    Such cold seas of silence! such room!
Such snow-light, such sea-light, confounded
    With thunders that smite like a doom!
Such grandeur! such glory! such gloom!
       Hear that boom! Hear that deep distant boom
          Of an avalanche hurled
          Down this unfinished world!

Ice seas! and ice summits! ice spaces
    In splendor of white, as God's throne!
Ice worlds to the pole! and ice places
    Untracked, and unnamed, and unknown!
Hear that boom! Hear the grinding, the groan
    Of the ice-gods in pain! Hear the moan
          Of yon ice mountain hurled
          Down this unfinished world.

Fairbanks to the Chandalar through Circle City and Fort Yukon

FROM *Ten Thousand Miles with a Dog Sled*

HUDSON STUCK

Hudson Stuck (1863–1920) was an intrepid Episcopal archdeacon who, between 1905 and 1910, traveled by dogsled to remote missions and Native parishes throughout Alaska. Stuck led the first successful expedition up Mount McKinley in 1913, which he chronicled in THE ASCENT OF DENALI *(1914). In* TEN THOUSAND MILES WITH A DOG SLED *(1914), excerpted here, Stuck recalls his rigorous adventures as he carried out his ministerial duties in the Alaska wilderness.*

The plan for the winter journey of 1905-6 (my second winter on the trail) was an ambitious one, for it contemplated a visit to Point Hope, on the shore of the Arctic Ocean between Kotzebue Sound and Point Barrow, and a return to Fairbanks. In the summer such a journey would be practicable only by water: down the Tanana to the Yukon, down the Yukon to its mouth, and then through the straits of Bering and along the Arctic coast; in the winter it is possible to make the journey across country. A desire to visit our most northerly and most inaccessible mission in Alaska and a desire to become acquainted with general conditions in the wide country north of the Yukon were equal factors in the planning of a journey which would carry me through three and a half degrees of latitude and no less than eighteen degrees of longitude.

The course of winter travel in Alaska follows the frozen waterways so far as they lead in the general direction desired, leaves them to cross mountain ranges and divides at the most favourable points, and drops down into the streams again so soon as streams are available. The country is notably well watered and the waterways are the natural highways. The more frequented routes gradually cut out the serpentine bends of the rivers by land trails, but in the wilder parts of the country travel sticks to the ice.

Our course, therefore, lay up the Chatanika River and one of its tributaries until the Tanana-Yukon watershed was reached; then through the mountains, crossing two steep summits to the Yukon slope, and down that slope by convenient streams to the Yukon River at Circle City.

We set out on the 27th of November with six dogs and a "basket" sled and about five hundred pounds' weight of load, including tent and stove, bedding, clothes for the winter, grub box and its equipment, and dog feed. The dogs were those that I had used the previous winter, with one exception. The leader had come home lame from the fish camp where he had been boarded during the summer, and, despite all attentions, the lameness had persisted; so he must be left behind, and there was much difficulty in securing another leader. A recent stampede to a new mining district had advanced the price of dogs and gathered up all the good ones, so it was necessary to hunt all over Fairbanks and pay a hundred dollars for a dog that proved very indifferent, after all. "Jimmy" was a handsome beast, the handsomest I ever owned and the costliest, but, as I learned later from one who knew his history, had "travelled on his looks all his life." He earned the name of "Jimmy the Fake."

Midway to Cleary "City," on the chief gold-producing creek of the district, our first day's run, we encountered the gold train. For some time previous a lone highwayman had robbed solitary miners on their way to Fairbanks with gold-dust, and now a posse was organized that went the rounds of the creeks and gathered up the dust and bore it on mule-back to the bank, escorted by half a dozen armed and mounted men. Sawed-off shotguns were the favourite weapons, and one judged them deadly enough at short range. The heavy "pokes" galled the animals' backs, however they might be slung, and the little procession wound slowly along, a man ahead, a man behind, and four clustered round the treasure.

These raw, temporary mining towns are much alike the world over, one supposes, though perhaps a little worse up here in the far north. It was late at night when we reached the place, but saloon and dance-hall were ablaze with light and loud with the raucity of phonographs and the stamping of feet. Everything was "wide open," and there was not even the thinnest veneer of respectability. Drinking and gambling and dancing go on all night long. Drunken men reel out upon the snow; painted faces leer over muslin curtains as one passes by. Without any government, without any pretence of municipal organisation, there is no cooperation for public enterprise. There are no streets, there are no sidewalks save such as a man may choose to lay in front of his own premises, and the simplest sanitary precautions are entirely neglected. Nothing but the cold climate of the north prevents epidemic disease from sweeping through these places. They rise in a few days wherever gold is found in quantities, they flourish as the production increases, decline with its decline, and are left gaunt, dark, and abandoned as soon as the diggings are exhausted.

The next day we were on the Chatanika River, to which Cleary Creek is tributary, and were immediately confronted with one of the main troubles and difficulties of winter travel in this and, as may be supposed, in any arctic or subarctic country—overflow water.

In the lesser rivers, where deep pools alternate with swift shallows, the stream freezes solid to the bottom upon the shoals and riffles. Since the subterranean fountains that supply the river do not cease to discharge their waters in the winter, however cold it may be, there comes presently an increasing pressure under the ice above such a barrier. The pent-up water is strong enough to heave the ice into mounds and at last to break forth, spreading itself far along the frozen surface of the river. At times it may be seen gushing out like an artesian well, rising three or four feet above the surface of the ice, until the pressure is relieved. Sometimes for many miles at a stretch the whole river will be covered with a succession of such overflows, from two or three inches deep to eight or ten, or even twelve; some just bursting forth, some partially frozen, some resolved into solid "glare" ice. Thus the surface of the river is continually renewed the whole winter through, and a section of the ice crust in the spring would show a series of laminations; here ice upon ice, there ice upon half-incorporated snow, that mark the successive inundations.

This explanation has been given at length because of the large part that the phenomenon plays in the difficulty and danger of winter travel, and because it seems hard to make those who are not familiar with it understand it. At first sight it would seem that after a week or ten days of fifty-below-zero weather, for instance, all water everywhere would be frozen into quiescence for the rest of the winter. Throw a bucket of water into the air, and it is frozen solid as soon as it reaches the ground. There would be no more trouble, one would think, with water. Yet some of the worst trouble the traveller has with overflow water is during very cold weather, and it is then, of course, that there is the greatest danger of frost-bite in getting one's feet wet. Waterproof footwear, therefore, becomes one of the "musher's" great concerns and difficulties. The best water-proof footwear is the Esquimau mukluk, not easily obtainable in the interior of Alaska, but the mukluk is an inconvenient footwear to put snow-shoes on. Rubber boots or shoes of any kind are most uncomfortable things to travel in. Nothing equals the moccasin on the trail, nothing is so good to snow-shoe in. The well-equipped traveller has moccasins for dry trails and mukluks for wet trails— and even then may sometimes get his feet wet. Nor are his own feet his only consideration; his dogs' feet are, collectively, as important as his own. When the dog comes out of water into snow again the snow collects and freezes between the toes, and if not removed will soon cause a sore and lameness. Then a dog moccasin must be put on and the foot continually nursed and doctored. When several dogs of a team are thus affected, it may be with several feet each, the labour and trouble of travel are greatly increased.

So, whenever his dogs have been through water, the careful musher will stop and go all down the line, cleaning out the ice and snow from their feet with his fingers. Four interdigital spaces per foot make sixteen per dog, and with a team of six dogs that means ninety-six several operations with the bare hand (if it be done effectually) every time the team gets into an over-flow. The dogs will do it for themselves if they are given time, tearing out the lumps of ice with their teeth; but, inasmuch as they usually feel consci-entiously obliged to eat each lump as they pull it out, it takes much longer, and in a short daylight there is little time to spare if the day's march is to be made.

We found overflow almost as soon as we reached the Chatanika River, and in one form or another we encountered it during all the two days and a half that we were pursuing the river's windings. At times it was covered with a sheet of new ice that would support the dogs but would not support the sled, so that the dogs were travelling on one level and the sled on another, and a man had to walk along in the water between the dogs and the sled for several hundred yards at a time, breaking down the overflow ice with his feet.

At other times the thin sheets of overflow ice would sway and bend as the sled passed quickly over them in a way that gives to ice in such condi-tion its Alaskan name of "rubber-ice," while for the fifteen or twenty miles of McManus Creek, the headwaters of the Chatanika, we had continuous stretches of fine glare ice with enough frost crystals upon it from condens-ing moisture to give a "tooth" to the dogs' feet, just as varnish on a photo-graphic negative gives tooth to the retouching pencil. Perfectly smooth ice is a very difficult surface for dogs to pass over; glare ice slightly roughened by frost deposit makes splendid, fast going.

Eighty-five miles or so from Fairbanks, and just about half-way to Circle, the watercourse is left and the first summit is the "Twelve-Mile," as it is called. We tried hard to take our load up at one trip, but found it impossible to do so, and had to unlash the sled and take half the load at a time, caching it on the top while we returned for the other half.

It took us half a day to get our load to the top of Twelve-Mile summit, a rise of about one thousand three hundred feet from the creek bed as the aneroid gave it. In the steeper pitches we had to take the axe and cut steps, so hard and smooth does the incessant wind at these heights beat the snow, and on our second trip to the top we were just in time to rescue a roll of bedding that had been blown from the cache and was about to descend a gully from which we could hardly have recovered it.

This summit descended, we were in Birch Creek water, and had we followed the watercourse would have reached the Yukon; but we would have travelled hundreds of miles and would have come out below Fort Yukon, while we were bound for Circle City. So there was another and a yet more difficult summit to cross before we could descend the Yukon slope. We were able to hire a man and two dogs to help us over the Eagle summit, so that the necessity of relaying was avoided. One man ahead continually calling to the dogs, eight dogs steadily pulling, and two men behind steadily pushing, foot by foot, with many stoppages as one bench after another was surmounted, we got the load to the top at last, a rise of one thousand four hundred feet in less than three miles. A driving snowstorm cut off all view and would have left us at a loss which way to proceed but for the stakes that indicated it.

The descent was as anxious and hazardous as the ascent had been laborious. The dogs were loosed and sent racing down the slope. With a rope rough-lock around the sled runners, one man took the gee pole and another the handle-bars and each spread-eagled himself through the loose deep snow to check the momentum of the sled, until sled and men turned aside and came to a stop in a drift to avoid a steep, smooth pitch. The sled extricated, it was poised on the edge of the pitch and turned loose on the hardened snow, hurtling down three or four hundred feet until it buried itself in another drift. The dogs were necessary to drag it from this drift, and one had to go down and bring them up. Then again they were loosed, and from bench to bench the process was repeated until the slope grew gentle enough to permit the regulation of the downward progress by the foot-brake.

The Eagle summit is one of the most difficult summits in Alaska. The wind blows so fiercely that sometimes for days together its passage is almost impossible. No amount of trail making could be of much help, for the snow smothers up everything on the lee of the hill, and the end of every storm presents a new surface and an altered route. A "summit" in this Alaskan sense is, of course, a saddle between peaks, and in this case there is no easier pass and no way around. The only way to avoid the Eagle summit, without going out of the district altogether, would be to tunnel it.

The summit passed, we found better trails and a more frequented country, for in this district are a number of creeks that draw supplies from Circle City, and that had been worked ten years or more.

At the time of the Klondike stampede of 1896–97, Circle City was already established as a flourishing mining camp and boasted itself the largest log-cabin town in the world. Before the Klondike drew away its people as a stronger magnet draws iron filings from a lesser one, Circle had a population of about three thousand. Take a town of three thousand and reduce it to thirty or forty, and it is hard to resist the melancholy impression which entrance upon it in the dusk of the evening brings. There lay the great white Yukon in the middle distance; beyond it the Yukon Flats, snow-covered, desolate, stretched away enormously, hedged here at their beginning by grey, dim hills. Spread out in the foreground were the little, squat, huddling cabins that belonged to no one, with never a light in a window or smoke from a chimney, the untrodden snow drifted against door and porch. It would be hard to imagine a drearier prospect, and one had the feeling that it was a city of the dead rather than merely a dead city.

The weather had grown steadily colder since we reached the Yukon slope, and for two days before reaching Circle the thermometer had stood between 40° and 50° below zero. It was all right for us to push on, the trail was good and nearly all down-hill, and there were road-houses every ten or twelve miles. Freighters, weatherbound, came to the doors as we passed by with our jangle of bells and would raise a somewhat chechaco pride in our breasts by remarking: "You don't seem to care what weather you travel in!" The evil of it was that the perfectly safe travelling between Eagle Creek and Circle emboldened us to push on from Circle under totally different conditions, when travelling at such low temperatures became highly dangerous and brought us into grave misadventure that might easily have been fatal catastrophe.

Our original start was a week later than had been planned and we had made no time, but rather lost it, on this first division of the journey. If we were to reach Bettles on the Koyukuk River for Christmas, there was no more time to lose, and I was anxious to spend the next Sunday at Fort Yukon, three days' journey away. So we started for Fort Yukon on Thursday, the 7th of December, the day after we reached Circle.

A certain arctic traveller has said that "adventures" always imply either incompetence or ignorance of local conditions, and there is some truth in the saying. Our misadventure was the result of a series of mistakes, no one of which would have been other than discreditable to men of more experience. Our course lay for seventy-five miles through the Yukon Flats, which begin at Circle and extend for two hundred and fifty miles of the river's course below that point. The Flats constitute the most difficult and dangerous part of the whole length of the Yukon River, summer or winter, and the section between Circle City and Fort Yukon is the most difficult and dangerous part of the Flats. Save for a "portage" or land trail of eighteen or twenty miles out of Circle, the trail is on the river itself, which is split up into many channels without salient landmarks. The current is so swift that many stretches run open water far into the winter, and blow-holes are numerous. There is little travel on the Flats in winter, and a snow-storm accompanied by wind may obliterate what trail there is in an hour. The vehicle used in the Flats is not a sled but a toboggan, and our first mistake was in not conforming to local usage in this respect. There is always a very good reason for local usage about snow vehicles. But a toboggan which had been ordered from a native at Fort Yukon would be waiting for us, and it seemed not worth while to go to the expense of buying another merely for three days' journey.

The second mistake was in engaging a boy as guide instead of a man. He was an attractive youth of about fourteen who had done good service at the Circle City mission the previous winter, when our nurse-in-charge was contending single-handed against an epidemic of diphtheria. He was a pleasant boy, with some English, who wanted to go and professed knowledge of the route. The greatest mistake of all was starting out through that lonely waste with the thermometer at 52° below zero. The old-timers in Alaska have a saying that "travelling at 50° below is all right as long as it's all right." If there be a good trail, if there be convenient stopping-places, if nothing go wrong, one may travel without special risk and with no extraordinary discomfort at 50° below zero and a good deal lower. I have since that time made a short day's run at 62° below, and once travelled for two or three hours on a stretch at 65° below. But there is always more or less chance in travelling at low temperatures, because a very small thing may necessitate a stop, and a stop may turn into a serious thing. At such temperatures one must keep going. No amount of clothing that it is possible to wear on the trail will keep one warm while standing still. For dogs and men alike, constant brisk motion is necessary; for dogs as well as men—even though dogs will sleep outdoors in such cold without harm—for they cannot take as good care of themselves in the harness as they can when loose. A trace that needs mending, a broken buckle, a snow-shoe string that must be replaced, may chill one so that it is impossible to recover one's warmth again. The bare hand cannot be exposed for many seconds without beginning to freeze; it is dangerous to breathe the air into the lungs for any length of time without a muffler over the mouth.

Our troubles began as soon as we started. The trail was a narrow, winding toboggan track of sixteen or seventeen inches, while our sled was twenty inches wide, so that one runner was always dragging in the loose snow, and that meant slow, heavy going.

The days were nearing the shortest of the year, when, in these latitudes, the sun does but show himself and withdraw again. But, especially in very cold weather, which is nearly always very clear weather, that brief appearance is preceded by a feast of rich, delicate colour. First a greenish glow on the southern horizon, brightening into lemon and then into clear primrose, invades the deep purple of the starry heavens. Then a beautiful circle of blush pink above a circle of pure amethyst gradually stretches all around the edge of the sky, slowly brightening while the stars fade out and the heavens change to blue. The dead white mirror of the snow takes every tint that the skies display with a faint but exquisite radiance. Then the sun's disk appears with a flood of yellow light but with no appreciable warmth, and for a little space his level rays shoot out and gild the tree tops and the distant hills. The snow springs to life. Dead white no longer, its dry, crystalline particles glitter in myriads of diamond facets with every colour of the prism. Then the sun is gone, and the lovely circle of rose pink over amethyst again stretches round the horizon, slowly fading until once more the pale primrose glows in the south against the purple sky with its silver stars. Thus sunrise and sunset form a continuous spectacle, with a purity of delicate yet splendid colour that only perfectly dry atmosphere permits. The primrose glow, the heralding circle, the ball of orange light, the valedictory circle, the primrose glow again, and a day has come and gone. Air can hold no moisture at all at these low temperatures, and the skies are cloudless.

Moreover, in the wilds at 50° below zero there is the most complete silence. All animal life is hidden away. Not a rabbit flits across the trail; in the absolutely still air not a twig moves. A rare raven passes overhead, and his cry, changed from a hoarse croak to a sweet liquid note, reverberates like the musical glasses. There is no more delightful sound in the wilderness than this occasional lapse into music of the raven. We wound through the scrub spruce and willow and over the niggerhead swamps, a faint tinkle of bells, a little cloud of steam; for in the great cold the moisture of the animals' breath hangs over their heads in the still air, and on looking back it stands awhile along the course at dogs' height until it is presently deposited on twigs and tussocks. We wound along, a faint tinkle of bells, a little cloud of steam, and in the midst of the cloud a tousle of shaggy black-and-white hair and red-and-white pompons—going out of the dead silence behind into the dead silence before. The dusk came, and still we plodded and pushed our weary way, swinging that heavy sled incessantly, by the gee pole in front and the handle-bars behind, in the vain effort to keep it on the trail. Two miles an hour was all that we were making. We had come but thirteen or fourteen miles out of twenty-four, and it was dark; and it grew colder.

The dogs whined and stopped every few yards, worn out by wallowing in the snow and the labour of the collar. The long scarfs that wrapped our mouths and noses had been shifted and shifted, as one part after another became solid with ice from the breath, until over their whole length they were stiff as boards. After two more miles of it it was evident that we could not reach the mail cabin that night. Then I made my last and worst mistake. We should have stopped and camped then and there. We had tent and stove and everything requisite. But the native boy insisted that the cabin was "only little way," and any one who knows the misery of making camp in extremely cold weather, in the dark, will understand our reluctance to do so.

I decided to make a cache of the greater part of our load—tent and stove and supplies generally—and to push on to the cabin with but the bedding and the grub box, returning for the stuff in the morning. And, since in the

deepest depths of blundering there is a deeper still, by some one's careless-
ness, but certainly by my fault, the axe was left behind in the cache.

With our reduced burden we made better progress, and in a short time
reached the end of the portage and came out on the frozen river, just as the
moon, a day or two past the full, rose above the opposite bank. One sees
many strange distortions of sun and moon in this land, but never was a
stranger seen than this. Her disk, shining through the dense air of the river
bottom, was in shape an almost perfect octagon, regular as though it had
been laid off with dividers and a ruler.

We were soon in doubt about the trail. The mail-carrier had gone down
only two or three times this winter and each time had taken a different
route, as more and more of the river closed and gave him more and more
direct passage. A number of Indians had been hunting, and their tracks
added to the tangle of trails. Presently we entered a thick mist that even to
inexperienced eyes spoke of open water or new ice yet moist. So heavy was
the vapour that to the man at the handle-bars the man at the gee pole
loomed ghostly, and the man ahead of the dogs could not be distinguished
at all. We had gone so much farther than our native boy had declared we
had to go that we began to fear that in the confusion of trails we had taken
the wrong one and had passed the cabin. That is the tenderfoot's, or, as we
say, the chechaco's, fear; it is the one thing that it may almost be said never
happens. But the boy fell down completely and was frankly at a loss. All we
could get out of him was: "May-be-so we catch cabin bymeby, may-be-so
no." If we had passed the cabin it was twenty odd miles to the next; and it
grew colder and the dogs were utterly weary again, prone upon the trail at
every small excuse for a stop, only to be stirred by the whip, heavily wielded.
Surely never men thrust themselves foolhardily into worse predicament!
Then I made my last mistake. Dimly the bank loomed through the mist,
and I said: "We can't go any farther; I think we've missed the trail and I'm
going across to yon bank to see if there's a place to camp." I had not gone
six steps from the trail when the ice gave way under my feet and I found
myself in water to my hips.

Under Providence I owe it to the mukluks I wore, tied tight around my
knees, that I did not lose my life, or at least my feet. The thermometer at
Circle City stood at 60° below zero at dark that day, and down on the ice it
is always about 5° colder than on the bank, because cold air is heavy air and
sinks to the lowest level, and 65° below zero means 97° below freezing.

My moose-hide breeches froze solid the moment I scrambled out, but not a drop of water got to my feet. If the water had reached my feet they would have frozen almost as quickly as the moose hide in that fearful cold. Thoroughly alarmed now, and realising our perilous situation, we did the only thing there was to do—we turned the dogs loose and abandoned the sled and went back along the trail we had followed as fast as we could. We knew that we could safely retrace our steps and that the trail would lead us to the bank after a while. We knew not where the trail would lead us in the other direction. As a matter of fact, it led to the mail cabin, two miles farther on, and the mail-carrier was at that time occupying it at the end of his day's run.

The dogs stayed with the sled; dogs will usually stay with their sled; they seem to recognize their first allegiance to the load they haul, probably because they know their food forms part of it.

Our cache reached, we made a fire, thawed out the iron-like armour of my leather breeches, and cutting a spare woollen scarf in two, wrapped the dry, warm pieces about my numbed thighs. Then we pushed on the eighteen miles or so to Circle, keeping a steady pace despite the drowsiness that oppressed us, and that oppressed me particularly owing to the chill of my ducking. About five in the morning we reached the town, and the clergyman, the Reverend C. E. Rice, turned out of his warm bed and I turned in, none the worse in body for the experience, but much humbled in spirit. My companion, Mr. E. J. Knapp, whose thoughtful care for me I always look back upon with gratitude, as well as upon Mr. Rice's kindness, froze his nose and a toe slightly, being somewhat neglectful of himself in his solicitude for me.

We had been out about twenty hours in a temperature ranging from 52° to 60° below zero, had walked about forty-four miles, labouring incessantly as well as walking, what time we were with the sled, with nothing to eat— it was too cold to stop for eating—and, in addition to this, one of us had been in water to the waist, yet none of us took any harm. It was a providential over-ruling of blundering foolhardiness for which we were deeply thankful.

The next day a native with a fast team and an empty toboggan was sent down to take our load on to the cabin and bring the dogs back. Meanwhile, the mail-carrier had passed the spot, had seen the abandoned sled standing by recently broken ice, and had come on into town while we slept and none knew of our return, with the news that some one had been drowned. The mail for Fairbanks did but await the mail from Fort Yukon, and the town rumour, instantly identifying the abandoned sled, was carried across to Fairbanks, to my great distress and annoyance. The echoes of the distorted account of this misadventure which appeared in a Fairbanks newspaper still reverberate in "patent insides" of the provincial press of the United States.

The next Monday we started again, this time with a toboggan and with a man instead of a boy for guide, and in three days of only moderate difficulty we reached Fort Yukon.

At the Foot of Denali

TIM MCNULTY

Northwest poet and nature writer Tim McNulty lives on Washington state's
Olympic Peninsula with his family. An active conservationist, his poems and
natural history articles have appeared in numerous periodicals, and he has
published several volumes of poems and a number of books about our country's
national parks. "At the Foot of Denali" is taken from his poetry collection
IN BLUE MOUNTAIN DUSK *(1992).*

At the edge of a storm
a few drops scatter over broken talus,
deepen the palm-smooth texture of shale:
  thin bands of rust, delicate
        trace of lichen—
so slightly,
and the wind blows it dry.

Above us the ice, blue
against a dark motionless sky.
A tumult stream buries itself,
its song
    a long steady windlike thing
lost beneath the glacier's edge.

In the early light
small patches of moss weave footholds;
        stonecrop
          wedged among banks of gravel
saxifrage:
some small nameless insect
  fluorescent-winged at its blossoms.

The birds and mammals have yet to be born,
salmon to try these ice-bound streams.
The trees have long ago turned back.
   And we come
slow and bedraggled, strung
together like beads on a thread.
   Long heaps of shattered rock,
   dark walls lifting into clouds,
     snow-streaked, wind-worn . . .

Come from the war dance on terrazzo floors,
come from the arms of strangers,
Cold one; come
as though this northern reach of wind and snow
were somehow
all that's left for earth.

As though this train of ice, slow
and barren miles
out to the plain where life begins,
were the first river.

And far down a doorstep valley
a people live in peace.

Dogmusher

RUBEN GAINES

Ruben Gaines (1913–1994) was a pioneer Alaskan broadcaster, poet, humorist, storyteller, and cartoonist. Alaskans remember one of his most delightful poetic characters, the sourdough giant Chilkoot Charlie, a Northern version of the Midwestern folk figure Paul Bunyan. Gaines was Alaska's fifth poet laureate, and lived many years in Anchorage. His work is anthologized in ALASKA *'76. "Dogmusher," written specifically for "The Great Land," an audio-visual presentation centered around a series of oil paintings by Rusty Heurlin, first appeared in print in Gaines's poetry collection* ON DISTANCE AND RECALL *(1980).*

The weather cold enough to suit you, boys?
I know, like you, that certain of life's joys
Are much to be preferred above some others
And fifty-odd below is one which, brothers,
We figure as among the least delights.
When days can't be distinguished from the nights
And vapor from the breath of dog and man
Surrounds our mid-Alaskan caravan
It truly seems this little crowd, you five
And me, are all the creatures left alive.
But loneliness and cold are just the price we pay
For living as we want to anyway:
A hundred miles, for better or for worse,
Of trapline, is our chosen universe;
It suits us well. And incidentally
These stunted spruce are lovely scenery.
They mean we won't be putting in the night
Along the trail again; the cabin is in sight.

The Sourdough Expedition, 1910

FROM *To the Top of Denali*

BILL SHERWONIT

Bill Sherwonit is a journalist, college instructor, photographer, and nonfiction writer. Born in Connecticut and educated as a geologist, he joined the now-defunct Anchorage Times *in 1982, first as a sportswriter and then as the paper's outdoor writer. His work has appeared in a variety of publications, including* Audubon, Climbing, National Wildlife, Outside, Summit, *and* Wilderness *magazines. In 1987, Sherwonit climbed to the summit of Mount McKinley. "The Sourdough Expedition, 1910" first appeared in his book* TO THE TOP OF DENALI: CLIMBING ADVENTURES ON NORTH AMERICA'S HIGHEST PEAK *(1990).*

Choosing the most significant mountaineering accomplishment in Alaska's climbing history is an imposing, if not impossible, task.

As Valdez physician and climber Andy Embick explains, "There are just so many categories to consider. Are you talking about big-wall climbs? First ascents? Solo ascents? Winter climbs? Comparing those different kinds of climbs is like comparing apples and oranges. It just can't be done."

Perhaps. But, believing it would be fun—and educational—to try, I conducted an informal and quite unscientific telephone poll of approximately twenty veteran Alaska mountaineers to see if those most devoted to climbing and exploring Alaska's high places could reach some consensus. I asked participants to name the mountaineering feat(s) they considered to be the most significant or noteworthy, with no limit on the number and types of choices.

The variety of responses was enormous. More than thirty expeditions received mention. Some, such as the first winter ascent of Mount McKinley by Art Davidson, Ray Genet, and Dave Johnston in 1967, are well-publicized mountaineering masterpieces. Others, such as John Waterman's five-month solo of Mount Hunter in 1978, have received little public attention but are considered classics within the mountaineering community.

From the many opinions offered, one expedition stood out from all the rest: the Sourdough Expedition of 1910. A handful of other climbs received as much mention, but none was so enthusiastically endorsed. The Sourdoughs were the first or second choice of about a third of all those polled.

Steve Davis's response was typical of Sourdough supporters. "It's phenomenal, what they did," said Davis, an Anchorage-based marine fisheries biologist and mountaineer, who has served several years on the American Alpine Club's board of directors. "The Sourdoughs pulled off one of the best pioneering efforts ever. Their ascent (from 11,000 feet to the summit of McKinley's 19,470-foot North Peak) was the equivalent of an alpine-style climb; they did it so quickly. And carrying a huge spruce pole, no less."

Jim Hale, a former McKinley guide and now pastor of the Talkeetna Christian Center, added, "For those guys to reach the top with homemade equipment and so little climbing experience, while hauling a spruce pole, is just incredible. It's superhuman by today's standards. Those guys had to be tough as nails."

More than any other group of climbers, past or present, the Sourdoughs seem to symbolize the pioneering spirit and adventurous nature of what is often called the Alaskan mystique. Over the past eight decades, their ascent has become the stuff of legend, and rightly so. This group of four gold miners challenged North America's highest peak with the most rudimentary gear and no technical climbing experience, simply to disprove explorer Frederick Cook's claim of reaching the mountain's summit in 1906 and to demonstrate that Alaskans could outdo the exploits—whether real or imagined—of any "Easterners."

That they succeeded in a brazen style uniquely their own delights Todd Miner, who calls their ascent a "climbing masterpiece." "To me, one of the most appealing aspects of the expedition is that it was a bunch of locals doing it," said Miner, an Anchorage mountaineer who also coordinates the University of Alaska Anchorage's Alaska Wilderness Studies Program. "It's a classic case of Alaskans showing Outsiders how it's done."

The expedition reached its literal high point on April 3, 1910, when Sourdoughs Billy Taylor and Pete Anderson reached the top of McKinley's 19,470-foot North Peak, widely recognized as a more difficult ascent than the higher—and ultimately more prestigious—20,320-foot South Peak. The Sourdoughs' reason for choosing the North Peak seemed quite logical at the time; the miners hoped that the fourteen-foot spruce pole, complete with a six- by twelve-foot American flag they'd lugged up McKinley, would be seen from Fairbanks and serve as visible proof of their conquest.

Taylor and Anderson made their summit push from 11,000 feet. Hauling their flagpole, they climbed more than 8,000 vertical feet and then descended to camp in eighteen hours' time—an outstanding feat by any mountaineering standard. (By comparison, most present-day McKinley expeditions climb no more than 3,000 to 4,000 vertical feet on summit day, which typically lasts ten to fifteen hours.) Yet the Sourdoughs' final incredible ascent is merely one chapter in an altogether remarkable story that for many years was steeped in controversy and, as historian Terrence Cole notes, "is still shrouded in mystery."

As seems to be the case with so many legendary Alaskan adventures, the Sourdough Expedition began with some barroom braggadocio. Or so the story goes. The expedition's leader and instigator was Tom Lloyd, a Welshman and former Utah sheriff who came to Alaska during the Klondike gold rush, eventually settling in the Kantishna Hills north of Mount McKinley.

In the fall of 1909, Lloyd and several other patrons of a Fairbanks bar joined in a discussion that focused on Frederick Cook's claim that he'd reached McKinley's summit in 1906. As the *Fairbanks Daily Times* noted in 1909, "Ever since Dr. Cook described his ascent of Mount McKinley, Alaskans have been suspicious of the accuracy of this explorer." Although Cook's account was later demonstrated to be a hoax, in 1909 there was still no definitive proof that he'd lied.

According to Lloyd's official account of the Sourdough Expedition, which appeared in *The New York Times Sunday Magazine* on June 5, 1910, "[Bar owner] Bill McPhee and me were talking one day of the possibility of getting to the summit of Mount McKinley and I said I thought if anyone could make the climb there were several pioneers of my acquaintance who could. Bill said he didn't believe that any living man could make the ascent."

McPhee argued that the fifty-year-old Lloyd was too old and overweight for such an undertaking, to which the miner responded that "for two cents" he'd show it could be done. To call Lloyd's bluff, McPhee offered to pay $500 to anyone who would climb McKinley and "prove whether that fellow Cook made the climb or not."

After two other businessmen agreed to put up $500 each, Lloyd accepted the challenge. The proposed expedition was big news in Fairbanks, and before long it made local headlines. In his official account, Lloyd admitted, "Of course, after the papers got hold of the story we hated the idea of ever coming back here defeated."

A seven-man party left Fairbanks in December 1909, accompanied by four horses, a mule, and a dog team. Their send-off included an editorial in the *Fairbanks Daily Times,* which promised, "Our boys will succeed . . . and they'll show up Dr. Cook and the other 'Outside' doctors and expeditions."

Original team members included Tom Lloyd, Billy Taylor, Pete Anderson, Charles McGonagall, C. E. Davidson, Bob Horne, and a person identified as W. Lloyd. But the latter three men quit before the actual climbing began, following a dispute between Tom Lloyd and Davidson, a talented surveyor/photographer whose role with the expedition, according to Cole, was "to map the route and keep track of elevations."

In his account of the Sourdough Expedition, Terris Moore writes that Lloyd antagonized Davidson after the first of the team's mountain camps had been established, further noting that one report mentions a fistfight. After that confrontation, Davidson departed for Fairbanks accompanied by Horne and W. Lloyd. The expedition was left with four members, all miners from the Kantishna District: Taylor was Lloyd's mining partner; McGonagall and Anderson each had worked several years for the two property owners.

The Sourdoughs spent most of February establishing a series of camps in the lowlands and foothills on the north side of McKinley. By the end of the month, they'd set up their mountain base of operations near the mouth of Cache Creek at an elevation of about 2,900 feet, which they called the Willows Camp.

On March 1, the team began "prospecting for the big climb," Lloyd wrote in his expedition diary. "Anderson and McGonagall examined the [Muldrow] glacier today. We call it the 'Wall Street Glacier,' being enclosed by exceedingly high walls on each side." Three days later, they set up their first glacier camp. Lloyd, who'd lost the barometer loaned him by Davidson, estimated the camp's elevation at 9,000 to 10,000 feet, but it was probably much lower. Team members then descended and spent the next several days cutting firewood and hauling it up the glacier, along with a wood-burning stove.

Traversing the Muldrow proved to be quite intimidating. As Lloyd explained in his diary:

For the first four or five miles there are no crevasses in sight, as they have been blown full of snow, but the next eight miles are terrible for crevasses. You can look down in them for distances stretching from 100 feet to Hades or China. Look down one of them and you never will forget it. . . . Most of them appear to be bottomless. These are not good things to look at.

Despite the danger of a crevasse fall, the climbers traveled unroped, a practice most contemporary McKinley mountaineers would considered foolhardy. There's no way to know whether the Sourdoughs' decision was made in ignorance or disdain for such protection. Years later, when asked why the team chose not to use climbing ropes, Taylor simply answered, "Didn't need them." Such an attitude seems to reflect the Sourdoughs' style. With the notable exception of their fourteen-foot flagpole, they chose to travel light.

The team had "less 'junk' with them than an Eastern excursion party would take along for a one-day's outing in the hills," wrote W. F. Thompson, editor of the *Fairbanks Daily News-Miner,* who prepared Lloyd's story for publication in *The New York Times.* The Sourdoughs' climbing gear consisted of only the bare essentials: snowshoes; homemade crampons, which they called creepers; and crude ice axes, which Lloyd described as "long poles with double hooks on one end—hooks made of steel—and a sharp steel point on the other end." Their high-altitude food supplies included bacon, beans, flour, sugar, dried fruits, butter, coffee, hot chocolate, and caribou meat. To endure the subzero cold, they simply wore bib overalls, long underwear, shirts, parkas, mittens, shoepacs (insulated rubber boots), and Indian moccasins. (The moccasins that the pioneer McKinley climbers wore were like Eskimo mukluks: tall, above-the-calf footwear, dry-tanned, with a moose-hide sole and caribou-skin uppers. Worn with insoles and at least three pairs of wool socks, they were reportedly very warm and provided plenty of support.)

Even their reading material was limited. The climbers brought only one magazine, which they read from end to end. "I don't remember the name of the magazine," Lloyd later commented, "but in our estimation it is the best magazine published in the world."

Other essentials included wooden stakes for trail marking and poles for crevasse crossings. The poles were placed across crevasses too wide to jump; the men then piled snow between the poles, which hardened and froze, creating a bridge over which the climbers could travel on snowshoes.

The team reached the site of its third and final camp on March 17, at the head of the Muldrow Glacier. Lloyd estimated the elevation at "not less than 15,000 feet," though later McKinley explorers determined the camp's altitude could have been no higher than 11,000 feet. The climbers spent the next several days digging a protective tunnel into the snow, relaying supplies from lower camps, cutting steps into the ice along what is now called Karstens Ridge, and enduring stormy weather.

On April 1, the Sourdoughs made their first summit attempt. But they were forced by stormy weather to turn back. Two days later, they tried again. Outfitted with a bag of doughnuts, three thermos bottles of hot chocolate (and caribou meat, according to some accounts), and their fourteen-foot spruce pole, Taylor, Anderson, and McGonagall headed for the summit at 3:00 A.M. Lloyd apparently had moved down to the Willows Camp; exactly why isn't clear, but he may have been suffering from altitude sickness. Unroped, without the benefit of any climbing aid other than their crude homemade crampons and ice axes, the three climbers ascended Karstens Ridge, crossed the Grand Basin—later to be named the Harper Glacier— and headed up a steep couloir now known as the Sourdough Gully.

A few hundred feet below the summit, McGonagall stopped. Years later, in a conversation with alpine historian Francis Farquhar, he explained, "No, I didn't go clear to the top—why should I? I'd finished my turn carrying the pole before we got there. Taylor and Pete finished the job—I sat down and rested, then went back to camp." Grant Pearson suggests otherwise in his book *My Life of High Adventure,* claiming that McGonagall fell victim to altitude sickness.

Taylor and Anderson continued on, however, still hauling their spruce pole. And sometime late in the afternoon, they concluded their unprecedented ascent by standing atop the North Peak's summit. Twenty-seven years later, in an interview eventually published in *The American Alpine Journal,* Taylor recalled that he and Anderson spent two and a half hours on top of the mountain, though the temperature reached as low as -30°F that day. "It was colder than hell," he reported. "Mitts and everything was all ice."

Before descending back to camp, the Sourdoughs planted their pole, complete with American flag. Said Taylor, "We . . . built a pyramid of [rocks] about fifteen inches high and we dug down in the ice so the pole had a support of about thirty inches and was held by four guy lines—just cotton ropes. We fastened the guy lines to little spurs of rock." Though they'd planned to leave their flagpole at the summit, the climbers were forced to plant it on the highest available rock outcropping, located a few hundred feet below the top.

Taylor and Anderson returned to the high camp late that night, completing their climb in eighteen hours. The next day, all members of the party were reunited at the Willows Camp. No attempt to climb the South Peak was made.

Their mission accomplished, Taylor, Anderson, and McGonagall returned to Kantishna. Lloyd, meanwhile, traveled to Fairbanks with news of the history-making ascent. Unfortunately, the Sourdough Expedition's team leader decided to mix fantasy with fact, and the team's true feat was transformed into an Alaskan tall tale. Returning to a hero's welcome on April 11, Lloyd proclaimed that the entire party had reached the summits of both the North and South Peaks. Furthermore, they'd found no evidence to substantiate Cook's claims.

Word of the team's success quickly spread. On April 12, the *Fairbanks Daily Times* published an account of the historic climb, and the story quickly made headlines around the country. According to historian Cole, "Congratulations poured in, including a telegram from President William Howard Taft."

Not everyone took Lloyd's word at face value, however. On April 16, *The New York Times* ran a story in which naturalist/explorer Charles Sheldon challenged Lloyd's claims:

> It is clearly the duty of the press . . . not to encourage full credibility in the reports of the alleged ascent until the facts and details are authoritatively published. Only Tom Lloyd apparently brought out the report, the other members of the party having remained in the Kantishna District 150 miles away; so we haven't had their corroborative evidence.

Despite such published doubts, *The New York Times* successfully bid for first rights to a detailed report of the climb. And on June 5, the newspaper devoted three pages of its Sunday magazine section to the Sourdough Expedition; the package included a story of the ascent written by W. F. Thompson plus Lloyd's own firsthand account, which featured entries from his daily record. A day later, the story ran in London's *Daily Telegraph*.

Even as Thompson was preparing his *New York Times* article, the challenges to Lloyd's account increased. Other evidence of the ascent was demanded, but photos taken during the expedition proved unsatisfactory. Lloyd felt enough pressure that he asked Taylor, Anderson, and McGonagall to repeat the climb and secure additional photos. In a little-known but fascinating adventure, the three climbers reascended McKinley in May. They reached Denali Pass (elevation about 18,200 feet) and took additional photographs of the mountain. Nearly forty years later, McGonagall recalled: "We didn't camp—we just kept going for three days—it was light enough and we were all skookum [an Indian word meaning strong or heroic]." The photos resulting from the second climb remain one of the Sourdough Expedition's many mysteries, because apparently they were never published.

With no solid proof to back up Lloyd's boasts, skepticism continued to build, such doubts being reinforced in part by the Sourdough leader's age and overweight condition; according to Taylor, Lloyd was "awful fat." Before long, the Sourdoughs were looked on no more favorably than Cook, the man they'd hoped to discredit. According to Cole:

> The contradictions in [Lloyd's] story and the fact that he supposedly admitted in private to some of his friends that he had not climbed the mountain himself, eventually discredited the entire expedition. Soon the Sourdoughs and their flagpole were regarded as just one more fascinating frontier tale, about as believable as an exploit of Paul Bunyan.

Back in Kantishna, the other Sourdough team members were unaware that Lloyd's false claims had caused their mountaineering feat to fall into disrepute. When interviewed in 1937, Taylor said, "He [Lloyd] was the head of the party and we never dreamed he wouldn't give a straight story. I wish to God we hadda been there. . . . We didn't get out till June and then they didn't believe any of us had climbed it."

Taylor also said that he didn't give prior approval to Lloyd's account of the climb that appeared in *The New York Times*. Yet on June 11, each of the Sourdoughs signed a notarized statement that "a party of four in number known as the Lloyd party" had reached the North Peak at 3:25 P.M. on April 3, 1910. Whether they knew in advance of Lloyd's fictitious account, or chose to go along with his claims because of some misplaced loyalty, none of the Sourdoughs publicly challenged their leader's story until years later.

(There's an interesting historical sidenote to the Sourdough Expedition. At least partly because of embarrassment about its role in the promotion of

Lloyd's story, the *Fairbanks Daily Times* organized its own McKinley expedition in 1912. Led by Ralph Cairns, the newspaper's telegraph editor, the party reached McKinley's base in late February. The climbers failed to find McGonagall Pass, which provides the easiest access to the Muldrow Glacier, and instead set up base camp on the Peters Glacier, following a route similar to that taken by Wickersham in 1903. Like the Wickersham party, the Cairns Expedition was turned back at about 10,000 feet by apparently unclimbable ice walls. On April 10, 1912, the *Times* ran a front-page story reporting the team's failure.)

A final blow to the Sourdoughs' believability was struck in 1912, when Belmore Browne and Herschel Parker reported that they saw no evidence of the fourteen-foot flagpole during their attempt to climb McKinley. Because Browne and Parker carefully documented their own ascent, great credibility was given to their point of view. In his report of the 1912 climb, Browne wrote:

> On our journey up the glacier from below we had begun to study the North Peak. . . . Every rock and snow slope of that approach had come into the field of our powerful binoculars. We not only saw no sign of the flagpole, but it is our concerted opinion that the northern peak is more inaccessible than its higher southern sister.

Though Browne intended only to disprove the Sourdoughs' claims, he ultimately paid them a great compliment by noting the greater difficulty faced in climbing the North Peak. Parker, meanwhile, was quoted as saying, "Dr. Cook didn't have anything on the Lloyd party when it comes to fabrications." Case closed. Or so it seemed at the time. The Sourdough story became generally accepted as nothing more than an Alaskan tale, until the following year.

In 1913, after a decade of unsuccessful attempts to reach the pinnacle of North America, an expedition led by Episcopal missionary Hudson Stuck placed all four of its members on McKinley's 20,320-foot summit. And en route to the top, they spotted the Sourdoughs' flagpole.

The climbers made their exciting discovery from the Grand Basin, located between the North and South Peaks. In his mountaineering classic, *The Ascent of Denali,* Stuck recalls:

> While we were resting . . . we fell to talking about the pioneer climbers of this mountain who claimed to have set a flagstaff near the summit of the

North Peak—as to which feat a great deal of incredulity existed in Alaska for several reasons—and we renewed our determination that if the weather permitted when we had reached our goal and ascended the South Peak, we would climb the North Peak also to seek for traces of this earlier exploit on Denali. . . . All at once Walter [Harper] cried out: "I see the flagstaff!" Eagerly pointing to the rocky prominence nearest the summit—the summit itself covered with snow—he added: "I see it plainly!" [Harry] Karstens, looking where he pointed, saw it also and, whipping out the field glasses, one by one we all looked, and saw it distinctly standing out against the sky. With the naked eye I was never able to see it unmistakably, but through the glasses it stood out, sturdy and strong, one side covered with crusted snow. We were greatly rejoiced that we could carry down positive confirmation of this matter.

When Stuck returned to Kantishna and told members of the Sourdough party about his team's sighting, "there was a feeling expressed that the climbing party of the previous summer [Belmore and Parker's group] must have seen it also and had suppressed mention of it." But Stuck concluded:

> There is no ground for such a damaging assumption. It would never be seen with the naked eye save by those who were intently searching for it. Professor Parker and Mr. Belmore Browne entertained the pretty general incredulity about the "Pioneer" ascent, perhaps too readily, certainly too confidently; but the men themselves must bear the chief blame for that. The writer and his party, knowing these men much better, have never [doubted] that some of them had accomplished what was claimed, and these details have been gone into for no other reason than that the honor may at least be given where honor is due.

It's especially worth noting that Stuck's party was the only group ever to verify the flagpole's existence. The next expedition to climb the North Peak, two decades later in 1932, failed to find any evidence of the pole.

Except for the one chance sighting, the Sourdoughs' story might always have been regarded as a tall tale. But thanks to the efforts of the 1913 expedition this group of skookum miners was finally and deservedly given credit for what Stuck called "a most extraordinary feat, unique—the writer has no hesitation in claiming—in all the annals of mountaineering."

Eighty years later, the Sourdoughs' achievement is still recognized as extraordinary. And certainly unique.

No Man's Land

FROM *Shadows on the Koyukuk*

SIDNEY HUNTINGTON, AS TOLD TO JIM REARDEN

Born in 1915 in Hughes, Alaska, on the banks of the Koyukuk River, Sidney Huntington is the son of an Athabascan mother and a white trapper/trader father. His fascinating life story is the subject of SHADOWS ON THE KOYUKUK *(1993), which Alaskan author Jim Rearden wrote from many taped interviews and conversations with his longtime friend, Sidney Huntington. Rearden, outdoors editor of* Alaska *magazine for twenty years and a field editor for* Outdoor Life *magazine for more than fifteen years, lives in Homer, Alaska. "No Man's Land" is excerpted from* SHADOWS ON THE KOYUKUK.

We were still trapping at Hog River in 1933 when I was eighteen. That fall I explored the Hog River-Pah River divide, part of what was called No Man's Land in the old days. The Pah drains into the Kobuk River in Eskimo country, and the divide between the Pah and Hog Rivers is fairly low. I found fair fur sign and decided to trap there. In November I put traps out along the upper Hog. A few days later, with thirty more traps in a backpack, I set out on foot from my Clear Creek cabin, planning to set more. I reached the last of my previously set traps about daylight. My traps had caught a few marten, which I hung in trees where I could pick them up on my return.

After I passed the portage trail, I started setting marten traps, following the right bank of the Hog. Hog River turns 180 degrees in a huge horseshoe; the Pah River portage takes off to the northwest from the approximate apex of the horseshoe.

By about three o'clock I had set all my traps. Encouraged by many fresh marten tracks, I headed home, backtracking and marking my trail with blazes on trees, broken branches, and other sign.

I didn't mind being alone. There was much to see—rabbit tracks, an occasional scurrying rabbit, a scolding red squirrel, a lethargic porcupine perched in a tree. A hawk-owl paced me in the treetops. Several ptarmigan leaped into flight along the stream. My snowshoes whispered through the dry snow, and I strode along, eyes busy, searching for tracks, which always told a story. The physical action felt good, and icy winter air in my lungs was like wine.

I had nearly reached the Pah River portage trail when I saw strange snowshoe tracks. Someone had followed me a ways, then had taken off on a direct line for the portage lake where most travelers camped because of sheltering timber and plentiful firewood. His stride was too long for me to step in his tracks; he was either going fast or he was a big man with long legs. I yelled a few times but received no answer.

I followed the tracks, thinking he must be camped at the usual site. Dark was near. I began to have a creepy feeling, remembering stories I had heard of missing Indians in this mountainous No Man's Land. To my knowledge, it had been decades since any Koyukon had disappeared in No Man's Land, but there were still stories. Before the turn of the century, no matter what happened to an Indian in No Man's Land—a fatal fall, freezing to death, a lethal encounter with a bear—Koyukon Indians assumed that Eskimos were responsible for the disappearance, and another story was born. Likewise, Eskimos blamed the Koyukon people for every Eskimo who failed to return from No Man's Land.

Although I was a bit nervous, I kept going. Soon I saw smoke. Although dusk was near, no light shone where the smoke was rising. No sled dogs barked. At the campsite I found the smoke was from ashes dumped from a stove. A tent had been pitched nearby. Dog and sled tracks led toward the Kobuk side of the range. It was evident that as soon as the stranger had reached camp, he had knocked his tent down, loaded his sled, and left.

I puzzled over this on the long hike home. That night my way was lit by a brilliant aurora that writhed in a huge curtain overhead, like a gigantic twisting rainbow. The reds, greens, and purples were brilliant, and great searchlightlike flashes punctuated the movements. I have heard that some people fear winters in the Far North because of the long, dark nights. In the Koyukuk, where clear skies in winter are the rule, nights are seldom really dark. It's only difficult to see when occasional heavy clouds cover the sky or when thick snow falls.

The aurora lights many winter nights, and so does the moon. The beauty of a full moon on a sparkling snowy landscape is difficult to describe: it can seem almost like full daylight, with tree shadows. Even the stars provide plenty of light for traveling on clear nights. Alaska's crystal air seems to magnify the millions of diamond-bright stars in the northern skies, and there is no background of city lights to dim their brilliance.

The following week, I went to see whether the mysterious visitor to the Pah-Hog portage had moved his camp down the Pah River a short way or had left the country. I walked eight miles to the Pah, where I poked around for awhile, following his snowshoe tracks. I concluded that the unknown person had taken up his traps and departed, despite the abundant fur sign.

A few years later, Jimmy, our brother Fred, and I made a dog team trip from Hog River to the Eskimo town of Kobuk to buy supplies. As the raven flies it is about seventy-five miles, and twice that distance by dog team. At Kobuk, trader Harry Brown asked me where I trapped.

"Usually on the Hog River, sometimes twenty or thirty miles above the Pah River portage," I answered.

"Who goes with you?" he wanted to know.

"I go alone" (Jimmy seldom trapped the area with me).

"What!" he exclaimed.

"I go alone," I repeated.

He then told me that several years earlier he had staked two Eskimos who had gone to trap at the Pah-Hog portage. They had soon returned, reporting "a big band of Indians traveling on the south bank of the Hog River."

"They said they had barely escaped with their lives," said Brown. "They told me that the Indians were hollering signals to each other."

I realized then that my yells had been heard, and like me, the Eskimos had remembered the stories of danger in No Man's Land and had fled. I wonder what their thoughts would have been had they realized that they had run from one youthful, medium-sized Indian, who was also somewhat spooked.

As a youngster I heard from my relatives and other Koyukon Indians many tales of the murder and violence of earlier years. Some of the stories dated to prewhite times, seven or eight decades before I was born. Many stories of murders by both Eskimos and Indians originated from the Zane Hills and Purcell Mountains, the rugged low mountains and hills that lie between the Koyukuk and Kobuk country—No Man's Land.

Neither Indian nor Eskimo controlled No Man's Land. Adventurous individuals who penetrated that remote area sometimes disappeared. Long before I was born, my uncle Frank, brother to my mother, went hunting in No Man's Land. Hog River Johnny, his brother, was to meet him there. When Johnny arrived at the meeting place, Frank was gone. Reading the tracks, Johnny could tell that Frank had arrived and met someone, but the trail disappeared and so did Frank. He was never seen again.

Years later a rumor drifted across the land: Eskimos from the Kobuk Valley had heard that Eskimos from the Selawik district had "taken" (killed) a man from the Koyukuk River. Based on the rumor, hunters from the Koyukuk, seeking revenge for the loss of Frank, supposedly went up the Dakli River and waited for some Eskimos to enter No Man's Land. After some weeks an Eskimo family arrived. Local legend had it that the Indians killed every member.

Old Toby, a Koyukon from the Kateel River country in the Koyukuk valley, died at an old age more than seventy years ago. His son, Young Toby, was one of the last of the Indians from the Kateel. Young Toby was also one of the great Koyukon song makers. During the early 1930s Young Toby told me this story:

> About 1850, Old Toby, then a young man, was hunting with a partner at the headwaters of the Kateel. The two men found evidence that strange hunters had taken game there.
>
> They consulted other Koyukon Indians. The group decided to send two of their finest hunter/warriors into the Kateel area before the prime fall hunting season. The Indians selected Old Toby and his partner for this assignment. Old Toby, a six-footer, was unusually tall for a Koyukon Indian.
>
> The two slipped into the headwaters region of the Kateel, making every effort to conceal their presence. While lying hidden in a brushy area one day shortly after their arrival, they noticed unusual movements of caribou on a high ridge of the Kateel valley. The animals trotted about nervously, as if human hunters were near.
>
> The two warriors studied a thick stand of spruce trees at the end of the ridge, about half a mile from the river. Nearby was a large lake that held a beaver lodge. They suspected that hunters were hiding in those trees—not Koyukon Indians, but Eskimos.
>
> Old Toby and his partner prepared themselves for a long stay in their hiding place. Only after darkness fell did they move from hiding to stretch and get a drink of water. They ate dried meat and fish, and lit no fire. Carefully, they observed what was happening.

On the afternoon of the third day after the unusual caribou behavior, a small bunch of the animals wandered off the high ridge. When they reached the end of the ridge near the timber, all but one suddenly bolted. A remaining caribou staggered about for a few moments as if hit by an arrow, then it fell. As darkness came, the caribou remained where it had fallen, but by the next morning it had disappeared.

That night Old Toby's partner moved upstream so he could get a closer view of the other side of the river the next day. At the end of that day, after dark, he rejoined Old Toby. "I saw two Eskimo hunters feasting on the caribou they killed," he reported.

"They have made a foolish mistake, taking that animal in the open, revealing themselves," Old Toby said. He smiled at his partner and added, "They're not going to leave, because the beaver lodge in that lake has six beaver—two old ones, two medium-size ones, and two small ones. They won't leave those fat animals alone. We will have our chance if we are patient. But we must be careful."

That night the two Koyukon warriors schemed, basing their plans on the presence of the six beaver. Before daylight, Old Toby's partner crossed the river to await the opportune time. He and Toby believed that only one Eskimo hunter would go to the lake to take a beaver, while the Eskimo who remained behind stood guard.

Sure enough, toward evening on the third or fourth day after the Eskimos had killed the caribou, Old Toby saw an Eskimo sneaking near the timber at the edge of the lake. At that moment Old Toby, still on the south slope of the valley, showed himself. Both Eskimos quickly spotted him. Old Toby simply stood in the open, a tall, ominous, distant figure. This frightened the Eskimos.

The Eskimo who had started for the beaver lodge quickly disappeared. The Eskimo standing guard was too busy watching Old Toby far across the valley to worry about his partner. Realization that it was a trick didn't dawn on him until too late. As he started to look behind himself, an arrow pierced his back.

Old Toby, still standing on the south slope, heard the signal he was awaiting—one beat on a dry tree. This told him that his partner had killed the lookout. Old Toby then crossed the valley and went to the lake, searching for the beaver-hunting Eskimo. At first he saw no sign of him.

A large fallen tree lay half in the water. Old Toby walked to the base of the tree. Stooping, he discovered slight but fresh disturbances; something or someone had crawled out on the trunk of the tree. He studied the water, but could see nothing.

He walked toward the beaver lodge. Near the lodge a point of land extended into the water; reeds grew at the water's edge. The grass was undisturbed. He walked to the point and silently looked in every direction. Still he saw no sign of the missing Eskimo. The growing darkness was making it hard to see anything.

Then he noticed a movement of the water, ever so slight, at the end of the point. Had he imagined that the water lifted? No, the surface really was lifting and falling. Could someone breathing underwater cause the ripple by expanding and contracting his chest? Old Toby peered at the reeds that protruded from the water, stem by stem. Poised, with arrow ready to fly, he detected a single reed that was moving with a slight rise and fall of water. Old Toby strained his eyes as he peered into the depths. There, finally, he made out the missing Eskimo, lying on the bottom of the lake with his feet and body inside one of the tunnels to the beaver house. The hollow reed held in his mouth formed a breathing tube.

Taking careful aim, Old Toby let his arrow fly, thus ending the hunt for the Eskimo interlopers.

I have heard Eskimos tell similar stories, almost legends, about the old days, when enemy Koyukon Indians were caught in No Man's Land. After about 1900, as whites came into the country bringing their laws with them, "disappearances" of Eskimos and Indians in No Man's Land gradually ceased. Travel between the Lower Yukon or Koyukuk valley into coastal Eskimo country now requires only a few hours by snow machine, and Indians and Eskimos commonly visit back and forth without fear. The violent deaths, fear, and hate are vestiges of the past.

Alaska

FROM *In the Shadow of Eagles*

RUDY BILLBERG, AS TOLD
TO JIM REARDEN

Rudy Billberg learned to fly in a Curtiss Robin in Minnesota in 1934. After a few years as a Midwestern barnstormer, he moved to Alaska in 1941, where he was a professional aviator for forty-six years. The Billbergs lived in Nome, in the Yukon River Athabascan village of Galena, and in several other bush towns and villages. His long and adventurous career as a pilot of bush planes and large carriers is chronicled in his memoir IN THE SHADOW OF EAGLES (1992), from which "Alaska" is taken; the book is a collaboration with his longtime friend, writer Jim Rearden.

In 1941, the interior Alaska town of Fairbanks was simple, uncrowded, charming. Log homes and buildings dominated. Weeks Field, the airport, was at the edge of town. The view of the great snow-clad peaks of the Alaska Range, 75 miles to the south, was breathtaking. The calm, dry climate was invigorating. Even today's bustling Fairbanks has a charm and a feel of the frontier that is lacking in most of Alaska's other larger cities. Fairbanks is at the end of the railroad that runs from the coastal town of Seward. Mining and furs had long fueled the town's economy. In 1941, a military buildup was under way. Fairbanks was and still is the hub of myriad tiny settlements in the vast Interior of Alaska.

That fall, Bessie, 13-month-old Cathy, and I flew as passengers in a Northwest Airlines DC-3 from Minnesota to Seattle. I didn't have the slightest idea that soon I would be piloting one of these mammoth wonders of the air. To us the DC-3 was the height of aviation technology and luxury. From Seattle, we booked passage on the Alaska Steamship Company's SS *Denali*. It was Bessie's first time aboard a ship, but I was an old-timer, having ridden from Seattle to Juneau and back in 1937.

The coastal mountains rise steeply from the sea along the Inside Passage of southeastern Alaska, dense conifer forests crowding their lower flanks. Above treeline, the lofty peaks are rocky and snow-covered. Forested islands, big and small, sprinkle the channels and straits.

As we traveled, we gawked up at the rugged coastal ranges of British Columbia and Alaska. I had never flown in such mountains, and I wondered: what kind of air currents would I encounter among these great peaks? I had heard other pilots speak respectfully of mountain flying.

From Juneau, after waiting two days for good weather, we flew in a twin-engine Lockheed 10-A to Whitehorse, Yukon Territory. We stayed there overnight, and the next day flew on Pan American Airways' Lockheed 14 (predecessor of the Lockheed Lodestar) to Fairbanks.

Immediately, we were delighted with Fairbanks, a small town not unlike our home area in Minnesota. Trees and plants were similar. Life was slow-paced, pleasant. Everyone was friendly.

I found the Wien Airways office a short distance from Weeks Field and checked in. "You're to be stationed at Nome," said the manager. "We'll fly you and your family there as soon as we can."

I knew little about Nome, and innocently I assumed it would be like Fairbanks. I was beginning to realize that Alaska was a bewildering land of vast reaches, varied climate, and primitive conditions. I certainly didn't realize that it was one-fifth the size of all the rest of the states combined. Or, that only about 75,000 residents occupied the entire Territory.

At that time, there were only about 100 airfields and 200 airplanes in all of Alaska. The airfields ranged from narrow, crooked, over-a-mountain goat tracks, to large, improved river bars. None was paved. No government program existed to build airports in Alaska until World War II. Airplanes included mainly Stinsons, Pilgrims, Travel Airs, Cessnas, Fairchilds, Bellancas, and a few Lockheeds—all cabin planes.

After the flight from Whitehorse to Fairbanks, I began to understand the vastness of the muskeg and forest. Current maps revealed many blanks—unmapped areas—in remote regions of Alaska. I was to learn that in the Interior, where I spent most of my years, temperatures can skid to 80 degrees below zero Fahrenheit in winter, and sizzle at more than 100 degrees in summer. Mosquitoes can be so abundant that they can kill an unprepared pilot forced down in the wrong place at the wrong time.

Huge herds of caribou wandered the mountains and tundra. Moose, too, lived in great numbers in this wild land. Black bears, polar bears, and brown/grizzly bears—the latter the largest of earth's land carnivores—are still abundant in Alaska. Silver-scaled salmon pour into many coastal streams annually in a proliferation of nature that seems unreal. Yet there are thousands of square miles of barrenness—high, rocky peaks that scrape the sky, and 10,000-year-old glaciers. The glaciers—rivers of ice—in their blue-ice splendor flow slowly down many of the mountains.

Daylight hours in summer are almost continuous, and in December at Fairbanks there are but four hours of light each day. Things Alaskan seem bigger and more violent than anywhere else. It is a challenging land that can break even the strongest, and a land of opportunity for the bold.

Two or three days after our arrival at Fairbanks, Wien pilot Bill Lund arrived from Nome. He flew a four-place Cessna Airmaster powered with a 145-horsepower Warner radial engine. We were to return with him to Nome, our new home. It was late October, and it had turned cold. All of the small ponds near Fairbanks were frozen over, and fresh snow lay on the higher peaks. Bill loaded us into the Airmaster and took off.

As we flew over the frozen landscape, I reflected on how that October day in 1941 was a mere 16 years after the first commercial flight between Fairbanks and Nome. The bold pilot of that pioneering flight was Noel Wien. He flew a Fokker F. III, a huge, single-engine monoplane that was 12 feet tall at the middle of its two-foot-thick cantilevered wing. Wien sat in an open cockpit in front of the wing and next to the 240-horsepower, six-cylinder, water-cooled BMW engine. That airplane could haul 1,200 pounds, and it flew at 90 miles an hour. In the cabin, separated from the pilot, the five passengers sat on upholstered chairs and a sofalike bench. The plush cabin had a carpeted floor, with glass flower-holders on the walls.

The airplane, built in Holland in 1921, had flown passengers for KLM airlines in Europe. For $9,500, Wien had purchased it in New York for Fairbanks Airplane Company. Disassembled, this European plane was shipped to Fairbanks via the Panama Canal. The Fokker had no brakes.

On June 5, 1925, about an hour before midnight, Wien coaxed the huge ship into the air and headed for 530-mile-distant Nome. He followed the Tanana River to the Yukon River. He then flew down the Yukon. He navigated by following rivers and locating other prominent land features on a map. There was no radio. There were no landing strips, as such, between Fairbanks and Nome.

His brother Ralph rode as mechanic in the after cabin with the passengers—a mining engineer and two women—and 500 pounds of baggage. Noel expected to find sandbars along the Yukon River in case he had to make an emergency landing. In fact, he planned to land on a sandbar at

Ruby, on the Yukon River, to refuel. But the river was high, and the sand-bars were all covered with water, including the one at Ruby.

Half an hour beyond Ruby, wondering where he could land to refuel, Wien flew into a storm. Remembering a small, cleared spot near Ruby, he turned back. He had no choice but to land in that clearing. The big, heavily loaded Fokker touched down in the clearing, which Noel soon learned was a baseball field. It then ran uphill, over the top of a rise, and started downhill. Having flown airplanes that had no brakes, I can imagine the helpless feeling Noel must have had as his plane ran into a soft spot and slowly nosed over onto its back. The Fokker's propeller was broken and the rudder damaged, but no one was injured.

The passengers went on to Nome by boat. Noel and Ralph Wien sent to Fairbanks for a new propeller, repaired the rudder, and with help from Ruby residents, righted the airplane. In a couple of days Wien took off and flew nonstop to Nome, where he landed on the parade ground of abandoned Fort Davis, an army camp established to provide protection for early gold diggers.

Noel Wien had broken trail. That Fairbanks-Nome flight was one of Alaska's great pioneer flights. To that point, fast travel time from Fairbanks to Nome in summer had been 15 days by boat. The three passengers who had traveled by boat from Ruby to Nome arrived one day after Wien's airplane.

Noel flew the Fokker nonstop back to Fairbanks. Two years later, in 1927, with a Hisso-powered Standard, he started regular air service from Nome to Fairbanks. After six months, he purchased from explorer Sir Hubert Wilkins the Detroiter II, a four-place cabin biplane, the fifth Stinson airplane built. With this plane he provided the first year-round air service between Nome and Fairbanks.

On our way to Nome with Bill Lund, I sat in the copilot's seat with a map on my lap. For the first couple of hours we followed big rivers, first the Tanana, then the broad, silty Yukon River, as had Noel Wien. Never had I seen a land with so few signs of man. Below me, here and there were dogsled trails. Occasionally, smoke rose from tiny log cabin villages on the river-banks. Stretched out before us lay America's last wilderness frontier, and I was excited. But I was also apprehensive. I was accustomed to surveyed land where section lines ran north and south and east and west—to seeing highways, railroads, and towns every few miles. Here were great forests, treeless tundra, huge river valleys, and, in the distance, snow-covered mountains with sky-scraping peaks.

In about two hours we arrived at Galena, a small Indian village on the north shore of the Yukon River. Bill landed on a big gravel bar near the village. The temperature was minus 30 degrees Fahrenheit and the bar was frozen solid—a perfect landing place.

After Bill refueled, we left the Yukon valley and flew across the Nulato Hills, the last barrier between the Interior and the Bering Sea. These are low but extremely rugged mountains. Peaks rise to about 3,400 feet, and they are slashed by heavily timbered deep canyons and steep ridges.

Being a flatlander, fresh from Minnesota, with a vivid memory of 49 in-flight engine failures, I peered into the canyons and looked at the steep ridges with much trepidation. "What on earth do you do if an engine quits when you're over this country?" I asked Bill.

He smiled grimly, shook his head, and shrugged.

"You must have top-notch equipment," I ventured, "and keep your engines up."

"We try," he said, noncommittally, "and we don't expect engine failure."

He wasn't speaking for me. I didn't see how I was going to fly in this rugged country.

We arrived at Nome five hours after leaving Fairbanks. This gold-rush town, 150 miles south of the Arctic Circle, lies on the south side of the mostly treeless, windswept Seward Peninsula. Constantly battered by Bering Sea storms, the sad-looking frame houses and other buildings appeared as if they had been sandblasted. Little paint remained. Many of the buildings had been hastily erected in the early 1900s. Some leaned, others sagged. Most looked as if they needed replacing. Even today, the sidewalks are boardwalks. In 1941, the streets were dirt-mud, at spring breakup. It was the bleakest town in the bleakest area I had ever seen. Even the poorest rural village I knew in Minnesota looked prosperous and comfortable by comparison.

Mining was the lifeblood of Nome. More than $100 million worth of gold had been wrested from Nome area mines in the four decades before our arrival. Mining had changed from one- or two-man operations with crude equipment to large-scale dredging efforts run by big companies. There were perhaps 30 working mines on the Seward Peninsula in 1941.

Because Wien Airways had yet to find a place for us to live, we had to check in to the Patterson Hotel. Our room overlooked the Bering Sea. Seven big ships were anchored offshore a couple of miles. Nome had no harbor. Lighters—small boats—were busily hauling freight ashore. There would be no more ships for eight or nine months, because ice on the Bering Sea prevents winter maritime traffic.

An icy wind constantly blew from the Bering Sea, and the curtains in our room at the ramshackle Patterson billowed out from the closed windows. Nome was a town of drafts. The doors of most buildings in Nome, including the Patterson, were warped, fitted loosely, and were often stuck.

After I looked about, I realized I had moved my family into a truly primitive frontier town. There was no plumbing. Water was delivered house to house in containers. Instead of flush toilets, every home had a honey bucket (chemical toilet). To me, most of the houses looked like shacks. Food and other living costs were astronomical. I was running low on money, and if we had to remain long, the hotel room was beyond our means.

I was discouraged and depressed. If we'd had enough money, I'd have turned around and gone back at least as far as Fairbanks. Happily, I didn't leave. Wien Airways soon found a comfortable little house for us on Steadman Street, and Nome grew on us.

When I started working for Wien, I thought that I would be flight checked very carefully by the company pilots. After that I expected to be gradually broken in to Alaskan flying. It didn't work that way.

Within a day or so after my arrival in Nome, Sig Wien took me with him on a flight to Deering, a small Eskimo community 140 miles north. We flew in the Cessna Airmaster in which Bill Lund had flown me and my family to Nome. Sig pointed out landmarks, this mountain and that, this river, that creek. He knew them all. I assumed I was on a round trip with him, but in his typical closemouthed way, he had a surprise for me. We landed at the Deering field, which was surrounded by tundra. The short, narrow, dirt runway was covered by enough snow to make landing a little touchy.

On the ground at Deering, Sig and I unloaded a couple of passengers and some freight. On this, my check ride with my new employer, I hadn't even touched the controls. Then Sig pointed to a Stinson Gullwing powered by a 245-horsepower radial Lycoming engine. "Take that and make a few landings," he said.

The Gullwing—named for its graceful wings—was popular in Alaska then. It was a strong airplane that could haul a good load, and it was very stable in the air. I know of no other airplane of the time that was nicer to ride in. Its takeoff performance wasn't as good as some, but it was passable. I gave the airplane a good walk-around preflight inspection, wiped frost off the wings, checked the fuel, and took off. It was a ratty-looking plane, as beat-up looking as some of the junk I had flown in my early flying years in Minnesota. To compensate, the engine ran well.

The runway at Deering was shorter than I was used to. I came in under power, settling pretty well and making good three-point landings, stopping with plenty of room. I thought I was doing fine as I made half a dozen touch-and-go landings.

As I taxied off the runway, a man came over to talk with me. He was perhaps five feet eight, mild-mannered and calm. He seemed concerned. "You're slowing that Gullwing too much," he said. Then he introduced himself. "I'm John Cross, and I fly around here too."

John Cross was a name I knew. He was an eagle who flew in Alaska's Arctic for many decades before and after World War II. Few arctic pilots have been so admired and loved. "Give her a little more speed on final," he advised.

"Yeah, but I gotta be able to stop," I answered.

"Try it," he said in his soft-spoken way. "You'll stop. You need that extra 5 or 10 miles an hour on final. Better that you run into the willows at the end of the runway at 5 miles an hour than fall out of the sky in a stall at this end."

He was right. I shot more landings and used a higher (and safer) approach speed, and I stopped in plenty of time. It wasn't necessary to slow down so much, or to land under power. So I was learning, and I was pleased that a really experienced Alaskan flyer was willing to give advice. Any pilot could have learned from John Cross.

After I had finished doing landings, Sig said, "Fly the Stinson back to Nome, will you Rudy?" He needed to fly the Cessna out of Deering.

"Oh, there are three passengers for you," he said, as a by-the-way.

"I don't know this country. What if I can't find Nome?" I blurted.

"Don't worry about it. These guys have mined here all their lives. They can show you the way," Sig promised.

I laid out the route to Nome on a map and worked out the proper compass course, then I loaded the three miners.

"You're new, aren't you?" one asked.

At my answer, he asked, "Think you can find Nome?"

"Sig says you guys know the way if I get lost," I half joked.

The instant we left the ground the guy in the front seat with me pointed and said, "Fly that direction." Then one of the guys in the back said, "No. Fly a little to the right of that." The third guy disagreed with both. "Look, I've flown this route with Sig lots of times. He always flies that way," he said, pointing off about 30 degrees from the route recommended by the second miner.

I followed my compass course and grinned to myself as the three miners argued about which direction we should fly. When we were about halfway, one of the guys in the back called up, "Why do you keep turning?"

I hadn't turned at all: I'd glued the proper course on the compass to the lubber line and hadn't deviated three degrees. In flight, as a plane passes geographic features, often perspective changes and it can appear that the airplane is turning.

The three miners were still arguing when I landed at Nome. Lesson one on Alaskan flying: don't count on passengers helping to find the way to a destination.

The next day, I was sent on a flight to Cape Prince of Wales with two passengers.

"Where do I land? What do I look out for?" I asked.

"Land on the beach—it's pretty good," I was told by the other pilots. "Sometimes the crosswinds are bad. What you really have to look out for is Cape Mountain, just southeast of Wales. A pilot or two, flying along the south side when winds were strong from the north, have been driven down onto the ice by the downdraft."

"It drove them onto the ice?" I asked.

"Yeah. They crashed," came the answer.

"You have to kind of watch for an updraft there too, so you don't get boosted into the clouds."

I knew virtually nothing about mountain flying and the winds encountered around mountains. I started on this trip with a lot of concern. I got over Cape Mountain and there was a strong north wind—just what I had been warned about. I stuck my nose into it and the plane started dropping. I turned back as quickly as I could.

I tried to go around it, but I didn't know how far out to sea I should go.

If I had known, I could have gone out half a mile or so and I would have been away from the downdraft. But I didn't know. I had been warned, I took heed, and I returned to Nome with my passengers.

Bob Long, Bill Lund, and the other Wien pilots chided me.

"All your ratings didn't get you through, huh?" one said.

"Nope, by God, they didn't," I said, and let it go at that.

At the time there was much subtle pressure exerted to push pilots into the kind of flying they shouldn't do. It was dollars talking, of course. Small flying services in Alaska have often been economically marginal, with every dollar being important. Also, I was the newest pilot, and tradition called for the old hands to try to scare hell out of me. I heard some hair-raising tales from them about the dangers of flying from Nome. I had been around enough pilots to know that the stories were aimed at disconcerting the new kid on the block. I acted impressed and almost scared, shook my head and said "by golly" a few times, and went on about my flying.

Gasoline, available at most trading posts, was expensive in the villages along the Arctic Coast. At Kobuk, a village northeast of Nome, for example, the trader sold a box of two five-gallon cans of fuel for $10. That sounds cheap today, but in 1941 that was high-priced gasoline. We were encouraged to load up heavily on fuel at our starting point, thus eliminating the need to buy at the outposts. To survive, small airplanes had to take advantage of every cost-saving device.

The day after having turned back, I flew the two passengers to their Cape Prince of Wales destination without difficulty.

My first six months of flying in Alaska were difficult for me. It was different from any flying I had ever done. I knew nothing about the venturi effect of high winds in mountain passes, how winds falling off a mountain can actually push a plane down, or how winds pushed upward from a long slope can lift a plane high into the sky. But I learned.

I also learned about bush residents who, with two-way radios, frequently called in and asked for a plane to fly out to pick them up. For someone who lived maybe 200 miles from town and 50 miles from the nearest neighbor and wanted to fly to town, the circumstances were usually urgent.

A woman up the coast from Nome radioed in one day requesting an airplane. "What's your weather?" she was asked.

"It's clear. Nice weather. Perfect," she answered. She was a damned prevaricator, and I risked my neck to find that out.

I took off in a Gullwing Stinson, and I wasn't very far from Nome when I had to choose between going under a low overcast and flying across the mountains, dodging clouds and peaks—a real iffy situation—or flying on top of the overcast. I had had 10 hours of dual instruction in instrument flying, so I knew the basics. I also knew how to use the radio range, the signal from Nome that instrument pilots used as a guide.

I followed out the northeast leg of the Nome radio range and climbed on top of the clouds, a foolish move with a single-engine airplane. I timed myself, saying, "OK, judging from the ground speed I was making at the beginning of the flight it will take me 90 minutes to get to the place from where the woman called. It'll be clear when I get there." I still believed her, even then.

When I was over the place where the woman lived, there was no sign of the ground. There was no hole in the clouds. I flew beyond, and found no change. I returned to Nome, arriving as a nasty storm was about to hit. I barely made it to the airport.

When I got in, I asked one of the other pilots about the woman and her radio call. "Oh hell, you can expect that," he said. "When they want to go, they want to go. They'll tell you anything to get you to come for them, and they figure you'll get there some way."

John Cross wasn't the only veteran Alaskan pilot to offer me valuable advice. Another pilot that I met at Nome, and who had a positive effect on my Alaska flying, was Gordon McKenzie. He flew for Mirow Flying Service, a Wien competitor.

McKenzie learned to fly with the British Royal Air Force in World War I. He barnstormed in Washington state before moving to Alaska to fly for several pioneer airlines—McGee Airways, Star, Woodley, and Mirow.

I was still wide-eyed and fresh to Alaska when I met Gordon. He was rough and tough, but outgoing and a happy-go-lucky back-slapper with a Scottish brogue. He was an exceedingly skilled pilot, and he knew the Nome–Anchorage route by heart.

Once, shortly after I arrived at Nome, I was holding on a flight to Fairbanks because of bad weather. In those early years I felt guilty when I didn't fly in bad weather, an attitude that soon changed. In roared Gordon in a Lockheed Vega, a hot airplane, and he was flying right on the deck. After he landed and got out, I walked over and said, "I'm supposed to fly to Fairbanks and don't know whether to buck this weather."

His answer was straightforward. "You won't make it."

Gordon's superior skill, quick thinking, and action once probably saved his life and that of his passenger. One day in 1942, McKenzie left Anchorage in a fast, narrow-geared Mirow Flying Service Lockheed Vega. He had one passenger, Al Polet, who lived in Nome. In the rugged Rainy Pass country, the usually reliable Pratt & Whitney Wasp engine failed. The choice of landing places was limited. Only the short, rock-strewn river bars of high altitude were available.

Gordon selected the bar that seemed best. He saw at once that a straight-on landing would be disastrous. The plane was certain to flip onto its back at high speed. He made a quick, and I think courageous, decision. Just before touchdown, he kicked the rudder to turn the Vega sideways. Thus, when the plane hit, the landing gear, not stressed for side load, was torn off, and the barrel-like fuselage of the Vega slid rather than tumbled. The fuselage, though broken in half, rumbled to a stop with neither man hurt.

I gradually started to learn what I needed to know from the various flights I made and from advice offered by Sig Wien, Bill Lund, Bob Long, John Cross, and Gordon McKenzie. I learned the names of the mountains and what they looked like from every side. Eventually, they became individuals, almost with personalities. I learned that when I saw a plume of snow flying from the tops of certain peaks, I didn't want to fly close because air turbulence would be bad. I learned that Nome weather can change unbelievably fast, as does any coastal weather.

I liked the freedom of the country and the people and their attitude. This was a land where a pilot was truly appreciated—not for the stunts he could fly, but for his ability to get in and out of short runways, for finding his way in bad weather, for providing a much-needed service for isolated people.

In the early 1940s, Nome was a true outpost, and there I learned a simple but basic lesson: real freedom lies in wilderness, not in civilization. If a man wanted to wander about downtown Nome with a pistol on his hip, hardly anyone would comment. There was some hard drinking, but Bessie and I stayed clear of the waterholes so it seldom affected us. I enjoyed clumping along the wooden sidewalks. Of course, in spring we had to wear rubber boots to cross the seas of mud that were called streets. I enjoyed becoming acquainted with the free-thinking, generous, hospitable people. I liked contemplating the wide difference between the two primary winter travel modes—dog team and airplane. Most people remained in town all winter. There was a stability and a friendliness that both Bessie and I liked.

Unfortunately, the stability didn't last.

A River Ran out of Eden

JAMES VANCE MARSHALL

*James Vance Marshall is a pseudonym for British novelist Donald Payne. His
best-selling novel,* A RIVER RAN OUT OF EDEN *(1962), is the story of Jim Lee, a
disillusioned white man who brings his Aleut wife, Tania, and their two
small children, Eric and Jess, to live on a deserted Aleutian Island. In this
selection, Eric is exploring his island home when he encounters a golden seal,
symbol of good fortune and prosperity for the Aleut people.*

The little boy had no difficulty in fording the river; the water was
barely up to his ankles. Then with many a backward glance to be
sure he was keeping the barabara in sight, he started up the bank.
In one hand were his father's binoculars, in the other a rhododen-
dron branch with which he flicked the melting medusas out of his
path. In twenty minutes he was on top of the highest sand dune.

The view was magnificent: behind him, the river snaking the slopes of
Komai; to his left, the estuary, with the barabara a pinpoint on its farther
shore (it was still in sight if he got it in the view finder of the binoculars, so
he hadn't *really* broken his promise); and in front of him, the vast expanse
of sea kelp, unbroken and brown as a salmon berry. He focused the glasses
on it.

He couldn't make out at first what was wrong; couldn't understand why,
in the view finder of the binoculars, the image of the kelp kept on blurring
and slipping out of focus. It seemed to be moving. It was several minutes
before he realized it really *was* moving, was undulating up and down in
wide-spaced rhythmic swells. Eric was fascinated. He lay face down on the
stones, legs wide apart, glasses riveted on the moving mosaic of kelp. All else
was forgotten; golden seals, parents, storm; he was rapt in his discovery, lost
to the world. He didn't see the great copper-colored cloud flooding out
against the wind from behind the spire of Komai; he didn't see the stir of

the sedge grass in the sirocco. Only when the sea kelp split and the spume came scudding inland and the waves began to pound the shore did he realize something was wrong.

He jumped up. He spun around. He saw the great cloud swallowing the sky. In terror he stood irresolute, like a sea bird poised for flight, a wind-torn papier-mâché silhouette dwarfed by the immensity of sea and cloud. Then he began to run.

Nine boys out of ten (nine hundred and ninety-nine town-bred boys out of a thousand) would have run for home, for the reassuring arms of their parents. But Eric ran for the sod hut, for the nearest of the dozen or so shelters built along the crest of the bank. That was the lesson his father had always drummed into him: "If you're out in a storm take shelter at once; never get caught in the open." The sod hut was nearer than the barabara, and so he ran for the sod hut.

He ran for his life, his feet sinking and slipping on the loose-packed stones, while about him the sky grew darker, the wind stronger, and the bank began to tremble to the pound of steepening waves. At last his goal was in sight—the squat mound of turfs sunk like an igloo into the ground. He was within a hundred yards of it when the light suddenly went out of the sky. A gust of wind knocked him off his feet. He didn't get up. He shook his head and crawled on. Beneath him the stones began to shift, and loose sand to stream in tattered pennants off the crests of the sand dunes. He kept his face close to the gravel and crawled on. It seemed a very long way to the shelter. After a while he began to doubt if he'd have the strength to reach it, but at last his fingers were clawing at the circle of sods.

He collapsed face down on the threshold, gasping for breath. And the first thing he noticed was the smell. For a second he drew back, uncertain. Then the gravel beat stinging against his legs, and he squirmed in quickly.

The sod hut was small and dark; it had no window or chimney; its door was simply a couple of movable turfs which Eric, from the inside, now hauled to to keep out the wind. As the turfs were pulled in, the moan of the storm faded, the last glimmer of light was snuffed out, and the smell—strong and fetid—rose pungently out of the dark. On the far side of the sod hut something moved.

The little boy peered into the darkness, suddenly afraid.

Twin orbs of fire swayed up from the floor, twin balls of red aglow like oriflammes in the dark. And Eric shrank back, appalled. Something was in the sod hut, some wild and terrible animal—perhaps a great brown bear with claws that could rip the guts from a caribou in a single slash. He spun around. He tore at the door turfs. Then he remembered the storm.

He stood very still, teeth clenched, eyes screwed tight. Waiting. But the wild and terrible animal didn't spring at him. Everything was motionless and very quiet—everything except his heart, which was pounding in frightened leaps between mouth and stomach, and after a while even the pound of his heart sank to a muffled, uncertain throb. Hesitantly he unscrewed his eyes, ready to snap them shut the moment the animal moved. But the orbs of red were motionless. The creature—whatever it was—kept to the farther side of the hut.

He peered into the blackness. At first he could see only the red of the eyes, but gradually as he became accustomed to the dark he could make out more: a shadowy mass, coiled and menacing, stretching almost a third of the way around the wall. The animal was large, but—to his unspeakable relief—it wasn't thickset and solid enough to be a bear. He began to breathe more easily.

After a while he became conscious of a faint persistent sound, a sound so low that it had been drowned up to now by the thud of his heart and the background moan of the storm. It was a sucky, slobbery sound, a sound he had heard before—years and years ago, when he was very small; it wasn't a sound be to frightened of; he knew that; its associations were pleasant. His fear ebbed a little. Perhaps the creature was friendly; perhaps it would let him stay; perhaps the hut was a refuge they could both, in time of emergency, share.

His mind seized upon the idea thankfully. He remembered a picture in one of his storybooks, a picture of a little boy (no older than he was) and all sorts of different animals lying together on a flood-ringed island; and he remembered his father reading the caption, " 'Then the wolf shall dwell with the lamb, and the leopard shall lie down with the kid; and the calf and the young lion and the fatling together,' " and he remembered his father explaining that in times of great danger—fire or flood, tempest or drought—all living things reverted to their natural (sinless) state and lived peacefully together until the danger had passed. This, he told himself, must be such a time.

He stared at the glowing eyes. And quite suddenly his fear was submerged in a great flood of curiosity. What *was* this strange red-eyed creature? It

was too big for a fox or a hare, and not the right shape for a bear or a caribou. If only he could see it!

He remembered then that somewhere in every sod hut his father had
cached matches and candles.

An older boy would have hesitated now. An older boy would have had
second thoughts and a legacy of fear. But to Eric things were uncompli-
cated. He *had* been frightened, but that was in the past; *now* he was curious. For a little boy of seven it was as simple as that.

He felt around the wall till his hand struck a metal box. He pried off
the lid. He found and lit one of the candles. A flickering light leaped around
the hut. And the little boy's breath stuck in his throat and he could only
stare and stare. For never in all his life had he seen anything so beautiful.

She lay curled up against the wall: a sinuous seven-foot golden seal, her
fur like a field of sun-drenched corn; and clinging to her teats, two soft-
furred pups.

"Ooooh!" he whispered.

Holding the candle high, his fear quite lost in wonder, he walked toward
her.

"Ooooh!'" he whispered. "You're beautiful. An' your babies."

One of the pups, frightened by his voice, fell away from its mother and
went snuffling round the floor. He bend down to pick it up.

The golden seal drew in her head. Her lips writhed back. Her eyes
turned suddenly dark.

"It's all right," the little boy said softly, "you needn't be scared. I know
what to do."

And very gently he picked up the pup and clamped it back on the teat.

A hint of hesitation or fear and she would have killed him. But his assurance took her aback; her head swayed this way and that like a cobra's, but
she didn't strike.

He looked at her brightly. "I bet you're hungry. Let's find something
to eat."

And he turned his back on her and started to forage inside the tin.

In it he found all manner of intriguing things: bandages, blocks of solid
fuel, and food—bars of chocolate and cuts of *beleek*—smoked salmon. He
didn't know how to use the fuel, but the food he sorted into two piles.

"The chocolate's for me," he told the golden seal. "The salmon's for
you."

She looked at him balefully. When he pushed the food toward her she didn't touch it. She watched his every move.

He stood the candle on the base of the upturned tin, and its flaring light threw shadows adance on the curve of the walls. He went to the door and eased out one of the turfs. But for a second only. For the storm was raging now with sustained malevolence, and the bank was a place of death, a battleground of wind and spume and ripped-up gravel and sand.

But inside the sod hut it was sheltered and almost cozy. The little boy and the golden seal lay on either side of the circle of candlelight and stared at each other.

And the hours passed.

Every now and then Eric pulled aside one of the turfs to see if the storm was easing off, but its violence remained unabated, hour after hour. Every now and then he renewed the candles—they burned fast in the eddying draughts. And in between times he ate chocolate, bar after bar of it. And every time he ate a bar of chocolate he laid out a salmon cut for the golden seal. At first she wouldn't look at it. But eventually, about the time that behind the storm clouds the sun was dipping under the ice—blink, she reached out her neck and sniffed at and tasted the nearest cut. She liked it. The little boy gave her more. And it was not very long before she was letting him put the fish into her mouth.

Come sundown, the temperature dropped sharply. The wind backed and the rain hardened to snow. Eric began to shiver. He unearthed the blankets, cached alongside the tin of provisions. There were two of them. He wrapped himself in one and the other he draped carefully over the golden seal.

And the hours passed, each slower and colder than the one before.

They lay on either side of the hut. Between them the guttering candle, outside the moan of the wind and the drifting up of the snow, and above the storm clouds the anemic stars creeping conspirator-like into a frightened sky. The night grew darker. The snow drifted higher. The candle burned lower. Its wick drooped into the melted wax. The flame was snuffed out. A pencil of smoke coiled up to the roof sods. And the little boy slept.

He woke in the small cold hours of the morning, stiff, uncomfortable, and trembling. The hut smelled of smoke, candle grease, fish and excrement, and the gravel was white with frost. He was lost and cold, and oh, so miserably alone. He tried to wrap himself more warmly into the blanket, but the blanket was all sides and ends—not big enough to keep out the cold. For a while he rocked to and fro, trying to comfort himself. Then he began to cry. He cried noiselessly, the tears welling out in a steady flood, salting his cheeks, trickling around the corners of his mouth, and dropping forlornly into a fold in the blanket. It was the loneliness that frightened him most.

On the far side of the hut the golden seal stirred. Her head swayed up; her eyes glowed warm and red.

Eric stopped crying. He stared at the eyes, mesmerized. Then unthinkingly, half asleep, half awake, his blanket dragging behind him, he crawled across to her. Awkwardly in the dark he snuggled against her. She was soft and warm and comforting. And she didn't snarl at him.

Soon his shivering, like his tears, died away. And it was not very long before he fell asleep, his face buried deep in the fine-spun gold of her fur.

During the night he slipped lower, and by dawn he was wedged against the warmth of her teats and her pups were snuffling hungrily. She nuzzled him aside. He fell to the ground; the cold and hardness of the stones jerked him awake, and he sat up, stretching and yawning.

The air in the sod hut was heavy and stale, and he went to the doorway and tried to ease out the turfs. They were stuck. He kicked them impatiently, and they cracked open, and ice, wind, and snow came swirling into the hut.

It was an unfamiliar world he peered out on. The sky hung low, a livid sheet wiped clear of coloring or cloud, and across it streamed the wind, a wind robbed now of its former malevolence but still strong enough to bowl a man off his feet and to drive in front of it a continuous veil of snow. The storm was dying, but it was not yet dead.

Thoughtfully Eric pulled back the turfs; thoughtfully he looked at the seal. And he was troubled. For it came to him that now the weather was improving his father would soon be starting to search for him, and didn't his father often go hunting golden seals—with a gun?

The idea appalled him. It was unthinkable that "she with the yellow hair" should be hurt. She was his friend. He sat down, head in hands, thinking. And after a while and with delightful clarity the answer came to him. He must make certain he found his father before his father found the golden seal, and he must make him promise never to hurt her.

Having hit on his plan, he was eager to be off. At the back of his mind was a nagging fear that his father might appear unexpectedly and shoot the seal before he had a chance to explain. He stuffed the last of the chocolate into his pocket, he fed the last of the fish to the golden seal, and as soon as he could stand against the ever lessening tear of the wind he set off for the barabara.

In the doorway of the hut he paused and looked back. His eyes met the golden seal's.

"Don't you worry," he said. "I'll see nobody shoots you."

The Tundra

JOHN HAINES

John Haines, American poet and writer, was born in Norfolk, Virginia, in 1924. After serving in the Navy during World War II, he enrolled in art school. Beginning in 1947, he spent nearly two decades homesteading in a log cabin near Richardson, Alaska. He is the author of several poetry collections, including WINTER NEWS *(1966),* THE STONE HARP *(1971),* THE OWL IN THE MASK OF THE DREAMER *(1993), and* FABLES AND DISTANCES *(1996), as well as a memoir,* THE STARS, THE SNOW, THE FIRE *(1989). He has received numerous writer's awards, including two Guggenheim Fellowships and a National Endowment for the Arts Fellowship. He currently lives in Anchorage. "The Tundra" originally appeared in* WINTER NEWS; *"The Way We Live" (on page 208) is taken from* THE STONE HARP.

The tundra is a living
body, warm in the grassy
autumn sun; it gives off
the odor of crushed
blueberries and gunsmoke.

In the tangled lakes
of its eyes a mirror of ice
is forming, where
frozen gut-piles shine
with a dull, rosy light.

Coarse, laughing men
with their women;
one by one the tiny campfires
flaring under the wind.

Full of blood, with a sound
like clicking hoofs,
the heavy tundra slowly
rolls over and sinks
in the darkness.

The Way We Live

JOHN HAINES

Having been whipped through Paradise
and seen humanity
strolling like an overfed beast
set loose from its cage,
a man may long for nothing so much
as a house of snow,
a blue stone for a lamp,
and a skin to cover his head.

Daughter of the Gold Rush

KLONDY NELSON

*Klondy Nelson came to Alaska in 1902 as a child and became an
accomplished writer, violinist, adventurer, and dog musher. Her
autobiographical* DAUGHTER OF THE GOLD RUSH *(1958), excerpted here,
recounts her early life and how she met and married Alaskan naturalist and
writer Frank Dufresne. Toodles, the woman referred to at the end of this piece,
was a dance-hall girl who had befriended Klondy as a child many years before.*

Dog teams blazed a thousand trails between the villages every
winter. Apart from the snow trails, there was no road between
Fairbanks and Nome. In summer the only highways were the
rivers.

Life on the Yukon began at spring breakup when the crash-
ing ice cakes swept down the raging flood waters toward the sea. The first
stern-wheel steamer followed close behind, its paddles thrashing the muddy
whirlpools, its stack belching spars and wood smoke. The Indian firemen
stoked the boilers with four-foot logs. The massive hull with its gingerbread
trimmings would zigzag across the river, following the shifting channel.
Deck hands with long red-and-white poles stood in the bow, sounding the
depths and shouting back to the pilothouse, "Deep six! Seven! No bottom!"

The captain steered his treacherous course by familiar landmarks on
either bank: an eagle's nest in a cottonwood snag, a high-pole cache, an
Indian cemetery on a hill, a burned stump that looked like a black bear.
With a blast on his whistle that echoed for miles, he would heave his lines
ashore at a native trading post, dump off provisions and take on sacks of
furs. Then he would churn on to the next settlement. Sometimes he would
pull up alongside the cut bank and buy a deckload of cordwood from a
homesteader who had cut it that winter on speculation. Rex Beach worked
this way one whole season, earning his grubstake to the Nome strike.

Behind the stern-wheelers came a whole flotilla of smaller craft, bound for the Bering seacoast—homemade naphtha launches, log rafts propelled by long sweeps, poling boats, dories and birchbark canoes. They looked graceful enough as they shot swiftly down the rapids, but it was a different story when they reached St. Michael and started back upriver against the mighty current. The slim canoes would ride the reverse eddies along the bank, the paddlers ducking their heads under the overhanging willows; but the bigger boats had to buck the main channel, and some of them never made it. Over the years St. Michael gradually became a graveyard of deserted ships that couldn't get home.

Frank's vessel, the *Beaver*, was a powerdriven houseboat with a tunnel bottom, and a canoe strapped on top of the cabin house for a tender. It was made specially for him by the Alaska Game Commission so he could navigate the shallow Yukon tributaries in search of wildlife violators. As soon as I could travel again, after our daughter Virginia was born, I made the downriver trip with him in the spring. Ginny was about six months old, and the first thing I did was to cover all the cabin windows with copper screening, to keep the mosquitoes out and keep Ginny in. My main problem was washing and drying Ginny's diapers. I thought I had a brilliant idea, stringing them on a deck clothesline, so the breeze would dry them in short order. An hour later when I went up to get them they were coal-black from the exhaust of the gasoline engine.

The *Beaver's* clean cabin, with its polished brass and freshly painted woodwork, was heavenly after the log hut in Fairbanks. We had a private bedroom, a living room and a galley, all completely shut off from the engine room and pilothouse. I made some gingham curtains for the windows, and the cabin looked like a little doll house inside. It was sheer luxury to toss the garbage overboard and watch it disappear, instead of keeping it in a slop bucket all winter. There was a real toilet that could be flushed with river water, and a hand pump in the sink. It was the first running water I'd ever had in Alaska.

The galley was so small that I could stand in one place and do everything—cook meals on a tiny oil stove for Frank and his engineer, Jack Warwick; wash the dishes in the sink, and bathe the baby on the galley table. I'd reach around behind me while I was holding her, take her bottle off the stove, carrying her a couple of steps to our stateroom and put her to sleep in the bunk. The vibration of the engine made her drowsy. She would sleep for hours at a time while I went up to the pilothouse with Frank and sat on a high stool, watching the ever-changing panorama of nature along the Yukon's banks.

At every turn of the river, flocks of waterfowl would skitter across the surface ahead of us and lift into the air, wheeling back overhead. Frank called their names off as he made notes in his field diary: whistling swans, mallard and pintail ducks, Canada geese, sandhill cranes. Sometimes, as we neared the mouth of a clear-water slough, I would glance upstream at what appeared to be a large driftwood snag among the water lilies. The snag would lift as our boat passed, and the head of a giant bull moose would emerge, its antlers dripping and its jaws chomping on a wad of moss it had just cropped from the stream bottom. In the morning—it was bright daylight by three A.M.—we would see hundreds and sometimes thousands of caribou standing on the bank, the forest of horns gleaming red in the early sunlight. They would wait until the *Beaver* was almost opposite them, then plunge into the river and swim across in front of us. We would have to slow the engine to avoid hitting them. They were so densely packed that Frank said he couldn't toss his hat in the water without hanging it on an antler.

Each Indian village we approached had racks of drying salmon lining the shores. Crude fish wheels turned with the current, and the floating fish boxes beside them were filled with king and coho and dog salmon, ling cod, pike and arctic shee-fish. Following the custom of the Yukon, we would pull up alongside and help ourselves to whatever we wanted for supper. If we preferred trout or grayling that night, we would poke the *Beaver*'s bow into a little side stream and tie up. Frank would set up his fly rod and cast from the deck. When the mosquitoes were too bad, I baited a hook with bacon and lowered it through the hole in the flush toilet. I caught a lot of fish that way.

As summer followed summer, I began to worry about Ginny. She was getting old enough to crawl around the boat. I knew that if she ever fell in the muddy Yukon, her clothes would instantly load with silt and she would never come to the surface again. I'd catch my breath in terror when we visited a native village and she toddled up to a chained Malemute dog, which was usually half wolf, and petted it without fear; but, for some reason, no dog ever attacked her.

One afternoon, while Frank was making a patrol with the canoe, I took Ginny up the hill to pick blueberries. She got ahead of me. Then I heard her calling, "Look, Mamma, a doggie!" She was trotting toward a feeding black bear. The bear lifted its head and took a step toward her. Fortunately I had Frank's rifle—he made me carry it when I went ashore—and I dropped the bear with my first shot. It weighed about 200 pounds, but I managed to kick and shove it down to the water's edge. Frank's only comment when he saw it was, "Well, I guess we'll have fresh meat for a change." But I knew he was proud of me.

I worried too about Ginny being taken ill, until the *Martha Angelina* began her mercy patrols up and down the Yukon. The *Martha* was a Government hospital ship, run by Dr. Curtis Welch. His wife, Lou, acted as nurse. The ship carried a full line of drugs and medical equipment for any emergency, and the service to the natives was free. When the moccasin telegraph sent word ahead that the *Martha* was coming, the natives would crowd at the river landings, eager for any attention. Old men with canes, withered crones, children, and mothers with babies would troop up the gangplank single file, to be treated for real or imaginary ailments.

One summer the Indian Service seemed to want everybody's tonsils removed. The natives appeared a little surprised at this drastic treatment, but they cooperated cheerfully because it didn't cost anything. During this period of mass operation the *Beaver* had tied up alongside the *Martha* at Nulato, while I went ashore to visit the trading post. As I started back to our boat I missed Ginny. After a frantic search through the village, I caught sight of a little towhead in the long file of Indian children, impatiently awaiting her turn. I yanked Ginny out of line just in time.

The natives were a little less eager to greet the Yukon dentist, Dr. Fromm of Nome, because he was a private practitioner and charged for his services. He had a collapsible dental chair and a portable drill which he operated with a foot tread, like an old-fashioned sewing machine. Dr. Fromm always figured it was simpler to pull a tooth than fill it, because he could take care of more patients that way.

The Yukon oculist was Dr. MacNab, who had sent to the States for a sample tray of ten-cent store eyeglass lenses. He had a canvas sign reading DOCTOR MACNAB with a big pair of spectacles painted under the name. When he landed at a village, he would examine a customer solemnly, fit a pair of lenses into a wire frame, set the spectacles on the native's nose and hand him a chart to read. Since few of the Indians knew how to read, the glasses were usually pronounced satisfactory. Dr. MacNab would then pocket his fee and depart for the next fish camp.

Dr. MacNab was doing especially well that summer because of all the mouse tracks. The mouse was the economic barometer of the Yukon. When mice were abundant in the summer, there would be feed for the fox and ermine and marten, and furs would be plentiful the following winter. Traders furnished credit to the Indians in proportion to the number of mouse tracks, and ordered heavier supplies for their posts. Even Frank was impressed enough to make a note in his diary, recommending a longer open season for trapping.

I loved our floating home on the *Beaver,* even though life was not always serene. One day the engine quit and the boat drifted onto a gravel bar, just barely under water. No amount of pulling and rocking could work it loose, so Frank decided to lighten the load. We set a couple of iron cots in the shallow water and piled everything on top of them, including Ginny and me. Frank and Jack Warwick worked the boat down the bar until she floated free, and scrambled aboard as the current caught her. I heard the starter whine, but the engine wouldn't fire. The boat drifted rapidly down the river and out of sight.

The Yukon was four miles wide at that point. I was perched with Ginny on a towering stack of oil drums, food cases and flour sacks, in a terrifying expanse of rushing water. The sand was being eaten away under the cot, and I could feel the pile teeter a little. By the time Frank started the engine and came back for us, I was shaking with fright, but Ginny was having the time of her life making paper boats and watching them bounce downstream.

As Ginny grew older, I could see more and more of my childhood self in her looks. She had curly flaxen hair and bright pink cheeks, and there was a little birthmark at the nape of her neck, just like Mother's and mine, that turned red when she was mad. She also had my knack of getting acquainted with strangers. When Frank stopped at a native village to tag beaver skins, Ginny played by the hour with the Indian children. I would wrap her legs with toilet paper, to protect them from mosquitoes. When Frank tooted the boat whistle, she would come back, smelling of fish oil and chewing a black piece of jerked moose meat.

Sometimes I went ashore and visited with the wives of the trading post agents, gossiping about some neighbor five hundred miles away or swapping recipes. Mona Muller, the half-Indian wife of the trader at Kaltag, had a different way of fixing salmon: she would loosen the skin back of the head, and peel it down over the tail in one piece. Then she'd remove the bones, season the chopped-up meat with strong wild onions and sage, stuff it inside the skin and bake it. Mrs. Rothaker at Iditarod made a delicious jam out of half-ripe blueberries, which tasted just like gooseberries. My favorite recipe, however, was Mrs. Fisher's at Ruby, and was called Cranberry Catsup. She picked the cranberries right behind her roadhouse, and added vinegar, brown sugar, spices and horseradish as for regular catsup, but this tasted better. She made it when Robert Service boarded with her at Dawson, and he was very fond of it.

Sometimes I stayed on the boat and helped Frank with the beaver skins. The natives would assemble on the bank as we tied up, and toss armloads of pelts on deck. Sometimes the bow would be heaped with a fortune in rich dark furs. Frank inspected them one by one, to make sure they were taken during the open season. If the fat on the pelt had gone rancid, it indicated that the animal had been trapped before the law allowed. But if all was well, the Indian would sign an affidavit, usually with an X. I would witness his mark, and Frank would clamp a serially numbered metal seal through the eye of the pelt; it could then be shipped to market. The beaver was the main source of revenue for the natives along the Yukon. We often tagged a half million dollars' worth in skins in a summer.

I enjoyed helping Frank with his wildlife work whenever he would let me, and I enjoyed it most of all when the work was a little dangerous. Occasionally when he stepped ashore, the trappers he challenged would put up a show of resistance, and without Frank knowing it I always kept the rifle handy, ready to back him up if necessary. The game violators were even more cunning than the foxes they trapped, so Frank had to be on the alert at all times. One afternoon, when we were chugging up the Yukon past the mouth of a tiny creek, Frank's quick eye spotted a crumpled white envelope bobbing downstream toward the main river. It didn't mean anything to me, but Frank stopped the boat at once. He slid the canoe off the deck, and I sat in the bow, holding the rifle across my lap, while Frank paddled silently upstream.

We moved so quietly that once I almost bumped my elbow against a cow moose drinking at the edge of the creek. We rounded a bend, and ahead of us was a small campsite. The trapper was as surprised to see us as if we'd dropped out of the sky. He had a pile of beaver pelts in his tent, and he swore up and down that he'd taken them during the open season, but Frank saw fresh blood on the skins and he said he'd have to seize the whole bunch. The trapper shook his head in sad surrender.

"Just one thing I can't figger out," he said. "How did you know I was here?"

Frank's eyes twinkled. "I got a letter."

Once we nearly ran into serious trouble. Frank had heard about some illegal furs around Rampart, and the Indians told him of a wild-looking white man camped at the mouth of Little Minook Creek. They said he threatened to kill anybody who landed on his beach.

Frank figured he'd better look into it. We could see the tent under the trees as we stopped at Little Minook. I watched Frank walk up the beach. Suddenly a man came out of the tent, wearing a fringed moose-skin jacket and a wide Stetson draped with mosquito netting. Without a word he pulled an ax out of a stump and started toward Frank. I grabbed our rifle, jumped off the boat and ran up the beach. Frank backed a couple of steps, reaching behind him with one hand as he faced the man, and called to me. "Hand me that gun quick, Klondy."

The man halted in his tracks. "Klondy?" he asked. "You ain't Warren Nelson's little girl?"

He strode toward me, handing Frank the ax as he passed him. "Here, you hold this." He grabbed my hand.

"By God, y'are Klondy! I can see Warren written all over ya." He pumped my hand, but I was too startled to say anything. "I was with your dad on the Third Beach Line. Ever hear him mention the Scurvy Kid? Why, I knowed ya since ya was a baby." He yanked me toward the tent. "Come on in and have some coffee," he said, adding absently to Frank, "you can come in, too."

The Scurvy Kid scaled his Stetson into a corner of the tent. He reminded me a spawned-out dog salmon, with a hooked nose and pock-marks all over his face and snag teeth protruding in all directions. He poured me a mug of inky liquid. I took a swallow and choked.

"That's plenty strong," I managed to say.

"By God," he said, "I like real coffee. This coffee they make nowadays, you might's well dip it out of a moose wallow." He poured a cup for himself, and let Frank get his own. "I like my coffee strong enough so's after I make it I got to rebore the pot."

He stood up, yanked a thin, oily strip of smoked salmon from the ridgepole, and handed it to me. "Here, by God, have some squaw candy." He started chewing on another piece, and Frank rose and pulled down a strip for himself.

"Sorry I busted in on you like this," Frank apologized, "but I was look-ing for a fur trapper."

"Trapper!" the Scurvy Kid snorted indignantly. "Hell, I'm a prospector. I hit some rich panning up the creek here, and I don't want no strangers nosin' around till I get a chance to file my claim."

"I'll be glad to record it for you," Frank offered, "as soon as I get back to my office in Fairbanks."

The Scurvy Kid looked at Frank as if he were seeing him for the first time. He turned to me. "Hell, Klondy, this dude you're hitched to's got a little sense, at that. I like a man with guts and go," he nodded. "Your dad had plenty of guts and go."

"He had plenty of go, all right," I said, with a dark look at Frank, "run-ning off and leaving his family all alone."

"That's what I mean, by God. He wasn't tied to no apron strings. He wouldn't stay in no swivel-chair office," he agreed, also casting a dark look at Frank. "He kep' on going, and he wouldn't stop for nothing. Why, him and me belonged to the vigilantes when we was here in Rampart. One time this gunfighter Wyatt Earp come into town, and your dad made him take off his six-shooters and hang 'em in Tex Rickard's saloon." His yellow teeth ripped off another chunk of squaw candy. "Tex run a nice saloon in Ram-part before he drifted down to Nome. He used to stage prizefights in back, just whipsaw planks and fellers fighting in their socks. Your dad and me hung around there all the time." He looked up at me suddenly. "How long since you seen your dad?"

I thought a moment. "Over ten years."

"Hell, I seen him just a couple of years ago," the Scurvy Kid said. "He come through here on his way upriver. He was following another gold rumor."

I didn't want to ask him, but I couldn't help it. "Where did he go?"

"A prospector don't never tell nobody where he's going," the Scurvy Kid snapped. "Prob'ly he didn't even know himself. But you'll catch up with him one of these days. You're bound to run into him again."

Somehow I knew in my heart the Scurvy Kid was right—sooner or later I would see my dad again. I hated him for deserting my mother. He was a braggart and a liar and he broke her heart, but nevertheless he was my dad. That night as I lay in my bunk on the boat, listening to the water lapping along the sides, the *Beaver* and the Yukon and even Frank seemed very far away. I was a little girl again. Dad was holding me in his arms—I could feel his pointed mustache tickle as he kissed me—and I knew I still loved him.

That summer we saw more and more airplanes buzzing overhead, flying up and down the Yukon. They would wag their fabric wings in greeting as they passed, but to Frank it was almost as though they were thumbing their noses. He was growing increasingly impatient with our slow and cumbersome means of travel, and he began referring to the *Beaver* as an old tub. We knew all the bush pilots by this time—A. A. Bennett and Ben Eielson and Bill Lavery, who took violin lessons from me, and Joe Crosson, of course. Frank recognized all the planes that flew over. "There's Joe now," he would say, "on his way to Nome." We'd be only a few more miles upriver when Joe would fly over again, heading back to Fairbanks. Frank would say, "I'm going to ask the Game Commission to trade in this tub," he'd threaten, "and get a plane."

"But Ginny couldn't go along in an airplane."

"Klondy," Frank said, pronouncing my name in that slow way which always warned me some bad news was coming, "you couldn't go along either, I'm afraid. There'd only be room for the pilot and me." He saw the hurt in my eyes, and he tried to console me. "But think how much shorter my trips would be."

"But think how many more of them you'd take," I said.

The airplane was changing Alaska rapidly. We'd talked with my old friend Roald Amundsen, and with Sir Hubert Wilkins, and they said it was inevitable. Dog drivers shook their fists at the fragile Jennies and Swallow biplanes, because they knew their own days were numbered. Already the pilots had taken most of their passenger business; now they were carrying furs and even starting to handle the mail. Resentment was building along the Yukon. Once, as we rounded a river bend at Koyukuk, we saw a float plane stuck on a sandbar. A crowd of boatmen and mushers lined the bank, jeering at the pilot. Nobody offered to row out and help, so Frank tossed the pilot a rope and towed him loose.

Even the roadhouse proprietors fought the airplane, since their business depended on feeding and lodging sled drivers. A few of them put up signs: NO DOGS OR PILOTS ALLOWED INSIDE. One day we stopped for lunch at Manley Hot Springs Roadhouse, run by Dan Green and his wife. Joe Crosson parked his plane at the landing and came in just as we were finishing. An old-time dog driver named Pretty Pete started ribbing Joe at once.

"That bailing-wire boxkite of yours wouldn't last two minutes in a blizzard," he scoffed. "You'll never get people to risk their necks in a cockeyed contraption like that."

"They're already doing it," Joe Crosson replied. He was a handsome-looking youngster, as dashing as Douglas Fairbanks, and he had a nice easy grin. "We've all got more business now than we can handle. The airplane's here to stay, Pete."

"That's right, Joe," Frank cut in. "It's going to be the making of Alaska someday. The Game Commission's even talking about getting one."

"Bosh," snorted Pretty Pete, slamming down his coffee cup in disgust. "It'll never take the place of the good old sled dog." He shoved back his chair. "Think I'll stroll over to the springs and take a hot bath."

"You going to take a bath, Pete," Dan Green asked slyly, "or just rent a towel?"

Everybody laughed, and Frank explained to me in a whisper that Pretty Pete was sweet on a girl who had taken over the bath-towel concession for the summer. A lot of sporting girls liked to hang around the hot sulphur springs in the summertime, waiting for the miners to come out after a bath—fresh, clean and feeling romantic. "Ain't she a little old for you, Pete?" Dan Green goaded.

"Maybe she's old"—Pretty Pete shrugged as he shuffled out the door—"but I ain't so young myself any more."

We started back to the *Beaver*, and I realized Ginny had wandered off again. Frank went down to the boat to help Jack untie and get the engine going, while I started calling. Soon Ginny came trotting along the plank walk from the bathhouse. I took her hand and we hurried to the landing. We were several miles downstream before I got around to asking Ginny where she'd been.

"I was talking to the lady that sells bath towels," she said. "She's a very nice lady."

"How did you happen to get acquainted with her?"

"She said I looked just like a little girl she used to know once, with the same golden curls and pink cheeks. She asked me who I was and I told her Virginia Dufresne, but she didn't know anybody by that name. She said whoever I was I bet I had a nice mommy and a nice home, and she told me to always be a good little girl and not come in this place any more."

"What was her name, Ginny?" I knew before I asked.

"I don't know, it didn't seem like a real name. A man came in and called her Toodles."

We stopped at Manley Hot Springs on the way back upriver at the end of the summer, but I was too late. Toodles had drifted on, and I never heard of her again.

The Birth of a Cabin

FROM *One Man's Wilderness*

RICHARD PROENNEKE AND
SAM KEITH

*Richard Proenneke, a World War II veteran, came to Alaska in 1950. After
working as a heavy equipment operator and repairman in Kodiak, he
followed his dream of building a log home in the wilderness. In 1968, at the
age of 51, the resourceful Proenneke single-handedly built his cabin, an
experience he describes in engaging detail in* ONE MAN'S WILDERNESS *(1973),
which he co-authored with Sam Keith, a Massachusetts writer. Proenneke still
lives in his cabin, far from roads, telephones, and neighbors, enjoying the
enviable, simplified lifestyle portrayed in his book.*

May *22d.* Up with the sun at four to watch the sunrise and the
sight of the awakening land. It seems a shame for eyes to be
shut when such things are going on, especially in this big
country. I don't want to miss anything. A heavy white frost
twinkled almost as if many of its crystals were suspended in
the air. New ice, like a thin pane of glass, sealed the previously open water
along the edge of the lake. The peaks, awash in the warm yellow light, con-
trasted sharply with their slopes still in shadow.

Soon I had a fire snapping in the stove, and shortly afterwards no longer
could see my breath inside the cabin. A pan of water was heating alongside
the kettle. That business of breaking a hole in the ice and washing up out
there sounds better than it feels. I prefer warm water and soap. Does a better
job, too.

Thick bacon sliced from the slab sizzled in the black skillet. I poured off
some of the fat and put it aside to cool. Time now to put the finishing
touches to the sourdough batter. As I uncovered it I could smell the fer-
mentation. I gave it a good stirring, then sprinkled half a teaspoonful of
baking soda on top, scattered a pinch of salt and dripped in a tablespoon of
bacon fat. When these additions were gently folded into the batter, it
seemed to come alive. I let it stand for a few minutes while bacon strips were
laid on a piece of paper towel and excess fat was drained from the pan. Then

I dropped one wooden spoonful of batter, hissing onto the skillet. When bubbles appear all over, it's time to flip.

Brown, thin, and light . . . nothing quite like a stack of sourdough hotcakes cooked over a wood fire in the early morning. Each layer was smeared with butter and honey and I topped the heap with lean bacon slices. While I ate I peered out the window at a good-looking caribou bedded down on the upper benches. Now that's a breakfast with atmosphere!

Before doing the dishes, I readied the makings of the sourdough biscuits. These would be a must for each day's supper. The recipe is much the same as for hotcakes, but thicker, a dough that is baked.

It was a good morning to pack in the rest of the gear. I put some red beans to soak and took off. Last night's freeze had crusted the snow and it made the traveling easier. About a mile down the lake shore a cock ptarmigan clattered out of the willow brush, his neck and head shining a copper color in the sun, his white wings vibrating, then curving into a set as he sailed. His summer plumage was beginning to erase the white of winter. "Crrr . . . uck . . . a . . . ruck . . . urrrrrrrr." His ratchetting call must have brought everything on the mountain slopes to attention.

The last load was the heaviest. It was almost noon before I got back to the cabin, and none too soon because rain clouds were gathering over the mountains to the south.

The rain came slanting down, hard-driven by the wind. I busied myself getting gear and groceries organized. Anyone living alone has to get things down to a system. Know where things are and what the next move is going to be. Chores are easier if forethought is given to them and they are looked upon as little pleasures to perform instead of inconveniences that steal time and try the patience.

When the rain stopped its heavy pelting, I went prospecting for a garden site. A small clearing on the south side of the cabin and away from the big trees was the best place I could find. Here it would get as much sun as possible.

Frost was only inches down so there would be no planting until June. Spike's grub hoe could scuff off the ground cover later on and stir up the top soil as deep as the frost would permit. I had no fertilizer. I suppose I might experiment with the manure of moose and caribou, but it would be interesting to see what progress foreign seeds would make in soil that had nourished only native plants.

By suppertime the biscuits were nicely puffed and ready to bake. There was no oven in the stove, but with tinsnips I cut down a coffee can so it stood about two inches high, and placed it bottom up atop the stove. On this platform I set the pan of three swollen biscuits and covered it with a gas can tin about six inches deep.

In about fifteen minutes the smell of the biscuits drifted out to the woodpile. I parked the ax in the chopping block. Inside, I dampened a towel and spread it over the biscuits for about two minutes to tenderize the crust. The last biscuit mopped up what was . . . mmm . . . left of the onion gravy.

When will I ever tire of just looking? I set up the spotting scope on the tripod. Three different eye pieces fit into it—a 25-power, a 40-power, and a 60-power. That last one hauls distant objects right up to you but it takes a while to get the knack of using it because the magnification field covers a relatively small area.

This evening's main attraction was a big lynx moving across a snow patch. I had seen a sudden flurrying of ptarmigan just moments before, and when I trained the scope on the action, there was the cat taking his time, stopping now and then as if watching for a movement in the timber just ahead of him.

I switched to a more powerful eye piece and there he was again, bigger and better, strolling along, his hips seeming to be higher than his shoulders, his body the color of dark gray smoke, his eyes like yellow lanterns beneath his tufted ears. Even from the distance I could sense his big-footed silence.

I went to sleep wondering if the lynx had ptarmigan for supper.

May 23d. Dense fog this morning. A ghostly scene. Strange how much bigger things appear in the fog. A pair of Goldeneye ducks whistled past low and looked as big as honkers to me.

After breakfast I inspected the red beans for stones, dumped them into a fresh pot of water from the lake and let them bubble for a spell on the stove. I sliced some onions. What in the world would I do without onions? I read one time that they prevent blood clots. Can't afford a blood clot out here. I threw the slices into the beans by the handful, showered in some chili powder and salt and stirred in a thick stream of honey. I left the pot to simmer over a slow fire. Come suppertime they should be full of flavor.

I took a tour back through the spruce timber. It didn't take much detective work to see how hard the wind had blown during the winter, both up and down the lake. Trees were down in both directions. That was something else to think about. Did the wind blow that much harder in the winter?

Hope Creek has cut a big opening into the lake ice. That could be where the ducks were headed this morning. Was it too early to catch a fish? I took the casting rod along to find out. The creek mouth looked promising enough with its ruffled water swirling into eddies that spun beneath the ice barrier. I worked a metal spoon deep in the current, jerked it towards me and let it drift back. Not a strike after several casts. If the fish were out there, they were not interested. No sign of the ducks either.

When the fog finally cleared the face of the mountain across the ice, I sighted a bunch of eleven Dall ewes and lambs. Five lambs in all, a good sign. A mountain has got to be lonely without sheep on it.

The rest of the day I devoted to my tools.

I carved a mallet head out of a spruce chunk, augered a hole in it, and fitted a handle to it. This would be a useful pounding tool and I hadn't had to pack it in either. The same with the handles I made for the wood augers, the wide bladed chisel, and the files . . . much easier to pack without the handles already fitted to them.

I sharpened the ax, adze, saws, chisels, wood augers, drawknife, pocket knife, and bacon slicer. The whispering an oil stone makes against steel is a satisfying sound. You can almost tell by the crispness of the sound when the blade is ready. A keen edge not only does a better job, it teaches a man to have a respect for the tool. There is no leeway for a "small" slip.

While I pampered my assault kit for building of the cabin, the sky turned loose a heavy shower and thundered Midwestern style. The echoes rumbled and tumbled down the slopes and faded away into mutterings. The shrill cries of the terns proclaimed their confusion.

The ice attempted to move today. Fog and thunder have taken their toll. I can see the rough slab edges pushed atop each other along the cracks. The winter freight will be moving down the lake soon, through the connecting stream and down the lower lake to the funnel of the Chilikadrotna River.

After supper I made log-notch markers out of my spruce stock. They are nothing more than a pair of dividers with a pencil on one leg, but with them I can make logs fit snugly. This is not going to be a butchering job. I can afford the time for pride to stay in charge.

I sampled the red beans again before turning in for the night. The longer they stay in the pot the more flavor they have.

The woodpile needs attention. I must drop a few spruce snags and buck them up into sections. Dry standing timber makes the best firewood.

Ho . . . hum. I'm anxious to get started on that cabin, but first things first. Tomorrow will have to be a woodcutting day.

May 25th. The mountains are wearing new hats this morning. The rain during the night was snow at the higher levels.

I built up the wood supply yesterday and this morning. There is a rhythm to the saw as its teeth eat back and forth in the deepening cut, but I must admit I enjoy the splitting more. To hit the chunk exactly where you want to and cleave it apart cleanly . . . there's a good sound to it and satisfaction in an efficient motion. Another reward comes from seeing those triangular stove lengths pile up. Then the grand finale! Drive the ax into the block, look around and contemplate the measure of what you have done.

Breakup is not the spectacular sight it was last year. A big wind would have cleared the thin ice out yesterday. As I loaded tools on the packboard this afternoon, the rotted ice began to flow past in quiet exit.

At the construction site several hundred yards down the lake shore, I found my logs were not as badly checked as I had first thought. The checking was only evident on the weathered sides. The logs were well seasoned and light in weight for their length.

When you have miles and miles of lake front and picture views to consider, it is difficult to select a building site. The more a man looks the fussier he gets. I had given much thought to mine. It sat atop a knoll about seventy-five feet back from a bight in the shoreline. There was a good beach for landing a canoe and a float plane also could be brought in there easily.

The wind generally blew up or down the lake. From either direction the cabin would be screened by spruce trees and willow brush. The knoll was elevated well above any visible high water marks. A shade over a hundred yards away was Hope Creek, and even though the water from the lake was sweet and pure, Hope Creek carried the best ever from out of the high places. At its mouth could usually be found fish, too.

There were two things that bothered me just a little, and I gave them serious consideration before making the final decision.

It was possible that after a continuous heavy rain and the resulting runoff from the mountains, Hope Creek could overflow and come churning through the timber behind me. If that happened, I felt I was still high enough to handle the situation. Perhaps some engineering would be necessary to divert the flow until the creek tamed down and returned to its channel.

It was also a possibility, though quite remote, that a slide or a quake might choke the Chilikadrotna River which was the drainpipe of the Twins. Any time the volume of water coming into the country was greater than what was going out, the lake level was going to rise. If the Chilikadrotna were to plug seriously, the country would fill up like a giant bath tub. I didn't like to think about that. Finally I decided such a catastrophe would rule out any site, and if a man had to consider all of nature's knockout punches, he would hesitate to build anywhere.

So I had taken the plunge and cleared the brush. I had grubbed out a shallow foundation, had hauled up beach gravel and had spread it to a depth of several inches over an area roughly twenty feet by twenty feet.

I felt I had made the best possible choice.

I stood with hands on hips looking at the plot of gravel and the pile of logs beside it. The logs were decked, one layer one way and the next at right angles to it so air could circulate all through the pile.

On that floor of gravel, from those logs, the home would grow. I could see it before me because I had sketched it so many times. It would be eleven feet by fifteen feet on the inside. Its front door would face northwest, and the big window would look down the lake to the south and west. It would nestle there as if it belonged.

A pile of logs. Which ones to start with? Why not the largest and crookedest for the two side foundation logs? They would be partly buried in the gravel anyway. Save the best ones to show off to the best possible advantage. I rolled the logs around until I was satisfied I had found what I was looking for.

One log in particular required considerable hewing to straighten. I must say black spruce works up nicely with ax and drawknife, a great deal like white pine. If I keep the edges of my tools honed, it will be a pleasure to pile up chips and shavings.

I bedded the two side logs into the gravel, then selected two end logs which I laid across them to form the eleven-by-fifteen foot interior. Next I scribed the notches on the underside of the end logs, on each side so the entire pattern of the notch was joined and pencilled. Everything inside the pencil patterns would have to be removed.

Four notches to cut out.

To make a notch fit properly, you can't rush it. Make several saw cuts an inch or two apart almost down to the pencil line and whack out the chunks with the ax until the notch is roughly formed. Then comes the finish work, the careful custom fit. I have just the tool for the job. At first I thought the character in the hardware store gouged me a little when he charged more than seven dollars for a gouge chisel (half round), but next to my ax I consider it my most valuable tool. Just tap the end of its handle with the spruce mallet and the sharp edge moves a curl of wood before it, right to the line. It smooths the notch to perfection.

The four notches rolled snugly into position over the curve of the side foundation logs beneath them.

Well . . . there's the first course, the first four logs, and those notches couldn't fit better. That's the way they're all going to fit.

Enough for this evening. The job has begun. It should be good going from here up to the eave logs and the start of the gable ends. Tomorrow should see more working and less figuring.

I wanted a salad for supper. Fireweed greens make the best and fireweed is one of the most common plants in this country. Its spikes of reddish pink brighten the land. They start blooming from the bottom and travel up as the season progresses. When the blossoms reach the top, summer is almost gone.

I went down along the creek bed where a dwarf variety grows. None were in bloom yet. I squatted among the stems and slender leaves and picked the tender plant crowns into a bowl. Then I rinsed them in the creek.

Sprinkled with sugar and drizzled with vinegar, those wild greens gave the red beans just the tang that was needed.

May 26th. I should have a fish for this evening's meal. It was a good morning to try for one down at the connecting stream.

There was still ice on the lower half of the lake. The way the ice was moving yesterday I thought the lake would be clear of it. Something is stalling the ice parade.

Traveling the lake shore, I nearly upended a time or two on the crusted snow. It was treacherous going. When I came to a good seat on the evergreens beneath a small spruce, I took advantage of it and proceeded to glass the slopes above the spruce timber.

First sighting was a cow moose with a yearling trailing her down country. While I watched them, I heard the bawling of caribou calves. It took me a few minutes to locate where all the noise was coming from. In a high basin I spotted seventy-five or more cows and calves. Across the lake ten Dall rams were in different positions of relaxation, and farther on down I counted eleven lambs and nineteen ewes. Satisfied that there was plenty of game in the country, I trudged down to the stream and followed along its banks, through the hummocks of low brush, until I came to where it poured invitingly into the lower lake.

I waded out a few steps. My boots did not leak, but almost immediately the chill seeped through the woolens inside them. I cast a few times, letting the small metal lure ride out with the current, then retrieving it jerkily with twitches of the rod tip. Several more casts. Nothing. Then it happened with the suddenness of a broken shoe lace.

As the lure came flashing towards me over the gravel, a pale shadow, almost invisible against the bottom, streaked in pursuit. Jaws gaped white, and the bright glint of the lure winked out as they closed over it. The line hissed, the rod tip hooped. The fish swerved out of the shallows, rolling a bulge of water before him as he bolted for the dropoff. He slashed the water white as I backed away with the rod held high, working him in to where he ran out of water and flopped his yellow spotted sides on the bank. A nineteen-inch lake trout. I thumped its head with a stone, and it shuddered out straight.

As I dressed it out, I examined its stomach. Not a thing in it. It is always interesting to see what a fish has been eating. Several times I have found mice in the stomachs of lake trout and Arctic char. Now how does a mouse get himself into a jackpot like that? Does he fall in by accident, or does he venture for a swim? Tough to be a mouse in this country. From the air, the land and the water his enemies wait to strike.

On the way back to the cabin I repaired the log bridge over Hope Creek. All it needed was shoring up with a few boulders rolled against the log bracings on each end. Easier to do now while the water was low.

I popped a batch of corn in bacon fat, salted and buttered it, and munched on it while I studied the sweep of the mountains. Before I left for the construction job, I shaped my biscuits, put them into a pan and covered them to rise for supper. Always have to think ahead with biscuits and a lot of other things in the wilderness.

If I can fit eight logs a day, the cabin will go along at a good rate. That's sixteen notches to cut out and tailor to fit. It is important to put the notch on the underside of a log and fit it down over the top of the one beneath. If you notch the topside, rain will run into it instead of dripping past in a shingle effect. Water settling into the notches can cause problems.

The sun shining on the green lake ice was so beautiful I had to stop work now and then just to look at it. That's a luxury a man enjoys when he works for himself.

I cut the trout into small chunks, dipped them into beaten egg and rolled them in corn meal. They browned nicely in the bacon fat and my tender crusted sourdoughs did justice to the first fish of the season.

May 28th. Frost on the logs when I went to work at six A.M. Had to roll many of them around to get the ones I wanted. Sorting takes time, but matching ends is very important if the cabin is to look right.

The wind helped the ice along today. The upper lake is nearly two-thirds ice-free now.

Had my first building inspector at the job. A Canada jay, affectionately known as camp robber, came in his drab uniform of gray and white and black to look things over from his perch on a branch end. The way he kept tilting his head and making those mewing sounds, I'd say he was being downright critical. I welcomed his company just the same.

May 29th. Only a few chunks of ice floating in the lake this morning. By noon no ice to be seen. Good to see the lake in motion again. It's even better to slip the canoe into the water and paddle to work for a change, gliding silently along over a different pathway.

My logs are not as uniform as they could be. They have too much taper. They make much more work, but just the same I like the accumulation of white chips and shavings all over the ground and the satisfaction that comes from making a log blend over the curve of the one beneath it as if it grew that way. Can't rush it. Don't want these logs looking as though a Boy Scout was turned loose on them with a dull hatchet.

This evening I hauled out Spike's heavy trotline, tested it for strength and baited its three hooks with some of the lake trout fins. I whirled it a few times, gave it a toss and watched the stone sinker zip the slack line from the beach and land with a plop about fifty feet from the shore. Let's see what is prowling the bottom these days.

Raining slightly when I turned in. There's no sleeping pill like a good day's work.

May 30th. A trace of new snow on the crags.

After breakfast I checked the trotline. It pulled heavy with a tugging now and then on the way in. Two burbot . . . a fifteen-incher and a nineteen-incher. A burbot is ugly, all mottled and big headed . . . looks like the result of an eel getting mixed up with a codfish. It tastes a whole lot better than it looks. I skinned and cleaned the two before going to work and left the entrails on the beach for the sanitation department.

The cabin is growing. Twenty-eight logs in place. Forty-four should do it except for gable ends and the roof logs. Really looks a mess to see the butts extending way beyond the corners, but I will trim them off later on.

Rain halted operations for a spell.

When I started in again, I made a blunder. My mind must have been on the big ram I had been watching. Just finished a notch, had a real dandy fit and was about ready to fasten it down when I noticed it was wrong end to! I tossed it to one side and started another. I guess a man needs an upset now and then to remind him that he doesn't know as much as he thinks he does. Maybe that's what the camp robber was trying to tell me.

May 31st. A weird-looking country this morning. The fog last night froze on the mountains giving them a very light gray appearance. That loon calling out of the vapor sounds like the spirit of Edgar Allan Poe.

The contrary log of yesterday carried over into today. I carefully fitted and fastened it down, and was selecting logs for the next course when I looked up and saw it was still wrong end to! How in the world did that happen? Two big ends together are proper but not three. I pried it off and flung it to the side. But why get shook up about it? Better you discovered it now than buried beneath a course.

Thirty-five logs in place. Nine to go and I will be ready for the gables . . . those tricky triangular sections on each end beneath the pitch of the roof. The roof logs and the ridge will notch over them. Babe said he could fly in some plywood for a roof. There would be room to spare in the Stinson but plywood seems too easy. I think I will stick with the pole idea instead. Run those spruce poles at right angles to the eave logs and the ridge, then decide the best way to cover them.

Snowing a few flakes as I worked. Cool weather is the best kind to work in, although rain makes the logs slick. Very few insects about. No complaints there.

I have a kettle of navy beans soaking for tomorrow. Babe says they must be at least fifteen years old. At that rate they will need a long bath. . . .

June 1st. Fog lifted early. This commuting to work by canoe is the best way yet.

Just fitted the jinx log into place when I heard a plane. It was Babe. I watched the T-craft glide in for a perfect landing on the calm lake. I've heard bush pilots say it is much easier to land where there is a ripple. Calm water distorts depth perception.

I shoved off in the canoe and rounded the point to meet him at Spike's beach.

Plenty of groceries this time. Fifty pounds of sugar, fifty pounds of flour, two gallons of honey, sixty pounds of spuds, two dozen eggs, half a slab of bacon, some rhubarb plants, plenty of mail, and some books . . . religious ones. I guess he has been working overtime on my philosophy from our last chat on the beach.

Babe had planted his potatoes yesterday. He was in a hurry. No time to visit. Wished he had time to inspect the building project. Next time he would. Right now he had a couple of prospectors to fly in somewhere. He would see me in a couple of weeks.

Mail from all over. Brother Jake is flying up and down that California country. How can he see it? Wish I could talk him into coming up here and staying a spell. We'd see some sights in that little bird of his.

Sister Florence is going to make a set of curtains for my big window. Dad is fine but he wishes I had a large dog with me. I've thought about a dog. It would mess up my picture taking for sure.

Sid Old is still soaking up the sun in New Mexico. The old boy has been off his feed lately. I could listen to him all day spinning his yarns about the early horse-packing days on Kodiak. Tying the diamond hitch . . . the cattle-killing bears . . .

Spike allows that he and Hope may drop in to Twin Lakes in August.

Spike not quite up to snuff these days either. Sam Keith writes that the kids in the junior high school where he is vice principal are like beef critters smelling water after a long drive. They smell vacation. Wish I could get him up here with that willow wand of his when the grayling are having an orgy at the creek mouth. . . . Good to hear from everybody. I guess part of man's root system has to be nourished by contacts with family and old friends.

The rhubarb plants should be put into the ground right away. Why not plant the whole garden patch while I'm about it?

I found the frost about four or five inches down. I drove the grub hoe into the soil as far as I could and stirred up the plot with a shallow spading. The loam seemed quite light and full of humus. I set out the rhubarb plants and watered them. Then I planted fifteen hills of potatoes, tucked in some onion sets and sowed short rows of peas, carrots, beets and rutabagas. Not much of a garden by Iowa standards, but it would tell me what I wanted to find out.

Finally back to the cabin building. I'm a better builder than I am a farmer anyway.

Thirty-eight logs in place and almost ready for the eave logs.

Where are camp robbers and the spruce squirrels? I miss seeing them. They are good companions, but work is really the best one of all.

A fine evening and I hated to waste it. The lake was flat calm and a joy to travel with quiet strokes of the paddle. My excuse was to prospect for some roof-pole timber near Whitefish Point. I found no great amount and I returned to this side of the lake.

June 3d. I am ready for the eave logs and the gables. Marked out the windows and door and will cut far enough into each log so that once the eave logs are on, I can get the saw back through to finish the cutting.

The gables and the roof have occupied much of my thoughts lately.

Up to this point my line level tells me the sides and ends are on the money. The course logs were selected carefully and I have done the hewing necessary to keep the opposite sides level as the cabin grows.

Five logs were very special. These were the twenty-footers, which along with the gable ends would be the backbone of the roof. Two would be eave logs, two purlin logs, and the last, the straightest, would be the ridge log.

In pondering how to go about the gables, I pictured to myself the letter A. It would take four logs, one atop the other and each one shorter than the one beneath, to make a triangle up to the ridge log height I planned.

The eave logs were the tops ones on the side walls. They would be different than the other wall logs in that they would overhang about a foot in the rear of the cabin and extend three feet beyond the front of the cabin, to hold eaves and porch roof.

The purlin logs were roof beams running parallel the length of the cabin, half way between the eave logs and the ridge log. The roof poles then would lay over them at right angles, from the ridge down across the eave logs.

Of course the ridge log still was not in place. To get it there, the fourth and shortest gable log would be spiked on top of the third one. The ridge could be seated on it, equidistant from the purlins. There would be a framework of five logs, two (or eaves) at the top of the walls, one (the ridge) at the peak, and two (the purlins) in between supporting the crossways roof poles.

The gable ends had to be cut to the slope of the roof. The slope could be determined with a chalk line. Drive a nail on top of the ridge pole, draw the string down along the face of the gable logs, just over the top of the purlins, to the eave nails. Chalk the line, pull it tight and snap it.

The blue chalk lines slanting down the gable logs would represent the slope of the roof on each side. The gable logs then could be cut at the proper angle of the letter A I had pictured.

The three-foot extension of the roof logs in front of the cabin would allow for three feet of shed-like entrance to the cabin.

That's the way the project shapes up. Let's see if we can do it.

June 4th. A good day to start the roof skeleton.

Another critic cruised past in the lake this morning, a real chip expert and wilderness engineer . . . Mr. Beaver. He probably got a little jealous of all the chips he saw, and to show what he thought of the whole deal, upended and spanked his tail on the surface before he disappeared.

Shortly afterwards a pair of Harlequin ducks came by for a look. The drake is handsome with those white splashes against gray and rusty patches of cinnamon.

My curiosity got the better of me and I had to glass the sheep in the high pasture. It was a sight to watch the moulting ewes grazing as the lambs frolicked about, jumping from a small rock and bounding over the green-ery, bumping heads. It was a happy interruption to my work.

I find I can handle the twenty-footers easily enough. Just lift one end at a time. With the corners of the cabin not yet squared off, there are some long ends sticking out on which to rest logs as I muscle them up to eave level and beyond. I also have two logs leaning on end within the cabin, and by adjusting their tilt I can use them to position a log once it is up there. The ladder comes in handy, too.

The two eave logs were notched and fastened down according to plan. I cut the openings for the big window, the two smaller ones and the opening for the door.

I placed the first gable log on each end, and it was time to call it a day.

The roof skeleton should get the rest of its bones tomorrow.

June 5th. Good progress today.

When you first think something through, you have a pretty good idea where you are going and eliminate a lot of mistakes.

I put up the gable ends, notched the purlin logs into them and fastened down the ridge log. It went smoothly. It's a good thing I put the eave log one higher than I had originally planned, or I would have to dig out for head room. Even now a six-footer won't have any to spare, and I won't have much more clearance myself.

The cabin is in a good spot. That up-the-lake wind is blocked by the timber and brush between the cabin and the mouth of Hope Creek.

As it now stands, the cabin looks as though logs are sticking out all over it like the quills of a riled porcupine. Much trimming to do in the morning. All logs are plenty long, so there will be no short ones to worry about.

June 6th. The time has come to cut the cabin down to size.

First file the big saw. Then trim the roof logs to the proper length. Trim the gable logs to the slope of the roof, and trim the wall logs on all four corners.

What a difference! Log ends all over the ground and the cabin looking like a once shaggy kid after a crew cut.

Now I have to start thinking about window and door frames, and the roof poles. I must find a stand of skinny timber for those. That means some prospecting in the standing lumber yards.

My cabin logs have magically changed form in the ten days since I cut the first notch. Only four full-length logs left, and only one of those half way decent. Before it's all over, there will be a use for all of them.

June 7th. I do believe the growing season is at hand. The buckbrush and willows are leafing out fast now. The rhubarb is growing, and I notice my onion sets are spiking up through the earth.

Those window frames have been on my mind. Decided to do something about it. First I built a saw-horse workbench, then selected straight-grained sections of logs cut from the window and door openings. Chalked a line down each side, and with a thin-bladed wide chisel I cut deep along the line on each side. Then I drove the hand ax into the end to split the board away from the log. Worked fine.

I smoothed the split sides with the draw-knife to one-and-three-quarter inches wide. The result was a real nice board, so I continued to fashion others. Put in place and nailed, they look first rate.

I finished the day cleaning the litter of wood chips. I mounded them in front of the door, beaver lodge style. Quite a pile for eleven days' work, enough to impress that beaver.

I have given a lot of thought to chinking. I think I will try mixing moss and loose oakum to cut down on the amount of oakum. If oakum with its hemp fibers can caulk the seams in boats, it should be able to chink logs.

June 8th. I moved my mountain of wood chips and shavings. Then I gathered moss and spread it on the beach to dry. There is still ice under the six-inch-thick moss in the woods. I used oakum in the narrow seams, and a mixture of oakum and moss where the opening was more than one-quarter of an inch. Straight oakum is easier to use. I will have a tight cabin.

June 9th. Today would be a day away from the job of building. I would look for pole timber up the lake.

I proceeded to the upper end of the lake where I beached the canoe on the gravel bar and tied the painter to a willow clump. A "down-the-lake" wind might come up, work the canoe into the water, and it would be a long hike to retrieve it.

I walked along the flat, crossing and recrossing the creek that had its beginnings in the far-off snows. I found a dropped moose antler, a big one, and decided to pick it up on the way back. There were fox tracks and lynx tracks in the sand, and piles of old moose droppings.

The rockpile was finally before me, a huge jumble of gray-black, sharp-edged granite chunks all crusted with lichens. It was a natural lookout that commanded three canyons. I set up my spotting scope, wedging the legs of the tripod firmly amidst the slim-fronded ferns that grew dagger-shaped in single clumps out of the rock crevices. Right off I spotted four caribou bulls grazing along the right fork of the creek bed. Then high on the slopes five good-looking Dall rams, one in a classic pose with all four feet together atop a crag, back humped against the sky.

Below them, four ewes moving in my direction. At mid-slope a bull moose on the edge of some cottonwoods was puling at the willow brush, changing black and brown as he swung his antlers amongst the foliage. I saw an eagle wheeling in the air currents, pinions stiffened like outstretched fingers. Ground squirrels whistled. Life was all around.

On the way back to the beach I stooped to nibble on last season's moss-berries. They were a little tart to the tongue. I picked up the moose antler and wondered where the other might be. To my surprise I found the mate not two hundred yards away. They made quite an awkward load to pack. It must be a relief to an old bull when the load falls off.

Just as I reached the canoe, it had to happen. An up-the-lake-wind! I battled against it for a spell, then decided to beach. Finding a warm spot in the sun I napped, waiting for the lake to flatten. It never really did, and I paddled back from point to point until I finally reached the cabin.

A good day. Only one thing I forgot . . . something for lunch.

June 10th. Bright and clear. I hear the spruce squirrel, but he stays out of sight. He likes to shuck his spruce cones in private. The blueberry bushes are nearly leafed out and loaded with bloom.

I finished chinking the cabin. Then I put a log under the bottom log in front, to plug an opening there. Did the same in back and chinked them both. Now I am ready for the roof poles which I will start cutting tomorrow.

The little sandpipers flying back and forth along the edge of the beach have a characteristic flight. A few quivering strokes of their wings, a brief sail, some more wing vibrations, and then wings rigid again as they glide to a landing and vanish. They blend in so well, they are invisible against the gravel until they move.

June 11th. I paddled up the lake to the foot of Crag Mountain. This would be a pole-cutting day.

Good poles were not as plentiful as I figured, and I worked steadily to get forty-eight cut and packed to the beach by noon. The mosquitoes were out in force.

To peel the poles I made a tripod of short sticks on which to rest one end of the pole while the other stuck into the bank, and put the drawknife to work. The bark flew.

June 12th. Today I finished peeling the poles, fifty in all, rafted them up and moved them down the lake to my beach. A good pile, but I doubt there will be enough.

June 13th. Rain. Wrote a batch of letters, not a job to do on a good day. It cleared in the late afternoon so I gathered sixteen more poles and peeled seven.

June 14th. Not a cloud in the sky. A cool morning but no frost. My garden is all up except the potatoes, and they should be showing soon. The green onions are more than three inches tall.

I peeled the remainder of my roof poles and trimmed the knots close. Now to put them on but how close? I decided on five inches center to center as they lay at right angles to the ridge log.

One side was nearly roofed and the other, about half. With only ten left, I must hunt more poles—about thirty if my calculations are right.

June 15th. I tried for a fish this morning at the mouth of Hope Creek. No luck. I did see the flash of a light-colored belly behind the lure. They are there.

I went pole prospecting below the creek mouth in the fine rain and cut fifteen . . . enough for one trip back up the lake. I tied the small ends side by side, ran the canoe into the butt-ends far enough to tie them to the bow thwart. It left me enough room to paddle from just forward of the stern. Worked real well . . . slow but effective transportation.

In the afternoon I finished the front end of the cabin roof and took count. I would need seventeen more poles. After scouting in the timber behind the cabin, I found seven.

A beautiful evening with a light breeze down the lake. A loon rode low in the water and trailed a wake of silver as it took flight.

June 16th. Where are my spuds? Maybe I planted them too deep.

Today I secured the roof poles over the gables and chinked them. A cabin roof takes time. A hundred poles to gather, transport and peel, trim the knots and notch them to fit over the purlin logs. I see where one more pole is needed. Soon I will be ready to saw the ends and fill the slots between the pole butts under the eaves. These fillers should be called squirrel frustrators. Give those characters an entrance and they can ruin a cabin.

June 17th. Up to greet the new day at 3:45 A.M. I am not sure of the time anymore. I have kept both my watch and clock wound but have not changed the setting. Now they are thirty minutes apart. Which one is right? No radio to check by. I don't miss a radio a bit. I never thought one was in tune with the wilderness anyway. A man is on his own frequency out here.

On the job at five-thirty. I sawed the roof pole ends off to a proper 18-inch overhang. Now I am ready for the chore of plugging the gaps between the roof poles on top of the wall logs. If varmints are going to get into my cabin, they will have to work at it.

The camp robbers are back. Four were near the cabin today. They are marked somewhat like king-size chickadees. I like the way they come gliding softly in to settle on a spruce tip and tilt their heads from one side to the other as if they are critical of what I am doing. Some have a very dark plumage, almost black.

Tomorrow should see the roof ready for the tar-paper, polyethylene and moss. I feel guilty about the tar-paper and polyethylene because they are not true wilderness cabin materials, but I am convinced that they will do a better job of keeping the weather out. Next I will finish the inside kitchen counter, table, bench and make stands for the water bucket and the wash basin. The more I think about it, I shall build a double deck bunk. Might have some company.

June 18th. Everything looks as though it had a bath last night. Must have been a good shower and I never even heard it.

My garden looks perky. Green onions five inches tall or more. Peas are up an inch. Everything growing first class but my spuds. Not a sign of them yet.

A check on the livestock before going down to the roof job. Two caribou bulls just up country from Low Pass Creek. Nothing else in sight. Should be a bear passing through one of these days.

I finished filling the slots between the roof poles and caulked joints with oakum. Then a strip of the oiled oakum down each side and over the gables. I chinked around the blocks on the outside and also caught the windows and door frame. Chinked all the corner joints of the logs. Any place I could get a table knife blade in, got oakum.

I was surprised to look up and see it raining on the other side of the lake. It was darkening fast. The rain was advancing on the double. A get-wet rain was upon me before I made it to Spike's cabin. Six o'clock by the Baby Ben. Time for the sourdough biscuits and those red beans.

Once I get my roof on, I can work on the cabin rain or shine.

I do believe this rain will help the blueberry crop. Seems to me there are more blossoms than last summer.

Twenty days to get the cabin to its present stage of construction. A lot of chips ago.

....

July 10th. I had the woodshed logs gathered on the beach when I heard the plane. Babe at last!

I left the poles high and dry and started the long paddle to the cabin.

I met Babe walking down the beach. As usual he was in a hurry. I hoped I hadn't held him up too long.

Four dozen eggs this trip, a full slab of bacon, some candy bars, a big heavy Stanley jack-plane dull and rusty as sin, but I could put it into shape and make the wood ribbons fly. No polyethylene. Babe said he might return later in the evening on the way back from a trip he had to make. I gave him the outgoing mail anyway, and off he went.

A seventeen-and-a-half-inch lake trout on the trotline. Enough for company.

Babe didn't come back.

July 11th. Calm. Perfect water for hauling my roof poles.

On the way back to the cabin site with the heavily loaded canoe, it started to rain. I beached the canoe well up on solid ground It was nice to have the tar-paper roof overhead. While the rain pattered, I sharpened the blade of the jack-plane and oiled it. Then I moved my log bench under the overhang and proceeded to make shavings. All the boards I had ripped for shelves, counter and table had to be planed on both sides and the two edges. Also the two-inch planks for the door. By the time I had finished, more shavings were piled up than I had ever made in a day before. I fitted the boards under the counter. The table will be ready to put together as soon as the glue arrives.

A light rain all afternoon. The mountains must be dry because there is no sign of running water yet.

A special treat for supper. Some of my green onions to spice up the salad of fireweed greens.

....

July 18th. High clouds moving fast from the south.

Fresh tracks of caribou and five-inch wolf tracks in the gravel not fifty feet from my new cabin. Now wouldn't that have been a sight?

I built a stove stand and a solid sawbuck while big cotton clouds formed down country.

The droning of a plane . . . Babe! In he came to make the first landing at my beach. I helped him back the tail end of the floats to rest on a spruce pole laid along the gravel. Then we tied her fast with a line.

The glue from brother Jake. That spelled progress. Plenty of mail. Still no polyethylene. Well, I've made up my mind. I'll just wait it out. Maybe next time it will come.

Babe spotted my peas [some nipped off just above the ground]. His eyes twinkled. "I like rabbit better than peas anyway," he said. "Don't you?"

He helped me finish the company dessert, a can of fruit cocktail. Then he was off for Lake Clark.

I spent the rest of the day reading mail and gluing boards and poles. I do believe the cabin is close to livable.

That rabbit really likes peas. He has a rough time of it in the winter, what with lynxes and fox ready to waylay him. I really don't need the peas. Let him have them.

July 19th. Today started in a very ordinary way, yet it was to be an extra-ordinary one.

I canoed down to the cabin. A good feeling to slide into my beach. I mounted the brackets for the kitchen counter and was just putting the finishing touches on a chair when I heard an unfamiliar sound. I listened and heard it again. Then I really came to life. The sound could be only one thing—wolves howling! They were on the hump. A low deep howl again and then one higher in pitch. The chair would have to wait. I took off up the trail towards my cabin log grove. I should be able to see them from there.

Surely enough, I saw two wolves in an easy lope coming down the trail off the hump and through the scattering of small spruce. Suddenly they vanished. I froze and waited. There they were again, going back up the trail, now walking, now breaking into a slow trot.

Why didn't I bring my scope? I decided to go back and get it. I flew through heavy brush and timber and had the scope all mounted before they were half way up the hump. It was a sight . . . the big one light with dark streaks on his back and sides, dark around his muzzle . . . the other a fourth smaller and light in shade. They traveled with tails down, long, lanky and loose with the fur bouncing on their backs. Then there were three. Another big one appeared. They stopped to smell a squirrel burrow, and as they did, their tails lifted slowly. I watched them climb up and over the top. After nearly fifty days of labor, it never really entered my mind that I could take a day off. As it turned out, I would today.

Back at the cabin I picked up the saw I had flung to one side in my wild dash to get a look at the wolves, intending to get back to work. I took one last peek through the scope, though, and there, no more than 100 yards from where the wolves had climbed, was a cow caribou. She was standing with her head down fighting insects. This seemed very strange.

I loaded my camera gear and started up the trail to the hump. Just before reaching the top I saw a reddish object in the low brush ahead. The wolves had made a kill. There were the remains of a young cow. The three wolves had nearly devoured her. All that was left was the backbone part of the rib cage, part of one front shoulder and most of the neck. The lower part of the head to the top of the eyes was eaten away. The lower jaw bones were stripped clean. Back straps and ribs all cleaned, too. The skin was badly torn and pulled down over the front leg as you would peel back a rubber glove. They had downed her fifty yards up the hill and scattered paunch, skin, and lungs along the trail to where she now lay.

The other caribou were nowhere to be seen. Wondering if I would see the killers again, I followed the trail high above Hope Creek, through patches of wild flowers. Many forget-me-nots, wild geraniums, dwarf fire-weed, paint brush, and wild celery. The breeze was at my back.

As I topped the ridge along a dry wash, a wolf came up from the other side, thirty or forty paces away. It was the light-colored one, staring at me head-on. She whirled and dropped over the edge. I scrambled forward to get a better look. She crossed a rocky slide and stopped on a grassy place to look back, tail down and head high. Then in a winking she was gone.

I walked the trail to the mouth of the big basin below the glacier, and sat down to glass the surrounding country. On a grassy slope was a big brown rock. Sometimes those big brown rocks move. I slipped out of my pack, lay on my stomach and studied the spot through the lenses. It moved. I saw a bear's head raise, his muzzle tossing and testing the wind. Maybe I could get some pictures.

By the time I climbed a steep pitch, the bear was digging for squirrels. I watched him chase a squirrel in a big circle. He sprawled on his belly and worked at something held between his forepaws. All the time I was taking pictures. He lumbered down by the noisy stream, up through a willow patch and bobbed on over the skyline.

The sun was warm and no insects about. I nearly fell asleep, thinking about what I had seen this day. I could have killed them all. I thought of the season that would soon open, of the men the season would bring to do just that, if they could. Kill, shake hands with the guide and stand with hands in their pockets while he skins out the hide or saws off the skull and antlers and perhaps a quarter or two of meat, not even bothering to open the carcass. The wolves had done a better job.

While I was away, the rabbit changed his menu. He cleaned half a row of rutabagas. Bet he never tasted them before, either.

....

July 31st. The last day of July and I don't believe I saw new snow during the entire month.

Today would be the day to set up the stove and do some more tin bend-ing. I dug the stove out of a corner of Spike's cabin. When I saw the old relic in good light, I almost chickened out of the project. It was the sorriest look-ing stove I ever saw. A half-inch gap along the sides under the top, one door hinge unstuck. I packed it down through the brush and put it on my stove stand. Then I put up my new stove pipe and made ready to touch it off.

First I packed a bucket of small rocks to put under the grate, then gravel to fill the grate. It would take a long time to get ashes enough to hold a fire. I stuffed in some shavings and some chips and struck a match. The flames grew out along the sides under the top and I thought this will never do. And then the smoke found the smoke stack and my troubles were over. In spite of its looks it did a fine job heating water. I was pleasantly surprised. Now to make it look professional I would need a Chinese hat for the top of the chimney pipe, so I got busy with tools and tin and had one on in short order.

Found a way to get paper and stickum off a gas can. Boil it in hot soapy water. The label is on to stay, but it can't stand that treatment.

I needed a big wooden spoon to dip hotcake batter onto the griddle. One spoonful, one hotcake. In the woodpile I found scraps of stump wood that looked suitable. It took no more than an hour to turn out a good-looking spoon. I must make a wooden bowl or two later on.

Cool breeze and the insects are no problem today.

Tomorrow is the big day. I will load all my remaining gear into the canoe and paddle down to my new home. A calm sea will help for this voyage.

August 1st. The lake dead calm. A perfect moving day. A camp robber, visiting me for breakfast, came inside. I wonder what his range is? Will he find me at the new cabin?

I worked clockwise around Spike's cabin, set out everything that I wanted to go and packed it down to the beach. Then I cleaned up the cabin that had been home, scrubbed the counter, the shelf and the woodwork of the stove stand. I glanced at Spike's sign and was satisfied I had complied. Everything in order and better than I found it.

I loaded the canoe and paddled down to my new quarters. Everything found its place and there was lots of room for everything, not a cluttered look at all. Some items to make, such as a knife holder to fasten on the wall.

Suddenly it happened, the worst accident of my cabin building career. The piece of wood I was working turned, and I raked my thumb with the newly sharpened ripsaw. Blood ran all over the place. I hurried down and stuck my thumb into the cold lake, watched the water turn from green to red, then doped up the gash, wrapped a rag around it, anchored it with a piece of tape and went back to work.

Burned my sourdoughs a bit on the bottom, but they were good anyway. It will take a few trial runs to get used to my antique range.

First night on my new bunk. Five inches of foam rubber will make it just about right. I can hear Hope Creek real plain. That will be a pleasant sound to go to sleep by.

The lake water is good, but now I pack it from Hope Creek and I think there is none better that I have ever tasted. I like to think of the high places it comes from.

I lit the Coleman lantern this evening. A bright friendly glow in the wilderness, the warmth of home.

August 2d. Best sleep in a long time. The sound of the waves lapping the gravel beach and the never-ending rustle of Hope Creek until freeze-up. No better sleeping pill.

The stove did a fine job on the hotcakes this morning and my wooden spoon is just right. Perfect-sized cakes every time.

I must have a stool outside to set things on when opening the door. A ten-inch slice from a twelve-inch-diameter log, and legs augered into one side. Gave the legs a flare so the stool wouldn't tip when I stepped on it. Why not a couple more thin slices from the log, and plane them smooth? Now I had place mats and hot pads to save my plastic table cloth.

That Babe! He landed and had things unloaded at Spike's cabin before I could get to him. We put the gear back into the plane and taxied down to my beach.

The polyethylene at last, more than enough, and plenty of grub. Also a package from my sister, Florence.

I watched Babe's eyes move with approval over the cabin walls. "A nice place," he said. "A real nice place."

"Like heaven," I said.

He just looked at me and slowly wagged his head.

I waved to him as he took off down country into the rainy fog, headed home.

Good news. Spike and Hope want me to take the stove from their cabin. They will bring in another one sometime. In nothing flat I was paddling down to get it. I took out some of the ashes before hauling it down, then out went that sorry-looking other monster, rocks, gravel and all. Some spikes into the top of my stove stand and the old reliable was soon in place. I scratched a match. She took off like a gut-shot cat. A welcome sound, as welcome as having one's wife return to full duty after an operation (I imagine).

The biscuits puffed up just right and baked to a turn. All is going well. Tomorrow I can work full time on roof.

....

August 4th. A surprise last evening as it was getting a bit on the dark side— Babe in the old Stinson. As soon as the prop stopped, out he bounced from his little door up forward.

"Man, am I ever tired." he said. "Been flying for ten hours. Moved the prospectors' camp to Farewell. Moved everything. Coming back it got so dark I couldn't see the gas gauge and the last time I saw it, the needle was on the wrong side of the glass."

He had some gas cached here. He would stay the night and gas up in the morning.

I had the fire going the next morning when Babe said, "Sure don't take long to stay all night here."

Suspenders hanging, Babe washed up. I could hear him sputtering water through his moustache. After hotcakes and bacon we hauled the gas that was cached in the brush and poured the fuel into the tank of the Stinson, which looked like a Greyhound bus compared to the T-craft. Big doors, big windows and room inside for five fifty-gallon barrels.

The old girl was balky at first. She had made many starts yesterday. The 120 oil made her stiff. A primer line had broken and, even after some repair work, still didn't prime too well. Finally she sputtered and shuddered into life. I watched her taxi out into the lake. She lifted easily. I wondered what they were thinking back in Port Alsworth when Babe didn't return last night.

Back to the roof job. It seems I have cleared two acres of moss and still the roof isn't covered.

Hard to believe, but I have all the moss in place at last. The cabin suddenly has even more character. This roof has helped more than any one thing to give the cabin a finished look. Now for the poles to hold down the moss. Four poles on a side will look better than three, I figure.

Babe brought in some fresh groceries that needed refrigeration. I had dug down a foot into the moss yesterday and found frost. Why not dig a hole and put in a gas can box, then use my moss carrying rack loaded with moss for a cover? I think that will do the job. I must put the thermometer in there to find out the temperature.

Clouding up down country. May bring rain tomorrow. I'll never hear it with all the moss on the roof to deaden the drops when they hit.

....

August 8th. Really had a time here this afternoon. I looked up from my letter writing to chew on my pen end and peer down the lake through the big window. For a moment I thought I was having hallucinations. Lots of motion and here comes a brown bear up my path.

He was nosing the gravel as he shuffled towards me, getting bigger all the time. He looked somewhat small for a brown, but he would have been big for a black. Abruptly he stopped and flipped his muzzle at the wind currents. I waited for him to wince as the man-scent struck him, and bolt with a crashing into the brush.

No such reaction at all. He just ambled unconcerned past my big window in the direction of the rear of the cabin. No more had he gone out of sight when I heard sounds that brought me right up out of the chair. That character was trying to climb up the corner of the cabin and on to my new roof!

This would never do. I slid the .357 magnum from its holster on the wall and stepped out the door. No bear could I see on the roof, so I yelled and touched off a round that exploded like a thunderclap.

It didn't have the expected result. Around the corner came the bear in four-paw drive. I scrambled for the door, pulled it shut and gripped a fist down hard on the handle.

The bear came slamming against the planks. I felt his weight bulging the upper door and heard the rake of his claws.

What kind of a bear was this? The noises he was making didn't sound friendly at all. In fact, they sounded downright psychopathic. His guttural complaints trailed off and I knew he was moving away. Through the small window I watched him poke towards the woodshed. He explored the area thoroughly, standing on his hind legs, teetering and snuffling along the front eave. He was one curious bruin.

Was he going to try climbing up the woodshed? Maybe it would take the heavy artillery to scare him off. I loaded the ought-six, opened the window and rested the barrel on the sill. Then I turned loose a rebel yell.

He must have been a reincarnation of Jeb Stuart. He spun with unbelievable quickness and came on like the cavalry. I drove a slug into the path in front of him, making the gravel fly. He put on the brakes, whirled in retreat, then stopped, rising to his full height as if trying to peer beyond the cabin logs and solve the strangeness there. Noiselessly he dropped to all fours with an almost fluid movement and was gone.

Less than five minutes later, here he came from another direction, this time towards the front of the cabin, stalking—silently and ominously.

I didn't like it at all. There was an orneriness about him I could feel. I couldn't have pets like this running around the place. The best thing to do would be to shoot him, skin him out and write a letter to Fish and Game.

He must have picked up warning vibrations. Off he went in a sudden huff, slinging his forepaws in pigeon-toed strides until the willows closed behind him. I checked the latch on my door and went back to my letter writing.

This evening I went on bear patrol. No sign of him. Just passing through, I hope. I think he has headed out of the country. I guess I made myself a pretty good door at that. One thing I can't understand though—if that character wanted in, how come he passed up the big window?

....

August 12th. The spruce boughs are glistening with rain-drops. The land had a bath last night.

Calm after the big blow of yesterday. I decided to take a trip down to the lower end of the lake. I could use a fish or two.

An easy paddle down. An Arctic tern sliced above, hovering to look me over, his breast picking up a pale blue cast from the water. Rags of fog strewn about the high peaks. I pulled the canoe up high on the gravel of the lower end. Fish were breaking. One that looked two feet long rolled on the surface. If I could only sink a hook into that one—but no luck after many casts. To make matters worse, the breeze was coming up strong and down the lake at that. One last try. I let the lure sink 'way down and twitched it towards me. Wham! A heavy fish but not much fight. More color than I have ever seen in a lake trout. Bright yellow fins and belly, big lemon spots against gray-green sides. This one should break my record of nineteen inches. I had my fish but now I was in trouble. Whitecaps all over the place and that seventh wave a big one. I could leave the canoe tied to the brush and high on the beach, then walk the three miles back, or give it a try.

I shoved the canoe out into the wind, crouched low with knees spread against the bottom. It was a battle. I finally made it to a bight in the shoreline near Low Pass Creek, and it was a relief to get behind the steep beach out of the wind. I slid the canoe into the shallows, tied her fast and gorged myself in a blueberry patch.

Still blowing. I tied one end of my long line to the bow and the other end about two-thirds of the way back towards the stern. Holding the line in the middle, I kept adjusting until the bow of the canoe was farther from shore than the stern, and started walking the beach. It worked real well for a time, until it got broadside to the wind and was blown ashore. Then I got in to paddle to the next favorable section of towing beach.

I was getting home, but it was a slow process. I got slowed down even more when I hit a section of no beach and big boulders. I took to the open water and battled my way.

As I passed the boss hunter's cabin, I saw something hanging on the meat pole, with birds flying around it. The fresh meat looked like a front quarter. No other sign of life around the cabin.

By the time I made my beach, I had had a workout. My trout measured nineteen inches on the nose. It was a female loaded with eggs.

I fried them in bacon grease with lots of corn meal, a dose of Tabasco sauce, some poultry seasoning, salt and pepper. When the eggs got hot, they commenced to pop like popcorn and flew every which way when I lifted the lid covering the pan.

They were different.

August 13th. It could rain today without too much trouble.

I made a paper towel rack out of some spruce stock. Two end pieces supporting a dowel that could be easily removed. Next I made a curtain rod out of a skinny piece of driftwood and hung the burlap curtains Sister Florence had sent.

Clean up my beach . . . that was a job that needed doing. I wanted to make it a beach that a pilot would enjoy coming into. I piled the driftwood in one pile, the rocks and boulders in another and waded out to pick the large stones from the bottom to pile them also. When I finished, I was sure I had the best plane landing place in both lakes.

A heavy fish splashed just out from the cabin. Have the sockeyes arrived? Must watch for them.

A little later I looked up from applying a coat of Varathane on my furniture to see a scarlet fish with a green head slice through a wave. It is the end of a long journey for them. They will spawn and die. Their escape from the can is a very brief reprieve.

This evening I sat on my driftwood pile admiring my cabin. Pale blue wood smoke rising up through the dark boughs of the spruce and beyond, looming huge and majestic, the jagged peak of Crag Mountain. The cabin was complete now except for the fireplace, and maybe later on, the cache up on poles. It was a good feeling just sitting and reflecting, a proud inner feeling of something I had created with my own hands. I don't think I ever accomplished anything as satisfying in my entire life.

Change

CHARLES J. KEIM

Writer and educator Charles J. Keim is a widely published author of award-winning magazine articles, short stories, and books. He and Hal Waugh, both big-game guides, co-authored FAIR CHASE WITH ALASKAN GUIDES *(1977). Keim was a professor of English and journalism and dean of the College of Arts and Letters at the University of Alaska Fairbanks, and through the decades he mentored many aspiring writers. Now retired, he lives in Washington state. He is the author of* CHANGE AND OTHER STORIES *(1976), from which this story is taken.*

The late spring sun already had been hard at work for several hours on the face of the glacier across the river valley when Arne Olsen threw the heavy comforter from his slight body and swung his feet to the cabin floor. The clock above the fireplace ticked away noisily, telling Arne what he already knew. It was 6 A.M. and time for breakfast.

When the spruce wood was crackling in the stove, he walked outside and held a wash pan and the coffee pot under a pipe that tapped off the creek to spill water into a stone basin he used during the summer to keep his food cool. Come freezeup, he'd use the well that he and his partner, Ross Ferrin, had dug alongside the cabin 60 years earlier and which still provided as good water as existed in the entire Alaska Range of mountains.

Water. That as much as gold had prompted him and Ross to stake the two adjoining claims. Maybe they could have scrabbled a better life out of richer gravels elsewhere, but water and the beauty of the place had anchored them there. Ross was gone now. He'd slipped out peacefully seven years earlier while lifting a shovel of gravel into the sluicebox. That's about the way he'd wanted it.

Arne had written a note to the Commissioner at Delta Junction, and then had buried Ross at the far edge of the large meadow below the cabin. In the winter the soft snow blanketed the land and the northern lights played their silent symphony across the sky. Spring and summer there always would be the song of the twin creeks, one clear, the other silty from a glacier and the mining higher up the mountainside. In all seasons moose and caribou would shamble out of the heavy spruce stands which bordered the meadow on both sides as did Silt Creek at the left and Clear Creek at the right below the cabin. And there always would be the view of the river and the mountains and the glacier beyond the open end of the meadow. Arne would rest near Ross, and the old man had mentioned this in the note to the Commissioner.

The note said other things—actually amounted to a will of sorts, something a person always figures to work around to doing, but puts off, what with one thing or another seeming to be more important. Arne had homesteaded the land around the claim and they had figured that Ross would homestead the meadow below, but with living in the cabin which was close for working the claim, it seemed easier to put off the other homesteading venture. Besides, Ross would have had to build and, for a time, live in another cabin, and the one they had put up together was plenty large for two, even more.

Arne's note said that when he was gone the authorities should sell his homestead to a person who would take care of it, keep up the mining and agree to tend the place where Ross and he would be resting. Seemed like he had figured things out right, even to specifying that the money from the sale of the place should go to the Pioneers Home down in Sitka to sort of help out the thinning ranks of their old friends there. There was contentment in that, too.

Arne pondered these things often, even talked to himself about them, like now while he pulled the coffee pot to the cool side of the stove, warmed up the blueberry syrup and fried a stack of six sourdough hotcakes and some bacon, meanwhile watching the sunlight creep from the base of the mountain, then cross the river and start moving toward the meadow. Soon the warmth would be on his doorstep, then climb the mountain to work on a glacier on that side, too. Silt Creek would rise then, for it had its beginnings at the glacier, shallowing in the mountain cold of the short spring and summer nights to just enough water to work the sluice and rising in a few hours of warmth until it raged down the mountain by midday, even rumbling giant rocks along its murky depth to discharge them at last on the river bed far below.

Arne reluctantly retrieved his ill-fitting teeth from a glass near the table, adjusted them, then forked four of the hotcakes from the stack. The other two would go to the squirrels that already were scratching around the house and adding their impatient chattering to the growing number of sounds from the awakening forest. Occasionally there was a discordant note as the sounds of the heavier traffic on the Richardson Highway four miles away would penetrate the valley. When he wished, Arne could tune out these sounds. They had grown over the years as the Fairbanks–Valdez Trail had metamorphosed into the Richardson Highway onto which funneled the commerce between Fairbanks, Anchorage, Valdez, the Yukon Territory border and other points.

Arne would watch the traffic for a while each Wednesday when he would walk over the well-worn ridge trail to the large mailbox set at the edge of the pavement. Then he would hasten back, grateful that the forest gradually would absorb the noise. He disdainfully would reject all proffers of rides during his rare, night-long walks into Delta Junction, but lately he grudgingly would admit to himself that he was finding it harder to turn them down.

Arne looked at the clock. Three minutes to seven. He poured a cup of coffee then reached across the table to switch on his radio. He would hear what was going on in Alaska, wash the dishes, shave, then impale the two hotcakes on a tree limb and head up to the diggings.

As his hand touched the switch, his eye caught the movement of a massive bull moose hurriedly lumbering up to the meadow below the cabin. The animal splashed through Clear Creek, crossed the meadow, then Silt Creek and disappeared into the forest. Arne half rose from his chair, hesitated for a moment as the radio announcer's voice began extolling the merits of aspirin, then the sourdough decisively switched off the set. He could hear the sound that had spooked the moose. Too slow for a plane.

More like a "cat" tractor, the old man thought. Maybe it's another tank.

Once the Army Arctic Indoctrination School at Fort Greely had sent a tank down the trail during maneuvers. It had parked near the Clear Creek edge of the meadow to get a commanding view of the braided river bed. Arne had talked to the tank fellows, told them how the tank could start erosion on the trail. Over coffee, one at a time in his cabin, the men figured they could cover the river just as well a little closer to the highway. Maybe they had forgotten, or new men were running the tank. Well, he would see.

Arne ate his breakfast, missing the news as he listened to the engine coming closer. A flock of ptarmigan flew part way across the meadow then flashed toward the river and out of sight. A curious raven flew about the meadow, waiting to see what was making the noise.

It was a cat, not a tank. The vehicle hesitated uncertainly before it approached Clear Creek. Arne let his fork and bacon drop from his hand when he saw that the cat was pulling a wanigan. Behind this small, house-like structure was tied an old truck, its bed piled high with gear.

The cat halted. Its pulsating roar echoed up and down the mountains as the skinner clambered down then walked toward the wanigan. The door opened and Arne, standing in his own cabin doorway now, watched the man carefully help down a woman. Then they slowly walked hand in hand to Clear Creek.

Arne was half way down the meadow by the time the man again had climbed aboard the cat and pulled the wanigan and truck to the level, tree shaded spot where the woman was standing. This was the best view of the valley, the peaks in front and behind, and Clear Creek flowed past the door. Ross had planned to put his cabin there.

Arne knew that it was useless to try to shout above the racketing of the diesel, but when the driver shut it off, the sourdough's "hold it there, hold it there" brought the couple around to face him. A little girl standing in the wanigan doorway rubbing her eyes as the sunlight touched her curly, yellow hair ran to the woman upon hearing the angry tone in the old man's voice.

Arne hadn't meant to shout, but his heart had begun pounding harder than ever when he had noticed that the wanigan was mounted upon freshly hewn sledges instead of wheels. These were no curious passersby. Young fellow was dressed in denims, and the crew cut head and neck were perched on broad shoulders and chest above a waist as slim as one of the birches. By now the little girl was clutching her mother's leg, tightening the woman's dress and accentuating the fact that the youngster soon would have a playmate.

With difficulty Arne restrained his heavy breathing and nodded to the trio.

"Morning. Kind of off the track, aren't you?"

The man, standing somewhat defiantly in front of the woman and girl, relaxed his face into an easy grin. Holding out his hand, he walked toward Arne.

"Hello. You're Arne Olson. They told me about you in Delta Junction. You were mining up on the mountainside the two times I came in to look over the land and get some soil for testing. We're going to be neighbors. We're homesteading 160 acres here."

Arne knew that he had flinched, so to cover up he stepped forward and used the same face he had used on Ross in winter poker games. He shook the firm hand then put both of his own back into his pockets. He knew that they were trembling and he wanted to shake them in the face of this fellow who said he was Don Ward and introduced the woman as his wife, Laura, and the girl as their daughter, Jan.

"Tough homesteading anyplace in Alaska," Arne said. "You need lots of money or another job."

"We know that. We've dragged our first home in with us to prove up on the homestead. We can clear our meadow with the cat, and get in some of our garden this season. I can get a moose this fall. It will be hard work, but our meadow is going to save us a lot of expensive clearing. We haven't got much money left, but we'll make out. I can cut logs for our home, and I might have a few tourist parties come in for fishing. Lots of grayling in the side-streams feeding the river, but then you know about that far better than I do."

Don looked expectantly at Arne, waiting for an answer. Then he picked up Jan.

"You're still sleepy," he said. "Kind of tough sleeping during that bumpy ride over the trail, but you'll do better tonight, sweetheart. We're home."

Arne and Ross had dealt with crises about the land before. But those had concerned claim jumpers and there hadn't been any women or youngsters involved. And after a few years there had been the law to fall back upon. Maybe if Ross had been there, Arne would have kept quiet now, thought it over a day or so and then talked to the intruders, but those final words "We're home," spoken to a youngster and a pregnant woman this young fellow had brought onto his land did it for Arne.

"What do you mean 'home,' 'our meadow,' cutting down trees, fishing parties and all that? Go somewhere else, closer to Delta Junction with all your ideas. This is my land." Arne pointed to the open end of the meadow. "Ross and I settled here before your dad was born. Now get out!"

Jan again clung to her mother's leg.

"Mr. Olson, we want to be friends. If I'd had more time I'd have climbed up to your diggings to explain the first time I came here. Why don't we have a cup of coffee and talk this over?"

Don stepped forward as though to guide Arne toward the wanigan.

"We'll respect the grave. The land was open to homesteading. I've filed for it and we're going to treat it right. The law is on our side, but we want you to understand."

Arne, fearfully remembering how he and Ross had won out when the law had been on their side, stepped toward the trio.

"I'm telling you to leave, and now." He shook his fist at the intruders, then turned and headed for his cabin.

He watched the cat nudge the wanigan into a better position, and Don unload the truck and cover the gear with a tarp. The squirrels chattered unceasingly for their hotcakes that day and Silt Creek rose and fell unnoticed for several more as Arne fretfully observed the hated activity in the meadow below.

He kept his peace until the morning when the sounds of chopping came from the Silt Creek edge of the meadow opposite the wanigan, and one of the isolated spruce trees that had grown larger than those in the groves fell in a long arc to the ground. Another fell before Arne could reach the axeman.

"What do you mean, cutting down the trees?" Arne demanded. "There's plenty of deadfall for firewood."

"That's what we've been using. But I figured that I'd better cut down the trees for the house logs now and drag them over near the wanigan before I clear the land and put in a garden. That way I can get them curing. We'll build next spring. Got time for a cup of coffee?"

"I've got time for nothing with you."

Don's hands tightened on the axe handle as he placed the Alaskan interpretation on the refusal which left little room for reconciliation. Then he shrugged and began limbing the tree. Arne watched for a moment, then looked about. He saw the piled slash from the other tree, firewood stacked neatly near the wanigan, the tarp-covered pole frame under which the Wards had stored their belongings, a hose tapping off Clear Creek to provide a steady trickle of water near the wanigan's door.

Overalls, large and small dresses and other clothing hung on lines which extended from a corner of the wanigan to a small spruce near the edge of the meadow. The woman was seated in the wanigan doorway showing magazine pictures to the girl while more washing water heated on a gasoline stove.

Then the solution to Arne's problem flitted through his mind infinitely faster than his sweeping look at the intruders and their activities. Just as quickly Arne dismissed it and angrily turned around and strode back to his cabin. That day he worked at the sluicebox, but there was small satisfaction in that, even when the cleanup yielded several ounces of gold. The trees continued to fall, and Arne felt himself shake as each new crash signalled another change in the meadow below.

Numerous long scars criss-crossed the more open part of the meadow like deeply worn game trails when Arne returned from his diggings one day. Don had dragged the logs alongside the wanigan where he could peel them in company with his family and add the bark to the fuel pile. That evening and for several others Arne could hear the steady chink, chink, chink of the pole-axe stripping the fallen trees as he fell into troubled sleep.

Rain awakened Arne early one morning. For a time it drummed steadily on the corrugated metal roof, and when the wind blew up the meadow to the cabin and the peaks behind, it played an unfamiliar tune while moving through the thinned ranks of the trees, seemingly complaining at the times of its greatest force that some of its harp strings were missing.

Arne pondered all this at breakfast, his hand cradled around the familiar coffee cup, but deriving little satisfaction from the warmth, aroma and taste. He gripped the cup more firmly when the racketing of the diesel suddenly broke the silence. Soon the cat crossed Clear Creek, lumbered into the wet meadow and stopped amid the logging ruts. The cat blade lowered, then scraped a long trail across the meadow toward Silt Creek. Don nudged the accumulated jumble of brush, rocks and rotted logs into the creek which by noon would be high enough to transport the mass into the already silty and debris-filled river far below.

Arne's anger, like the debris in front of the cat, mounted higher and higher as the scar lengthened. He crashed the cup to the floor and hastened to intercept Don before he would begin a second cut across the land.

Don cut the diesel when the old man planted himself in the cat's path and peremptorily signalled Don to come to him.

"Good morning, Arne."

Don's politeness, his seeming lack of contrition for what he was doing, intensified Arne's fury.

"Good morning, hell!" Arne shouted. He moved closer to Don. "Do you know what you're doing?"

"Clearing my land."

"Clearing *my* land, you mean. Get out of here now before you cut it all to hell. I've seen your kind before. A lot of you come to Alaska all fired up to be pioneers. You cut down trees, clear some of the land, then get tired of your little game and clear out."

"Not all of them, Arne."

"Lots of them."

"I plan to stick."

"Yeah? Then find some land of your own. All the room in Alaska, and you have to park on what's rightfully my land, and start cutting it all up."

"Arne, let's get something straight. You've been using the land one way every time you've shovelled some gravel into your sluice. And that's all right. You and your kind opened the country. But it can't stay the same. We're building where you left off. If I wouldn't homestead here, somebody else would. There has to be change."

"Don't lecture me. Clear out, or you'll wish that you had."

Don shrugged. Then he restarted the diesel and, when Arne remained standing in its path, carefully steered around him, isolating the old man on a tiny island between the two clearing swaths.

That afternoon on the edge of his own property Arne carefully diverted a part of Silt Creek into Clear Creek. At noon when Don dipped a pail into Clear Creek he brought up a silty mixture unfit for drinking or other uses before long settling.

The channel widened and dumped more silt into Clear Creek. The Wards endured the silty water until the day before wash day, then Don closed the channel with the cat. When Arne returned from his digging and saw what Don had done, his emotions at first balanced between anger and stubborn determination to cut another channel. The balance began shifting when he noticed with a twinge of regret that the washing flapping on the line below his property was gray and dingy and that the woman was carrying another pail of the as yet somewhat silty water to the tubs beneath the tree. But Don had trespassed to close the channel, and in the sourdough's absence had cleared a great expanse of the meadow and now was working the cat near Ross's grave. Well, he'd clear Ward out of there!

Arne seized his old Model '95 Winchester from the caribou rack above the fireplace and hastened toward the tractor. He was drawing deep gasps of air when he had almost reached the grave site and he drew an even deeper one when he noticed that Don carefully had constructed a neat, white birch pole enclosure around the grave and skirted the plot a wide margin while clearing with the cat.

Arne looked toward the tractor which Don was working in his direction approximately 75 yards away. Then the old man's attention came back to the grave when his eyes caught a slight movement in the untended meadow grass near the wooden marker. Seated there was the little girl, watching him wide-eyed like a caribou calf. She was leaning on one arm; the other was moving into position to enable her to scramble to her feet.

She sat upright as Arne's eyes caught hers then switched from her solemn little face to the shiny object near the marker. It was a glass jar with aluminum foil crimped around it and holding an assortment of tawny colored Coltsfoot flowers, red-purplish Dwarf Fireweed, and Pink Plumes.

"What are you doing there?" Arne asked gruffly and really louder than he had intended because by now the noise of the approaching tractor was intensifying, arousing earlier emotions.

The girl sprang to her feet and, as she dodged under the birch poles, Arne seized her arm to get an answer to his question—to settle his puzzlement. Then he felt a strong grip on his own arm, the one that still held the rifle. Surprised, he relaxed his grip on the struggling girl who ran to the edge of Clear Creek.

"You deal with me, Olson, instead of punishing my wife and child!" Don sharply snapped down Arne's arm and the Winchester fell to the ground.

Arne did not struggle, but poured his strength into the bitterness of his words.

"Tried to soften me up with that fence and putting your girl to pick a few flowers." The old man glared at Don then looked downward briefly as the younger man's grip on his arm intensified at the words. Arne's eyes traveled in an instant from Don's hand to the neatly patched pant leg then to Don's foot encased in an ancient paratrooper's boot which he had planted on the barrel of the rifle.

"The fence and flowers were my wife's idea. Now get this straight. We're homesteading here. We're going to stay!" Don levered the cartridges from the gun and handed it to Arne. "We haven't the money or the time now to take this to court. You can divert all of Silt Creek into Clear Creek and we'll still stay, even if I have to haul water from another creek and melt snow in winter. Now get off my land!"

The girl was standing by Clear Creek as Arne slowly walked toward his cabin. She clenched her little hands and stared at the old man, and when their eyes caught he could read the anger and fright in her face which was besmudged on each cheek where she had wiped away her tears.

Arne still could see those eyes as he dug another small channel from Silt Creek to Clear Creek, this time higher up on rockier ground where the digging was harder, but there was less danger of erosion and where the cat would have to contend with boulders if Don again would try to undo his work. As he worked Arne had ample time to ponder the scene which had occurred at the grave. When the milky water began racing into Clear Creek, Arne even test panned some of the gravel he'd dug, and he found a bit of color.

Arne heard the cat at work early in the morning after he had linked the two creeks. His first impulse was to hasten down the slope with his rifle, but his anger, memory of the girl's face, Don's snapping the rifle from his hand, the dingy wash all coupled with the warmth of the bed dissolved his resolution. For a long time he lay there, tracing and retracing the corrugated pattern of the ceiling and pondering the events of the past few days. But dammit, he was protecting his land as Don claimed he was doing with the meadow. Then Arne heard the squeal of the cat blade as it began working among the boulders. An unusually loud noise brought him from his bed. From the window he could see Don examining the cat blade and its lifts. Arne saw the small figure suddenly throw his hands despairingly into the air then drop from shoulders that sagged now like one side of the damaged blade as Don backed the machine protestingly down to the meadow. One end of the blade dragged like the broken wing of a ptarmigan.

The sunlight had just begun crossing the river when Arne heard Don's old truck cough into life and move to the cat. Don worked for a time on the blade and its lift, then Arne saw him hoist a large piece of the machinery into the truck bed, wave goodbye to his wife and daughter and head toward the ridge trail, evidently to Delta Junction and a welding shop.

"Good," the old man grunted aloud, but remembering meantime Don's badly worn boots, the patched denims and his remark about no money. Arne pulled on his hip boots, shouldered his shovel and hastened toward the creek. He'd dig out a very shallow part of the channel Don had filled before he'd broken the tractor. Silt Creek would rise when the sun would reach the glacier behind his cabin and even the smallest rivulet soon would wash away the loose dirt and rock and scour out the old channel.

Arne discovered that Don, naturally enough, had filled in the channel next to Silt Creek first. Good, Arne thought. I'll leave the plug there while I dig the rest. Soon he was working approximately 10 feet from an as yet shallow Silt Creek and moving toward turbulent Clear Creek. As he neared that stream, Arne found the boulder that had broken the cat. At first glance the rock looked small enough, and from the seat of the cat must have looked smaller yet. Arne could tell from its slope that, just like an Arctic Ocean iceberg, the major portion was out of sight. The Silt Creek water pouring through the new channel had swirled around this obstruction, widened the channel considerably and deposited a bed of oozy silt before it continued racing at a sharper angle to Clear Creek.

Arne stooped to pick up a small piece of metal evidently broken from the cat and lying at the edge of the bank that dipped sharply into the ooze filled bowl. As he raised the metal to study its fracture, his right foot slipped in the rubble of the slope and he was forced to drop the metal and his shovel and run heavily down the incline to maintain balance.

Arne's momentum slowed as he splashed through the ooze, and he stopped when he had moved approximately eight feet into the cloying mess. Winded, he stood there for a moment, then experience told him to move out fast as his feet began to sink even deeper. Here was a quicksand of sorts built up from the silt deposited by the channel water which also had turned the clayey bottom into a heavy, tenacious gumbo that successfully had defied the strength of the stream.

Unruffled, but still tired from his jolting run in his heavy boots, Arne put an arm around each side of his leg then locked his fingers together behind the knee. As he pulled upward he carefully worked the leg back and forth.

Arne's foot moved upward in the boot. He locked his fingers more tightly. Then the movement of the boot widened its muddy prison a bit and lifted slightly. Arne continued working the leg and pulling upward. As he did so he sensed more than he really felt that his other leg was sinking more deeply into the muck. He locked his fingers behind the knee of that leg and began pulling upward. The leg he partially had freed again sank into the muck, not quite as deeply as before. Back and forth, right leg, left leg, unlock, lock, up a bit, sink a bit the old man worked, but he was tiring now. The perspiration rolled down his as yet unshaven face and he took a hurried swipe at it, leaving a muddy, dripping smudge across his lips and chin.

He straightened up for a moment to ease his back. As he did so he noticed a tiny, harmless looking thread of water moving across the mucky surface toward him. Before the thread reached him, it spread into tiny hairs as it followed the depressions on the surface of the muck. Then it was gone. Arne watched, and as he watched his legs sank deeper. Another thread of water, a wider thread, moved toward him. It, too, broke up in small webs and disappeared. But the next one was larger and began cutting a tiny channel toward Arne then disappeared around his boots. Silt Creek was building up. Each new surge of water was working at the plug between the creeks, wearing it down.

Arne pulled again and this time he heard the sucking noise of the water that had raced across the mud and disappeared beneath him.

Well, he'd been stuck before. He'd have to pull his legs from the boots and belly crawl and roll across the muck to safety. He'd lose the boots, but they were old ones anyway.

Too old. He unclenched his fingers to permit his right leg to pull free from the boot, and as he pulled the boot tore at the knee, the ripping sound of the fabric coming clearly to Arne's ears for a moment before the ooze rushing into the boot swallowed the sound.

For the first time, then, Arne felt fear. It gripped him for a moment like the cold ooze that filled around his leg. Then the fear left as his body heat killed the chill.

He carefully pulled his left leg free from its boot and deliberately fell with a splash onto the now watery surface of the muck. His fall pushed a tiny wall of water upstream, but the water coming downstream soon countered the movement and pushed its force against and then around Arne.

He wiped at the muck on his face and pulled on the imprisoned leg, but the movement merely forced the water from the broken boot and compacted the silt more firmly around the foot and calf. He placed his fingers in the rip and pulled. The boot tore neatly around his leg, separated, and left his leg imprisoned in what now was a tall overshoe.

Arne splashed over on his back into the deepening water and reached into his muddy pocket for his knife. It was gone. He splashed back to a belly position and tried to crawl, the effort driving both arms deep into the ooze. He rested for a moment, turtlelike, his neck and head raised above the level of his body. He moved his head back and forth, desperately looking for a branch, a log, anything to put under his body. The shovel was there, out of reach. He saw something else downstream on the opposite bank of a now muddying Clear Creek. It was the little girl, watching Arne as solemnly as she had earlier near Ross's grave.

"Get help," he wanted to shout, then the absurdity of the desire stopped him. Very soon the channel would be too badly eroded to block off with a shovel. Who could pull him out, a pregnant woman surely too far along even to cross Clear Creek?

Arne struggled again and momentarily freed his hands and arms. He turned his body as far as he could to face the girl and at the same time enable him to fall back on unchurned mud. Both legs were sinking more deeply. He reared his muddy body upward and splashed back into the rising water. When his eyes cleared, the girl was gone. Frightened at the sight of me, Arne thought, then coughed. He had opened his mouth, but he hadn't shouted, and he'd swallowed mud and water.

The water was fluttering his shirt now, ballooning it. Again he raised his body and tore the garment from him. It grounded for a moment, then the waves created by his splash downward pushed it reluctantly toward Clear Creek. Arne watched the shirt accelerate as it neared Clear Creek then whisk from his sight as another object, then two, entered it. The girl and her mother were stumbling over the rocky bank of Clear Creek, the girl leading, the mother following and trailing a piece of clothesline to which three tiny stockings still were securely pinned.

Again Arne raised his body, not so high this time because there was no unchurned mud on which to place his arms, and the water was higher and he was tired. The mother placed the girl on a large rock, waved an admonitory finger and said something Arne couldn't hear above the gurgling of the channel water and the singing of Clear Creek. Then the woman moved upstream, above the confluence of the channel and the creek and almost from Arne's sight.

She'll never make it across Clear Creek, Arne thought. Then the action he witnessed in the next few tortuous minutes came in broken, muddy yet related sequences as he fought the water and the mud and his growing inclination to just let things happen.

The woman picked up a stout stick, tied the rope around her body, then held the loose gathers in her hands. She threw the rope around a large boulder and as she entered the creek and pushed and probed and leaned with the stick she slowly paid out the gathers. Arne saw her fall once and he groaned aloud; she had no business risking two lives for that of an old man.

"Stay there," he shouted as she rose from the water, the stick gone and her dress plastered to her round body, still holding onto the taut rope. When Arne had floundered twice more, she was across, resting for a moment, then letting go of the remaining gathers of rope and its loose end and pulling it from around the boulder on the opposite side of the creek toward her.

When she reached the edge of the bank above Arne, he splashed around in the sharpening current to face her. She hurriedly picked her way down the incline as the water again swung his body to face downstream. Then she was just a few feet away and throwing him the loop she had knotted at the end of the rope. The other end still was knotted above her distended waist. Arne fought to place the loop over his head and under his arms. She moved downstream until the rope tautened between them and across her back. She sat down and braced her feet against a boulder. Arne stood. As his legs sank deeper into the mud and water his eyes traveled the length of the taut rope, up to the woman's face, her eyes. The water gurgled around Arne's buttocks and he heard that sound and the blessed caw-caw of a raven and the breeze in the spruce and still their eyes held. Then he could see that she was breathing hard, almost gasping, and she flicked her eyes downward for a second to look at her belly and then again at the old man. And Arne lowered his eyes for an instant to look at his body sinking deeper, deeper into the mud and water.

"Tie it around a stone," he cried. "I'll pull myself out." His body would be anchored by the rope so he could rest beside Ross, and Arne was almost ready to rest now.

He felt the rope bite into his shoulders and back and he saw that the woman still was sitting down and bracing against another stone. He grasped the rope with both hands for balance and strained to free the unbooted leg. When that reluctantly came loose he dug the freed foot alongside the imprisoned one to widen the hole around the boot. Then he again strained to pull out the bootless foot. The woman braced against another stone to take up the bit of slack. Then Arne deliberately fell into the water that was deep enough now to flow over his back. Its chill would sap his strength further, but help to push his straining body downstream toward the woman and shock him into action for a time at least.

Arne fought then with the last of his strength to save his life and to help that woman on the bank. He clawed into the mud and water and pushed with his free leg as the water rose higher and higher—killing him, yet its force helping him, too.

Then he was free, not gradually, but all at once as his leg pulled from the boot and his frantic clawing and steady pull of the rope brought him up the channel bank.

Arne grasped the dry stones, retched, dragged himself higher, then lay still in the almost stupefying combination of warm sun and earth and exhaustion.

He felt a slight tug on the rope, another more insistent one, and he wanted to ignore them both, but coupled with a third tug was a moan that was louder than the gurgling, steadily rising water in the channel. Arne had heard that moan before—once in the cabin of an Indian friend in the Copper River Valley and a second time at the Black Rapids Roadhouse.

He raised his head. The woman was sitting near a large boulder. Her need reached out to Arne and brought him slowly to his feet. When he was certain of his equilibrium, he looked again. The woman had tugged the rope from her body and thrown back her head while her fingers dug into the unyielding gravel.

Arne lurched drunkenly toward Clear Creek, pulling the loop from his body while his filthy trousers restricted his movement. He looked for a moment at the cold water, then at the girl who was standing on the stone where her mother had placed her.

He lowered himself deliberately into the stream shallows above the confluence, and the cold waters shocked and cleansed his body.

"Tell your daddy the rest of his family is at my cabin," he croaked to the girl. He returned to the woman and helped her there.

Volcano

NANCY LORD

*Writer Nancy Lord came to Alaska in 1973; she lives in Homer, a small town
on the eastern shore of Cook Inlet, from which three active volcanoes on the
western shore can plainly be seen. She fishes for salmon at her summer fish
camp on Cook Inlet, where she whistles to keep bears away. Lord's work has
appeared in a number of magazines and anthologies, including* Left Bank,
Mānoa, Alaska Quarterly Review, *and the* WILDLANDS ANTHOLOGY. *In
1991 she was a winner of* Sierra *magazine's nature writing competition. She
is the author of two collections of stories,* THE COMPASS INSIDE OURSELVES
(1984) and SURVIVAL: STORIES *(1991), from which "Volcano" is taken.*

Julia sat on the living room rug, sewing a button on one of Dave's shirts.
It was warm for April—what Dave called a bluebird day—and the sun
pouring through the window made her perspire. She unbuttoned the
neck of her blouse and rolled up her sleeves. An Alaskan tan was the
idea of getting warm through a window, even if the glass blocked out
the actual tanning rays.

Fifty-two years old, and she still had good skin. With all the days she'd
spent working in the fields and around the yard, she'd never had too much sun.

A dark spot in the corner of the window caught her eye. It was moving,
fast—a line of black cloud pushing across the clear sky. It wasn't like any
weather she'd ever seen. *Fire!* She tucked her needle into the shirt's cuff and
went to the door.

The mushroom shape was just like all the drawings she'd ever seen of
nuclear bomb explosions. It rose straight up in a column and then billowed
out into a horizontal cap. The sight was so foreign, unnatural, and yet—it
was strangely familiar, as though a lifetime of living with the possibility had
prepared her. She shut the door and snapped on the radio. Although she
couldn't put a name on what she felt, she knew it wasn't fear.

On the radio, the man was saying it over and over again. Volcano, volcano, volcano. The mountain, which had been puffing wisps of steam for
months, had blown its top. They didn't know anything more. They were

checking with authorities. Stay tuned. The ash was heading this way. It was a good idea to stay inside.

Julia watched the dark cloud sweep east until it passed over the sun, blocking it entirely. Not even a pale circle shone through. The cloud fell like a curtain, cutting off the distance; she could barely make out the grove of cottonwoods at the bottom of the hill. And then the ash began to fall, dirtying the last patches of snow, blotting out all color.

The man repeated the news. They were trying to get more information from the authorities. The best advice they had was to stay put indoors. Don't drive your car. The air filter will clog up.

Julia rolled down her sleeves and resumed her button-sewing. She wasn't going anywhere. She never did go far from the homestead. How could she, when the animals needed to be fed, the cow milked, the chores done? At most, she drove to town three times a week to deliver milk and eggs.

She glanced at the calendar beside the refrigerator. It was marked into blocks—two weeks on and two weeks off. That had been the pattern of Dave's life for years now. Two weeks at Prudhoe Bay, two weeks at home on the homestead. He had only been gone for three days.

She pictured Dave at work, wearing his hardhat, tending some oil-drilling machinery, all of his mind on what he was doing. If he looked up, he'd see the frozen Arctic stretching away to the horizon. He wouldn't know that back home, his fields and home were being buried under volcanic ash.

So there.

Julia snipped her thread. In the dark she could hardly see it, but she didn't want to turn on a light. She sat on the couch and watched the ash fall, like a fine, crystalline snow, past the windows. Pompeii, wasn't it, that was buried in ash, everything neatly preserved, with people curled up sleeping, or sitting at their tables with bowls of food? Ash, or the blast of hot air that shot across the land, crisping everything in its path?

The man on the radio still didn't have much information. The ash was clogging the equipment at the power plant. It was getting into the turbines and damaging them. They were going to have to be shut down. The station would be off the air. There would be no electricity.

And then it was gone. The radio was silent, the refrigerator ground to a stop. She turned off the radio. Her good citizenship—turning off what she could, to save the power system from a surge whenever the electricity came back on—was automatic.

Julia lay on the bed beneath the skylight and watched the ash fall. It settled onto the glass in a coating of small, dark grains. Then a stream avalanched off the roof above and slid down the glass, clearing a path.

She thought, *I can't do anything about a volcano.*

The sky through the cleared track was the deep gray of old tar paper. A night sky, starless, here in the middle of the day, at—she glanced at the clock beside the bed—11:18, but it had said that for more than an hour. She kept forgetting.

She pulled a blanket over her. She missed the familiar sounds she never heard until they stopped. The click of the digital clock as it flipped from one minute to the next. The rattle of the refrigerator. The hum of the lights. The static and occasional chatter of the CB radio that she left on for company more than for messages. Her house had never been so quiet.

She listened to her breathing. She imagined that the volcano kept blowing, belching, spreading its insides across the country. What could you do about a volcano? You couldn't escape it. You couldn't put it out, or clear the ash away as though it were snow.

Over on the bureau, Julia could just make out the children's graduation pictures. She knew them by heart; she didn't need light to see them. David's was cropped around his shoulders so that he looked handsome and whole. You couldn't see the arm that was gone, mangled in a mower when he'd been trying—so hard—to be the man on the homestead, doing more than a boy should have had to do. He did all right with his hook, down in San Diego, considering. Sharon's picture gave her more pain. Even in her smile, you could see the discontent. Sharon couldn't wait to leave the homestead. Oregon, California, Texas. Julia wasn't sure where her daughter was anymore. She only knew for certain that she wasn't anywhere near cows, muddy roads, or volcanoes.

Without electricity, Dave couldn't reach her. He could phone their friends who lived down on the road, but they couldn't call through by CB radio. Not without electricity.

Julia swung her legs down and walked across the room to the window. Everything she saw, across the fields to the forests and the inlet below, was gray, like a grainy newspaper photograph shot in poor light. Hummocks of dead grass rose and fell into valleys of old snow, the whole hillside as neutral as if it were all one material, like a child's papier-mâché model. The forests were several shades darker, but gray, too—not green—and blurry, as though wrapped in heavy fog. The inlet was lost within the same clouds that obscured the sky—clouds that streaked to the sea the way rainstorms sometimes do. It was colorless—this still photo—absent even of the headlights of cars winding up the coast road, the spots of boats on the water. Everyone was shut down, saving their engines, waiting.

She thought about the chickens in their shed, the cow in the barn. Both doors were open to the yard. If she'd been smart, she'd have shut them earlier. That, and she'd have drawn water and filled every container in the house, instead of sewing that foolish button.

Dave will never wear that shirt again. Julia tried out the thought. It was reasonable. When they came for bodies, when it was all over, they wouldn't bother with household possessions and personal effects. The crew of men with masks over their faces would dig down through the ash, searching for a door or window. They'd find her in bed, under the darkened skylight.

Already, she had trouble picturing Dave. She tried to focus on the face beneath the hardhat. Smiling, his cheeks bunched up, but then he let his face go, and creases sagged from beneath his eyes and at the edge of his mouth.

Julia rummaged through a drawer and came up with a blue bandana. She tied it around her neck. Downstairs, she put on her jacket, pulled the bandana up to cover her mouth and nose, and squeezed through the door.

The air smelled like rotten eggs.

Julia crossed the yard. She tried to pick her feet straight up instead of scuffing; still, they raised clouds of dust. Her eyes stung. She narrowed them until she was looking through the flutter of lashes. In her mouth, ash ground between her molars like leftover polish after a dental cleaning.

The cow was lying down in her stall. She shifted her weight from one hip to another but didn't get up. Julia talked to her for a minute. She told her she would shoot her before she let her suffocate or starve. She owed her that. She pulled the barn door shut and flattened herself against it, thinking, *He's never here when things happen.*

The spring before, someone had set the next hill on fire. The yellow flames, like something alive, had raced through the dead grass toward their homestead. She'd joined the neighbors, beating at the fire with shovels, until her hands were blistered and raw. The flames nearly made it to the fenceline. When Dave's two weeks were over, her hands were healed, and new grass had grown up to cover the burn.

In the fall, alder banks slid down and blocked their road. Wind blew the chimney off. Later, snowstorms struck; she shoveled, plowed, chained up the truck to get through. By the time Dave came back, everything was cleared and repaired. It was no good wanting to tell him, *It was too much work for me. You should have been here.* The weather would already have turned to rain, snow melted into nothing.

In the chicken house, the chickens were quiet. Julia crouched in their doorway and saw them all roosted together in the far corner, their feathers fluffed out. They thought it was night.

The kitchen clock gave the same stopped time. Julia knew it would never run again. What was time, anyway? Twenty-seven years on the homestead. All those years of coping, taking charge of what needed to be done. Was this what she'd been waiting for?

She found a damp washcloth in the bathroom and wiped the grime from her face. Her eyes still hurt, and she made herself cry to wash them out. She liked what she saw in the mirror. This was how she should look in the end— quiet tears, no hysteria, stoicism mixed with regret. She raised a hand to arrange a lock of hair more tragically. It was thick and stiff, coated with volcano dirt.

She tied the bandana over her head. The look was right.

In the kitchen, Julia pulled out a chair and sat at the table. The things she'd meant to do—baking bread, vacuuming, walking the west fence to see where the moose had knocked it down—were no longer possible. She supposed she could always light a candle to see by; she could continue her mending. That was what she always did—continue, go on, as though nothing ever changed.

She didn't move to light a candle. She sat and thought. *It has come to wanting a disaster that is beyond anything I can handle. A volcano is bigger than both of us.*

Through the front window, the clouds changed to a lighter shade of gray. A dark edge broke abruptly to a sliver of blue. The cottonwoods sharpened within their ghostly outlines. Julia turned away from the window.

The refrigerator rumbled as its motor started up; the house began to hum. Julia ignored the sounds. Her eyes were on the wall calendar. She studied it and smoldered.

Tales of the North

SHEILA NICKERSON

Poet and novelist Sheila Nickerson lives in Juneau. A former poet laureate of Alaska, Nickerson has been the editor of Alaska's Wildlife *(the periodical of the Alaska Department of Fish and Game), writer-in-residence at the Alaska State Library, and an instructor at the University of Alaska Southeast. She has written seven volumes of poetry and, most recently, a memoir,* DISAPPEARANCES: A MAP: A MEDITATION ON DEATH AND LOSS IN THE HIGH LATITUDES *(1996). Her poem "Tales of the North" (1975) captures the magic and beauty of everyday life in Alaska.*

I live where trees are dressed in strands of moss
And Christmas is forever.
The porcupine is near at hand,
A raven in my ear.
A bearskin comes to school
(three can climb inside).
A seagull turns the sky.
The waxwings happen each November,
And oranges from islands of Japan.
Cranberry, crowberry, cucumber, currant—
We eat the index of the woods;
And when the mountains have grown dark
With fiddleheads all folded into sleep,
We are the children of the rain
With unexpected blossoms in our mouths
And have the stories of the totems
Sprouting ferns from fallen faces.
Trawlers slip away in fog
And secret places wait
Behind the frozen waterfalls
And in the caves of trees.

The moss grows thick upon my roof
And winter is immense.
In the long tunnels of remembering
Safe beneath the wind
I count my unknown store,
Listening to the wingbeats of the dark.

Whalescape

Ann Fox Chandonnet is a poet and nonfiction writer. Born in Massachusetts, Chandonnet has lived in the Anchorage area since 1973. Her seven poetry collections include PTARMIGAN VALLEY *(1980),* AURAS, TENDRILS *(1984), and* CANOEING IN THE RAIN *(1990). Her poetry is anthologized in several volumes. "Whalescape" first appeared in the Oregon poetry annual* CALAPOOYA COLLAGE *(1993).*

> *We become rooms for whatever almost is.*
> *It speaks in us, trying.*—William Stafford, "ANSWERERS"

I. 10 p.m., Barrow, September

A landscape unto itself,
undulating black dunes.
No huddled corpse,
but a reclining rubber Buddha,
a captured continent
that croons "tide flats" to the nose.
A dusky rose, a bayside chapel,
a Gulliver napping among puny gawkers,
a fallen star.
     (A fallen star.)

The line snaps twice as they ease her onto the bar,
49 feet of tradition—
Inupiaq heat and light,
pink butter and black meat;
a tail 20 feet long,
a tongue like a rawhide futon.
    (Like a rawhide futon.)

271

The crew claiming this hoard
clambers aboard the slippery, upturned hull
where they perch, honing cutting spades with steel's kiss.
Toddlers sledding sleek prune hide are shooed away.
Now the first layered slabs of muktuk
are peeled away like turfs,
then towed to one side.
  (To one side.)

Suddenly a blade releases a surge of clear fluid
and in the flood a glittering missile form.
A baby leaps into our galvanized midst,
seems to cry out—
a single bleat pierces the stillness.
  (A single bleat.)

SOMETHING cries out.
Perhaps it's only a shrill of shock and regret,
a psychic scream,
the instant letdown of my female sorrow.
"My namesake," says a proud whaler,
half turning to the crowd.
The moment is a dream
spotlighted by kliegs.

Amnion sinks into the sand,
and the pale pink cord—a hawser, a dryer exhaust—
is neatly severed.
  (Neatly severed.)

With gentle care, the biologist on duty tugs the 5-foot fetus
away from the danger of the flensers' long knives
to document its perfection.
"They breed in March," he offers
to the circle of rapt faces.
The pearl gray calf steams in the 10 degree air
but neither breathes nor stirs.

Forgetting cold feet,
women shoulder forward in sympathy, curiosity,
donkeys at the manger.
"Good eating," says one.
   (Good eating.)

I seek communion at the other end of the scene,
between polka-dotted lips.
The bowhead rests on her back and right shoulder,
a serene and languid odalisque
with pinto-spotted flanks.
The phalanx of baleen on her upper jaw
thrusts stiffly into the night—
ten-foot pampas,
black palm fronds,
dark, tapering keys and fringes coated with rime.
Arctic breeze plays them like a wind chime—
a tinkling just audible above the surf,
A siren tune, an icy dirge.
   (An icy dirge.)

II. Noon, the following day.

Laboring all night, the crew penetrates to the core.
With hooks they haul forth the minotaur, the liver—
quivering lobes enough to fill a bathtub.
Body heat threatens the spoils,
scarlet bubbles already boiling around black boots.
The meat is porous—lava boulders.
The blubber is strawberry ice,
darkening in the air to beefy red.
   (Beefy red.)

Now they are felling the black forest,
hacking out plates of baleen
from obdurate stumps.
Hatchets swing again and again.

Later they'll clean up the 600 horny slabs—
first pare with a jackknife,
then steelwool, then Mop 'n Glo;
scrimshaw, initial,
offer to tourists for $10, $12 a foot.
Females have the prettiest hair, they say.
  (The prettiest hair.)

Meanwhile, gulls keen overhead,
awaiting their turn at the board,
and every yard stacks up its winter hoard,
its alphabet blocks of plenty.
  (Plenty.)

Berrying

Anchorage resident Ann Fox Chandonnet is a poet and nonfiction writer. She grew up in Massachusetts and moved to Alaska in 1965. The author of thirteen books, her poetry has been published in several anthologies, as well as seven of her own poetry collections. "Berrying" is taken from Chandonnet's collection THE WIFE AND OTHER POEMS *(1978).*

Warm lips against my palm:
my son gulps raspberries,
afraid to lose a one.
A tiny bird, perched on a root,
trying not to tumble into this
pit of decayed vines and thorns,
he waits for my hand to regurgitate food.

"Berries, berries," he chirps
whenever his mouth finds itself empty.
From the first currants—
ruby lavaliers dangling in bogs or
strung beneath Devil's Club's spiny leaves—
to the last soggy rasps,
to blueberries up on the mountain,
low bush cranberries in mossy thickets,
rose hips like schools of scarlet octopi—
it's "berries."

275

Sheer content:
finding a low cane
and picking for himself—
disdainfully removing hulls.

We go down toward Little Peter's Creek
in a July drizzle,
he in backpack,
me in jeans, boots, coat, hat.
We lean into the cliff,
picking currants before they drop,
the creek mumbling,
thorns and bugs zeroing in,
the ground giving way,
a chorus demanding "berries,"
and black bears—somewhere.

Sheer content.

Lost

FROM *The Stars, The Snow, The Fire*

JOHN HAINES

John Haines is a poet, essayist, and teacher who trained as a painter and sculptor. For more than twenty years he homesteaded in the Alaska wilderness. He is the author of several major collections of poetry and an autobiography, LIVING OFF THE COUNTRY *(1981). His essays and poems have appeared in numerous publications, including* The Hudson Review, Kayak, Oberlin Quarterly, Harper's, The Living Wilderness, *and* Ironwood. *"Lost" is excerpted from a memoir of his Alaska homesteading years,* THE STARS, THE SNOW, THE FIRE *(1989).*

Now and then people disappear in the far north and are never heard from again. For various reasons: they are lost, drowned or frozen to death. It was common enough in early days when so many were traveling the country on foot and by water and often alone. Yet in recent memory whole planeloads of people have dropped out of sight, the fuselage with its frozen bodies found years later in a snowdrift on a remote mountainside.

I remember one spring morning when a group of men came down the road at Richardson. We watched them as they searched the roadside thickets and probed the snowdrifts with poles. They were looking for an old woman who had left her house near Big Delta a few evenings before, and had not come back. Family and neighbors thought she may have walked in her half-sleep into the nearby river, to be swept away under the ice. But they couldn't be sure. They went on down the road, a scattered troop of brown and grey soon lost to view in the cold sunlight.

And there was the fellow who disappeared from his Quartz Lake trapline a few winters back. Said to be a little strange in his head and mistrustful of people, he had been long absent in the bush when a search was begun by his brother and the police. Though the country was flown over and searched for weeks, he too was never found alive. But two or three years later someone hunting in the backcountry came upon a pair of legbones and some scraps of blue wool cloth with metal buttons. Most of the bones had been carried off by animals, and is was impossible by then to say who he was or what had happened to him.

There are people lost in more ways than one. Like the man named Abrams, active for a while in the Birch Lake area many years ago. Despondent over something or other, he walked away from camp one late winter day and did not come back. No one followed him then, but he was found eventually in an old cabin up on one of the Salcha River tributaries, dead. He had cut both his wrists, and bled to death lying in a makeshift bunk.

I was told once of the end of a man whose name will have to be Hanson, since I cannot remember his real name. He drove mail by dogsled in an early day, out of Fairbanks and up the Tanana beyond Big Delta. It was sixty below zero one January day when he stopped at McCarty Station on his way upriver. He was urged not to continue, but to stay at the roadhouse for a day or so and wait for a promised break in the weather. An experienced man, he decided to go on. He was well-dressed for it, and carried a good robe on his sled. But his dogs whined in the foggy, windless cold, and would rather have stayed.

A few days later his dogs came back, dragging the sled behind them, but without Hanson. The cold had broken by then, and men went out, following the sled trail back upriver. Some thirty miles on they found Hanson crouched beside a stack of driftwood, his arms folded on his chest, and his head down. He did not move or speak when they walked up on him. One of the men touched him, and found that they had been calling to a stone. At his feet were the charred makings of a fire that had never caught.

Though I have never been lost in the woods, I have known that momentary confusion when a strange trail divided or thinned out before me, and I have stopped there on a hillside in the wind-matted buckbrush and willows, wondering which of the many possible roads I ought to take. I have come home late through the woods at night and missed my trail underfoot, to stand undecided, listening for something in the darkness: the wind moving aloft in the trees, the sound of a dry leaf skittering over the snowcrust, or the sudden crashing of an animal disturbed.

Fred Campbell told me once of being shut in by fog on Buckeye Dome one fall day, a fog so thick he could not see the ground at his feet. He lost all sense of place and time, and wandered that day in an endless and insubstantial whiteness. It seemed to him at times that he was not walking on earth, but was stranded in a still cloud, far from anything he could touch or know. Toward evening the sun burned a hole in the mist, and he found his way down into familiar woods again.

That lostness and sinking of things, so close to the ordinariness of our lives. I was mending my salmon net one summer afternoon, leaning over the side of my boat in a broad eddy near the mouth of Tenderfoot. I had drawn the net partway over the gunwale to work on it, when a strong surge in the current pulled the meshes from my hand. As I reached down to grasp the net again I somehow lost hold of my knife, and watched half-sickened as it slipped from my hand and sank out of sight in the restless, seething water.

Poling upriver in the fall, maneuvering the nose of my boat through the slack, freezing water; or wading over stones and gravel in the shallow current, while the boat tugged behind me at the end of a doubled rope; or again, as I floated down on the turbulent summer water, swinging my oars in response to the drift-piles looming swiftly ahead: how easily I might be spilled and swept under, my boat to be found one day lodged in driftwood, an oar washed up on the sand, and myself a sack weighted with silt, turning in an eddy.

A drowsy, half-wakeful menace waits for us in the quietness of this world. I have felt it near me while kneeling in the snow, minding a trap on a ridge many miles from home. There, in the cold that gripped my face, in the low, blue light failing around me, and the short day ending, in those familiar and friendly shadows, I was suddenly aware of something that did not care if I lived. Or, as it may be, running the river ice in midwinter: under the sled runners a sudden cracking and buckling that scared the dogs and sent my heart racing. How swiftly the solid bottom of one's life can go.

Disappearances, apparitions; few clues, or none at all. Mostly it isn't murder, a punishable crime—the people just vanish. They go away, in sorrow, in pain, in mute astonishment, as of something decided forever. But sometimes you can't be sure, and a thing will happen that remains so unresolved, so strange, that someone will think of it years later; and he will sit there in the dusk and silence, staring out the window at another world.

Slade's Glacier

ROBERT F. JONES

Novelist and nature writer Robert F. Jones lives in Vermont. He has traveled widely in the Far North to hunt, fish, backpack, and canoe. His eleven books include the award-winning UPLAND PASSAGE: A FIELD DOG'S EDUCATION *(1992) and* SLADE'S GLACIER *(1981). In this excerpt from* SLADE'S GLACIER, *Jack Slade, rugged Alaskan homesteader and hunting guide, makes a discovery, assisted by his able wife, Josey, and their friend, Charlie Blue, a Tlingit shaman.*

Charlie spent the night curled in front of the barrel stove, naked except for his bearclaw necklace—the twin of mine—and his mukluks. He was wrinkled all over, like one of those Chinese fighting dogs you see now and then in the photo magazines, all drooped and folded skin so that when another dog grabs one in a fight, it can't get hold of anything vital. He snored in a great rolling cacophony of roars, grunts, gurgles and wheezes, sometimes sounding like a ravening wolf, sometimes like a giant raven. Even our dogs, who usually spent the night growling and snapping at one another, fell silent in awe. At first we could not sleep, but then his snoring took on a kind of rhythm, as if one were dozing at the edge of a great waterfall, or high on a beach where a storm was playing itself out among the rocks below.

We awoke to the smell of frying bear bacon and bubbling oatmeal. Charlie stood at the stove, singing at the top of his voice in what I took to be Tlingit.

"Up! Up!" he yelled on seeing us stir. "Daylight in the swamp! Let's eat and then I take you into the glacier, show you your own forever cache of dog meat."

He was as good as his word. After we'd eaten, he led us up over the frozen scree slope to the blue face of the glacier itself, and on into a deep crevasse. It was dark and dank in there, slippery going.

"Here," said Charlie. "Here is the entrance." He smiled and ducked his head and crawled inside the twisting vertical ice-edged slot that gaped between the boulders. We followed.

The dark dissipated quickly into a pervasive blue light, day permeating the height of glacier above us, filtered as through a thick lens carved from pure corundum. Muck and ice water soaked our knees, but soon the twisting passage angled upward, and we clawed our way along, using elbows and toes and the waning friction of wet mukluks until we began to skid more than we climbed.

"Grab this," said Charlie. I groped and felt a curved projection, cold as the ice but grooved to accept the clutch of my fingers. I heaved myself up on it and reached back for Josey. Above us through the blue shadows, I could see an irregular ladder of these semicircular protuberances, some closer together, others a short leap apart. Then it came to me: this was ivory.

Above us, hundreds of feet of ice above us, the sun broke through the cloud and the intensity of the light in the tunnel went up by megalumens. Through the ice wall, I saw dim shapes from which the ivory circles grew, slope-backed, thick-legged, elephantine, hairy. We were climbing a ladder of mammoth tusks. A smell of rotting meat wafted down the tunnel from the exposed flanks of animals long buried, creatures wandering on crusted earth-covered ice in the thawing of that time, who crashed through into the crevasses, caught these many millennia in the deepfreeze of my glacier.

"Chaw a hunk," said Charlie, grinning. He had whittled a sliver of mammoth meat from the exposed flank, close to the ice where it was still fresh. I took it and chewed. The meat was rich and red and, as it thawed in my mouth, it tasted sweet. It could have used some salt and pepper. Josey tried some and agreed.

"We'll have to bring some back to the cabin," she whispered as Charlie climbed ahead. "Mammoth tartare!"

Farther up, my eyes growing accustomed now to the fact of frozen prehistory within the ice, I discerned the shape of a huge, bobtailed cat, broke-legged on its back, its foot-long fangs angling out so that one of them stuck through the ice and served as a convenient handhold. Above it, barely visible, the figure of a giant dog—a dire wolf, no doubt victim of the thaw.

Cave bears, giant sloths, long-horned bison, marmots the size of calves; here a great beaver grinning bucktoothed out of the wall, its ears rotted, its eyes like floating opals; there a small and ugly horse no bigger than a

Labrador retriever with a square, unfinished head and the stripes of a quagga.

Our voices, as we murmured awestruck in this miraculous gloom, echoed down the twisting tunnel, rose back to our ears as far-off hisses, so that it was easy to imagine the dead creatures themselves muttering and sighing in their icy jail, denied the freedom of entropy.

We emerged finally into a cavern. The light was much brighter now and half-thawed bones littered the floor. The sour smell of cold rot pervaded the room, such as one whiffs on opening a long-uncleaned freezer. The legs, tails and flanks of animals showed through the ice, in some places masked by only a shallow film of it, in others protruding through into the open air.

"Plenty meat here," Charlie said. "Good meat too. These animals no longer live on the earth, but they are not poison. Many times I feed them to my dogs, eat the meat myself. It's good! Rich meat! Good as whale meat!"

His voice echoed and reechoed through the cavern and down the long tunnel we had followed. The ice creaked and groaned in response. Josey squeezed my hand and I too was fearful that Charlie's decibels would bring the whole glacier tumbling down around our ears. The few times we had shot a rifle near the ice, we had sent small seracs snapping and tumbling down the glacier's snout.

"But this meat you better not eat," he said, his voice falling to a whisper. He led us over to the far corner of the cavern and pointed up into the gloom. Staring down at us through the blue ice was a human face. It was that of a white man, heavily mustachioed, his eyes not much darker than the ice that locked him in his grave. On his head was a sombrero with a chin strap stretched taut by his gaping jaw, his mouth wide open as if he were still yelling with the fall down the crevasse that had killed him. His broken limbs were clad in what appeared to be a heavy chain-stitched wool sweater, corduroy trousers stagged into cleated leather boots, and around his neck a set of smoked glasses of the sort Arctic explorers use to prevent snow-blindness. One hand had melted free of the ice at some previous time and it groped out into the air above us, fleshless, but with a few cold-withered tendons still clinging to the clawlike bones.

"That's Doctor Moran," whispered Charlie. "A great shaman in his own country, but worse than a fool up here."

"Did you know him?" Josey asked.

"Like a brother," Charlie answered. "A stubborn, younger brother who will not listen. This was in the days of the Stampede, '98 or '99, and I was down on the coast then. I was very poor, trying to live like a white man. Doctor Moran had bought a map that showed lost gold fields in the mountains behind the glacier. He asked me to guide him and his men over the ice. The men he had picked himself after much searching in New York, where he came from. One man knew all about rocks. Another how to build tools of steel. A third could bend tin into useful shapes. They all knew how to read. They all were very big and very weak, though Doctor Moran said they had worked hard at exercise before leaving their homes. I didn't know what exercise was. To me, it meant living. They were stupid as well as weak. I told Doctor Moran that there was no gold over the glacier. 'How do you know?' he asked. 'Would I be here in Gurry Bay, poor and listening to nonsense, if there were?' I answered.

"But I agreed to take them over the ice. For dogs they had six large, weak ones from New York. Saint Bernards and Newfoundlands, I learned they were called. They were bigger than wolves but weak as wolf puppies when their eyes are still closed and they wiggle and whine in the den smelling of sour milk and spittle. Each of the men had a thousand pounds of food and equipment. They also had a great huge motor-driven sled that was so heavy that they left it on the beach. Such fools have rarely come to this country, though recently we have been seeing more of them.

"We came up the river to the glacier. They pulled everything up on top. Days passed, weeks passed. Then it was all up there and they found the dogs could scarcely move the sledges. Blizzards blew in off the sea. They waited them out. The sun broke through and the men began to turn red, their skin peeling away in long slippery tatters. Some went snowblind. More storms. The men began to go mad. They found one strangled out on the ice. His partner said a 'glacier monster' had appeared out of the driving snow and attacked them.

"Weeks passed, then months. Soon it was winter again and still they were on the glacier. Men walked out into the storms to die. You will find them somewhere here in the ice. When their food was nearly gone—though there was plenty of food just a day's march on snowshoes off the glacier, down in the protected valleys, as you two have seen—they decided to make a final dash across the ice to the valley of the lost gold. I told them there was no gold. They called me a fool and a liar.

" 'If you go ahead in weather like this, you will fall into the mouths of the ice bear,' I told them. They went ahead. I went back. You see what became of them."

He sighed and reached up to touch the bony fingers.

"The only 'glacier monster' was in their bellies. The hunger for gold."

We set to work cutting slabs of mammoth meat from the protruding flesh and skidded a good-sized pile of it back down the passageway. Charlie helped us carry it to the cache and stow it. There was enough now to tide us through the rest of the winter, dogs and humans alike.

"That ivory is valuable," I told Charlie as he harnessed his dogs and prepared to leave downriver.

"*Vraiment, certes!*" he bellowed. "Do you need money? Do you need a thousand professors from a thousand museums from all over creation pouring in here to examine those carcasses? Try that fox scent I gave you. It is quieter."

He whipped up his lean, wolf-eyed team and slithered out onto the frozen Alugiak, the Aurora arching and surging above him as he sang and roared his way into the nearly-always night.

The next day, while Josey went out on snowshoes to hunt willow ptarmigan along the Alugiak, I stayed behind to mend a binding on the sled runner. When I was finished, I went back up into the cavern. The day was bright and the light much more intense than on our earlier visit, and I counted fully two dozen mammoths buried in the ice, ranging in size from an infant as big as a Buick to great tuskers with ivory that possibly weighed two hundred pounds the side. The herd must have crashed through the ice in panic, pursued perhaps by a pack of dire wolves. In the big cave, I avoided Doctor Moran's eyes and picked up the tip of a tusk that had cracked off and fallen to the floor. It was smooth and heavy, the color of old gold; a shard of the dead past in that eerie underwater light: palpable antiquity.

Chenega

TOM SEXTON

Tom Sexton, Alaska's current poet laureate, is the author of several books of poetry, including THE BEND TOWARD ASIA *(1993) and* A BLOSSOM OF SNOW *(1995). A longtime Alaska resident, he is a Professor Emeritus of English at the University of Alaska Anchorage, now retired, and for years he served as poetry editor of the* Alaska Quarterly Review. *His poem "Chenega" concerns the Good Friday Earthquake of 1964 and its devastating effect on a small Athabascan village on the Kenai Peninsula. It is reprinted from* THE BEND TOWARD ASIA.

Imagine a woman who was still a child
when the tidal wave destroyed Chenega.
For her Good Friday might always be
that day God, like a drunken father,
turned his face from her without a word.
On that day, she is always climbing
a steep slope behind the village
to escape the surging wave that swallowed
the church and those who gathered there to pray.
When she lifts her crying daughter
from her cradle, she must see the frenzied water
and hear the dead calling from the harbor.
The wave is a raised fist
always hovering at the edge of her dream.

Exit Glacier

PEGGY SHUMAKER

Poet Peggy Shumaker lives in a log house near Ester, Alaska, and is a professor in the MFA program in creative writing at the University of Alaska Fairbanks. She was born in California and grew up in Tucson, Arizona, where she received her education in creative writing at the University of Arizona. In 1989, she received a Poetry Fellowship from the National Endowment for the Arts. Her poem "Exit Glacier" appears in her third collection of poetry, WINGS MOIST FROM THE OTHER WORLD *(1994).*

When we got close enough
we could hear

rivers inside the ice
heaving splits

the groaning of a ledge
about to

calve. Strewn in the moraine
fresh moose sign—

tawny oblong pellets
breaking up

sharp black shale. In one breath
ice and air—

history, the record
of breaking—

prophecy, the warning
of what's yet to break

out from under
four stories

of bone-crushing turquoise,
retreating.

Murder on the Iditarod Trail

SUE HENRY

Anchorage mystery writer Sue Henry teaches at the University of Alaska
Anchorage. She is the author of the award-winning MURDER ON THE
IDITAROD TRAIL *(1991), which won the Macavity Anthony Award and became*
a made-for-TV movie, and its sequel, TERMINATION DUST *(1995). This excerpt*
is the first two chapters of MURDER ON THE IDITAROD TRAIL, *which takes*
place during the annual Iditarod Trail Sled Dog Race from Anchorage
to Nome.

Date: Sunday, March 3
Race Day: Two
Place: Between Skwentna and Finger Lake checkpoints (forty-five miles)
Weather: Clear skies, light to no wind
Temperature: High 8°F, low 4°F
Time: Late afternoon

The Iditarod Trail out of Skwentna, Alaska, ran easy and level, bending its way northwest for miles through snow-covered muskeg. Without strong winds to erase them, the tracks of sled runners were still visible in the late afternoon light. The musher watched them flow beneath his sled. A day and a half into the thousand-mile sled-dog race to Nome, he was among the leaders in a field of sixty-eight participants. His sixteen dogs were eager to run, well rested from a four-hour stop in Skwentna. But, riding the runners behind his sled, George Koptak fought fatigue. An hour of poor sleep at the last checkpoint had not been enough. His body demanded more. He'd spent thirty-one hours on the trail, most of it standing up, pushing the sled or pumping behind it.

Checkpoints in a long-distance race offer little rest for competitors. Once fed, tired dogs almost immediately curl into tight tail-to-nose balls in the snow and sleep. The musher must haul water, cook another batch of dog food for a trail feeding, repack equipment, find something to eat (though his hunger often seems inconsequential compared to his need for rest), and, finally, lie down for a ragged hour's sleep.

Excitement, anticipation, and nerves left over from yesterday's start had continued to feed a certain amount of adrenaline into Koptak's system, as had the knowledge that some of the most difficult challenges in the race must soon be met and overcome.

Now the tired musher leaned forward over the handlebars of his sled, trying to find a semicomfortable way to rest on top of his sled bag. Although the trail was level, it was not smooth, and the bow caught him under the ribs, gouging with every bump. He straightened, stretched his shoulders to relieve the ache between them, pumped for a while with one foot, then the other, and talked to his dogs to keep awake.

At the site of the old, abandoned Skwentna Roadhouse, the trail plunged down onto ice and followed the frozen river for a while before climbing the opposite bank to enter the spruce and alder forest surrounding Shell Lake. Though the sun had set, light lingered on the snow. Knowing it would soon be dark, he stopped his team on the riverbank before going onto the ice.

He snacked his dogs, tossing them frozen whitefish. After munching a few handfuls of trail mix, heavy with nuts and chocolate, he drank half the hot coffee in his metal thermos, filled at the checkpoint. Locating his headlamp, he checked the batteries and fastened it in place. Twenty minutes later he was heading upriver.

For half an hour, the coffee kept him awake. Then, as he came up off the ice and into the trees, fatigue caught him again. He drifted in and out, catching a few seconds of sleep at a time, as the team snaked its way along the trail between the trees in a steady, almost hypnotic rhythm.

When he jerked awake to the dangerous reality of the narrow, winding trail, he was afraid. Dark had fallen quickly among the trees. He switched on his headlamp, losing his perspective and night vision in the process. The trail became a tunnel, closing in around him.

The dogs, stretched out for almost forty feet in front of the sled, were rarely all visible at the same time along the twists and turns of the trail. Like fireflies, strips of reflector tape on the harness winked back at him when hit by his light. Low-hanging tree limbs flashed by overhead, making him duck, though most were beyond reach. He knew the agony of having wood lash cold flesh and had seen mushers come into checkpoints with swollen, battered faces—the result of a moment's inattention.

The trail curved perilously close to trees as it swung back and forth through the forest. The sled, responding to the centrifugal pull, slid toward these as if attracted by a magnet. If he didn't quickly throw his weight to control the slide, he risked slamming into the trunks, which bristled with small limbs and sharp broken branches that could scratch and tear at face, clothing, and sled.

One brush against a tree trunk ripped a hole in the sled bag. In the next small clearing, he stopped, knowing he must repair that hole or risk having essential gear fall through and be lost. He searched through his supplies for a needle and dental floss, standard temporary repair material, and squatted beside the sled to attempt the chore.

Trees closed off most of the sky. Only the circle of light from his head-lamp, focused on the needle and the tear, was real. Everything else disappeared, even the dogs, the trail. He nodded drowsily, then jerked awake, forcing himself to attention, opening his eyes wide.

After a few minutes of working without mittens his fingers grew numb with cold and he could no longer feel the large needle. He stopped and put his hands under his parka, wool shirt, and long underwear, directly on the warm flesh of his belly. Waiting for feeling to return, he leaned his head against the side of the sled bag and closed his eyes.

He threw his head back with a start, the headlamp casting a narrow arc of light over the sled and trees beyond it. His hands were warm, but more than anything he wanted to lay his face back against the sled. Refusing to give in, he stood up. His back and legs had cramped slightly, and he stomped around the sled to stretch them. The dogs raised their heads, waiting for his word, but he still had to complete the repair. Slowly he finished the stitching and repacked the needle with care so as not to lose it in the snow.

He did not understand why he was so exhausted and wondered vaguely if he was ill. Dulled reflexes and reactions were more common at the end of the long trail. He had always been able to adjust to the early pace, shake off sleepiness. Coffee usually helped, but this time it was not working.

Coffee. Pulling out the thermos, he drank all but a few swallows of the still warm brew, determined to wake up. Whistling up the dogs, he continued down the trail.

Within minutes his eyes were closing again. His head lolled against one shoulder, then the other. The world turned to fog. He could hardly hold on to the sled. Summoning a gigantic effort, he took the thermos from the bag on the back of the sled, uncapped it, stuffed the cap into the bag, and finished the coffee. Before he could put it away, it slipped from his hand and bounced behind him to lie forgotten in the trail.

The dogs followed an abrupt turn to the right. A large tree loomed ahead, so close to the trail that the swing dog on the left brushed her flank against it as she passed. Koptak fell forward across the drive bow, aware of nothing. As the sled, out of control, whipped into the turn, it slid solidly into the tree, mashing a stanchion and cracking the left runner. The musher, body limp, mercifully unconscious, was thrown directly against the trunk, face first.

His headlamp shattered as it hit. So did his nose and cheek. A wicked, foot-long limb projected from the side of the trunk. Cold and sharp, it entered his closed right eye and pushed through his brain until it hit the back of his skull. There it stopped. His body hung against the trunk of the spruce until his weight broke the limb and he fell slowly onto the trail.

A half-hour later, the corpse was starting to stiffen. The next driver, curious about a thermos picked up three turns back, swung into the curve. Horrified but unable to stop, he felt the lurch as his runners passed over the heap he recognized as his friend.

Date: Sunday, March 3
Race Day: Two
Place: Between Skwentna and Finger Lake checkpoints (forty-five miles)
Weather: Clear skies, light to no wind
Temperature: High 8°F, low 4°F
Time: Midevening

Forty-five-year-old Dale Schuller had not set out from Skwentna with any premonition of impending tragedy. If anything, his expectations for the rest of the Iditarod ran high. He had every reason to suppose he had as good a chance of winning as anyone in the race.

The start in Anchorage the day before had been clean for everyone, though soft snow had slowed the pace somewhat. Warm temperatures had brought enough snow so the city had not had to truck it in to Fourth

Avenue. Schuller had drawn number nine in the starting lineup, and the trail to Eagle River, fifteen miles away, had still been in good shape when he hit it, not yet churned up by the feet of over a thousand sled dogs from the sixty-eight teams. He sympathized with the last forty mushers. The year before he had been number thirty-two. Now, though he had passed and been passed by mushers as they jockeyed for position, he was moving consistently and well.

In Eagle River the teams had been loaded onto trucks and transported twenty-five miles to Settler's Bay for restart. This avoided crossing the Knik and Matanuska rivers, which sometimes weren't frozen on the first Saturday in March.

After restart, the run across the Knik Flats to Rabbit Lake and Skwentna had been uneventful. It had felt good to step off the sled for a couple of hours' rest, but the ground had seemed to go on moving slightly as Schuller fed and watered his dogs and completed the necessary chores.

This was his seventh year of mushing, his third attempt at this greatest of all dog-racing challenges. His team was well seasoned, just at their peak, with over fifteen hundred training miles behind them. He had won the Knik 200 and come in third in the Kuskokwim 300, both good mid-distance races. The prize money was security. But with two local sponsors solidly behind him, money was not the problem it had been in earlier years. The huge cost of running a kennel, obtaining the best equipment, and paying entry fees would not put him in debt this year.

All of his dogs were running well and eagerly. Comet, his veteran lead dog, was behaving like the lady she was, keeping to the trail and ignoring distractions with dignity. She had a good head, was here to do a job, and knew it. Pepper, her three-year-old son, was running for the first time this year and, so far, had managed to hold his own. The sixteen other dogs were healthy and strong, the pick of his kennel.

When they pulled up off the river ice, Schuller had tensed slightly as the trees closed in around them, but he soon relaxed into the rhythm of the curves, enjoying his driving skill and the response of his team. It caught him off guard when Comet made a seemingly senseless error.

For no apparent reason she missed a sharp right turn and led the first half of his dogs off the trail to tangle themselves in the trees. Schuller thought he saw a light on the trail ahead but dismissed it in his surprise and frustration. Swearing, he stepped hard on the brake and dug in the snow hook before leaping forward to assess the situation, concerned with the danger of strangulation for a dog snarled in its harness.

The dogs yelped and struggled, trying to free themselves from branches and brush. "Whoa. Easy there. Down, Comet. Easy girl." From what he could see, they were tangled but safe and not going anywhere without help. Reaching the turn they had missed, he stopped. The light from a headlamp flashed across his face.

Bill Turner, who had left Skwentna only a few minutes ahead of him, sat in the trail. Another musher lay across his knees. There was little left of the musher's face. Blood covered the front of his parka, and a great splash of it stained the snow under the bloodstained tree trunk.

"What the hell happened?" Schuller asked, striding forward quickly and dropping to his knees in the snow beside them. Removing his headlamp, he directed its beam more closely as he stripped off his mitten and laid his fingers along the soft hollow beneath the musher's jaw. There was no pulse.

"It's George," Turner said stiffly. His pale face reflected the light, his eyes huge with shock. "He m-must have lost it on the corner and hit the tree. God, Dale, I r-ran over him."

Schuller could hear Turner's teeth click together as he tried to talk. "I can't find his team. Wh-where's his dogs?"

"You looked?"

"Yeah. But I c-couldn't let him just . . . lay here in the snow. I knew you'd be along pretty close behind me, so I waited."

"Sit still. I'll be right back." Schuller rose and returned to his sled. Unzipping the sled bag, he removed his sleeping bag and a pint of brandy he carried with his personal gear.

Critical accidents were not common. No musher had ever died on the trail in a race. Bones were broken, skin lacerated, joints dislocated occasionally, and a few dogs died as a result of accident or illness, but traumatic human death was not a serious concern for racers. Their largest fear was of injury or damage to equipment that would make it impossible to continue and isolate them in the emptiness of the Alaskan winter. Food for the team and musher could run short before they could be located and a rescue accomplished. That sort of close call was possible in this sport, where blizzards could blow up in hours, last for days, and force the Iditarod's flying support into idleness.

Schuller drew a deep breath, marshaling his strength, knowing he would have to make the decisions. Turner was, justifiably, in shock. George Koptak had been a friend and mentor to the younger man; they'd both been obsessed with sleds and distance. For over two years they had raised and trained dogs together in Teller, an Eskimo village outside Nome. George had run the Iditarod many times, but this was Bill's first try and, Schuller hoped, not his last. It was like losing family for the twenty-six-year-old rookie to lose George. To be the one to find him dead in the trail had to be devastating.

Taking his sleeping bag and brandy, Schuller walked back to the bloody tree.

"Here, take a hit of this." He forced Turner's cold fingers around the bottle and raised it to his lips. The younger man choked down a swallow or two, coughed before he took a third, and handed the brandy back.

"What are we gonna do?"

Schuller looked down again at George's body. "We're gonna get him to Finger Lake, Bill. We can't leave him here." He thought of the wolves that periodically stole dog food during the race. "We'll put him on my sled in my bag, since we don't have his. But you'll have to help me get him on. Maybe we'll find his team on the way in."

He took a long pull of the brandy and shoved it into his parka pocket. Hell, I'm in shock myself, he thought.

They worked the body into Schuller's sleeping bag and lashed it to his sled. It took over twenty minutes to untangle the traces and straighten out both teams.

Before they left, Schuller tied his red bandana to the trunk of the tree as a marker. After the race, he promised himself, I'm coming back to cut down this damn tree.

Willow Was Her Name

DIXIE ALEXANDER

Dixie Alexander is an Athabascan Indian writer and beadwork artist who lives in North Pole, Alaska, south of Fairbanks. Her prose includes an essay about her grandmother, a skin sewer and beadworker, in FROM SKINS, TREES, QUILLS AND BEADS: THE WORK OF NINE ATHABASCANS *(1985). Her poem "Willow Was Her Name" is reprinted from the* Alaska Quarterly Review *(1986).*

Willow was her name
I needed her roots
the touch her soul the earth

Some stayed natural
some were dyed
some were split
but the coil stayed whole

Born again one day by these hands
that coil her into beautiful baskets

Willow was her name
when winter winds blow
she'll sway bare from side to side
but the beauty is still there

Nomadic Iñupiat, for Kappaisruk

SISTER GOODWIN

Sister Goodwin, an Inupiat Eskimo writer and teacher, was born in Kotzebue, Alaska. She is married to Tlingit writer, editor, and Native activist Andrew Hope III. Her poems have appeared in the San Francisco Chronicle, Loon Lark *magazine (Sitka),* Nalahat Review, Maize, *and the* Alaska Quarterly Review. *"Nomadic Iñupiat, for Kappaisruk" is taken from her poetry collection* A LAGOON IS IN MY BACKYARD *(1984).*

Illivaaq
  how many times
mom & dad took us
out of school
  one month ahead
ahead of the coming water
     we rode on an
oaken sled over spring ice
  the dogs excited as
children
        race without directions
east to Illivaaq
opening up the summer home
  is a special thirst
saved for the nomadic change
     we drank the freshness
of the new-fallen snow
       the last of the year
we ran
as the snow crunched under us
we felt

we touched
happy to be home again
we ran across both creeks
on the rocky shore
we ran up to the top
of the hills named
for each of us
we ran over to the
old drifted up scow
we couldn't wait for Nelsons
to move to their camp
from Napaatauchaaq
  how many games of
norwegian ball kept us happy
we held onto driftwood boats
on a pole making waves on a
calm arctic shoreline

Agvagaaq
  summer home for grandparents
the spruce is tall
  roots for baskets & carved dish
      you bounced on a
  wild duck carved of driftwood
      while the owls
  just sat around
watching
      big robins
    fly by tree to tree
golden eagles & hawks glide
on a quiet wind current

Kitikliquagaaq
  fall season
  where we pick barrels of berries
& dine on kutugaq a wild duck

Qugluktaq
  last berry camp
  last duck hunting camp
evening becomes a reality
        as the first hours of
  darkness
hold a blanket over the sun
  the northern lights fill up
the sky with a bright speeding
  polar force
legends are remembered from
parents of parents & retold
        how special for
a whole family to sit
together
reminiscing laughing planning
for the winter
always the squirming children
        sit wide-eyed for hours
  listening to old-time powers
hushed by folks telling them
        the bears outside will hear
them laugh and come to take
        them away

fall
a glint
a last chance to take home the earth
a beginning of subdued sleep

Southeastern Alaska

FROM *Alaska Blues*

JOE UPTON

Joe Upton is a commercial fisherman who lives and writes on Bainbridge Island, Washington. He has fished in Maine, off Chile, and in Alaska's Inside Passage, and he participates in the annual early summer salmon season in Alaska's Bristol Bay. He is the author of AMARETTO *(1985), tales of Maine's herring fishery;* JOURNEYS THROUGH THE INSIDE PASSAGE *(1992), chronicles of the legendary waterway; and* THE COASTAL COMPANION *(1995). His first book,* ALASKA BLUES: A FISHERMAN'S JOURNAL *(1977), excerpted here, won several awards; it is an autobiographical account of the life of a commercial fisherman in Southeast Alaska.*

A man in a boat could travel for weeks in Southeastern Alaska and never find a town. The coast, like the coast of British Columbia, is deeply indented with inlets winding back into a mountainous and forbidding interior. The several major islands, and countless smaller ones, form a maze of channels and passages between the ocean and the mainland. In the northern part of the region, glaciers lie at the head of most of the mainland inlets, and they discharge ice all year round.

A vast part of the area is thickly forested, without settlements or towns, little changed since the arrival of white men. Almost all the land is owned by the federal government in the form of national forests, and little is available to individuals.

There are a few towns, none large. Each has a few miles of roads, but except for Haines, in the far north, none of the towns are connected to anyplace else or to each other, except by air or water. The industries are fishing and logging, both fairly seasonal. Only the capital, Juneau, has a true year-round economy and escapes the seasonal nature of life in much of the area.

Tourism is now increasing, as many people travel through the area each summer on the ferries and cruise ships that pass almost daily during the season. But most of those people are going farther north or preparing to fly south. There is little to keep them in Southeastern Alaska, and I'm sure that after a while their trip just fades into a blur of islands, all the same, overcast days, and a few towns busy with canneries or sawmills.

Scattered in little coves and harbors far from the towns that are big enough to have fish plants, mills, schools and stores are a few roadless fishing communities that still enjoy a sleepy existence. One of these, Port Protection, was discovered and named by Captain George Vancouver when he anchored there on a gloomy and windy evening in September, 1793, after searching for a harbor in failing light and deteriorating weather. He named a nearby point and its small harbor Point Baker, after his lieutenant.

Today Port Protection and Point Baker each has a general store and homes built under the trees around the bay. All told, the population in the winter might reach 60 people. There are no roads, phones, electricity or other services. The nearest town is 50 miles away by plane or boat. Once a week a mail and freight boat makes a stop. The woods are thick, the homes are built hard by the water, and behind the homes the forest rises dark and tall. Even paths are few, and usually just used by dogs. For most people, skiffs are the way to get around.

Except for the storekeepers, all the men fish, mostly only for salmon. In the winter the men are all home; in the summer they're scattered from the bay out front to points up and down the whole coast. Their fleet ranges from skiffs to seiners, and when the fish run, it's a busy time.

Then the population of the area doubles and triples, as boats from the south and from other parts of Southeastern Alaska make one or the other of the two communities their base of operations for the season. Many boats have been going to Port Protection and Point Baker for years with their friends and sometimes with their families; when the fishing period is over, or in the evenings, the floats of the communities are almost towns in themselves.

But it's a rush too, for the peak of the run may pass the area in just a few days, and when the fish run, it seems as if there aren't enough hours in the day for everything that you have to do.

But then comes the fall; the outside boats leave, and the local boats straggle back home. By the first of November, everyone is pretty much tied up for the winter. In the winter the days are short, with a pale sun low in the sky. Many homes are hidden by the trees and don't feel the sun from November until March. It isn't a bitter winter—rarely will the bay freeze—but the weather is poor and the snow lies on the ground for weeks at a time. In the summer, as many as two and three planes a day land in the bay, bringing people and supplies, but in the winter it's dead quiet, and weeks will pass with only the mail boat to break the monotony.

Despite the short days and gloomy weather, many of the local residents prefer the winter. Salmon season's a rush and the winter can be a welcome change, with time to work on a cabin or boat, visit neighbors or just sit inside when the weather's poor. It's not a fast life, but there's enough to do just to keep going. Many of the residents have spent time in the larger towns and wouldn't think of ever going back.

April 24. A peach of a day, fresh and clear with light northerlies. Sam couldn't wait this morning, so over the side he went, to swim ashore to the point and run through the woods barking until we went ashore, too. We have the whole cove to ourselves. A half-mile away, through a narrow tidal channel, is the settlement of Point Baker, but here there's hardly a sign of man. The cabin we built a few summers ago is high on a point with water on three sides, but hidden from view by the trees. It's just 12 by 16 feet with a sleeping loft above and storage out back, but that's fine for the three of us. I pulled the boards off the windows and laid a fire as Susanna took off through the woods to check on her garden spot. Flying squirrels had found their way into the cabin and chewed on the food, but otherwise all was tight and dry. Spent day in unloading the boat and just settling in. I sat for a bit in the evening with the sun dying brilliant in the hills across the strait, our boat riding easily in the cove below, Sam asleep at my feet, and Susanna beside me. If there are any fish at all, we'll just stay here and fish.

April 25. Fair again. Spent the day in the garden with Susanna and Sam. Spring's late up here, but already the days are getting longer and the first buds are appearing, so we planted anyway and strung up some old net to keep the dog out. If we have to go out to the coast, it'll be too late to plant by the time we get back.

A neighbor came by tonight, said not to waste our time fishing here; most of the local boats left last week for the coast. Guess we'll have to go, too, but don't much want to. Built this place so we could get off the boat once in a while, and every year since, we've had to travel farther and farther to fish.

April 26. Wind southeast at 25 knots with spits of rain. Spent the day in boat work: changed the oil and went over the trolling gear, made all ready to travel in the morning. Back to the cabin, where I found Susanna had baked rolls, bread and even two pies for the trip, but I don't think she wants to go any more than I do. Sam fell down from the loft last night. He climbs up the ladder to sleep with us, then gets hot in the night and circles around for a cooler spot. Heard a great crash and looked around with the flashlight. Finally spotted him asleep under the table downstairs; he probably fell seven feet and never even woke.

April 27. Weather continued southeasterly with squalls. Gathered up wife and dog and tried for early start, but ran into a friend while taking water at Port Protection, and spent the morning drinking coffee and catching up on the winter's gossip. Missed the tide and spent a dirty afternoon bucking down Sumner Strait toward the ocean. The outside route looked gray and mean, so we headed up Shakan Bay and back into the trees and rockpiles of El Capitan Passage. It's a longer and more tedious route, but it puts off that outside business for a while longer. This time of year it's still almost winter out in the Gulf of Alaska, and I take the sheltered routes every chance I get. Ran through Dry Pass at the very last light, through channels with no room even for two boats to pass, the trees almost meeting above. At 11 P.M. slipped past the rock at the entrance to Devilfish Bay and dropped the hook in five fathoms, soft bottom, the night black and rainy. Shut down to the roar of falls close at hand; above us, pale snow on the steep hills. Untraveled country out here; passed only one boat all day.

April 28. The day came overcast and found us swinging at anchor in a little landlocked bay with trees rising steeply to snow on all sides. In the shallows ducks traded back and forth, and off our stern three seals played, diving and swimming under the boat. Soon we'll be in the outer islands, with the ocean close around the point, and such peace will be rare, so we savored it this morning, dawdling over breakfast, Susanna looking through the glass at the ducks with her bird book out. But miles to go, so we went down the long channel at 10, while watching the depth recorder for signs of fish as we passed into island-choked Sea Otter Sound. The country grew ever wilder and more remote, with steep-sided islands and lonely inlets, and only an occasional logged-over slope to show the hand of man. Ran all the old spots with the sounding machine, but not a sign of fish or feed, either. Anything at all and I would have stayed, but it just looked dead. Saw one boat and he was running, too, so I guess it's the big waters for sure; can't put it off.

Passed the ruins of a nameless settlement in narrow Tuxekan Passage, already the wind darkening the water to the southwest. The Gulf of Esquibel opened up ahead for 20 miles of rolling in the trough, with bleak dark islands, gnarled trees and forbidding rocky shores on all sides. The closer we get to the coast, the wilder the country gets. A rain squall passed over us, blotting out the shores and causing squealing on the radio. Finally, at 5 P.M., the fjordlike opening of Steamboat Bay on Noyes Island appeared out of the mists, and we passed inside to tie up, the fourth boat out at the float of a disused cannery. Vicious williwaws buffeted us from the mountains above; a neighbor says no one has left the bay in three days.

Baited up and laid out all my gear for the morning anyway, while Susanna and Sam headed off for the woods. She beat me four hands straight at cards after dinner. As I write this, in the stillness between the gusts I think I can hear the boom of the surf on the outer coast of the island three miles away.

April 29. Day came at 3 A.M., with violent squalls heeling us over at the float. Pulled on oilskins and ran a long bow line out to the float, then back in that sack for some good winks with the eerie whine of the wind loud around us. I'd rather be in here than swinging on the hook somewhere and worrying about dragging. Slept late, and no one even started an engine; you can lie in your bunk right here and listen to the weather report howling in the rigging. Fed the minks last night, I guess—not a bait left on the hooks this morning. You're falling down on the job, Sam.

Out in the wind and rain for a long walk with Susanna and Sam. Sam's good company these long harbor days, and he gets us out of the boat. Lying in the bunk rainy day after rainy day, with the wind shaking the rigging, can get to you after a while. Walked past rows of bunkhouses and outbuildings, their paint peeling and windows broken. Huge scows for fish trapping, with steam winches to haul the heavy trap anchors, were lying on the beach, rotting and broken. Around the curve of the beach we walked, until the cannery seemed tiny. Later, dinner and more cards, with wet clothes drying over the stove. That cabin back at Baker looks pretty good tonight.

April 30. Gray and cold, with engines starting up on all sides at 5 A.M. I put on two wool shirts and followed the *Anatevka,* skippered by Doug, a fishing friend of seasons past. Headed out to Cape Ulitka, where the ocean pours around the point and meets the outgoing tide. That's a dirty spot; we almost turned around right there. The swells on the outside were 15 feet high, mean and ominous in the early morning light with a wind chop on top. Ran out to the 30-fathom edge and went back into the trolling cockpit to start dropping my gear. A mile and a half away loomed the dark wall of Noyes Island, clouds low on the hills and the shores lost in the spume and mists of the heavy breaking seas. They call this the Gulf of Alaska, but it's the North Pacific Ocean, and the shores show the effects of the winter gales: bare rock extends up over a hundred feet from the water without a trace of vegetation, and above that what trees there are grow twisted and stunted from the constant gales. It's a wild spot to fish, but when the fish come by, a fellow can do well even in a small boat—if the weather will let him fish. They're traveling fish, running south along the Pacific Rim and headed for all the major rivers up and down the West Coast; I doubt that one in five is headed for an Alaskan stream. We snag a few on the way by. My boat is well built and I trust it, but those are big waters out there, and I fish with an eye over my shoulder, for the weather can blow up in a hurry, and then getting through the rip at the cape can be a desperate struggle.

First day of the season, and the kid is all thumbs. Always there are the little bugs to work out after the winter and working on gear, but today I lost a whole line—lead, flashers and all, cut off by the stabilizer dragging back too far. Susanna and Sam pretty much stayed in the bunk, so I was back in the cockpit trying to hang on, fish, and steer the drag by memory.

I was disgusted by 3 P.M., and the weather was doing things to boot, with spitting rain and a freshening breeze to the southwest. Looked around to see the *Anatevka* close, but no other boats in sight. We crossed tacks just then and I waved that I was picking up; Doug was picking up, too. By then the tide had carried us miles to the south and we figured we might as well just go around the island.

If you only see Cape Addington once, it should be on such a day. The wind was coming on hard and running against the tide, and the cape, a long rocky arm, was almost lost in the mists as the heavy seas beat against its rocky sides. That's an evil place, and we gave it plenty of room in order to stay clear of the tide race, but even so, it was a wild hour before we were around. Once, on top of a big one, I took a long look around. To the south the water was white and the sky dark. A quarter-mile away, Doug labored heavily through the rip, but beyond that we were alone. There was nothing but the sky and the troubled sea. We rounded the cape, finally, and after that the rest seemed easy—an hour's run along a bold shore, then in through the steep swells at Cone Island to tie to the little float at Kelly Cove on Noyes Island. The crew rowed ashore, and I poured out a stiff drink and started in on the mess on the back deck. Seven fish for the day—just about covered our losses.

May 1. Up at 5 A.M. to a pale clear morning, not a tree moving around the cove. Under way at once, but I didn't trust the weather much. Heavy swells at the entrance; idled through with the tide pushing us on. Fished Veta Bay and Granite Point and had a dozen by noon, when it blew up southeast and we had to give up. Had a good long walk on beach this windy afternoon, though. Susanna says she's going to Hawaii this time next year. Don't blame her much. Haven't met too many people that really like Noyes Island in the spring. Don't like it myself, but it pays the bills.

May 2. Actually fished a full day—Cape Chirikoff for 18, and most were large kings at $1.20 a pound! Gear, finally, more or less fishing well.

Weather continued southeast. Lousy but fishable. It's exciting to get into a bite of kings—king salmon—and maybe get two or three on a line. Had a couple like that today, but mostly it's just standing back there in the cockpit, wedged in, watching your depth on the meter and watching the lines for a hit. Lost what looked like a 40-pounder today—dammit—had him right up to the boat, ready to lay that gaff alongside his head, and he just took off and broke the leader. Pulled up three useless hooks today—solid duranickel and bent back straight like coat-hanger wire. Should have bought stainless steel. Sometimes I think that if you land 50 percent of the fish you hook, you're doing pretty good. But God, it hurts to lose those big babies—that one today was a $50 bill.

May 3. Couldn't believe it—bright sunshine and no wind until the afternoon westerly; can this be Noyes Island? Fifteen fish, too, and Susanna even went back there with me for a couple of hours and landed five—how do you like that? Then, on the way in, found a big glass float, covered with weeds and kelp, but unbroken. Wrote in the log book in capital letters: BIG DAY. Topped it all off with a hot shower at the buying station in the cove.

Working on the Edge

SPIKE WALKER

Spike Walker worked for nine seasons as a crewman aboard crab boats in the Alaskan fleet. He has also worked in the offshore oil fields of Louisiana and Texas, on the Mississippi River as a certified commercial deep-sea diver, and as a logger in Washington, Oregon, Idaho, and Alaska. He currently lives in Oregon, but returns each year to Alaska to fish for halibut. He is the author of WORKING ON THE EDGE *(1991), the definitive portrait of the dangerous occupation of a high-sea crab fisherman from which the following excerpt was taken.*

After vacationing for several months in the South 48, I returned to Kodiak once more and took a job aboard the eighty-six-foot crab boat *Elusive*. After an opelio crab season off the Pribilof Islands in the Bering Sea, I spent a peaceful and contented summer packing iced-down loads of salmon between the fleets fishing in the isolated bays around Kodiak Island and the canneries in the village of Kodiak itself. When the king crab surveys carried out in the Bering Sea revealed that surprisingly few harvestable king crab remained there, I decided to fish the fall crab season in the waters around Kodiak Island.

The day before the opening of the fall king crab season, three other crewmen and I worked in a miserable wind-driven rain to load our crab pots. We craned them aboard, bound them with chains, and stored a ton or so of frozen herring bait in our freezer. Then we packed our foodstuffs aboard and secured our deck for running.

But it was rough weather, and several of the crab boats that had gone before us radioed back that a fifty-knot wind was blowing outside, with sixteen-foot seas pounding in against Chiniak Head. It had been years since I'd seen such seas so close to land, but since our course was to be different from that of much of the rest of the fleet, we left the safety of Kodiak in spite of the weather report.

Our plan was to take the somewhat-protected waters from Kodiak to

Ouzinkie and Whale Pass. Yet we had hardly begun the journey when the weather found us. The seas just outside Kodiak's city limits were stacking up higher than any of us on board could recall. And when we passed out from behind the close protection of Near Island, a fast-breaking surf drove into our starboard side, throwing our bow a full twenty degrees off course.

Once committed, there was nothing to be done in the narrow channel. Veer to port and you ran smack into Kodiak Island, only a few hundred feet away. A turn to starboard—and into the waves—also would have taken us on the rocks. A skipper might eventually pound his way around the end of Long Island and out its channel, but that would mean running the entire one-hundred-mile length of Kodiak Island broadside to the high winds and hard-driving seas. Running in the trough with a tall load of king crab pots is one of the most unstable of open-sea maneuvers.

Our radios were mounted on the ceiling overhead, and now they squawked with the chatter of ship captains trying to round Cape Chiniak. I stood with my crewmates in the wheelhouse while our skipper navigated. Ahead of us, we could see the *Kodiak Queen,* with skipper Jack Johnson at the helm. Now as we watched, all 155 feet of her black steel hull lumbered up and over an exceptionally steep wave crest, then disappeared completely into the canyonlike wave trough ahead. She showed herself again as she rose over the steep slope of the next wave. Searing winds stripped draining seawater from her superstructure and blew it into silvery gray veils of mist.

"Oh, I like this!" said MacDonald to no one in particular as we plunged headfirst over the crest of one mountainous wave.

"We could always go back and call it a season," I offered, holding on for dear life.

"Yah, I might just decide to dump this load off in Chiniak Bay and go back and tie up and take you all out for a night on the town, too, but I wouldn't bet on it," replied MacDonald, his voice tightening as another wall of breaking white water closed on us.

The wave struck our starboard with a resounding thud, knocking the vessel sideways for several fathoms. We braced ourselves and held on as a gusty, irregular rhythm of waves broke completely over the ship. Each time, a flood of seawater drained off the ship's superstructure, temporarily blurring our vision.

But our skipper hung fast to his commitment and remained steady to his course until we eventually pounded our way around the last red swing buoy. Then, with the force of the seas directly on our stern, we shot ahead and soon passed through the narrow slot called Ouzinkie Pass. Now we were no longer fighting the wind and seas, and the force of the storm pushed us along on a remarkably level ride. Leaving our skipper to navigate through the narrow waters of Whale Pass, my crewmates and I went below and sacked out in our staterooms.

Now married, the father of four, and a much respected captain in these Alaskan waters, MacDonald was introduced to commercial fishing more than a decade before while working in a management-training program in a large grocery store chain down on the Oregon coast. He "hated the work," he recalls, being indoors all the time, with no hope of significant profit or adventure. Then a friend offered to take him fishing for a trip as a paid deckhand aboard a shrimp boat.

MacDonald was earning about $130 a week when he rode out of Charleston Harbor near Coos Bay on the Oregon coast for the first time. The shrimp fishing at the time was red-hot and soon Tom MacDonald found himself "making two hundred dollars a *day!* I couldn't believe there was that much money in the whole world!" he recalls. He held his own on deck, and by journey's end his friend offered him a full-time position on board the vessel.

The lure of the money and the sense of freedom and independence of a fisherman's life were too much for MacDonald. When he arrived back in port, he quit the management-training program on the spot. Already, the thought of returning to the regimentation and confinement of such a job seemed incomprehensible. He would never live that kind of life again. And with ever increasing success, he would go on to run, own, or captain such ships as the *Betty A., the Ironic,* the *Sleep Robber,* and now the modern and immaculately kept crab boat *Elusive.*

It was well past midnight when we powered clear of the tip of Raspberry Island. Then, swinging to port, we set a course parallel to the rugged green radar outline of Kodiak Island. And with bruising twelve-foot waves lifting and pushing us on a roller-coaster ride, we sailed down Shelikof Strait.

Tom MacDonald had taken the ship the entire way by himself, and at about 1:00 A.M. he decided to turn in for a few hours rest, leaving me responsible for the ship and crew for a three-hour graveyard shift. Calling it quits, he retired with only a few parting words. "Well, she's all yours. . . . Night."

Actually, I had volunteered for the duty. The late-night shift had always been one of my favorite duties aboard ship. It was a quiet time when I could be left alone with my own thoughts and dreams. As I sat alone in the captain's chair in the wintry blackness, my eyes moved habitually between the green face of the radar screen to my left and the seas dead ahead, while a huge sea launched the vessel down the western side of Kodiak Island.

I was deep in my own thoughts when a frantic voice leapt from one of the radio sets mounted overhead. "Mayday! Mayday! Mayday! Help! We're in trouble! Mayday! This is the *City of Seattle!* We're in trouble! Can anybody out there hear me?"

I yanked the microphone from the radio set overhead and was about to call back when another voice cut in.

"Yes, sir, we can hear you! What's your position?"

"Mayday! Mayday! We're going down!" came back the frantic voice.

Then I jumped in.

"What's your damned position? Give us your loran readings!" I yelled.

"We're in trouble! We're going down! Our bow's under water right now!" replied the voice.

Then he seemed to gather himself, and in a trembling voice, he said, "Our position is four-three-five-four-nine-point-three and three-two-three-one-three-point-five!"

I turned to our map table, and soon I had him pinpointed. He was just two miles due east from us—only minutes away.

As I hurried into the skipper's room, I fought to control the urgency in my voice. "Hey, Tom! We've got a Mayday and he's right here beside us!"

In one motion, Tom rose and leapt to his feet. He paused at the map table long enough for me to show him the distressed vessel's exact position, then he hopped nimbly into the captain's chair and cranked the ship hard to starboard. "Go get the rest of the crew," he ordered.

Then the stirring voice of the frantic fisherman leapt again from the radio set. "We're putting on our survival suits now! We're abandoning ship!"

Ahead of us, concealed by the darkness, drifted the 105-foot crab boat *City of Seattle.* She was reportedly adrift without power or lights. Her interior was aflame, and she was sinking steadily. It would be difficult to locate her.

As we closed on the area, several of us donned our rain gear and ventured out onto our bow. Lying against the bow railings, we searched the chilly black night around us for a sign of the foundering vessel.

In our wheelhouse, Tom MacDonald continued the dialogue with the skipper of the *City of Seattle.*

"You got any flares on board?" he asked.

"Negative," the voice shot back. There was a pause. "Hey you! You with the blue deck crane! You're going right by us now! You're right beside us!"

The fishing vessel *Cougar* was nearby. Perhaps it was the *Cougar* they had spotted.

Then MacDonald switched on the entire array of our ship's huge mast lights and began making frantic circles across the face of the sea, weaving in and out and over and down the passing waves.

Suddenly, out of the corner of my left eye, I caught the movement of smoke streaking across the water, whipped there by the thirty-knot winds. "There it is, Tom" I yelled, pointing. "Twenty degrees off the port bow! She's burning! See the smoke?"

"By God, you're right!" he answered, resetting our course.

The crew on board the sinking crab boat had been through their own private and unknowable ordeal. It had been a long night for skipper and owner Gary Wiggins. All night, he had idled ahead into storm-generated waves that broke directly over the bow, then washed through the entire deckloads of pots before slamming into the tall steel wheelhouse with a hellacious shudder.

Then, just before midnight, a huge wave struck with a loud bang, knocking the vessel sideways.

The sleeping crew of the *City of Seattle* came alive and pandemonium broke out. Several greenhorn deckhands began running back and forth in the wheelhouse, screaming that they were going to die.

"Shut up! Shut up!" screamed Wiggins. "We're trying to get our position off!"

A crewman was sent forward to check out the bow, and he returned shortly to report that the fo'c'sle and bow deck were covered with some two feet of steadily rising water. The skipper ordered his crew to put on their survival suits.

Wiggins went below to survey the damage. When he opened the engine-room door, he was driven back by a deadly cloud of smoke and Freon gas. Regardless, he rushed below and tried without success to put the generator back on line. But he soon grew too sick to continue.

One crewman held his breath and ran down the stairs into the engine room to see what could be done. When he showed again at the top of the stairs, he was down on his knees, crying from the eye-burning Freon.

When the lights went out, the greenhorn crewmen panicked again. "What are we going to do?" they screamed. "What do we do now?"

"Go topside and get the raft ready!" shot back Wiggins.

"Let's go, honey," said Wiggin's wife. "Let's get off this thing!"

But the main engines were still running, and Gary Wiggins hesitated. "No!" he shot back. "You go! I'm going to stay with her and see if I can save her!"

No one would ever know with certainty what caused the bow to begin to sink, but Gary Wiggins later surmised that the seawater flooding over the bow started pouring into the engine room through electrical conduit pipes that ran the full length of the hull. "When the water rose, it eventually hit the four-hundred-and-forty-volt electrical panel," he told me, "and knocked everything off line—pumps and bilges and lights."

For a time, the engineer could hear the generator running. It sounded as though it was racing out of control. Then the lights and power flickered out altogether, and the *City of Seattle* was cast adrift without power to steer by, or light by which to see or be seen.

Our mast lights threw an icy blue beam of light across the ever-changing face of the cold black sea and the drama unfolding before us. The scene left us silent, awestruck, and transfixed.

The *City of Seattle* was packing a fair-sized load of crab pots. Tied to one another and chained to the deck, the seventy-odd fully rigged crab pots weighed some sixty thousand pounds. Shiny new buoys could be seen gleaming from inside crab pots that had never been fishing. As the forward compartments of the ship's hull continued to flood with seawater, the bow settled noticeably, and ocean waves began to break across her deck. The vessel's tall, steel wheelhouse was mounted high over the stern. And as the bow slowly sank, the stern rose and the wheelhouse facing out over the long forward deck began to tilt ahead in unison. Well off on our starboard, rolling heavily in the late-night swells, idled the fishing vessel *Cougar*. She was standing by to pick up the survivors.

With smoke billowing from the wheelhouse and seawater rising steadily over the deck, the stern of the *City of Seattle* began to tilt upward sharply, exposing the rudder and propeller.

No sooner had the young crew of the *City of Seattle* finally finished launching their life raft than its sea anchor became tangled in her props. When several greenhorn crewmen once again started to panic, it was Wiggins's wife who cut the line and set them free.

With his wife and crew safely aboard the *Cougar,* skipper Gary Wiggins and one other experienced deckhand finally abandoned ship. One by one, they leapt from the angular tall column of stern steel, their bright red survival suits gleaming in our mast lights.

You could see how the stern was thrust up and down by the waves. The two men fell about twelve feet through the night air and were swallowed briefly by the sea. Beneath the surface, Wiggins heard the *thump-thump-thump* of the diesel engines aboard the waiting ships.

Then, just as suddenly, he was on the surface again. He swam wildly through the jet black sea, fighting against the suck and surge of the *City of Seattle*'s stern as it plunged up and down. Wiggins would never forget the fear, the adrenaline, and the long, sweeping valleys of sea. But as he approached the *Cougar,* he noticed that she, too, was heavily loaded with crab pots and was rolling sharply in the steep and irregular seas.

As he drew near, the huge steel hull of the *Cougar* leapt high and free—then fell into a trough. She rose, staggered, and fell. Seawater spilled over her bulwarks. The vision terrified Wiggins, and he thought, I don't even want to get close to this boat! But he knew he had to. As he drew closer to the *Cougar,* he could hear the flush and pop of water sucking at the ship's hull.

Then as he maneuvered to within arm's reach of the ship's hull, he saw a big, bearded crewman reach down for him. "All I can remember is that I swam alongside the *Cougar,* and this big bearded guy, and I mean *big,* grabbed me by the back of the neck and with a deep grunt gave me a pull. The next thing I knew, I had landed clear across the deck and was crumpled up in the corner of a crab pot stacked there."

As he lay there panting with exhaustion on the wet wood of the deck, Wiggins could heard the rhythmic flush of water escaping through the ship's scuppers. Then there was a metallic clip as the ship rolled high and the flaps flipped shut.

The large bearded man was none other than Kodiak's Steve Griffing—"Big Steve" to his friends. Standing six eight and weighing 285 pounds, he was exactly the right kind of man for the job. Griffing would soon play a major role in another dramatic rescue attempt that same season.

On board the *Elusive,* we stood by to assist. As the skipper and crew of the *Cougar* maneuvered to pick up the men, our skipper, Tom MacDonald, decided to try and save the *City of Seattle* itself. He disappeared into his stateroom and when he reappeared, he was wearing a diver's wet suit.

MacDonald grabbed a shot of line off the back deck, tucked it under one arm, and climbed out onto the outermost peak of our leaping bow. He sat down and began pulling on his flippers. With the wind filling my ears and spray hissing against my rain gear, I had to yell to be heard.

"Just what in the hell do you think you're going to do, Tom?"

Tom lifted the mask to his mouth and spit on the inside of it to prevent the glass from fogging. Then he turned, pointed to the deck boss sitting at the helm inside the wheelhouse, and yelled, "Tell him to keep this big bastard away from me, or he'll squish me!"

Then, suspended out over the water, Tom balanced himself on the lonely, plummeting tip of our bow. The bow carried him up and up until its momentum peaked and it began its free-fall descent once again.

He adjusted his mask and turned back to me one last time. "Feed the line to me as I go!" he yelled. "I'm going to try to climb up on the bow of that ship. When I do—*if* I can—then tie our two-inch hawser line off on your end and signal me and I'll drag it over to me. Let's see if we can't hook on to that big bastard and drag her into shallow water before she sinks!"

Then as the ship lunged forward into another wave, he clutched his face mask in one hand and the line in the other and fell forward into the sea. MacDonald went under momentarily, came up trailing the 5/8-inch crab-pot line, and set out stroking mightily toward the foundering *City of Seattle.*

While our young crew looked on, our deck boss reversed the throttle and backed the ship slowly away. Then we watched together as our gutsy skipper swam through the undulating sea to the foundering ship. It was a true act of daring, and I did my best to feed him the line free of tangles.

Soon MacDonald swam into a pool of diesel fuel. It was a horrid experience. The fumes filled his sinuses, and the waves washed the oily film over him, coating him repeatedly.

Several hundred feet of ocean away, the huge steel bow of the sinking ship leapt and rolled like a thrashing beast. Up it rose, a full ten feet out of the ocean, dumping untold tons of seawater from its flooded deck. Then it plunged straight down and vanished beneath the waves.

When MacDonald reached the leaping hull of the *City of Seattle,* he paused and backpedaled, as if to evaluate the situation. His body seemed dwarfed by the huge moving wall of steel rising and plunging before him.

For several minutes, MacDonald stood off from the reeling bow, gauging its rhythm. Then he swam closer, knowing that if he was sucked beneath the ship, he would be crushed and that none of us would be able to come to his aid. One could see the calculation in his manner. Then in one motion, he reached out and caught the bow railing. As the bow leapt skyward, MacDonald clung to the outside of the railing and was swept perhaps twelve feet into the night. As I watched, he disappeared into an emerald green flood of seawater draining from the deck and pouring down over him. And then I saw him come under the strain of the rushing current and the burdensome weight of the water, and match them.

As the bow plunged back toward the sea, MacDonald clambered over the railing and clung to the anchor winch and chain as ensuing waves did their best to wash the bow clean of him. Then, during a lull in the wave action, he stood and signaled me. I tied the end of the crab-pot line to the thick two-inch hawser line, then fed it to him as he pulled the expensive high-test hawser line over to himself and tied it off on the *City of Seattle*'s anchor mounted on the point of her bow. When the bow buried itself in another wave, MacDonald floated free of the deck and set out swimming for the *Elusive.*

He was puffing heavily as we pulled him up and over the side. At his adamant instructions, we peeled his wet suit top from his back and stood back as he raced, dripping, through the galley and up the stairs into the wheelhouse, where he threw the engine in gear and began the tow.

He pointed us toward Uganik Bay. Once inside the bay, MacDonald intended to tie the *City of Seattle* alongside the *Elusive* and just run both ships aground. He figured the *City of Seattle,* riding as low in the water as she was, would be the first to strike bottom. When the sinking vessel was resting safely on the beach, he planned to cut her loose and back away. The *City of Seattle* was worth more than a million dollars, and we knew the successful completion of such a task could earn us hundreds of thousands of dollars in salvage fees. But we had no sooner begun our tow when she started shearing from side to side off our stern, veering first one way and then the other. They were long, helter-skelter runs and they made the *Elusive* shudder and shift in the water.

Each time the *City of Seattle* came to the slack end of her run, our thick hawser line stretched elastically, wringing seawater from her expensive fabric like drops from a twisted towel. Then a mile or so off Miner's Point, the bow of the *City of Seattle* nosed toward the bottom and the megaton strength of the hawser line broke suddenly and it collapsed limply across the pot stack on our back deck.

We could only stand by then and wait for the *City of Seattle* to sink.

For Gary Wiggins and his wife, watching from the wheelhouse of the *Cougar*, the sight of the sinking vessel was a sobering one. No one would ever know exactly what caused the ship to begin taking on water, but a lifetime of planning and working and fishing and saving had gone into building the crab boat. Nearly everything Wiggins owned was on the boat. His wife and family could attest to the endless months Gary had spent at sea. He'd been at home no more than three weeks out of the entire previous year.

"Oh, God, it's gone!" said the skipper's wife as the ship went down.

Then the bow of the *City of Seattle* suddenly reappeared on the surface. The ship was floating vertically through the ocean water, with only the top few feet of her bow showing above the surface. Her bow rose and fell in front of the *Cougar* like a whale breaching for a better look, as if to offer up some nostalgic pose or to say goodbye. Then it disappeared altogether as the ship went down for good.

Fatigued from the ordeal, and deeply disappointed at the failure of our salvage efforts, our exhausted crew fell heavily into their bunks. Without comment, our wet and disgusted skipper returned the *Elusive* to her original course down the length of Shelikof Straits.

Flying for 1002

FROM *Navigations*

TED KERASOTE

Naturalist, writer, and adventurer Ted Kerasote has traveled extensively,
exploring the natural world. A resident of Wyoming, he is the author of
BLOODTIES *and* NAVIGATIONS *(1986). "Flying for 1002," excerpted from*
NAVIGATIONS, *concerns the Arctic National Wildlife Reserve (ANWR) and*
the controversial possibility of oil exploration there.

Cleaning the Helio Courier's windshield is a rite of the morning. Don Ross, the assistant manager of the Arctic National Wildlife Refuge in northeastern Alaska, stands on the wheel strut of the orange and white, single engine plane and sprays a sweet smelling paste on the cockpit's Plexiglas. The cold Arctic breeze flays the paper towel he rubs over the windows. Don has red hair, turning blond with age (he's almost 40), and an understated R.A.F. moustache. In another time his blue eyes would have searched for German fighters from the cockpit of a Spitfire. Now, a participant in the Department of the Interior's 1002 study, he helps spot grizzly bears, caribou, and musk ox in the foothills of the 19-million-acre refuge, a hunk of country the size of the state of Maine.

The 1002 study (everyone pronounces it "ten-oh-two") was mandated by the Alaska National Interest Lands Conservation Act of 1980 (ANILCA), which in turn was birthed out of the Alaska Native Claims Settlement Act of 1971 (ANCSA). It is designed to investigate the sensitivity of the refuge's wildlife to projected oil drilling. Seismic exploration is taking place on the coastal plain of the refuge during the winters of 1984 to 1986. By September of 1986 the Secretary of the Interior must submit the data from both the geological and biological surveys to Congress, which will then have the unenviable task of deciding whether to allow further petroleum development in an area that has been called by one biologist of the

U.S. Fish & Wildlife Service "the most untouched and pristine coast left in northern Alaska."

So, hoping to demonstrate that the mammals, birds, and fish who live in the refuge might be adversely affected by the extensive industrial corridors that would usurp their home grounds, Don cleans his windshield, adjusts the tracking antennas on his wings, loads Larry Martin and Tom Wilners, the biological technicians, into his plane, squeezes me in the back (observer), and taxis down the gravel runway of Barter Island—home of a D.E.W. line station, the Inupiat village of Kaktovik, and the main scrambling strip for entry into ANWR, the United States' second biggest, least spoiled and, some feel, most endangered wild country. Everyone has a war.

We head inland at 3000 feet. The desolate, spiny mountains of the Brooks Range lie ahead, the ice of the Arctic Ocean retreats behind. Below, the shadow of our plane crosses the pale-green, muskrat-brown tundra. Water lies everywhere: six major rivers, hundreds of ponds, and a horizon-to-horizon sheen of bog. Odd that the north slope of Alaska is, in meteorologic terms, a semi-desert. Still, one must take into account that less than 10 inches of precipitation fall annually, collecting above the permafrost and producing the spongy terrain that is so difficult to walk or build on, the despair of backpackers and civil engineers alike. Ideal country for caribou, though, who travel across it effortlessly on their big splayed hooves and long legs, give birth on its barrenness, and eventually die here, leaving the occasional antler as a memento to a life that is an enduring fast.

The beeps begin as we fly over the foothills. Don loses altitude. Larry peers from the starboard window, squinting into the sun. Tom, next to me in the rear of the plane, bends over a topographic map and puts an X on an anonymous looking hillside. Circling—now the peaks of the Brooks Range off the wing, now the ice of the distant ocean—we search for the radio-collared bear.

"There it is!" Larry's voice crackles on the headphones.

We stare at the drainage to which he points and sweep our binoculars over the tundra. Don loses more altitude and suddenly we see two hamsters, one larger than the other, grazing slowly, heads lowered to the ground.

"Sow and cub," says Larry.

Tom marks the information.

It seems that one could reach out the plane window and pick up the two blond rodents in his palm. Grizzly bears? Lower we glide. Don throttles back and coasts along the hillside. When we're five hundred feet above the bears, the sow and cub flee. Now they look like bears, but still in miniature, toy-shop size. We pull out before they ever become *Ursus arctos,* the largest carnivore left on the good green earth.

We head west along the foothills, finding bears in every drainage, 22 in all. We see a pair of wolves, white and black, who run, tails between their legs, through the scrub willow at the approach of the plane, and soon thereafter a couple musk ox, their shaggy coats making them appear, from 1000 feet, like the caparisoned horses in a child's cavalry. Round about noon we cross into Canadian airspace, only to discover that the coastal plain of the Yukon looks no different from the coastal plain of Alaska. It's just as vast, just as flat, and just as marked by an endless repetitive series of polygons, created when the tundra freezes, cracks, and heaves upwards, giving the northern landscape a geometric and wrought appearance that would please a theist. It's also just as marked for development as the adjacent hinterlands of Alaska.

Dome Petroleum, Esso, and Gulf Canada have sunk exploratory wells in the Beaufort Sea, and Esso has proposed a pipeline to transport crude up the Mackenzie River Valley. Gulf, on the other hand, has proposed a harbor for Stokes Point on the north shore of the Yukon. Dome would also like to see a harbor on the coast and has eyed Kings Point, just south of Herschel Island. Here Peter Kiewit Sons Co. Ltd., a multinational firm based in the U.S., has proposed a quarry, using the rock to build artificial islands for drilling structures in the Beaufort Sea. The access road Kiewit would construct, as well as a proposed all-weather highway connecting Kings Point with the Dempster Highway, further to the south, would transect the migration of the Porcupine Caribou Herd.

Moreover, the Stokes port and quarry are within the boundaries of the 15,000-square-mile area of the northern Yukon that was withdrawn from appropriation in 1978 and which was designated for national park status in 1984. The delays in finalizing the park boundaries have stemmed from the unresolved land claims of the Inuvialuit (Eskimo) and Dene (Indian), and the lack of a comprehensive development package that would balance extracting energy resources with preserving a subsistence culture. The delays, however, have made industry impatient, and the result has been the far-reaching plans for the Yukon coast. Taken one by one, such developments could prove benign in their impact. But strung together into an interlocking web of arctic industrial centers and transportation corridors, they could seriously affect the free movements of the great herds of wild northern deer, according to Ken Whitten, a caribou biologist with the Alaska Department of Fish and Game. One of his colleagues and one of Alaska's most well-known caribou researchers, Ray Cameron, has also expressed concern over the long-range effects of extreme North Slope development. In a recent issue of *Arctic,* Cameron noted the "haphazard matrix of roads, pipelines and facilities" that have characterized the expansion of Prudhoe Bay and the consequent loss of caribou habitat that has occurred. If a large percentage of the Arctic Slope were developed in a similar unplanned manner, Cameron believes that the ". . . loss of access to favorable calving areas might . . . be catastrophic to calving caribou, their offspring . . . and, ultimately, to the herd itself." A third caribou biologist, the Canadian George Calef, has also found the prospect of development on the caribou's traditional calving grounds a threatening prospect. In *Caribou and the Barrenlands* he has written:

> At the time of birth cows are more wary than at any other season; they will flee if disturbed and try to lead their calves away, even before the young ones are dry and steady on their feet. Any concentrated human activity on the calving grounds would interfere with the cow's all-important early maternal behaviour: cleaning the calf, nursing, and forming the vital cow-calf bond. If cows abandoned the traditional calving grounds for less favourable areas, fewer calves would survive. Therefore the calving grounds of all the herds should be made inviolable wildlife sanctuaries, off-limits to all industrial activity and transportation corridors.

Would that the world were so simple. Years have gone into the making of an international caribou treaty that must take into account the needs of animals, Native hunters, the state government of Alaska, the territorial government of the Yukon, and the federal governments of the U.S. and Canada. The treaty continues to be negotiated and the issues remain complex—so complex (and the stakes so high) that the Canadian Minister of Indian and Northern Affairs, John Munro, decided to temporarily reject both Gulf's and Peter Kiewit's proposals, pending the creation of a master development plan for the northern Yukon. [In 1984 limited industrial activity was sanctioned within the boundaries of the new national park.]

If the caribou who annually cross this web of proposed industrial corridors only stayed put, everyone whose livelihood revolves around their habits might have an easier time. But the Porcupine Herd is as migratory as a flock of oceanic birds and has been since long before a neat international boundary was drawn down the 141st parallel.

The herd's journey begins in March as small bands of deer leave the forested valleys of the central Yukon and the country surrounding the Arctic Village. Grouping together, they walk to the coastal plain of the northeastern Yukon and the Arctic National Wildlife Refuge. Here, free from predation by wolves as well as harassment by insects, which in late May still haven't hatched, the cows drop their calves and begin to graze on the new tundra shoots—a rich carpet of high quality nutrients that, in the case of the Arctic National Wildlife Refuge, lies over what has been called by the *Oil & Gas Journal* "Alaska's biggest known untapped structure," perhaps rivaling Prudhoe Bay in yield. By late July the caribou retrace their route to the Yukon and the mountains on the south side of the Brooks Range and there, pawing through the snow for lichens, spend a dark and ruminative winter, reflecting on whatever caribou reflect on while chewing their cuds.

Whether these northern deer (not to mention the grizzly bears, musk ox, wolves, swans, phalaropes, old squaw, arctic char, bowhead whales, seals, and polar bears who also make the north coast their home) can adapt to major changes on their home range as well as some of their southern cousins have—the whitetail deer, for instance—no biologist can yet say. And that's precisely what the 1002 study is designed to find out, with its radio collars on newborn calves, its hundreds of hours of air time (at $185 an hour), and its research camps spread across the coastal plain.

In the Helio we bank west, climb, and in the distance spy a helicopter over the ocean, making its way back to Barter Island. It's probably the boys from Western Geophysical, who have a weather port camp next to the D.E.W. line station. Outfitted with hot and cold running water, several thousand pounds of canned food and beer, and a library of video movies, they, too, are doing their bit for 1002. Come the winter of 1984, another exploration company, Geophysical Services, Inc. (GSI), a Dallas-based firm, will also be on the coastal plain, laying seismic line from Caterpillar-drawn sled trains. Of the eight geophysical study proposals submitted to U.S. Fish & Wildlife, only this one was chosen by Keith Schreiner, regional director for the Service's Alaska region. His reasoning was based on public commentary, which stressed that, if the coastal plain must be explored, unnecessary duplication of the seismic work should be avoided. In addition, Schreiner felt that GSI's plan showed the highest degree of technical adequacy and environmental sensitivity.

Prudential as his reasoning was, his decision to allow any ground survey at all brought much criticism from the native, scientific, and environmental communities. Cat-trains have left their mark on tundra from the Mackenzie River to Barrow, and, despite the fact that the seismic crews of GSI will be monitored by Fish & Wildlife observers, many Alaskans, particularly those in the village of Kaktovik, felt that the refuge, a hilly region often blown clear of snow, will be permanently scarred. Although a less injurious helicopter seismic survey was proposed, it was rejected primarily because the data it would produce might not be as accurate as the information generated with ground techniques. However, not a few participants in the environmental impact hearings felt that the choice of a ground survey over a helicopter one sprang from Washington and not Anchorage and was born in the Department of the Interior's current leaning toward development. In short, if the coastal plain of ANWR were scarred by exploration, it would be a less likely candidate for protection and a more likely shoo-in for use as an energy reservoir when Congress makes its decision in 1986.

Even though the impacts of a ground survey may be of concern to recreationists in the rest of Alaska and Outside, few of these people will feel the results of the seismic exploration as keenly as the residents of Kaktovik who live off the animals of the refuge. Loren Ahlers, a former D.E.W. line worker and a resident of Kaktovik for 12 years, is one who uses the refuge often. Married to an Inupiat woman and the father of two children, he now supervises the Kaktovik powerhouse, water delivery, and sewage and trash pickup. A big man with dusty blond hair and blue eyes, Ahlers has a deep voice and a soft, self-effacing handshake. His house faces south toward the refuge and the Brooks Range, and looking in that direction from the warmth of his living room, he spoke of what the country meant to him. "I fish in there." He nodded to the south. "Hunt caribou, moose. . . . I camp in there. And now they're letting cat-trains in because the government has subsurface rights." Likening the federal government to a colonizing power, Ahlers concluded glumly, "We don't control our own destiny."

In a June 21, 1983, public hearing held in Kaktovik, Marilyn Akiak echoed Ahlers' sentiments and expressed what other villagers feel: "I don't know how the rest of Alaska is, but I know it's very cold, and the weather up here is very bad. I mean, you can go for days, be fogged in, or you can go for days being windblown. . . . Half the time these roads aren't open, and half the time the stores don't keep their shelves stocked. . . . Once you're out of something, you're just out of it. And we can't just hop in the car and run to the grocery store like you people can, go pick up a head of lettuce or a side of meat or a pound of bacon. . . . I mean, we have to sit here and wait, we have to wait for the weather. Our life revolves around the weather and the land . . . and . . . the animals."

Yet, some residents of Kaktovik find the prospect of oil development and its spinoffs not all that gloomy. Marx Sims, who has lived in the village for 20 years and has operated a hotel for backpackers, river runners, and now exploration crews, didn't testify against development at the public hearings. In fact, he is expanding his operations. Looking at the construction materials stacked between his family's home and the guest bunkhouse, he said, "Development is inevitable. So I'm gearing up for it. Television, electricity, heat," he continued, "have become a necessity. People need the jobs to pay for these developments. If the electricity goes off, people don't have wood stoves or gravity space heaters." A strong wind came off the ice of the Beaufort Sea and blew the fur-trimmed hood of Sims' parka. Jamming his hands into his pockets, he added, "As the youngsters get an education this'll become a city just like any other city, only with a different weather pattern."

A few days later, Archie Brower, the then mayor of Kaktovik, took a few minutes to push his chair away from his cluttered desk. Looking over his black spectacles and reflecting on the changes taking place across Barter Island, Brower said, "Even my kids hardly understand Eskimo."

The decline of Inupiaq culture is sad to see, yet it didn't begin with seismic exploration. American whalers bringing firearms and alcohol to the Beaufort Sea in the 1890s, trader Tom Gordon who came to Barter Island in 1923, and the building of the D.E.W. Line System during the Cold War all played a role in drawing Eskimos into a cash economy and tying them to a worldwide culture. Since oil was discovered on the North Slope, the ties have become more enduring and the ways of subsistence hunting more difficult to follow. Certainly since June of 1983, the choices for the village of Kaktovik, once a fairly isolated community, have become more complex.

In that month the Arctic Slope Regional Corporation finalized a land swap with the Department of the Interior. ASRC surface rights in the Gates of the Arctic National Park were traded for subsurface rights on 92,160 acres of federal land in the refuge, the surface rights of which were owned by Kaktovik Inupiat Corporation. (Brower, acting as Kaktovik Corporation head and not as mayor, had given his provisional approval of the trade in an Anchorage meeting. No village forum was held and the trade was completed without the benefit of input from Kaktovik.) The expected happened. ASRC began negotiating with Chevron, USA, Inc. for lease and exploration rights, and their hope is to sink three wildcat wells by the winter of 1985.

Certainly everyone in Kaktovik stands to benefit if an oil facility is placed on the acreage in question. Yet the same block of land is often used by the Porcupine Caribou Herd for calving. Undoubtedly the herd will find another calving grounds, unless that land is also being used for petroleum development. We then are faced with the scenario described by the biologists Whitten, Cameron, and Calef: 140,000 caribou with no place to go, or at least no place that meets their unique nutritional and reproductive requirements. And so, like many of us who now meet the wilderness via the interface of technological assistance, the Inupiats find themselves in a double bind—how to extract one natural resource without destroying another. Sooner or later it's a question each of us must answer . . . or avoid.

After enjoying another half-hour of Maple Leaf skies, we cross back into Stars and Stripes country and drone westward to Barter Island where we sit on the ground fogbound, for a day. When we're able to fly again, we head eastward—this time in a Beaver piloted by Patrick Valkenburg, a biologist at Alaska's Department of Fish & Game who is helping to photograph the post-calving aggregation of the Porcupine Herd. When we're about 90 miles out from Kaktovik, we notice that a fuzzy disease has appeared on the horizon. Spreading beneath us, it flows, congeals, and sends off long fingers of colony bacteria at a dizzying rate.

Patrick banks and descends. When he straightens the aircraft, we can see that the disease is composed of individual caribou—the Porcupine Herd itself, massed on the coastal plain near Beaufort Lagoon. Numbering close to 100,000 animals now, the aggregated herd of bulls, cows, and calves looks to be 10 miles broad and 10 long. Large parts of the herd graze peacefully; other groups, several thousand animals at a time, hurry toward the mountains or the sea. Wind waves of refracted light shimmer across the tundra and bend the legs of the deer so that they appear to swim through a translucent and rolling surf.

We circle and drink the view. We might be looking at a school of silver-sides through a scuba mask or the ghosts of a billion passenger pigeons. But we're not. We're looking at one of the largest herds of mammals left in North America, a herd that travels hundreds of miles across tundra and mountains while we to the south sit at our desks, work in factories, read newspapers. And yet, what is below remains a herd. It's impossible to imagine that there are individually bonded cows and calves down there, with distinct smells, voices, discomforts, pleasures, and deaths.

Patrick drops a little lower to give us a more intimate view. Now we can see tiny, three-week-old calves amidst the melee of adults. I try to pick out one calf and one cow and focus on them. But my attempt fails. The cow and calf I've singled out blend into those around them and are replaced by another and another seemingly identical cow and calf. I'm left with what Alaska always leaves me with when viewed from the air: the same white and black wolves, the same stolid musk ox, the same patient, rooting, and unremarkable bear. Yet confronted by the vast herd below, something not connected to the dry notebook and pen I hold in my hand, but lodged within my chest, loses its footing, clutches, and stops. I'm carried east with the herd. Is there any person so civilized who would not go along?

We accompany their wanderings for only two days, photographing their aggregation on the windswept plain filled with marigolds and daisies. Then they head east with determination. And we return west to Kaktovik. As we climb from the airstrip and head toward the bank of fog on the horizon, the empty tundra still seems to vibrate with the passing of the deer. No one talks for a few minutes as we gaze out the windows at the last stragglers of the herd and the features of the coastal plain passing beneath us like a map: There the Arctic Ocean, there the Aichilik River, there the obvious line from the Mackenzie Delta to Prudhoe Bay where a pipeline and road may someday run, enabling many of us to get closer to the wilderness while inevitably changing what we came to see.

Below, a small white spot catches my eye—again bacteria-like and inconsequential. Raising my binoculars, I focus on the white fleck and discover two swans nesting on the tundra, perfectly alone and at ease on the coast plain of ANWR, birthed out of ANILCA, child of ANCSA, studied under 1002, another X among the many data bits, heading to Washington, far far away.

IV

The Hunt

The Mammoth Hunters

ESKIMO LEGEND

"The Mammoth Hunters" is an Eskimo hunting tale of the prehistoric past as told by Michael Peglirook from KOBUK RIVER PEOPLE *(1961) by J. L. Giddings, published by the University of Alaska Studies of Northern Peoples, Fairbanks.*

Now and then, mammoths come around. One time, near the Salmon River, a man was out hunting. His name was Ataogoraachuak. He was hunting marmots in the mountains. He wasn't wearing any boots, he never wore them while hunting on the rocks—he was barefoot. That time of year the marmots were fat. In a while Ataogoraachuak had caught two marmots, and he ate them both. But while he was up on the mountain the weather got foggy. He stayed on the mountain trail, and when he looked down the creek he saw some great big animal walking along, as though it was floating, barely touching the ground. He could see its breath.

Ataogoraachuak trailed this animal, which was floating just above the ground. And then he saw that three men were following the animal, tracking it. The men had spears and they too were walking along without touching the ground. And soon, two of the men walked right up to Ataogoraachuak while the third man went on following the big animal. The two fellows said to Ataogoraachuak, "Our companion will catch up with that mammoth just up ahead."

"I don't want to go see it," Ataogoraachuak said.

The two men thought Ataogoraachuak was lazy and offered to pay him to go down and see the mammoth. "If you go down there to the mammoth," they said, "you'll become a great shaman. You'll always know where bears hole up in the wintertime. You'll be a great seer."

But Ataogoraachuak didn't want to go down. He said, "If you will fix it so I can cut jade and drill it with my little finger, I'll go."

To Ataogoraachuak's great surprise, the men said, "Sure, okay, it's done. From now on, you'll be able to drill jade with your little finger."

So, they all walked down the path and soon they got to the mammoth. It was lying dead by a lake. This was a great, huge animal with long curved ivory tusks growing out of its head.

The three men, who walked without touching the ground, went to work divvying up the mammoth.

Now the three hunters said to Ataogoraachuak, "Go and fetch some wood and build a fire so we can cook mammoth meat."

Ataogoraachuak got the wood, all nice and dry, and piled it up, but when he tried to light it, it acted like green wood and wouldn't burn. And when the wood wouldn't burn, one of those hunters took off his clothes and walked to the lake. Then he went under the water and fetched some wood. And when he got back with wood from the lake, right away he built a fire with it and it burned like it had kerosene on it. Then the three hunters started to eat, and when they'd eaten some, they put some meat in their packsacks. Before they set out, they told Ataogoraachuak, "Go on home, and when you've walked a ways, turn around and try to look at us."

So Ataogoraachuak started home, and in a while he looked back at the three fellows, and they were up in the air! They were walking with their packsacks up in the air!

Now, when Ataogoraachuak got home, he took out some jade and found he could cut it and drill it with his little finger. Everyone in his village knew then he was a great shaman.

Those fellows that hunt the big animal with ivories live up in the air, halfway to the sky above us. They too are oldtime shamans. From the past. When the weather is bad around here, those fellows go hunting. When the weather is fine, and clear, they stay home. Only shamans can see them. The name of the big animal with ivories is *kilyigvuk.*

Aghvook Comes

FROM *Island Between*

MARGARET E. MURIE

Margaret E. Murie is a respected writer and environmentalist. She arrived in Alaska in 1911 at age nine and later married Olaus Murie, the biologist, and spent many years exploring the Alaska wilderness with him. The author of several books, Murie today lives in Wyoming. "Aghvook Comes" is taken from her novel, ISLAND BETWEEN *(1977), set on St. Lawrence Island in the icy Bering Sea, where the Siberian Yup'ik Eskimos have lived for several thousand years. This excerpt is about one of the most important events of the islanders' year—the whale hunt.*

All his life, Toozak was sure, he would remember his first winter of hunting as a long misery of early rising in cold dawns, of stumbling down to the shore behind the older ones while a cruel icy wind bit at him, before the blood in his sleepy veins was yet warmed.

Now it was spring and dawn came earlier, but the hunters made up for that by rising in the middle of the night, so as to be out hunting with the first light; the wind was still cruel. Toozak wondered if he were the only one who noticed these things. Of course he kept it to himself; a hunter only thinks of the urgent doings of the chase, and all one heard now in the village was Aghvook and Ivick, whale and walrus. Of all the moons, this one was the most important.

Apangalook, with calm, strong steps, walked up and down before his boat through the dark hours of each night to guard it from visits of rivals who might pray to the evil spirits to give him bad luck in the hunt; then he roused his crew before daylight and set out for the long hours in the boat. Day after day this went on, and there were no whales. And all the while Toozak lived with that awful knowing that there was one soul praying to bring them bad luck! Yet he dared not tell Apangalook. He could only keep on offering his own young prayers. Certainly this was something to make one grow out of childhood quickly. Toozak felt old these days.

. . . .

The edges of the ice floes were bluer than the blue flowers which bloom on the sandspit in July, as blue as the flowers and as green as their leaves. A laughing little breeze made deep blue ripples in front of the boat; the sky was that same blue, and mountains of white clouds like giants' ningloos were sailing about up there. A male sawbill duck flew right in front of Toozak's face. He waved his paddle but missed him, and the other boys laughed. The duck was chasing a female, round and round, climbing into the air, streaking downward.

As the crew sailed and paddled steadily out toward more open water, they heard geese passing high overhead. Now a flock of puffins came swishing by, close to the water, and behind them, a cloud of Least Auklets! Whee-ee—the auklets again! Every man in the boat shouted and laughed, nodded to his neighbor, waved greetings to the auklets. Spring was really come, then—the auklets were back, and hunters could carry boiled meat in the whaling boats. Not until the auklets came was this permitted.

Hi-hi, winter was gone! Birds, clouds, sunshine, blue ripples and blue floats of ice all proclaimed it. A little flock of plovers flew over the boat. Toozak wondered how it felt to be one of those swift-flying ones. They made his heart lighter somehow. He stroked along easily. The very boat seemed lighter since the sun had come out and they had seen the birds. If only they could see—"Ah-eee." Toozak dropped his paddle, jumped to his feet, started to point, snatched his hand back as though he had burned it, then, clasping both hands behind his back, nodded his head to the left and said in a small trembling voice, "There is Aghvook."

Instantly, they were all paddling like demons! Toozak paddled too, but still trembling. Kulukhon brought the walrus-stomach sail about and sat with eager face, holding the line and watching Apangalook for orders.

Poor Toozak! He breathed a great sigh. What a narrow escape! He had had the good fortune to see the first whale, and then had nearly insulted him by pointing a finger at him. Aghvook and the all-powerful Keyaghunuk who sent him were so easily offended, every consideration must be shown them. Toozak's heart pounded in his throat. He paddled fiercely, not even glancing at Tatoowi who paddled beside him. One of the great moments of life had just come and his thoughts were whirling like a flock of kittiwakes. Only this he realized: they must paddle and watch Apangalook for orders, and perhaps Keyaghunuk would listen to their prayers rather than to those of that handsome evil one back in the village.

They were fairly flying over the smooth dark sea, and there was the tall plume of Aghvook's breath, much closer than the first time. He was traveling almost toward them, heading north along the island coast. Every man was tense, putting every ounce of strength into his strokes. Aghvook disappeared. "Slower now," spoke Apangalook softly, "see where he comes up next."

Kulukhon took in the sail. Quietly they slid along; even their breathing seemed too loud. "Whoosh"—only fifty yards away, a fountain of hot steam rose into the air, and up came a great black back which gleamed a moment in the sun. The crew held the boat motionless and waited for the black hulk to sink again.

Apangalook's eyes were like the stars of a cold winter sky; his thick lips were pressed into a flat line; the veins in his temples throbbed. He looked at Pungwi in the bow, and Pungwi looked back at him and nodded. "This time we try," said Apangalook softly, and the boat shot forward again. Pungwi rose in the bow, planted his feet solidly, examined once more the ivory head of his harpoon, the lines leading from it. From the tail of his eye, he could see that Timkaroo and Tatoowi were poised to drop their paddles and throw over the three pokes.

They paddled on in the course Aghvook had taken. Toozak had by now gotten the signal poke, a special inflated sealskin, fastened to a slender pole which he held up as high as he could and waved, and then lashed in the stern behind his father's seat. He glanced back over the water and ice and saw that two boats back there already had their pokes up; they had seen the signal and would be coming.

Toozak had no time to look further. Aghvook was almost under them. Up came his wet breath again. "Oh, hoh," spoke Apangalook sharply. Swiftly he swerved the boat to the left of the whale and yet more swiftly they paddled. Pungwi lifted his long harpoon over his head; right up almost onto the whale's shoulder the boat sped, then Aghvook's back began sliding up out of the water, and Pungwi struck. He meant that harpoon to go clear through Aghvook's eight inches of blubber and stay there, and that is what it did. At the same instant Timkaroo and Tatoowi, both sitting on the right side, threw over the pokes of Pungwi's harpoon.

Aghvook went down like a rock, flicking his enormous flukes as he went and enveloping his hunters with a great salt wave. But they could not notice that. Timkaroo was watching the coil of rope as it payed out. To get caught in that meant sure death. Tons of mighty flesh were pulling that line down, deep under. The rest of the crew were paddling furiously to get clear. Under the water went the pokes. Pungwi's harpoon was holding so far!

Apangalook now raised his paddle straight up into the air and shouted out with a great voice, "Wo-ho-ho, ho-ho."

Again he raised his paddle high and "Wo-ho-ho, ho-ho" rang out, again. Apangalook's boat had struck a whale. Toozak began to feel younger!

Now the chase began.

Two pokes and a long black back were up again and through the water they raced. Aghvook was towing them along at a furious speed. Apangalook's face was set, but gleaming with excitement as he steered to keep them free of the line. White spume flew from the boat's bow; the breeze of their passage whistled in their ears. Toozak felt he was being carried along in a mad dream, a sorcerer's dream; things had become too exciting to be real. They all sat quiveringly alert, paddles poised, streams of sweat pouring down over their faces. After all the thought and planning, the songs and sacrifices, here they were, actually in the midst of a battle with Aghvook, the greatest beast.

Pungwi lifted his great stone-tipped spear, but they all knew they could not hope to spear Aghvook yet; they had to have help, more harpoons, more pokes.

Toozak hardly dared look around, but he sensed boats coming up behind them. First came Wohtillin's, its crew swaying in unbelievable speed, taking in their sail and approaching from the other side of the whale, Ozook poised in the bow. Ozook, father of that Walanga, ignorant of his son's doings, about to help kill Apangalook's whale! Aghvook perhaps realized now that he was pulling more than his own weight. He slowed a bit, and in that moment Wohtillin's boat sped up close and Ozook struck.

Ozook was one of the best, and they needed the best this day. Two true strikes. Down went Aghvook, and this time Wohtillin's crew was backing frantically away from the tumult of his descent. For he was angry now. Something was bothering him too much. The great hulk rolled and shook as it went down and raised the sea into real waves.

Both boats pulled their lines straight and the men breathed a moment, for now Aghvook had six pokes fastened to him and it would be harder and harder to stay down. Come up he must, and here were the rest of the boats now, four of them, Irrigoo's first, holding off to the side, ready to come in and strike.

So it went. Hours of racing headlong behind the angry giant, far out westward, till the island began to lose its height; back again, straight for shore, and toward floating ice cakes, where everyone was breathless, and Apangalook's were not the only lips which moved in silent pleading with the great Spirit. If the whale dove under one of those, the line must be cut, and the quarry, with lines, pokes, and harpoons, would all be lost.

And crueler yet, all knew that the loss, thus, of a whale once struck would mean loss also of a member of the captain's family. So it had always been. This fear was forever with them and froze their hearts into a cold misery whenever Aghvook headed toward ice. Even in the loose slush ice there was plenty of danger from fouled lines, and every paddle was busy. Toozak shivered and at the same time felt sweat running down his cheeks. It seemed that he was living years of his life flying along over that blue water.

Aghvook had three boats on him now and still it went on; the breeze increased a little, the white clouds scudded faster in the blue sky; the sea was darker. Kittiwakes cried overhead, the puffins, murres and auklets skimmed back and forth, and fulmars, the whale birds, had also sensed the thing which would interest them and glided and wheeled about on quiet wings, watching that queer scene. A long blackness streaking through the water with upright seals wavering along on top of it, and racing along behind, three boats with six stiff figures in each one—so it looked to the fulmars' eyes. It also looked like a big meal for fulmars before long!

Toozak was really surprised when he came out of the trance of excitement and realized it was still daylight when Aghvook was finally tired and the lances of Pungwi and Ozook could find his heart. They were fortunate. They had been able to lance the whale on one of his trips toward shore, so that towing in was not the back-breaking long ordeal it sometimes was. They had seen many other whales blowing during that day but the boats had stayed with Apangalook. They knew his whale was a big one and it would take all their forces to get him in.

Now Apangalook stepped to the bow and from the outside of his charm bag took two beaked eye-shields of young mukluk skin, fastened one on his own forehead, handed the other to Pungwi. This was a day of triumph for these two; it was only right that the people should be able to see who had struck the whale.

Aghvook floated there, harmless, wonderful great hulk, great gift to Inuit. The boats floated about at a little distance. What a good feeling, now, for all the crews, to drop paddles and slump in their seats and rest a bit while Apangalook did the next thing. Toozak and Tatoowi found time to look at each other now, and smile, and Toozak felt all the worries and all the old age flying away. He felt good inside for the first time in weeks, and he would be so glad to smile into Walanga's face when they brought Aghvook in!

The boat was paddled slowly to Aghvook's side, just in front of his tail, and started slowly around, close to the black body. Apangalook raised his paddle and shouted, "Wo-ho-ho"; slowly they paddled along to Aghvook's head. "Wo-ho-ho." Around they slid to the other side of his head. "Wo-ho-ho." Along the side, close to the flukes again, once more Apangalook's voice rang out over the water, "Wo-ho-ho!"

Now to work. Some cutting up must be done before they towed him in. Keen-edged stone blades, fastened to long handles, now came into every man's hand, and all the boats clustered about, against that quiet body. All life, all fierceness was gone from it; it had become merely a mass of food, of building material, of fuel, for the small lively creatures clustered about it.

Everyone was cutting. Of course Apangalook and his crew would have half the slabs, and all flukes and flippers, eye, and nostrils. Apangalook himself leaned over and carefully removed the eyes, the nostrils. The center part of the fluke was cut out and leaned carefully in the very bow of the boat. Behind this, Apangalook and Pungwi carefully laid the eyes, in the bottom of the boat, behind these, the nostrils, then the flippers, and finally, a little astern of the middle of the boat, the ends of the flukes. In Apangalook's boat, things were always done in exactly the proper manner.

Now they were ready to fill the boat with slabs, with long sections of baleen, and finally to tow the rest of the monster in, the pokes still attached and helping to hold him up. And Apangalook did not forget to present two slabs of skin and blubber each to the old men who were in the other boats. It would be dangerous to be forgetful of the old.

They were perhaps a mile and a half from shore, and everyone bent to his stroke with a will, and the sails went up again. They were all tasting in anticipation the excitement in the village, the joy of women and children, the delicious flavor of success in hunting—also the delicious flavor of munktuk. Feasting and song and unrestrained mirth there would be on Sevuokuk this night.

The fifth and last boat to arrive at the scene of the chase took its place next to the whale's head and fastened its line firmly into the body. The fourth boat came next, then the third, then Irrigoo's boat, then Wohtillin's, and leading the whole line, Apangalook's.

Approaching the land, Apangalook and his crew raised their paddles and shouted the call of triumph, "Wo-ho-ho, ho-ho," and again, when they were very close in and could see all the eager crowd on shore, loudly, happily, they sang out, "Wo-ho-ho-ho-ho."

None shouted more loudly than Toozak.

....

Toozak opened his eyes just a little. Apangalook knelt there, shaking him. "Come boy, you cannot get Iviek in your sleep. The north wind still blows; everyone will be out on the ice. Assoonga has broth ready for us."

Toozak opened his eyes wide and scrambled out of his furs. In place of the dream fox running over the tundra, a great black walrus loomed in his mind. This was the day—perhaps this day he would become a hunter. Assoonga was there, smiling, holding out to her son trousers and sox of reindeer skin. He pulled them on. She brought outer trousers and boots of sealskin, tucking fresh insoles of dry grass into the boots, then came inner and outer parkas of deerskin and mitts of dogskin. Toozak pulled them all on in a dreamy manner, and with his thoughts running ahead of him out onto the ice, drank broth in the same manner.

All the hunters were setting out; from every house they came, tramping across the smooth shore ice of the cove, climbing like furry animals over the heaped rough ice the pack was fast piling up at the edge of the solid ice, and which was making a straight line between the two headlands of the village cove. Toozak hurried after his father and Timkaroo, Timkaroo, the already-experienced hunter. He had often enough mentioned that to Toozak. Toozak set his lips and hurried.

On the heaped ice ridge they stopped and gazed out at ice, solid fields of it, broken only here and there by small black pools of water between the angles of great floes. Otherwise there was simply whiteness, rough and glinting. The great pack had arrived. As far as they could see, the ocean had become a great white field, quiet and solid.

Apangalook jumped down onto the pack ice. He glanced back at the island; fog hung over the slopes, almost down to the beach, but out over the ice were gray clouds scudding along with the north wind. Toozak knew that his father would watch that fog; so long as it hung low, the wind was pushing the pack tighter and tighter against the island and hunters were safe on the ice.

Over the white field the men spread out, quietly, quickly, eyes busy. Each hunter carried on his back a sealskin bag. Through the cover of the bag lay a stout stick. In one hand he carried his harpoon, six feet of strong wood bound well with baleen, an ivory harpoon head already stuck into the plug in the end of it and fastened to the hundred-foot coil of walrus-hide rope which the hunter carried in his other hand. This coil was tied about in several places with short pieces of baleen, to keep it from springing wide open into a trap for the hunter.

Rapidly and silently they traveled. Toozak was breathing hard. He *would not* be the last one! Still, "No danger of that," he thought. He glanced quickly back over the ice and laughed aloud. "Yahoh the lazy one is far behind; here he comes, shuffling like a great bear, always the last out on the ice, and the first one in at night! What would the people think if Yahoh came out first, one day?"

Toozak crawled cautiously over a jumble of broken ice and looked into an opening—black water with a clear green rim around its edge where it reflected the ice. Toozak noted all this but his attention was on a ripple in the water not far from him, a ripple which suddenly burst to release a huge bewhiskered face! Ongtopuk, the big male walrus!

He knew that Ongtopuk would only breathe once and go down again when he sensed something crouching there on the ice. Toozak's heart was pounding, but there were no other hunters very near and he got ready, poised, harpoon in hand, coil of rope thrown down on the ice. When Ongtopuk parted the black pool a second time, Toozak with one mighty thrust buried the harpoon head in that black muzzle.

Down went Ongtopuk with the five-inch piece of ivory deep in the soft flesh of his nostrils, and the hundred feet of rope began paying out swiftly, with the little baleen strips snapping as the rope broke them.

Yet swifter was Toozak. The instant he made his strike, the harpoon shaft was thrown behind him out of his way. He let out a great shout, "Come! Here is Iviek! Come quickly," even while he ducked his head and brought his sealskin hunting bag over it, onto the ice at his feet, pulled out the ivory-pointed stick from under its flap, and stuck the sharp point into the ice through the loop which marked the end of the curling rope. He knelt, holding that stick in the ice with all his strength.

All in an instant. In another instant Ongtopuk in his great rush had reached the end of the line, a great wounded hulk on the end of the line, with slender Toozak bearing back, his teeth set, then Timkaroo and Apangalook and many others there in a rush. Toozak's shout had brought them. Timkaroo knelt beside his brother, holding the stick. Apangalook stood ready with his own coil and harpoon. Quietly they watched. In a few seconds the poor whiskered face appeared again and received Apangalook's harpoon beside Toozak's, and they had another line on him. The next time, Timkaroo's harpoon drove home.

Ongtopuk was now desperate. With all this coming up and going down so quickly he had not been able to breathe properly. So at last he came up, blowing and snorting and breathing in great gasps; he simply must have more air. He could not go down again, and he hung there at the edge of the ice, a helpless creature. Apangalook handed his stone-tipped spear to Toozak. "Here, boy, it is your walrus. Strike for his heart."

Toozak took the spear, braced himself, set his teeth (oh, to make a clean stroke with Timkaroo watching!), drove the point through that black side. Ongtopuk's mouth opened with a terrible roar and blood gushed in a great stream from his side. Toozak looked around at Timkaroo, a bit dazed. Timkaroo's eyes were full of thoughts. "You may be a hunter, some day," he murmured, and smiled.

Now the work had only begun. By this time there were more helpers. Stout Pungwi, clever with the ivory ice pick in one end of his harpoon shaft, began chopping a rope-hold in the ice twenty feet back from the edge; he soon had a hold under which the rope was led. Two others dug solid stances for their harpoons, one back from the ice-hold a few feet, one a little to the side and halfway to the edge. Apangalook, with Toozak watching carefully, had cut two big slits in the skin of Ongtopuk's head. Through this he tied one end of the rope and it was led around the two harpoons and under the hold in the ice, and now everyone began to pull, slowly, steadily, minute after minute, sweat pouring off their faces, until at last Ongtopuk, that great hulk, came slowly, slowly over the edge of the ice.

Apangalook made the first cut. With his stone knife he cut straight down the walrus's breast. There was nothing, thought Toozak, that his quiet father did not know how to do. They pulled out the stomach, a great bag, all that two men could manage. "But we fix that a little bit," laughed Pungwi. "Hunting has some pleasures."

Pungwi slit the stomach, reached in with bare hand and, grinning, pulled out juicy clams and mussels, all nicely shelled and steaming. Every hunter did the same, and squatting there on the ice, rested and feasted. "Ongtopuk ate well," laughed Apangalook. "Now we are hungry too. This stomach will soon not be too heavy for you to drag alone, Toozak, but drag it carefully; it will make a fine drum someday."

Apangalook licked the delicious juice from his fingers, pulled on his mitts. This was not the time to sit and tell stories. He set to work again, Toozak close beside him, watching and doing just as he did, pushing back for future pleasure the crowding thoughts of the big thing which had happened to him this day on the ice. Tonight, on the sleeping platform, he could live it all over.

The hide, the layer of fine blubber, a little meat underneath, these were the slabs they cut off, each one all that a man could drag on a rope. On each man's bag hung many little coils of mukluk rope for just this work. Trip after trip they made to the solid shore ice, depositing the meat; it would be divided among all who had helped haul Ongtopuk up.

Toozak's walrus was not the only one caught that day. The opening he had discovered was quite large and into it came walrus and seal from all about. Live in the water they could and did—swimming about in that dark world under the ice, but always watching their breathing holes; from far off they could see the light filtering down in certain places. This meant air and life to them and there they must go, often to find, with the air, not life, but death. Inuit were on the ice today, and they must have much meat, much oil, many skins, else the year could be horrible.

Of course Yahoh harpooned nothing, but he was on hand to hold a rope in his hands and appear to haul up several walrus. "I wonder," said Timkaroo to Toozak, "how he makes so much sweat pour down his face, when one cannot see his muscles move when we pull!"

"Oh, he uses a lot of strength grunting," answered Toozak quickly. "Didn't you hear? He grunted louder than anyone when Apangalook gave the signal to pull."

Toozak had a warm feeling inside. This was wonderful, Timkaroo laughing with him, Toozak, as with an equal! He even felt warm toward that fake, Yahoh. He had furnished the joke for them to laugh about together. Toozak bent fiercely to his work. "It is good to have a Yahoh, perhaps," he thought as he pulled a big slab along, "else we would have to search for something else for our fun."

People must always have fun.

The fog stayed over the mountains all day long. On the ice pack, with daring, with skill, with strength, with hard, hard work, the hunters kept steadily on. This was the time. Over the pack near every opening, walrus and big seals were hauled out just as Toozak's had been hauled.

Timkaroo left the meat cutting long enough to harpoon a fine ribbon seal at a small breathing hole, and that was a great thing, for the pretty things would be there in the pack only a few days and then they would not be seen again until they came in spring, traveling north. Toozak saw his brother hauling the beautiful seal rapidly to shore.

Ah-hah! Timkaroo is not feeling the sting of this bitter north wind right now. He is thinking only of what a fine present he has for that round-faced Ega. Such a clothes-bag should make her feel warm toward him.

While the north wind held, there was no rest. Toozak finally added the walrus stomach to the growing pile of meat on the solid shore ice. He noticed that up on the shore old Ikmallowa and Iyakatan were slowly walking, up and down, standing a bit, walking again, always watching. They were the guardians; they had a task, watching the ice, the sky, the currents, the wind. So long as hunters were out there some older men would be watching from shore.

Toozak trudged back to the walrus again. Timkaroo was pulling out the great length of intestine, running his hand along it, squeezing the contents out upon the ice. He then took the hundred-foot-long tube, divided it in three, braided it; now it was ready to be carried home and hung up until Assoonga needed it for rain parkas and snowshirts.

Timkaroo looked up into the weary young face and laughed, "Ho, hunter boy, lots of fun to get Ongtopuk, eh? And lots of work too! Warm ningloo will feel pretty good tonight. Here is your walrus heart. What is happening?"

From beyond them they heard a shout, taken up from group to group and followed by sudden motion in every place. Timkaroo grasped his brother's arm and pointed. Over on the shore the two old men were slowly waving their white snowshirts and the hunters also could see now the fog was breaking and lifting.

"We have plenty of time yet," said Timkaroo. "They are waving *slowly*. But come along."

From far out over the pack, gray-white now in the deepening dusk, bulky black figures came, dragging slabs of precious meat behind them. The two old men stood still and waited; bitter cold it was for them, but they would watch until every hunter was safe on the shore ice. A good day on the ice would then be finished and along with the weary hungry hunters they too would go to the warm ningloos. The women would be waiting to help them out of sweat-soaked, ice-hung clothing and to serve them good food.

Toozak almost staggered across the rough ice, but his heart was glowing. He had made his first big catch and now was qualified to go upon the ice, able to care for himself, and his brother was treating him as an equal. He came up to the old men, and his grandfather, Ikmallowa, laid a hand on his shoulder. "Ah, so here is a new hunter, carrying home his first head of Iviek!"

Ikmallowa, by his words, had accepted Toozak the boy as Toozak the man. Nothing more could be added to this day!

Yet when the men were rid of their wet clothes, Toozak and his father, weary as they were, must still do one more thing. They carried in the great tusked head of Ongtopuk from the passageway and laid it by the centerpost. Behind them came Assoonga, carrying a little wooden bowl in which was some nunivak, the green tundra plant, and Tokoya, kneeling, took a pinch of greens from the bowl and placed it between the walrus's lips while all the others stood silent. Thus was the walrus spirit fed and appeased and more walrus in future hunting assured to Toozak.

So also must the house idol be fed. As after every ceremony, Tokoya now rose and crossed over to the front wall of the house where hung the carved wooden man with his hungry, smiling teeth. She rubbed a bit of nunivak against these clenched teeth, her long braids hanging back from her smooth round cheeks as she reached up. Toozak, tired as he was, noticed that his sister was becoming good to look at.

At last they could rest and eat and become warm clear through. What delicacies Ongtopuk provided! Clams from his paunch, slices of mangona, heart and liver and kidneys. The young folks could not eat any of the heart, lest they get bad sores from little scratches, but in the big platter, and in plenty, were other fine things. From the cheeks of the walrus Assoonga cut rich slices, being careful not to cut near the lips of course, for that would cause the lips of him who ate that part to twitch, and likewise she was careful not to get too near the ear, for the spirit who sent the meat to their shores must not be rendered deaf to their prayers.

"Did you bring in the breast bones? Ah, those soft bones, they are fine to chew!"

"Yes, we brought in everything good," answered Apangalook. "See, here is the last rib; that is a good one. Toozak, be careful not to eat near this rib, else you will have pains in your side when exercising." Apangalook laughed as he took the piece of rib and bit off juicy bites of raw meat. He smacked his lips loudly. Such good food deserved proper appreciation. He had forgotten cold and the weariness of long hours on the ice.

He looked about at his family, squatted in a happy circle on the floor about the platter. Heat and glow from two lamps in the corners made everything comfortable There was Ikmallowa, worn, almost nodding over his meat, but content after his long watch; there was Assoonga's lively little old mother Yokho, cutting up a piece of liver and feeding choice bits to fat little Sekwo, who accepted all the nice bites her grandmother handed her in an absent-minded manner, all the while gazing in round-eyed wonder at her brother Toozak, who had suddenly become a hunter and left his boyhood behind. Apangalook watched Sekwo's eyes and smiled. He too could gaze with proud eyes at his sons, so quickly had they changed from small boys swinging bird bolas and netting crabs to strong men able to hold their own on the ice. Any father would feel good!

Apangalook's eyes went clear round the circle, back to his Assoonga of the happy glance, busy cutting more pieces of heart on the end of the platter, and Tokoya, round and supple and smooth of skin. His family, well fed, in warmth and safety. Apangalook was well satisfied this night.

Spearing Grizzly Bears

FROM *Shadows on the Koyukuk*

SIDNEY HUNTINGTON, AS TOLD TO JIM REARDEN

*The son of an Athabascan Indian mother and a white trapper/trader father,
Sidney Huntington grew up along the banks of the Koyukuk River in Alaska's
remote interior. His remarkable life story is the subject of* SHADOWS ON THE
KOYUKUK: AN ALASKAN NATIVE'S LIFE ALONG THE RIVER *(1993), which
Alaskan author and editor Jim Rearden wrote from many taped interviews
and conversations with his longtime friend, Sidney Huntington. "Spearing
Grizzly Bears," from that book, describes what he believes is the last
traditional Koyukon grizzly bear hunt with a spear.*

When war came in December 1941, at the Japanese bombing of Pearl Harbor, Jenny and I had six children—
Franklin, Marie, Electa, Arnold, John, and Leonard.
Nevertheless, I went to Anchorage to enlist in the Army. I
had never seen such turmoil. People crowded the streets;
construction continued day and night, with trucks and tractors running
continuously.

At the Army recruiting office, I completed a questionnaire. The recruiter
left and returned shortly with a civilian, who said, "I understand you can
work with metal."

"Yes, I've done a little sheet metal work," I replied. Charlie Swanson had
taught me some of the basics at Batza River, and I had once worked for a
short time helping on a sheet metal job at Galena.

"We need sheet metal workers at Fort Richardson," he said. "You don't
have to go into the Army. We'll give you a draft classification that will keep
you out of the service."

"But I want to do my share," I said. During World War II every able-
bodied Alaskan wanted to help his country.

"You can help best by working for us as a sheet metal worker," he
answered.

I went to work at Fort Richardson near Anchorage as a sheet metal roofer on January 1, 1942. One week later I was promoted to sheet metal roofing foreman. I worked all spring and all summer, night and day, for as many hours as I could stand. I bought a house in Anchorage, and Jenny and the kids joined me. I had never lived under such stress. People were everywhere, crowding and pushing. We stood in lines to buy clothing, food, and cigarettes. Everyone was in a hurry. Living was expensive, although I was making more money than I had ever dreamed of making.

That fall, as I put roofs on military buildings, hundreds of flocks of geese flew over. With every flock heading south I'd raise my eyes and remember the sweet silence of the Koyukuk, the smell of spruce forests, the yelp of sled dogs, and thousands of square miles of beautiful, unpeopled land. Those great Vs of birds and their wild calls seemed to be telling me, "Sidney, you weren't bred to live like this. You don't belong in this crowded place."

Finally, I went to the colonel in charge of the base. "I've got to leave, Colonel," I told him.

"Why? You're doing a good job."

"I've trained a man to do my job."

I was unable to express my strong feeling of homesickness, but somehow he understood. He called Galena, where a new Air Force base was under construction, and found me a job as foreman of an oiling truck and a crew of twenty men. With relief and gratitude, I agreed to take the job. Jenny and I sold our Anchorage house and moved to Galena.

At Galena I was only a ten-minute walk from the Alaskan wilds where I had lived most of my life. I renewed my ties with the forests and streams by hunting, trapping, picking berries, and fishing in my off-hours.

The Galena Air Force Base was originally a Civil Aeronautics Authority (today the Federal Aviation Administration) airfield. During World War II, it was the first stop for Russian pilots flying American lend-lease warplanes from Fairbanks to Russia. During the war, I saw as many as 132 Bell Airacobra (P-39) fighter planes parked there, awaiting improved weather so they could fly to Nome. Altogether, the Russians accepted 7,929 American warplanes at Fairbanks and flew them to Nome via Galena. From Nome, the planes flew across the Bering Straits to Siberia, then to the Eastern Front, where they flew in combat against the Germans.

The Air Force decision to build at Galena created a boomtown on the north bank of the Yukon River, 575 river miles from the Bering Sea. About thirty-five people lived in Galena in 1941 at the start of construction. With the influx of people, the quiet village became a noisy tent city. During wartime, Galena's population ballooned to at least 3,000.

The Air Force first arrived in Galena via the Yukon River with six barges full of tractors, trucks, and cranes. Twenty soldiers were dumped on the beach with that heavy equipment. They had no blankets and no housing. The Koyukon people of Galena took those GIs into their homes as if they were their own kids, including the commanding officer, a Lieutenant O'Neil. The men slept and ate at the homes of Native families, while they ran the tractors, cranes, and trucks to build the airfield.

The Galena Native homes were mostly small, simple log cabins, but they were warm and open to these hardworking young men. They became homes away from home for the soldiers, and many close relationships were forged.

That winter, soldiers built a huge domed airplane hangar. To bolt the girders in place, they worked 150 feet in the air from buckets lifted by draglines, never losing a day of work, no matter how cold or how windy. I saw them working at −58 degrees. Those rugged men became highly respected for their accomplishments during the time they lived at Galena. Some of them fell in love with Alaska and our way of life. Upon discharge from the service, many settled in Alaska and married Native girls.

Life changed for many local residents who found permanent jobs at the Galena Air Force Base. From seasonal trapping and commercial fishing, with a consequent seasonal income, they converted to a partial cash economy with year-round income. Most continued to largely depend upon game and fish for food.

In 1939, the last boat that Jimmy and I whipsawed lumber for and built at Hog River was the thirty-two-foot *Koyukuk*. She was long and skinny, with a five-foot beam and a reverse-curve bow. With the twenty-horsepower Kermath marine engine we installed, the *Koyukuk* could make about twenty miles an hour, fast for the time.

Jimmy's personal Pearl Harbor on December 7, 1941, was the death of his wife Celia that day, from tuberculosis. Jimmy and Celia had a daughter, Christine. Three years later Jimmy married Flora Charles. In time they had seven children, but Jimmy and Flora split up, and Jimmy kept all the kids and later married Marion, a girl from Koyukuk, who helped Jimmy raise all those kids plus an adopted daughter. When Jimmy and Marion split up, he never remarried.

In 1943, with the *Koyukuk,* Jimmy started towing rafts of floating gasoline barrels from Nenana to the Air Force base at Galena where the fuel was needed for Russia-bound warplanes. The barrels were held together with two-by-four frames, and some of the rafts held as many as 2,000 fifty-five-gallon drums. Jimmy towed these rafts down the Tanana River to the Yukon River, then down the Yukon to Galena.

At Galena, the army picked four drums at a time out of the water with a dragline. Thousands of those barrels, empty and full, were eventually scattered around Galena, along back trails and in the woods. Alaskans nicknamed gasoline drums "tundra daisies," for they seemed to sprout everywhere in the Territory.

In the spring of 1943, after sticking to my wartime jobs at Anchorage and Galena for seventeen months almost without a break, I applied for a month of leave and mushed a dog team from Galena to the headwaters of the Huslia River, a tributary to the Koyukuk. I wanted to make a lone hunt for beaver. After the stress of wartime work, the hunt and the solitude were more important to me than any money I would make. But on the way, at Cutoff, I encountered Louis Golchik, a Koyukon elder, who was dying of tuberculosis, and he asked me to take him with me.

"Sidney, it will be my last hunt, for I don't have long to live," he said. "I promise I won't be in your way."

"Sure, Louie," I agreed, for he was a wonderful old man. "If you'll take care of camp, I'll do the rest."

We traveled by dogsled, pulled by two of my poorest dogs and three dogs given to me by Steven Attla. Attla was leaving for military service, and he had to get rid of his dogs before he left. Upon reaching our destination we killed the dogs, and, after breakup, drifted back downriver in canoes we made with spruce frames carved with axe and knife, and covered with canvas I had hauled in the sled.

During our hunt we lingered over many evening campfires when I should have been hunting, because the failing Louis wanted to share his memories. During that time he told me of the last Koyukon winter spear hunt for grizzly bear. He had been one of the hunters.

....

I have hunted with several older Koyukon men who sometimes talked about the old ways and the old days, including Johnny Oldman, Little Sammy, Edwin Simon, and Louis Golchik. Many aspects of old Athapaskan culture are almost unknown because of a taboo against talking about them. In modern times, many elders have been reluctant to talk because they don't want to be considered superstitious, for some of their beliefs would be so labeled today. Another compelling reason for silence was humility. Because he was dying, Louis Golchik was willing to talk about forbidden subjects.

For many years, out of respect for the elders, I have not discussed many of the old beliefs or repeated stories I heard. But most of the elders I once knew are gone, and many young Koyukon people are unaware of the old beliefs. I am in my last years and I would like to see preserved a few of the old beliefs and stories.

Early Koyukon hunters never talked about big game animals in the presence of a woman. This was a cultural taboo, and was particularly true for the brown or grizzly bear. Their respect for "the big animal," as the grizzly was always obliquely referred to, was close to fear. This is not surprising, considering that the early hunters had to face this, the largest and fiercest North American land carnivore, with nothing more than a spear or bow and arrow.

That some Koyukon people deliberately sought the grizzly bear with a spear has always amazed me. Hunting a grizzly with a spear required detailed planning and preparation. The spear handle, upon which the hunter's life depended, was the most critical part of the preparation. Before venturing after a bear, spear in hand, the hunter had to know if the spear could withstand the powerful blows of a grizzly bear's paws.

The handle, helve, or length of the spear, always cut in July, was made from a birch tree growing on level ground. The best birch for a handle grows near a river where large spruce trees provide shade from the hot summer sun. Slow-growing trees not more than two and a half inches in diameter were sought. The bark had to be pinkish brown, with no loose bark. Very small, clean, horizontal lines on the growing birch were a sign of its strength. A suitable birch tree was cut, leaving about a foot-long stump.

To test the grain and the quality of the wood, a piece was cut from above the section to be used as a handle. An axe was placed dead center across the end of the sample and hammered in a short way with a block of wood.

If the birch didn't split, the axe was removed and wedges of hard dry spruce were driven into the cut. If the birch still didn't split, it was considered suitable.

The birch handle was then burned with the bark on. Heat was driven from the outside into the center of the wood, tempering it. After the bark was burned off, the pole was hung from the butt end to dry in the shade in an out-of-the-way spot where no woman could see it.

After many weeks of drying, it was again tempered by fire, with the shine being slowly burned off. The end on which the point was to be fastened was narrowed. The handgrip was left full size.

The handle was then tested by beating it on a large tree that had the bark peeled from it. After beating it in every way possible that might break it, the pole was placed over a fire to see if expansion of the wood revealed any cracks. Even a hairline crack was sufficient evidence of weakness to discard a handle. Only a handle that passed all of these tests was considered suitable for a spear.

Both the point, often made from a sharpened bone from a grizzly, and a crossbar were attached with wet rawhide. As rawhide dries, it shrinks. This tightened both the crosspiece and the point so that both were rigidly attached. The crosspiece, fastened about nine inches from the tip, acted as a stop, preventing the spear from entering the bear too far.

When the grizzly was hunted during summer or fall, the hunter most often went alone, for more than one hunter could distract a bear, making him more unpredictable. The hunt was ruined if a woman learned about it—for that put a curse on the hunt that could cost the hunter his life. Sometimes a woman, learning of a hunt, warned the man. "Don't go. We've heard of your plans." When that happened, the hunter canceled the hunt.

If, after many days of a summer hunt, a hunter failed to locate a bear, the bear was telling him that he (the bear) had the advantage. Perhaps, the hunter would believe, someone had talked or bragged about the hunt. If all went well and a lone hunter sought the big animal in summer or fall, he tried to find it on hard ground atop an open ridge. In spring or fall, frozen ground was acceptable, although it is sometimes slippery. The hunter had to select a place with ground on which the end of the pole would not slip after the spear had entered the bear's chest.

The grizzly bear fears no other animal. In encounters with man, he normally goes on his way in peace. But when challenged, surprised, or angered, he may attack. His great strength and size, his huge teeth, and his five- to seven-inch-long claws make the grizzly a formidable killer. A grizzly can break the neck of a moose with one swat, and a big grizzly can carry a 1,000-pound moose in his jaws.

In snow-free months, early Koyukon hunters seeking an encounter with a grizzly approached the bear and taunted it by shooting it with blunt arrows. This angered the animal, and usually it charged. The hunter held his ground. From a full charge the bear habitually reared on hind legs within reach of the spear tip. The hunter quickly plunged the point into the animal's chest. Instantly, the hunter jammed the end of the spear handle against the ground and held it there, literally for dear life. The bear pushed forward—it never retreated. Both front paws beat upon the spear handle. The bear sometimes pivoted on the cross bar, and circled as he tried to reach the hunter. The harder he tried, the more damage the spear point did to his lungs and/or heart, and soon the grizzly toppled to the ground, dead or dying.

Early in this century a photographer arranged to take movies of a Koyukon hunter killing a grizzly in this manner. All went well until the bear charged. The photographer lost his nerve and fled while the Indian killed the bear, so he failed to get pictures of the actual killing. He did return shortly to take still photographs of the bear and the small Indian with a spear. The spear, tipped with sharpened bone made from the forearm of a bear, was only five to five and a half feet long—shorter than the Koyukon hunter who used it. I once saw one of these pictures hanging on a wall in an old building at Tanana.

Austin Joe and Chief Paul, two Koyukon hunters from Koyukon Station, decided to make a winter hunt for grizzly with a spear. Both had helped take bears from a den about ten years earlier. This was to be their last great test, the end of an era, for they realized that no Koyukuk Indian was likely to make such a hunt ever again. The knowledge of how to make such a hunt, and the tradition of making them, had nearly died out.

To the old Koyukon people, killing a grizzly with a spear was the supreme test of a man as an individual, and as a hunter. A winter hunt for a grizzly in its den was more complex than a summer hunt, for it required cooperation of at least three skilled, strong, and agile hunters. To kill one or more grizzlies at a den tested a hunter for speed, quickness, and character.

His actions determined whether he could control fear, if he were a liar, whether he could keep his mouth shut, and whether he was a braggart.

The hunt the failing Louis Golchik described for me occurred about 1917, and I believe it was the last successful Koyukon winter spear hunt for grizzly. Here is his story:

> That fall Chief Paul asked Tom Patsy and me to accompany him to 3,000-foot Heart Mountain (its base is in the shape of a heart), about forty miles up the Koyukuk River. His purpose was to hunt (with rifles) black bears for meat while they were feeding on blueberries, fattening themselves before winter.
>
> After we had killed a black bear, Chief Paul told us that we had been chosen to prepare for the supreme test of a Koyukon hunter—to take a "big animal" from its den with a spear.
>
> "You are the fastest and strongest young men on the Koyukuk and lower Yukon," Chief Paul said. "You will be the fast men on this last great spear hunt for the 'big animal.' " Both of us were relatively small, 5 feet 7 inches tall and weighing about 135 pounds, but strong.
>
> I had never been so honored, but I couldn't discuss the honor—that would have been bragging. I knew stories of famous hunters who had speared the "big animal" both in the Koyukuk valley and in the Nulato and Kaltag areas, but no Koyukon hunter ever admitted that he had taken, or helped take, a "big animal" with a spear.
>
> Chief Paul explained the rigid requirements: not one word of the hunt could be mentioned. Idle talk could cost us our lives. We were not to ask how the old-timers hunted "the big animal" because no real hunter who had killed a bear would talk. A braggart wasn't worth listening to.
>
> "When the time comes, two of us will teach you," said Chief Paul. That surprised me. "Where is the other hunter?" I asked.
>
> "He is finishing some secret work. You know him. You will meet him this winter about one month before we try to take a 'big animal,' " Chief Paul answered.
>
> When the black bear hunt ended, Chief Paul told Tom and me to keep in shape by running to toughen our muscles. "I want you to secretly practice the pole vault, too," Chief Paul said. We were to constantly think about what we had to do to beat the "big animal" in order to be real men and proud Indians like our forefathers.
>
> "Even when you defeat others in running or wrestling, never say you are faster, stronger, or better. That might hurt people's feelings. It might also give you problems during the hunt," Chief Paul warned.

Chief Paul told me that a message would reach me in early December telling me where to go, and I was to travel by foot to a place somewhere on the Kateel River to meet the other hunters. I left the Yukon River that fall and stayed with my sister, Martha Cleever, and her husband on the Koyukuk River below the Dulbi River. Tom Patsy spent the fall at Chips Island, in the Koyukuk River, below the Kateel River.

In December, word came that Chief Paul wanted me to travel to Chips Island, so I set out on snowshoes, camped one night, and arrived next day. I was in the best physical shape of my life.

At Chips Island, I met five people—Tom Patsy, Austin Joe, Chief Paul, and Andrew Paul, Chief Paul's son. I will not mention the name of the other man, because it could embarrass relatives who are still living. He had bragged about taking a "big animal" single-handed with a spear.

Chief Paul spoke to us. "Austin Joe has found the den of a female 'big animal' with two almost-grown cubs. Tomorrow we'll cross over to the Kateel [a river that flows into the Koyukuk from the west]. There we'll practice at an old bear den, and you will learn what must be done." Austin Joe had also carefully prepared the spear for the hunt, following all the old traditions.

After a walk of a day and a half to the old den, we rehearsed carefully. Each of us had a role, and each of our lives depended on the quickness, bravery, and ability of the others.

To test Tom's and my pole-vaulting ability, a big fire was built of spruce boughs. Each of us had to vault through the flames while wearing a fur parka. A scorched parka would have disqualified us for the spear hunt for "the big animal."

Both of us qualified.

When we were ready for the hunt, the wind was wrong, blowing from the east. Because of the location of the den, we needed a north wind, and the stronger the better. After waiting a day or two for the right wind, we camped within a mile of the den. The following day we studied the den from a distance, becoming familiar with the approach, and planning the route each of us had to follow to reach our positions at the den.

The last evening before the hunt we told traditional stories of long-ago hunts, tales handed down from generation to generation. Included were stories about hunters who had died when their spear hunt for the "big animal" went wrong.

Conditions were perfect at daylight next morning. A light wind blew from the north, and the temperature was mild, about 0. We didn't eat breakfast because we feared conditions would change if we delayed. Chief Paul gave last-minute instructions, and the five of us swiftly moved to the occupied den.

Tom Patsy, the fastest, carried an eight-foot vaulting pole of tough, dried birch. He dashed to the den entrance, vaulted over it and drove his vaulting pole across the den mouth. I followed and quickly drove my pole into place so that the two poles formed an X across the den opening. "Big animal" dens usually have dry loose soil at the entrance, which permits poles to be driven into the ground so they won't slip easily.

The two vaulting poles Tom and I held functioned as a gate, keeping the "big animals" in the den until the man with the killing spear was ready. The commotion we caused by vaulting into position and closing the den with our vaulting poles brought the old female to the mouth of the den almost as soon as the poles were in place. In front of the den, Austin Joe quickly cut a hole in the ground into which the handle end of the killing spear could be planted. Meanwhile, Chief Paul talked to the "big animal" in a language unknown to me. I was later told it was bear talk.

Would the "big animal" accept the spear? Perhaps we would have to use one of the two .30-30 rifles we had brought. If the "big animal" didn't accept the spear, there could be many possible reasons: Did someone brag? Had word of our hunt somehow leaked? Had a woman seen the spear? Did any woman know about the hunt?

While Austin Joe dug the hole, Andrew Paul and the other man joined Tom and me in holding the gate poles to prevent the "big animals" from pulling the poles in or pushing them out. Austin Joe finished the hole and Chief Paul set the spear handle into it and braced himself. "Let the first one out," he called. We pulled our poles back, opening the den, and the big female rushed directly into the spear held by Chief Paul. The spear entered the "big animal's" chest. The crossbar held the animal off so that her powerful claws and teeth could not reach him.

Chief Paul held the handle firmly in the hole in the ground, and with a mighty heave, using the momentum of the charging "big animal," threw it right over himself. The big female flew about twenty-five feet downhill, with its chest organs ripped to shreds, and landed with a thud. It rolled a few feet and lay dying.

The instant the big female left the den, Tom and I jammed our poles back into the ground to re-form the gate. Two nearly grown cubs remained in the den.

Now the test: Chief Paul handed the spear to the man who had bragged about taking a bear single-handed with a spear. Chief Paul spoke, "I helped take a 'big animal' once with a spear. I never talked about it before. I know this is my last 'big animal'—the one you see lying there, dead. This could be your last one too. Now you try, because I don't believe you ever took a 'big animal' with a spear.

"We never told you that we were going to try to take the 'big animals' with a spear because we were afraid you would talk. Maybe you wouldn't go with us. I want to demonstrate to these men how not to brag, and why no Koyukon should talk about taking 'big animals' with a spear, trying to make a big man of himself."

Obediently, the man accepted the spear. He tried to get the young "big animal" at the mouth of the den to accept it. To test the "big animal," he placed the point of the spear under its mouth, near the throat. The "big animal" slapped the spear aside. This meant he sensed fear in the man holding the spear. If the weapon had passed his face without the "big animal" slapping it aside, it would have meant that the man holding the spear was brave enough to handle that "big animal."

The "big animal" pushed the blade aside not once, but twice, indicating that the man was afraid. Then Austin Joe grabbed the spear, saying, "You lie. You never took a 'big animal' by yourself with a spear. This one tell us. I never took one either, but I never lie. Now watch this."

With that Austin Joe called, "Open the den." Tom and I pulled our poles clear. One of the "big animals" charged. Austin Joe set the spear and the charging "big animal" impaled himself upon it. Like the old female, the big cub was thrown through the air with lungs and heart shredded. The dying "big animal" landed far downhill, near the adult.

Austin Joe handed the bloody spear once more to the braggart, with the same results. The last "big animal" in the den pushed the blade aside.

Then the spear was handed to one of the younger people. The third "big animal" charged and impaled himself, and the spearman tossed it down the hill to join the first two dead animals.

"One of the younger people," was, of course, Louis. Old Louis Golchik refused to brag, even though he knew he was near death.

For many years the eighteen-inch-long metal blade from the spear used on that hunt was displayed in the home of trader Dominic Vernetti at Koyukuk Station. With lingering belief, Louis told me, "That spear point would not be good for another hunt. Too many women's hands have touched it. Too many people have seen it."

Louis Golchik died a few weeks after we canoed down the Huslia River at the end of our beaver hunt.

Jenny and I were divorced in 1944. We remained friends, and we both stayed close to our children. Later that year I married Angela Pitka, a

Koyukon girl of eighteen. Tall and strikingly beautiful, she was a woman of great determination and ability. She lost both of her parents early in life, and was raised by an older sister and an aunt.

In 1945, at war's end, Angela and I moved from Galena to Hog River, where I took up my old life on the trapline. I took enough fur so we had some cash. I killed enough game and caught enough fish to permit us to eat and live well. Ours was a simple wilderness life, much as I had lived for years before the war.

In some ways, those years on the trapline with Angela were the best of my life. She helped me whipsaw lumber so I could build boats. She cut firewood, helped run the traplines, and caught, cut up, and dried fish. She often stayed alone while I was off running distant traplines or working at other jobs, which I was forced to do in order to make enough to take care of our growing family. Every year we had a new baby. First came Roger, then Elma, Carl, Annie, and Agnes. There were to be more.

A Moose Calling

JOHN HAINES

John Haines is a poet, essayist, and former poet laureate of Alaska. He has taught at the University of Montana, the University of Washington, and at the University of Alaska Fairbanks as poet in residence. "A Moose Calling" originally appeared in a collection of his poetry, WINTER NEWS *(1966).*

Who are you,
calling me in the dusk,

O dark shape
with heavy horns?

I am neither cow
nor bull—

I walk upright
and carry your death
in my hands.

It is my voice
answers you,

beckoning, deceitful,
ruse of the hunter—

at twilight,
in the yellow frost

I wait for you.

Of Traps and Snares

FROM *The Stars, The Snow, The Fire*

JOHN HAINES

*John Haines, originally from Virginia, has spent the past four decades, off
and on, living in Alaska. After World War II, he homesteaded in a log cabin
in Interior Alaska, living off the land. From that experience he wrote* THE
STARS, THE SNOW, THE FIRE *(1989) and* LIVING OFF THE COUNTRY *(1981). For
his books, poetry, and essays, Haines has received numerous prestigious awards.
"Of Traps and Snares" is from* THE STARS, THE SNOW, THE FIRE.

The lore of traps and snares. The old handbooks are filled with talk of
lures and sets and skills. The subject has its own fascination, and to
one attracted to life in the woods this knowledge seems essential and
good, something handed down, useful, and binding in time. The
world may fail us, the markets crash, and the traffic stand still. But
with a good axe in hand, a gun, a net, a few traps—life will go on in the old,
upstanding ways.

If we don't have steel traps, and are otherwise cut off from the tools of
commerce, we can always make deadfalls. Men made them in early days
when hardware was scarce and expensive; they made them out of whatever the country provided, from logs and stones. Abandoned, these native
materials soon fell to rot and were added to the soil and covered with snow.
Steel cable and copper wire can also be done without. When white men
first came into the country, late in the century, they found the Indians
catching marten and rabbits and other small animals in snares made from
sinew, or from strands of halibut twine they had gotten from traders on the
coast.

The plain vocabulary of this woods-lore hardly conceals a native harshness. Sooner or later the thinking man considers the barbaric means for
what is plainly a kind of murder: the steel jaw and the wire noose, the choking and the crushing, the cutting and tearing of the wet skin from the cold

body of the dead beast. And the end in view: selling the fur so that others may be rich and clothed beyond their natural right.

In all that hardness and cruelty there is a knowledge to be gained, a necessary knowledge, acquired in the only way it can be, from close familiarity with the creatures hunted. A knowledge of blood, of sinew and gut; of the structure of joint and muscle, the shape of the skull, the angularity, the sharpness or roundness of nose and ears and lips and teeth. There is passion in the hand that pulls the pelt and strokes the fur, confident that it knows as second nature all the hinges and recesses of the animal body. But however close that familiarity, something is always withheld; the life of the animal remains other and beyond, never completely yielding all that it is.

So much can be said about it from one conviction or another, the attitudes easily become partisan and intractible. There is the coarseness too often found in those who follow the trade, especially where mere cash is the end in mind. And yet to some fortunate individuals there have been few things more deeply attractive than this seasonal pursuit of the wild. It is life at its fullest, uncertain and demanding, but rich with expectation. The wilderness is open, and whoever enters it knows the satisfaction of being at ease in a country he calls his own. The land belongs to him and to no one else. He can go where he likes, following his own trail through the spruce bogs and across the dry birch hills, a pathway tramped in the snow, to stop at nightfall in his own snug camp.

It will never be an easy life, the gift comes with its hardships firmly attached: the occasional poor season and bad luck, the missed hunt, the weariness and disappointment; long days alone in the snow and frost with no sure reward for the time spent. Some things make sense only in the light of their personal necessity, and what that necessity is to be we choose for ourselves.

I ran a trapline periodically for over twenty years in interior Alaska. That old, persistent dream, fed by the old tales, the worn books: to be alone in the snow with my dogs, tending the traps and snares. The trail before me, and the life of the animals I sought, secret and apart from my own.

It was part of the homestead life there at Richardson, on the bluff hills above the Tanana River east of Fairbanks. It was something else to do, and at times it brought in that small amount of money we needed. But it was in some ways an unlucky time to be a trapper; fur prices were low, and for most of those years the country hadn't much fur in it.

My first winter alone in the cabin at Richardson, when I was still in my twenties and knew nothing at all about living in the North, I went out with an older neighbor named Fred Allison one afternoon in November to set snares for rabbits. Allison was that increasingly rare survivor from early days, having mined and teamstered, driven mail, trapped and roughnecked his forty-odd years in the north. Now he was tending bar in the roadhouse at Richardson two miles down the road. From behind the counter he watched me with his one good eye, curious how I, a quiet and uncertain youth from the city, was finding my way in a new country. While I did occasional chores for him and we met from time to time in conversation, he would tell me things that he knew and that he thought would be good for me to learn. And now he was going to show me, convinced, perhaps, that I would never learn otherwise. He had spent his own young days in the woods in eastern Canada, and knew what it was to live on rabbits and grouse when nothing else was on hand. Nearly seventy, limping and slow in his walk, I think he was glad in his last, lame years to have something to do outside the tame routine he had come to, feeding coal to the kitchen range, answering the gas pump bell and waiting on infrequent customers in the bar.

We went down into the woods below the roadhouse, toward the river. It was growing late in a dry fall, the ground was frozen, and a few inches of grainy snow bent down the small grasses and lay thinly on the moss. There were plenty of rabbits that winter, and their trails were beaten through the willows and birches; a maze of neighborhood pathways crossing and inter-rupting each other, and to the unskilled eye going nowhere at all.

We tramped around in the woods, while Fred swore and muttered to himself, half-confiding to me some of the secrets of rabbit-snaring. Finally he chose a place, an opening in the willows where a rabbit path was con-fined by the brush around it. As I stood aside and watched him, he found a dead willow standing nearby, broke from it a section about three feet long and stripped it of branches. It should be dry rather than green, he explained in a voice indefinably Scots or Nova Scotian, "Because, you see, your rabbit might stop to nibble the green stick, and he wouldn't go into the snare."

We had brought with us a few lengths of thin copper wire. Fred took a piece of the wire, and in one end of it he made a sliding noose, three inches or so in diameter. He wound the other end of the wire midway on the stick and made it tight. Then, kneeling down in the snow beside the path and disturbing the ground as little as possible, he carefully worked the stick into the brush above the rabbit path, so that it was fixed firmly there, the noose hanging down a few inches above the snow. Explaining with a word or two what he was doing—"Now you see . . ." He arranged other dry sticks around the snare, on either side and above it, and two small stubs beneath it. Satisfied, he got to his feet with a grunt, and we both stood and looked at the snare.

There was only one way through that opening now. A rabbit would come in the night and find its way partly blocked. The chances were that it would not go back, but put its head into the snare, try to go on, and be caught, to choke and freeze in a short time. The colder it was, the better. But you had to be careful about the way you did it. The snare must be short enough that the rabbit could not turn easily when caught and bite the wire. Sometimes one of them would get a foot into a carelessly set snare, and eventually break the wire and get away.

Soon enough I saw how it was done, standing beside Allison in the snow, while his strongly hooked red nose dripped snot, and the cold, grey dusk deepened around us. "There now, my boy," he said, pleased with what he had done. "Come back in the morning, and you'll find a rabbit!"

We set four or five snares that afternoon, all within a small space of ground where the rabbit sign was thickest. It was nearly dark when we walked out of the woods to the roadhouse for supper. When I came back the following day, sure enough, I found two rabbits frozen in the snares. They were bunched up in the torn brush, contorted, feet in the air, their eyes turned to ice.

From then on, whenever I wanted a rabbit, for myself or for my dogs, I went out and set a few snares. But it wasn't always as easily done as that first time. As long as the rabbits were abundant no great cunning was needed to catch them. But when they were scarce they seemed to become cagey and shy. They would stop and go back, or find some way around the snare rather than go through it. Great numbers made them careless, or they were too busy chasing each other in the dark to notice the wire.

There was a fox in the neighborhood then. We saw him sometimes from the roadhouse when he came up from the river at dusk to hunt rabbits in the birchwood. One evening when I went down to look at my snares, I met the fox in my trail. I saw him coming across an open field beyond the woods, his dark red form stepping surely and alertly through the clumps of snow-covered grasses. I stopped and stood quietly where I was, half in among the trees. The fox did not see me, but trotted to within five feet of me before he caught my scent and crouched down on the snowpath, uncertain. Suddenly his big yellow eyes blazed up at me, and he turned and fled.

I caught that fox in a trap a few weeks later. It was my first attempt. I followed Allison's advice, using a fresh piece of rabbit for bait. I set the trap carefully in the snow at the base of a large spruce tree near where the fox had been hunting, and covered it with a thin sheet of paper. The trap chain with its chunk of dead wood for a drag was concealed in the snow beside it. I sprinkled some fresh snow around the set to cover my tracks, and left it there for several days. I came back one mild, sunlit afternoon to find the fox caught fast in the trap by one of its hind legs. He had not run far, but was still tugging on the chain where it had tangled in the brush, trying to get free. The skin of his caught leg was broken and bloody, and his eyes had a baffled and wounded look.

What to do. Allison had told me how to kill him. I was not to shoot him, for that would make a hole in the skin and diminish its value. The best way was to knock him out with a sharp blow across the bridge of his nose. While he was unconscious I should grab him and break his neck. Allison told me how. I was skeptical and a little afraid, but I was also determined to learn.

I found a stout, dry stick in the willows around me; the fox was backed into the brush, silently watching me. I got myself close enough, reached out with my stick, and hit him a good rap in what I thought was the right place. To my surprise, but just as Allison said he would, the fox suddenly stiffened and fell.

He would not stay that way long, so I quickly kneeled down in the snow. I seized the unconscious fox by his forelegs and drew him into my lap. Holding him there with one hand, I grasped his muzzle tightly in my other hand and twisted his head as far around as I could, until I felt the neckbone snap, and a sudden gush of blood came from his nostrils. A shudder ran through the slender, furred body, and then it was still.

I released him and got to my feet. I stood there, looking down at the soiled, limp form in the snow, appalled at what I had done. This is what trapping meant when all the romance was removed from it: a matter of deceit and steel set against hunger. But I had overcome my fear, and I felt something had been gained by that.

For the rest of that winter I set a trap only now and then. I worked on my cabin, mended clothing, and read the few books I had with me. I spent many hours visiting the older residents with whom I became friendly, listening to their tales of works and days. As spring came on and heavy snow came to the hills, I went out on my snowshoes, roaming ever wider into the country, taking more and deeper note of the woods around me and all that would become the ground of my life.

I left Richardson the following fall, after another summer of clearing and building. For a time I was back in the world of cities and people, of books and schools—another part of the forest with its own snares and deceptions. I returned early one May with a young wife, resolved now to live the homestead life as fully as I could. I was thirty years old, and I found my world again, house, yard and wilderness, more or less as I had left it. Allison had moved away, retired to the state of Washington, and the roadhouse had new owners. The road to Fairbanks had been straightened and paved in my absence, and there were a few new settlers on the road out from town; but the Tanana River and the country to the north and south of us had not changed, still unsurveyed, quiet and empty of people.

It was a good time to be in the woods, one of those periodic years of abundance in the north. The rabbits were thick, at the peak of their cycle, and everything else in the woods was bound to flourish. We came upon lynx everywhere we went, in the hills and in the swamps. There were big ones, small ones, females with kittens. The sheer richness of it was astonishing. Rabbits bounded away underfoot, and the big, tawny-grey lynx seemed nearly as tame as tabbies; they moved deliberately across the trails and through the clearings, or sat blinking by the roadside in the evenings, as if they were stunned by the abundance of food. That winter Fred Campbell, one of the old Richardson trappers, caught fifty lynx in snares, and Hans Seppala across the Tanana caught another forty-five or fifty in traps. That was a lot of fur animals to take out of one country, but Campbell justified it, claiming that in a year or so the big cats would be gone anyway, starved and eating each other when the rabbits died off.

Two years later there was hardly a lynx left in the country and scarcely a rabbit to be found. When I took up trapping again, determined to make it a serious part of my life, it was at the poorest time in a decade. Poverty gripped the woods, and when the fall snow came there was nothing to be seen in it but a few squirrel tracks, or now and then an ermine or mouse-hunting fox. Even moose became scarce for a while, as if they too had been driven by some great famine to a farther country.

I was alone then for the most part, marriage and the wilderness having come to their parting. I had myself, four dogs, a couple of sleds, harness and snowshoes, a few books and a passion for the country. I set out to learn what I could and prepare myself for a long life in the woods.

For a time I set my traps along the Tanana and in the old roads around Richardson and Tenderfoot, within easy miles of home. Very little immediate reward came of all my walking and searching, a perplexed peering into the snow. But I was schooled all the same. I learned to read animal sign, the snowmark of foot and tail and wing. In some uncanny and prehuman way it was like beginning a new language, each detail and accent of which had its special meaning. It led me step by step into a world I seemed to have known once but had forgotten, shadowy and haunted by half-realized images from the past. I found my way there, somehow assured, though alone and separated from all I had grown up with, that I was in my right place, performing the right tasks.

Now and then I caught an ermine or a fox. I snared a big lynx in one of my foot trails near the river. I tried to catch rabbits again as I had once done so easily, setting my snares wherever I found a solitary track. But the country proved to be barren of fur, and I saw that no amount of time and work would change that. I realized that I would have to go much farther and find another country away from the river and the highway.

I hung my traps for a season or two. Working in the fall and in the spring, when I had time and the days were longer, I began building a system of trails and camps in the only country available to me then, the boggy creeks and spruce ridges northwest of Richardson. This was the Redmond Creek country, draining west from the Banner watershed; it was higher and wetter than home, and dominated by the broad height of Banner Dome, a bare and windy summit from which you could look down into the Salcha River drainage and north toward the Yukon itself. It was a country deeply marked by the overgrown trails and wagon roads of the gold rush, and walking these for any distance I was sure to come sooner or later on a fallen cabin or the partly cribbed remains of a prospect hole with a rotting ladder standing there in the brush as if ready for use. The country had been partially burned over, hunted over and trapped over during those hectic and destructive years, and it was never really rich in game and fur afterwards. But there were moose in it now, undisturbed by hunters, and always a few marten on the ridges and a rare lynx prowling the willow thickets in the creek bottoms.

Surveying this country by foot and snowshoe, chopping and blazing, plotting and building, I made for myself a personal domain of which I was the sole ruler and working occupant. By the time I was done with it, or as much done as one ever is with such things in the woods, I could claim at least thirty miles of trail laid out north, east and west along the ridges and benches. Much of this was cut wide and straight enough to take the sled and dogs, with here and there a roughly blazed footpath striking off into some part of the country where I found it necessary to go. I put a lot of care into making those trails, and I take some pride in knowing that most of them are still there, sound and true. A trail through the woods is made for a purpose; and if it is important enough it is worth the time spent to do it well—or so I thought as I sighted a way through the birches to the next rise, and checked behind me to see that the way was clear and the grade as easy as I could make it.

With daily and seasonal use these trails became in their own essential way a part of the homestead, an extension of the yard. As naturally as leaves falling, came the inevitable places to rest while traveling, to view the hills or to look for a moose; favorite clearings, windfalls to gather firewood from, patches in which to pick blueberries and cranberries. All things encountered along a trail might be of use—a dry snag for kindling, a dead birch for the bark that held it upright, a dry leaf floor under aspens for a crop of mushrooms in late summer. In no time at all the trails acquired their home legend of past kills and other memorable events—here a bear was feeding early in the summer, and there last fall a bull moose stripped a spruce sapling of its branches with his horns. There were caches built in the trees, items placed for use at a later time, tent poles and berry buckets. By the stream-crossings and waterholes I left tin cans upside down in the brush to use for a drinking cup on hot summer days. In a few seasons the country became worn and familiar like a neighborhood, though spread over many miles of birch hills, alder thickets and black spruce bogs. The trails were hard going in places, the ground wet, the summer-thawed moss exhausting to walk over, and the hills sometimes long and steep, but it was my own made place. The labor of it occupied me the better part of three years, but I have known and done few things more satisfying. I contemplated the map with a sure sense that I knew where I was in that far corner of North America.

I had no competitors in all that country. There were few people trapping anywhere in those years, and around Richardson only two of the old, dedicated and solitary kind were left. Hans Seppala kept to himself in the flat Clearwater country across the Tanana where he had been for the better part of thirty years, his only access to the world a river boat in the summer and a dogteam in the winter. Fred Campbell owned the hills northeast of Richardson, but his trapping days were at an end; the big year of the lynx had been his last, and he took a meager solace in his memories. When he died late one fall toward the end of the 1950s I considered taking over his old trapline and adding it to my own. We had talked about it once or twice, skirting what was for him the painful admission that he could not keep it any longer. But he wanted money for what he had, and I had none to give him. There was not much left of it by then, in any case—two tumbledown cabins, some rusty traps, and the forty to fifty miles of trails he had maintained for nearly forty years, away north behind Buckeye Dome, and all the way to McCoy Creek on the Salcha drainage. It was good marten country, remote, and uninhabited by any other trapper; but the distance was greater than I wanted to travel, and by then I was well into my own territory. It would be enough.

To make the most of this widespread country I had two choices. One was to build cabins, more or less permanent camps at convenient distances, though each of these might occupy part of a summer's work. The other was to brave the cold and camp in the open under a canvas lean-to or in a small tent. This was not always the extreme hardship it might appear to be, though at thirty and forty below zero it was always an adventure. If nothing else it toughened one for the life and made the encounter with the wilderness just that much closer and deeper. But after a few experiences camping in the cold, in a worn eight-by-ten-foot wall tent with a sheet-iron stove, sleeping out, or "siwashing," as it used to be called, I chose to build a cabin, both for the comfort of it and for the sense of a permanent place that it gave me.

Along the way I rebuilt two ancient and disused cabins left behind many years before by old residents in the country. One of these was a tiny square hut of a thing with a dirt floor and sod roof on a low bluff near the mouth of Tenderfoot Creek, six miles upriver from the homestead. Though it was too small to be more than a temporary camp, for three or four years it was useful to me as a fishing camp and as a shelter while trapping. The other cabin, tilted and barely standing when I found it, was in Issacson Flat, a few miles up Banner Creek and over a long steep hill from home. I patched up these two camps, furnishing each of them with a bunk and a stove, a few pots and dishes. They would be there with a rick or two of firewood, available to me at the end of a long day if I needed them. But I used these two camps only now and then, and the country around them was seldom good for trapping.

And then one rainy fall my second wife and I built a small, snug cabin on a wet bench above one of the creeks that drained off Banner Dome, several miles north of the homestead. We worked three hard months building that place; the rain turned into snow, and the bark froze to the timber before the roof was on, but it was worth it. The cabin, with four dog houses and a meat rack, was well-placed, with a good view into a grassy flat, in a good country. There were moose in the creeks and marten on the hills, the big dome above the cabin, making a high, far sound in the wind.

It is often true that the best things we do in some strange way take place within us long before we come to the ground itself. The physical domain of the country had its counterpart in me. The trails I made led outward into the hills and swamps, but they led inward also. And from the study of things underfoot, and from reading and thinking, came a kind of exploration, myself and the land. In time the two became one in my mind. With the gathering force of an essential thing realizing itself out of early ground, I faced in myself a passionate and tenacious longing—to put away thought forever, and all the trouble it brings, all but the nearest desire, direct and searching. To take the trail and not look back. Whether on foot, on snow-shoes or by sled, into the summer hills and their late freezing shadows—a high blaze, a runner track in the snow would show where I had gone. Let the rest of mankind find me if it could.

Stopped briefly in a still fall afternoon, resting while on a hunt, I looked north from a high and open slope to another range of hills—what lay beyond them? What did I hear once of that distant and rocky prominence someone had called "The Butte"? I studied my favorite map with its legend of watersheds and old trails, its numerals and lines of elevation. The names

I read there spoke to me: Caribou, Deep Creek, Deadwood, Monte Cristo. Each name, each creek, each wooded rise of ground led on to another. I might, at a long stretch of fancy, have gone all the way north to the Yukon. I would build another camp a day's travel on, and another beyond that, until I reached the great river, or as far as I wished to go.

Or, again, I could as easily turn south. I remember thinking one fall with excitement and conviction that we should go across the Tanana, into the foothills of the Alaska Range, and make another country there. No one had trapped and hunted there in recent years—think of being so close to those high ridges whose snowline we watched each fall as if we gazed into some far Tibet. There were caribou and grizzlies there, and who knows what fabulous country to roam in.

They were big and indefinite dreams never realized, though I could imagine them down to the last detail—the camps I would build, the trails I would cut, the fall hunt coming on early near timberline. But for me finally there were limits. Things at home also had their claim on me—that other world of books, and of thoughts that went far beyond such immediate things as hunting and trapping, into a country of their own. I would stay where I was and make the most of what I had.

The trapping year had its own calendar, and everything fitted a niche in the months and days. The far north summer passed quickly, a round of gardening and berry-picking, of fishing and wood-cutting—a chopping and hauling and stacking that never stopped for long under the great span of daylight. In late August darkness returned, with the glitter of frost in the mornings. Fall came on with its ice and color, with the late rush to dig potatoes and gather in the garden and greenhouse crop. The river channels shrank, the water slowly cleared of silt, and pan ice clung in the eddies. Fishing ended with the nets dried and put away, the boat hauled out on a sandbar and secured for the winter. With luck, the hunt was over and a moose was hanging in the shade. The last swans passed overhead with distant cries, and the woods were quiet.

Snow came and melted, and came again, a patchy whiteness over the fallen debris of summer. Sometime in October the first good snowfall came and remained on the ground; anything that moved upon it left its sign to be read. November came, and the snowfall deepened with the cold, falling at night far below zero. I would go for a long hike over the hills one day to look at the fur sign, or I might see while hunting late that the marten were in good number that year. At home I sorted traps and looked over snares, deciding what to do. I felt the season steady on its downward track as I paused there, weighing my choices: three months' travel in the dark, or a winter at home with my books and thoughts. The two things squared off— needs and wants. My decision to trap sometimes came almost as an after-thought. I had a moose down somewhere back in the hills, and in no time a marten or two would find it and attempt to feed on the meat while it was hanging in the woods. I set a couple of traps then and there. The signs looked good, and besides I had to come and haul the meat home, didn't I? The sled was taken from storage, the harness checked and mended. The dogs were restless.

My traps were a scattering of sizes and sorts, from the small #1 jumps I used for marten, to the larger double-spring Victor and Newhouse made for fox, for coyote and beaver. Some of these had teeth—ugly, grim-looking things that were dangerous and hard to set. I had bought a few of them out of a bin in Fairbanks once, years before I knew what I needed and wanted; others were given to me, or I found them in one place or another. They piled up, in boxes at home or hung from nails on the wall of a camp. To save myself some of the work of packing them, I often left my marten traps hanging in trees along the trail, to be used the following season. They got a little rusty there in the weather, but it didn't seem to matter. And once because I found the advice in a book, I boiled all my traps in a strong brew made from spruce twigs and bark. This was supposed to rid the traps of their metal odor and to protect them from rust. Maybe it did, but to the marten and lynx I trapped it seemed of no importance one way or the other.

Whatever was needed, the country always provided somehow—out of its soil and snow, and from those found tools, the dulling coils and edges men leave behind. I made lynx snares from strands of old windlass cable rescued from a dump on one of the mining creeks. Time in the late fall afternoons when the long grey light filled the porch windows, and I sat there unraveling cable, working with cutters and pliers, while my thoughts strayed outward to the river below the house and returned to the task at hand. Five or six strands were about right, twisted together and knotted at the ends in a figure eight. Sometimes I found it best to heat the wire over a flame to make it easier to work with or to change its color; the brightness burned to a dull metallic blue or grey, and was not so easily seen in the woods. When I had ten or a dozen snares made I wound them into small coils, tied them together, and hung the bundles from nails on the workshop beams. I had other snares that were factory-made, with fancy metal locks, but I found them to be too long for most uses and wasteful of wire. I cut them down, making two out of one. Great numbers of snares were needed, for many would fail and be lost in the woods.

I went on foot, packing my gear for the day, or I went with the dogs overnight and for longer. The dogs went with a yelping rush when they could, or until they were winded, and there were times I preferred to trudge along at my own pace, to stop and spend some time in a new terrain. Or I might take the dogs and sled for a few miles, tie them, and go on afoot or with snowshoes. The snow might be deep or shallow, the season warmer than usual, or colder than the year before with long spells of wind and drifted trails. The best winters were those in which snowfall was light, and the worst cold passed in a few days' time—"The finest kind of trapping winter," as one old Finn trapper liked to put it.

However I came to it, from hints in books, or from the remarks of old neighbors, I understood quite early that I should not trap the country too hard. There was once a common attitude, and I suppose it may still be found, that one could move into a country, trap it of everything on four legs, and then move on. But that would not do for me. Though my awareness of these things was still half-formed, I seemed to have had it in me as an instinct to care for the country that I might live in it again. Most animals in an unsettled land are not trap shy. It is possible to catch every marten and mink in the country, and the same will be true for lynx. A country trapped too hard, as my own Redmond creeks and hills had once been, may take a long time to recover, and a man living there will face lean years of his own making. As I watched the woods and listened to the talk of old trappers, I saw that it was best to leave a little seed in the country, and to trap according to the scarcity and abundance of the fur sign. It was all too uncertain at best; too many things intervene to make any cropping of the wild a secure and reliable thing, as if life had no purpose beyond our own uses for it. That year of great abundance may return, and the woods flourish; but the rabbits will leave us again some day, and nothing we can think of to do will bring them back until they are ready.

The trapping year turned on the winter solstice, a twilight world of

lasting shadows and soft grey light. A cold sun clearing the mountains far
to the south, the daylight hardly begun when it ended. I became a creature
of the dusk, to be out early and home late, to begin in the dark and end in
the dark. A trudging and packing, watching, and marking off the days.
December went by, January and February. Perceptibly the days grew longer
and the light stayed, though the cold often remained, deepening at nightfall. Marten season closed, beaver season opened and ran until April. A
quickening came to the woods, felt in the long light and the sudden days of
warmth. My mind began its return from snow and darkness to sunlight
once more, to seeds and pots of earth.

And then with the onset of thaw in late spring, it was over. The traps
were pulled, hung up or stored away, the snares gathered in from the woods.
I made my last trip with the sled and dogs over a softening trail, and put
away harness and sled for the summer. The furs were counted and admired,
the money already spent in mind. Some new things learned, some disap-
pointments. Decisions for next year: a new trail needed to a farther creek,
and a cache to be built there. One of the dogs has been acting up. So, as the
sun gains power, and water drips from the cabin eaves, another year.

As I write this now, many things come to mind, half-buried under the
stored-up debris of the years: scraps from books, words of advice, murmurs,
glimpses into forgotten days and habits. I want to make a great list of them,
as if in a moment they would pass from my mind forever.

The catalogue is endless. I begin with water sets and trail sets, with blind
sets and cubby sets, with drowning stones and balance poles. The vocabulary clinks with chains and rasps with nooses. The exercise of an ancient
cunning, schooled in the forest so far back that its origin is forgotten, the
ruses handed down by voice and page, or rediscovered by the hand and eye
in practice. So innocent a device as a "stepping stick," a length of dry willow,
casually dropped across the trail, to lie there much as nature might have
felled it; the trap set just beyond it and to one side, so that the forefoot of
the animal comes squarely down as it walks or lopes along.

I hear these words from a dead man's journal: "I will first describe the
most successful set I know of. . . ." A dead log spans a gully; it is so old that
the bark has slipped and fallen, and the branches rotted away. But halfway
across there is one dry stub standing crookedly in the air. And from it a
round noose is suspended, propped above the log to bar the way. Something

will cross there, who knows what; but come snowfall and a moonless night, we may find the creature hanging.

"A rabbit's head hung in a hollow tree. . . ." My list tells of baits and how to use them, of spoiled fish and rotted guts. How once on someone's advice I dragged a ripe chunk of moose paunch behind me for a couple of miles, setting traps as I went. It worked, too. Every marten that crossed my trail turned and followed it. I saw that foxes and coyotes liked to dig through the snow on river bars for a dead salmon stranded in the fall. So I buried a piece of fish in the snow where I saw old tracks, and set my trap above it; I covered it all with snow and hoped for a little wind.

"This scent is made as follows: take equal parts of rabbit, skunk and muskrat, with two mice added, chop fine, place in a covered jar and allow to stand in the sun. . . ." And so the baits are refined into lures and scents, to the pungency of beaver castor chopped and ground, the reek of soured meats, of urine saved and droppings preserved. Rich and disturbing, the whole obscene and fascinating craft and science of it, set down, stored away in mind, to be searched out one day when its use is needed.

So many intricate methods of death, brooded upon and perfected. Once in an old book I found a chapter called "The Art of Pulling Hearts." It told how to kill small animals by reaching with a deft hand under the ribcage where the heart jumped and pounded—and with a sure pull downward the heartstrings snapped.

I became reasonably skilled at what I did, almost as if I'd been born to it, and this sometimes gave me trouble. I could not avoid thinking of the animals I caught, and of my own motives and craft. I lay awake at night, watching my trail in the snow overhead, and saw myself caught in a trap or snare, slowly freezing to death. I felt the cold grip of the metal, the frost in my bones. A pair of great yellow eyes seemed to stare at me from the darkness, and looked into my soul. Very likely I bestowed on the creatures more capacity for pain and suffering than they possess, but there was no way to be sure of this. Their lives and deaths haunted me like a wound in my own flesh.

Especially painful things would sometimes happen. Once on the river I caught a neighbor's dog in a coyote snare. He was long dead when I found him, the wire drawn up so tightly around his neck that his head was nearly severed from his body. The snow and torn brush gave evidence of a terrible struggle. I removed the snare from his neck with difficulty, and dragged the frozen body onto the mid-channel ice to let the river have him. I told myself that it was not my fault; the neighbor, who lived several miles away, was careless and let his dogs run loose in the country. Nevertheless, my regret over it was so keen that I set no more snares on the river close to home.

It was partly because of this persistent identification that I did not often attempt to trap beaver, though they were fairly common on the river sloughs. I disliked the idea of it to begin with, they were such hardworking animals, the engineers of the woods and waters, and too often pitted against careless men with their traps and guns, their roads and culverts. But at the same time, beaver were one of the few furs consistently worth money on the market, and three or four good pelts in those days would buy a lot of beans and bacon.

I caught my first beaver late one spring in a small pond on lower Tenderfoot. I put in a lot of time for that beaver, walking the six miles both ways from Richardson in a cold wind. I had little experience in it, and knew mostly what I had read and had been told by other trappers. And what it amounted to was work.

Snow covered the pond ice, and the beaver house was a large, irregular mound in the still-wintry landscape. I had a two-inch chisel mounted on a heavy six-foot pole. With this and a small shovel to clear the ice chips as I worked, I cut a hole two or three feet down in the ice. The brown pond water, released from its ice prison, surged up, foaming and bubbling, filling the hole to its brim. Sometimes the water kept on coming, staining the snow and flooding the ice around me. When that happened, I retreated to the shoreline where I cut some brush and poles to stand on while I continued to work with my chisel, making the hole large enough to take my trap.

I used the standard #4 beaver trap and baited it with a fresh piece of aspen. Other baits might be used—cottonwood was best, but willow would do, and aspen was handy close to the pond. From spruce poles cut near the pond I built a rough sort of tripod, nailed and wired together. The trap was set at the bottom of this, the bait stick nailed above it and blazed with the axe so that the white wood showed through the green bark to attract a beaver in the murky water. The entire contraption was let down into the water until the lower half of it, with trap and bait, was below the ice and resting on the bottom of the pond. The water in the open hole soon froze in the subzero air, and the set was fixed like concrete until I came next time to chop it loose.

All this had to be done with care, and at the right distance from the shoreline and the beaver house, or the work would go for nothing. After cutting a hole and testing the depth with a stick, I occasionally found that the water was too shallow. There was nothing for it then but to move farther out on the ice and try again. A twig standing up from the pond bottom, or a troublesome growth of weeds, might set off the trap before a beaver found it. Beaver were scarce on the ponds, and to me in my inexperience they seemed to be exceptionally wise. Twice I pulled up a trap to find it sprung and the bait stick gone.

But I came one bright morning to find my beaver at last. It came out of the water at the end of the trap chain, drowned and dripping. I looked at it there on the sunlit ice with mingled triumph and regret. It was big and dark, and must have weighed nearly forty pounds. It made a wet and heavy load in the basket going home to Richardson over the hill.

Sometime later I tried to catch beaver in the Tanana. I had chosen a new beaver house built on the bank of a slough below the mouth of Banner Creek, and marked it with a stick in the fall so that I could find it again in the spring. The Tanana overflowed many times that winter; a tremendous, multilayered sheet of ice built up on the slough, spilling over the shoreline, so that it seemed nothing could be alive beneath it. The beaver house itself was out of sight under the ice and impacted snow. But beaver season came, and I was going to try it.

Not far from where I thought the house was, and in what I thought would be the deepest part of the channel, I cut my way with the big chisel through six feet of ice before I struck water. Ah! I thought, as I stood there perspiring in the cold, while the ice-clear river water bubbled up in the hole—that should do it! But when I searched the depth with a long pole to see how much room I had, I found that I had reached only a two-foot pocket of water trapped in the ice, and there was more ice beneath. I gave it up, disgusted. The beaver in that house must have starved that winter, frozen in, unable to reach their food. Unlucky beaver.

It was hard work and low wages. Some of the old people used to say that there were few things more demanding. To stand out there in that amazing frost and handle the burning iron, often with thin gloves, or nothing at all on your hands, if the work must be done with care. Cold hands and cold feet, numbed and aching fingers. Nothing to eat all day but a frozen dough-nut, or a piece of dried meat and a handful of snow. As Fred Campbell would sometimes say of himself as he danced up and down beside his trail on a cold morning, trying to stay warm, "whining like a pup" for the frost— "it was *that* cold!"

And it was not the cold alone, though that could be brutal enough. Trav-eling on the river ice and in the creek bottoms, there was always danger of stepping into overflow water and getting wet to the skin. Many a Far North trapper could tell of breaking through thin ice and plunging into knee-deep water, of the race to shore to build a fire, to warm and dry himself. If you got anything frozen out there, far from home and shelter, it was just too bad.

I have an image of myself bent over on the ice in Tenderfoot, my nose feeling as if it was about to split open in the minus-forty-degree frost; curs-ing, muttering to myself, as I tried with thick mitts or dead fingers to get that damned trap set just right. And come back days or weeks later to find no animal caught, but wind and snow over the set, the bait gone, the trap sprung, and nothing there at all for the time and work.

There were quiet days at home, in camp, skinning marten. The small carcass thawed overnight in a cool part of the cabin. In the morning I began with a knife, working down from the tail and back legs, pulling the skin from the cold, still partly frozen body. A small-bladed knife was best around the toes and head. When the nose and lips came free, I stretched the wet skin inside out on a narrow board made for that purpose, and tacked it there, a thin splint holding the tail down flat.

I dried the skins carefully away from the heat, turning them on the boards, making the best of the work. And then with a few of my best furs I caught a ride to Fairbanks one morning—a long, cold ride in the back of someone's pickup, maybe. I made the rounds of the furbuyers in town, finally taking a price, never enough, but something, enough to buy a few things we needed. With a sack of groceries I caught a ride home through the dark on the long, empty highway.

If success in the woods can be put into numbers, or measured at all with its many hidden rewards, my own was never great, but varied according to the fur supply and the time I was willing to give to trapping. In one good winter I have record of, I caught twenty marten, a couple of lynx, and one or two foxes. I was paid less than $300 for these when I sold them. That was a lot of money to us then, two-thirds of the year's income. And as I say that, I realize again how little we needed to live on in those years, and how important that little could be.

Not long ago, while stopped in a small settlement in Yukon Territory, I saw a local notice of fur prices for the coming fall. As I glanced over the list, I was astonished. $350 for a prime lynx! $250 for a red fox. Coyote to $150. And so on down to the always reliable marten, mink and beaver. I thought back to my own days with envy. We were lucky to get $30 for a lynx, and the average was $15. You could hardly give away a fox skin, and except for the occasional bounty money, coyote were better left in the woods. As I turned away from the price list, I felt as if I'd spent a good part of my life in a bleak and impoverished age.

But as necessary as it seemed to be, and as welcome as the money was, I never really liked selling my furs. They were more to me than money—the satisfaction of a good job done, and the clean fur shining in the light. I felt the pride had gone into my pocket when they were sold.

I think of myself during those years as a passionate amateur, an intense and respectful intruder on an ancient domain. My trails and cabins were real, the dogs and much else, and I lived much of the time as if no other life or work could ever matter. But trapping was not for me the single, lifelong occupation it has been for others. I would yield to them the greater claim— masters and serious men in their own right, as many of them have been. But what I did had its own seriousness, and I learned from it what I wanted. Another lifetime, perhaps, I might have remained and let the wilderness take me.

When some of the adventure of it had worn off, and we had another source of income, I did not trap again. But it was always there, a thing I could do if I had to, though my dogs were gone, sleds and harness sold, and fur prices lower than ever.

If I consider it now, with many details forgotten, prices and much else put aside, what I return to is the deep wonder of it. How it was to go out in the great cold of a January morning, reading the snow, searching in the strongly slanted shadows for what I wanted to see. And there were books to be read there, life-histories followed sometimes to their end: a bit of fur matted in the stained ice, the imprint of an owl's wing in the snow.

A strange, mixed enjoyment. The smell of something victorious, to have worked that hard in the cold, and gotten something for my labor. To have outwitted that creature, set the trap or snare, and caught it. To discover by morning light something that lived and moved by night, and of which I had known nothing before but a footpad left in the snow.

There might come that morning after a storm when I went with snow-shoes to break out a trail in the deep drifts and wind; all the tree limbs bent over with snow, and no trail to be seen, the traps buried out of sight. It was far, far back in time, that twilight country where men sometimes lose their way, become as trees confused in the shapes of snow. But I was at home there, my mind bent away from humanity, to learn to think a little like that thing I was hunting. I entered for a time the old life of the forest, became part fur myself. Sometime there may come to us in a depleted world, the old hunter's dream of plenty. The rich country, full of game, fish and fur, bountiful as it once was. The bear, the moose, and the caribou. The woods are thick with rabbits; the marten crossing and recrossing, their paired tracks always going somewhere in the snow under the dark spruces. And carefully, one foot before the other, the round, walking track of the lynx: they never seem to hurry. Beaver in the ponds, a goshawk beating the late winter thickets like a harrying ghost; and now and then the vague menace of a wolf passing through.

This, or its sometime shadow: the country dead, and nothing to see in the snow. Famine, and the great dream passing.

Bear, and More Bear

FROM *The Cheechakoes*

WAYNE SHORT

*Wayne Short came to Southeast Alaska as a boy in 1946 to homestead
on Admiralty Island, an experience that he recounts in his two memoirs,*
THE CHEECHAKOES *(1964) and* THIS RAW LAND *(1968). In "Bear, and More
Bear" from* THE CHEECHAKOES, *twenty-year-old Wayne and his family live
among the giant brown/grizzly bears of the island.*

Several nights went by without incident, then late one night Duke
woke me, and said: "There's something fooling around in the
woodshed." I climbed out of my sleeping bag and pulled on a wool
shirt. Old Spot was whining softly at the door. The woodshed was
actually a lean-to, open at the end, built against the side of the
house. I pushed Spot away and eased the door open a crack. In the dim
moonlight I saw the indistinct shapes of two bears eating our deer. My heart
quickened and began to pound. Their unpleasant, musky odor filled my
nostrils, and I shivered uncontrollably. I quietly closed the door and turned
to Duke.

"Bears," I whispered. "Get your oh-six ready. I'll ease the door open and
hold the light on them for you."

When he was ready I slowly opened the door once more—and flicked
on the light. Both bears looked up from their eating straight into the light.
I was in front of Duke and I jumped aside and yelled: "Shoot!"

Spot broke between Duke's legs just as he pulled the trigger, and the
shot went through the woodshed roof. The bears exploded into action,
coming within a few feet of us as they ran out of the shed and across the
garden to disappear into the brush.

It had happened so quickly, Duke did not have time for another shot.
Spot followed as far as the garden and stopped to bark for a couple of hours,

thus showing the intruders that they had scared him not at all. Ma was calling from inside the house, and lighting a lamp. Pap and Dutch were wanting to know what the shooting was about.

The deer had been badly chewed, a fact that made us wonder how we could possibly have slept while the carnivores munched and cracked bones only a few feet away. The next three nights we boys took turns standing watch, but the bears did not appear. On the fourth night, after we had said, "We must have scared the devil out of them—they won't be back," they came and, this time, with a friend.

Dutch heard them, and woke Duke and me. We pulled on our boots first, for the last time I had run outside barefooted and stepped on a nail. Pap heard us and asked, "What's up, boys?" "Bear!" I said, and pushed the growling Spot into one of the back bedrooms and closed the door. Then Duke and I took rifles from the rack on the wall and stepped quietly to the back door. We had rehearsed just what we would do if the marauders came back, so each man knew his job and there was no confusion. Dutch had the five-cell flashlight, but he did not turn it on until we eased the back door open. Duke and I stepped quietly out into the back yard and waited several paces apart. When Dutch's flashlight went on, three brownies were so busy working on the one mangled deer carcass we'd left for bait, they hardly looked up. Duke and I put our sights upon the two front ones and shot. One went down immediately, but the other two lunged off the porch and started across the garden, one carrying the deer carcass in his mouth much like a dog might carry a rabbit. Dutch ran out of the doorway and kept the beam of his light upon them. One was obviously wounded. Duke and I got them in our sights and began shooting again. The wounded one went down in Ma's cabbage patch and the one with the deer dropped it and ran into the woods roaring and bellowing at the top of his lungs. Duke and I both claimed to have hit him.

As we stood there a moment getting our breath, Dutch turned with the light and saw the brownie on the porch trying to get to its feet. He screamed for us to shoot, and we wheeled together and each put a shot into the massive head. Ma and Pap were lighting lamps and calling to us, and Dutch went back to explain what had happened. Duke and I walked out to the garden to where the other bear lay. I put the muzzle of my rifle against the big head and fired. We were learning.

Out in the woods the wounded brownie continued to roar. From the sound we could tell he was slowly circling the house.

"I wouldn't go back there after him now, for all the money in the world," Duke said, shivering.

"Me either," and I thought of all the terrifying tales I'd heard and read about wounded brown bears.

We went back to the porch where the others stood looking at the brownie that lay there flooding the floor with its blood. The wounded bear kept roaring with rage out in the woods and I felt a shiver go down my spine. Tomorrow we'd have to take old Spot, trail the bear and kill him, but I sure didn't relish the chore of going into the brush after him.

The next day, after we had dragged the brownie from the porch and skinned it, we took our rifles and, with Spot in the lead, set out on the wounded bear's trail. It had circled the house at a distance of perhaps seventy-five yards, then veered and crossed the creek. We took it slow and easy, our eyes on Spot who had an extraordinary nose for a terrier. The trail turned and twisted with no set direction; sometimes we found blood, sometimes not. At last we came to a thicket of blueberry brush, devil club, and small stunted cedar.

"I'll lay odds," Pap said, "that he's holed up in there."

Spot, nose still to the trail, limped into the thicket and was soon lost from sight. A minute later we heard him barking; it was not his excited yip-yip bark.

"What do you boys think?" Pap asked.

We all agreed that he had found the bear, and that it evidently represented no danger.

"Well, let's spread out a little," Pap said, "and take it slow and easy."

Sixty yards inside the thicket we found Spot sitting on his haunches looking at the dead bear, already starting to stiffen. We all breathed a big sigh of relief.

When we got home we began skinning out the bear we had killed in the garden; both brownies had long, dark-brown hair, and we decided to smoke-tan their hides and put them on the front-room floor. The one we had already would go on our bedroom floor. But now we were back facing our old problem: what to do with the carcasses. Both bears weighed in excess of seven hundred pounds, we guessed, the larger one possibly eight hundred pounds. To haul them out into the woods would be inviting their cronies to another feast—and that, we decided, we could do without. At last Pap suggested that we bury a "deadman" on the beach in front of the house for a tail-hold, then with block-and-tackle we could drag the carcasses out to where the high tide would float them. Then it would be no job to tow them out into the bay with the skiff and outboard motor. We did this and, when we were through with the chore, Duke spoke for all of us when he said: "I've had about all I want of bears for a while."

Late September is a time of change; summer has gone, and winter is not too far ahead. It is a time of equinoctial storms and sudden rain squalls. By October the morning air is crisp and, up high, the ridges show frost. The deer begin to move downward just ahead of the frost line, and this is the best time of the year for the hunter.

During the late summer we had brought in silver salmon, called *cohos,* and Ma had canned several cases of them. We had invested in a home-canning machine and twenty-five cases of cans; we intended to fill the rest of the cans with venison, ducks, geese, and with clams from the nearby clam bed on the spit at Deer Island. We also had some special enameled cans for crab meat, and we built several crab pots and set them out in the bay. Although in many ways we were green to this country, we had come from a farm and knew how to put up winter food. Venison would take the place of beef and pork, and the big, fat Sitka blacktail bucks were plentiful. We boys were doing all of the game hunting and packing—and we loved every minute of it. Ma and Pap began putting it up for winter use.

Venison chops and roasts were canned and processed, the scraps ground and made into hamburger and chili, which were also canned. Pap had several big crocks and one of these held salted king salmon sides that we'd put down in the early fall to be soaked out and smoked or baked at a later date. The other crocks were for corned venison and sugar-cured venison hams. It is surprising how much like pork venison tastes when it is smoked and later fried or baked. We ordered side pork out from town on the mailboat, then ground and mixed it equally with venison. This made a delicious sausage, which we seasoned and either packed for smoking into small cheesecloth bags that Ma made, or else made into patties and partly fried before packing them into a large crock and covering the patties completely with lard. Either method kept the meat well and it could be used as needed.

Paul Stromgren had shown us how to make a deer-call, and we began using it with great success. A call will bring a doe within range, nine times out of ten. It will also bring a buck as rutting season nears, but he is much more cautious and will rarely show himself if there is any cover. It will even bring a brownie who, with a shortage of salmon in the streams, has developed a taste for venison. Duke found this out one day as he was sitting upon the edge of a muskeg blowing his deer-call.

The day before on this same muskeg, he had called up a particularly fine buck and killed it. Now he was back, trying for another. He had blown the call off and on for some minutes but nothing had shown. He put out his cigarette and was ready to leave when a strange musky odor came to his nostrils. As he sat there trying to identify it, he became aware of something at his back, and at precisely the same moment he recalled the odor of the brownies we'd killed. Something touched his back, and then he could hear the bear sniffing the dried deer blood of yesterday's buck. He wished suddenly that he'd changed his wool hunting shirt. His reaction was to jump up and run, but he knew better than that. He glanced at his .30/06 leaning against a rotten stump three feet away—it might just as well have been a mile. Then, as his self-control was about to break, he recalled Paul's words: *If a brownie ever gets you dead-to-rights, don't move! Don't move an eyelid; movement is what sets them off.*

For several long minutes he sat there with the hot breath of the bear on his neck as it continued to sniff him. His reprieve finally came when a fawn called from across the far side of the muskeg. The bear moved away a few yards, and ever so slowly Duke turned his head and saw the animal for the first time. It was big—larger perhaps than any of the ones we had killed. When the brownie had moved off fifty yards, Duke eased to his left and got his rifle. He slipped a cartridge into the chamber with trembling fingers and sat there quietly watching the bear until it was out of sight.

A week later we had a still closer call. We had by now slashed out a fair trail across the peninsula to Murder Cove. On this particular morning I had elected to stay home, and the rest of the family set out on the weekly trip to the cannery to collect the mail. They moved along the trail single file, Duke in the lead with the only rifle, then Ma, Pap, and Dutch.

They were midway along the trail when, without warning or apparent provocation, a huge brownie rose up from behind a log where it had been lying and charged straight for them. When Duke first saw the animal, it was perhaps thirty-five feet away, and by the time his rifle came to shoulder it was almost upon them. He flipped off the safety, and shot. The bullet hit the animal squarely in the chest, staggered it, but still it came. He shot twice more into the chest, but each time it recovered from the smashing impact of the 220-grain bullet and came on resolutely. Finally he shot it in the head and for the first time it went down. But the next moment it was up again. Duke put another shot again into the massive head and was now hardly a barrel's length away. As the brownie slid forward to the ground it knocked Duke backward and he too went down.

He twisted on the ground and threw the remaining cartridge into the chamber, but it was not needed; it was all over. The whole thing had taken less than a minute during which the rest of the family had scarcely moved.

I have been told by some that a female brownie does not attain any real size; this female's hide, however, squared eleven feet, and we estimated she weighed somewhere near twelve hundred pounds. It was the largest brownie I have seen in this part of the country, and by far the largest bear any of us were to kill in several years of hunting these carnivores. And it brought to our attention another facet of the strange, unpredictable behavior of these animals. The bear had been waiting behind the large log, watching the trail. Had it been waiting for a deer to pounce upon, or had it become separated from a cub and turned its frustrations upon the first moving thing it saw? But there was one thing we did know: the head shots had put the bear down!

When first we had decided to come to Alaska, we boys had read every article we could find on brown bears. I still remember one of the things almost always preached: *Never* shoot a brown bear in the head, for its brain is located at the base of the sloping skull and so protected by thick bone that the bullet will glance off.

This is pure fiction. I do not know what started the story that a bullet would glance off a bear's skull. Perhaps the perpetrator made a bad shot; again, it might have resulted from the use of one of the old slow-moving calibers. At any rate, it is certainly untrue of today's high-speed rifles—except perhaps in rare instances. It is true that a bear's skull is long and sloping, and that its brain is well protected from a frontal shot. But this certainly does not mean that it is invulnerable; a modern rifle will shatter the bones of the head to such a degree that the nerve centers are bound to be seriously affected. An enraged brownie with its heart shot out is still a dangerous animal. It may travel a hundred yards before bleeding to death, and an animal that has time to do this is easily capable of killing its foe before dying itself. But a head shot, as a rule, will put a bear down, if it does not kill it outright, thus giving the shooter time for another shot. An ear shot such as Dutch had made accidentally with his little .25/20 illustrated how easily a bear may be killed if hit squarely in the ear. The record shows that a surprising number of brownies have been killed by a shot in the ear from a .22 rifle.

Shortly after this encounter we made a rule that has served us well: *If the bear is inside the safety margin, and appears dangerous—shoot it in the head.* And we all carried .30/06 rifles when we thought we might run into a brownie. It is my opinion that a man is foolish if he hunts with a rifle any smaller. All of us have killed brown bears with everything from a .22 Hornet on up, but it was only because it was all we had to shoot with at the time. With a smaller caliber rifle one must stand fast and place his shots. But sometimes a man does not have the time, and he must shoot by instinct alone.

The first occasion on which I had a chance to test my speed with a rifle—and my courage as well—was very nearly my last. It happened shortly after Duke's encounter with the big she-bear on the trail. I was deer hunting and was packing in a nice buck I had taken. I was still unfamiliar with the ridges behind Surprise Harbor, and in the vastness of the woods I got turned around. I knew, however, that all the streams in the country led eventually to the beach, and I decided to follow out the first creek I came to.

Before I came to a creek I ran into several acres of windfalls, the result of an exceptionally bad storm some years before. In my ignorance I thought I might cross the downed timber without too much difficulty, but soon I found it would be practically impossible to cross the obstacle course with the deer upon my back. I had turned about and was starting back, when suddenly I heard brush cracking on the far side of a log pile. It never entered my mind that it might be anything but a deer; and, likewise, I did not consider how I could find my way back to the spot if it was a deer and I killed it. I slipped off the safety on my rifle, and stepped quietly around the end of the log pile.

There, facing me, not fifteen feet away, was a brownie. We stared at each other for a long moment. I did not want to shoot at such short range if it was at all possible to avoid it. But the bear apparently wasn't going to be the first to turn away; the scent of the freshly killed buck upon my back must have been enticing. The hair of the brownie's hump began to rise, and my finger tightened on the trigger. At its first lunge I shot at the massive head.

The next moment I was knocked sideways and the crushing weight of the deer came down on top of me. I lifted my head slowly and looked around. The brownie was several yards away, watching me malevolently and coughing blood. My right hand still gripped my rifle, but with the weight of the deer upon my back I dared not try to reload and move into a position to fire. I lay still, scarcely breathing, and wondered how hard I had hit the bear. From what I could see I'd missed the head and hit the throat. My thoughts went to old man Hasselburg at Mole Harbor who had been so badly mauled by a brownie.

The coughing continued for several long moments, then finally the huge head began to drop. I waited until the animal had fallen to the ground, then slipped slowly out of the deer-pack. I did not really begin to breathe freely until I had put another bullet into the big head. I was bruised but not so much as scratched.

And it was not just Duke, Dutch, and I that seemed to draw brownies; eventually both Ma and Pap had their troubles with them. Pap, while goose hunting in the high grass flats of Murder Cove, almost stepped on a dozing bear that rose up and came straight for him. He quickly dispatched it with a number-two shot; a 12-gauge shotgun is a formidable weapon at short range. The following summer Ma was to kill a big brownie that had dominated the creek while the rest of us were away fishing. After two days without water she rigged herself a shooting bench on the back porch. She waited patiently until Mister Brownie ambled out into sight, then clobbered him with an extraordinary shot in the head.

After killing so many bears in the vicinity of Surprise Harbor, we began to breathe more freely, although we never went into the woods unarmed. We were to have encounters with them from time to time throughout the years to come, but never again would they trouble us to the extent they did that first fall.

The Moose Kill

MARGARET G. MIELKE

Minnesota-born poet Margaret Mielke raised five children with her husband in Peter's Creek, north of Anchorage. An indefatigable booster of Alaskan poets, Mielke was named the state's first poet laureate in 1963. Her poems have appeared in Harpoon *magazine, in* Alaska '76, *and in the Alaskan writers' issue of* Northward Journal. *"The Moose Kill" was published in* THE FIRST ANTHOLOGY OF CONTEMPORARY ALASKAN POETRY *(1956).*

This is something I would have the boys remember:
The moose kill in Alaska each September.
The annual trip by dory to horizon land
Across the water, where the pastel mountains stand;
Leaves of copper scaled and shiny
On the sponge-moss ground.
The padded oars, the queer excitement of no sound.
The spotting of the animal against a distant space,
Our beating temples, and the moose's homely face,
The long, long aim and quick, quick shot, releasing blood,
The work of men and knives and axe that turn it into food.
The heavy quarters that with pride we load
With provider's knowledge that the meat is good.
This knowing that when snow is crowding white
There will be roasts and steaks and stews at night.
The journey home, the beaching on home shore,
The lifting of the quartered meat again, the chore.
The pride and climax of getting what we went for;
The wife's one look, knowing whom it's meant for.
Then the hunting stories, the telling and the swapping;
Sawing steaks and cutting roasts, and then the wrapping.

The final storing in the locker that is cold;
The neat and packaged moose now looks like gold.
There is not a chance the boys will not remember—
No one could forget moose season in Alaska in September.

The Battle of the Giants

FROM *Look to the Wilderness*

W. DOUGLAS BURDEN

W. Douglas Burden is the author of LOOK TO THE WILDERNESS *(1960), from which "The Battle of the Giants" is taken.*

The Siwashing expedition had come to an end and Henry Lucas and I had made ourselves gloriously comfortable in Bill Kaiser's log cabin at the edge of Skilak Lake.

Bill—big, smiling, easygoing—seemed bursting with happiness to have company. He was talkative. On the other hand, I was hungry for reading material and was soon absorbed in some old *Saturday Evening Post*s. Since this was not to Bill's liking, he disappeared down a trap door and emerged with some potent rhubarb wine. As a result, we soon found ourselves engaged in an enthusiastic shooting competition. Naturally, we were all proud of our prowess and at the outset were quite evenly matched, but by the simple expedient of drinking one drink for their two I soon gained an advantage and finally won.

The shooting led to stories of the great bear and particularly of the giant Kenai moose we were about to pursue. The Kenai moose is the largest of his tribe, far larger than his Canadian cousin. His horns not infrequently weigh a hundred pounds and on rare occasions have a spread of six feet. A moose is a very easy animal to shoot, particularly during the rutting season when he seems to be devoid of fear. Thus the prospect of hunting them offered little challenge. However, when Bill began to bet that we could not get a six-foot head I promptly took him on and told Henry I would not pull the trigger on any animal with a spread of less than seventy-two inches. The situation had suddenly changed. Bill had put an entirely different complexion on our hunt, for we had now set a mark for ourselves that would be far from easy to fill.

For the remainder of the day we made preparations for a trip which we planned on a thoroughly luxurious level. In contrast to our mountain adventures, we would have the very best of wilderness homes, an Indian tepee and, in addition, ample food and bedding.

That night I sat up late reading and at dawn we were off again, rowing down a wave-tossed lake toward the great moose flats.

These so-called moose flats are a broad alluvial plain that slopes off gently northwestward from the base of the Kenai Mountains to Cook Inlet. Rivers from the melting snows meander across this incline which, with its potholes and ponds and swamps and eskers, glacial boulders and curving sand hills, bears all the characteristics of a true glacial morain. Except for Bill Kaiser's cabin, there was no human habitation in the vast stretch of land between Kenai Lake and the tiny Indian village of Kenai where the Kenai River empties into Cook Inlet.

At noon we landed on a sandy beach. The country had been burned over years before and presented a bleak and dismal aspect. However, the great burn brought into being a young succulent growth of willow and quaking aspen that produced the largest moose in the world.

We had heavy loads to pack over the ten-mile portage to the Funny River, where we planned to camp. The trail was blazed with bleached moose horns which over the years had been hung on the dead trees to make the way. Underfoot it was firm from long years of travel by man and beast.

Now that we had left the mountains, I was back in my woods clothes. For comfort in the bush, nothing is more important than proper footgear, and I had the very best knee-high Eskimo sealskin boots and smoke-tanned moccasins lashed tight around the ankles. Over my underwear I wore flannel pajamas, the legs of which emerged under the trousers and hung loose and tattered over the skin boots so as to drain off the water from the wet grass on the outside. A sloppy sight, perhaps, but a perfect combination.

While we were packing in, a swollen-necked young bull disputed our passage, giving evidence the rut was on. He walked to within thirty feet of us, the hair on his spine standing on end. We yelled at him again and again and in abusive language ordered him out of there. We even threw stones, all to no avail. Finally we made a big detour and left him where he was.

In the late afternoon, a white moose horn emerging from a pile of debris caught my eye. A brown bear had killed a big moose, as they often do during rutting when an old bull is sleeping against a tree. The bear had eaten his fill and then tried to cache the carcass. Sticks, stone, moss and grass had been scratched up and heaped over the remains—all but one horn.

It was a dismal place, this kill lair of the brown bear. As I thought of the tremendous strength and size of these giant moose, I tried to imagine how even a great bear could lay him low—what power to break a neck so swollen for battle! Henry told me he had once seen a brownie in pursuit, a thundering onslaught at a running moose. They had disappeared behind some spruce, so he did not see the kill, but when he arrived the bull was dead—his neck broken.

For a week Henry and I hunted hard. We had breakfast at daybreak and started immediately afterwards, with a bit of the inevitable sourdough bannock to munch on at noon. Every day we saw moose that were too many to count, some with large heads, but each day we returned empty-handed, exhausted by the soft muskeg and endless stretches of spruce that lay in littered confusion all over the land like piles of jackstraws. Nothing we saw even remotely approached horns with a six-foot spread.

The black flies were bad whenever the wind dropped and for these demons we were well prepared with Stockholm tar spiced with citronella. What a joy it was to smear on this revolting mess! It made Henry darker than a Cree and I was not far behind.

Henry was a man dedicated to his task. He spoke little; even under cross-questioning his answers were brief and to the point. Rarely did he permit himself an anecdote.

Only once do I remember a question of abstract curiosity. Our tepee was pitched in a thick sheltering grove of young spruce at the edge of Funny River. I had gone out to cut some more wood, for there is nothing more pleasant than a bright fire on a frosty autumn night. As I returned with an armful and saw the tepee glowing with warm flame, it seemed that no other shelter in the world makes such an inviting home on a cold wilderness night. It is nest and safety and comfort and warmth all combined. Outside is hostile darkness and perhaps storm and wind, rain or snow. Inside is peace and security—brightly lit and toasting, with an endless draft of pure air that comes in the bottom and carries the smoke out the top but which, because of the inside flap, never touches the occupants.

I had dumped my load just inside the entrance and was seated on a raised bedding of logs and boughs while Henry cooked more of his execrable bannocks. After he was through cooking, I added some wood to the flame, building the fire up Indian style so that we would have plenty of light while eating. In the ever-moving flames playing on his strong features, Henry's keen, mobile face was a study; sensitive but with repose and nobility, a face that somehow seemed to belong to this stupendous land. A tin plate was on my knees and I was spreading a thick layer of jam to soften some hard-fried bannock when Henry suddenly turned to me and said, "Douglas, what is fire?" I was surprised and flattered that he should have turned to me with a question that primitive man, forever struggling against darkness and cold, must have asked himself for countless eons. For a long time I gazed into the flames, not knowing how to answer. Finally I murmured, "Henry, fire is energy in the process of being released." This was a tough one, but I added, "Energy is latent in all things—even a piece of rock." I knew he would not understand the word "latent" but I went ahead anyway. "When you set fire to wood, the energy in that piece of wood is released in the form of heat and light." I didn't know what more to add. I felt inadequate to the occasion and failed completely to bridge the gap in our backgrounds. Henry lapsed into silence and disappointment. I wished somehow that I could have answered adequately a question that this lone trapper must have pondered many times.

The following day we were up and off as usual, striding over strewn jackstraws, sinking deep in the soggy lowland moss, and scouting endlessly from every high ridge with the telescope. We worked westward into lower country and at about two o'clock we suddenly saw our moose, his white horns looming large against the broken bracken on which he was lying. Two cows stood guard nearby. He was about three quarters of a mile away on an open ridge facing our way. There was no chance of getting any closer unseen, for between us was a broad expanse of swamp grass. Henry and I were stretched on our stomachs among the prone spruce poles. For a full five minutes Henry studied him through my thirty-power hunting scope. Then he said, "Maybe seventy-two inches—too far be sure." He had a measuring tape in his pocket and, still lying low, he marked out seventy-two inches on a dead spruce log with his hunting knife so as to fix the width in his mind.

We lay there from 2:30 to 4:15 and during all that time the great bull never moved. Henry looked at him through the scope. I looked at him, then

Henry looked again. He was in love with my scope and hated to yield it to me even for a few minutes. Finally he said, "I think him seventy-two inches. We try get him." The sun came out for a while. The wind dropped and the black flies were at us. With the cows still standing guard, we could not move, but now that Henry had given his verdict we were filled with excitement.

At 4:15 we heard some grunting beyond the ridge. Evidently a challenge, for the bull got to his feet and strode away from us over the ridge. That was our chance.

As soon as he and his two cows were out of sight, we jumped up and sprinted across the intervening marshy ground. Long before we reached the ridge where he had been lying I was panting hard, but Henry gave me no respite. We pushed on to the top of the ridge, where we found ourselves confronted with a rare spectacle. The terrain before us was like a stadium closed in by ridges sloping down to the level ground in the center. The bronze-brackened ridges were covered here and there with stands of golden aspen shimmering in the late evening light. Moose were everywhere— young and old, cows and bulls, some alone, some in groups. We started to count them but soon gave up and concluded later there were at least three hundred in sight.

We looked for our big bull with his light-colored flat-lying horns, but he was nowhere to be seen. Then we noticed to our right, at the upper end of the amphitheater, another giant moose. He was standing alone with ears erect, looking out over the floor of the arena. Except for size and magnificence of appearance, he was totally different from the animal we were after; his horns were dark with enormous upturned palms and a forest of brow tines as big as a man's forearm.

He stood, motionless and alone, king of the herd. His very aspect carried such defiance we instinctively felt this was a young animal at the peak of his power. Then he grunted a deep-throated challenge again and again, all the time looking fixedly toward the open end of the low encircling hills at something we could not see. Finally came the answer and a moment later our white-horned giant strode magnificently into view and stood there, head high, accepting the challenge. Immediately Henry said, "Shoot! Shoot!" I was still panting from hard running and, though utterly galvanized by the entire situation, I fired, and, happily, missed. The roar of the 9.5mm Mannlicher reverberated through the amphitheater, but even against the silence the explosion had no more effect on that gathering than the buzz of a mosquito. Not one animal moved away, they did not so much as look in our direction.

Instead, they seemed to be watching the two giants on the floor of the arena as though knowing something important was about to take place. Again Henry said, "Shoot!" "No," I said, "let's watch." Henry could stand it no longer. "Come," he whispered, and started to move down the slope.

The two bulls were a hundred yards apart but they had marked each other as leaders and were slowly advancing for battle. Moose were on all sides as we sped down the slope. One cow was so close I could see the erect hair on her spine and thought she was certain to charge.

At the bottom of the slope was a log where we rested. We were now not more than fifty yards from the center of the arena. On the far ridge and to the right were several dark congregations of animals and I noticed some of the younger bulls were taking advantage of the preoccupation of their seniors.

I had the feeling we had invaded the privacy of the most primitive and prehistoric of all the deer family—nothing was to be allowed to disturb it. We might as well have been on Mars, so little did our presence influence the behavior of this primeval gathering.

The two bulls were closing the gap between them. But there was no haste, no sudden rush. Their strides were slow and measured and dignified. Heads down, their necks were arched and bulging. They moved with great deliberation, sweeping their heavily pronged antlers ponderously from side to side with each forward step. I knew their eyes were bloodshot with angry fire.

These animals were no alien species. The attack was not to devour. Yet the will of each to destroy the other was deep in their blood. It was an urge as basic as sex itself—a part of the aggressive drive to dominate.

The two great bulls were now within a few yards of each other. Theirs had been a noble advance. Neither animal had in the slightest degree hastened the majestic rhythm of his forward march. Their great heads and enormously swollen necks were still swinging heavily when I became aware of an almost stifling stillness that fell abruptly on that wild assembly. It was like the final moment of quiet before the storm. I glanced at the surrounding hills. Not a single moose was moving. All stood stock-still, gazing down on the arena. We were witnessing something out of the dim and distant past—something not many civilized men would ever witness.

And then it happened: the resounding clash of antlers backed with nearly fifteen hundred pounds of taut sinew and bursting muscle. The mighty forward surge of two great beasts came to a dead stop. For seconds the contenders were so equal the battle seemed motionless—nothing but straining muscles thrusting forward against equal thrust. Forelegs were tucked under the belly, hind legs braced far back.

At that moment I noticed for the first time the fighting advantage any moose has if his eyes and forehead are well protected with a fine array of brow tines. The younger bull had that protection. The older bull did not have it and soon blood was dripping from his head. For a moment he drew back slightly and then plunged forward again with all his might. The younger animal reeled backward a few paces and I could see how careful he was not to expose his flank to battering horns whose prongs could have driven into his lungs or pierced his intestines.

When moose fight it is often to the death and woe betide any animal that falls, for then the victor uses his sharp hoofs to cut his adversary to shreds. Now the bulls broke apart and as they did so the old one reared and slashed out with his foreleg, striking the young bull's chest.

It was a lightning play that I had seen once before when a spikehorn moose struck at a wolf. The old fellow drew blood but immediately the young bull closed again and there was a great straining back and forth; the soft earth became chewed and muddy as they circled and slashed, seeking some momentary advantage.

Yet in all the maneuvering and hard fighting, there was something about the old bull's behavior that was never completely convincing. Perhaps, I thought, he sensed his age and limitations. Perhaps he counted on his faithful cows to stand by him even in defeat, but whatever it was, I could not help feeling that here was a gladiator—fighting, defending, but without the determination to kill. Several times he broke off the engagement as if to say "enough is enough," and each time the younger bull came at him again harder than ever.

It is rare, I imagine, that animals so committed quit the field of battle. Yet sometimes an old veteran may decide to do just that. But how was it to be done? With horns thrusting against him, how could he escape? How turn aside without exposing his flank to impalement? But his was a beautiful maneuver, executed with consummate skill. The old bull broke loose the grip of horns, reared high like a stallion about to strike, and then with smooth, almost unbelievable agility, turned in the air and fell back to earth in full retreat, exposing only his rear end for a brief moment. The very instant he landed, he trotted off with head still high. Meantime, the victor stood his ground, not deigning to pursue. The hot breath was streaming from his nostrils. He called several times but no answer came. Among all the moose in that amphitheater there was no movement. I, too, felt immobilized. Now Henry came to his senses as if pulled out of a dream. "Come," he said. It was difficult to rise but when I did, I looked once more over that arena. The victor still stood like a statue even though some of the moose on the surrounding hills were beginning to move again. "Come," repeated Henry. We took off across the field of battle right under the nose of the victor, ran as hard as we could up the ridge, out of the stadium, and onto a broad open area of aspen and spruce. For more than half a mile we ran—when Henry suddenly stopped and pointed. There directly ahead, about a hundred and fifty yards away, was our bull. He was facing away from us, an impossible shot. The two cows, still with him, had seen us, for their ears were up and both had swung around toward us.

When you have been pursuing an animal for a long time and finally catch up with him in a situation where you are certain of a kill, the thought often comes over you to let him go and sometimes you do, for killing then seems wrong. But now, I had no qualms; I wanted that spread more than I had ever wanted anything before. The whole situation had built up to a final climax. The hunt had gotten into our blood. Henry had never secured a seventy-two-inch head. This might be his record as well as mine.

I was still panting hard when I dropped on one knee and moved the safety catch with my thumb. At that moment the old bull swung his head to see what the cows were looking at. In doing so, he exposed his vulnerable neck. I have missed many easy shots in my day. But though this one was far from easy and by all odds the most important shot of my early years, the bullet went home and the big bull fell and never moved again. When we reached him, he was dead. What a magnificent animal! For a moment I knew remorse at destroying a creature so fine. Yet the bull was past his prime, was on the decline, and I consoled myself with the thought that he probably had not had too long to live. Now he was down, his fine white horns shone against the bracken, and there was Henry dancing around him. He pulled the measuring tape from his pocket, fluttered it in the breeze, then jigged about as if daring himself to take the measurement.

Finally Henry sidled up to the wide-spread antlers, placed the end of the tape on the widest prong and asked me to hold it there. Then he ran it out across the total spread and held it for a while without daring to look. He had his thumb at the exact measurement and when at last he took courage and glanced at it, the reading was exactly seventy-two inches. With that my silent Henry burst into cheers and fairly jumped for joy.

We had won our bet and attained our goal and eventually these horns were duly recorded in *Records of Big Game.*

It was a tough trip home in the dark but by ten the next morning we were back with our bull. It was warm and the raw skin, meat, and horns attracted clouds of flies. But I was so proud of my animal I decided to portage the horns myself, no matter what they weighed or how bad the flies, and this I did with packboard and tumpline all the way to camp and then another ten miles to Skilak Lake.

Then came a trip down the foaming rapids to the little Indian village of Kenai. Shooting rapids is always exciting and this wild ride made a glorious end to our adventures. Henry and I had gotten along beautifully. Never had there been the slightest misunderstanding between us. He was a lone-wolf type and I had enough of those feelings myself to have a wonderful sense of kinship with him. Endless days of tough terrain, bad food, and often extreme physical exhaustion measure a man as few things do, and Henry had been grand. It was hard to imagine that we would not meet again.

I wanted to express my appreciation with something other than cash. As we clambered together down the loam cliff from Kenai village and mingled with the Indians boarding a launch for the run up Cook Inlet to Anchorage, I had a sudden inspiration. Digging into my packsack, I pulled out my beautiful telescope and said, "Henry, this is yours. I want you to have it. I will enjoy thinking of you using it." His answering smile was marvelous to see, and when he took the telescope I sensed a certain mistiness in his eyes that told me his heart was happy. He tried to speak, "Douglas . . ." and then he turned and walked away without another word. At the top of the bank he stopped. A moment later, the deep throbbing of a heavy-duty engine shattered the quiet and I was off in an unseaworthy launch overloaded with Indians, waving good-by to a wonderful guide by the name of Henry Lucas.

Moon of the Returning Sun

FROM *Shadow of the Hunter*

RICHARD K. NELSON

*Richard K. Nelson is a cultural anthropologist, educator, and writer who has
lived among the Koyukon Athabascan and Eskimo peoples. He is the author of
many books, including* HUNTERS OF THE NORTHERN FOREST, HUNTERS OF THE
NORTHERN ICE, *and* MAKE PRAYERS TO THE RAVEN *(1983). His 1989 book,*
THE ISLAND WITHIN, *won the John Burroughs Nature Writing Medal. An
Alaska resident for many years, Nelson currently lives in Sitka. "Moon of the
Returning Sun" is from his collection of short stories,* SHADOW OF THE HUNTER
*(1980); it concerns the lives of a group of Inuit (Eskimo) villagers in the
Alaskan Arctic through the seasons of the year.*

I t was near dawn, a few days past the New Year. A half-moon, low
above the northern horizon, threw gray light across a featureless
expanse of snow and ice. Featureless except for the silent cluster of
houses set atop a low cliff where the tundra ended and long drifts
sloped away to the ice-covered Arctic Ocean. The houses made up a
small Eskimo settlement called Ulurunik, "where-the-bank-crumbles."
Thin streamers of smoke, glowing pale in the moonlight, trailed from each
house and diffused into a haze above the ocean ice.

A large husky sat near the edge of the bank, its outline dimly silhouetted against the horizon. Then it stretched forward, lifted its head in a gentle
arc, and began a deep, moaning howl. Its voice started low and hollow, rose
slightly in pitch, then dropped and faded. The dog howled again, this time
higher and louder, its head thrown back and wavering slowly from side to
side. The third time it howled several dogs nearby rose to their feet and
added their voices. This aroused still others, and the chorus spread, like a
drift before a growing wind, until almost every dog in the village was howling. Their sound, eerie yet wild and beautiful, carried for miles through the
clear, frigid air. After several minutes it faded away except for the shrill barks
and howls of a few diehard pups. Silence closed back over the land.

A midwinter day was about to begin. Toward the southeast, pale blue
was gradually spreading along the horizon, where flat tundra plain met

arching sky. The sun would never appear above the horizon on this day, nor on many more that would follow. For more than two months each year it remained hidden from sight, unable to climb above the curved edge of the earth. Even during this season, however, the twilight was strong enough to create a "day" several hours long. What little light there was, the Eskimos appreciated to its fullest.

The dog that began the howling was one of eleven tethered alongside a small frame house that was almost buried under a broad snowdrift deposited by the prevailing northeasterly gales. On one side a trough dug through the snow led to a small door that opened into a very low hallway. A second door at the far end of the hallway gave entry to the single large room in which the family of Kuvlu lived.

The dawn light was still too faint to be seen through the small window in the east wall of the house, but the dogs' spirited howling had awakened an old man, Sakiak, father of Kuvlu. He knew despite the darkness that it was morning, so he lay on his side, head braced on one hand, waiting for the sleepiness to leave him. No one else had awakened. He could barely make out a large bed near the south window where Kuvlu, his wife Nuna, and two of their smaller children slept. Three more children occupied another bed, and an older son, Patik, used a small mattress on the floor. Sakiak, whose wife had died many years earlier, also slept on the floor.

He could hear a breeze blowing gently in the stovepipe, and he hoped it would grow no stronger. Some mornings the house rumbled and shook as if there were an earthquake, but it was only *nigiqpak,* the northeaster, which howled across the tundra so often at this season. If the wind remained light today, Sakiak would go far out onto the ocean ice to hunt.

He felt around near his bed until he found a match, which he struck against the wall and used to light a kerosene lamp. The flame caught quickly, and yellow light filled the room, which was dingy and unpainted, cluttered everywhere with the necessities of life. In addition to the beds there were several chairs and box stools, a table, containers filled with clothing, and a large iron-topped stove. Sakiak pulled several chunks of seal blubber from a box, put them into the stove, and let the glowing embers set them afire. The blubber sputtered and burned with a hot, smoky flame that quickly drove the chill from the house.

Nuna slipped out of bed, set a kettle of water on the stove, and picked up a caribou skin she had begun scraping the day before. "Perhaps you will hunt," she said in a low voice, as if she were talking to herself. "It is possible," he answered. Men were usually indefinite when they spoke of hunting, because the fickle moods of weather and ice too often mocked their plans. Sakiak ate cold slices of boiled caribou meat left from the night before, dipping each one into a saucer of fermented seal oil to give it flavor. When he finished, he drank the cup of strong coffee that Nuna had set before him.

She used the remaining hot water to make a pot of black tea, which she poured into a battered thermos. Sakiak slipped the thermos into a cylindrical pouch made from caribou hide with the thick fur inside. This pouch would help keep the tea hot, since a thermos alone was inadequate when the temperature was far below zero. He packed the thermos, a few biscuits, and a small frozen fish into an oblong sealskin bag that he always carried when he hunted. The bag also contained binoculars, an ammunition pouch, matches, a sewing kit, and a seal-pulling harness.

Sakiak opened the door and stepped into the dark hallway. Supercooled air rushed into the house, condensing instantly to a thick cloud of steam that spread along the floor. He returned in a moment, carrying a voluminous bundle of clothing, all made from caribou hide. Two of the children, who had awakened, sat quietly watching as he pulled a pair of bulky fur pants over his cloth trousers. He slipped his feet into fur-lined inner boots and tugged his outer boots over them. Then he put on two wool shirts, a nylon jacket, and a knit watch cap. Over it all he pulled a bulky parka, its fur turned inside and white cloth covering the scraped skin outside.

The caribou hide clothing was light and comfortable, but its loose fit and thick fur made Sakiak look almost twice his normal size. A ruff of stiff-haired wolverine fur encircled his wrinkled face. He smiled at the children and gave one of them a pinch with his stumpy, leather-skinned fingers before turning to leave. On the way to the door he picked up his hunting bag, gloves, and fur mittens.

Moments later he emerged from the long hallway, now carrying a rifle in a homemade sheath of white canvas. He straightened up outside the door, peering into the early twilight. Needles of cold stung his face, and each time he drew breath a deep minty chill spread down his throat into his chest. "*Alapuu!*" he spoke to himself. "Cold!" It was thirty-five below zero, with a gentle breeze from the east lending added chill to the air. He pulled his gloves on before his fingers numbed but stuffed his mittens into the sealskin hunting bag. His hands would perspire if he wore mittens during the long walk out onto the ice.

Sakiak stood atop the hard drift beside Kuvlu's house. The moon was low above the northern horizon, its white profile drawn sharp against the deep black sky. Millions of stars stippled the heavens, each one standing out clear and unwavering. These were good signs. If the horizon was hazy and the stars twinkled erratically, it forewarned of a gale that could crack and move the sea ice. Looking southeastward, Sakiak saw the black sky lighten to pale blue. Gold streaks flowed upward from the invisible sun, illuminating a few wisps of high cloud. If the east wind held, he thought, tomorrow would be bitter cold. But this was a good day to hunt.

He turned and walked along a hard-packed sled trail that led to the edge of the village and onto the frozen ocean. There were lights in several houses now, but Sakiak was the first man out to begin his day's activities. Only the dogs watched him pass, aroused by the noisy squeaking of snow beneath his steps. He was careful to stay clear of the chain-tethered animals, knowing they might lunge at any stranger who passed within reach. Some dogs stood up to bark or growl as he walked by. Most, however, remained in a tight curl on the snow, breathing into the thick bushes of their tails and conserving the warmth of their bodies.

Beyond the last house, the trail followed a gently sloping ravine that opened onto the snow-covered beach. The trail split at the ocean's edge, one fork going north along the coast and the other heading out onto the sea ice. Sakiak chose the seaward trail. He walked with short, brisk steps, rather stiff-legged and somewhat bent at the waist. His hunting bag and rifle were slung horizontally on his back, each suspended from a strap that passed across his chest and shoulders. He carried a long iron-pointed staff, or *unaaq,* that he would use primarily for jabbing the ice to test its safety.

For the first half-mile the ice was almost perfectly flat, except for a few low hummocks, or ice piles, where the floes had moved and been crushed the previous fall. The surface was also punctuated by the minor undulations of snowdrifts, packed hard as a wooden floor by the pounding winds. Sakiak's practiced eye could tell which drifts had been shaped by the cold northeasters and which by the warmer south winds. If fog or a blinding snowstorm caught him, he would navigate by watching, or even feeling, the configuration of the drifts.

Shortly, he reached the first high ridges of piled ice. He picked his way up the side of a huge mountain of tumbled slabs and boulders, from which he could look far out over the pack. When he stood at the top, he scanned the vast expanse of snow-covered ice that stretched beyond him. It was still gray twilight, but in the crystal air and brightness of snow the sea ice stood out sharply to the distant horizon. From his lofty perch, Sakiak looked over an environment that appeared totally chaotic and forbidding. Huge ice piles and ridges interlaced the surface everywhere, encircling countless small flat areas and occasionally fringing a broad plain of unbroken ice.

To the unpracticed eye this jumbled seascape would have seemed utterly impenetrable and unattractive. But to the Eskimo it held a different promise. He would find an easy trail by weaving among the hummocks, crossing them at low places. And he would find his prey, the seal, that now swam in dark waters beneath the pavement of ice. For although this world appeared silent and lifeless, the sea below was rich with living things. The currents carried millions of tiny planktonic organisms, the basis of a long chain of biological interrelationships. Larger invertebrates and fish fed upon the drifting clouds of krill, and they in turn fell prey to warm-blooded animals that rose to the surface for air. Seals lived all winter among the congealing floes, gnawing and scratching holes through the ice to reach the air above or rising in the steaming cracks. And, on the ice surface, polar bears and Eskimos stalked the seals.

Sakiak searched the pack with his binoculars, their cold eyepieces stinging his skin. He was attentive to minute details, hoping to pick out the yellowish color of a polar bear's fur against the whiteness of the snow. He looked also for the fresh black lines of cracks and for rising clouds of steam that would mark open holes and leads. Long minutes passed before he took the binoculars from his eyes, satisfied that there were no bears or open places in the area. The ice was packed firm against the coast and would not move today unless the wind or current changed. It was a perfect time for an old man to wait for a seal at its breathing hole.

In a moment Sakiak was down from the ice pile, walking seaward again along the sled trail. About a mile out from the coast he passed the frozen carcasses of two old dogs, half-covered by blown snow. They had been shot early in the winter by their owner, who was replacing them with strong pups. This fate awaited all dogs that outlived their usefulness, for though Eskimos appreciated their animals they could ill afford the luxury of emotional attachment to them. Sakiak had used dogs all his life, but like all the older hunters he often preferred to walk. Animals frequently saw or heard a dog team long before they could detect a lone man afoot, so it was better to hunt this way. If the kill was heavy, a man could drag part of it home and return with a team for the rest.

The trail wound and twisted across the ice, which made it long but relatively smooth. Still, it crossed many ridges that the Eskimos had laboriously chopped and smoothed to make the passage as easy as possible. About two miles out the trail entered a field of very rough ice, with some ridges forty to sixty feet high. Broad slabs of ice four feet thick had been tossed on end and pushed into the air like huge monuments that towered high above a man's head. The far edge of this rough area was marked by a single ridge that stretched unbroken for miles, its direction generally paralleling the distant coast. The outer face was a sheer wall of pulverized ice, ground flat and smooth by the motion of the pack.

Sakiak sat down to rest and cool off beside this ridge. His long walk had generated too much warmth, and if he did not stop he would begin to perspire. He knew that moisture robbed clothing of its warmth, so he always tempered his labors during these cold months to avoid overheating. The long ridge where Sakiak rested marked the outermost edge of the landfast floe, an immobile apron of ice that extended far out from the land. An early winter gale had driven the ice against the coast and caused it to pile so high and deep that the entire floe had become solidly anchored to the bottom of the ocean. The ice beyond it was the mobile Arctic pack, which moved according to the dictates of current and wind.

Hunters knew that landfast ice rarely moved during the winter unless a tremendous gale arose, with an accompanying high tide that lifted the ice free of the bottom. Landfast ice meant safety because it would not drift away, carrying men out to sea with it. But the pack was different. Hunters who ventured onto it were suspicious and watchful, constantly checking wind and current to be sure the ice would not break away from the landfast floe. If this happened, and it sometimes did, they would be stranded beyond a widening lead, an open crack that blocked their return to shore. Men who drifted away often died without seeing land again.

A week earlier, powerful onshore winds had driven the pack against the landfast ice, where it had remained without moving ever since. Sakiak would now decide if it was safe to go beyond the final grounded ridge. He walked along its edge until he found a narrow crack covered with dark, thin ice. With the point of his *unaaq,* he chiseled a fair-sized hole through it. Then he cut a bit of sealskin thong from his boot tie, chewed it until it was moist, and dropped it into the black water. The white thong sank slowly downward until it cleared the bottom edge of the ice, then drifted off eastward, toward the land. Finally it was enveloped in the blackness.

Sakiak stood up and looked out onto the pack. The current flowed from the west, from the sea toward the land, gently but with enough force to hold the ice ashore against opposing pressure from the easterly breeze. He had studied the movements of ice throughout his life, and he remembered well the lessons taught him by old hunters during his youth. With this knowledge and experience he could judge to near perfection the mood of the pack. Today it would be safe, so long as the wind and current pushed against each other. He would look for breathing holes somewhere not far from the landfast ice, where he could scurry to safety if conditions changed. Old men knew there was no point in taking chances. "The ice is like a mean dog," they warned. "He waits for you to stop watching, and then he tries to get you."

Sakiak climbed to the top of a nearby ridge and scanned the pack with his binoculars. Jagged lines of hummocks pierced sharply into the brightening sky. The day was now full and blue, brilliant refracted twilight glowing high above the seaward horizon. He smiled as he squinted into the brightness. Indeed, it was *Siqinyasaq tatqiq,* "moon of the returning sun." But the cold needling his cheekbones reminded him that it was still midwinter, and that he must work fast to hunt before darkness closed over the sky again.

He saw no hint of life on the pack, but the configurations of ice told him where best to look for it. Just beyond a low ridge several hundred yards away there was a long plain of flat ice, its color and lack of snow cover indicating that it was not more than three feet thick. This would be an ideal place to search for the breathing holes of seals, because they were easy to see on such ice. The sled trail had ended at the edge of landfast ice, so he picked out an easy route before heading toward the flat. Younger hunters often failed to reconnoiter in this way, considering it a waste of time. But instead of moving faster they were forced to clamber laboriously over the rough ice, and they often came home bruised and exhausted.

It was not long before Sakiak stood at the edge of the big flat. Its surface was completely free of snow but was covered everywhere with large, fluffy crystals of frost, some so thin and feathery that they shivered in the breeze. They were made flexible by salty moisture from the ice, which prevented them from freezing hard, and when Sakiak walked on the frost his tracks were slushy despite the intense cold. This was why ice hunters wore boots soled with waterproof seal hide, which kept their feet dry on the moist surface.

He moved quickly along one side of the flat, searching for the telltale signs of a breathing hole. Presently he stopped, looking at the ice nearby. He saw a little group of thin ice chunks frozen into the surface, scattered in a circle about a handbreadth in diameter. When this ice was newly formed, a seal had broken up through it to breathe, leaving a small opening with bits of ice around it. The hole was never used again, but this frozen scar remained.

If the seal had continued to use such a hole as the ice thickened, it would have looked quite different. Each time the animal returned, water would slosh out over the ice and freeze, eventually building up a small, irregularly shaped dome with a little hole in its top. By scratching and gnawing, the seal kept this dome hollow inside, like a miniature igloo. Beneath this structure the hole widened into a tunnel through the ice, large enough to accommodate the seal's body when it came up to breathe. The Eskimos called such breathing holes *allus*.

Sakiak walked to the far end of the flat without seeing an *allu* or even another scar. So he turned back, following a low ridge that flanked the opposite side. He had not gone far when he spotted an *allu* just a few yards from the base of the ridge. It was very large and nearly cone-shaped, so he knew at a glance that it had been made by the huge *uguruk*, or bearded seal. He bent low, stiff-legged, moving his trunk from side to side and peering into its opening. The interior was very dim, but he could make out its round entryway, covered by a layer of dark gray ice. This was a disappointing find. The ice was almost a day old, indicating that the seal was not using this *allu* often.

If the days were longer he might wait there, for a bearded seal was a fine catch indeed. But with few hours of daylight he needed a hole that was visited more frequently. He would remember this *allu*, and if the ice did not move he might check it again to see if the seal returned. Sakiak memorized the shape of the ridge nearby so he could easily guide himself to this spot another day.

Breathing holes were often somewhat clustered, so he looked carefully around the area. Seeing none, he climbed the ridge to inspect a small flat on its opposite side. He was surprised to find that the flat was cut by a broad crack, perhaps ten yards across, covered with newly frozen ice. The crack, which must have opened during the past week's storm, made a jagged swath across the flat and sliced cleanly through a ridge on its far side. Sakiak marveled at the power of moving ice, which could split a heavy ridge into two sections as a man would cut through blubber with his knife. The crack probably ran for miles, and there would almost certainly be a few breathing holes in its covering of young ice. It also offered Sakiak an easy trail through the hummocky areas.

Sakiak made his way down the ridge and onto the frozen crack. He followed it across the flat, through the chasm of the split ridge, and onto another flat. There he saw what he was looking for. Almost in the middle of the crack was a nearly perfect little dome, the *allu* of a ringed seal, or *natchiq*. He peered closely into its opening and saw deep black inside. "It's good," he murmured softly to himself. The blackness was a circle of open water with a transparent skin of new ice forming at its edges, just a few inches below the quarter-sized opening of the *allu*. Not an hour before, while Sakiak walked out across the landfast ice, a seal had risen here to breathe.

There was no time to waste. For all he knew, the animal might be heading for this hole now, and he was not ready for it. He slipped off his hunting bag and rifle, laying them on the ice together with his *unaaq*. Then he went quickly to the nearest hummock and kicked free two blocks of ice for a stool and footrest. After carrying them back, he again inspected the interior of the *allu*. Its opening was slightly off center, and the tunnel appeared to angle somewhat away from the vertical. From this Sakiak knew which direction the seal would face when it came to breathe, and he would angle his rifle slightly for the deadliest possible shot.

Now he placed the two ice blocks about a foot from the hole, along its southeast side. He calculated automatically, almost without thought, the effects of wind and light. There was enough brightness to create a faint shadow, which must not fall across the hole. And he must not sit upwind lest the seal be frightened by his scent. He also preferred to face away from the biting chill of the breeze. He emptied his hunting bag onto the thick ice alongside the crack and pulled his rifle from its canvas sheath. The bag would insulate and cushion his stool while the sheath insulated the footrest. Eskimos always took pains to minimize loss of heat from their bodies in every way possible, and Sakiak knew the wait would be a cold one even in the best circumstances.

He placed his *unaaq* on the thick ice, where its shadow would not be visible from below, and he adjusted the ice blocks so they could not jiggle or squeak noisily. Then he sat down on one block and put his feet on the other, so that his legs were held straight out before him, Eskimo fashion. He could sit this way for many hours without tiring. When he was seated atop the ice blocks, his menacing presence could not be detected by a seal looking up through the glowing translucence of the gray ice.

The bolt of his rifle clicked loudly in the brittle cold as he thrust a shell into the chamber. Then he placed the weapon crosswise over the tops of his boots, where it was least likely to compress his clothing and cause chilling. Its muzzle faced the *allu* but did not hang over where the seal might see it. He had taken the precaution of standing a flat chip of ice alongside the little opening to screen his intrusive shape from the seal's eyes as it rose to breathe.

Now he would wait.

It was impossible to know when the seal would appear. In fifty winters of hunting at breathing holes, Sakiak had learned not to think too much of time. It might be fifteen minutes, perhaps an hour. Perhaps many hours. Sometimes the animal never returned.

Sakiak knew of old men who, in times of starvation, had waited beside an *allu* for twenty-four hours. Nowadays the young men refused to hunt at breathing holes, preferring to wait until a wide crack or lead formed so they could shoot seals in the open water. When Sakiak was a boy the men had relied upon harpoons, which could not be thrown far enough to strike a seal swimming freely out in a lead. But a harpoon was as good as a rifle for hunting at breathing holes, perhaps better. When a seal was harpooned, a line attached to the point ensured that the animal would not sink or be carried away by the current.

Young men said that breathing-hole hunting was too cold, that it involved too much waiting. The old men said only that people must eat. They had learned the art of enduring patience, as if they could merge their thoughts with the timeless physical world that surrounded them. Life, after all, was a game of waiting. One could not expect that the weather, ice, and animals would do a man's bidding. If a man would live, he must persist, wait, endure.

Sakiak was enveloped in still silence, interrupted only by the occasional buffeting of wind against his parka hood. His breath condensed on the ruff around his face and on his scraggly moustache, coating each hair with thick white frost. He could feel the immensity of the pack surrounding him, its quiet, latent power.

Radiant amber flowed up the wall of the sky before him, hinting of warmth in some distant world, while the pervasive cold drew closer around his body. Time faded away to a dim consciousness at the core of the hunter's mind.

Twilight grew and spread slowly southward, then edged toward the west. The fullest light of midday came, then imperceptibly began to fade. Sakiak drew his arms from the sleeves of his parka and held them against his body for warmth. He was shivering. Frost had collected on his eyelashes and brows. Occasionally he poked a bare hand up through the neck of his parka and held it against his cheek to warm the stiff, numb flesh. His toes felt large and icy cold. Perhaps the temperature was falling, he thought. Indeed, it was now minus forty, but the wind was fading as it grew colder.

Sakiak wished he had brought the boy along. His grandson Patik was old enough to hunt and could make the seal come to the *allu* where he waited. If he walked in a broad circle around Sakiak, he would frighten the seal away from its other holes and force it toward the hunter's station. Had the ice been perfectly smooth, Sakiak could have accomplished this alone by finding every breathing hole in the area and urinating on it. The powerful scent would frighten the seal away, leaving it only the hunted *allu* to use. It was funny to think how a seal must plunge away in frightened surprise when it smelled urine in its *allu*. But in rough ice many breathing holes were concealed in open spaces beneath hummocks and snowdrifts, where a man could never find them.

Almost two hours had passed. A growing ache spread up Sakiak's legs and back, but he dared not move to relieve the discomfort. The seal might be near enough to hear any noise transmitted through the ice to the water below. So he moved only his head and arms, even then very carefully.

It was also important to watch the surrounding ice in case a polar bear happened to approach him. Bears would occasionally stalk a man, if they were so thin and hungry that starvation drove fear out of them. But today it seemed there was no life anywhere, except for the silent lives beneath the pack. Sakiak wondered how deep the water under him might be. And he thought the current could soon shift and flow from the east, as it always did when intensely cold air moved in off the great expanse of land that stretched eastward away from the coast.

He was now shivering hard, and he wondered if his shaking might jiggle the ice stool, making a noise that would scare away the seals. He smiled, thinking what a great joke that would be after such a long, cold wait!

But beneath him at that moment a seal torpedoed through the black-gray water, darting and arcing in pursuit of the fleeting silver of fishes. It dodged between the blue and emerald-green walls of ice protruding down-ward beneath the hummocks. Huge inverted ice mountains blocked its path, but it sensed them and turned away before striking invisible barriers deep in the blackness.

In the freedom of its dense medium, the seal could ignore the encum-brances of gravity. It swam on its side, then upside down, then coasted to a stop in midwater. There it hung quietly in the dark silence, drifting slowly with the current, like a footloose star in the vastness of space. But this space was far from an empty void. Nervous shoals of fish left glowing trails as they spun and needled through luminescent plankton. Tiny jellyfish pulsed and parachuted, trailing delicate streamers beneath them. And, far below, crabs littered the bottom, waiting for those above to die and become their food.

For more than a minute the seal remained motionless, ignoring the fish that swam too near. It was in need of air and was listening. Then it suddenly whirled and shot upward toward a circle of white that glimmered faintly in the high distance.

When it reached the underside of the ice, the seal turned slowly beneath the circle. It hesitated a moment, then swam slowly upward into the narrow passage. Reaching the surface, it poked its nose out for an instant, sampling the air, then dropped again. The air was fresh and stinging of cold. It rose again, emerging into the bright igloo of ice, globed eyes wide and black, nostrils flaring and closing.

In the silence of the pack, after a long wait, the seal's approach was startling and exciting. Sakiak first heard, almost sensed without hearing, a pulsation of the water inside the *allu*. Then he saw water flow through the opening and over the ice outside, where it instantly froze to a fresh glaze. This water was forced up ahead of the seal as it rose from below.

Sakiak heard scratching as the seal cleared away newly formed ice at the tunnel's upper opening. He quickly slipped his arms into the sleeves of his parka, then remained perfectly still. The cold had vanished. Shivering ceased as warmth spread from mind to muscle.

He fixed his eyes on the *allu,* consumed with intense concentration. His lips moved slightly, almost imperceptibly. "Come seal," he whispered, asking the animal to give itself to him. "Come. . . ." It was only a thought this time.

In a moment the seal obeyed Sakiak's will. It took a first short, hissing breath, smelling the air for signs of danger. He did not move. He expected the brief silence that followed, knowing the next breath would be a deep one.

Whoosh!

It was a long, drawn-out hiss that sent a misty spray from the opening. This noise was loud enough to drown out the sound of Sakiak's movement as he reached down and picked up his rifle from his legs. He was careful to spread his arms so his clothing would not scrape noisily, and he was still before the deep breath was finished.

Whoosh!

Again the animal breathed. Sakiak lifted his rifle and held it vertical, with the thumb of his upper hand against the trigger. Again he waited, as the second breath stopped.

Whoosh!

On the third breath he moved his rifle straight above the *allu,* its muzzle inches from the opening. His face was expressionless. His resolve was complete. Without a second's hesitation, he deliberately squeezed the trigger.

For the seal, breath cut short. A sudden *crack!* only half heard before the world was shut out in closing clouds of black.

For the hunter, a sudden deafening explosion. The *allu* split and shattered. Fragments of ice dyed crimson. The seal bobbing on the pulse of water, grotesque and broken, instantly detached from the reality of life.

Sakiak ran to fetch his *unaaq.* Using its sharp point, he chipped the rest of the *allu* away, then snagged the animal with the metal hook on its other end. The seal was still quivering, so he held it until movement stopped. With the knife he carried on his belt he slit the skin of its upper lip, then he pushed the loop end of his seal-pulling harness through this cut and fastened it around the animal's nose.

This done, Sakiak held the line under one foot while he chiseled the hole until it was large enough so he could pull out the seal. If he had not secured the seal quickly with a line, it might have been carried off by the current. In thicker ice, where the seal would enter through a long, cigar-shaped tunnel, this would be unnecessary; winter-killed seals were buoyant from their thick layer of blubber, so they would float well up into the tunnel where the current could not take them away.

Finally Sakiak pulled the seal out onto the ice. It was completely limp and flexible, like a sack full of liquid. Blood flowed and coagulated on its skin, freezing in thick layers around the wound. It was large for a ringed seal, about four feet long and weighing perhaps a hundred pounds. And its hide was deep black, patterned with small whitish circlets. The *Inupiat* called a dark seal like this *magamnasik.*

The warmth of excitement that had flared inside Sakiak died quickly, and he found himself shivering again. Before starting back he should eat something and drink the hot tea in his thermos. Eskimos knew that food kindled heat inside a man's body, so it was important to eat well and often during the cold hunts. Heavy steam billowed from the thermos when he opened it. He drank quickly, feeling the hot liquid flow down his throat to the cold pit of his stomach. Refreshed, he took the hard-frozen fish he had brought along and peeled off its skin. Then he cut it into small sections and hungrily ate the raw chunks. Its oily fat would bring him quick warmth and energy.

More hot tea and a couple of frozen biscuits finished his meal. When he had drunk his fill of tea he spilled the remainder out onto the snow, staining its white surface yellow brown. It made sharp, crackling noises as it immediately froze to a brittle crust. He felt deep appreciation for the food and for the seal he had killed. He could remember his grandfather chanting thanks to an abiding spirit that helped him, but Sakiak thanked the Christian God with a short prayer in Eskimo.

He rested for a few minutes, looking at the distant sky. The light was fading, and he had a long walk before him. Perhaps in a few days he would return to this *allu*. Often several animals used one hole, and they might eventually come back in spite of the damage done to it. But now there was little time to waste. Sakiak lighted a cigarette and put his equipment back into the hunting bag. When this was finished he took his knife and made a long slit down the seal's belly. Then he cut a wide slab of blubber from the abdomen and both flanks, laying it aside on the ice. Along each side of the slit he made a series of holes in the hide, and through these he laced a piece of heavy cord, sewing the animal back together. Removing the blubber made it almost ten pounds lighter, and ten pounds would make a noticeable difference to an old man pulling a large seal home over the ice.

Now he slung his hunting bag and rifle case across his back, placed the strap of his seal-pulling harness around his chest, and began walking toward the landfast ice. The limp seal, still warm inside, slid along easily behind him. Sakiak had pulled hundreds of seals this way, however, and he knew that its weight would grow as he crossed the piled ice.

Once, when he was young and strong, Sakiak had shot two bearded seals weighing several hundred pounds apiece and decided to pull both of them home. He cut every bit of meat from one animal, discarding the bones, skin, and entrails. Then he removed the entrails of the other, stuffed the meat of the first seal into the empty carcass, and sewed the skin back together. The load was still very heavy, and he had pulled late into the night before reaching the settlement, completely exhausted.

Thinking of that experience seemed to lighten his load, and soon he could see the edge of the landfast ice. This was good, because he wanted to be off the pack while there was still fair light. He was taking a long route, because by weaving back and forth he could stay almost entirely on flat ice. In spite of the deep cold he soon became overheated from pulling, and so he decided to rest at the base of a small ridge.

He was about to sit down on a large ice boulder when he noticed what appeared to be an *allu* in the flat ice some distance away. Curious, and hoping to find a place to hunt another day, he walked quickly to it, leaving the seal behind. Even before he reached it he could tell that something was wrong. The little dome was partially caved in, and along one side the ice had been dug away. He knew immediately what had happened. "Ah, *nanuq!*" he whispered. Wandering away from the hole was a set of broad footprints, the track of a polar bear. It was not fresh. A haze of frost crystals already filled the prints, showing that a day had passed since they were made.

Sakiak inspected the tracks again and again, looking off in the direction they faced. The bear had hunted at this *allu* and, like him, had found success. It first dug around the dome until the ice was very thin. Then it filled the excavated area with snow scraped from the ice, so the seal could detect no change as it came up inside. Finishing this, it stood beside the *allu* at a right angle to the wind, awaiting the seal's return. Eventually, perhaps many hours later, the bear heard its prey breathing within the dome. In an instant it smashed the surrounding ice with both paws, simultaneously crushing the animal's skull. Then it pulled the seal out onto the ice, squeezing it through a hole so small that many bones broke inside the lifeless body. So it was that Eskimo and polar bear hunted the same animal in almost the same way.

The hole was now frozen over. Flecks of blood spotted the bear's tracks, showing that it had carried the seal away to eat it elsewhere. Sometimes bears slept long and soundly in the rough ice near a kill site, digesting the meal before moving on. Sakiak saw darkness moving up the eastern sky and looked away along the tracks. The bear might be somewhere nearby, or it might be far away over the ice horizon. From the age of the tracks he suspected it had moved on, but he would follow them for a short distance to look for more signs.

Several hundred yards away, near a broad field of rough ice, he found the seal's carcass. The bear had eaten only its skin and blubber, leaving the rest behind to be gnawed by the little white foxes that so often followed bears. They had already eaten half the meat, showing that many hours had passed since the bear's meal. The bear must have been fat and in its prime; otherwise it could not afford to eat only the choicest parts. Sakiak was sure now that it was far away, but he climbed a ridge and scanned the surrounding floes for a long time to be sure. Seeing nothing, he returned to his seal and resumed his trek toward the landfast ice.

Now he was careful to look behind him every few minutes, to be sure no bear was following. Bears often followed a man's trail over the sea ice, especially if it was scented with the blood and oil of a seal. Sakiak knew men who had felt a tug on their seal-pulling harness as they dragged their catch home in the dim hours of evening. They turned to see a white bear, ready to stake claim to the animal. Old-timers often warned the young hunters to slip out of the harness quickly and grab for their rifles if ever they felt something strange while pulling a seal.

A man named Takirak, who lived in the neighboring village of Utqeavik, had an unexpected encounter with a bear when Sakiak was still a boy. He was setting fox traps on the landfast ice and carried only a long knife. A skinny bear appeared nearby, looking as if it might attack him. Takirak was a brave man who knew much of animals, so he handled the bear wisely. He drew his knife and walked threateningly toward it, speaking in a firm, low voice. "Go away, bear, or I will cut up your handsome face." The animal backed away, but it persisted in following as Takirak walked homeward. Each time it came too near, he threatened it again. Finally, when they drew within earshot of the village's howling dogs, the bear ran off and did not return.

It was not long before Sakiak reached the ridge that marked the edge of landfast ice. He followed it southward until he found the sled trail, and there he rested briefly before heading landward. Twilight was fading rapidly now, and distant ridges loomed mysteriously in the growing gloom of evening. The trail crossed many low ridges, and Sakiak found himself becoming warm and a little tired. Fortunately the snow had been pounded slick by the passage of many dog teams over the previous months, so the carcass slid along easily. In any case, old men, like old dogs, were tough and long-winded. The young were faster and had more brute power, but they often tired long before their elders.

Sakiak thought of these things as he trudged across the silent floes. He was alone, one small old man on the vastness of an ice-covered sea. The breeze had died away to an occasional puff, and his footsteps squeaked loudly in the steel-hard cold. Beads of perspiration covered his forehead, just inches from the rime of thick frost that whitened his parka ruff. He melted ice droplets from the long whiskers of his moustache by holding his tongue against them, refreshing himself with the cold moisture. Ahead he could see the village, sharp and black against the snow-covered tundra that swept away to meet the sky. Smoke from the chimneys rose, then flattened out in a thick haze that hung over the houses.

Soon he was crossing the last stretches of flat ice that fringed the shore. It had been a long, slow walk from the edge of the landfast floe, and Sakiak thought fondly of the comfort that awaited him. Nuna would have hot tea ready, and stew made from caribou meat. Behind him the last streaks of flaming gold spread widely along the sea horizon beneath the overarching blackness of night.

He could see a dog team returning home amid a chorus of envious howls and challenging barks from tethered animals. Someone was hauling in large blocks of freshwater ice cut from a tundra lake near the village. He wondered if any hunters had killed caribou today far inland where tall willows broke the sweeping wind. Fresh tongue and heart, boiled together in a large pot, would await the families of the lucky ones.

Sakiak walked slowly up the ravine that ended atop the bank and followed the trail toward Kuvlu's house. Children of all sizes ran out to walk beside him, asking endless admiring questions. "Where did you catch the seal?" "Did you see a bear?" "Will you eat the seal's boiled intestines tonight?" Sakiak said little, letting the older children invent answers for him. He loved to hear the laughter of children and was always happy when they ran to meet him. Someday, perhaps, they would hunt to feed him when he no longer walked out over the ice.

Migalik, a young man, was feeding his dogs when Sakiak passed. "Ah, Sakiak, you have killed a seal. *Azahaa,* you're a man!"

"And you," he answered, "perhaps you have traveled today." Migalik said he had gone far south along the coast, nearly to Qayaqsirvik, searching for polar bears. But he saw nothing except a few wolverine tracks and a fox caught in one of Nauruk's traps. The two men talked briefly, their conversation raptly followed by several young boys who wished they could hunt instead of spending their days inside the village school. Some of the boys had already killed their first animals and passed the meat out among the old people to ensure luck as they grew to manhood.

When the men had told each other the events of their day's hunting, Sakiak pulled his seal the rest of the way home. His grandchildren, bundled in parkas that were miniature replicas of his own, ran out from the house to meet him. He joked briefly with them, then told the oldest boy to pull the seal in for his mother to skin and butcher. When she finished, he was to carry a piece of its meat to Saatuk, the old woman who lived in a sod hut at the far end of the village.

Sakiak stood looking out over the sea ice. He wondered about the bear whose tracks he had followed. It was a big one, with meat that would drip with fat and a pelt that might bring a handsome price indeed. He did not think about killing it, lest he bring bad luck upon himself. Tomorrow would be very cold and still, perhaps so cold it would be wise to stay at home. But he would like to walk out and look for the bear.

The moon, enormous and brilliant white, was lifting itself into the southern sky. Long gray shadows stretched out over the snow. The sea ice emerged again from darkness, looking distant and utterly detached from the world of the land. Sakiak brushed a shower of sparkling frost crystals from the ruff of his parka, turned, and disappeared into the long hallway of the house.

The Ten-Footed Polar Bear

ESKIMO LEGEND

"The Ten-Footed Polar Bear" is an Eskimo tale retold by John Smelcer in his collection of traditional Native stories, THE RAVEN AND THE TOTEM *(1992). Smelcer, an educator, writer, and publisher, was adopted into an Ahtna Athabascan family as a small child. He lives in Anchorage.*

A long the northern coast of Alaska, there once lived a Ten-Footed Polar Bear. It spent much of its time in the water swimming between icebergs off the ice pack hunting seals and so it was rarely seen by Eskimos. No one knows why it had ten feet instead of four like all other bears, but it did. It had five feet on each side and when it walked or ran all five feet on one side moved forward and then the other side followed.

Because he had so many legs, when the Ten-Footed Polar Bear ran, he would sometimes get his feet all tangled up and then he would fall down. This is why he spent so much time in the water, because there he was not so clumsy.

A long time back, before there were white men in the arctic, a great Eskimo hunter was hunting seal on the ice pack. He had killed a seal and was dragging it a long distance across the frozen landscape on his journey home to his village.

All of a sudden he came upon a strange sight. In the snow was the track of a polar bear, or many polar bears. He could not be sure. He had heard the strange stories of the Ten-Footed Polar Bear which hunted far away from the villages and was rarely seen by Eskimos, but he didn't believe there was such a bear.

He continued on his way still pulling the dead seal with one arm while the other held his long spear. Then the man heard the ten feet of the Ten-Footed Polar Bear making tracks in the snow just behind him. He stopped and looked over his shoulder. Coming over a tall snowdrift close by, was the polar bear. The hunter was frightened. He had never seen a Ten-Footed Polar Bear and he didn't know what to do!

Quickly, he released the dead seal and ran, still holding his long spear. The great bear ran after him with his ten heavy paws barely sinking in the snow. It stopped for a minute and ate the seal, but then followed after the scared hunter.

The man saw two big blocks of ice close together. He ran towards them and hid there. But the Ten-Footed Bear smelled his scent and ran straight at him, tripping over his clumsy feet on the way.

The wind was blowing the snow all over and for a moment the man could not see the bear, nor could the bear see the man. The hungry polar bear climbed on top of the ice and fell in between the two ice blocks. It landed upside down and got its feet all tangled up when it tried to get up.

The Eskimo hunter took his heavy spear and threw it with all of his strength and hit the Ten-Footed Bear in the heart. Its ten great feet waved back and forth in the air as it desperately tried to get up. But soon it was dead.

The hunter cut off all ten of the bear's feet and took them to his village, but no one believed that he had killed the Ten-Footed Polar Bear. Since that time, though, no one has ever seen such a strange and mysterious polar bear in the arctic.

Moose: Season of the Painted Leaves

FROM *Shadows on the Tundra*

TOM WALKER

*Tom Walker, a photographer and writer, has lived in Alaska for thirty years.
He has worked as a game warden, a wilderness guide, and a log home builder.
Walker is the author of several books, including* WE LIVE IN THE ALASKA BUSH
(1977), HOW TO BUILD THE ALASKA LOG HOME *(1984),* SHADOWS ON THE
TUNDRA *(1990),* RIVER OF BEARS *(1993), and* ALASKA'S WILDLIFE *(1995). His
photographs and articles have appeared in many publications, including*
Audubon, Field & Stream, Outdoor Life, *and* National Geographic.
This selection is taken from SHADOWS ON THE TUNDRA.

The grating of the stovepipe as the wall tent shifted in the wind roused me from a fitful sleep. Only dim outlines were visible against the opaque white canvas. It was five o'clock and the sun had not yet risen.

By this time yesterday we were halfway up the valley searching for the bull moose we had come here to kill. Today there was no need to get up. I could curl into a ball, relax, and ease my aching back. For the first time in weeks I could linger in the warmth of the worn sleeping bag and drift to the music of the dawn wind through the forest.

Later, magpies calling from the meat pole brought me fully awake. Tree shadows groping across the tent showed the sun was high, the sky clear after days of rain and snow. Close by, a woodpecker hammered on a dead tree.

It was seven-thirty. Feeling vaguely guilty for sleeping in, I sat up and started to dress. I shivered into a wool shirt and the blood-stained jeans that I had worn yesterday. Despite two pairs of socks, the shoepacs were cold, the liners frozen. I pulled on a down vest, then a down jacket.

Sitting on the edge of the cot, I opened the Yukon stove and smoothed the ashes with a stick. From a pile next to the stove, I sorted dry spruce twigs, broke them into small pieces, and piled them on the ashes. The night before I had whittled fuzz sticks from a piece of kindling; these I now pushed under the branches. Over the branches I laid several sticks of kindling. I scratched a match on the side of the stove and lit the fuzz sticks. The fire caught and spread rapidly, smoke puffing back into the tent. I adjusted the flue, closed the door, and opened the draft.

The water bucket in the corner near the tent door had a half-inch lid of ice. I dipped water into the boil pot and put both the pot and bucket on the stovetop. As I untied the tent flap and ducked outside, two magpies skittered away from the hanging meat.

Smoke and sparks belched from the stovepipe. The tall pipe, reinforced with wires tied to the tent's supporting poles, jutted through a metal sleeve set into the canvas. The tent was safe from fire, even in the wind.

I walked to the meat pole to check the damage. The birds had pecked through the cheesecloth; swarms of black flies would appear to feed on the exposed meat as the day warmed. From a sack on the ground I took a can of black pepper and rubbed generous amounts into the meat. The flies would avoid these places.

Not a cloud blemished the sky. Southbound flocks of sandhill cranes calling in their peculiar way circled overhead. The mountaintops to the west, in sharp contrast to the azure sky, were covered with fresh snow. Below the snow line, yellow birch and green spruce mingled with patches of scarlet and white tundra.

I strolled about the clearing, stretching and enjoying the crisp, scented air. I checked the heavy moose rack and the silver tag hanging from the skull plate. The supplies hung in the tree, the extra gear was covered with a tarp. All was in order. I went back inside.

The tent smelled of woodsmoke, dirty socks, and (faintly) rutty moose. The warmth, always a surprise in a tent, felt good after the cold wind. I shivered up against the stove. The popping and cracking of the fire couldn't mask the cry of ravens sailing over the treetops. John, sleeping bag around his waist, sat up on his cot. He looked haggard and worn.

"Coffee ready yet?" he said.

"You don't need coffee. You need a transfusion."

"That bad, huh?"

"Yep. Death warmed over," I replied. "I don't know how your poor wife does it. She must not see well in the morning."

John rather crudely disparaged my ancestry but at least he began to dress. The tent now smelled of sweaty, week-old underwear.

I took off my vest and stoked the stove. The boil pot bubbled, so I poured two plastic cups full of instant coffee. John accepted his cup as a starving man would food. I splashed the rest of the water into the wash basin. Behind me John was sputtering. I heard something about "tattoo remover" and "coffee fit to strangle a moose." There were only two table-spoons in each cup. I ignored his ingratitude.

After washing up, I started breakfast. I refilled the boil pot and put it on the stove next to the stovepipe. Beside it I placed another pot of water, for oatmeal. Next to that went the folding-handle skillet, with a slab of mar-garine in the middle. I took half of a moose backstrap from a small cloth bag beneath the table, picked off a few hairs and bits of lichen, and cut six small steaks. I rolled these in a mix of flour and pepper, and when the mar-garine begin to sizzle, I placed them in the skillet.

When the cereal water rolled to a boil I dumped in oatmeal, raisins, and brown sugar. While I tended the meat and stirred the oatmeal, John mixed up a cup of powdered milk. He poured a large dose in his coffee.

The smell of frying meat filled the tent. We'd had ten days of breakfasts of oatmeal and coffee; coffee and oatmeal. Now fresh meat . . . and oatmeal and coffee. I served the steaks on sectioned, plastic plates. We both ate rav-enously, cutting the meat with our sheath knives, forking down big bites. I ate four steaks, John two. Then came bowls of gluey oats washed down with my thick hot coffee. The meal took hardly any time to prepare and even less to eat. Dessert was dried apricots and prunes.

Over cleanup I asked John if he would like to go for a hike to look around the country. His "Hell, no" was not unexpected. He was tired. So was I, but a clear autumn day was not to be ignored. While gathering a lunch of cheese, pilot bread, and gorp, I gave him a rough idea of my planned hike. I told him to keep an eye on the meat and what to do if the birds or flies got to it. I also warned him to watch for bears that might trail in on the wind-borne meat scent.

In my daypack went camera, film, rain jacket and chaps, spotting scope, waterproofed matches, and lunch. I hung my binoculars around my neck, snapped my vest closed over them, donned a blue watchcap, picked up my rifle and started out. I was glad to be alone. I liked John, had hunted with him twice before, but living nose-to-nose with anyone can get old. Free time on such a trip seldom arises until after the kill.

The trail from camp, winding through a forest of birch and spruce, led down onto the river valley and west toward the distant hills. Alone, for the first time in days, I felt the old tingle. The wilderness was mine, alive and sweet, charged with mystery and magic.

Despite the sun, I had to walk fast to stay warm. Underfoot the trail was frozen firm. Alert for any sign of life, I crunched along through a woods alive with the rustle of branches and a blizzard of autumn leaves. Nothing would hear me over the clatter of wind and trees.

One mile from camp the trail climbed a knoll commanding a view of the river valley and the two small lakes to the north. Here I left the trail, walking a few yards to a clearing, dropped my pack to the ground, and began to glass, intent on finding moose in the clearings below. John and I had sat here many times while searching for his moose and had seen a few young bulls and several cows. A mile upriver, ravens circled where John had killed his moose. When the wind died for a moment I could hear them calling. Several perched on the willows, others were wheeling on the wind. I suspected that many more were on the ground, fighting over scraps and entrails. I pictured a few magpies, their long tails flicking nervously, hopping about trying to steal from the ravens.

The bluffs and slopes along the river shimmered in the wind and morning light. The lakes below stood gray and stark, frozen perhaps for the next seven to nine months. Almost at once I spotted movement in the trees near the smaller lake. It was a cow moose. She moved with deliberate steps, head up, ears erect, searching the way ahead for the shapes that bite. I watched her for some time, but only when she stopped to look back did I see the bull that followed. He was lighter than she, a tawny beige. Only his lower hind legs were the typical dark brown. If motionless, he would have been extremely difficult to see in the birch and sere grass, despite his white, palmated antlers.

I was glad no one sat at my side needing directions to the bull. Hunters fresh from urbania seldom see an animal unless it's standing in the open. Looks like the cover of *Field & Stream*. They even pay a guide and rely on another's bushcraft to find it. Over the years I've trained myself to look for a turn of horn, a section of haunch, an unusual profile, a shadow, a color out of place, a difference in texture. This talent, developed through application of energy and interest, became my most remarked upon skill.

"Man! How did you see that moose?" Usually I'd laugh to myself. Great eyesight? Me? Right. Worn eyeglasses since I was six. Twenty-one hundred, uncorrected. Blind as a bat without specs. Seeing is all a matter of tuning in, of knowing what to look for. But I enjoyed the praise. Didn't mind being Natty Bumppo. *Hawkeye.*

Directions to the quarry usually went like this: "Do you see that large spruce at the end of the stream where it runs into that pond? . . . No, not that one. The spruce, the evergreen . . . right . . . the one that looks like a pine. . . . Okay, now follow up the tree about halfway. . . . Move your binoculars slowly . . . then at that point swing left along that crooked branch . . . right . . . the one that has a Y at the end. It has no needles. . . . Now, look at the hillside beyond it. There, just off the end of the branch, next to that small aspen . . . yes, the tree with the smooth, green bark . . . is the bull moose. Only his head and neck show. His body is hidden by willows. . . . Still don't see him? . . . Let's try again. Put down your binoculars and look with your bare eyes. . . . Now, then, do you see that large spruce at the end of the . . . "

Seeing how well this bull blended in, I remembered a time on the Wood River when I spotted a white patch in the timber about a mile from camp. The patch was the size of a pie plate and did not move. At first I thought it a snag or scarred tree but something seemed out of place. I set up the scope and watched the spot for over half an hour. There *seemed* to be some slight movement but nothing definite. After forty minutes of peering through the 35x spotting scope, I saw the shape disappear, then reappear. *Antler.* I knew it. I watched some more. It moved again. I called the hunter over to look through the scope. He was skeptical. I insisted it was a moose. He mumbled something about "ghost moose." That did it. We'd make a stalk.

The timber over there proved extremely thick and hard to hunt. We snuck around it and through it without seeing a thing. I felt certain a bull was bedded somewhere close and had let us walk by. We tried one more time . . . and walked right into a bull rising huge from his cover. One shot at forty feet and the hunt was over. We walked up and looked down. I couldn't resist. "A rare ghost moose."

This bull by the lake wasn't that hard to see. The two moose stood looking at each other. The cow had probably been harried throughout the previous night, or at least since dawn. The bull would have followed her every move, insisting, demanding, prodding, as only a bull moose can. But if she wasn't receptive, it wouldn't have done him much good. With her eyes on the bull, the cow lowered her head and began to feed.

Some moments passed before the bull, antlers held low and at an angle, moved forward. At the first movement the cow stopped feeding. At every other step, the bull's chest would contract, and his mouth open, breath vapor trailing on the wind. I could hear nothing at first but in a lull came the deep grunt of his courting.

"Unk . . . Unk . . . Unk . . ." He approached the motionless cow.

Echoing from a forest on a frosty morn, this traveling call alerts other moose to a bull's presence. Moose locate one another by scent and sound. When transient bulls rake their antlers through the brush, they are doing more than "polishing." Like grunting, antler thrashing can be heard at a considerable distance. A cow might run moaning to the caller, or wait for the bull to home in on her powerful musk. Another bull will answer by thrashing *his* antlers. A transient bull will go toward the sounds in anticipation not just of battle but also of the cows consorting there.

The cow watched the bull approach, then turned away. She trotted several paces, stopped, and urinated. The bull, silent now, came close to scent the flow. The cow straightened and walked away. She was safe for a moment. The bull would not follow, for he was trapped. Trapped by a solid wall of scent, a wall of fire and lust and challenge. His head went down, nostrils to the damp soil. With powerful jabs of his right front hoof, then with his left, he dug and pawed at the ground. The stiff-legged strokes worked the soil into mud. He stopped, smelled the ground again. I imagined the pungent odor. Powerful, searing. To a bull moose in rut, arousing. In an instant his head came up, antlers back, muzzle thrust skyward, lip curled back revealing lower teeth. The *flehmen*. The lip curl. The male display triggered by scent. His head moved slowly from side to side, displaying, reacting in the primal way.

The bull now lowered his head to dig at the ground with his antlers. First the tines on the left side, then the tines on the right. He jabbed and dug, then stomped and pawed, faster and faster, enlarging the wallow. He stopped, moved over the puddle and urinated into it, then lay down like a dog to roll and rub until mud dripped from his neck and shoulders. He stood up and smelled the wallow. Again he pawed at the mud before working it with his antlers, lashing madly with both palms. Once he backed and lunged at the wallow with the fullness of his strength.

The bull stopped, head up, in classic pose. Soil and moss clung to his shoulders, thick black water dripped from the muddied antlers. He seemed to hear something, or perhaps he remembered the cow now gone from sight. In a moment he trotted after her.

I got to my feet, chilled through by the freshening wind, and picked up my pack and rifle. Careful to avoid twigs and grasping limbs, I moved as quietly as possible through the shintangle above the lake.

It felt fine to be alone, free of the shadow behind. One thing about guiding, you learn to ignore the sounds behind: the jacket scraping a bush, the heavy step, the subdued cough. You are aware, too, that the man has a loaded rifle in his hands, and no matter how many times you check to see that the chamber is empty, you constantly worry. I long for days like these, free to stalk the woods and follow a whim, alone in the magic.

I skirted the lake, avoiding the thick brush and ice-over puddles. Downwind from the wallow I stopped in the scent of moose. Far enough from the source to enjoy it, I inhaled the familiar pungency. Closer to the wallow—or moose—one whiff could turn my stomach. Here, now, at this distance, the scent of musk (not unlike the smell of crushed spruce needles) brought memories of forest stalks, glimpses of beasts moving through shadow, racks scraping brush, and antler crashing against antler.

I thought of the bull I once watched in the Brooks Range. After digging a wallow, he walked to a small black spruce where he vigorously rubbed his neck and shoulders until all the branches within reach were crushed, not only leaving his scent in the tree but also grinding into his own hide the clinging scent of evergreen.

I remembered, too, the day near Ship Creek, in the mountains east of Anchorage, when I'd first smelled the musk. I thought it revolting, as indeed in full potency it can be, but here, on this day, the aroma was sweet, light, and good, even exciting. I wanted to follow these moose, stalk close, watch their most intimate acts.

The wallow was to be avoided, so I circled partway up the hill to parallel the moose trail. With the wind in my face I knew the moose would not get my scent or hear me, but I had to move with caution so that I would not be seen. If careful, I would have a good chance to get close.

I crept along until the forest thinned at the edge of a bog. I stopped in the shadow of a tall spruce to carefully study the treeline across the clearing. I double-checked every bush, branch, shadow, and shape. Just as I thought it safe to cross the bog, I saw movement, only a slight flicker, but movement all the same. It could have been a squirrel or bird but I had to be sure. I stared hard, then, *there,* at the edge of the bog under the willows growing tight against the spruce, I saw it again.

I sank to the ground and crawled carefully under the spreading branches of a spruce. Leaning against the trunk, using one hand, I worked my binoculars from beneath my vest and focused them on the spot. It took shape as the ear of a cow moose, and from that I could pick out the entire form. Behind her I picked out the curve of antler in the thick brush.

I knew from other long waits that once bedded like this, the moose could be still for hours, perhaps until evening, or at best, early afternoon. I watched awhile, then decided to sneak away to find a place where I could wait without fear of being detected but still be close enough to know if the moose began to move. I crawled from my hiding place until far enough away to stand up without being seen. Some distance up the hill I found a good place to sit. The ground was hard and dry, the trees blocked the wind but not the sun's feeble warmth. A place to sit, wait, and enjoy the solitude.

Solitude. I crave it. I love to be out like this, the wind tussling the branches, the squirrels chittering in the trees, the fresh air sharp in my lungs. Air so new it tastes like mountain water. My senses brighten. *Moose nearby.* Frost sparkling in the shadows. Blueberries to pick. *Life,* it all screams. All my life I have been an outsider, a nonmixer, feeling I never really belonged. Yet here, in the forest near the wild ones, I'm most alive.

My back and shoulders ached from the loads of moose meat packed in yesterday. I've always had mixed feeling about shooting a moose, or any animal for that matter. I'll want or need the meat—and antlers if hunting with another—but I don't enjoy the kill, butchering, or pack. The stalk is the hunt. The work begins when the trigger is pulled. But the meat is always so good, so palatable, that it alone puts pressure on the trigger finger. A winter without moose meat, or other wild meat, in the cache or freezer is like a winter without snow. When you've got it, you tire of the monotony, but without it you wither longing for it.

Yesterday we had been out before dawn, walking the river trail, moving slowly, looking to the front, rear, and sides, as we had so many times in the preceding ten days. An hour after sunrise we came to the crest of a small rise. After all the days of hunting in wet, miserable weather, we finally spotted a good bull moose. Below us were a cow and two bulls, not a quarter-mile away. One of the bulls was a two-year-old, a Mulligan (nicknamed for the stew), and the other was a giant, sporting antlers I guessed to spread over sixty-five inches.

We watched the three moose walk into the timber. When they did not at once reemerge, we stalked down the slope through light brush to a point near where we'd last seen them. We moved with utmost caution, taking great pains not to make a sound. At the edge of the willows we hunkered low. The light breeze carried a hint of rutty moose.

In whispers we discussed our options, finally agreeing to try and call the moose into the open. While John raked a stick through the brush to mimic the sound of antlers, I'd imitate a bull's challenge call.

Cupping my hand to my mouth, I grunted deep, sharp—an angry challenge. Once. Twice. Three times I called. At my signal, John worked the stick through the brush. In a moment I hushed him. I called again, then stopped. The seconds ticked by. In the timber a squirrel chattered. Just as I began to think the moose had moved on, from across the thicket came the crash of antlers. Grabbing John's stick, I copied the sound. The bull called, once. He was coming.

John, at my gesture, slipped a cartridge into the chamber and snicked on the safety. The bull would be close. Maybe time for just one shot.

Long moments passed without sound. I worried that the bull had sensed us. If agitated, he'd come crashing through the willows. After a while, I took the chance, uttered the Judas call, the low, lustful tones of a cow. Almost at once, to our left, a branch snapped.

"Unk . . . Unk . . . Unk . . ." and the heavy-antlered head of the bull loomed over the willows close by.

"Stand up slowly," I whispered, "and when he sees you, he'll watch a moment, then turn to run. Shoot through the shoulders as he turns."

John stood. I ducked out of the way. The bull stared across a gap greater than just the few yards between us. He blinked. Not understanding. Where was the challenge? The seductive temptress? Perhaps I gave him greater capacity for thought than he possessed, but as he turned to flee, just before the bullet struck, I thought I saw a look of resignation born of comprehension. Betrayed by deceit set against lust.

John had his moose rack, his life-long dream come true. The first thing he did was measure the antlers. Sixty-two inches across. He had me take his picture with the moose. Every conceivable angle. A whole roll of film and part of another. He could not believe *the size of those antlers*.

Instead of the satisfaction that I'd have felt ten years before, I felt tired, quietly depressed. I fought against it, didn't like the feeling, and didn't understand it. Instead of pride in my woodcraft skills, I felt sadness. We had not cheated but worked hard, and fairly, to kill this moose. It had not been easy. We had hunted each day, every day, regardless of weather. Other than the binoculars and the gun, our only tools were our mental capacities. No vehicles, airplanes, or technology. We'd sought the bull on his own ground, in as basic a way as reasonable. I'd always felt remorse at an animal's death but this confusion I couldn't grasp. Something had gone from hunting. The stalk still carried the energy-high and excitement . . . but the *kill?* Vaguely I wished the bull alive.

I'd come to judge the quality of a hunter on many things but mostly on how he or she reacted to the kill. Some people could see nothing of interest in the wilderness except as a place to shoot an animal, or set a hook in a fish's mouth. Others found great beauty, wonder, and magic in all nature. Flowers, berries, birds, bear, moose, sheep—all were equal and wonderful. I enjoyed these hunters best. John fit somewhere in the middle of the extremes. He liked the country and wildlife, but he was strongly geared one way. His elation was typical. I'd hoped for more.

The best hunters always seem deeply moved by the kill, comprehending fully what they have done. Many temper their elation with quiet respect for the animal. These are the hunters that, at some point in their lives, have come to grips with the inherent contradictions in recreational hunting. They never use euphemisms like "take," "harvest," "collect." They say "kill." They know exactly what they do and don't mask it with wordplay. I have hunted with only a rare handful of such hunters. At the kill each was deeply moved, and one, a woman, cried. Each time I saw their deep emotion I walked away and fiddled with gear, to give them time alone. I knew what they felt. But I also knew that if they had to do the whole thing over, they would kill again.

Butchering John's moose was the usual labor, sweat, and struggle with an unwieldy bulk. I knew a few tricks but it still was work. John, helping the best he could, held up a leg, or pulled on the hide as I cut and skinned. The real struggle was to keep the meat clean despite the ease with which it would pick up dirt. First we rolled the moose onto its back. No, *rolled* sounds too easy. We *worked* the moose onto its back, struggling with the antlers to get them pointed down and back. Just this struggle prompted John to say, "How the *hell* are we ever going to pack this out?" Hours later, in the darkness of early night, he'd know.

Beginning at the throat, I cut a long line through the skin from neck to anus, using the first and middle fingers of my left hand to guide the blade away from the tender flesh over the viscera. I then cut into the throat, severing the windpipe. Next I cut through the flesh along the neck to the sternum. I used the packsaw to separate the bone.

Cautiously, again using my fingers to guide the blade, I cut the animal open from sternum to anus. Steam and hot smells poured from the cavity. There was little blood. I moved to the trachea, cut a fingerhole for my left index finger, and pulled backward, slicing it from the neck as I worked toward the lungs. John spread the ribcage while I reached in awkwardly to cut the lungs loose. Much blood here. The bullet had passed through both lungs, breaking ribs on entry and exit. I strained to loosen the diaphragm. The carcass kept tipping over and I had to push with my knees to keep it upright. I put down my knife and grasped the windpipe with both hands and pulled backward with all my strength, spilling the heart, lungs, and diaphragm from the chest cavity onto the complex stomach. I stopped to sharpen my knife.

Next I began to cut the stomach away from the abdominal cavity. The four-part stomach, like a water-filled balloon, refused to stay in one place. One slip with the knife and the meat would have been tainted with spilled rumen. We pulled, tugged, pushed, shoved, and swore the stomach out of the way. I cut around the anus, freeing the lower alimentary tract. John and I grabbed the windpipe and pulled the entire system from the body cavity. With a knot of grass I wiped away the blood that pooled along the backbone. The moose was cleanly field-dressed.

We took a break. While I again sharpened my knife, John took more pictures. He said that he wanted pictures of the gutted moose to show his friends that didn't approve of, or understand, hunting. He wanted to show how he obtained his meat and that he used the entire animal. He also wanted to show that all the meat we eat begins this way, be it fish, fowl, beef, pork, or mutton. Rather stridently, as if talking to his intended audience, he explained that few people understand, that few people would eat steak if they first had to kill and butcher the animal. Perhaps he had a point, but I doubted many people would look at his pictures and get it.

I started to skin the moose before John finished talking. I began at the right rear hock and made the opening cut down the leg. With John's help, it wasn't long before we had the skin loosened on one side. We were careful to keep the half-skinned animal on its hide and off the ground, away from lichen, leaves, and dirt. Though I'd been careful, a few hairs clung to the meat. Before turning the moose over we severed the head from the body by cutting through the spine at the last vertebra below the skull. It took both of us to carry the antlered head away from the carcass.

We rolled the moose over, maneuvering the carcass to keep it on the hide. Fifteen minutes later the moose was fully skinned and cooling. We finished the job by removing the lower legs at the first joint. I cut away three legs in the time it took John to do one. He had a hard time finding the joint. One by one we tossed the lower legs into the brush. At this point the white and red carcass looked unremarkably similar to a full steer in a butcher shop.

With John's help, and a sharp knife and saw, I segmented the moose into eight sections: the four quarters, the two rib halves, the neck, and a pile of loose meat that included the backstraps and tenderloins. John didn't want the kidneys, heart, or liver. Some hunters consider these delicacies, but not John. A light steam rose from the rapidly cooling meat.

John, wiping the blood from his hands, surveyed the mountain of meat. Meat that would be choice and tasty because of proper, expeditious care. The moose smelled only faintly of the rut. John looked at me and shook his head. "You never answered me," he said. "How the *hell* are we ever going to get this out of here?"

I laughed. A pair of gray jays flew over and landed in a nearby spruce. Their chirping joined in my laughter, as if to say: "Stop talking. *Show* him. We're hungry."

Sitting alone in the clearing waiting out the day, I thought of yesterday's hunt, and the heavy loads of meat packed in. I thought of many things. Food. Home. Daughter. Approaching winter. Chores that needed doing. Good times. Women. Bad times. Hunters in general. John in particular. Bears. (No matter how deep in thought, or sound asleep, I stir at the slightest sound.) Thoughts of people, places, and things seldom recalled. I thought a great deal about the moose we killed, the species in general, and the ethics of hunting. Questions. Always the nagging, persistent, draining questions.

In midday I drifted off to sleep. A while later I awoke hungry. I lunched on cheese, hardtack, and a few handfuls of gorp, washed down with icy water from my poly bottle. After ten days of Monterey Jack on pilot bread—Cheese Supremes, as John called them—I wished for something more. Wished I'd fried up some extra meat to bring along. (That's *exactly* what I did do, I reminded myself, but I had eaten it at breakfast.)

Afterward I shoved my gear back into my pack. I'd waited out moose many times before, as long as ten hours while the moose napped and ruminated. I wanted to see the mating ritual again. See the act that galvanized these usually placid creatures. While I slept the sun had slanted toward the west and I sat shivering in the shade. I looked at my watch. Two hours until dark.

Just then the call of a bull moose echoed in the timber. *Damn. I'd blown it.* The call came from north of the clearing. The moose must have moved while I napped. I slung the pack over my shoulder and hurried off, anxious not to lose them. Partway down the slope I forced myself to stop. Take your time. Go slow. The call could have been a different bull. Full of anticipation, I continued more cautiously. Moving from bush to bush, looking right and left for any sign of movement, I crept to the edge of the timber. *The bull was there.* He stood motionless over his bed, the cow beside him, both looking toward the north. I drew closer to crouch behind a small spruce. From there I could watch the moose and see the entire clearing. The air hung heavy with the pungent mixed odor of moose and spruce, the primal scent of lust and combat.

From the north came another call followed by the snapping of limbs and an angry snort. A bull was coming.

The cow whined low and took several steps toward the sounds. Her suitor watched this treachery, then took a few deliberate steps past her and into the open meadow, positioning himself between her and his rival.

"Unk . . . Unk . . . Unk . . ." In familiar cadence the bull approached. The light-colored bull grew excited, pawed the meadow, and shook his antlers. The cow moaned again, provoking him. He rushed at her, driving her back, making her wait, demanding her fealty.

A timber cracked at the far end of the clearing. Over the willows there, I could see the head and antlers of a fine, big bull, at least the equal of the one before me. There would be combat.

The new bull stood unmoving, looking down the clearing at the cow and bull. I glassed his heavy, swollen neck, the puffy eyes, and spreading antlers. One palm had an enormous rent in the upper half, a result of damage done when in the velvet. Brokenhorn, the challenger.

He seemed to ponder the situation, evaluate the moose before him. After a long moment he decided. He raked his antlers hard through the willows, back and forth, up and down, breaking limbs and tearing one whole plant from the ground. He grew agitated. Heavy limbs snapped as he worked the brush harder. I could hear sudden exhalations.

The light-colored bull, Tawny, began to respond. In ritual pattern, he rocked forward in slow paces, antlers swaying side to side. He walked to a willow and thrashed the brush with his antlers. He pawed the ground, slashed the willows, working himself into a fury.

Brokenhorn stopped to watch. Grunted once. Then walked into the meadow in a stiff-legged, head-swaying threat display. Tawny stepped forward to meet him.

The two approached in slow, rolling steps, their antlers swinging in rhythm. Step by step, foot by foot, like sumos approaching in polite but lethal ritual, the bulls closed, ready to test antler against antler, strength against strength, courage against courage. For the cow.

Seldom had I seen two such prime bulls armed with similar, multitined antlers. These heavy racks, driven before rut-swollen necks and massive shoulders, could be deadly. Because of the potential carnage, large bulls will not battle small bulls. A close-up antler display usually determines dominance. Perhaps this day dominance would be gained only through death.

Head to head, moaning softly, twisting racks side to side, left to right, up and down, the bulls stopped inches apart, trying to intimidate one another. I could see the white of Brokenhorn's eye as it rolled to fix upon the tines wagging inches away.

Moments passed. The forest was silent and still, without even the cry of jay or squirrel to break the tension. Several yards from the bulls, the cow stood watching, waiting.

I heard a sharp grunt. I looked back. The bulls had backed up, one pawed the ground. Jabbing hard at the soil, Tawny grunted. Brokenhorn responded with a charge.

The bulls crashed together, quick feints bringing the antlers flush together, palm against palm, tine between tine. In a flurry of body movement, muscles straining, legs dancing, the two sought for advantage, whirling, twisting, turning, thrusting back and forth. Hindquarters low and driving, mud and grass flying from splayed hooves, the bulls fought for purchase. Power and beauty. Grace tangled with violence.

The bulls tore apart, only to come smashing together again, neither seeming to gain advantage from the impact. Tines were aimed just inches from eyes; one unparried thrust could take an eye. Heads low, shoulders driving—parry and thrust, push and shove—they tested each other, each ready to strike at weakness.

Slowly the moss and lichen under their hooves was churned into mud. It made the difference. Brokenhorn slipped in the muck just enough for his adversary to gain ground and begin forcing him backward. With hind legs driving, and all the strength of a half-ton of moose focused behind his antlers, Tawny forced Brokenhorn back. Brokenhorn tried to stem the onslaught but could not. His legs and spine buckled each time he planted his rear hooves. For a brief moment he checked the thrust, seemed to gain strength, only to be thrown off-balance by a slight twist of his adversary's antlers. Back they came until they fought only a few yards from my hiding place.

With locked antlers the bulls crashed into the willows, separated, and stood looking at one another. Somehow, perhaps by his posture, I knew that Brokenhorn was beaten.

After a short pause, Tawny charged. Just fifteen yards from me, Brokenhorn, reeling under the attack, turned to flee. His opponent seized the advantage and slammed into Brokenhorn's shoulder. He went down, crashing hard into the willows, snapping a two-inch-thick spruce tree like a matchstick. He was up in the instant and running hard into the timber, his antagonist in close pursuit.

The sounds of the chase gradually receded into the distance. The meadow was empty now. Sometime during the fight, the cow had stolen away. I listened for sounds, but other than the soughing wind, all was peaceful.

Shaken, I stood up. I tried to swallow, my mouth dry as paper. I took a deep breath and looked around. I felt the wind on my face, the cold in my body, my pantlegs soaked from kneeling in the wet muskeg. The air was heavy with musk. The sun had set and a faint twilight gathered in the timber. Ravens called in the distance.

Taking four long steps, I reached out to touch a smashed willow; ten steps and I fingered the shattered spruce. Spots of blood congealed on willow leaves. Tufts of hair clung to spruce branches. I took the two-inch-thick sapling between my hands and tried to break it. I could not. I scuffed at the muddied ground, at the hoof prints filling with dark water. I stood there a long time, looking, thinking, memorizing.

In the lengthening shadows I started toward camp. The forest smelled of dead leaves, of mould and decay. I stumbled in the dark until I cut the trail to camp. On the path I slowed. I stopped on the lookout knob to stare at Polaris, the first star I'd looked at in a week, perhaps in a lifetime. I looked down at the river shining silver in the fading light, listened to its rush eastward. Then, far away north, over the tall trees, a bull moose called: once, twice, and again.

Tôrnârssuk (Ursus maritimus)

FROM *Arctic Dreams*

BARRY LOPEZ

Naturalist Barry Lopez, one of the foremost literary artists of his generation, frequently addresses the interconnections of the natural and human worlds in his work. He is the author of such celebrated works as OF WOLVES AND MEN *(1978),* WINTER COUNT, CROSSING OPEN GROUND, CROW AND WEASEL, FIELD NOTES, *and* ARCTIC DREAMS *(1986), which won numerous awards including the American Book Award. Lopez lives in Oregon. "Tôrnârssuk (Ursus maritimus)" is excerpted from* ARCTIC DREAMS.

The seascape was almost without color beneath a low gray sky. Scattered ice floes damped any motion of large waves, and fogs and thin snow showers came and went in the still air. The surface of the water was the lacquered black of Japanese wooden boxes.

Three of us stood in the small open boat, about a hundred miles off the northwest coast of Alaska, at the southern edge of the polar pack in the Chukchi Sea. I and two marine scientists were hunting ringed seals that cold September day. In the seal stomachs we found what fish they were eating had eaten; and from plankton samplings we learned what the creatures the fish ate were eating.

We had been working at this study of marine food chains for several weeks, moving west in our boat across the north coast of Alaska, from the west end of the Jones Islands to Point Barrow. At Barrow we boarded a 300-foot oceanographic research vessel, the *Oceanographer,* and headed out to the Chukchi Sea. Each morning for the next two weeks our boat was lowered from the deck of this mother vessel and we worked in the sea ice until evening.

We had been hunting seals intensively for three days without success, Twice we had seen a seal, each time for only a split second. We moved slowly, steadily, through the ice floes, without conversation, occasionally raising a pair of field glasses to study a small, dark dot on the water—a piece of ice? A bird? A seal breaking the surface of the water to breathe? It is not so difficult to learn to distinguish among these things, to match a "search image" in the mind after a few days of tutoring with the shading, shape, and movement that mean *seal.* Waiting in silence, intently attentive, was hard to learn.

We were three good sets of eyes, hunting hard. Nothing. A fog would clear, a snow squall drift through. In the most promising areas of the ice we shut off the engines and drifted with the currents. The ice, despite its occasional vertical relief, only compounded a sense of emptiness in the landscape, a feeling of directionlessness. The floes were like random, silent pieces of the earth. Our compass, turning serenely in its liquid dome, promised, if called upon to do so, to render points on a horizon obliterated in slanting snow and fog.

We drifted and sipped hot liquids, and stared into the quilt-work of gray-white ice and ink-black water. If one of us tensed, the others felt it and were alert. Always we were *hunting.* This particular habitat, the number of cod in the water, the time of the year—everything said ringed seals should be here. But for us they weren't.

Late summer in the sea ice. Eventually the cold, damp air finds its way through insulated boots and wool clothing to your bones. The conscious mind, the mind that knows how long you have been out here, importunes for some measure of comfort. We made a slow, wide turn in the boat, a turn that meant the end of the day. Though we still watched intently, thoughts of the ship were now upon us. Before this, we had camped on the beach in tents; now a hot shower, an evening meal in light clothing at a table, and a way to dry clothes awaited us. In the back of your mind at the end of the day you are very glad for these things.

My friend Bob saw the bear first: an ivory-white head gliding in glassy black water 300 feet ahead, at the apex of a V-wake. We slowed the boat and drew up cautiously to within 30 feet. A male. The great seal hunter himself. About three years old, said Bob.

The bear turned in the water and regarded us with irritation, and then, wary, he veered toward a floe. In a single motion of graceful power he rose from the water to the ice, his back feet catching the ice edge at the end of the movement. Then he stepped forward and shook. Seawater whirled off in flat sheets and a halo of spray. His head lowered, he glared at us with small, dark eyes. Then he crossed the floe and, going down on his forelegs, sliding headfirst, he entered the water on the other side without a splash and swam off.

We found our way to him again through the ice. We were magnetically drawn, in a fundamental but perhaps callow way. Our presence was interference. We approached as slowly as before, and he turned to glower, treading water, opening his mouth—the gray tongue, the pale, violet mouth, the white teeth—to hiss. He paddled away abruptly to a large floe and again catapulted from the water, shook his fur out, and started across the ice to open water on the far side.

We let him go. We watched him, that undeterred walk of authority. "The farmer," the whalers had called him, for his "very agricultural appearance as he stalks leisurely over the furrowed fields of ice." John Muir, on a visit to the same waters in 1899, said bears move "as if the country had belonged to them always."

The polar bear is a creature of arctic edges: he hunts the ice margins, the surface of the water, and the continental shore. The ice bear, he is called. His world forms beneath him in the days of shortening light, and then falls away in the spring. He dives to the ocean floor for mussels and kelp, and soundlessly breaks the water's glassy surface on his return, to study a sleeping seal. Twenty miles from shore he treads water amid schooling fish. The sea bear. In winter, while the grizzly hibernates, the polar bear is out on the sea ice, hunting. In summer his tracks turn up a hundred miles inland, where he has feasted on crowberries and blueberries.

Until a few years ago this resourceful hunter was in a genus by himself: *Thalarctos.* Now he is back where he started, with the grizzly and black bear in the genus *Ursus,* where his genes, if not his behavior, say he belongs.

What was so impressive about the bear we saw that day in the Chukchi was how robust he seemed. At three years of age a bear in this part of the Arctic is likely spending its first summer alone. To feed itself, it has had to learn to hunt, and open pack ice is among the toughest of environments for bears to hunt in. This was September, when most bears are thin, waiting for the formation of sea ice, their hunting platform. In our three days of diligent searching, in this gray and almost featureless landscape of ice remnants so far off the coast, we had seen but two seals. We were transfixed by the young bear. We watched him move off across the ice, into a confusing plane of grays and whites. We were shivering a little and opened a thermos of coffee. A snow shower moved quickly through, and when it cleared we could barely make him out in the black water with field glasses from the rocking boat. A young and successful hunter, at home in his home.

He had found the seals.

Dall

FROM *Cowboys Are My Weakness*

PAM HOUSTON

Writer Pam Houston has been a river guide, a big-game hunting guide, and a teacher. Her work has appeared in many magazines, including Mademoiselle, Mirabella, *and* The Gettysburg Review. *"Dall" is taken from her collection of short stories,* COWBOYS ARE MY WEAKNESS *(1992).*

I am not a violent person. I don't shoot animals and I hate cold weather, so maybe I had no business following Boone to the Alaska Range for a season of Dall sheep hunting. But right from the beginning, my love for Boone was a little less like contentment and a little more like sickness, so when he said he needed an assistant guide I bought a down coat and packed my bags. I had an idea about Alaska: that the wildness of the place would enlarge my range of possibility. The northern lights, for example, were something I wanted to see.

After the first week in Alaska I began to realize that the object of sheep hunting was to intentionally deprive yourself of all the comforts of normal life. We would get up at three A.M., and leave the cabin, knowing it would be nearly twenty-four hours, if not several days, before we would return. Everything depended upon the sheep, where they were and how far we could chase them. Boone was a hunter of the everything-has-to-be-hard-and-painful-to-be-good variety, and there was nothing he liked better than a six- or seven-hour belly crawl through the soggy green tundra.

The weather was almost always bad. If it wasn't raining, it was sleeting or snowing. If the sun came out, the wind started to blow. We carried heavy packs full of dry and warm clothing, but if we saw some sheep and started stalking them, we had to leave our packs behind so that we'd be less conspicuous, and often we didn't return to them until after dark. We got our feet wet very early in the day. We carried only enough water so that we were always on the edge of real thirst. We ate Spam for lunch every day, even though smoked baby clams and dried fruit would have weighed considerably less in our backpacks. It seemed important, in fact, not to eat any fruits and vegetables, to climb up and down the steepest part of every mountain, and to nearly always get caught out after dark.

Boone and I were a good team, except when we fell into one of our fights, which were infrequent but spectacular. In Alaska we seemed to fight every time we had a minute alone, and those minutes were rare with a series of hunters who were scared of the bears and half in love with Boone's macho besides.

When Boone got really mad at me, when his face puffed up and his temples bulged out and he talked through his teeth and little flecks of spit splattered my face, it was so comic and so different from his guidely calm that I was always waiting for him to laugh, like it was all a big joke that I hadn't quite gotten. And when he grabbed me so hard he made me yell or threw me on the bed or kicked my legs out from under me it always felt less like violence and more like a pratfall. Like we were acting out a scene, waiting for some signal from the audience that the absurdity of Boone's actions had been properly conveyed.

Several times in my life I've sat with women, friends of mine, who reveal, sometimes shyly, sometimes proudly, bruises of one kind or another, and I know I've said, "If it happens one time, leave him." I've said, "It doesn't matter how much you love him. Leave him if it happens one time." And I've said it with utter confidence, as if I knew what the hell I was talking about, as if violence was something that could be easily defined.

It was never that clear-cut with Boone and me. For all the shoving around he did, he never hit me, never hurt me really. I'm big and strong and always tan, so I don't bruise easily. And I was always touched, in some strange way, by the ambivalence of his violent acts; they were at once aggressive and protective, as if he wanted not to hurt me but just to contain me, as if he wanted not to break me but just to shut me off.

We took four hunters out that season, one at a time for fourteen days each, and gave them the workout of their lives. We hiked on an average of fifteen miles a day, with a vertical gain of between four and five thousand feet; roughly equivalent to hiking in and out of the Grand Canyon every day for two months. At first confused by my presence and ability, the hunters would learn fast that I was their only ally, the one who would slip them extra candy bars, the one they could whine to.

"Aren't you hungry?" they'd whisper to me when Boone was out of earshot.

And I'd say, "How about a little lunch, Boone?" and Boone would look at me exasperated.

"We're hunting, baby," he'd say, as if that explained everything. "We'll eat as soon as we can."

We did the dishes with stream water that had so much silt in it that they looked muddier every time we washed them. The cabin was only eight by ten and we took turns standing in the center of the floor over the washbasins to brush our teeth, and then one at a time we got ready for bed. Two half-cots/half-hammocks folded out of the wall into something like bunk beds. The hunter slept in the top bunk and I got the bottom. Boone spread his ground pad and sleeping bag on what was left of the floor.

Every night we'd wait until the hunter started to snore and then Boone would climb into my bunk and we'd make slow and utterly silent love. There was barely enough room for my shoulder blades across the cot, barely enough room for both of our bodies under the hunter's sag, but we managed somehow to complete the act and I discovered, for the first time in my life, that restraint can be very sexy.

Boone would usually fall right asleep and I'd be so tired from the day's hunting that I'd sleep too, even crushed like that under the weight of him. Sometime before three-thirty we'd wake up, stiff and numb, and he would slip out of my bank and onto his knees on the floor. He'd stay there, kneeling for a while, rubbing my temples or massaging my fingers until I fell asleep again. When the alarm went off he was always buried in his sleeping bag, everything covered but one arm reaching toward my cot, sometimes still up and on the edge of it.

I don't think any of the hunters knew what was going on except for Russell, who got so crazy for Boone in his own way that he was afraid to leave Boone and me alone, afraid he'd miss a moment of intimacy, afraid even to fall asleep at night. One night, close to climax, we bumped Russell hard, hard enough so that I felt it right through Boone. Boone lay still for a long time until we all fell asleep, and we never even finished making love. The next night we waited forever for Russell to start snoring, and even when he did I thought it sounded forced and fake but Boone seemed convinced by it and he crawled into my bed and made himself so flat like a snake against me that I couldn't tell my movements apart from him.

We hunted in grizzly-bear country, and on cloudy nights when the transistor could pick up the Fairbanks station we'd always hear of another mauling, or another hunter's body that Fish and Game couldn't find. We didn't go anywhere without rifles, and when our bush pilot found out I didn't have a gun he pulled the smallest .22 pistol I'd ever seen out of his pocket.

"It won't stop a bear unless you put it inside his mouth," he said. "But it's better than nothing at all."

And then he told a story just like all the other stories. In this one a bear took a man's scalp off with one swipe of the paw, and then the bear crushed his skull against a tree trunk, and then he broke his back against a rock.

But it wasn't the fear for my life that I thought would get to me, it wasn't the fighting or the hard work or the bad food. The only thing I really worried about in Alaska was how I'd feel when the hunt was successful, how I'd feel watching the animal go down: the period of time, however short, between the shooting and the dying.

Boone told me it wouldn't be as bad as I expected. He told me our hunters were expert marksmen, that they would all make perfect heart-lung shots, that the rams would die instantly and without pain. He told me that the good thing about hunting Dalls was that you always harvested the oldest rams because they were the ones with the biggest horns, they were the ones whose horns made a full curl. Boone said that most of the rams we would shoot that season would have died slow painful deaths of starvation that winter. He said when they got weak they would have had their guts ripped out by a pack of wolves, sometimes while they were still alive.

Boone talked a lot about the ethics of hunting, about the relationship between meat eaters and game. He said that even though he catered to trophy hunters he had never let his hunters shoot an animal without killing it, and had never let them kill one without taking all the meat. The scraps that had to be left on the carcass became food for the wolves and the eagles. It was the most basic of spiritual relationships, he said, and I wanted so much to believe him that I clung to his doctrine like hope.

But I still always rooted for the sheep. Whenever we got close I tried to send them telepathic messages to make them turn their heads and look at us, to make them run away after they'd seen us, but so often they would just stand there stupidly and wait to be shot. Sometimes they wouldn't move even after the hunter had fired, sometimes even after the dead ram had fallen at their feet.

It was at those times, in the middle of all the hand clasping, the stiff hugs and manly pats on the back, that I wondered how I could possibly be in love with Boone. I would wonder how I could possibly be in love with a man who seemed happy that the stunning white animal in front of us had just fallen dead.

The first sheep that died that season was for a hunter named James. James owned a company that manufactured all the essential components of sewage-treatment plants. He was jolly and a little stupid and evidently very rich.

On the first day we were all together, James told us a story about going hunting with six other men who all had elk permits. Apparently they all split up and James came upon the herd first and shot six animals in a matter of seconds. I tried to imagine coming into a clearing and seeing six bull elk and shooting all of them, not leaving even one.

"I knew if I just shot one they was gonna scatter and we'd lose them," he said. "They was standing real close together and I knew if I just let the lead fly, I'd dust more than one."

For the first ten days of James's hunt we had so much rain and such low clouds that the sheep could have been on top of us and we wouldn't have seen them. Our clothes had been wet for so long that our skin had started to rot underneath them. Each morning we put our feet into new plastic bags.

On the eleventh morning the sun came out bold and warm. During the cloudy days the short Alaskan summer had slipped into fall, and the tundra had already started to turn from green and yellow to orange and red.

Boone said our luck would change with the weather, and it wasn't two hours and six or seven miles of hiking before we'd spotted five of the biggest rams Boone had ever seen in the valley.

They were a long way from us, maybe three miles horizontal and three thousand feet up, the wind was squirrelly, and there was no real cover between us and them. Our only choice was to go right up the creek bed on our bellies and hope we blended with the moving water and the slate-colored rocks. The bed was steep for a couple of hundred yards, and there were two or three waterfalls to negotiate, and I thought we were going to lose James to the river once or twice, but we all made it through the steep part only half soaked.

Then we were in the tundra with almost no protection, and we had to crawl with our elbows and our boot tips, knees and stomachs in the mud, two or three inches per advance, wet, cold, dirty.

I thought how very much like soldiers we looked, how very much like war this all was, how very strange that the warlike element seemed to be so much the attraction.

The crawling took most of the day, and it put us in a good position for the afternoon feeding. We got behind a long low rock outcrop where we could get a good look at the rams, and sure enough, they had started coming down off the crags they bedded on during the day. Four of the five were full curls, all with a lot of mass and depth. We couldn't get any closer without being seen, so all we could do was lie on the rocks in our wet clothes and wait for them to graze in our direction.

Every half hour Boone would raise his body just enough to see over the ridge that protected us. He'd smile and give us the thumbs-up. Three more hours passed and the numbness which had started in my feet had worked its way up above my knees. Finally, Boone motioned for James to join him on the ridge. For the first time in hours I moved, getting up on my elbows to see the rams grazing, no more than a hundred yards away. I watched James try to position himself, try to breathe deeply, try to get the best hold on the gun. Boone was talking softly into his ear and I could only hear fragments of what he was saying—"very makeable shot," or "second from the right," "one chance," "get comfortable"—and I tried to imagine some rhythmic chant, some incantation, that would sanctify the scene somehow, that would make what seemed murderous holy. Then the shot exploded in my ears and one of the rams ran back up the mountain toward the crags.

"Watch him for blood!" Boone said to me. And I set my binoculars on him but he was climbing strong and steady. I was pretty sure it was a clean miss but I didn't say so because I didn't want James to get another shot, and the other four rams were still standing, staring, trying to get our scent, trying to understand what we were and what we were doing on their side of the mountain.

James was in position to shoot again.

"What do you see?" Boone asked me.

"I haven't got a look at him from the front," I said, which was true, even if beside the point.

James relaxed his hold on the gun. A gust of wind came suddenly from behind us and the rams got our scent. Just that fast they were climbing toward the fifth ram, and in seconds they were out of shooting range.

"He's clean," I said. "You must have shot over his back."

"Okay," Boone said to James. "We're gonna let them get a little ahead and then we're gonna follow them up to the top. Baby, I want you to stay here and watch the bottom. Watch the rams, watch our progress. Once we get to the top we're going to start to move south along the ridge. I want you to stay a few hundred yards ahead of us. I want you to keep the rams from coming down."

It was another three thousand feet to the top of the ridge. The rams topped out in twenty-five minutes. Boone and James hadn't gone a quarter of the way. I knew that if the rams would just keep going, if they would drop down into the debris on the other side, Boone and James would never get to them before dark. I watched two rams butt horns against the darkening sky and I thought that maybe the reason why the ewes and the lambs lived separately was that the rams were not so different from the hunters after all, and in some strange way I was consoled.

"Go on," I thought at them again and again, but they stayed there, posed on the skyline while the men got closer.

Finally Boone and James were at the top, about six hundred yards from the rams. But the rams saw them first and started back down on my side. If I wanted to do as Boone told me, it was time to start walking. I sat in the tundra and slowly pulled on my gloves. I knew Boone could see me from up there. I knew he would know if I didn't do my job. I took a step toward where the rams were coming down, and then another. I had their attention, and they stalled nervously on the mountainside between the hunters and me. I sat down to change my socks, which were soaked and suddenly annoying. When I stood back up I watched the five rams, one at a time, slip down into the valley floor in front of me.

It was after dark when Boone and James got down off the mountain. We decided to camp there and look for the rams again early in the morning.

I made some freeze-dried chicken stew and instant chocolate pudding.

Right after dinner we met Brian. He approached our camp at dusk, hollering for all he was worth so we wouldn't think he was a bear and fire. He walked and talked and looked like a Canadian lumberjack, but sometime during the evening he confessed to being from Philadelphia.

Brian was a survival specialist. He taught survival courses in Anchorage and nationwide. When he finished his two-week solo hunt he was off to the Sonoran desert to teach people how to jump out of helicopters with scuba gear on. He was the only man I met in Alaska who said nice things about his wife.

Brian carried Jack Daniel's in a plastic bottle that said "emergency provisions" in six different languages. He told us about his students; how they were required to solo for three days at the end of his course; how he gave them each a live rabbit to take with them so they could have one good meal. He hoped they would dry some jerky. He hoped they would stitch a hand warmer together with string made from the sinews in the rabbit's legs.

"But it never works," he said, "because companionship is a very special thing."

We all thought he was going to say something dirty, and we waited while he took a long hit off the bottle.

"I check on them sometime during the second day," he said. "They've all built little stone houses for their rabbits, some of them with mailboxes. They've given their rabbits names, and carved their initials into pieces of bark and hung them above the little doors."

We all sat there for a minute without saying anything, and then the conversation turned back to the usual. A brown bear that continued to charge after six rounds with a .300 Winchester. A bull moose that wouldn't go down after seven shots, and then after eight. A bullet that entered a caribou through the anus and exited through the mouth.

I looked across the fire in time to see Boone, out of chewing tobacco, stick a wad of instant coffee between his cheek and gum. Brian passed the bottle again, his rifle across his knees, a bullet in the chamber. He said he had followed grizzly prints the last mile and a half to camp, big ones, indicating at least a seven-foot bear.

I wanted to go to bed, but the tent was almost one hundred yards from the fire, and I knew I'd never get Boone away. I was tired of hunting stories, tired of chewing tobacco and cigars and the voices of men. I was tired of bear paranoia: of being afraid to spill one drop of food on my clothing, afraid to go to the bathroom, afraid to really fall asleep. I was tired of being cold and wet and hungry and thirsty and dirty and sweaty and clammy and tired of the sand that was in our eyes and our mouth and our food and our tent and even the water we drank and of the wind which blew it around and was incessant.

We never saw those five big rams again, but on the second-to-last day of James's hunt we got close enough to some new rams for another stalk. We had the wind in our favor but only a few hours till dark. We crawled like soldiers for what seemed like a long time, the only sound besides the river James's rhythmic grunting every time he lifted his belly out of the mud.

We got into shooting position with just enough light, Boone talking softly into James's ear, James positioning his body, then his rifle, then his body again.

There were eleven rams in front of us, eight high and three low. At least four or five of them were full curls. I was trying to decide which one was the biggest when the gun fired sharp and loud, and then fired again.

"Don't shoot again!" Boone said, his voice angry. "Watch that ram."

And we all watched as one of the five lower rams ran down the gravel bed, his front legs splayed and awkward.

"Let me shoot again," James said. "Let me shoot at another one."

"We need to see if the one you shot at is hit," Boone said, calm again.

"He ain't hit," James said.

"He *is* hit," I said.

"At this point I can't tell," Boone said.

James cocked his gun.

The ram hobbled farther down and out of our view. James and Boone kept talking, talking themselves into the fact that the ram wasn't injured, but I knew it was. I knew it the way a mother knows when her child's been hurt.

"That ram's been hit," I said again. "I just don't know where."

First one and then three other rams ran down to join the first.

"I didn't see any blood," Boone said. "I think he's okay."

"He's not okay," I said, loudly now. "Do you hear me?"

Both men turned suddenly, as if remembering my presence for the first time, and then just as suddenly turned away.

"Let's see if we can get closer," Boone said. And then, after all that crawling, Boone stood up and strode across the moraine towards where the five lower rams had disappeared. James and I followed. The eight rams above us watched for a minute and then started climbing, slowly but steadily, up to the top of the ridge. The sun had set behind that ridge hours ago, but the Alaskan twilight lingered and lit the backdrop as the rams, one by one, topped out and filled the skyline, each one a perfect black silhouette against a bloody sky.

One of the five lower rams ran up to join the herd on the skyline. We came over a ledge and saw three more, not fifty feet below us.

"This is my kind of shot," James said.

"Not yet," Boone said. The three rams walked out in full view. None of them was bleeding.

"The first two are full curls," Boone said. "Fire when you're ready."

"We're still missing one ram," I said. "The injured ram is still down there."

Boone didn't even turn around. His hand silenced me. The gun fired again and the first ram went down.

"Dead ram!" Boone said.

I remember thinking I shouldn't watch, and I suspect everything would have been easier from then on if I hadn't. But it wasn't the way Boone had said it was going to be.

The ram was hit in the hindquarter, leaving him very much alive but unable to stand. For ten or twelve seconds he tried to drag himself across the glacier on his front feet, and then, exhausted, he gave up and started rolling down the glacier, rolling, in fact, right for a crevasse.

"Stop, you son of a bitch!" James yelled. "Stop, you motherfucker!"

The ram was still alive, twitching and kicking its front legs, when it fell several hundred feet to the bottom of the crevasse, irretrievable, even for the wolves, even for the eagles. We all watched the place where it had fallen.

"Jesus fuckin' Christ," James said.

That's when the injured ram, the first injured ram, limped out from the place we couldn't see below us and started to run, or tried to run, across the glacier. It was faltering now, dying, and we could see the blood running down between its front legs. Without a word to either of us, Boone grabbed James's gun and took off at a dead run across the glacier. Even fatally injured, the ram made better time on the ice than Boone, but just before the ram topped out above him he aimed and made a perfect heart-lung shot and the ram fell, instantly dead.

Of course we'd left our backpacks miles behind. Boone sent me back for them alone, and I clutched the little gun in my pocket as if it would help me. I walked right to the backpacks, in the near total darkness, something that even Boone himself couldn't have done. I had learned, by then, to make mental markers each time we left the packs, to find a mark on every surrounding horizon so that even after dark the spot could be relocated.

The temperature had dropped thirty degrees in thirty minutes, and I dug for my down coat and put it on over my wet clothing, and headed back toward James and Boone.

I found them just by following the smell of the dead ram. We were all without flashlights, and Boone decided it was too dark to butcher.

"We'll gut it and come back for it tomorrow," Boone said. "If the bears don't get it, the meat won't spoil."

"Fuck the meat," James said. "Let's cut the horns off the son of a bitch and get the hell out of here."

It was true dark now and James was getting nervous about bears. He had the safety off his gun and he kept spinning around every time a chunk of ice rolled down off the glacier.

"That's against the law," Boone said. "Come help me gut this ram." He turned to me. "You stay close."

I found out later about Alaska's wanton waste law, designed to protect the wilderness from trophy hunters like James. I also found out later the reason the ram smelled so awful. He died so slowly his adrenaline had lots of time to get pumping; James's first shot hit him in the gut and by the time he finally died his insides were rotten with stomach acid.

That night, though, the smell just seemed like a natural part of the nightmare. Even when they were finished gutting and we all started gingerly down the glacier, the smell of the ram came off Boone like he was the one who'd been shot in the gut. For the first time ever, I wouldn't hug him. He saved me from slipping once by grabbing my hand and left the smell all over my glove. It was worse than sour milk, that smell, worse than cat piss, worse than anything.

We walked for over an hour and I could tell by my marks on the skyline that we hadn't even gone a half a mile.

"This is crazy," I said. It was so dark that we couldn't see the dirty ice we walked on. "One of us is going to wind up in a crevasse with that ram."

"Maybe we should sit for a couple hours," Boone said. "If we sit for three or four hours it will start getting light."

"I think we should keep walking," James said.

Neither option was good. We were wet and cold already, we smelled like dinner for a bear, we had one real gun and a hunter who couldn't make an accurate shot at thirty yards. But we were alive and whole and together, and each careful step I took into the blackness made my heart race.

"We'll sit until we get so cold we have to move again," Boone said.

We piled up, nearly on top of each other. I opened three cans of sardines.

"That's perfect," Boone said. "The bear will think he's getting surf and turf."

We did okay for the first half hour. There had been a light cloud cover at sunset but now a million stars dotted the moonless sky. Boone was the thinnest, and he started to shiver first. We moved even closer together.

My fantasies were simple. A long hot shower. A plate of vegetables. A bed with sheets. TV. I thought of my mother, our last conversation by satellite telephone from North Pole, Alaska, where I assured her there was no real danger, and she told me about an actor, Jimmy Stewart or Paul Newman. "He used to be an avid hunter," she said, "and now he's a conservationist. He's done a hundred-and-eighty-degree switch." And I stood there for five dollars a minute listening to myself tell her that conservation and hunting are not antithetical, listening to myself use words like "game management," words like "harvest" and "herd control."

"This," I said out loud, "is wanting to love somebody too much."

"Here come the lights," Boone said, and even as he said the words a translucent green curtain began to rise on the horizon. Then the curtain divided itself and became a wave and the wave divided itself and became a dragon, then a goddess, then a wave. Soon the whole night sky was full of spirits flying and rolling, weaving and braiding themselves across the sky. The colors were familiar, mostly shades of green, but the motion, the movement, was unearthly and somehow female; it was unlike anything I'd ever seen. I was suddenly warm with amazement. I pressed my body harder into Boone's.

Early the next morning we went back for the ram. I shot a roll of film while James and Boone hugged and shook hands over it, while they picked up the horns and twisted the now stiff head from side to side, and then shook hands again. They were happy as schoolboys and I understood that what we had accomplished was more for this moment than anything, this moment where two men were allowed to be happy together and touch.

James flew back to Fairbanks the next morning, giving Boone and me our first day together in more than two weeks. We needed to take another hundred pounds of food up to the cabin for the hunter who was already on his way, and bring the garbage back down to the strip. With the six miles of packing each way from the airstrip we had a full day, but I was hoping we'd have time for a nice lunch once we got up there, hoping we'd have time for some loud, rowdy sex before we had to load up our packs and come back down.

The sun came out for our walk to the cabin, and when we got there I made Boone lunch and a couple of drinks. I mixed the Tang and water separately from the rum so the drinks would taste real. I added extra butter to the freeze-dried food, some dehydrated Parmesan, some parsley flakes.

I can't remember how the fight started, or why we disagreed. I only remember the moment when we stepped, as we always did, out of ourselves, and into the roles from which we fight.

"I spent the whole day trying to make everything nice for you," I said, hearing the script in my head, already knowing the outcome of the scene.

"What did you do?" he said. "Boil water?"

And he was right, what I had done was boil water, and there still might have been a way of saving the day if it hadn't been for the fact of those parsley flakes, if it hadn't been for the fact of that Parmesan cheese.

"Go to hell," I said.

"What was that?"

"Fuck you."

And then he was there, in my face, temples bulging. He grabbed my neck and twisted it into an unnatural position. I felt one of the lenses fall out of my glasses, felt something pinch between my shoulder blades, and I screamed, trying to channel all the pain into my voice so he'd let go, and it worked. But then he came back at me, grabbed my shirt around my neck and twisted it.

"If you hurt me again," I said, "I'll shoot you." It was sort of a ridiculous thing to say, on many levels, not the least of which being that the gun in my pocket, the one that Bill had given me simply out of pity, wasn't big enough to kill a ptarmigan unless you hit it in exactly the right place. I remembered another argument of months before, where I'd said I wouldn't shoot a rapist and infuriated Boone, and I tried to decide if what was happening was somehow worse than rape, and I knew even then that Boone would never really hurt me and I would never really shoot him, loving him like I did. And I decided it was just something I said because it seemed like the next logical line in the drama, but it made Boone wilder.

He ripped my coat off and took the little gun out of my pocket. He knocked me onto the floor of the cabin and then picked me up and threw me out the front door. My knee hit the rock that was the doorstop. He threw my backpack out after me, and then my bag of dirty clothes. The wind coming off the glacier picked up one of my T-shirts, a couple of pairs of underwear, and scattered them across the tundra, which was finally, I noticed, all red and gold.

"Give me my gun," I said, as if that were the issue.

"You won't have it," he said. "And don't ask again."

Stupid in his anger, he walked to the river, leaving his rifle a few feet away from me. I stared at it for a minute and thought about my previously nonviolent life. Only rednecks and crazy people had fights with guns, people in the inner city, people on late-night news shows.

But I was fascinated by us with our dramatics, and somehow bound to the logical sequence of the scene. I picked up the rifle, carried it into the cabin, hid it under a foam pad on the bunk bed, and sat on it.

"Where is it?" he said, minutes later. "Did you touch it?" I knew in his anger he thought he might have misplaced his gun. He crashed around the cabin and then outside.

"Where is it?" he said again.

"Give me my gun," I said.

This undid him. He ripped his gun from under me.

"If you messed up the scope . . ." he said. I eased into the corner as he examined the scope. If it had moved a fraction, even if only in his mind, I was in big trouble. We had gone too far this time, and at that instant I didn't know if and how we'd ever get back. He put his rifle down and took a step toward me.

"Don't come near me," I said.

"Now don't get upset," he said, suddenly all control and condescension.

"Just get yourself together." He patted my knee. "Take it easy now," he said. "Take a deep breath."

That was when my hiking boot moved, it seemed, all by itself and my Vibram sole connected with his thigh and I pushed with all the strength I had and sent him hurtling backwards across the cabin into the woodpile and the stove. A shelf crashed down on his head when he hit the wall. My foot hung in the air and I stared at it, amazed at its power, amazed at my life's violent act.

Then Boone was up and coming across the cabin at me and I just balled up and let him throw me out the door again, let my knee make contact with the rock. I gathered my clothes around me, pulled my backpack over my legs to block the wind.

Boone stayed inside, shouting things I only half heard. "You're out," he said at one point. "In more ways than you know."

I thought I ought to be horrified at myself, but I felt okay, light-headed, almost elated. He was stronger but I was strong. I looked again at my boot and flexed the muscle in my leg.

His tirade ended in some kind of a question I couldn't hear but guessed was rhetorical. I said something I couldn't resist about the shoe being on the other foot, and then laughed out loud so suddenly that he came to the cabin door and stared at me.

It was going to be dark in a few hours and I didn't think Boone would let me in the cabin, so I gathered up my underwear and started down towards the airstrip, where we had a tent set up. I knew it was a bad time of night to be walking alone in bear country, but after two long weeks without even seeing one bear, the grizzly had started to seem a bit like a creature of everybody's mind.

My knee was swelling to almost twice its normal size, but as long as I watched where I was walking, and didn't let it bend too far, it didn't really hurt. It was because I was looking down, I guess, because I was walking carefully, that I got so close to the bears before we saw each other.

It was a sow, six or seven feet tall, and two nearly full-grown cubs. They were knee-deep in blueberries, rolling and eating and playing. When I saw them they weren't fifty yards away.

I froze, and reached for my little gun before I remembered that Boone hadn't given it back. I took one step backwards and that's when mama saw me. The sun was just setting, and the late-afternoon light shone off their coats, which were brown and long and frosted at the tips. Mama stood on her hind legs, all seven feet of her, and then the cubs stood too and looked my way. They couldn't smell me, I knew, and they were trying to. Mama's ears went back and I thought, "Here she comes," but then she raised one giant paw in the air and swung it at me like a forehand, and then all three bears ran up into the mountain.

Boone and I took three more hunters out that season and we got them each a ram. All three hunters made perfect heart-lung shots. All three rams died instantly, just like Boone said.

One of our hunters, a man named Chuck, was kind and sincere. He got his ram with a bow and arrow from thirty yards away after a ten-hour stalk that was truly artistic. Chuck seemed to have an unspoken understanding with the wildlands and I was really almost happy for him when the ram went down, and I would have shaken his hand when he and Boone got finished jumping up and down in each other's arms if he had wanted to shake mine.

Boone told me I would get used to watching the rams die, and I have to admit—not without a certain horror—that the third killing was easier than the second, and the fourth was easier yet again.

I got thinner and harder and stronger and faster, turning my body into the kind of machine I couldn't help but be proud of, even though that had never been my goal.

Boone and I stopped fighting after the day we hiked to the cabin, but we also stopped talking; what we had left between us was hunting, and making love. I knew as soon as we got back to the lower forty-eight it would be over between us, and so I spent each day hiking behind him, measuring the time by quantity and not quality. It was like sitting by the bedside of a dying friend.

The nights got longer and longer, and we spent a lot more of them stuck out and away from the cabin. But the clouds were always thick and low, and even on the nights I tried hard to stay awake the northern lights never came again.

It was late September when we finished. The snow line was below four thousand feet and it was getting well below zero every night, and we'd been camped on the airstrip for three days waiting for the bush plane. The last hunters had flown out days before, and Boone and I had closed up the cabin in silence, like animals preparing for winter.

It had been hours, maybe days, since we'd spoken, so the sound of Boone's voice out of the darkness, out of somewhere deep in his sleeping bag, startled me.

"You know, none of those rams had an ounce of fat on them," he said. "There's not one of them would have lasted through the winter."

"Well," I said. "That's something."

"I've been doing this for years," he said, and at first I thought he was going to say, "And it still isn't easy to watch them die," but he didn't.

"You really hung in there," he said.

"Yeah," I said. "I did."

"But it made you stop loving me," he said. "Even so."

Somewhere up the mountains the wolves started moaning and shrieking. I hadn't told Boone about the night I saw the bears, but the scene had stayed right with me; I couldn't get it out of my mind. It was the power of the mother bear's gesture, I guess, the power and the ambivalence. Because the wave of her paw was both forbidding and inviting. Because even though I knew that she was showing me her anger, I also knew that somewhere in her gesture, she was asking me to come along.

Sheefish Time

FROM *The Last Light Breaking*

NICK JANS

Nick Jans is a writer and teacher who has lived for over a dozen years in Ambler, Alaska, an Eskimo village in the northwest Arctic, 300 miles from the nearest highway. His essays and poems have appeared in publications including Christian Science Monitor, Rolling Stone, GEO, National Fisherman, *and* Alaska Quarterly Review. *"Sheefish Time" is reprinted from his book of personal essays,* THE LAST LIGHT BREAKING: LIVING AMONG ALASKA'S INUPIAT ESKIMOS *(1993).*

After a hundred casts, I'd stopped thinking; I drifted off into the rhythm of cast and retrieve as the Kobuk River flowed by in the bright arctic midnight. The water was low and clear, dimpled by rising grayling. I was after something bigger—sheefish, a race of giant whitefish that inhabits only a few dozen river systems in northern Alaska, Canada, and Siberia. Here in the remote Kobuk and neighboring Selawik drainages, the fish are arguably the largest anywhere. Twenty to thirty pounders are common, and the world all-tackle record of fifty-three pounds, caught in 1986, came from the upper Kobuk.

I was anchored at the edge of an eddy, where the current spilled off a bar and pooled green. I'd caught fish here several times over the years, and I'd already seen a couple rolling on the surface tonight. But sheefish are moody; they might refuse to strike for hours, even days. Then again, they might suddenly erupt into a frenzy—especially late on a clear July night. And so I cast again and again, waiting. I could feel the *tap-tap-tap* of my heavy spoon brushing the sandy bottom, and its flutter as I jigged it upward. If a strike came, it would be on the settle. If not, I'd cast again.

Here, at the edge of the western Brooks Range, time isn't measured in hours or minutes; there are other rhythms, larger and less definite. Part of being here is learning to empty yourself of clocks, to see time as it's measured by the land—an endless pattern of cycles and momentary abundances.

There's a time when blueberries ripen, another for caribou to migrate. This was the time when sheefish run upriver. They were here, and so was I. That was all I needed to know.

I was paying attention to something else—the Jade Mountains reflecting the evening sun, or a widgeon paddling by—when it came. There was the thrum of my lure working as it swung in the current, the occasional tap of the bottom, then an electric *tugtugtug WHAM,* and my line and heart were singing with the rod's bow. Ten yards out, there was the bright bulge of a fish coming up, and a boil the size of a washtub—a big female, broad and heavy with eggs. Her tail and backfin thrashed against the sharp weight in her mouth, and she exploded downstream, hissing my line away, fifteen-pound test barely enough to take the pressure. Twenty yards. Thirty. Finally I brought her back, pumping and reeling, giving line when she ran, until I had her under the boat. As I reached for the gaff, she made a last surge for the bottom, nearly taking my rod. At last I got the lower jaw and hoisted her aboard—a bright, bucket-mouthed fish of twenty pounds.

I looked up to the mountains, out over the tundra, and downriver, where clouds were turning the color of blood. The willows caught the wind, bowed and flashed silver, and a flight of mergansers whistled overhead without swerving.

Sheefish have always been creatures of mystery; early French Canadian explorers called them *poissons inconnus,* unknown fish. Only in the past twenty years have biologists, notably Ken Alt of the Alaska Department of Fish and Game, filled most of the gaps in our knowledge. Still, sheefish refuse man's attempts to breed them successfully in hatcheries.

In both appearance and habit, sheefish seem to be a mongrel blend of species. They've been called "tarpon of the north" often enough that the comparison has become stale; true, they're big, square-jawed and silvery, and leap when hooked. But sheefish also run up rivers to spawn, as salmon do. Their voracious, predatory instincts seem to be borrowed from pike or bass. On the table, the rich, delicate, pinkish-white flesh tastes like a cross between halibut, trout, and crab. Only the fins are all whitefish.

Because sheefish are constantly on the move, finding them is most of the battle. Most sheefish migrate each spring from their winter homes in brackish estuaries to spawn in clear, swift river currents far upstream. Kobuk River sheefish, for example, swim as much as three hundred miles to their spawning beds near the Pah River. The run starts after the ice breaks up in late May or early June, and fish gradually work their way upstream until they reach the spawning grounds by late August. They don't dig redds (spawning beds) as salmon do, but broadcast their eggs over clean gravel as the males add milt. A thirty-pound female (the males are half as large) may drop 350,000 eggs. After spawning, the fish run downstream with the first ice floes to winter in Hotham Inlet, an arm of the Chukchi Sea. There they gorge on ciscos and smelt, fattening up for the next year's run. Along with king salmon, they are among the largest and longest-lived anadromous species; they may swim for twenty years.

Traditionally, the Inupiat seined for sheefish in the summer as the fish made their way upriver, and dangled hooks made of bear teeth and ivory through holes in the ice in winter. The rich, oily flesh and eggs of spawning females were especially prized as food for both people and dog teams. In early fall, whole fresh fish were buried ungutted in a leaf-lined pit to age several weeks. This "stink fish," eaten raw, had a cheeselike texture and a certain aroma that made it a special delicacy. In the past twenty years, rod and reel fishing has become the favored method for harvesting sheefish, especially among the upper Kobuk Eskimos.

Although sheefish as a rule don't feed in fresh water, they'll hit a well-presented lure at any time of year—if the water's clear enough, and if they're in the mood. Most fish lie deep through the day, moving little and refusing all offerings. In the late evening they begin to stir. Some continue their journey upstream, while others cruise along dropoffs or gravelly runs, rolling on the surface now and then. Eskimo anglers on the Kobuk usually start fishing around midnight, warming up with a fire and coffee when the action slows.

On a good night, you don't need a fire to keep warm. I recall a July evening twelve years ago, fishing a deep pool downstream from Ambler. I rode the thirty miles with two Eskimo friends in their plywood skiff. Low clouds scudded overhead, spattering rain. When we reached the spot, two other boats from the village were already pulled against the steep gravel beach. We waved—everybody knows everybody here—and rigged our rods. A hundred yards upstream, one man was leaning back, his rod bent double. Half-watching as I tied on, I saw him beach what looked like a silver log. I tossed my two-ounce Krocodile fifty yards into the current, counted as it sank, and began a slow jerk and flutter retrieve. *Whunk.* Something slammed in, tore off downstream, and snapped my line in one rush. Hands shaking, I reeled in what was left, tied on a new lure, and remembered to set my drag this time. Two casts later, I landed a fifteen pounder, and nailed its twin on the next try. Up and down the beach, everyone was catching fish. I cast again, felt a tap, and set the hook. The next thing I knew I was running down the beach, reel screeching, trying to save line.

Three hours later, the action ended as if someone had thrown a switch. Had the fish moved off or just stopped striking? The river flowed past, smooth and gray in the mist. My arms were wooden, my back drenched in sweat as I collected my fish and carried them two at a time to the boat. I'd kept six and released over a dozen, the smallest ten pounds, the largest somewhere between thirty-five and forty.

As we skimmed upstream toward home, the sun filtered through the fog, casting the world in silver light. "What time is it?" one of my friends asked. I looked down at the boat bottom, bright with fish. The light, diffused and timeless, seemed to flow from them. Sheefish time, I whispered to myself.

Two with Spears

C A R O L Y N   K R E M E R S

Carolyn Kremers is a musician, teacher, poet, and nonfiction writer who lives in Fairbanks. Her poems have appeared in Alaska Quarterly Review, Denali Alpenglow, permafrost, The Prose Poem, Runner's World, Steam Ticket, *and elsewhere. Her first book of nonfiction,* PLACE OF THE PRETEND PEOPLE: GIFTS FROM A YUP'IK ESKIMO VILLAGE *(1996), describes her experiences teaching in a remote Yup'ik Eskimo village, as well as her love of flute playing and her strong attachment to the Alaskan wilderness. "Two with Spears" is from her unpublished poetry manuscript* THERE ARE FISH AT THE MOUTH OF THE RIVER.

I.

No one else has said
her gaze is like a peregrine's.
Startled, she sees again
the ragged pass at Arrigetch,

the sudden bird, silent, steady,
coming deep from fog, coming
at eye-level. Feather-breasted: grey-white-
grey-white-grey. Seated now

at the crowded lunch table,
she wants to kiss the neck
so big and bare beside her.
Hot room. His throat smooth

in a cool green jacket.
She cannot look,
needs not to want to glide
over him, like a peregrine,

suddenly soft
and near in fog.

II.

He asks to visit. Walking
she wants to touch
palms, line up life-lines,
press his pulse to hers.

His fingers, by her side,
seem small. She looks away.
When at last he takes her
hand on this fall morning,

brown earth touches
a pale moon. If he had learned
to walrus hunt, she might feel
calluses, but he lives

in two worlds. The white one
claims his hands. She asks
his Inupiat name, delights
in the story: how his namesake

killed nine polar bears,
two with spears. He asks
if he might take her shooting,
wants to show her why he switched

from a rifle to a pistol. A moose
must get very close, he says, so close
you can look into its eyes
as it gives itself up.

III.

Like the jagged peaks at Arrigetch
and clear sky, they touch
with awestruck fingers.
Even mistranslated,

the Athabascan name stuns.
Awestruck, outstretched.
Outstretched, awestruck.
He wraps his hunger

around the legs he says can reach
another time-zone. She sucks
his small fingers, lets them play
between her teeth. She remembers

looking down from a Cessna
over tundra more wide
and green than she had ever seen,
how it lay sprinkled with white dots

like daisies, like unpainted
Easter eggs. Swans,
nesting tundra swans.
Sometimes they unfurled

their hundred elegant wings in a freedom stretch
that, later, she feared
she might not know again.
Is this how it happens?

Beyond the window,
another snow flies.
After years of broken glass,
is this how it happens?

Peregrine, Moose, Raven, Swan.
Polar Bear, Walrus, Bearded Seal.
Peregrine, Moose, Raven, Swan.
Polar Bear, Walrus, Bearded Seal.

IV.

He says his daughter
has chicken pox, misses evenings
with Dad, the way they usually
walk around the block

to Pasta Bella's for dessert.
He tells how he asks for *espresso*
and the machine whirrs, while his hazel-eyed
child swings her legs and orders

cheesecake with blueberries.
"Store-bought blueberries," she says,
and grins. "Real ones
are better." He tells her

what he did in school that day,
she tells him, and sometimes
they trade jokes. "Oh, Dad,"
she says, "you're so silly."

He says he worried she'd miss
Halloween, but she got well
enough to walk a few blocks in the paws
of a cat with a long black tail.

His wife's friend from Kotzebue
stitched it. And last year
in Ohio, when this little person
who means everything to him

was in second grade, she said,
"I know what, Dad.
Let's go as Eskimos."
So they did.

V.

This is the night the moose comes:
deep holes, long scuffs
in the snow. A full moon lights
the long domed veil

and she knows.
She will never leave.
When she goes, if she does, something
will stay. He says white people

think they know the future.
They live by calendars
in their heads. He laughs.
He tells how his uncle

taught him to steady the trigger
and the seal. "Live now,"
his uncle said, in Inupiaq.
"Look now."

VI.

"Did you put out food
for the moose?" he asks,
lying fully clothed on her bed.
She laughs. She likes to talk

with him this way.
"I could never do that,"
she says, "unless the moose
was starving." She knows better

than to feed wild animals.
"I wouldn't want to make
a moose a pet." His eyes settle
on the distance. "My father

used to ride the back
of a polar bear," he says. "Kids
in the village took turns. My father says,
even now, he remembers

how it felt to jump up and grab the fur—
'Hang on!'—while the bear
flopped on its belly and slid
downhill like a pancake.

A hunter had shot
the bear's mother, not knowing
she had a cub. When he saw,
he took it home.

One day, an Air Force officer
from Tin City came
to Wales. He saw the half-grown cub
and shot it, just like that."

VII.

They will find the beach
that she has always wanted
to visit, he says, and they will walk it,
looking for what has washed up.

She knows
that whatever he discovers,
he will give to her, or to someone,
because he gives away

everything. He says
he'd like to see her
in the long white dress,
the sleeveless cotton dress,

that she has always wanted
to wear on that beach,
bare-footed, toes teasing
turquoise water. They will walk

a long time, he says,
breeze ruffling her silvered hair,
until Raven flings them
down into sand and up

into wide, wide, sky.

Beautiful Meat

FROM *A Place Beyond*

NICK JANS

Nick Jans is a teacher and writer living in Ambler, an Eskimo village in Alaska's northwest Arctic. An avid outdoorsman, he's traveled over fifty thousand wilderness miles by snowmachine, small boat, and on foot. His first book, THE LAST LIGHT BREAKING: LIVING AMONG ALASKA'S INUPIAT ESKIMOS, *was published in 1993. His essays and poems have appeared in many publications, including* Rolling Stone, GEO, Christian Science Monitor, Gray's Sporting Journal, *and* Alaska *magazine. "Beautiful Meat" is taken from his second book,* A PLACE BEYOND: FINDING HOME IN ARCTIC ALASKA *(1996).*

We climb a tundra bank above the river, and Clarence grunts, "Bear." I follow his nod to not one bear but four, less than two hundred yards away, against a tundra knoll. Heads down, they're feasting on blueberries, packing on winter fat. Since grizzlies are almost always loners, I know this must be a family—a sow with three grown cubs. I size things up. The wind is perfect, and there's enough cover for a stalk. I sprint back to the boat for camera gear, and sling my rifle just in case. Clarence shrugs and lights a Marlboro. He makes it clear he's staying right here.

Bending at the waist, I hustle forward, then drop down and crawl. When I ease over the rise, they're only forty yards away—the sow and one cub grazing, the other two sprawled out on the tundra. One has its front paws splayed in the air, twitching with bear dreams.

I brace my camera and burn through a roll of film. The light is perfect. Dwarf birch and willow flicker red and yellow, rattling in the wind. A raven's cry echoes from a distant line of spruce. I'm aware of all this, and of my luck in being here. These aren't the Denali Park or McNeil River bears you see posing on calendars and postcards. Bears around here are used to being hunted, and are almost impossible to approach. I'm sure my being this close depends on stealth rather than goodwill, and, like most good things, it won't last long. Five minutes becomes ten. One more shot, I tell myself, and keep going.

All at once the cubs get agitated, standing like circus bears, backs straight. Then *woof,* the sow rears up. Maybe the wind swirled on me, or maybe the raven is to blame. I only know the bears are about to bolt— probably straight away, though there's no telling. I flatten out and snake backward, trying to duck behind cover.

But the sow drops down and lopes straight for me, huffing, her three two-hundred-pound teenagers in tow. It's not an all-out charge, but they're clearly locked on to my shape. Maybe they mistake me for a caribou. Maybe, too, this sow is that one bear in a hundred that doesn't avoid trouble. Either way, I'm on the hot seat. Any one of the cubs, each the size of an adult black bear, could break my neck with one swat. I back down the rise and out of sight, then sprint for the boat, waders flapping, camera clutched in one hand.

I know, I know. You're not supposed to run from bears, any more than you should run from a dog that's chasing you. I've stood my ground before. But it's only a couple hundred yards to safety. And hey, face it. This isn't one bear. It's a damn stampede.

I still have a good lead by the time I reach Clarence. "Here they come," I pant. "Let's get going." I'm keyed up, but clearheaded. There's no real danger, I know; the river is just another fifty yards. We can trot over, jump in the boat, and shove off. Clarence shakes his head, and stubs out his cigarette.

"Naah," he says. The bears are bounding straight toward us, mouths agape, shoulder humps rippling. Now they're too close to outrun. Clarence snaps back the bolt on his Ruger carbine, chambering a round. "I think I'll hunt one," he murmurs. "They look faat." He seems as calm as a woman picking over avocados in the supermarket, but I see him leaning forward, getting ready. I should have known better.

I'm trapped—not by the bears so much as by my friendship with Clarence. Moments like this define who he is, and all he is: an Inupiat hunter, part of a centuries-old tradition. Whenever we travel together, it's understood, of course, that we're hunting for whatever's in season—in other words, for whatever is "faat." Trying to talk him out of shooting makes as much sense as jumping between wolves and caribou, shouting for the madness to stop.

I knew all this from the start, but mistook Clarence's reluctance for lack of interest. He was, in easygoing Eskimo fashion, letting me go because I pushed ahead. Now it's his turn, and one man's photo opportunity is another's pot roast. I realize, with sinking heart, that I've unwittingly pimped this peaceful little family straight into Clarence's sights.

We're at the crest of a sandy knob, and the bears are thirty feet below us, moving slower now. We can't see them, but the sow's grunts and the crackle of willows tell us they're closing in. I know that if Clarence shoots, I have to join in. Clarence's rifle, though semiautomatic, is a real peashooter, with a bullet half the size of mine. No one in his right mind faces down a pissed-off bear with a .223. Except Clarence, maybe. He'll tell you a smaller bullet wastes less meat.

Suddenly the sow rears up before us. Her chest fills my scope. I have a flashing image of an old-time Inupiat hunter dashing in low to plant a bone-tipped spear. Instead, Clarence's carbine crashes, and I hear my own .243 erupt. The bear staggers, then topples backward, dead before she hits the ground. The cubs mill about. One bluffs a charge, and then they retreat, crashing downhill through the brush.

Clarence lowers his rifle. "She was pretty mad," he says. "Trying to get you for sure." He reassures me that the cubs are old enough to be on their own. There's no use arguing. I'm not too fond of either Clarence or myself just now.

The sow lies on her back, eyes glazing. We break her down, skinning quickly together, Clarence taking over on the butchering cuts. Working with a three-inch pocketknife, he severs joints and tendons with the effortless grace of a surgeon, rendering the carcass into neat, surprisingly bloodless packages: quarters, ribs, slabs of fat from the pillow on her rump. Even the spine is cut into chunks; paws are delicacies to be shared among village elders. "Beautiful meat," Clarence murmurs gently as he works. "Beautiful."

We leave only the badly worn hide, entrails, a few scraps. The head, as always, stays here. Clarence was careful, too, before he started skinning, to cut away "the worm," or cartilage beneath the tongue. Though he doesn't explain, I know these are precautions against the bear's spirit following us home. As we head up the windswept Kobuk, there's little to say. Somewhere behind us, there must be a place where all the ghosts wait. I can feel them gathering.

V
.....

Survival

The Wolfmen and the Hunter

E S K I M O   L E G E N D

"The Wolfmen and the Hunter" is an Eskimo legend retold by Edward L. Keithahn in ALASKAN IGLOO TALES *(1945). In 1923, Keithahn and his wife arrived in the remote Arctic village of Shishmaref, where they taught school, herded reindeer, and operated a cooperative store. The couple spent many enjoyable evenings "in the cozy igloos of their new friends" listening to age-old Eskimo tales.*

There was once a family consisting of a father, mother and two sons who lived alone at the mouth of a long river. Shortly after the boys had reached young manhood the parents suddenly died and left them alone. The brothers never left the old home but stayed there and made their living by hunting for seal in their kayaks.

Just across the river from their igloo, the boys one day saw a silver fox digging a hole which was to be her den. Instead of killing her, the boys daily brought her food and the fox became quite tame and unafraid of them. Early in spring a litter of fox puppies were born and when they came, the boys helped the old fox feed them by bringing birds and fish and seal meat to the den.

One day when the pups were almost grown, the two brothers were out sealing when they saw two strange kayaks approaching. The eldest brother wished to talk with the strangers but the younger one sensed danger and paddled home alone after having warned his brother to no avail. When he got to the igloo he prepared the evening meal and then sat down to wait for his brother. But the brother did not come. Night came and still no brother. The young hunter was so worried that he neither ate nor slept.

In the morning when he was about to start in search of the missing brother, a little old woman came to the igloo. "You want to know about your brother so I will tell you," she said. "Those men that you saw in the kayaks were not men. They were wolves and they killed your brother!"

When the young hunter heard this he was very sorry for his lost brother and wished to avenge his death at once. The old woman continued: "Go up the river to its source and there you will find an igloo. A little farther on is a village, and in the second igloo lives your grandmother. She can help you if you wish to find the wolfmen."

"And who are you?" asked the young man, after he had thanked her.

"I live just across the river," said the old woman, smiling. "I am very grateful to you and your brother for feeding my family." Then she left the igloo without giving the boy a chance to speak further. "It must be the silver fox," thought he, for they had fed none other.

After breakfast the young hunter got into his kayak and started paddling up the river. When he reached its source he found an igloo as the old woman had said he would. Here he left his kayak and went on until he came to the village. In the second igloo he found his grandmother who was very glad to take him in, so he made his home with her. She soon told him everything about the village. The chief man of the village had a son who was a great hunter and a very beautiful daughter who was married to two husbands. Strangely, these two men spent most of their time away from the village.

The young hunter soon became acquainted with the chief's son and the two often went hunting together. Every time they hunted, the young hunter killed game before the chief's son did. This caused the latter to admire the young man and they became fast friends.

From the day of the hunter's arrival in the village, the two husbands of the chief's daughter had been missing. In fact the people believed them to be dead. In the meanwhile the daughter and the young hunter had fallen in love with each other and when she finally was convinced her other husbands were dead, they were married.

Winter had begun and one day while the young hunter was visiting his grandmother, she said to him, "When the winter is half over, your wife's former husbands will return from the moon. You should be on your guard for they are the wolves that killed your brother!"

When the young man heard this he was at first greatly alarmed but when he thought of his dead brother he was glad that his chance for vengeance would soon come. After that he slept with one eye open and grew more cautious as the winter went on.

One day in mid-winter the wolfmen returned but their wife warned the hunter in time for him to grasp his bow and arrows and flee to his grand-mother's igloo. When he came in, the grandmother said, "You must return to the small igloo where you left your kayak. In the igloo is a spear which you must take and stick into the ground. When you have done that come back to me."

The young man did exactly as his grandmother had instructed but no sooner had he stood the spear upright in the ground than two wolves appeared and started after him, running swiftly. He dashed away and ran with all his speed for the village. Just as the wolves were about to drag him down he reached his grandmother's igloo. Then, turning quickly, he shot two arrows and ran through the door. "You have killed the wolfmen!" shouted the old woman. He could not believe he had been so lucky and when he opened the door to see if it were true, they were gone. But when he went to his wife's igloo, there before the door lay the two wolves, dead.

Great happiness now filled the young man's heart for he had not only avenged the death of his brother but had destroyed his dangerous rivals as well. But when he went inside to tell his wife that he had killed her two hus-bands she began to weep, pitifully. "Are you sorry that I have killed your husbands who were wolves?" asked the young man. Then he showed her the bodies of the wolves and his wife forgave him. This was the first time she had known that they were wolves in the form of men and now she knew why they disappeared together for long periods of time. Needless to say, the young couple lived happily ever after.

Let Us Die Trying

FROM *Two Old Women*

VELMA WALLIS

Velma Wallis is a Kutchin Athabascan from Fort Yukon, Alaska, a small community situated just upriver from the confluence of the Yukon and Porcupine Rivers. A subsistence trapper, hunter, and fisher, Wallis wrote the award-winning best-seller TWO OLD WOMEN *(1993), based on her mother's traditional oral stories. In this excerpt, "Let Us Die Trying," two elderly Athabascan women, Ch'idzigyaak ("Chickadee") and Sa' ("Star"), have been abandoned by their people during a time of starvation.*

Ch'idzigyaak sat quietly as if trying to make up her confused mind. A small feeling of hope sparked in the blackness of her being as she listened to her friend's strong words. She felt the cold stinging her cheeks where her tears had fallen, and she listened to the silence that The People left behind. She knew that what her friend said was true, that within this calm, cold land waited a certain death if they did nothing for themselves. Finally, more in desperation than in determination she echoed her friend's words, "Let us die trying." With that, her friend helped her up off the sodden branches.

The women gathered sticks to build the fire and they added pieces of fungus that grew large and dry on fallen cottonwood trees to keep it smoldering. They went around to other campfires to salvage what embers they could find. As they packed to travel, the migrating bands in these times preserved hot coals in hardened mooseskin sacks or birchbark containers filled with ash in which the embers pulsated, ready to spark the next campfire.

As night approached, the women cut thin strips from the bundle of babiche, fashioning them into nooses the size of a rabbit's head. Then, despite their weariness, the women managed to make some rabbit snares, which they immediately set out.

The moon hung big and orange on the horizon as they trudged through the knee-deep snow, searching in the dimness for signs of rabbit life. It was hard to see, and what rabbits existed stayed quiet in the cold weather. But they found several old, hardened rabbit trails frozen solid beneath the trees and arching willows. Ch'idzigyaak tied a babiche noose to a long, thick willow branch and placed it across one of the trails. She made little fences of willows and spruce boughs on each side of the noose to guide the rabbit through the snare. The two women set a few more snares but felt little hope that even one rabbit would be caught.

On their way back to the camp, Sa' heard something skitter lightly along the bark of a tree. She stood very still, motioning her friend to do the same. Both women strained to hear the sound once more in the silence of the night. On a tree not far from them, silhouetted in the now-silvery moonlight, they saw an adventurous tree squirrel. Sa' slowly reached to her belt for the hatchet. With her eyes on the squirrel and her movements deliberately slow, she aimed the hatchet toward this target that represented survival. The animal's small head came up instantly and as Sa' moved her hand to throw, the squirrel darted up the tree. Sa' foresaw this, and, aiming a little higher, ended the small animal's life in one calculating throw with skill and hunting knowledge that she had not used in many seasons.

Ch'idzigyaak let out a deep sigh of relief. The moon's light shone on the younger woman's smiling face as she said in a proud yet shaky voice, "Many times I have done that, but never did I think I would do it again."

Back at the camp, the women boiled the squirrel meat in snow water and drank the broth, saving the small portion of meat to be eaten later, for they knew that otherwise, this could be their last meal.

The two women had not eaten for some time because The People had tried to conserve what little food they had. Now they realized why precious food had not been given to them. Why waste food on two who were to die? Trying not to think about what had happened, the two women filled their empty stomachs with the warm squirrel broth and settled down in their tent for the night.

The shelter was made of two large caribou hides wrapped around three long sticks shaped into a kind of triangle. Inside were thickly piled spruce boughs covered with many fur blankets. The women were aware that, although they had been left behind to fend for themselves, The People had done them a good deed by leaving them with all their possessions. They suspected that the chief was responsible for this small kindness. Other less noble members of the band would have decided that the two women soon would die and would have pilfered everything except for the warm fur and skin clothing they wore. With these confusing thoughts lingering in their minds, the two frail women dozed.

The moonlight shone silently upon the frozen earth as life whispered throughout the land, broken now and then by a lone wolf's melancholy howl. The women's eyes twitched in tired, troubled dreams, and soft helpless moans escaped from their lips. Then a cry rang out somewhere in the night as the moon dipped low on the western horizon. Both women awoke at once, hoping that the awful screech was a part of her nightmare. Again the wail was heard. This time, the women recognized it as the sound of something caught in one of their snares. They were relieved. Fearing that other predators would beat them to their catch, the women hurriedly dressed and rushed to their snare sets. There they saw a small, trembling rabbit that lay partially strangled as it eyed them warily. Without hesitation, Sa' went to the rabbit, put one hand around its neck, felt for the beating heart, and squeezed until the small struggling animal went limp. After Sa' reset the snare, they went back to the camp, each feeling a thread of new hope.

Morning came, but brought no light to this far northern land. Ch'idzig-yaak awoke first. She slowly kindled the fire into a flame as she carefully added more wood. When the fire had died out during the cold night, frost from their warm breathing had accumulated on the walls of caribou skins.

Sighing in dull exasperation, Ch'idzigyaak went outside where the northern lights still danced above, and the stars winked in great numbers. Ch'idzigyaak stood for a moment staring up at these wonders. In all her years, the night sky never failed to fill her with awe.

Remembering her task, Ch'idzigyaak grabbed the upper rims of the caribou skins, laid them on the ground and briskly brushed off the crystal frost. After putting the skins up again, she went back inside to build up the campfire. Soon moisture dripped from the skin wall, which quickly dried.

Ch'idzigyaak shuddered to think of the melting frost dripping on them in the cold weather. How had they managed before? Ah, yes! The younger ones were always there, piling wood on the fire, peering into the shelter to make sure that their elders' fire did not go out. What a pampered pair they had been! How would they survive now?

Ch'idzigyaak sighed deeply, trying not to dwell on those dark thoughts, and concentrated instead on tending the fire without waking her sleeping companion. The shelter warmed as the fire crackled, spitting tiny sparks from the dry wood. Slowly, Sa' awoke to this sound and lay on her back for a long time before becoming aware of her friend's movement. Turning her aching neck slowly she began to smile but stopped as she saw her friend's forlorn look. In a pained grimace Sa' propped herself up carefully on her elbow and tried to smile encouragingly as she said, "I thought yesterday had only been a dream when I awoke to your warm fire."

Ch'idzigyaak managed a slight smile at the obvious attempt to lift her spirits but continued to stare dully into the fire. "I sit and worry," she said after a long silence. "I fear what lies ahead. No! Don't say anything!" she held up her hands as her friend opened her mouth to speak.

"I know that you are sure of our survival. You are younger." She could not help but smile bitterly at her remark, for just yesterday they both had been judged too old to live with the young. "It has been a long time since I have been on my own. There has always been someone there to take care of me, and now . . ." She broke off with a hoarse whisper as tears fell, much to her shame.

Her friend let her cry. As the tears eased and the older woman wiped her dampened face, she laughed. "Forgive me, my friend. I am older than you. Yet I cry like a baby."

"We are like babies," Sa' responded. The older woman looked up in surprise at such an admission. "We are like helpless babies." A smile twitched her lips as her friend started to look slightly affronted by the remark, but before Ch'idzigyaak could take it in the wrong way Sa' went on. "We have learned much during our long lives. Yet there we were in our old age, thinking that we had done our share in life. So we stopped, just like that. No more working like we used to, even though our bodies are still healthy enough to do a little more than we expect of ourselves."

Ch'idzigyaak sat listening, alert to her friend's sudden revelation as to why the younger ones thought it best to leave them behind. "Two old women. They complain, never satisfied. We talk of no food, and of how good it was in our days when it really was no better. We think that we are so old. Now, because we have spent so many years convincing the younger people that we are helpless, they believe that we are no longer of use to this world."

Seeing tears fill her friend's eyes at the finality of her words, Sa' continued in a voice heavy with feeling. "We are going to prove them wrong! The

People. And death!" She shook her head, motioning into the air. "Yes, it awaits us, this death. Ready to grab us the moment we show our weak spots. I fear this kind of death more than any suffering you and I will go through. If we are going to die anyway, let us die trying!"

Ch'idzigyaak stared for a long time at her friend and knew that what she said was true, that death surely would come if they did not try to survive. She was not convinced that the two of them were strong enough to make it through the harsh season, but the passion in her friend's voice made her feel a little better. So, instead of feeling sadness because there was nothing further they could say or do, she smiled, "I think we said this before and will probably say it many more times, but yes, let us die trying." And with a sense of strength filling her like she had not thought possible, Sa' returned the smile as she got up to prepare for the long day ahead of them.

Lost Face

J A C K   L O N D O N

*Jack London (1876–1916) was born in San Francisco and came to Alaska in
1897 during the Klondike gold rush. Though he stayed in the Northland only
a few short months, his experiences there fired his imagination and his
writing. Now Jack London's name is invariably associated with pioneering
adventures in Alaska and the Yukon. He is best known for his novels,
including* The Call of the Wild *(1903),* The Sea Wolf *(1904), and* White
Fang *(1906). "Lost Face" is set during the days of Russian Alaska. It was first
published in the* New York Herald *in 1908, and was subsequently included
in his collection of short stories called* Lost Face *published in 1910.*

It was the end. Subienkow had traveled a long trail of bitterness and
horror, homing like a dove for the capitals of Europe, and here, farther away than ever, in Russian America, the trail ceased. He sat in the
snow, arms tied behind him, waiting the torture. He stared curiously
before him at a huge Cossack, prone in the snow, moaning in his pain.
The men had finished handling the giant and turned him over to the
women. That they exceeded the fiendishness of the men the man's cries
attested.

Subienkow looked on and shuddered. He was not afraid to die. He had
carried his life too long in his hands, on that weary trail from Warsaw to
Nulato, to shudder at mere dying. But he objected to the torture. It offended
his soul. And his offense, in turn, was not due to the mere pain he must
endure, but to the sorry spectacle the pain would make of him. He knew
that he would pray, and beg, and entreat, even as Big Ivan and the others that
had gone before. This would not be nice. To pass out bravely and cleanly,
with a smile and a jest—ah, that would have been the way. But to lose control, to have his soul upset by the pangs of the flesh, to screech and gibber
like an ape, to become the veriest beast—ah, that was what was so terrible.

There had been no chance to escape. From the beginning, when he
dreamed the fiery dream of Poland's independence, he had become a puppet
in the hands of fate. From the beginning, at Warsaw, at St. Petersburg, in

the Siberian mines, in Kamchatka, on the crazy boats of the fur thieves, fate had been driving him to this end. Without doubt, in the foundations of the world was graved this end for him—for him, who was so fine and sensitive, whose nerves scarcely sheltered under his skin, who was a dreamer and a poet and an artist. Before he was dreamed of, it had been determined that the quivering bundle of sensitiveness that constituted him should be doomed to live in raw and howling savagery, and to die in this far land of night, in this dark place beyond the last boundaries of the world.

He sighed. So that thing before him was Big Ivan—Big Ivan the giant, the man without nerves, the man of iron, the Cossack turned freebooter of the seas, who was as phlegmatic as an ox, with a nervous system so low that what was pain to ordinary men was scarcely a tickle to him. Well, well, trust these Nulato Indians to find Big Ivan's nerves and trace them to the roots of his quivering soul. They were certainly doing it. It was inconceivable that a man could suffer so much and yet live. Big Ivan was paying for his low order of nerves. Already he had lasted twice as long as any of the others.

Subienkow felt that he could not stand the Cossack's sufferings much longer. Why didn't Ivan die? He would go mad if that screaming did not cease. But when it did cease, his turn would come. And there was Yakaga awaiting him, too, grinning at him even now in anticipation—Yakaga, whom only last week he had kicked out of the fort, and upon whose face he had laid the lash of his dog whip. Yakaga would attend to him. Doubt-lessly Yakaga was saving for him more refined tortures, more exquisite nerve-wracking. Ah! That must have been a good one, from the way Ivan screamed. The squaws bending over him stepped back with laughter and clapping of hands. Subienkow saw the monstrous thing that had been per-petrated, and began to laugh hysterically. The Indians looked at him in wonderment that he should laugh. But Subienkow could not stop.

This would never do. He controlled himself, the spasmodic twitchings slowly dying away. He strove to think of other things and began reading back in his own life. He remembered his mother and his father, and the little spotted pony, and the French tutor who had taught him dancing and sneaked him an old worn copy of Voltaire. Once more he saw Paris, and dreary London, and gay Vienna, and Rome. And once more he saw that wild group of youths who had dreamed, even as he, the dream of an inde-pendent Poland with a king of Poland on the throne at Warsaw. Ah, there it was that the long trail began. Well, he had lasted longest. One by one, beginning with the two executed at St. Petersburg, he took up the count of the passing of those brave spirits. Here one had been beaten to death by a jailer, and there, on that bloodstained highway of the exiles, where they had marched for endless months, beaten and maltreated by their Cossack guards, another had dropped by the way. Always it had been savagery—brutal, bestial savagery. They had died—of fever, in the mines, under the knout. The last two had died after the escape, in the battle with the Cossacks, and he alone had won to Kamchatka with the stolen papers and the money of a traveler he had left lying in the snow.

It had been nothing but savagery. All the years, with his heart in studios and theaters and courts, he had been hemmed in by savagery. He had purchased his life with blood. Everybody had killed. He had killed that traveler for his passports. He had proved that he was a man of parts by dueling with two Russian officers on a single day. He had had to prove himself in order to win to a place among the fur thieves. He had had to win to that place. Behind him lay the thousand-years-long road across all Siberia and Russia. He could not escape that way. The only way was ahead, across the dark and icy sea of Bering to Alaska. The way had led from savagery to deeper savagery. On the scurvy-rotten ships of the fur thieves, out of food and out of water, buffeted by the interminable storms of that stormy sea, men had become animals. Thrice he had sailed east from Kamchatka. And thrice, after all manner of hardship and suffering, the survivors had come back to Kamchatka. There had been no outlet for escape, and he could not go back the way he had come, for the mines and the knout awaited him.

Again, the fourth and last time, he had sailed east. He had been with those who first found the fabled Seal Islands; but he had not returned with them to share the wealth of furs in the mad orgies of Kamchatka. He had sworn never to go back. He knew that to win to those dear capitals of Europe he must go on. So he had changed ships and remained in the dark new land. His comrades were Slavonian hunters and Russian adventurers, Mongols and Tatars and Siberian aborigines; and through the savages of the New World they had cut a path of blood. They had massacred whole villages that refused to furnish the fur tribute; and they in turn had been massacred by ships' companies. He, with one Finn, had been the sole survivors of such a company. They had spent a winter of solitude and starvation on a lonely Aleutian isle, and their rescue in the spring by another fur ship had been one chance in a thousand.

But always the terrible savagery had hemmed him in. Passing from ship to ship, and ever refusing to return, he had come to the ship that exploded south. All down the Alaskan coast they had encountered nothing but hosts of savages. Every anchorage among the beetling islands or under the frowning cliffs of the mainland had meant a battle or a storm. Either the gales blew, threatening destruction, or the war canoes came off, manned by howling natives with the war paint on their faces, who came to learn the bloody virtues of the sea rovers' gunpowder. South, south they had coasted, clear to the myth land of California. Here, it was said, were Spanish adventurers who had fought their way up from Mexico. He had had hopes of those Spanish adventurers. Escaping to them, the rest would have been easy—a year or two, what did it matter more or less?—and he would win to Mexico, then a ship, and Europe would be his. But they had met no Spaniards. Only had they encountered the same impregnable wall of savagery. The denizens of the confines of the world, pained for war, had driven them back from the shores. At last, when one boat was cut off and every man killed, the commander had abandoned the quest and sailed back to the North.

The years had passed. He had served under Tebenokoff when Michaelovski Redoubt was built. He had spent two years in the Kuskokwim country. Two summers, in the month of June, he had managed to be at the head of Kotzebue Sound. Here, at this time, the tribes assembled for barter; here were to be found spotted deerskins from Siberia, ivory from the Diomedes, walrus skins from the shores of the Arctic, strange stone lamps, passing in trade from tribe to tribe, no one knew whence, and, once, a hunting knife of English make; and here, Subienkow knew, was the school in which to learn geography. For he met Eskimos from Norton Sound, from King Island and St. Lawrence Island, from Cape Prince of Wales, and Point Barrow. Such places had other names, and their distances were measured in days.

It was a vast region these trading savages came from, and a vaster region from which, by repeated trade, their stone lamps and that steel knife had come. Subienkow bullied and cajoled and bribed. Every far journeyer or strange tribesman was brought before him. Perils unaccountable and unthinkable were mentioned, as well as wild beasts, hostile tribes, impenetrable forests, and mighty mountain ranges; but always from beyond came the rumor and the tale of white-skinned men, blue of eye and fair of hair, who fought like devils and who sought always for furs. They were to the east—far, far to the east. No one had seen them. It was the word that had been passed along.

It was a hard school. One could not learn geography very well through the medium of strange dialects, from dark minds that mingled fact and fable and that measured distances by "sleeps" that varied according to the difficulty of the going. But at last came the whisper that gave Subienkow courage. In the east lay a great river where were these blue-eyed men. The river was called the Yukon. South of Michaelovski Redoubt emptied another great river which the Russians knew as the Kwikpak. These two rivers were one, ran the whisper.

Subienkow returned to Michaelovski. For a year he urged an expedition up the Kwikpak. Then arose Malakoff, the Russian half-breed, to lead the wildest and most ferocious of the hell's broth of mongrel adventurers who had crossed from Kamchatka. Subienkow was his lieutenant. They threaded the mazes of the great delta of the Kwikpak, picked up the first low hills on the northern bank, and for half a thousand miles, in skin canoes loaded to the gunwales with trade goods and ammunition, fought their way against the five-knot current of a river that ran from two to ten miles wide in a channel many fathoms deep. Malakoff decided to build the fort at Nulato. Subienkow urged to go farther. But he quickly reconciled himself to Nulato. The long winter was coming on. It would be better to wait. Early the following summer when the ice was gone, he would disappear up the Kwikpak and work his way to the Hudson Bay Company's posts. Malakoff had never heard the whisper that the Kwikpak was the Yukon, and Subienkow did not tell him.

Came the building of the fort. It was enforced labor. The tiered walls of logs arose to the sighs and groans of the Nulato Indians. The lash was laid upon their backs, and it was the iron hand of the freebooters of the sea that laid on the lash. There were Indians that ran away, and when they were caught they were brought back and spread-eagled before the fort, where they and their tribe learned the efficacy of the knout. Two died under it; others were injured for life; and the rest took the lesson to heart and ran away no more. The snow was flying ere the fort was finished, and then it was the time for furs. A heavy tribute was laid upon the tribe. Blows and lashings continued, and that the tribute should be paid, the women and children were held as hostages and treated with the barbarity that only the fur thieves knew.

Well, it had been a sowing of blood, and now was come the harvest. The fort was gone. In the light of its burning, half the fur thieves had been cut down. The other half had passed under the torture. Only Subienkow caught Yakaga grinning at him. There was no gainsaying Yakaga. The mark of the lash was still on his face. After all, Subienkow could not blame him, but he disliked the thought of what Yakaga would do to him. He thought of appealing to Makamuk, the head chief; but his judgment told him that such appeal was useless. Then, too, he thought of bursting his bonds and dying fighting. Such an end would be quick. But he could not break his bonds. Caribou thongs were stronger than he. Still devising, another thought came to him. He signed for Makamuk, and that an interpreter who knew the coast dialect should be brought.

"Oh, Makamuk," he said, "I am not minded to die. I am a great man, and it were foolishness for me to die. In truth, I shall not die. I am not like these other carrion."

He looked at the moaning thing that had once been Big Ivan, and stirred it contemptuously with his toe.

"I am too wise to die. Behold, I have a great medicine. I alone know this medicine. Since I am not going to die, I shall exchange this medicine with you."

"What is this medicine?" Makamuk demanded.

"It is a strange medicine."

Subienkow debated with himself for a moment, as if loath to part with the secret.

"I will tell you. A little bit of this medicine rubbed on the skin makes the skin hard like a rock, hard like iron, so that a cutting weapon cannot cut it. The strongest blow of a cutting weapon is a vain thing against it. A bone knife becomes like a piece of mud; and it will turn the edge of the iron knives we have brought among you. What will you give me for the secret of the medicine?"

"I will give you your life," Makamuk made answer through the interpreter.

Subienkow laughed scornfully.

"And you shall be a slave in my house until you die."

The Pole laughed more scornfully.

"Untie my hands and feet and let us talk," he said.

The chief made the sign; and when he was loosed Subienkow rolled a cigarette and lighted it.

"This is foolish talk," said Makamuk. "There is no such medicine. It cannot be. A cutting edge is stronger than any medicine."

The chief was incredulous, and yet he wavered. He had seen too many deviltries of fur thieves that worked. He could not wholly doubt.

"I will give you your life; but you shall not be a slave," he announced. "More than that."

Subienkow played his game as coolly as if he were bartering for a fox skin.

"It is a very great medicine. It has saved my life many times. I want a sled and dogs, and six of your hunters to travel with me down the river and give me safety to one day's sleep from Michaelovski Redoubt."

"You must live here, and teach us all of your deviltries," was the reply.

Subienkow shrugged his shoulders and remained silent. He blew cigarette smoke out on the icy air, and curiously regarded what remained of the big Cossack.

"That scar!" Makamuk said suddenly, pointing to the Pole's neck, where a livid mark advertised the slash of a knife in a Kamchatkan brawl. "The medicine is not good. The cutting edge was stronger than the medicine."

"It was a strong man that drove the stroke." (Subienkow considered.) "Stronger than you, stronger than your strongest hunter, stronger than he."

Again, with the toe of his moccasin, he touched the Cossack—a grisly spectacle, no longer conscious—yet in whose dismembered body the pain-racked life clung and was loath to go.

"Also the medicine was weak. For at that place there were no berries of a certain kind, of which I see you have plenty in this country. The medicine here will be strong."

"I will let you go downriver," said Makamuk, "and the sled and the dogs and the six hunters to give you safety shall be yours."

"You are slow," was the cool rejoinder. "You have committed an offense against my medicine in that you did not at once accept my terms. Behold, I now demand more. I want one hundred beaver skins." (Makamuk sneered.) "I want one hundred pounds of dried fish." (Makamuk nodded, for fish were plentiful and cheap.) "I want two sleds—one for me and one for my furs and fish. And my rifle must be returned to me. If you do not like the price, in a little while the price will grow."

Yakaga whispered to the chief.

"But how can I know your medicine is true medicine?" Makamuk asked.

"It is very easy. First, I shall go into the woods———"

Again Yakaga whispered to Makamuk, who made a suspicious dissent.

"You can send twenty hunters with me," Subienkow went on. "You see, I must get the berries and the roots with which to make the medicine. Then, when you have brought the two sleds and loaded on them the fish and the beaver skins and the rifle, and when you have told off the six hunters who will go with me—then, when all is ready, I will rub the medicine on my neck, so, and lay my neck there on that log. Then can your strongest hunter take the ax and strike three times on my neck. You yourself can strike the three times."

Makamuk stood with gaping mouth, drinking in this latest and most wonderful magic of the fur thieves.

"But first," the Pole added hastily, "between each blow I must put on fresh medicine. The ax is heavy and sharp, and I want no mistakes."

"All that you have asked shall be yours," Makamuk cried in a rush of acceptance. "Proceed to make your medicine."

Subienkow concealed his elation. He was playing a desperate game, and there must be no slips. He spoke arrogantly.

"You have been slow. My medicine is offended. To make the offense clean you must give me your daughter."

He pointed to the girl, an unwholesome creature, with a cast in one eye and a bristling wolf tooth. Makamuk was angry, but the Pole remained imperturbable, rolling and lighting another cigarette.

"Make haste," he threatened. "If you are not quick, I shall demand yet more."

In the silence that followed, the dreary Northland scene faded from before him, and he saw once more his native land, and France, and once, as he glanced at the wolf-toothed girl, he remembered another girl, a singer and a dancer, whom he had known when first as a youth he came to Paris.

"What do you want with the girl?" Makamuk asked.

"To go down the river with me." Subienkow glanced her over critically. "She will make a good wife, and it is an honor worthy of my medicine to be married to your blood."

Again he remembered the singer and dancer and hummed aloud a song she had taught him. He lived the old life over, but in a detached, impersonal sort of way, looking at the memory pictures of his own life as if they were pictures in a book of anybody's life. The chief's voice, abruptly breaking the silence, startled him.

"It shall be done," said Makamuk. "The girl shall go down the river with you. But be it understood that I myself strike the three blows with the ax on your neck."

"But each time I shall put on the medicine," Subienkow answered, with a show of ill-concealed anxiety.

"You shall put the medicine on between each blow. Here are the hunters who shall see you do not escape. Go into the forest and gather your medicine."

Makamuk had been convinced of the worth of the medicine by the Pole's rapacity. Surely nothing less than the greatest of medicines could enable a man in the shadow of death to stand up and drive an old woman's bargain.

"Besides," whispered Yakaga, when the Pole, with his guard, had disappeared among the spruce trees, "when you have learned the medicine you can easily destroy him."

"But how can I destroy him?" Makamuk argued. "His medicine will not let me destroy him."

"There will be some part where he has not rubbed the medicine," was Yakaga's reply. "We will destroy him through that part. It may be his ears. Very well; we will thrust a spear in one ear and out the other. Or it may be his eyes. Surely the medicine will be much too strong to rub on his eyes."

The chief nodded. "You are wise, Yakaga. If he possesses no other devil things, we will then destroy him."

Subienkow did not waste time in gathering the ingredients for his medicine. He selected whatsoever came to hand such as spruce needles, the inner bark of the willow, a strip of birch bark, and a quantity of mossberries, which he made the hunters dig up for him from beneath the snow. A few dozen roots completed his supply, and he led the way back to camp.

Makamuk and Yakaga crouched beside him, noting the quantities and kinds of the ingredients he dropped into the pot of boiling water.

"You must be careful that the mossberries go in first," he explained.

"And—oh yes, one other thing—the finger of a man. Here, Yakaga, let me cut off your finger."

But Yakaga put his hands behind him and scowled.

"Just a small finger," Subienkow pleaded.

"Yakaga, give him your finger," Makamuk commanded.

"There be plenty of fingers lying around," Yakaga grunted, indicating the human wreckage in the snow of the score of persons who had been tortured to death.

"It must be the finger of a live man," the Pole objected.

"Then shall you have the finger of a live man." Yakaga strode over to the Cossack and sliced off a finger.

"He is not yet dead," he announced, flinging the bloody trophy in the snow at the Pole's feet. "Also, it is a good finger, because it is large."

Subienkow dropped it into the fire under the pot and began to sing. It was a French love song that with great solemnity he sang into the brew.

"Without these words I utter into it the medicine is worthless," he explained. "The words are the chiefest strength of it. Behold, it is ready."

"Name the words slowly, that I may know them," Makamuk commanded.

"Not until after the test. When the ax flies back three times from my neck, then will I give you the secret of the words."

"But if the medicine is not good medicine?" Makamuk queried anxiously.

Subienkow turned upon him wrathfully.

"My medicine is always good. However, if it is not good, then do by me as you have done to the others. Cut me up a bit at a time, even as you have cut him up." He pointed to the Cossack. "The medicine is now cool. Thus I rub it on my neck, saying this further medicine."

With great gravity he slowly intoned a line of the "Marseillaise," at the same time rubbing the villainous brew thoroughly into his neck.

An outcry interrupted his playacting. The giant Cossack, with a last resurgence of his tremendous vitality, had arisen to his knees. Laughter and cries of surprise and applause arose from the Nulatos, as Big Ivan began flinging himself about in the snow with mighty spasms.

Subienkow was made sick by the sight, but he mastered his qualms and made believe to be angry.

"This will not do," he said. "Finish him, and then we will make the test. Here, you, Yakaga, see that his noise ceases."

While this was being done, Subienkow turned to Makamuk.

"And remember, you are to strike hard. This is not baby work. Here, take the ax and strike the log, so that I can see you strike like a man."

Makamuk obeyed, striking twice, precisely and with vigor, cutting out a large chip.

"It is well." Subienkow looked about him at the circle of savage faces that somehow seemed to symbolize the wall of savagery that had hemmed him about ever since the Czar's police had first arrested him in Warsaw. "Take your ax, Makamuk, and stand so. I shall lie down. When I raise my hand, strike, and strike with all your might. And be careful that no one stands behind you. The medicine is good, and the ax may bounce from off my neck and right out of your hands."

He looked at the two sleds, with the dogs in harness, loaded with furs and fish. His rifle lay on top of the beaver skins. The six hunters who were to act as his guard stood by the sleds.

"Where is the girl?" the Pole demanded. "Bring her up to the sleds before the test goes on."

When this had been carried out, Subienkow lay down in the snow, resting his head on the log like a tired child about to sleep. He had lived so many dreary years that he was indeed tired.

"I laugh at you and your strength, O Makamuk," he said. "Strike and strike hard."

He lifted his hand. Makamuk swung the ax, a broad ax for the squaring of logs. The bright steel flashed through the frosty air, poised for a perceptible instant above Makamuk's head, then descended upon Subienkow's bare neck. Clear through flesh and bone it cut its way, biting deeply into the log beneath. The amazed savages saw the head bounce a yard away from the blood-spouting trunk.

There was a great bewilderment and silence, while slowly it began to dawn in their minds that there had been no medicine. The fur thief had outwitted them. Alone, of all their prisoners, he had escaped the torture. That had been the stake for which he played. A great roar of laughter went up. Makamuk bowed his head in shame. The fur thief had fooled him. He had lost face before all his people. Still they continued to roar out their laughter. Makamuk turned, and with bowed head stalked away. He knew that thenceforth he would be no longer known as Makamuk. He would be Lost Face; the record of his shame would be with him until he died; and whenever the tribes gathered in the spring for the salmon, or in the summer for the trading, the story would pass back and forth across the campfires of how the fur thief died peaceably, at a single stroke, by the hand of Lost Face.

"Who was Lost Face?" he could hear, in anticipation, some insolent young buck demand. "Oh, Lost Face," would be the answer, "he who once was Makamuk in the days before he cut off the fur thief's head."

To Build a Fire

JACK LONDON

Popular novelist Jack London (1876–1916) started out writing short stories for magazines such as The Atlantic Monthly, *but it was his sweeping adventure sagas,* THE CALL OF THE WILD *(1903),* THE SEA WOLF *(1904), and* WHITE FANG *(1906), which were based on London's brief experience in Alaska and the Yukon during the Klondike gold rush, that brought him fame. "To Build a Fire" was first written for children and published in* Youth's Companion *in 1902. London revised the story for adult readers for* Century *magazine in 1908, and subsequently published it in a collection of stories,* LOST FACE, *in 1910.*

Day had broken cold and gray, exceedingly cold and gray, when the man turned aside from the main Yukon trail and climbed the high earth-bank, where a dim and little-travelled trail led eastward through the fat spruce timberland. It was a steep bank, and he paused for breath at the top, excusing the act to himself by looking at his watch. It was nine o'clock. There was no sun nor hint of sun, though there was not a cloud in the sky. It was a clear day, and yet there seemed an intangible pall over the face of things, a subtle gloom that made the day dark, and that was due to the absence of sun. This fact did not worry the man. He was used to the lack of sun. It had been days since he had seen the sun, and he knew that a few more days must pass before that cheerful orb, due south, would just peep above the sky line and dip immediately from view.

The man flung a look back along the way he had come. The Yukon lay a mile wide and hidden under three feet of ice. On top of this ice were as many feet of snow. It was all pure white, rolling in gentle undulations where the ice jams of the freeze-up had formed. North and south, as far as his eye could see, it was unbroken white, save for a dark hairline that curved and twisted away into the north, where it disappeared behind another spruce-covered island to the south, and that curved and twisted away into the north, where it disappeared behind another spruce-covered island. This dark hairline was the trail—the main trail—that led south five hundred miles to the Chilcoot Pass, Dyea, and salt water; and that led north seventy miles to Dawson, and still on to the north a thousand miles to Nulato, and finally to St. Michael, on Bering Sea, a thousand miles and half a thousand more.

But all this—the mysterious, far-reaching hairline trail, the absence of sun from the sky, the tremendous cold, and the strangeness and weirdness of it all—made no impression on the man. It was not because he was long used to it. He was a newcomer in the land, a *chechaquo,* and this was his first winter. The trouble with him was that he was without imagination. He was quick and alert in the things of life, but only in the things, and not in the significances. Fifty degrees below zero meant eighty-odd degrees of frost. Such fact impressed him as being cold and uncomfortable, and that was all. It did not lead him to meditate upon his frailty as a creature of temperature, and upon man's frailty in general, able only to live within certain narrow limits of heat and cold; and from there on it did not lead him to the conjectural field of immortality and man's place in the universe. Fifty degrees below zero stood for a bite of frost that hurt and that must be guarded against by the use of mittens, ear flaps, warm moccasins, and thick socks. Fifty degrees below zero was to him just precisely fifty degrees below zero. That there should be anything more to it than that was a thought that never entered his head.

As he turned to go on, he spat speculatively. There was a sharp, explosive crackle that startled him. He spat again. And again, in the air, before it could fall to the snow, the spittle crackled. He knew that at fifty below spittle crackled on the snow, but this spittle had crackled in the air. Undoubtedly it was colder than fifty below—how much colder he did not know. But the temperature did not matter. He was bound for the old claim on the left fork of Henderson Creek, where the boys were already. They had come over across the divide from the Indian Creek country, while he had come the roundabout way to take a look at the possibilities of getting out logs in the spring from the islands in the Yukon. He would be in to camp by six o'clock; a bit after dark, it was true, but the boys would be there, a fire would be going, and a hot supper would be ready. As for lunch, he pressed his hand against the protruding bundle under his jacket. It was also under his shirt, wrapped up in a handkerchief and lying against the naked skin. It was the only way to keep the biscuits from freezing. He smiled agreeably to himself as he thought of those biscuits, each cut open and sopped in bacon grease, and each enclosing a generous slice of fried bacon.

He plunged in among the big spruce trees. The trail was faint. A foot of snow had fallen since the last sled had passed over, and he was glad he was without a sled, travelling light. In fact, he carried nothing but the lunch wrapped in the handkerchief. He was surprised, however, at the cold. It certainly was cold, he concluded, as he rubbed his numb nose and cheekbones with his mittened hand. He was a warm-whiskered man, but the hair on his face did not protect the high cheekbones and the eager nose that thrust itself aggressively into the frosty air.

At the man's heels trotted a dog, a big native husky, the proper wolf dog, gray-coated and without any visible or temperamental difference from its brother, the wild wolf. The animal was depressed by the tremendous cold. It knew that it was no time for travelling. Its instinct told it a truer tale than was told to the man by the man's judgment. In reality, it was not merely colder than fifty below zero; it was colder than sixty below, than seventy below. It was seventy-five below zero. Since the freezing point is thirty-two above zero, it meant that one hundred and seven degrees of frost obtained. The dog did not know anything about thermometers. Possibly in its brain there was no sharp consciousness of a condition of very cold such as was in the man's brain. But the brute had its instinct. It experienced a vague but menacing apprehension that subdued it and made it slink along at the man's heels, and that made it question eagerly every unwonted movement of the man as if expecting him to go into camp or to seek shelter somewhere and build a fire. The dog had learned fire, and it wanted fire, or else to burrow under the snow and cuddle its warmth away from the air.

The frozen moisture of its breathing had settled on its fur in a fine powder of frost, and especially were its jowls, muzzle, and eyelashes whitened by its crystalled breath. The man's red beard and mustache were likewise frosted, but more solidly, the deposit taking the form of ice and increasing with every warm, moist breath he exhaled. Also, the man was chewing tobacco, and the muzzle of ice held his lips so rigidly that he was unable to clear his chin when he expelled the juice. The result was that a crystal beard of the color and solidity of amber was increasing its length on his chin. If he fell down it would shatter itself, like glass, into brittle fragments. But he did not mind the appendage. It was the penalty all tobacco chewers paid in that country, and he had been out before in two cold snaps.

They had not been so cold as this, he knew, but by the spirit thermometer at Sixty Mile he knew they had been registered at fifty below and at fifty-five.

He held on through the level stretch of woods for several miles, crossed a wide flat of nigger heads, and dropped down a bank to the frozen bed of a small stream. This was Henderson Creek, and he knew he was ten miles from the forks. He looked at his watch. It was ten o'clock. He was making four miles an hour, and he calculated that he would arrive at the forks at half-past twelve. He decided to celebrate that event by eating his lunch there.

The dog dropped in again at his heels, with a tail drooping discouragement, as the man swung along the creek bed. The furrow of the old sled trail was plainly visible, but a dozen inches of snow covered the marks of the last runners. In a month no man had come up or down that silent creek. The man held steadily on. He was not much given to thinking, and just then particularly he had nothing to think about save that he would eat lunch at the forks and that at six o'clock he would be in camp with the boys. There was nobody to talk to; and, had there been, speech would have been impossible because of the ice muzzle on his mouth. So he continued monotonously to chew tobacco and to increase the length of his amber beard.

Once in a while the thought reiterated itself that it was very cold and that he had never experienced such cold. As he walked along he rubbed his cheekbones and nose with the back of his mittened hand. He did this automatically, now and again changing hands. But, rub as he would, the instant he stopped his cheekbones went numb, and the following instant the end of his nose went numb. He was sure to frost his cheeks; he knew that, and experienced a pang of regret that he had not devised a nose strap of the sort Bud wore in cold snaps. Such a strap passed across the cheeks, as well, and saved them. But it didn't matter much, after all. What were frosted cheeks? A bit painful, that was all; they were never serious.

Empty as the man's mind was of thoughts, he was keenly observant, and he noticed the changes in the creek, the curves and bends and timber jams, and always he sharply noted where he placed his feet. Once, coming around a bend, he shied abruptly, like a startled horse, curved away from the place where he had been walking, and retreated several paces back along the trail. The creek he knew was frozen clear to the bottom—no creek could contain water in that arctic winter—but he knew also that there were springs that bubbled out from the hillsides and ran along under the snow and on top of the ice of the creek. He knew that the coldest snaps never froze these springs, and he knew likewise their danger. They were traps. They hid pools of water under the snow that might be three inches deep, or three feet. Sometimes a skin of ice half an inch thick covered them, and in turn was covered by the snow. Sometimes there were alternate layers of water and ice skin, so that when one broke through he kept on breaking through for a while, sometimes wetting himself to the waist.

That was why he had shied in such panic. He had felt the give under his feet and heard the crackle of a snow-hidden ice skin. And to get his feet wet in such a temperature meant trouble and danger. At the very least it meant delay, for he would be forced to stop and build a fire, and under its protection to bare his feet while he dried his socks and moccasins. He stood and studied the creek bed and its banks, and decided that the flow of water came from the right. He reflected awhile, rubbing his nose and cheeks, then skirted to the left, stepping gingerly and testing the footing for each step. Once clear of the danger, he took a fresh chew of tobacco and swung along at his four-mile gait.

In the course of the next two hours he came upon several similar traps. Usually the snow above the hidden pools had a sunken, candied appearance that advertised the danger. Once again, however, he had a close call; and once, suspecting danger, he compelled the dog to go on in front. The dog did not want to go. It hung back until the man shoved it forward, and then it went quickly across the white, unbroken surface. Suddenly it broke through, floundered to one side, and got away to firmer footing. It had wet its forefeet and legs, and almost immediately the water that clung to it turned to ice. It made quick efforts to lick the ice off its legs, then dropped down in the snow and began to bite out the ice that had formed between the toes. This was a matter of instinct. To permit the ice to remain would mean sore feet. It did not know this. It merely obeyed the mysterious prompting that arose from the deep crypts of its being. But the man knew, having achieved a judgment on the subject, and he removed the mitten from his right hand and helped tear out the ice particles. He did not expose his fingers more than a minute, and was astonished at the swift numbness that smote them. It certainly was cold. He pulled on the mitten hastily, and beat the hand savagely across his chest.

At twelve o'clock the day was at its brightest. Yet the sun was too far south on its winter journey to clear the horizon. The bulge of the earth intervened between it and Henderson Creek, where the man walked under a clear sky at noon and cast no shadow. At half-past twelve, to the minute, he arrived at the forks of the creek. He was pleased at the speed he had made. If he kept it up, he would certainly be with the boys by six. He unbuttoned his jacket and shirt and drew forth his lunch. The action consumed no more than a quarter of a minute, yet in that brief moment the numbness laid hold of the exposed fingers. He did not put the mitten on, but, instead, struck the fingers a dozen sharp smashes against his leg. Then he sat down on a snow-covered log to eat. The sting that followed upon the striking of his fingers against his leg ceased so quickly that he was startled. He had had no chance to take a bite of biscuit. He struck the fingers repeatedly and returned them to the mitten, baring the other hand for the purpose of eating. He tried to take a mouthful, but the ice muzzle prevented. He had forgotten to build a fire and thaw out. He chuckled at his foolishness, and as he chuckled he noted the numbness creeping into the exposed fingers. Also, he noted that the stinging which had first come to his toes when he sat down was already passing away. He wondered whether the toes were warm or numb. He moved them inside the moccasins and decided that they were numb.

He pulled the mitten on hurriedly and stood up. He was a bit frightened. He stamped up and down until the stinging returned into the feet. It certainly was cold, was his thought. That man from Sulphur Creek had spoken the truth when telling how cold it sometimes got in the country. And he had laughed at him at the time! That showed one must not be too sure of things. There was no mistake about it, it *was* cold. He strode up and down, stamping his feet and threshing his arms, until reassured by the returning warmth. Then he got out matches and proceeded to make a fire. From the undergrowth, where high water of the previous spring had lodged a supply of seasoned twigs, he got his firewood. Working carefully from a small beginning, he soon had a roaring fire over which he thawed the ice from his face and in the protection of which he ate his biscuits. For the moment the cold of space was outwitted. The dog took satisfaction in the fire, stretching out close enough for warmth and far enough away to escape being singed.

When the man had finished, he filled his pipe and took his comfortable time over a smoke. Then he pulled on his mittens, settled the ear flaps of his cap firmly about his ears, and took the creek trail up the left fork. The dog was disappointed and yearned back toward the fire. This man did not know cold. Possibly all the generations of his ancestry had been ignorant of cold, of real cold, of cold one hundred and seven degrees below freezing point. But the dog knew; all its ancestry knew, and it had inherited the knowledge. And it knew that it was not good to walk abroad in such fearful cold. It was the time to lie snug in a hole in the snow and wait for a curtain of cloud to be drawn across the face of outer space whence this cold came. On the other hand, there was no keen intimacy between the dog and the man. The one was the toil slave of the other, and the only caresses it had ever received were the caresses of the whip lash and of harsh and menacing throat sounds that threatened the whip lash. So the dog made no effort to communicate its apprehension to the man. It was not concerned in the welfare of the man; it was for its own sake that it yearned back toward the fire. But the man whistled, and spoke to it with the sound of whip lashes, and the dog swung in at the man's heels and followed after.

The man took a chew of tobacco and proceeded to start a new amber beard. Also, his moist breath quickly powdered with white his mustache, eye brows, and lashes. There did not seem to be so many springs on the left fork of the Henderson, and for half an hour the man saw no signs of any. And then it happened. At a place where there were no signs, where the soft, unbroken snow seemed to advertise solidity beneath, the man broke through. It was not deep. He wet himself halfway to the knees before he floundered out to the firm crust.

He was angry, and cursed his luck aloud. He had hoped to get into camp with the boys at six o'clock, and this would delay him an hour, for he would have to build a fire and dry out his footgear. This was imperative at that low temperature—he knew that much; and he turned aside to the bank, which he climbed. On top, tangled in the underbrush about the trunks of several small spruce trees, was a high-water deposit of dry firewood—sticks and twigs, principally, but also larger portions of seasoned branches and fine, dry, last year's grasses. He threw down several large pieces on top of the snow. This served for a foundation and prevented the young flame from drowning itself in the snow it otherwise would melt. The flame he got by touching a match to a small shred of birch bark that he took from his pocket. This burned even more readily than paper. Placing it on the foundation, he fed the young flame with wisps of dry grass and with the tiniest dry twigs.

He worked slowly and carefully, keenly aware of his danger. Gradually, as the flame grew stronger, he increased the size of the twigs with which he fed it. He squatted in the snow, pulling the twigs out from their entanglement in the brush and feeding directly to the flame. He knew there must be no failure. When it is seventy-five below zero, a man must not fail in his first attempt to build a fire—that is, if his feet are wet. If his feet are dry, and he fails, he can run along the trail for half a mile and restore his circulation. But the circulation of wet and freezing feet cannot be restored by running when it is seventy-five below. No matter how fast he runs, the wet feet will freeze harder.

All this the man knew. The old-timer on Sulphur Creek had told him about it the previous fall, and now he was appreciating the advice. Already all sensation had gone out of his feet. To build the fire he had been forced to remove his mittens, and the fingers had quickly gone numb. His pace of four miles an hour had kept his heart pumping blood to the surface of his body and to all the extremities. But the instant he stopped, the action of the pump eased down. The cold of space smote the unprotected tip of the planet, and he, being on that unprotected tip, received the full force of the blow. The blood of his body recoiled before it. The blood was alive, like the dog, and like the dog it wanted to hide away and cover itself up from the fearful cold. So long as he walked four miles an hour, he pumped that blood, willy-nilly, to the surface; but now it ebbed away and sank down into the recesses of his body. The extremities were the first to feel its absence. His wet feet froze the faster, and his exposed fingers numbed the faster, though they had not yet begun to freeze. Nose and cheeks were already freezing, while the skin of all his body chilled as it lost its blood.

But he was safe. Toes and nose and cheeks would be only touched by the frost, for the fire was beginning to burn with strength. He was feeding it with twigs the size of his finger. In another minute he would be able to feed it with branches the size of his wrist, and then he could remove his wet footgear, and, while it dried, he could keep his naked feet warm by the fire, rubbing them at first, of course, with snow. The fire was a success. He was safe. He remembered the advice of the old-timer on Sulphur Creek, and smiled. The old-timer had been very serious in laying down the law that no man must travel alone in the Klondike after fifty below. Well, here he was; he had had the accident; he was alone; and he had saved himself. Those old-timers were rather womanish, some of them, he thought. All a man had to do was to keep his head, and he was all right. Any man who was a man could travel alone. But it was surprising the rapidity with which his cheeks and nose were freezing. And he had not thought his fingers could go lifeless in so short a time. Lifeless they were, for he could scarcely make them move together to grip a twig, and they seemed remote from his body and from him. When he touched a twig, he had to look and see whether or not he had hold of it. The wires were pretty well down between him and his finger ends.

All of which counted for little. There was the fire, snapping and crackling and promising life with every dancing flame. He started to untie his moccasins. They were coated with ice; the thick German socks were like sheaths of iron halfway to his knees; and the moccasin strings were like rods of steel all twisted and knotted as by some conflagration. For a moment he tugged with his numb fingers, then, realizing the folly of it, he drew his sheath knife.

But before he could cut the strings, it happened. It was his own fault or, rather, his mistake. He should not have built the fire under the spruce tree. He should have built it in the open. But it had been easier to pull the twigs from the brush and drop them directly on the fire. Now the tree under which he had done this carried a weight of snow on its boughs. No wind had blown for weeks, and each bough was fully freighted. Each time he pulled a twig he had communicated a slight agitation to the tree—an imperceptible agitation, so far as he was concerned, but an agitation sufficient to bring about the disaster. High up in the tree one bough capsized its load of snow. This fell on the boughs beneath, capsizing them. This process continued, spreading out and involving the whole tree. It grew like an avalanche, and it descended without warning upon the man and the fire, and the fire was blotted out! Where it had burned was a mantle of fresh and disordered snow.

The man was shocked. It was as though he had just heard his own sentence of death. For a moment he sat and stared at the spot where the fire had been. Then he grew very calm. Perhaps the old-timer on Sulphur Creek was right. If he had only had a trail mate he would have been in no danger now. The trail mate could have built the fire. Well, it was up to him to build the fire over again, and this second time there must be no failure. Even if he succeeded, he would most likely lose some toes. His feet must be badly frozen by now, and there would be some time before the second fire was ready.

Such were his thoughts, but he did not sit and think them. He was busy all the time they were passing through his mind. He made a new foundation for a fire, this time in the open, where no treacherous tree could blot it out. Next he gathered dry grasses and tiny twigs from the high-water flotsam. He could not bring his fingers together to pull them out, but he was able to gather them by the handful. In this way he got many rotten twigs and bits of green moss that were undesirable, but it was the best he could do. He worked methodically, even collecting an armful of the larger branches to be used later when the fire gathered strength. And all the while the dog sat and watched him, a certain yearning wistfulness in its eyes, for it looked upon him as the fire provider, and the fire was slow in coming.

When all was ready, the man reached in his pocket for a second piece of birch bark. He knew the bark was there, and, though he could not feel it with his fingers, he could hear its crisp rustling as he fumbled for it. Try as he would, he could not clutch hold of it. And all the time, in his consciousness, was the knowledge that each instant his feet were freezing. This thought tended to put him in a panic, but he fought against it and kept calm. He pulled on his mittens with his teeth, and threshed his arms back and forth, beating his hands with all his might against his sides. He did this sitting down, and he stood up to do it; and all the while the dog sat in the snow, its wolf brush of a tail curled around warmly over its forefeet, its sharp wolf ears pricked forward intently as it watched the man. And the man, as he beat and threshed with his arms and hands, felt a great surge of envy as he regarded the creature that was warm and secure in its natural covering.

After a time he was aware of the first faraway signals of sensation in his beaten fingers. The faint tingling grew stronger till it evolved into a stinging ache that was excruciating, but which the man hailed with satisfaction. He stripped the mitten from his right hand and fetched forth the birch bark. The exposed fingers were quickly going numb again. Next he brought out his bunch of sulphur matches. But the tremendous cold had already driven the life out of his fingers. In his effort to separate one match from the others, the whole bunch fell into the snow. He tried to pick it out of the snow, but failed. The dead fingers could neither touch nor clutch. He was very careful. He drove the thought of his freezing feet, and nose, and cheeks, out of his mind, devoting his whole soul to the matches. He watched, using the sense of vision in place of that of touch, and when he saw his fingers on each side the bunch, he closed them—that is, he willed to close them, for the wires were down, and the fingers did not obey. He pulled the mitten on the right hand, and beat it fiercely against his knee. Then, with both mittened hands, he scooped the bunch of matches, along with much snow, into his lap. Yet he was no better off.

After some manipulation he managed to get the bunch between the heels of his mittened hands. In this fashion he carried it to his mouth. The ice crackled and snapped when by a violent effort he opened his mouth. He drew the lower jaw in, curled the upper lip out of the way, and scraped the bunch with his upper teeth in order to separate a match. He succeeded in getting one, which he dropped on his lap. He was no better off. He could not pick it up. Then he devised a way. He picked it up in his teeth and scratched it on his leg. Twenty times he scratched before he succeeded in lighting it. As it flamed he held it with his teeth to the birch bark. But the burning brimstone went up his nostrils and into his lungs, causing him to cough spasmodically. The match fell into the snow and went out.

The old-timer on Sulphur Creek was right, he thought in the moment of controlled despair that ensued; after fifty below, a man should travel with a partner. He beat his hands, but failed in exciting any sensation. Suddenly he bared both hands, removing the mittens with his teeth. He caught the whole bunch between the heels of his hands. His arm muscles not being frozen enabled him to press the hand heels tightly against the matches. Then he scratched the bunch along his leg. It flared into flame, seventy sulphur matches at once! There was no wind to blow them out. He kept his head to one side to escape the strangling fumes, and held the blazing bunch to the birch bark. As he so held it, he became aware of sensation in his hand. His flesh was burning. He could smell it. Deep down below the surface he could feel it. The sensation developed into pain that grew acute. And still he endured it, holding the flame of the matches clumsily to the bark that would not light readily because his own burning hands were in the way, absorbing most of the flame.

At last, when he could endure no more, he jerked his hands apart. The blazing matches fell sizzling into the snow, but the birch bark was alight. He began laying dry grasses and the tiniest twigs on the flame. He could not pick and choose, for he had to lift the fuel between the heels of his hands. Small pieces of rotten wood and green moss clung to the twigs, and he bit them off as well as he could with his teeth. He cherished the flame carefully and awkwardly. It meant life, and it must not perish. The withdrawal of blood from the surface of his body now made him begin to shiver, and he grew more awkward. A large piece of green moss fell squarely on the little fire. He tried to poke it out with his fingers, but his shivering frame made him poke too far, and he disrupted the nucleus of the little fire, the burning grasses and tiny twigs separating and scattering. He tried to poke them together again, but in spite of the tenseness of the effort, his shivering got away with him, and the twigs were hopelessly scattered. Each twig gushed a puff of smoke and went out. The fire provider had failed. As he looked apathetically about him, his eyes chanced on the dog, sitting across the ruins of the fire from him, in the snow, making restless, hunching movements, slightly lifting one forefoot and then the other, shifting its weight back and forth on them with wistful eagerness.

The sight of the dog put a wild idea into his head. He remembered the tale of the man, caught in a blizzard, who killed a steer and crawled inside the carcass, and so was saved. He would kill the dog and bury his hands in the warm body until the numbness went out of them. Then he could build another fire. He spoke to the dog, calling it to him; but in his voice was a strange note of fear that frightened the animal, who had never known the man to speak in such way before. Something was the matter, and its suspicious nature sensed danger—it knew not what danger, but somewhere, somehow, in its brain arose an apprehension of the man. It flattened its ears down at the sound of the man's voice, and its restless, hunching movements and the liftings and shiftings of its forefeet became more pronounced; but it would not come to the man. He got on his hands and knees and crawled toward the dog. This unusual posture again excited suspicion, and the animal sidled mincingly away.

The man sat up in the snow for a moment and struggled for calmness. Then he pulled on his mittens, by means of his teeth, and got upon his feet. He glanced down at first in order to assure himself that he was really standing up, for the absence of sensation in his feet left him unrelated to the earth. His erect position in itself started to drive the webs of suspicion from the dog's mind; and when he spoke peremptorily, with the sound of whip lashes in his voice, the dog rendered its customary allegiance and came to him. As it came within reaching distance, the man lost his control. His arms flashed out to the dog, and he experienced genuine surprise when he discovered that his hands could not clutch, that there was neither bend nor feeling in the fingers. He had forgotten for the moment that they were frozen and that they were freezing more and more. All this happened quickly, and before the animal could get away, he encircled its body with his arms. He sat down in the snow, and in this fashion held the dog, while it snarled and whined and struggled.

But it was all he could do, hold its body encircled in his arms and sit there. He realized that he could not kill the dog. There was no way to do it. With his helpless hands he could neither draw nor hold his sheath knife nor throttle the animal. He released it, and it plunged wildly away, with tail between its legs, and still snarling. It halted forty feet away and surveyed him curiously, with ears sharply pricked forward.

The man looked down at his hands in order to locate them, and found them hanging on the ends of his arms. It struck him as curious that one should have to use his eyes in order to find out where his hands were. He began threshing his arms back and forth, beating the mittened hands against his sides. He did this for five minutes, violently, and his heart pumped enough blood up to the surface to put a stop to his shivering. But no sensation was aroused in the hands. He had an impression that they hung like weights on the ends of his arms, but when he tried to run the impression down, he could not find it.

A certain fear of death, dull and oppressive, came to him. This fear quickly became poignant as he realized that it was no longer a mere matter of freezing his fingers and toes, or of losing his hands and feet, but that it was a matter of life and death with the chances against him. This threw him into a panic, and he turned and ran up the creek bed along the old, dim trail. The dog joined in behind and kept up with him. He ran blindly, without intention, in fear such as he had never known in his life. Slowly, as he plowed and floundered through the snow, he began to see things again—the banks of the creek, the old timber jams, the leafless aspens, and the sky. The running made him feel better. He did not shiver. Maybe, if he ran on, his feet would thaw out; and, anyway, if he ran far enough, he would reach camp and the boys. Without doubt he would lose some fingers and toes and some of his face; but the boys would take care of him, and save the rest of him when he got there. And at the same time there was another thought in his mind that said he would never get to the camp and the boys; that it was too many miles away, that the freezing had too great a start on him, and that he would soon be stiff and dead. This thought he kept in the background and refused to consider. Sometimes it pushed itself forward and demanded to be heard, but he thrust it back and strove to think of other things.

It struck him as curious that he could run at all on feet so frozen that he could not feel them when they struck the earth and took the weight of his body. He seemed to himself to skim along above the surface, and to have no connection with the earth. Somewhere he had once seen a winged Mercury, and he wondered if Mercury felt as he felt when skimming over the earth.

His theory of running until he reached camp and the boys had one flaw in it: he lacked the endurance. Several times he stumbled, and finally he tottered, crumpled up, and fell. When he tried to rise, he failed. He must sit and rest, he decided, and next time he would merely walk and keep on going. As he sat and regained his breath, he noted that he was feeling quite warm and comfortable. He was not shivering, and it even seemed that a warm glow had come to his chest and trunk. And yet, when he touched his nose or cheeks, there was no sensation. Running would not thaw them out. Nor would it thaw out his hands and feet. Then the thought came to him that the frozen portions of his body must be extending. He tried to keep this thought down, to forget it, to think of something else; he was aware of the panicky feeling that it caused, and he was afraid of the panic. But the thought asserted itself, and persisted, until it produced a vision of his body totally frozen. This was too much, and he made another wild run along the trail. Once he slowed down to a walk, but the thought of the freezing extending itself made him run again.

And all the time the dog ran with him, at his heels. When he fell down a second time, it curled its tail over its forefeet and sat in front of him, facing him, curiously eager and intent. The warmth and security of the animal angered him, and he cursed it till it flattened down its ears appeasingly. This time the shivering came more quickly upon the man. He was losing in his battle with the frost. It was creeping into his body from all sides. The thought of it drove him on, but he ran no more than a hundred feet, when he staggered and pitched headlong. It was his last panic. When he had recovered his breath and control, he sat up and entertained in his mind the conception of meeting death with dignity. However, the conception did not come to him in such terms. His idea of it was that he had been making a fool of himself, running around like a chicken with its head cut off—such was the simile that occurred to him. Well, he was bound to freeze anyway, and he might as well take it decently. With this new-found peace of mind came the first glimmerings of drowsiness. A good idea, he thought, to sleep off to death. It was like taking an anesthetic. Freezing was not so bad as people thought. There were lots worse ways to die.

He pictured the boys finding his body next day. Suddenly he found himself with them, coming along the trail and looking for himself. And, still with them, he came around a turn in the trail and found himself lying in the snow. He did not belong with himself any more, for even then he was out of himself, standing with the boys and looking at himself in the snow. It certainly was cold, was his thought. When he got back to the States he could tell the folks what real cold was. He drifted on from this to a vision of the old-timer on Sulphur Creek. He could see him quite clearly, warm and comfortable, and smoking a pipe

"You were right, old hoss; you were right," the man mumbled to the old-timer of Sulphur Creek.

Then the man drowsed off into what seemed to him the most comfortable and satisfying sleep he had ever known. The dog sat facing him and waiting. The brief day drew to a close in a long, slow twilight. There were no signs of a fire to be made, and, besides, never in the dog's experience had it known a man to sit like that in the snow and make no fire. As the twilight drew on, its eager yearning for the fire mastered it, and with a great lifting and shifting of forefeet, it whined softly, then flattened its ears down in anticipation of being chidden by the man. But the man remained silent. Later the dog whined loudly. And still later it crept close to the man and caught the scent of death. This made the animal bristle and back away. A little longer it delayed, howling under the stars that leaped and danced and shone brightly in the cold sky. Then it turned and trotted up the trail in the direction of the camp it knew, where were the other food providers and fire providers.

The Cremation of Sam McGee

ROBERT SERVICE

Robert Service (1874–1958), an English-born Canadian author, is best-known for his poems and ballads of frontier life in the Far North. Among his books are SONGS OF A SOURDOUGH *(1907),* BALLADS OF A CHEECHAKO *(1909),* THE SPELL OF THE YUKON AND OTHER VERSES *(1907), and* BAR-ROOM BALLADS *(1940). "The Cremation of Sam McGee" is a theatrical tall tale of the frontier. It first appeared in* SONGS OF A SOURDOUGH *(1907).*

There are strange things done in the midnight sun
*   By the men who moil for gold;*
The Arctic trails have their secret tales
*   That would make your blood run cold;*
the Northern Lights have seen queer sights,
*   But the queerest they ever did see*
Was the night on the marge of Lake Lebarge
*   I cremated Sam McGee.*

Now Sam McGee was from Tennessee,
        where the cotton blooms and blows.
    Why he left his home in the South to roam
        'round the Pole, God only knows.
He was always cold, but the land of gold
        seemed to hold him like a spell;
    Though he'd often say in his homely way
        that he'd "sooner live in Hell."

On a Christmas Day we were mushing our way
        over the Dawson trail.
    Talk of your cold! through the parka's fold
        it stabbed like a driven nail,

If our eyes we'd close, then the lashes froze
      till sometimes we couldn't see,
  It wasn't much fun, but the only one
      to whimper was Sam McGee.

And that very night, as we lay packed tight
      in our robes beneath the snow,
  And the dogs were fed, and the stars o'erhead
      were dancing heel and toe,
He turned to me, and "Cap," says he,
      "I'll cash in this trip, I guess;
  And if I do, I'm asking that you
      won't refuse my last request."

Well, he seemed so low that I couldn't say no;
      then he says with a sort of moan,
  "It's the cursed cold, and it's got right hold
      till I'm chilled clean through to the bone.
Yet 'taint being dead—it's my awful dread
      of the icy grave that pains;
  So I want you to swear that, foul or fair,
      you'll cremate my last remains."

A pal's last need is a thing to heed,
      so I swore I would not fail;
  And we started on at the streak of dawn;
      but God! he look ghastly pale.
He crouched on the sleigh, and he raved all day
      of his home in Tennessee;
  And before nightfall a corpse was all
      that was left of Sam McGee.

There wasn't a breath in that land of death,
      and I hurried, horror-driven,
  With a corpse half hid that I couldn't get rid,
      because of a promise given;
It was lashed to the sleigh, and it seemed to say:
      "You may tax your brawn and brains,

But you promised true, and it's up to you
    to cremate these last remains."

Now a promise made is a debt unpaid,
    and the trail has its own stern code.
    In the days to come, though my lips were dumb
    in my heart how I cursed that load!
In the long, long night, by the lone firelight,
    while the huskies, round in a ring,
    Howled out their woes to the homeless snows—
    Oh God, how I loathed the thing!

And every day that quiet clay
    seemed to heavy and heavier grow;
    And on I went, though the dogs were spent
    and the grub was getting low.
The trail was bad, and I felt half mad,
    but I swore I would not give in;
    And I'd often sing to the hateful thing,
    and it hearkened with a grin.

Till I came to the marge of Lake Lebarge,
    and a derelict there lay;
    It was jammed in the ice, but I saw in a trice
    it was called the *Alice May.*
And I looked at it, and I thought a bit,
    and I looked at my frozen chum;
    Then "Here," said I, with a sudden cry,
    "is my cre-ma-tor-eum!"

Some planks I tore from the cabin floor,
    and I lit the boiler fire;
    Some coal I found that was lying around,
    and I heaped the fuel higher;
The flames just soared, and the furnace roared—
    such a blaze you seldom see,
    And I burrowed a hole in the glowing coal,
    and I stuffed in Sam McGee.

Then I made a hike, for I didn't like
 to hear him sizzle so;
  And the heavens scowled, and the huskies howled,
   and the wind began to blow.
It was icy cold, but the hot sweat rolled
 down my cheeks, and I don't know why;
  And the greasy smoke in an inky cloak
   went streaking down the sky.

I do not know how long in the snow
 I wrestled with grisly fear;
  But the stars came out and they danced about
   ere again I ventured near;
I was sick with dread, but I bravely said,
 "I'll just take a peep inside.
  I guess he's cooked, and it's time I looked."
   Then the door I opened wide.

And there sat Sam, looking cool and calm,
 in the heart of the furnace roar;
  And he wore a smile you could see a mile,
   and he said, "Please close that door.
It's fine in here, but I greatly fear
 you'll let in the cold and storm—
  Since I left Plumtree, down in Tennessee,
   it's the first time I've been warm."

There are strange things done in the midnight sun
 By the men who moil for gold;
  The Arctic trails have their secret tales
   That would make your blood run cold;
The Northern Lights have seen queer sights,
 But the queerest they ever did see
Was the night on the marge of Lake Lebarge
 I cremated Sam McGee.

Nimrod

FROM *Home Country*

ERNIE PYLE

Ernie Pyle (1900–1945) was born in Dana, Indiana, and gained fame as a World War II war correspondent because of his popular realistic dispatches from the front lines. He was killed by Japanese gunfire on Ie, west of Okinawa, near the end of the war. His stories, HERE IS YOUR WAR *(1943) and* BRAVE MEN *(1944), were widely read at publication. In the 1930s, Pyle had visited Alaska, and he was delighted by the spectacular beauty of the landscape and the humor of the people. His pre-war columns, including the material about Alaska, were posthumously published in* HOME COUNTRY *(1947), from which "Nimrod" is taken.*

All the way from Seattle I'd been hearing about Nimrod. According to the story, Nimrod was an Alaskan woodsman who lost his teeth, killed a bear, took the bear's teeth and fashioned a crude false plate for himself, and then ate the bear with its own teeth. So, at Eagle, I went to sit at the feet of the great Nimrod and hear the epic yarn in his own words.

I found the story true in its larger elements, but its purveyors had neglected a number of small facts. They neglected, for instance, to state that Nimrod was not an uncouth creature of the wilds, but a cultured gentleman from Maine who still spoke with a Boston drawing-room accent about thirty-nine years in northern isolation. And they didn't mention the fact that Nimrod was an experienced artisan, who could do any sort of minute mechanical work with his hands. Making a set of false teeth was no great task for him.

Nimrod was living way up the creek out of Eagle, and he and his partner were working at a little gold and cutting some wood. The year was 1905. That winter the wolves got in and destroyed all the cache of meat, leaving them with nothing but vegetables and canned foods. Nimrod got scurvy. Within a few months there wasn't a tooth in his head, so he decided to make himself some teeth. He knew how.

For the four front ones he used mountain-sheep teeth. He said they were almost like human teeth, except longer, so he just filed them down. Back of these, four on each side, he used caribou teeth. And for the grinding molars, bear's teeth. Just one on each side—a bear's back tooth is so large it takes the place of two human teeth.

He made his plate of aluminum, drilled out holes for the teeth, set them in, and then worked the warm aluminum back over to hold them tight. It took him a month. He made both uppers and lowers. And he wore them for nearly twenty-five years. He told me he ate a lot of bear meat with them, but not the bear the teeth came from. Eventually a Seattle dentist offered to make him a set of real teeth in exchange for those homemade ones. Nimrod sent in his specifications, and back came the store teeth. He was still wearing them now, after seven years, and the "teeth of the wild" were on display in a Seattle dental shop.

Nimrod's real name was Ervin Robertson. He got the nickname when he was a boy in New England. He was a jeweler by trade for fifteen years in the East before he made the break for Alaska in the '98 days. For more than a third of a century he lived in a cabin "up the crick" from Eagle. He hunted and fished and cut wood and played at gold, but nothing much ever came of anything. Now he was living in a tiny old log cabin in Eagle, a streetless riverbank village of eighty-five people, not more than a dozen of them whites.

Nimrod was one of those perplexing human question marks you find now and then in far spots of isolation. Buried, by choice. But he had never let himself slip into shoddy ways, as most self-exiles do. His speech was professionally precise. He wore a neatly laundered gray shirt with long collar points, and blue trousers with belt and suspenders. He was freshly shaved, and meticulously clean. He apologized for his appearance, said he hadn't cleaned up today, and he kept standing while he talked.

His ancestral tree went back to Scotland, and he still had the family crest between tissues in a cardboard folder. He had scads of relatives in New England, and corresponded with them regularly. I asked why he went to Alaska in the first place, and he said he joined the gold stampede in the hope of making a thousand dollars. He needed that much to develop his ideas for an airplane. "If I had had a thousand dollars I'd have flown long before the other fellows," he said. "But I'm not much nearer to my accomplishment than I was forty years ago." He laughed as he said it, but the note of failure in his voice made it a poignant thing.

Nimrod made his living now by creating small things. He fashioned beautiful hunting knives, and fine gold-wire puzzle rings, and he repaired watches. He was a crack rifle shot, and an ardent hunter. He said he hadn't hunted much in the last year because he had been so busy in the shop. The truth was, he hadn't been able. Constantly he made those little excuses. They were perfectly plain to you as he made them, but you wouldn't let on for anything.

Nimrod had been Outside only once in forty years. He probably would never go again. But forty years of isolation had not corroded him. He was still just as polite, just as gay, just as neat, just as gentle as the day he arrived to make a thousand dollars.

The Flood

FROM *Shadows on the Koyukuk*

SIDNEY HUNTINGTON, AS TOLD TO JIM REARDEN

Alaskan Native Sidney Huntington was born in 1915 on the banks of the Koyukuk River in Alaska's Interior, the son of an Athabascan mother and a white hunter/trapper father. His adventurous life story is the subject of SHADOWS ON THE KOYUKUK: AN ALASKAN NATIVE'S LIFE ALONG THE RIVER *(1993), which was written in collaboration with Alaskan author Jim Rearden. In "The Flood," thirteen-year-old Sidney, confronts the hazards of spring breakup of river ice.*

Usual breakup time for the Koyukuk is mid-May, but in 1928 it was late May when at last the ice began to move slowly down the river. But it jammed and stopped moving almost immediately. Those huge, thick, rough blocks of ice, many weighing dozens of tons, were simply too big to float easily downstream. The extremely cold winter had frozen the ice to an unusual thickness and it piled up in a shifting, grinding mass.

Next day the ice moved again, but downstream from our cabin the blocks formed a dam, causing the frigid, rushing water to flow over the bank. "Getting dangerous, Jim," Charlie said, anxiously watching the rising water.

"Sure is," said Dad. "Let's get everything out of the cabin. Put what we can on the roof, the rest in the cache." We scurried, and in an hour the cabin was empty.

Our bearproof cache was a platform fourteen feet above ground in a large spruce tree that had a trunk about two and a half feet in diameter. We always kept some food, and usually a few furs, in this cache. When the flood threatened, we stored more food, winter clothing, caribou-skin sleeping bags, an extra stove, traps, tools, and guns there. We knew these valuables would be safe, for that tree had to have been growing there for a century or more.

Our cabin perched on a point of high, gravelly ground, well above any flood level within memory. With the huge ice jam, we figured water might reach the cabin door, maybe even flood the floor. In case the water rose high enough to force us to leave, we put emergency supplies in my new boat and chained the dogs nearby. We had cut a trail to the lakes behind our cabin. That trail could provide an escape route to a hill three-quarters of a mile away, beyond the lakes.

The ice dam shifted. For about three hours, a whole river of ice rushed past our log home. The sight was spectacular. Thick chunks as big as a house tumbled by, rolling, grinding against one another and against the river bottom. Geysers of water spurted high. Ice chunks, forced onto the bank, sheared trees like matchsticks. The sharp edges of ice and the force of the current plowed the bank away. Some giant pieces of ice ran as far as ten feet up on the bank. The noise was a continuous rolling thunder. Jimmy's eyes were as big as egg yolks and mine must have been too.

Again the ice jammed downriver. The rising water soon floated huge hunks of ice and spread them out along the riverbanks. Trees snapped like toothpicks and crashed into the jumble of ice and flooding water. As the water reached our cabin, we boosted the dogs ahead of us and climbed onto the roof.

Before our astonished eyes the water rose swiftly to the level of the roof. Hastily, we piled everything we could, including the whining dogs, a .22 rifle, some clothes, and a little food, into my new boat, the fishnet skiff, and into a canoe. We could scarcely believe that the river could rise so rapidly; it had come up the last four feet in less than two hours. As we paddled toward the hills, we knew that our cabin would soon float. We didn't worry about our cache, for that big tree had survived many a flood.

Upon reaching the hill, we unloaded the supplies we had hastily gathered and waited for a few hours. Then we tried to paddle back to the cabin, but the current, even in the lake, was too swift for us. Muskrats rode swirling ice chunks along the shoreline. They too had been washed out of their houses.

Returning to the hill, we spent two days and a night listening to the destruction. It sounded as if Hell had broken loose along the Koyukuk. Trees crashed to the ground as they were struck by the ice. Great chunks of ice collided and scraped against one another, creating a never-ending roar. Ice rubbing against ice produced high-pitched screeches and low growls.

Suddenly ice downstream broke free and the water dropped swiftly. The level fell so fast—six feet in a few hours—that we wondered whether there would be enough water to float my boat (the heaviest of the three) back through the portage. We loaded up and headed back, reaching the portage without difficulty. I went first, paddling the canoe, but a tangle of fallen trees and huge ice chunks blocked the way.

We went back to another short portage and a creek that flowed into the river half a mile above our cabin. That route was clear, so we followed the openings. Flood water was just emptying from the creek when we arrived at the river. Ice chunks, some as big as our cabin, were stranded high along the banks among the scrubby streamside willows. As we waited on the wet, sloppy shore, our boat nearly went aground. As the water dropped we had to keep moving it into deeper water.

Despite the sogginess we found some half-dry wood and coaxed a fire into burning, to heat some food and coffee and to drive the damp chill from our bones. The river was still choked with ice, so we had to wait for it to clear. Along the banks, ridges of debris indicated that the water had been eight feet or more above normal high-water mark. Tired, we dozed off, sprawled atop our gear in the boat because the ground was too wet to sit on or lie on. We walked down the bank of the Koyukuk, hoping to see our cabin downriver, but piles of ice blocked our view.

Early next morning we maneuvered out of the creek and into the Koyukuk, which was now clear of big ice chunks. Drifting downstream, we avoided the smaller pieces of ice that still floated about. Charlie figured the ice that pushed onto the banks was now sliding back into the river.

Where our cabin had been, we found only a huge pile of ice. And the cache tree had disappeared. Everything we owned, except what we had in the boats, was gone—furs, food, traps, guns, tools, winter clothing—everything. Gone. A clean wipeout: even the gasoline for the *Vixen* was gone.

We were in shock. To Jimmy and me it was almost as if the world had come to an end. We had accomplished so much in our winter on the trapline, and now everything we needed to survive as trappers was gone. Fortunately, we were carrying the money received from selling furs at Tanana.

We drifted downstream to where we had stored the *Vixen* and she too was gone. We found the frayed end of her bow line attached to a freshly splintered spruce stump. Gone too was the barge that we had pushed upriver.

The scene along that desolate stretch of river remains etched in my mind. Broken branches, splintered stumps, downed trees, mud, freshly gouged cutbanks, melting dirty ice chunks—all gave the impression that the world was now a broken-up, filthy, miserable swamp. We were all silent.

We drifted thirty miles downriver to our old cabin at Hog River, where Mom's grave was. No ice jams had formed along that part of the river and water hadn't even gone over the banks. Old Mike Laboski and Ben Keilly had lived in our cabin there while trapping along Hog River that winter, and were getting ready to pull out when we arrived.

"Well, we've at least got a cabin now," Dad said to us, with a sad smile. "That's a start."

Mike and Ben had extra food, which they agreed to leave. Charlie examined the supplies, looked the cabin over, and made up his mind.

"I'm going to stay and prospect here this summer. You and the boys go on out and get us reoutfitted," he suggested to Dad.

They talked briefly and decided that the three of us would take the small boats downriver to Nulato where we would try to acquire another powerboat for our return. Somehow, we had to catch enough salmon to feed the dogs for another winter. Charlie was unenthusiastic about fishing on the Koyukuk. Fishing on the Yukon was far easier and much more productive.

"Let's see what happens," Charlie said. "I'm sure everything will come together before fall. You have lotsa good friends. I'm not going to worry." We decided that in the fall we would fix up our old store and cabin at Hog River where we would live during the next few years while trapping. We left our lead dog with Charlie for companionship and took the others with us.

"I think it's awful to leave Charlie behind like this," I said to Dad.

"Charlie has the gold bug," Dad explained. "He's wanted to find gold ever since he hit the Dawson country thirty-five years ago. He wants to prospect Sun Mountain." Sun Mountain was a nearby ridge that Charlie had often talked about.

We left old Charlie on the riverbank as we drifted downstream. He wore a wide-brimmed hat, a canvas jacket, worn pants, and rubber-bottomed leather shoepacks. His gray hair showed below his hat, and his weathered face showed calm determination. I hated to leave him, and wondered if we would ever see him again. He waved once, then stood watching until we rounded the first bend. I thought he looked lonesome.

Drifting downstream we stopped at likely lakes and back sloughs to hunt muskrats with the .22 rifle. At Koyukuk Station we learned that Nulato and Koyukuk Station residents had also experienced a bad flood at breakup. We weren't surprised, for breakup floods aren't unusual along the Yukon River.

Trader John Evans told us that Joe Stickman had pulled a boat off the ice that might be the *Vixen*. Encouraged, we went on to Nulato to see Joe. He owned a large powerboat with a twelve-horsepower four-cylinder Universal engine—a big engine for those days. He had used it to pull the runaway boat ashore below Nulato. Sure enough, he had salvaged our *Vixen*. She had been found perched atop a drifting block of ice. One side was caved in, the propeller and rudder were sheared off, and the pilot house was gone, but the engine seemed undamaged.

"How much do I owe you, Joe?" Dad asked.

"Is $10 too much?" Joe asked. Joe had paid two men $5 each to help him, and he had used some gasoline in towing the *Vixen* ashore.

Ed Allard was about to take the mail boat up the Koyukuk on its first trip of the year, so Dad sent along some grub and a note for Charlie. We pitched a tent on the beach beside the *Vixen* two miles below Nulato and set up a saw pit so we could whipsaw the lumber we needed. John Tilley and Bill Dalquist loaned us tools and we worked long hours to rebuild the ice-battered boat.

Joe Strickman liked the twenty-foot boat I had built so well he asked Dad if he could buy it. "It's Sidney's boat. You'll have to talk to him about it," he told Joe.

I was playing baseball with the Nulato team one day when Joe came to see me. "I'd like to buy your boat, Sidney," he said.

"How much will you give for it?" I asked.

"Old Ambrose makes big gas boats for $150. Your boat's a lot smaller. How about $100?" he offered. One hundred dollars was a fortune to me.

"My wife wants that little boat pretty bad. She wants to use it for fishing."

I thought about it. His wife, Lucy, was always good to us. Just that day she had treated us to a big feed of fried king salmon. And Joe had helped us by saving the *Vixen*. Nevertheless, I hated to sell my boat.

My turn came to bat. After my base hit, a line drive into left field brought me around second and third bases. Joe caught up with me again after I crossed home plate.

"How about it?" he asked.

"All right," I said. "I don't really want to sell it, but you helped us. Now it's my turn to help you."

I was learning that life wasn't all dollars and cents—that business can be tinged with feelings for the other guy. After all, I could build another boat.

In about five days we launched the *Vixen*. Her engine ran fine, and she didn't leak. She had no cabin, but that could wait.

A trader at Nulato, Pop Russell, knew we had been wiped out and that we were low on cash. He had heard we were going to fish for salmon, so he offered to buy dried dog (chum) salmon from us for six cents a pound. He had a mail contract, and he needed enough dried fish to feed his mail team.

Russell's offer was an opportunity for us to earn money, but we would have to work hard. We knew nothing about making a fish wheel, which is how we planned to catch our fish. Johnny Sommers and Charlie Evans offered to help us. Local fishermen agreed that Devil's Island would be a good site for a fish camp, and no one claimed the island, about four miles below Nulato, as a fishing location.

In two days we collected raft logs for the fish wheel, as well as some green poles. With plenty of help and advice from experts, we built the fish wheel the next day.

The fish wheel is a simple device Two wire baskets and two paddles, like four spokes on a wheel, radiate from a large wooden axle. River current turns the device, and as it rotates, the baskets scoop fish from the river and deposit them in a collecting box. The fish wheel is effective because salmon follow the riverbank as they swim upstream toward spawning grounds. When placed directly over a place where salmon pass, each revolution of a basket has a chance of picking up fish.

We used the *Vixen* and our canoe to move the fish wheel to Devil's Island, where we cut brush to clear space for a camp and a smokehouse. The story of our being wiped out at Batza Creek had spread up and down the river. Travelers on the Yukon stopped to see us and have coffee; many pitched in to help for a while. In a few days we were ready to fish.

We set the fish wheel to turning and almost immediately started catching chum salmon. Charlie Evans taught us how to cut the fish for dog food and Jimmy and I quickly learned the technique. We cut and split the fish and kept Dad more than busy hanging them on the drying racks we had built. With practice we were able to process 800 six- to eight-pound salmon a day. One dried male chum salmon from the Yukon weighs from a pound to a pound and a half; females weigh from six to eight ounces. A salmon's weight varies with the distance the fish is from salt water. By the Fourth of July, we had 5,000 salmon dried or hanging on the drying racks. We smoked some of the choicer fish to eat ourselves.

Jimmy and I wanted to participated in the festivities of the Fourth of July at Nulato. That morning we began working very early and cut and split 500 salmon. Then we paddled our canoe upstream to Nulato, where we competed in races, baseball, jumping contests, and other games.

A dance that night capped the celebration. "It's time you started dancing, Sidney," said Lily Stickman, Joe's younger sister, as she grabbed me by the collar and dragged me onto the dance floor. And dance I did! After that they couldn't keep me off the dance floor.

Jimmy and I paddled back to camp late that night. It was light, so we immediately set about cutting and splitting the afternoon catch of 350 salmon. The days of July fled, and soon we had prepared 10,000 chum salmon. We needed at least 2,500 to feed our own dogs during the coming winter. The remainder were promised to Pop Russell.

A friend gave me two fine young sled dogs. Toby Patsy gave Jimmy another. (Patsy wrote "Eagle Island Blues," a song popular along the Yukon, and eventually a popular recording all over the United States.) With the addition of these three our team numbered eight, which Dad thought was too many, so Jimmy and I split and dried another 500 salmon to make sure we would have enough food.

We bundled up Pop Russell's 6,000 pounds of dried fish and hauled them to his warehouse. Our income from the fish was about $360. We were still short of the $3,000 needed to pay for a year's outfit (roughly the equivalent of $25,000 today). We had about $2,000 combined from sale of furs at Tanana the previous winter and from the salmon sold to Pop Russell. Dad didn't want to ask for credit, and decided we should try to manage on what we could pay for. We could go to Hughes for supplies by dogsled if need be.

When Dad gave Pop his list, Pop snorted, "Hell, I thought you said you lost everything last spring. This won't take you through half the winter."

"I don't want to put anything on the books, Pop," Dad said.

"Don't worry about it. I'll give you what you need. Pay what you can. I'll catch up with you next spring. Keep some money so you can buy winter gear if you need to," he advised. We left Nulato owing him $1,400, a huge debt in 1928. Pop Russell was a prince.

Another bit of sweetening came when my uncle Hog River Johnny found our barge in a back slough at Cutoff. He arranged for Ed Allard to tow it to us with the mail boat on his downstream run. My uncle had heard we were fishing to make a stake; he knew we would need the barge on our return to Hog River.

We left Nulato on the first day of August, our barge loaded with a good winter outfit, plenty of good dogs, good grub—everything. As usual, everyone in Nulato was on the beach to see us off. We traveled day and night, moving northeast up the beautiful Koyukuk. Dad, Jimmy, and I took turns steering. Memories of the sodden, ice-smashed desolation we had left the previous spring grew dim. The riverbanks now appeared normal, with high green grass, leafed-out trees, clear tributaries, and clean-washed sand and gravel beaches.

We arrived at Hog River in four and a half days. Charlie recognized the Model T engine's steady roar long before we came into sight. Wearing a mile-wide smile on his weathered face, he stood on the bank waiting in the exact spot we had left him the previous spring. He was thin, and his long uncut gray hair almost flowed over his collar, but he cheerfully said, "I never doubted that you'd come back with a good outfit."

I often think back to that challenging year filled with learning experiences for two boys, and realize how from those events I learned that hard work and determination pay off. Eventually, I began to view that period as a wonderful time.

Brother Wolverine

MARY TALLMOUNTAIN

Mary TallMountain, a Koyukon Athabascan from Nulato, Alaska, was adopted as a child by white parents. As a teen, she felt displaced and sought to rediscover her Native American heritage. Her work has appeared in THERE IS NO WORD FOR GOODBYE *and* MATRILINEAL CYCLE *(1990). "Brother Wolverine" first appeared in* MATRILINEAL CYCLE *and was collected in* RAVEN TELLS STORIES: AN ANTHOLOGY OF ALASKAN NATIVE WRITING, *edited by Joseph Bruchac (1991).*

girl child
they took you so far away
upriver I hear
the mailboat whistle
my heart jumps
waiting for words from you

snaa',
I miss you
when the children shout
down by the slough and
when I see leaves of *k'eey*
dance in the white wind

in pictures you sent
you wear the fawnskin parka
I sewed with little sinew stitches
by the light of our coal-oil lamp
around your face I see
the gray ruff of Wolverine

he has *yega* of power
his ruff can stop
the winter winds
from freezing your breath
into needles of ice—
I give you his fur

Wolverine, we call *Doyon*
the Chief,
snarled in my trap—
bared his teeth, bit the air
it was his last battle
he came home with me

Brother Wolverine
let your fur warm my girl child
guard her in far strange places
make her fearless like you
do not let her forget us
Brother Wolverine

---

snaa' = little child
k'eey = birch tree
yega = spirit

The Village Is Taken

FROM *The Wind Is Not a River*

ARNOLD A. GRIESE

*Arnold A. Griese grew up on an Iowa farm, earned a degree in foreign service
at Georgetown University, and eventually taught school in the Athabascan
village of Tanana. His children's books include* THE WAY OF THE PEOPLE,
AT THE MOUTH OF THE LUCKIEST RIVER, ANNA'S ATHABASCAN SUMMER, *and*
THE WIND IS NOT A RIVER. *In this excerpt from* THE WIND IS NOT A RIVER
*(1978), two Aleut children barely escape capture when their village on the
Aleutian island of Attu is invaded by the Japanese army in June 1942.*

For a moment Sasan did not move. Everything was again just as it
had been a short time ago. Just as it had been when they first
crawled into the ditch to rest. Everything was quiet except for the
sound of the south wind blowing through the grass. The low
clouds still covered the mountain peaks, just as before. But in that
short time, Sasan's world had been turned upside down. News of the bombing, just a few days ago, had made her feel sad for the men who had died.
But the war and the bombing had seemed so far away; not a part of her
world. Her island was far out in the ocean. The thick fogs, heavy rains, and
strong winds kept all ships away except for the one or two that brought supplies each year. Yet now, on this Sunday morning, enemy soldiers had
landed. In another hour they would capture the village. Then the island
would no longer belong to her people.

Sasan did not think long about these things. In a moment she stood up
and spoke. "Our island is in danger. We must do something."

"What can we do?" asked Sidak. "Even if we could warn the men in the
village, they have no guns. They could not fight against so many."

Sasan answered, "We cannot warn them. It is too late and there is only
one trail. We will have to follow them and see what happens. Then we can
decided what to do next."

Just as they were ready to start, the loud call of a raven came from somewhere ahead. At the same moment a sudden cold gust of wind swept off the snow-covered mountain peaks, whipped against Sasan's dress, and sent a shiver through her body.

"We can start now," she said, and they began walking.

No bushes grew along the trail, and the new grass was not yet tall enough to help hide them. Sasan stopped from time to time to make sure they did not follow too closely after the marching soldiers.

When they reached the hill overlooking the village and the harbor, they stopped and crawled behind a large rock to watch. Sasan had come to this same place many times before to be by herself. From here she could see the houses standing along the shore of the harbor, sheltered from the strong winds by East Peak on one side and West Peak on the other.

Now as she watched, everything was still quiet and peaceful. But it would not be so for long. Already the soldiers had formed a line in back of the village. The line ran from the church at one end, nearest East Peak, to the school at the other end. It was already too late for anyone to escape into the mountains. Another line of soldiers was moving along the beach in front of the village. When the two lines met, there would be a circle of soldiers all around it. Everyone would be trapped inside this circle.

Sasan and Sidak watched and listened for a sign that someone in the village had at last seen the danger, but nothing happened. The soldiers seemed to move without making a sound. "Why doesn't someone see them?" she asked herself. Sasan's heart pounded as she watched and waited. "Are all the people still in church?" she wondered.

They did not have much longer to wait and wonder. A shot rang out in the morning air, then another. Sasan felt her brother's hand against her arm, but her eyes did not leave the village. People started pouring out of the houses and out of the grass-covered barabaras next to the church. Some of the older people still used these as homes. They all ran together into groups and stood staring at the soldiers. The soldiers walked with their rifles pointed straight ahead, making the circle smaller and smaller.

Sasan had almost forgotten that Sidak was with her. When he whispered, "Do you suppose any of the men got away?" it surprised her and she jumped.

Before she could answer, another shot rang out. It seemed to come from the school, which sat off by itself, next to the stream that emptied into the harbor. Two soldiers ran inside the school, their rifles ready. One more shot came from inside, then all was quiet again.

Sasan's eyes turned back to the people in the village. By this time the soldiers had pushed them together into one tight circle. The women, some holding babies, stood in the middle along with the younger children. Around the outside the men stood facing the soldiers. The soldiers held their rifles pointed at the men. The end of each rifle held a knife blade and these were almost touching the circle of men.

Sasan could hear nothing, and for a moment nothing seemed to be happening. No one moved. Then suddenly, a soldier raised his rifle in the air and brought it down against one of the men. The man fell backward into the crowd and two other village men grabbed at the soldier and his rifle. Sasan heard a shot, then saw other soldiers rush in and push the two village men back inside the circle.

Sidak's fingers tightened on Sasan's arm again as he said, "I have seen enough. I will go down and stand together with the men of the village."

Sasan felt her own anger grow as she watched the enemy soldiers. But she answered, "You must not go. As you see, the men can do nothing against so many. And what can they fight with? There is only one gun and that is in the school."

When he did not answer, Sasan looked and saw the anger on his face. The hand still holding her arm trembled as he said, "Would you want me to just sit here and watch them kill our people?"

She answered, "Remember, we may be the only ones who are still free. We must plan well what we do."

Sidak said no more and their eyes turned back to the village. Chief Joseph now stood facing one of the soldiers. This one was dressed differently and had a sword hanging from his side. The two of them talked. After a short time, Chief Joseph turned toward his people. Then the soldiers moved back and the people walked slowly to their homes.

After all the families were back inside, the soldiers began to gather around the one who was dressed differently. He seemed to be their leader. Just then, out of the corner of her eye, Sasan saw one of the village men run from his house and dash towards the barabaras over by the church. He was almost there before one of the soldiers saw him. He quickly aimed his rifle and there was the sound of a single shot as the man disappeared into the heavy grass between the houses. Sasan could not see if he had been hit. Soldiers swarmed over to the spot. Others moved in close to the other houses to make sure no one else tried to escape. A moment later the man came out with his hands over his head. Two soldiers pushed him forward with the blades of their rifles. They marched him toward the school where their leader was waiting.

After the man and the soldiers disappeared into the school, Sasan said, "You see, it does no good against so many."

Sidak's next words put a new fear in to Sasan's heart. "We will see. Tonight in the darkness I will use my knife against the enemy."

Sasan answered quietly, "You are too young. And even if you did kill one of them, what good would that do?"

"I will not just sit here and wait," he answered back. "I will do something."

A firmness that her brother had never before heard came into Sasan's voice. "You are angry," she said. "But you will obey me as you promised Grandmother you would. You must do nothing without telling me first." Then she said more gently, "Together we will think of a way to free our people."

Sidak spoke no more, but his face was still filled with anger.

Hours passed as the two lay by the rock on the hilltop, watching and saying nothing. The sky stayed cloudy and by midafternoon the wind had shifted to the north, bringing with it a lower layer of clouds and heavy rain showers from off the sea. The north wind also brought the sound of heavy waves crashing against the rocks at the harbor's mouth. From time to time Sasan would look over and see the waves throw themselves against the rocks, sending water and spray in all directions. But most of the time her eyes were on the village.

The people were all still in their homes. A machine gun now stood at each end of the village; one next to the church, the other near the school. And there were soldiers everywhere. Two sat by each gun and watched. Some were marching at both the front and the back of the village to make sure no one came outside. Others were busy chopping away the dead beach grass in back of the houses so that anyone trying to run away into the mountains could be seen by the guards. Still others were rolling wire out from the school and putting up a searchlight next to one of the machine guns.

Sasan saw all this: the many soldiers, the machine guns, the searchlight, and her people waiting helplessly inside their houses. She saw all this and said, "It will be hard to free our people even after it is dark."

Sidak answered angrily, "Grandmother was wrong!"

"Why do you say that?" she asked.

Without looking at her he said, "Grandmother made us learn the Old Ways, but what good are they to us now? Will knowing how to use the bidarki help us fight the enemy? Will these ways help us free our people?"

Sasan answered quietly, "Do not mock. These ways can help us even now."

Sidak gave a short laugh. "They can help us? How?"

"Our ways have taught us how to find food and to live off the land. We will use what we have learned. We will stay hidden from the enemy soldiers as our people hid from their enemies long ago."

Before Sasan could go on Sidak asked, "And what good will it do for us to be free on our island? To be free while our people are held against their will in their own houses?"

Sasan looked over at her brother. His eyes were still on the village. She went on, "How many times has Grandmother told us the story of our men who lived long ago? What they did when the Russians forced them to hunt? They did not try to kill. They had only spears and the Russians had guns. No, they waited until the Russians were not watching, then they took their families and ran off into the hills. The people on the islands to the east did not learn to wait and many of them were killed."

When Sasan had finished, Sidak took his eyes off the village. He looked at her and said, "Tonight after dark, I will go down into the village and free the men. Then they can take their families and go into the mountains where the soldiers cannot find them."

Sasan thought for a time about what her brother had said, then answered, "It is one of the things we might do to help. But we cannot do it tonight."

"Why not tonight?" he asked.

"You have seen the soldiers, the machines guns, and the light. It will not be easy to get into the village and free our people. We must have a plan."

There was now anger in her brother's voice as he said, "I have a plan. I will go first to the barabaras. There the soldiers cannot see me as well. I will go to Chief Joseph. His two oldest sons can help me free the other men."

Sasan listened but would not agree. "Surely the soldiers will put locks on the doors. How will you open them? And what of the machine gun and the light, which are right next to the houses?" She stopped but not long enough for her brother to answer. "No, we will wait and think more about these things. If we do go, we must not fail."

Sidak's eyes were once more on the village. "I will not wait too long," he said.

These last words angered Sasan. She stood up behind the rock and said, "We have other things to do now. It is late. The rain clouds are already moving in from the sea, and we have no food and no shelter for the night."

Sidak stood up too but did not look at her. She went on, "We will go back to the camp first and make ready to live off the land."

Little more was said as they walked back over the trail to Sarana Bay. It was late and a light rain was falling when they finally heard the sounds of the sea. As they came to the last bend in the trail, Sasan, who was walking in front, stopped, turned around, and whispered, "It is best we leave the trail here and make sure there are no soldiers in the camp."

Crawling through the grass they soon came to a low mound. Here they could look and listen without being seen. Sasan peered out over the top and saw low clouds and fog rolling in over the waters of the bay. Wind rattled the dry grass on top of the mound and a sudden gust splattered rain against her face. All at once she felt terribly tired and hungry. Her wet clothes chilled her body, and she hoped with all her might the enemy soldiers had not found the summer camp.

Their boat was still there, high up on the beach where she and Sidak had left it the night before. There were no other boats to be seen. Everything seemed to be just as they had left it this morning. Still she was not sure. Motioning her brother to stay, she started walking to their house, carefully looking around as she went. When she opened the door and stepped inside, there was just enough light to tell her nothing had been moved. Next she went outside and walked along the sandy beach. There were no tracks since the last tide.

When she was sure of everything, she called to Sidak. As he walked towards her, she saw that he, too, was wet, tired, and hungry. Her earlier anger was forgotten. She smiled and said, "We will have a warm, dry place tonight."

Sidak, too, had forgotten his anger. He smiled back but said nothing.

"I know you are hungry," Sasan said, "but we must save the food we brought with us last night. Come, it is still light enough to look for sea urchins along the beach."

They found many of these round shellfish on the rocky beach above the creek. As they found some, they ate. The spiny shells cracked easily on the rocks, and they swallowed the yellow insides right from the shell. Sasan did not mind the taste. Grandmother had made her eat them since she was a baby.

Devil's Canyon

FROM *Wager with the Wind*

JAMES GREINER

James Greiner (1933–1992) moved his family to Alaska in 1965 and settled in Fairbanks. For many years he was the curator of the University of Alaska Fairbanks Museum, as well as a bush pilot, wilderness guide, and naturalist. He wrote two books: THE RED SNOW *(1980), a fictionalized natural history of an Alaska wolf pack, and* WAGER WITH THE WIND: THE DON SHELDON STORY *(1982). This excerpt is from* WAGER WITH THE WIND, *a stirring account of one of Alaska's best-known bush pilots.*

The Susitna River was first explored in 1834 by a Russian named Málakov, who recorded it in his field journal as the Sushitna, a word meaning "sandy river" in the gutteral dialect of the Tanaina Indians of the southern interior. When he saw it, the river, like a tattered ribbon of gray satin, sought the sea 260 miles from its source at the foot of a vast crevasse-scarred glacier in the then unnamed Alaska Range. Its fresh though silty waters mingled with the North Pacific in a broad maze of stinking tidal flats, 24 coastal miles from a place that would someday be called Anchorage.

With the exception of spring, when the flow becomes bloated with snow runoff, black drift logs, and rotted ice, the river is placid enough, and its journey to Cook Inlet is half over as it passes the village of Talkeetna. Here, it is already braided with countless side channels and split by willow- and driftwood-covered islands of scoured gravel. The river's deceptively slow current is accentuated by roiling boils, the occasional rhythmic slapping of some bank-bound sapling, and the monotonous splash of collapsing silt bars. The riverbed, like the desert, changes with each passing minute of every year.

In most places below its confluence with the shallow and swift Chulitna, five miles above the approach to Sheldon's backyard airstrip, the river, known to Alaskans as the "Big Sue," is at least one-half mile in width. There is, however, a place 65 miles above Talkeetna where this generous breadth shrinks to a measly 50 to 70 yards between vertical rock palisades. Here, during late spring, the Susitna's 6,750,000-gallon-per-minute flow attempts to surmount itself in a roaring dervish of hissing gray spume. The U.S. Army Corps of Engineers is planning to construct a power plant in this five-mile stretch of turbulent waters called Devil's Canyon.

A rank profusion of pink fireweed and blue lupine nodded on the high cutbanks of the river near town, and countless tons of salmon were moving upriver. Sheldon had been almost content with the transport of itinerant fishermen, miners, and homesteaders during the weeks that had followed his rescue of the nude woman from the Talkeetna River.

The arrival of the northbound train, an event of regular though transient interest, took on new dimensions one July afternoon in 1955. Sheldon noticed that a crowd had gathered on the planking near the station almost before the engine jarred to a stop and braked against the slight grade. Resting on a special flatcar like some huge landbound ark was a bright yellow boat, with its bow decked over and two formidable-looking engines in its capacious stern section. The detachment of U.S. Army scouts that presided spelled property of Uncle Sam.

As the 50-foot boat was being off-loaded, Sheldon joined the group of curious spectators and found that little if any information was being offered by the Army as to why the boat was there or what it would be used for. Speculation was the order of the day, and Sheldon had already heard several rumors when he spotted a casual acquaintance—a lieutenant with the Search and Rescue Section at Fort Richardson in Anchorage. The lieutenant was busy checking a sheaf of dog-eared papers.

"Hi! How've ya been?" grinned the pilot.

"Good, Don. How's yourself?"

"Great. Hey, what's the deal here? You guys goin' fishin'?"

The officer glanced once more at his paperwork and allowed that the boat was to be used in an attempt to chart navigable watersheds in the Susitna Drainage.

Sheldon was incredulous. "Hey, you don't mean you're going to attempt to run this thing up the Susitna and through the canyon?"

The lieutenant, who had never seen Devil's Canyon, missed the surprise in Sheldon's voice. His reply was curt and precise.

"That's exactly what we plan to do, and the sooner we can get under way, the better."

There wasn't time for Sheldon to appraise the real chances of such a mission on such short notice, and even if there had been, he was sure that the officer was not particularly interested in his homespun opinions. He did, however, have a very vivid picture of Devil's Canyon and had serious doubts about the possibility of the mission's success.

"Lookee, I've got a heck of a lot of fishing traffic up that way in the next few days. I'll check on your progress from time to time."

With the boat successfully launched, the small detachment of eight scouts that comprised the crew cast off. The powerful engines churned the current-roiled river, and the boat disappeared from view around the first upstream bend. Sheldon had flown over the five-mile stretch of boiling water in Devil's Canyon many times. It was a very familiar landmark to the pilot. From the air, the canyon's sheer rock walls, rising to 500 and 600 feet, produced an awesome corridor, the bottom of which is always in shadow. Above the canyon, the air was characteristically turbulent.

"The current there is so swift and heavy that even the salmon get beat to death trying to swim upriver."

The day after the scouts started up the Susitna, Sheldon flew over the river to make a casual check on the progress of the boat, but he did not see it. On the second day, he was curious, a trait that to date has accounted for not only his promptness in times of trouble but his own personal safety as well. This time, with two elderly fishermen aboard his Aeronca Sedan en route to Otter Lake north of Talkeetna, he deliberately flew up the Susitna. As he reached the flume below the fast water, he banked sharply to the left and rolled the portly Aeronca Sedan up on its ample side. Something at the periphery of his vision caught his attention, and he made a second swing to get a better look. What he saw made his skin crawl.

"I was shocked to see pieces of yellow wreckage floating down the river. I had a feeling this was a fresh wreck, and they'd really gotten clobbered. I saw barrels of gasoline bobbing around here and there. The wreckage was strewn downriver to a point almost 25 miles below the canyon, and it consisted mostly of bright yellow chunks of the boat's hull and other debris—but no people."

Sheldon continued the ten miles to Otter Lake, off-loaded his passengers, and quickly retraced his path to the tail of the Devil's Canyon rapids. He dropped down to a point just above the jagged rim of the canyon. After making several passes in the seething air, he spotted a group of men huddled on a narrow ledge of wet rock in the shadows at the base of the north wall. Even from his vantage point, he could tell that they were in bad shape and in desperate need of assistance.

"They were in a terrible condition—cut up and barely managing to cling to the shelf of rock. Their clothing was literally torn off, and a few of them still had life jackets on. These were also in shreds. They had apparently floated down about 60 percent of the canyon, a distance of roughly 3 miles."

Because he knew the place so well, Sheldon could rapidly appraise his chances of retrieving these men, and they looked poor. The canyon walls at their top were but a scant 200 yards apart, and the river was a succession of hissing combers broaching over house-size boulders in the river bottom. His chances were not only poor but probably nonexistent, for the Aeronca weighed only a scant 1,400 pounds empty and would be tossed like a tiny cork even if he somehow managed to land it on the surface of the river below, a feat that at the moment looked impossible. To drop onto the surface of the rapids here would be suicide because the floats needed a flat surface upon which to dissipate the forward momentum of the airplane. Sheldon needed little or no imagination whatsoever to visualize the results of running headlong at 65 miles per hour into any one of the tumbling white crests of water that surely towered up to 6 feet above the surface of the river.

"There was no place to land below them; it was just more of the same terrible rough water. I did a 180-degree turn, and about a quarter mile above the guys, I spotted a slick, high-velocity stretch of river that looked like it might be big enough. I made a couple of passes to try it on for size and then set myself up for an up-canyon approach to the place. It looked mighty small."

As Sheldon dropped the Aeronca below the tops of the canyon's walls, he found himself flying in a narrow alleyway of wet spruce and vertical rock. The plane rocked with the turbulence produced by the unstable air of the canyon, and he carefully adjusted his glide path. The floats were causing the airplane to respond to the controls in a delayed manner, due to a lowered center of gravity. This reaction is normal and in a routine landing produces no problems. But in this case, control of the airplane was everything, and Sheldon hitched forward as far as his seat belt would allow to gain every inch of forward visibility.

Even before the floats touched down, spray and mist from the river surface were streaking the Plexiglas windshield of the Aeronca. Sheldon fought the compulsion to firewall the throttle plunger and climb away from the terrifying spectacle of the gray water. Then he was down.

Sheldon was landing against a 30-mile-per-hour current, and the airplane decelerated at an alarming rate. When an airplane is moving through the air at an airspeed of 90 to 100 miles per hour, the control surfaces—ailerons, rudder, and elevator—work at optimum efficiency because the forward motion of the plane through the air and the slipstream blast of the rotating propeller produce the rush of air over the wings and tail surfaces. An airplane out of its design element and on the ground or water is much more difficult to control, primarily due to the fact that only the rush of air produced by the propeller provides forward velocity. In addition, an airplane on floats is infinitely less maneuverable than one on wheels or even skis, and as a result, the Aeronca became an unresponsive death trap as it almost immediately began to accelerate downriver with the current.

"The nose wanted to swing in about every imaginable direction, but somehow I managed to keep it pointed upriver with the throttle. I was floating backward at about 25 miles an hour, the windows were fogged, and I couldn't see where I was going."

Sheldon was certain of one thing—that behind him was the beginning of the heavy stretch of boiling rapids he had seen from the air only seconds before. At that moment, he was like a blindfolded man rolling backward toward a cliff in a brakeless car he could not steer. Sheldon will never forget those moments that elapsed so rapidly they precluded panic.

"As the plane backed into the first of the combers, I felt it lurch heavily fore and aft. It was like a damned roller coaster. The water was rolling up higher than my wing tips, beating at the struts, and I could barely see because of the spray and water on the windows. All of a sudden the engine began to sputter and choke, and I knew it was getting wet down pretty good. If it had quit, I'd have been a goner, but it didn't."

Suddenly, through the Aeronca's side windows, he saw the Army scouts on the small rock ledge. They stared, openmouthed, as the airplane backed past them. And now the most critical and delicate aspect of the entire rescue began.

"After spotting the men, I had to stop the airplane's backward motion, which I did with full throttle, but I knew my problems had only begun.

Without damaging a wing on the rocks, I had to get the airplane close enough to the ledge for the guys to jump out onto the float and get aboard. If they missed, in their condition, they'd drown for sure. I jockeyed around and finally got the wing angled just enough to get one of them on the left float and still keep myself from turning downstream."

Once aboard the float, the grateful GI managed to balance-walk long enough to get into the cabin of the Aeronca while Sheldon was already making his next move.

"Because of the heavy current and extremely rough water, it was impossible for me to taxi upriver, let alone take off in that direction, so all I could do was continue to float backward as I had been doing. It was a mile and a half downstream to the end of the rapids, and that first trip was one of the longest rides on a river that I've ever taken."

Once below the rapids, Sheldon was able to turn the plane and make a downriver takeoff. He would make three more of these landings for there were still six men on the ledge, and he could only remove two at a time due to the need to keep the plane as light as possible for maximum maneuverability.

After miraculously returning to the rapids three more times, without damage to the airplane, himself, or the stranded scouts, he turned his attentions to the search for the eighth man.

"I flew upriver, looked and then looked some more. I still saw a lot of debris but no eighth man. I was just about ready to go back for another load of gas when I finally spotted him. The guy had dragged himself out of the river, and he was about 18 miles below the canyon. He had floated all that way hanging onto a piece of debris, and when I got to him, he was a shock case and could barely crawl aboard. The water was about 55 degrees, and he was all skinned up and bruised but had no broken bones."

The rescue at Devil's Canyon had been a marvel of efficiency. It was but one of many such feats that Sheldon would perform over the years. Many would be of a milder cast, while some would exceed the events that had transpired that day at Devil's Canyon. Today, Don Sheldon is well aware of the part that luck played in the four landings and subsequent takeoffs, for not even he could gauge the depth of the water as it plunged over the jagged rocks in the floor of the Susitna, yet somehow his floats missed them all four times.

Sheldon neither expected nor received financial compensation for the rescue. The U.S. Army, in a formal ceremony, awarded him a citation, which stands as a constant reminder of his close association with the military organization. It reads as follows:

CITATION FOR
ALASKA CERTIFICATE OF ACHIEVEMENT
TO
MR. DONALD EDWARD SHELDON
CIVILIAN AVIATOR—TALKEETNA, ALASKA

The Alaska Certificate of Achievement is awarded for meritorious achievement while assisting in the evacuation of an eight-man patrol of the United States Army on the 9th and 10th of July 1955. Mr. Sheldon, having information that a patrol was operating in the area in which he was flying, and knowing the treacherous nature of the rapids on the Susitna River, made an aerial check to determine the patrol's progress. Spotting debris in the water, and realizing that the men might be in trouble, he continued his search and located the patrol upstream on the bank of the river. At possible risk of life, Mr. Sheldon guided his aircraft between towering canyon walls and landed in the river. He then proceeded to fly the first group to Talkeetna, so that an injured man could be given medical attention. Returning to the river three times, he continued the evacuation of the patrol in semi-darkness to bring the last member to Curry at 0300 hours in the morning. His humane efforts prevented possible exposure and extreme difficulties for the members of the patrol. Seeking neither acclaim nor reward, Mr. Sheldon had willingly and voluntarily pitted his skill and aircraft against odds in behalf of the U.S. Army personnel. His intrepid feat adds lustre to the memory of those stalwart pilots whose rare courage and indomitable spirit have conquered the vastness of Alaskan Territory, and merits the deepest respect and admiration of every member in the United States Army Alaska.

Today, when asked what aspect of the entire Devil's Canyon episode he remembers best, Sheldon smiles thinly.

"I guess it would have to be the expressions on those guys' mugs as they crawled aboard my old floatplane."

March 1: -148°

from Minus 148°

A R T   D A V I D S O N

Art Davidson is a nonfiction writer and outdoorsman with more than three decades of Alaskan experience. He was a member of the expedition that completed the first winter ascent of Denali (Mount McKinley) in 1967. Davidson's diary of that harrowing climb, MINUS 148°: THE WINTER ASCENT OF MT. MCKINLEY *(1969) is one of the best-known pieces of modern mountaineering literature. "March 1: −148°," excerpted from that book, involves climbers Dave Johnston, Ray Genet (Pirate), Gregg Blomberg, Shiro Nishimae, George B. Von Wichman (orthopedic specialist), John Edwards, and the author.*

Note: The expedition is split between Denali Pass and the 17,300-foot camp. With no means of communication, each group has no way of knowing what is happening to the other group. The narrative follows Dave, Pirate, and Art at Denali Pass, while diary entries written by Gregg, Shiro, George, and John during the isolation imposed by the wind record the course of events and the trend of their emotions.

17,300 FEET: GREGG, JOHN, SHIRO, GEORGE

Gregg's diary:

A frightening thing is developing, but let me start from this morning. Shiro got up early, and although there was some wind we decided to give it a go. We started off with Shiro and George and John and me roped in twos. From the time we started it was apparent we wouldn't get far. The winds aloft were howling. After a few hundred yards John pooped out, and I went ahead to tell the others. When I caught them George unroped to go back with John, and I roped in with Shiro. The idea was to go up and see that the others were all right. When we approached the pass it was evident why the others had not descended. The wind was howling like crazy. I tried to lead up to the pass but was turned back by the wind. We then traversed to a spot that we thought was directly under their bivouac site. Shiro went up and tried twice, but the wind was so fierce it was impossible. The wind was coming from our direction, and if we went one step too far it meant not getting back again.

Shiro tried another place . . . the same. . . . We retreated rapidly. Once, when Shiro had come back, I asked him what he saw. He said: "Three sleeping bags. They are in their sleeping bags." When we were just about back in camp he told me all he saw was one sleeping bag, lying up against the rock and flapping in the wind.

Shiro surmises the three are on the leeward side of the rock, covered with the parachute, with possibly two in one bag. All I know is that they must have made it back to the bivouac site, and are in a bind. If I could have reached them—they were less than a hundred feet away—we could have told them that the wind wasn't as bad on this side of the pass. We could have told them to make a try.

It's a bad situation . . . winds up to a hundred miles per hour, possibly more. It's a whiteout up there. . . . I pray at this point that they make it through. . . . They must make it through.

Much later Shiro confided: "When I saw only one sleeping bag I was certain they were dead. I told Gregg I saw three. He is very emotional. I thought maybe dangerous to alarm him. He might lose his mind."

DENALI PASS: ART, DAVE, PIRATE

The wind woke us. The wildly whipping parachute billowed and snapped with reports like those of a bullwhip or rifle. The wind blasted against the rocks we were nestled among with a deafening eruption of noise; crosscurrents in the storm fluctuated its pitch to a groan or a prolonged whine. A dull, aching pressure along my backside was the cold, pressed into me by the wind.

I twisted in my sleeping bag to grope for the loose section of parachute thrashing me from behind. The moment I caught it my hands were pierced with cold; groggy with sleep, I'd forgotten that the nylon, like everything else outside our sleeping bags, was about −40°. The cold sank into my fingers while the parachute, jerking and cracking erratically, resisted my attempt to anchor it. As soon as I managed to gather the slack material under me, the weight of my body holding it down, I shot one hand under an armpit and the other into my crotch for warmth. I was out of breath from the effort.

Drawn tighter, the parachute made less noise, and I was able to relax for a few moments. My fingers, aching inside from being deeply chilled, began to gradually rewarm with strong tingling sensations. I pressed the length of my body against Dave to be warmer on that side, and I felt Dave shift inside his bag, trying to press against me. I snuggled close to him and lay quietly for a long time, hoping I'd fall asleep again, as if not thinking about the wind and cold would make them disappear.

I couldn't sleep, and the wind only grew more vicious. I tried to ignore the cold along my backside, away from Dave, but when the first shiver ran through my body I turned to check the sleeping bag where it touched my back. To my horror it was no thicker than its shell, two pieces of nylon. The wind had pushed the down away. I could hardly believe it possible that the parachute, designed to resist wind, was letting the wind and cold eat through it and into my sleeping bay.

The parachute began cracking again. "Oh, hell," I mumbled. The cracking meant a portion of the parachute had broken loose again. Feeling I didn't have the strength for another attempt at anchoring it, I curled up in my bag, shivering occasionally, waiting for something to happen; I didn't know what. After what seemed like several minutes but was probably only a matter of seconds, I heard Pirate trying to tie down the parachute.

"Art." Pirate's voice sounded far off and unfamiliar. "Help me hold it."

Hearing his voice made me realize that the three of us had been awake for more than an hour before anyone had spoken. Burrowed into my sleeping bag, I didn't want to budge from its security, false as it was, for even a moment. While I was deciding whether to help Pirate or prolong my rest, I felt Dave get to his hands and knees and begin wrestling with the parachute, which was now pounding his head and back as it billowed and cracked back in rapid succession. Yanking and cursing, Dave managed to pull part of it around him again, only to have it whip off as soon as he settled down into his bag.

"Look, we gotta get outa here!" Dave yelled.

"Where? We'd never make it down!" I said, grabbing onto the piece of parachute that Pirate was clinging to. "Maybe it's a morning wind that'll die down."

"Morning wind?" Dave looked at me with disbelief. "It's a bloody hurricane, you fool! I'm checking the other side of the rocks."

"Awwghaaaaa. . . ." Pirate growled, staring up into the wind.

Instead of getting completely out of his bag, Dave tied the drawstring at the top tight around his middle. With his legs still in the sleeping bag and his arms free, he lurched toward the crest ten feet away. I was horribly apprehensive. If he lost his grip on the rocks he could easily be blown off the mountain. On the other side we'd never hear him again if he called for help. How far was he going? Maybe he'd be hidden behind a rock where we wouldn't be able to find him if we needed his strength. Besides the logic of my fear, I recoiled emotionally against Dave's leaving because it seemed to break our trust; it violated a fundamental law of survival—stay together.

"Dave," I cried. "Wait! I think it's safer here."

"Stay if you want!" he hollered back. "This wind's bad, and I'm gettin' out of it!"

"Where are you going?" Dave didn't hear me. "It's exposed over there!" He had disappeared over the crest.

Since my mittens were too bulky to grip the parachute, I pulled thick wool socks onto my hands; my fingers were nearly numb already. I was astonished as I looked up to see Pirate holding the parachute with his bare hands. Just as I yelled at him to get something over them, one of my socks started to slip off. Pulling it back on, I shifted position, and the wind seized the wind parka I had been sitting on. Inside its main pocket was the tape recorder I had been using for the physiological testing, but at that moment I was much more concerned about the loss of the half dozen cookies I'd stashed in the pocket. One moment the parka had been next to me, then I saw it whirling through the air, fifty, a hundred feet up, sailing in the direction of McKinley's summit.

With Dave gone, his loose end of the parachute caught the wind, and this threatened to rip the entire piece of nylon from our grip. We gave up trying to wrap the parachute around us; the pull on our arms wrenched our whole bodies as we clung to it to keep it from escaping. The parachute was our only shelter.

"My hands are bad!" Pirate's voice was weak, almost a whimper. His face was drawn up into a hideous, painful grin. Ice caked his beard.

"Bring them in!" I yelled, though his head was only inches from mine. His fingers felt like chunks of ice against my stomach.

"They're stiff!"

"Move them!" I reached for a better grip on the parachute. It slipped. I lunged. Pirate caught it as it whipped past him. He winced in pain.

"Aw, the hell with it!" Pirate sighed. As he let loose, the parachute twisted through the air. It snagged on a rock. I saw it starting to rip, then it was gone.

For the first time I noticed the sky. It was a blue wall, smashing into the mountain. Thin pieces of cloud shredding—everything grew blurred. My eyes were watering and stinging from squinting into the wind. Compared to anything I had ever experienced, this wind was like another element. It was as if gravity had shifted and, instead of holding us down, was pulling us across the landscape.

Pirate began digging his hands in under my parka. The top of my bag had fallen open to the wind. As I pulled it shut, I fell against Pirate. We grabbed each other.

"Hold onto me!"

"Art, let's get into one bag."

"How? There's no room. . . . Give me your hands." I felt his icy fingers grabbing the skin around my middle. My bag had opened again, and to keep the wind from getting to me Pirate pushed himself over the opening. I just leaned against him, trying to catch my breath. Shivering, teeth chattering, my whole body was shaking with cold.

"Pirate, it's no good!" Wind was coming into my bag. We were both losing our warmth. "Each in his own bag . . . it's better."

"I can't feel my fingers!"

"Put 'em between your legs!"

"I don't want to lose my hands!"

I remembered Dave. If it was less windy on the other side of the rocks, he would have come back to tell us. If it was just as windy, I thought he would have returned to be with us. Something must have happened to him. But maybe he had found a sheltered corner. How could he abandon us?

"Pirate, let's try the other side!"

"Naw . . . the wind's everywhere!"

We huddled together, hunched upright in our sleeping bags, wedged tightly between two rocks. Whenever we relaxed the wind caught us, started us sliding along the ice which gradually sloped away, and forced us to push and fight our way back up into the rocks. Leaning against Pirate didn't make me any warmer, but it was comforting—I wasn't alone. We didn't talk. I could breath more easily with my head inside my bag. I wondered what the others were doing down in the cave. Shiro's cough, Gregg's foot, John's swollen ear—it was too frightening to think about.

Beneath me I felt the ice sliding. Slipping onto my side, I brought an arm out in time to grab Pirate's knee. I pulled myself back against the rocks. My arms trembled from exhaustion. Pirate stared blankly out of his bag. His head turned slowly toward me with a groggy nodding motion. Was he slipping into a stupor? I wondered whether I looked as awful.

"It's no use here," I sighed.

I could barely keep myself up against the rocks. There was nothing I could do for Pirate. Maybe Dave had found a safe spot. I had to check the other side of the rocks, but that would be deserting Pirate. Yet there was no way I could help. How could I just leave him? I had to do something for myself!

"I'm going over." He didn't move. "Pirate," I yelled, "I'm going after Dave!"

His head shook from side to side as he half mumbled, half shouted, something I couldn't understand. I grabbed at the rock above me and pulled myself up the slope. Another rock; its sharp cold cut through the wool socks. Another pull. I reached the crest. To my tremendous relief I saw Dave crouched on the ice only about fifteen feet away. His back was toward me.

"Dave!" He couldn't hear me. I worked a little closer to him. The wind threatened to throw me off the crest. Beyond lay bare glacier where I'd never catch anything to hold onto if I was blown from the rocks.

"Dave!" This time he turned and saw me. I was out of breath and must have been gasping as much as yelling. "Is it better where you are?"

"What? . . . It's the same. Go back!"

I didn't want to go back, and waiting here on the crest was impossible because it was completely exposed to the wind. Before I'd decided which way to go, a cross-current gust caught me. I grabbed for rocks. One came loose. I caught another one nearer Dave. Somehow the sock on my left hand had blown off. I shoved the bare hand into my sleeping bag. The other hand held onto a rock. The wind flung and tossed my body as though it were weightless.

My right hand ached with cold from gripping the rock, and my forearm began cramping from the strain. I couldn't go back into the wind, but neither could my right hand cling to the rock much longer. The only other rock I could reach was three feet to my left, near Dave. My numb right hand had become so dead that I couldn't feel the rock it held onto. My shivering body seemed on the verge of going into convulsions.

I tried to think. If I lost my grip, I'd be blown across the ice. My mind was racing. I had to grab for the rock near Dave with my left hand: it was bare, no mitten or sock. It would be frozen. I had to. Suddenly, my bare hand shot out to grab the rock. Slicing cold.

I saw Dave's face, the end of his nose raw, frostbitten. His mouth, distorted into an agonized mixture of compassion and anger, swore at me to get a glove on. I looked at my hand. It was white, frozen absolutely white.

I pulled my body onto the rock. Dave was only five or six feet away on the ledge he had chopped in the slightly sloping ice.

"Christ, Art." His voice cracked. "You froze your hands!"

I pushed off from the rock, letting the wind throw me against Dave. He flung his arms around me. All I could do was lie across him, wheezing and shaking, trying to catch my breath.

"Man," he said, "we gotta dig in!"

17,200 FEET: GREGG, JOHN, SHIRO, GEORGE

John's journal:

The pass as roaring windy, and we had our first real concern for the summit party. . . . Change of wind. Raven flew down buttress! Hypothesis concerning summit party: perhaps they had not gone to the summit the previous day, and had gone today. . . . Weather worsening rapidly all afternoon. Flying clouds, but mountain looked magnificent all afternoon. Blue shadows, yellow snow. . . . Shiro saw one sleeping bag against the bivouac rocks. At the time Gregg thought Shiro had seen three, but had misheard under the roar of the wind, and was rather profoundly disturbed when back in camp Shiro said he had seen only one. . . . Very tired and anxious for the three. I am pretty sure they will break out despite the weather and come down tonight despite the whiteout. If not, we are in serious trouble, indeed.

Sheldon flew in late this afternoon, low around the igloo, with landing lights on. Some discussion as to the significance of this flight, but probably a reconaissance before the storm. Had Ray been in radio contact with

Anchorage and given an emergency to Sheldon, or was this flight on his own or on someone else's account before the onset of the storm? George very apprehensive about storm. Solemn. There is not much we can do about it but wait for the others to move down. But if they don't? I have no great apprehension for the three above yet. I think they will fight their way down, that is, if they are all well. Art's altitude sickness? But then we may have seven days before Sheldon can take us out.

Gregg's diary continued:

It's evening. We all stayed in case there is a need to help one of the others down. The wind has descended to this altitude, and we are huddled in the snow cave with a large mouth covered by a tent, weighed down with rocks which we hope will hold. If they come down tonight, we will be crowded, but we will be a happy crowd. If they make it back tonight, we will descend tomorrow as quickly as possible.

The wind is from the southeast, right into the tent, but it will hold unless things get worse. Those guys only had a bunch of lunch, one stove full of gas, a pot, their sleeping bags, and the parachute with which to cover themselves up.

Please God, let us hear their voices. Let them descend unharmed. Give them a break in the wind and the wisdom and stamina to use it.

What can we do? I suppose the best is the prayer above. I am thankful that Shiro wanted to come down yesterday, or we would have probably been caught in the same trap. How proud and stupid we all are.

Edi [Gregg's wife], you can't imagine how I long to be in your arms, to lay my head in your lap while you stroke my hair. This is nothing new. I had been longing to be with you since I started. I think you can tell by this journal. All my love, honey. Don't worry. I'll still call you about the fifth of *this month.* Good night. Pray for a happy morning.

With the provisions and personal reserves they have they could probably last two more days at the longest, but practically speaking they must make it down tonight or tomorrow morning at the latest. If they had only known today that the wind wasn't as bad on this side of the pass. Oh, pray to hear their voices urgently wanting to come inside.

On the bright side, they are the strongest of us. Dave and Art have plenty of experience. Ray has good sense. They're all tough as nails. With a tiny break in the wind, they can't help but make it! Thank God the wind is dying down here, and pray it is there. Oh Lord, what anguish we are all suffering for our friends' safety.

DENALI PASS: ART, PIRATE, DAVE

Dave cradled Pirate's feet against his belly and massaged them gently until they began to rewarm.

"Dave," I said, "you know you saved us out there." My words sort of hung in the air. They sounded hollow, and Dave bit at his lip self-consciously. I didn't say more, but my eyes followed Dave with admiration and a kind of love as he tucked Pirate into his bag and then reached for the stove.

For more than an hour I had clung to the ledge on the ice, feeling the frostbite blisters swell on my hands and watching helplessly while Dave dug a cave in the ice. Just before he had completed it, Dave had collapsed from exhaustion; by then Pirate had pulled himself together, and despite his hands and feet, which were beginning to swell with frostbite blisters, he had somehow made it over the crest to finish hollowing out the cave. Dave had recovered enough strength to help me through the small hole in the ice which was the entrance to our new home.

Now inside our cave, Dave leaned on his elbows, and steadying the stove with one hand, he prepared some food with his free hand. In this cramped chamber under the ice cooking was more miserable than it had ever been in the last four weeks; Dave had quietly accepted the job because his were the only hands capable of working the stove. At least he had found some good food to fix—four pound-and-a-half cans of ham, bacon, and peas which had been cached by a previous expedition among the rocks we had bivouacked against. Since our pot had blown away, he heated the ham in its own can, then used the can to melt water in.

Flattened against the wall while Dave cooked in the middle, I realized how small our cave was. At the wide end there was barely enough room for our shoulders, and at the narrow end our feet in our sleeping bags were heaped on top of each other. Because of the rocks behind us, Dave and Pirate had been unable to make the cave long enough for us to stretch out completely. Over our feet the ceiling was about a foot and a half above the floor; toward the larger end there was just enough height to turn or lie on our sides with one shoulder touching the ice on the floor and the other touching the ice on the ceiling. We were quickly learning that our every movement bumped the next person. This cave certainly wasn't pleasant or comfortable by ordinary standards, but it kept us safe from the wind, and that was all that mattered, for the moment.

Dave looked for his journal and found it missing. We had lost too much to the wind—the use of four hands and two feet, an incalculable amount of body warmth, two packs with half our food in them, the parachute, my wind parka, and—perhaps our greatest loss—the foam pads which would have insulated us from the ice and helped to keep our bags dry. Yet we felt secure. We were supplied with enough gas to make water for another day, maybe two more days if we stretched it. With four lunches left, and three remaining cans of food, we needn't worry about starving.

That night ham and hot water were a feast, not filling, but delicious nonetheless; it was our first warm food since leaving the cave down at 17,200 feet more than thirty hours before. My hands had become so inflexible that Dave had to place each bite of ham—there were five of them—in my mouth, then tip the can to my lips to let me drink. Eating made us giddy with pleasure and almost got us feeling warm.

We were actually exultant, not from any sense of conquering the wind, but rather from the simple companionship of huddling together in our little cave while outside in the darkness the storm raged through Denali Pass and on across the Alaska Range. We agreed that the wind coming out of the northwest was funneling through the pass at least 130 miles per hour. We remembered that a wind of such velocity, combined with the −30° to −45° air temperature outside our cave, created an equivalent wind-chill temperature somewhere off the end of the chart; the last figure on the chart was −148°.

"One hundred and forty-eight degrees below zero."

It was frightening to say, but the worst was over, we thought. In the morning the wind should slack off; we would descend, greeting the others at 17,200 feet with the news that we had made the summit; we would get off the mountain and go home. We wanted to believe the climb was over, that in a couple of days everything would be warm and easy again. Yet the wind, howling and pounding the slope overhead, reminded us that we couldn't move until it died down. We talked of the cave as our refuge, but the suspicion that we were being held captive in the ice must have entered each of our minds as we fell asleep listening to the wind.

Possessing the Land

FROM *Road Song*

NATALIE KUSZ

*Natalie Kusz and her family came to Alaska from Los Angeles in 1969 when
Natalie was six years old. She graduated from the University of Alaska, and
her work has won several writing awards. In her memoir* ROAD SONG *(1990),
Kusz writes of the struggles she and her family endured. In this excerpt,
Natalie is living with her mother and siblings in Fairbanks when a terrible
accident occurs. Kusz now lives in St. Paul, Minnesota.*

Christmas passed, and Mom went into town every day—for water,
or to do laundry, or to get the mail—but no check arrived from
my father. He wrote often, including short notes to each of us,
and he said he had sent his first paycheck down just two weeks
after he started work. It was good money, he wrote, enough for
stove oil and groceries and for the instruments in hock. When he came
home, we would finish my violin lessons, and we'd start on the younger
kids, too, and we would play together the same songs we had sung on the
way up the Alcan and then after that at the campgrounds all summer long.

That first check never did come. Mom wrote back that it must have
been lost, and could he get them to print another. When was the next one
due, she asked. She would try to stretch things out until it came.

The redemption time was running out on all our things at the pawn-
shop. We had one violin left to pawn, the one my grandfather had given to
Dad before I was born, when Dad had driven from L.A. to New York and
brought the old man home with him. In Polish, it was a *Benkarty,* a wide,
barrel-chested French violin, aged reddish-brown under its lacquer. It was
for a master, made to play fast and ring loudly, its neck rounded and thinner than most, the back of its body all a single piece of maple. The wood
and varnish had aged and crystallized so smoothly that when my father
tuned it and began to play, each string he stroked resonated acutely with the

sounds of the others. To pay the interest on the other things in hock, my mother took the *Benkarty* in to the pawnbroker, telling him she would be back for it soon. "It's my husband's," she said, trusting this Russian man to keep the violin safe, if only for sake of the old country and my father's Slavic tongue. She could not know then that the man would sell the *Benkarty* before its redemption date, or that she and my father would never get it back. At the time, the clearest thing for her was the extra cash she got for it, and the powdered milk and the gas she was able to buy that afternoon.

Mom arranged her days carefully around the hours I was in school. Her glasses had broken across the bridge one morning when she had come inside and set them to thaw on the woodstove, so she walked me to the bus stop wearing prescription sunglasses and then fastened my sisters and brother into the truck and drove into town, scraping ice from the windshield as she steered. I know from her journal that she was afraid, that she padlocked the cabin door against the vandalism recently come into town, that she counted her time out carefully so she would be home in time to meet my afternoon bus. She reminded me and made me promise that, should she be late one day, I would take Hobo to Paul and Kevin's and wait there until she came for me. "Okay, Mommy," I said then, and turned to pull Hobo's ears.

"No, listen to me, Natalie." Mom held my arm until I looked up. Behind the dark lenses her eyes were invisible, but her cheeks were white, and her lips very nearly the same color. "This is not a joke," she said. "Now don't forget what I'm saying. You must go to the boys' if I'm late. This is very important."

"It's okay," I repeated. I looked into her glasses. "I'll remember."

On January 10, only Hobo met me at the bus stop. In the glare from school-bus headlights, his blue eye shone brighter than his brown, and he watched until I took the last step to the ground before tackling me in the snow. Most days, Hobo hid in the shadow of the spruce until Mom took my bag, then he erupted from the dark to charge up behind me, run through my legs and on out the front. It was his favorite trick. I usually lost my balance and ended up sitting in the road with my feet thrown wide out front and steaming dog tongue all over my face.

Hobo ran ahead, then back, brushing snow crystals and fur against my leg. I put a hand on my skin to warm it and dragged nylon ski pants over the road behind me. Mom said to have them along in case the bus broke down, but she knew I would not wear them, could not bear the plastic sounds they made between my thighs.

No light was on in our house.

If Mom had been home, squares of yellow would have shown through the spruce and lit the fog of my breath, turning it bright as I passed through. What light there was now came from the whiteness of snow, and from the occasional embers drifting up from our stovepipe. I laid my lunchbox on the top step and pulled at the padlock, slapping a palm on the door and shouting. Hobo jumped away from the noise and ran off, losing himself in darkness and in the faint keening dog sounds going up from over near the Horners' house. I called, "Hobo. Come back here, boy," and took the path toward Paul's, tossing my ski pants to the storage tent as I passed.

At the property line, Hobo caught up with me and growled, and I fingered his ear, looking where he pointed, seeing nothing ahead there but the high curve and long sides of a Quonset hut, the work shed the Horners used also as a fence for one side of their yard. In the fall, Paul and Kevin and I had walked to the back of it, climbing over boxes and tools and parts of old furniture, and we had found in the corner a lemming's nest made from chewed bits of cardboard and paper, packed under the curve of the wall so that shadows hid it from plain sight. We all bent close to hear the scratching, and while Paul held a flashlight I took two sticks and parted the rubbish until we saw the black eyes of a mother lemming and the pink naked bodies of five babies. The mother dashed deeper into the pile and we scooped the nesting back, careful not to touch the sucklings, for fear that their mama would eat them if they carried scent from our fingers.

It seemed that we had spent most of the fall looking out just like that for shrews and lemmings. Oscar and Vic had cats, and Paul and Kevin had three German shepherds, and one or another of them usually found a rodent to play with. Oscar's cats would catch a shrew in their teeth, holding tight to the skin behind its neck until its eyes swelled out and it stopped breathing. The boys and I squeezed the cats' jaws, screaming, "You're not even *hungry*," until the teeth parted and the shrew dropped into our palms. If we were fast enough, it was still alive, and we pushed its eyes back in and let it go. The dogs worried a lemming in their mouths, dropping it out on occasion and catching it back into the air, over and over again until it couldn't move and was no longer any fun. When we caught the dogs doing this, we beat their ears with walking sticks, but usually we were too late and had to bury the thing under moss.

The dogs were loud now beyond the Quonset, fierce in their howls and sounding like many more than just three. Hobo crowded against my legs, and as I walked he hunched in front of me, making me stumble into a drift that filled my boots with snow. I called him a coward and said to quit it, but I held his neck against my thigh, turning the corner into the boys' yard and stopping on the edge. Paul's house was lit in all its windows, Kevin's was dark, and in the yard between them were dogs, new ones I had not seen before, each with its own house and tether. The dogs and their crying filled the yard, and when they saw me they grew wilder, hurling themselves to the ends of their chains, pulling their lips off their teeth. Hobo cowered and ran and I called him with my mouth, but my eyes did not move from in front of me.

There were seven. I knew they were huskies and meant to pull dogsleds, because earlier that winter Paul's grandfather had put on his glasses and shown us a book full of pictures. He had turned the pages with a wet thumb, speaking of trappers and racing people and the ways they taught these dogs to run. They don't feed them much, he said, or they get slow and lose their drive. This was how men traveled before they invented snow-mobiles or gasoline.

There was no way to walk around the dogs to the lighted house. The snow had drifted and been piled around the yard in heaps taller than I was, and whatever aisle was left along the sides was narrow, and pitted with chain marks where the animals had wandered, dragging their tethers behind. No, I thought, Kevin's house was closest and out of biting range, and someone could, after all, be sitting home in the dark.

My legs were cold. The snow in my boots had packed itself around my ankles and begun to melt, soaking my socks and the felt liners under my heels. I turned toward Kevin's house, chafing my thighs together hard to warm them, and I called cheerfully at the dogs to shut up. Oscar said that if you met a wild animal, even a bear, you had to remember it was more scared than you were. Don't act afraid, he said, because they can smell fear. Just be loud—stomp your feet, wave your hands—and it will run away without even turning around. I yelled "Shut up" again as I climbed the steps to Kevin's front door, but even I could barely hear myself over the wailing. At the sides of my eyes, the huskies were pieces of smoke tumbling over one another in the dark.

The wood of the door was solid with cold, and even through deerskin mittens it bruised my hands like concrete. I cupped a hand to the window and looked in, but saw only black—black, and the reflection of a lamp in the other cabin behind me. I turned and took the three steps back to the ground; seven more and I was in the aisle between doghouses, stretching my chin far up above the frenzy, thinking hard on other things. This was how we walked in summertime, the boys and I, escaping from bad guys over logs thrown across ditches; step lightly and fast, steady on the hard parts of your soles, arms extended outward, palms down and toward the sound. That ditch, this aisle, was a river, a torrent full of silt that would fill your clothes and pull you down if you missed and fell in. I was halfway across. I pointed my chin toward the house and didn't look down.

On either side, dogs on chains hurled themselves upward, choking themselves to reach me, until their tethers jerked their throats back to earth. I'm not afraid of you, I whispered; this is dumb.

I stepped toward the end of the row and my arms began to drop slowly closer to my body. Inside the mittens, my thumbs were cold, as cold as my thighs, and I curled them in and out again. I was walking past the last dog and I felt brave, and I forgave him and bent to lay my mitten on his head. He surged forward on a chain much longer than I thought, leaping at my face, catching my hair in his mouth, shaking it in his teeth until the skin gave way with a jagged sound. My feet were too slow in my boots, and as I blundered backward they tangled in the chain, burning my legs on metal. I called out at Paul's window, expecting rescue, angry that it did not come, and I beat my arms in front of me, and the dog was back again, pulling me down.

A hole was worn into the snow, and I fit into it, arms and legs drawn up in front of me. The dog snatched and pulled at my mouth, eyes, hair; his breath clouded the air around us, but I did not feel its heat, or smell the blood sinking down between hairs of his muzzle. I watched my mitten come off in his teeth and sail upward, and it seemed unfair then and very sad that one hand should freeze all alone; I lifted the second mitten off and threw it away, then turned my face back again, overtaken suddenly by loneliness. A loud river ran in my ears, dragging me under.

My mother was singing. *Lu-lee lu-lay, thou little tiny child,* the song to the Christ Child, the words she had sung, smoothing my hair, all my life before bed. Over a noise like rushing water I called to her and heard her answer back, Don't worry, just sleep, the ambulance is on its way. I drifted back out and couldn't know then what she prayed, that I would sleep on without waking, that I would die before morning.

She had counted her minutes carefully that afternoon, sure that she would get to town and back, hauling water and mail, with ten minutes to spare before my bus came. But she had forgotten to count one leg of the trip, had skidded up the drive fifteen minutes late, pounding a fist on the horn, calling me home. On the steps, my lunchbox had grown cold enough to burn her hands. She got the water, the groceries, and my brother and sisters inside, gave orders that no one touch the woodstove or open the door, and she left down the trail to Paul's, whistling Hobo in from the trees.

I know from her journal that Mom had been edgy all week about the crazed dog sounds next door. Now the new huskies leaped at her and Hobo rumbled warning from his chest. Through her sunglasses, the dogs were just shapes, indistinct in windowlight. She tried the dark cabin first, knocking hard on the windows, then turned and moved down the path between doghouses, feeling her way with her feet, kicking out at open mouths. Dark lenses frosted over from her breath, and she moved toward the house and the lights on inside.

"She's not here." Paul's mother held the door open and air clouded inward in waves. Mom stammered out thoughts of bears, wolves, dogs. Geri grabbed on her coat. She had heard a noise out back earlier—they should check there and then the woods.

No luck behind the cabin and no signs under the trees. Wearing sunglasses and without any flashlight, Mom barely saw even the snow. She circled back and met Geri under the windowlight. Mom looked toward the yard and asked about the dogs. "They seem so hungry," she said.

Geri looked that way and then back at my mother. "No. Paul's folks just got them last week, but the boys play with them all the time." All the same, she and Mom scanned their eyes over the kennels, looking through and then over their glasses. Nothing seemed different. "Are you sure she isn't home?" Geri asked. "Maybe she took a different trail."

Maybe. Running back with Geri behind her, Mom called my name until her lungs frosted inside and every breath was a cough. She whistled the family whistle my father had taught us, the secret one he and his family had used to call one another from the woods in Nazi Germany. "*Dodek, ty-gdzie,*" the tune went, "Dodek, where are you?" She blew it now, two syllables for my name, high then low, then a lower one, quick, and another high slide down to low. Her lips hardly worked in the cold, and the whistle was feeble, and she finished by shouting again, curling both hands around her mouth. "Come on," she said to Geri. "Let's get to my cabin." The three younger children were still the only ones home, and Mom handed them their treasure chests, telling them to play on the bed until she found Natalie. Don't go outside, she said. I'll be back real soon.

Back at the Horners', Geri walked one way around the Quonset and Mom the other. Mom sucked air through a mitten, warming her lungs. While Geri climbed over deeper snow, she approached the sled dogs from a new angle. In the shadow of one, a splash of red—the lining of my coat thrown open. "I've found her," she shouted, and thought as she ran, Oh, thank God. Thank, thank God.

The husky stopped its howling as Mom bent to drag me out from the hole. Geri caught up and seemed to choke. "Is she alive?" she asked.

Mom said, "I think so, but I don't know how." She saw one side of my face gone, one red cavity with nerves hanging out, scraps of dead leaves stuck on to the mess. The other eye might be gone, too; it was hard to tell. Scalp had been torn away from my skull on that side, and the gashes reached to my forehead, my lips, had left my nose ripped wide at the nostrils. She tugged my body around her chest and carried me inside.

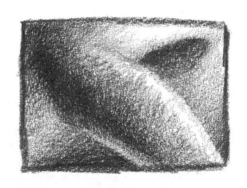

VI

The Animal People

The Man and the Loon

ATHABASCAN LEGEND

"The Man and the Loon" is an Athabascan legend retold by Peter Kalifornsky in his book A DENA'INA LEGACY: THE COLLECTED WRITINGS OF PETER KALIFORNSKY *(1991), which won an American Book Award. Kalifornsky (1911–1993), a Tanaina Athabascan from Kenai, Alaska, was a storyteller and scholar dedicated to preserving the history and language of his people, the indigenous people of the Cook Inlet region.*

One man had a wife and a young boy. The husband became blind and they were hungry. People would give them some food, but that woman would not give this food to her husband. He was starving and beginning to lose strength.

He said to his wife, "Give me my bow." And she gave it to him. He said, "I whittled it down to make it easier to draw back the bowstring. If it shoots well, take me out hunting," he told her.

And they went out with their son. She took him to his brush camp. She built a fire.

And then a caribou appeared in the clearing. "Try out your bow," the woman said, and she pointed him toward it and he shot it. But she didn't tell him he killed the caribou. She would cut off a piece of that caribou and roast it for herself and eat it. And the man would smell it. When he said, "What do I smell?" she would say to him, "Those are only greasy rocks that have been heated."

One day she said, "Tomorrow I will take you out. Maybe we will find some game." And the next morning she took her husband out into the woods, and she told him, "You stay right here." And she took his bow and left him to starve. And then she went back to the brush camp and roasted meat for herself and ate.

The man hollered out for her, but she was gone. And he began feeling around there, and he made a wooden cane for himself. And then he vowed, "I will survive, whatever happens."

He turned in one direction and walked that way. He heard a loon calling, and he walked in the direction of the loon. And he came out to the edge of the water. He felt the water with his staff. He stooped and he drank some water.

And Loon swam up to him. Loon said to him, "What are you doing?" and the man told him what had happened to him. Loon said, "Good. I will help you, but you will have to pay me."

The man said, "What can I pay you with? I am a poor man. All I have is this vest with dentalium shells."

"Good," Loon said. "I'll dive down with you three times. When I come back up with you, open your eyes and look closely."

The first time Loon surfaced with the man, he could see slightly. After the next time he could see better. The third time they surfaced he could see well.

"Can you recognize the places we surfaced each time?" Loon asked.

"Yes," the man said, "over there the first time and there the second time, and over here the third time."

"Good," Loon said, "try to remember this place here. By this landmark you will return to your camp. From this place go that way, and you will return to your camp."

And the man left, and as he approached his camp, he began to crawl. His wife was roasting something again. She saw him. She said, "Loved one! I too had gotten lost and have just gotten back."

"What is that smell?" he asked her.

"It is just those greasy rocks."

When she said that, he said, "That is what I killed when we arrived here. And you did not give me anything to eat." And he grabbed a sharp, broken rock, and he pierced her eyes. And he said to that boy, "You love your mother more than me. You stay with your mother."

And he left them. He returned to the village and he told the people the story. He told them, "I paid Loon with a dentalium vest, a white beaded vest."

The Prince and the Salmon People

T L I N G I T　　L E G E N D

John Smelcer, an Anchorage poet, publisher, and lecturer, is the author of
A Cycle of Myths *and* The Raven and the Totem *(1992). "The Prince
and the Salmon People," a popular Tlingit tale retold by Smelcer, is taken
from* The Raven and the Totem.

In the days of long ago, there was a prince named Yaloa who lived with
his parents in a village upriver from the sea. Yaloa was a member of the
killer whale clan, and it was a tradition of his people to be taught the
ways of the sea by his mother's brother. Yaloa was not very interested
in this, but wanted to learn the ways of the eagle and so he spent a
great deal of time trying to catch eagles.

Yaloa's mother wanted him to learn the ways of the killer whale clan and
urged him to practice the ways of the river and the sea. Yaloa wanted to
please his mother and so he learned to catch salmon, but his heart was not
in it. Instead, Yaloa tried to catch eagles most of the time.

Once, he was lucky and caught a very large salmon. His mother was
proud of him and she carefully cut and dried it for him to show his uncle
when he came to teach him the ways of the sea. Yaloa's mother told him that
he must return the bones of the salmon to the river where it was caught, as
was the custom of their people.

Yaloa did not want to do this and had his younger brother take the
bones to the river. His brother was not careful and only some of the bones
were returned to the river.

The next year the salmon run was very small and the people of the
village did not have enough salmon to feed themselves. That winter starvation threatened Yaloa and his people. His younger brother was very hungry

and so Yaloa gave him a piece of dried salmon that his mother was saving.

When his mother saw that part of the salmon was missing, she thought that Yaloa had selfishly eaten it while the rest of the village starved. Yaloa ran away in shame to the river. Some people called to him from their canoe and took him to the land of the salmon spirits. His mother, not knowing what happened, thought that he must have drowned in the river.

Yaloa lived with the salmon people for a year and they taught him the ways of the salmon and why it was important to return all of the salmon's bones to the river. When this was not done, the salmon people suffered and would not return to the river. Because Yaloa had not returned all of the big salmon's bones to the river, the chief of the salmon people was very sick. This was the reason why the salmon run had been very poor.

Soon it was time for the salmon to return to the river and Yaloa went with them in the shape of a salmon. The people of Yaloa's village caught many fish and Yaloa was caught by his mother. She did not recognize him until she saw that he was wearing Yaloa's necklace. A shaman was asked to change Yaloa back to his human form, and in a few days he was human again.

Since Yaloa had learned so much about the salmon people, he went to find the missing bones so that the chief of the salmon people would be well again, and so that the salmon would return in large numbers. Yaloa taught his people all that he had learned from the salmon people. He taught them how to observe the rituals which pleased the salmon people.

In honor of his return and because of the knowledge he gave his villagers, a feast was given for Yaloa. Yaloa wanted to have many eagle feathers to give to his guests, so once again he went to hunt eagles. This time he used the skills taught to him by the salmon people. Yaloa turned himself into a salmon and when an eagle swooped down to get him with his sharp talons, Yaloa quickly turned back into a human and grabbed the eagle.

Although Yaloa caught many eagles this way, he was not happy because he longed to return to the salmon people. The day before the feast Yaloa changed himself into a salmon again and swam down the river to the salmon people's village and never went back to his mother's village.

The Man Who Became a Caribou

ESKIMO LEGEND

"The Man Who Became a Caribou" is a popular Eskimo cautionary tale retold by Edward L. Keithahn in his book ALASKAN IGLOO TALES *(1945). Keithahn and his wife first arrived in Alaska in 1923 at the remote Arctic village of Shishmaref, where they spent many fascinating winter evenings listening to Eskimo storytellers.*

There was once a hunter who had a wife and two small sons. With them lived his mother-in-law, who unhappily found fault with everything he did. At night even, when she thought he was asleep, he often heard her berating him to his wife, telling her that he was a poor provider and not to be compared with other men in any way. Although his wife never found fault with him, nor heeded what her mother said about him, life became so miserable for the poor hunter that he decided to leave. He gave instructions that all his nets, snares, spears, bows and arrows, harpoons and boats should be preserved for his boys when they grew up and that they should be instructed in their uses. His wife cried bitterly when he told her he was leaving but his mind was made up. He kissed her and the two little boys goodbye and started on his way.

Once alone on the tundra he began to feel very bitter toward life. Of all things on earth it was worst to be a human being, he thought. As he wandered aimlessly about he espied a large flock of ptarmigan feeding carefree on the tundra. All about them were berries, green leaves and seeds. The ptarmigan all looked fat and contented. "Oh, if only I were a ptarmigan," said the man, "I would be happy!"

The longer he watched the ptarmigan the more his desire grew and when the flock rose like a snow-white cloud and swept away he followed them. Somehow he had a vague hope that there was a chance that they might take pity on him and cause him to become a ptarmigan. But each time that he caught up to the flock they would spread their wings and sail away. All day long he followed them hopefully. Just at sundown the flock rose over a little hill and disappeared on the other side.

When the hunter reached the spot where they had disappeared he estimated the distance that they would probably fly and just where the flock should have settled he saw a little village. So he went to the village and walked straight to the kazhgie. Inside were many men and boys and a few women. As he entered one man who seemed to be the leader or chief man of the village addressed him saying, "Why is it, stranger, that you have followed us all day?"

The hunter now saw that these were the ptarmigan in human form, so he answered, "It is because I should like to be one of you." Whereupon the leader said, "Our lives are not as pleasant as they may seem to you. Although we are always warm and have plenty of food, we are constantly in danger of our lives. We are preyed upon by birds of the air, and by beasts, as well as by men. Surely you would not like to be one of us!"

The hunter had not thought of these things which he recalled were true enough so he gave up the idea of becoming one of them. The people were very kind to him and gave him a white deerskin to lie upon and a brown one for a cover. As he was very weary from his long walk, the hunter fell to sleep instantly and knew nothing more till morning.

When the first rays of the morning sun shone over the hills the man awoke. The village and all of its inhabitants had disappeared! He looked for his brown deerskin and in its place was a brown ptarmigan feather. Then he looked for the white deerskin and under him was a white ptarmigan feather. His bed had been but two feathers, yet he had kept warm all night.

Again the hunter began to walk aimlessly about, letting his feet carry him where they would. He had not got far when he saw a pair of rabbits frisking among the willows. He watched them for a long while as they fed and played carefree on the grass. "I believe I should be happy if I were a rabbit," thought the discontented man. "I will follow them and perhaps they will pity me and cause me to become a rabbit like themselves."

But as he approached them, they sped away like the wind. He followed them only to find that whenever he came near they would bound away. Just at sunset the two rabbits ran up a little hill and disappeared over the other side. When the hunter reached the spot where he had last seen them he looked down into the valley before him and there he saw a lone igloo. He went down to it and inside he found two old people getting ready to spend the night. They gave him his supper and when he had eaten, the old man asked, "Why have you followed us all day?"

The hunter told his troubles and ended by saying he had noticed how happy and carefree they seemed and that he wanted to be like them.

"You would not be happy if you were a rabbit," said the old man, sadly. "At times we are most miserable. Large birds of the air hunt us, to kill and eat us. Foxes and wolves lie in wait for us. Even the mink and weasel take our children. Surely you would not wish to be a rabbit!"

The hunter was convinced that the rabbits' lot was not so pleasant as he had supposed, so he troubled them no further. At bedtime he was given a sleeping-bag and in a short time was fast asleep. The early morning sun was shining when he awoke. He felt warm, yet the igloo, the old people and even his sleeping-bag had disappeared. He was alone, lying on the bare earth.

Once more the hunter started on his quest of a happy life. Presently he saw a large herd of caribou grazing contentedly on the hillside. He went closer and noticed how fat and healthy they all were. In their very numbers he saw security. There was no visible reason why he should not be contented if he were only a caribou. So he started towards the herd in hopes that they might let him join them and be a caribou. Yet as before, upon his approach the animals moved away to another spot and he had nothing left to do but follow again. All day long he followed the herd till at evening the deer went over a hill and disappeared from view.

The hunter climbed to the top of the hill and looking down before him saw a village of many igloos and in the center stood a large kazhgie. He bent his steps towards the kazhgie and upon entering found it to be full of men, one of whom they looked upon as a chief or leader.

Food was brought for the hunter and when he had eaten, the leader came to him and said, "Hunter, why have you followed us all day without either bow and arrow or a spear?"

"I did not wish to kill any of your people," answered the hunter. "I want to become a caribou and live with you."

"But why should you wish to become a caribou when you are already a man?" asked the leader.

Thereupon the hunter told his tale of woe and when he had finished, the people felt so sorry for him that they decided he could become one of their number. The next morning the hunter awoke at sunrise. The village had disappeared and all about him were caribou, kicking away the snowy cover and eating the moss that they uncovered. He looked at himself and sure enough, he was a caribou, too!

Now the hunter was happy for the first time in many years. He broke away the snow with his sharp hoofs and ate the tender white moss that lay beneath. He felt fine but at the same time he noticed he was losing weight steadily. Finally when he had become so thin that he was worried, he went to the leader and asked for advice.

"I eat all day long," said the hunter, "but I grow thinner every day."

"That is because the change of food does not agree with you," said the leader. "Whenever you eat moss, think of something you liked when you were a man." The hunter tried this plan and in a short time was large and strong again.

Everything went well with the hunter thence-forward except at times when the herd was suddenly frightened and ran wildly away. On these occasions the hunter was left far behind. Try as he might he could not keep up with the fleet-footed caribou. One day when the herd was being pursued, the leader noticed the hunter far behind and went back to him. "Why is it you cannot keep up with the herd?" asked the leader.

"It is because I lose time when I look at my feet and footing," answered the hunter.

"Never mind your feet when you are running," returned the leader. "A caribou looks only at the horizon when he runs."

The next time when they were chased by the wolves the hunter held up his head and looked at the horizon. He found it easy thereafter to keep up with the fastest deer.

Each night when the herd went into camp for the night, it was the habit of the leader to tell the hunter what would happen on the following day so that he would know what to do and not be afraid. One evening the leader called him to his side and said, "I will tell you about the hunters. There are two kinds. One we call the black hunter and the other we call the white hunter. The black hunter is our enemy and from him we always flee. He kills for pleasure and does not take care of his meat but leaves it to rot on the tundra. You will know him for he looks black against the horizon and when you cross his trail, his tracks prick your feet like needles. The other hunter is not really white. He is clear like water and takes good care not to waste his meat. We always try to help the white hunter."

A few days later a black object was seen on the horizon. The herd immediately took flight and as they ran, the hunter felt something prick his feet. He knew that he had crossed the black hunter's trail. When the herd was far away and out of danger the deer grazed as contentedly as before.

The following day a white hunter was seen approaching. The leader went among the deer and, selecting two fat young bucks, told them to graze at the edge of the herd, which they did without question. Then the remainder of the herd wandered a short distance away and left the two bucks to the white hunter.

This occurrence worried the hunter very much but that night in the kazhgie the leader comforted him, saying: "Our boys will soon be home so do not worry." He hardly had finished when the sounds of laughter and talking came to their ears and shortly in walked two young men.

"Did the white hunter skin you properly and take good care of the meat?" asked the leader.

"Yes," returned the young men. "His knife was sharp and everything was done properly."

"It is well," smiled the leader and the young men went to their evening meal.

As the happy years went by and the hunter was now an old caribou he began to think about his former life as a man. He wondered if his mother-in-law was dead and if his wife had remarried and if his boys had grown to be strong men. As he thought of these things a desire came to him to return to his old home by the sea, so he went to the leader for advice.

The leader sympathized with the hunter and gave him instructions to follow, but warned him it would be hard to become a man after being a caribou for so many years.

So the hunter bid his caribou friends goodbye and started off towards his old home. As he got nearer the homes of men he passed by many snares and pitfalls set for caribou but he knew them and went by unharmed. But as he approached his former home he began to think about his wife and boys, forgetting all about the dangers about him. All at once he felt himself caught in a snare and could go no further. He knew that to struggle would only make matters worse so he lay down and waited quietly. Soon two young men came up and when they saw a caribou in their snare they shouted joyfully. But when they approached to kill the deer it spoke to them in the voice of a man and they became so frightened that they could not move.

"Please take me out and skin my head," asked the caribou.

For a long time the boys could not move but finally when the request had been repeated many times, one of the boys began to skin the head. When they saw there was a man inside the skin, they completed the task and the old hunter went home with the young men.

Great was his surprise and joy when his wife recognized him as her long-absent husband. She had never been remarried, expecting every day that he would return. The old mother-in-law was long since dead and the two young men who had snared him were his own sons grown to manhood.

The old hunter was at last happy to be a man but it is said that he didn't live many years as his chest was much deformed from walking like a caribou.

The White Seal

RUDYARD KIPLING

Rudyard Kipling (1865–1936) was a short-story writer, poet, and novelist, whose classic works are still popular today. Born in India of British parents, Kipling was a journalist with the Civil and Military Gazette *of Lahore. His best known works include* THE JUNGLE BOOK, CAPTAINS COURAGEOUS, KIM, *and many poems, ballads, and stories. Although he lived briefly in the United States before settling in England, there is no evidence that Kipling ever visited Alaska. "The White Seal," set on St. Paul Island in the Bering Sea, is taken from* THE JUNGLE BOOK *(1895).*

> *Oh, hush thee, my baby, the night is behind us,*
> *And black are the waters that sparkled so green.*
> *The moon, o'er the combers, looks downward to find us*
> *At rest in the hollows that rustle between.*
> *Where billow meets billow, there soft be thy pillow;*
> *Ah, weary wee flipperling, curl at thy ease!*
> *The storm shall not wake thee, nor shark overtake thee,*
> *Asleep in the arms of the slow-swinging seas.*
> —Seal lullaby

All these things happened several years ago at a place called Novastoshnah, or North East Point, on the Island of St. Paul, away and away in the Bering Sea. Limmershin, the Winter Wren, told me the tale when he was blown onto the rigging of a steamer going to Japan, and I took him down into my cabin and warmed and fed him for a couple of days till he was fit to fly back to St. Paul's again. Limmershin is a very odd little bird, but he knows how to tell the truth.

Nobody comes to Novastoshnah except on business, and the only people who have regular business there are the seals. They come in the summer months by hundreds and hundreds of thousands out of the cold gray sea; for Novastoshnah Beach was the finest accommodation for seals of any place in all the world.

Sea Catch knew that, and every spring would swim from whatever place he happened to be in—would swim like a torpedo-boat straight for Novastoshnah, and spend a month fighting with his companions for a good place on the rocks as close to the sea as possible. Sea Catch was fifteen years old, a huge gray fur-seal with almost a mane on his shoulders, and long, wicked dog-teeth. When he heaved himself up on his front flippers he stood more than four feet clear of the ground and his weight, if anyone had been bold enough to weigh him, was nearly seven hundred pounds. He was scarred all over with the marks of savage fights, but he was always ready for just one fight more. He would put his head on one side, as though he were afraid to look his enemy in the face; then he would shoot it out like lightning, and when the big teeth were firmly fixed on the other seal's neck, the other seal might get away if he could, but Sea Catch would not help him.

Yet Sea Catch never chased a beaten seal, for that was against the Rules of the Beach. He only wanted room by the sea for his nursery; but as there were forty or fifty thousand other seals hunting for the same thing each spring, the whistling, bellowing, roaring, and blowing on the beach were something frightful.

From a little hill called Hutchinson's Hill you could look over three and a half miles of ground covered with fighting seals; and the surf was dotted all over with the heads of seals hurrying to land and ready to begin their share of the fighting. They fought in the breakers, they fought in the sand, and they fought on the smooth-worn basalt rocks of the nurseries; for they were just as stupid and unaccommodating as men. Their wives never came to the island until late in May or early in June, for they did not care to be torn to pieces; and the young two-, three-, and four-year-old seals who had not begun housekeeping went inland about half a mile through the ranks of the fighters and played about on the sand-dunes in droves and legions, and rubbed off every single green thing that grew. They were called the holluschickie—the bachelors—and there were perhaps two or three hundred thousand of them at Novastoshnah alone.

Sea Catch had just finished his forty-fifth fight one spring when Matkah, his soft, sleek, gentle-eyed wife, came up out of the sea, and he caught her by the scruff of the neck and dumped her down on his reservation, saying gruffly: "Late, as usual. Where *have* you been?"

It was not the fashion for Sea Catch to eat anything during the four months he stayed on the beaches, and so his temper was generally bad. Matkah knew better than to answer back. She looked round and cooed: "How thoughtful of you! You've taken the old place again."

"I should think I had," said Sea Catch. "Look at me!"

He was scratched and bleeding in twenty places; one eye was almost blind, and his sides were torn to ribbons.

"Oh, you men, you men!" Matkah said, fanning herself with her hind flipper. "Why can't you be sensible and settle your places quietly? You look as though you had been fighting with the Killer Whale."

"I haven't been doing anything *but* fight since the middle of May. The beach is disgracefully crowded this season. I've met at least a hundred seals from Lukannon Beach, house-hunting. Why can't people stay where they belong?"

"I've often thought we should be much happier if we hauled out at Otter Island instead of this crowded place," said Matkah.

"Bah! Only the holluschickie go to Otter Island. If we went there they would say we were afraid. We must preserve appearances, my dear."

Sea Catch sunk his head proudly between his fat shoulders and pretended to go to sleep for a few minutes, but all the time he was keeping a sharp look-out for a fight. Now that all the seals and their wives were on the land, you could hear their clamour miles out to sea above the loudest gales. At the lowest counting there were over a million seals on the beach—old seals, mother seals, tiny babies, and holluschickie, fighting, scuffling, bleating, crawling, and playing together—going down to the sea and coming up from it in gangs and regiments, lying over every foot of ground as far as the eye could reach, and skirmishing about in brigades through the fog. It is nearly always foggy at Novastoshnah, except when the sun comes out and makes everything look all pearly and rainbow-coloured for a little while.

Kotick, Matkah's baby, was born in the middle of that confusion, and he was all head and shoulders, with pale, watery-blue eyes, as tiny seals must be; but there was something about his coat that made his mother look at him very closely.

"Sea Catch," she said at last, "Our baby's going to be white!"

"Empty clam-shells and dry sea-weed!" snorted Sea Catch. "There never has been such a thing in the world as a white seal."

"I can't help that," said Matkah, "there's going to be now"; and she sang the low, crooning seal-song that all the mother seals sing to their babies:

> *You mustn't swim till you're six weeks old,*
> *Or your head will be sunk by your heels;*
> *And summer gales and Killer Whales*
> *Are bad for baby seals.*
>
> *Are bad for baby seals, dear rat,*
> *As bad as bad can be;*
> *But splash and grow strong,*
> *And you can't be wrong,*
> *Child of the Open Sea!*

Of course the little fellow did not understand the words at first. He paddled and scrambled about by his mother's side, and learned to scuffle out of the way when his father was fighting with another seal, and the two rolled and roared up and down the slippery rocks. Matkah used to go to sea to get things to eat, and the baby was fed only once in two days; but then he ate all he could, and throve upon it.

The first thing he did was to crawl inland, and there he met tens of thousands of babies of his own age, and they played together like puppies, went to sleep on the clean sand, and played again. The old people in the nurseries took no notice of them, and the holluschickie kept to their own grounds, so the babies had a beautiful playtime.

When Matkah came back from her deep-sea fishing she would go straight to their playground and call as a sheep calls for a lamb, and wait until she heard Kotick bleat. Then she would take the straightest of straight lines in his direction, striking out with her fore-flippers and knocking the youngsters head over heels right and left. There were always a few hundred mothers hunting for their children through the playgrounds, and the babies were kept lively; but, as Matkah told Kotick, "So long as you don't lie in muddy water and get mange, or rub the hard sand into a cut or scratch, and so long as you never go swimming when there is a heavy sea, nothing will hurt you here."

Little seals can no more swim than little children, but they are unhappy till they learn. The first time that Kotick went down to the sea a wave carried him out beyond his depth, and his big head sank and his little hind-flippers flew up exactly as his mother had told him in the song, and if the next wave had not thrown him back again he would have drowned.

After that he learned to lie in a beach-pool and let the wash of the waves just cover him and lift him up while he paddled, but he always kept his eye open for big waves that might hurt. He was two weeks learning to use his flippers; and all that while he floundered in and out of the water, and coughed and grunted and crawled up the beach and took cat-naps on the sand, and went back again, until at last he found that he truly belonged to the water.

Then you can imagine the times that he had with his companions, ducking under the rollers; or coming in on top of a comber and landing with a swash and a splutter as the big wave went whirling far up the beach; or standing up on his tail and scratching his head as the old people did; or playing "I'm the King of the Castle" on slippery, weedy rocks that just stuck out of the wash. Now and then he would see a thin fin, like a big shark's fin, drifting along close to shore, and he knew that that was the Killer Whale, the Grampus, who eats young seals when he can get them; and Kotick would head for the beach like an arrow, and the fin would jig off slowly, as if it were looking for nothing at all.

Late in October the seals began to leave St. Paul's for the deep sea, by families and tribes, and there was no more fighting over the nurseries, and the holluschickie played anywhere they liked. "Next year," said Matkah to Kotick, "you will be a holluschickie; but this year you must learn how to catch fish."

They set out together across the Pacific, and Matkah showed Kotick how to sleep on his back with his flippers tucked down by his side and his little nose just out of the water. No cradle is so comfortable as the long, rocking swell of the Pacific. When Kotick felt his skin tingle all over, Matkah told him he was learning the "feel of the water," and that tingly, prickly feelings meant bad weather coming, and he must swim hard and get away.

"In a little time," she said, "you'll know where to swim to, but just now we'll follow Sea Pig, the Porpoise, for he is very wise." A school of porpoises were ducking and tearing through the water, and little Kotick followed them as fast as he could. "How do you know where to go?" he panted. The leader of the school rolled his white eyes, and ducked under. "My tail tingles, youngster," he said. "That means there's a gale behind me. Come along! When you're south of the Sticky Water [he meant the Equator], and your tail tingles, that means there's a gale in front of you and you must head north. Come along! The water feels bad here."

This was one of the very many things that Kotick learned, and he was always learning. Matkah taught him to follow the cod and the halibut along the under-sea banks, and wrench the rockling out of his hole among the weeds; how to skirt the wrecks lying a hundred fathoms below water, and dart like a rifle-bullet in at one port-hole and out at another as the fishes ran; how to dance on the top of the waves when the lightning was racing all over the sky, and wave his flipper politely to the stumpy-tailed Albatross and the Man-of-war Hawk as they went down the wind; how to jump three or four feet clear of the water, like a dolphin, flippers close to the side and tail curved; to leave the flying-fish alone because they are all bony; to take the shoulder-piece out of a cod at full speed ten fathoms deep; and never to stop and look at a boat or a ship, but particularly a row-boat. At the end of six months, what Kotick did not know about deep-sea fishing was not worth the knowing, and all that time he never set flipper on dry ground.

One day, however, as he was lying half asleep in the warm water somewhere off the Island of Juan Fernandez, he felt faint and lazy all over, just as human people do when the spring is in their legs, and he remembered the good firm beaches of Novastoshnah seven thousand miles away, the games his companions played, the smell of the sea-weed, the seal roar, and the fighting. That very minute he turned north, swimming steadily, and as he went on he met scores of his mates, all bound for the same place, and they said: "Greeting, Kotick! This year we are all holluschickie, and we can dance the Fire-dance in the breakers off Lukannon and play on the new grass. But where did you get that coat?"

Kotick's fur was almost pure white now, and though he felt very proud of it, he only said: "Swim quickly! My bones are aching for the land!" And so they all came to the beaches where they had been born, and heard the old seals, their fathers, fighting in the rolling mist.

That night Kotick danced the Fire-dance with the yearling seals. The sea is full of fire on summer nights all the way down from Novastoshnah to Lukannon, and each seal leaves a wake like burning oil behind him, and a flaming flash when he jumps, and the waves break in great phosphorescent streaks and swirls. Then they went inland to the holluschickie grounds, and rolled up and down in the new wild wheat, and told stories of what they had done while they had been at sea. They talked about the Pacific as boys would talk about a wood that they had been nutting in, and if any one had understood them, he could have gone away and made such a chart of that ocean as never was. The three- and four-year-old holluschickie romped down from Hutchinson's Hill, crying: "Out of the way, youngsters! The sea is deep, and you don't know all that's in it yet. Wait till you've rounded the Horn. Hi, you yearling, where did you get that white coat?"

"I didn't get it," said Kotick, "it grew." And just as he was going to roll the speaker over, a couple of black-haired men with flat red faces came from behind a sand-dune, and Kotick, who had never seen a man before, coughed and lowered his head. The holluschickie just bundled off a few yards and sat staring stupidly. The men were no less than Kerick Booterin, the chief of the seal-hunters on the island, and Patalamon, his son. They came from the little village not half a mile from the seal-nurseries, and they were deciding what seals they would drive up to the killing-pens (for the seals were driven just like sheep), to be turned into sealskin jackets later on.

"Ho!" said Patalamon. "Look! There's a white seal!"

Kerick Booterin turned nearly white under his oil and smoke, for he was an Aleut, and Aleuts are not clean people. Then he began to mutter a prayer. "Don't touch him, Patalamon. There has never been a white seal since— since I was born. Perhaps it is old Zaharrof's ghost. He was lost last year in the big gale."

"I'm not going near him," said Patalamon. "He's unlucky. Do you really think he is old Zaharrof come back? I owe him for some gulls' eggs."

"Don't look at him," said Kerick. "Head off that drove of four-year-olds. The men ought to skin two hundred to-day, but it's the beginning of the season, and they are new to the work. A hundred will do. Quick!"

Patalamon rattled a pair of seal's shoulder-bones in front of a herd of holluschickie, and they stopped dead, puffing and blowing. Then he stepped near, and the seals began to move, and Kerick headed them inland, and they never tried to get back to their companions. Hundreds and hundreds of thousands of seals watched them being driven, but they went on playing just the same. Kotick was the only one who asked questions, and none of his companions could tell him anything, except that the men always drove seals in that way for six weeks or two months of every year.

"I am going to follow," he said, and his eyes nearly popped out of his head as he shuffled along in the wake of the herd.

"The white seal is coming after us," cried Patalamon. "That's the first time a seal has ever come to the killing-grounds alone."

"Hsh! Don't look behind you," said Kerick. "It *is* Zaharrof's ghost!

I must speak to the priest about this."

The distance to the killing-grounds was only half a mile, but it took an hour to cover, because if the seals went too fast Kerick knew that they would get heated and then their fur would come off in patches when they were skinned. So they went on very slowly, past Sea-Lion's Neck, past Webster House, till they came to the Salt House just beyond the sight of the seals on the beach. Kotick followed, panting and wondering. He thought that he was at the world's end, but the roar of the seal-nurseries behind him sounded as loud as the roar of a train in a tunnel. Then Kerick sat down on the moss and pulled out a heavy pewter watch and let the drove cool off for thirty minutes, and Kotick could hear the fog-dew dripping from the brim of his cap. Then ten or twelve men, each with an iron-bound club three or four feet long, came up, and Kerick pointed out one or two of the drove that were bitten by their companions or were too hot, and the men kicked those aside with their heavy boots made of the skin of a walrus's throat, and then Kerick said: "Let's go!" and then the men clubbed the seals on the head as fast as they could.

Ten minutes later little Kotick did not recognize his friends any more, for their skins were ripped off from the nose to the hind-flippers—whipped off and thrown down on the ground in a pile.

That was enough for Kotick. He turned and galloped (a seal can gallop very swiftly for a short time) back to the sea, his little new moustache bristling with horror. At Sea-Lion's Neck, where the great sea-lions sit on the edge of the surf, he flung himself flipper over head into the cool water, and rocked there, gasping miserably. "What's here?" said a sea-lion gruffly; for as a rule the sea-lions keep themselves to themselves.

"*Scoochnie! Ochen scoochnie!*" ("I'm lonesome, very lonesome!") said Kotick. "They're killing *all* the holluschickie on *all* the beaches!"

The sea-lion turned his head inshore. "Nonsense!" he said; "your friends are making as much noise as ever. You must have seen old Kerick polishing off a drove. He's done that for thirty years."

"It's horrible," said Kotick, backing water as a wave went over him, and steadying himself with a screw-stroke of his flippers that brought him up all standing within three inches of a jagged edge of rock.

"Well done for a yearling!" said the sea-lion, who could appreciate good swimming. "I suppose it *is* rather awful from your way of looking at it; but if you seals will come here year after year, of course the men get to know of it, and unless you can find an island where no men ever come, you will always be driven."

"Isn't there any such island?" began Kotick.

"I've followed the *poltoos* [the halibut] for twenty years, and I can't say I've found it yet. But look here—you seem to have a fondness for talking to your betters; suppose you go to Walrus Islet and talk to Sea Vitch. He may know something. Don't flounce off like that. It's a six-mile swim, and if I were you I should haul out and take a nap first, little one."

Kotick thought that that was good advice, so he swam round to his own beach, hauled out, and slept for half an hour, twitching all over, as seals will. Then he headed straight for Walrus Islet, a little low sheet of rocky island almost due northeast from Novastoshnah, all ledges of rock and gulls' nests, where the walrus herded by themselves.

He landed close to old Sea Vitch—the big, ugly, bloated, pimpled, fat-necked, long-tusked walrus of the North Pacific, who has no manners except when he is asleep—as he was then, with his hind-flippers half in and half out of the surf.

"Wake up!" barked Kotick, for the gulls were making a great noise.

"Hah! Ho! Humph! What's that?" said Sea Vitch, and he struck the next walrus a blow with his tusks and waked him up, and the next struck the next, and so on till they were all awake and staring in every direction but the right one.

"Hi! It's me," said Kotick, bobbing in the surf and looking like a little white slug.

"Well! May I be-skinned!" said Sea Vitch, and they all looked at Kotick as you can fancy a club full of drowsy old gentlemen would look at a little boy. Kotick did not care to hear any more about skinning just then; he had seen enough of it; so he called out: "Isn't there any place for seals to go where men don't ever come?"

"Go and find out," said Sea Vitch, shutting his eyes. "Run away. We're busy here."

Kotick made his dolphin-jump in the air and shouted as loud as he could: "Clam-eater! Clam-eater!" He knew that Sea Vitch never caught a fish in his life, but always rooted for clams and sea-weeds, though he pretended to be a very terrible person. Naturally the Chickies and the Gooverooskies and the Epatkas, the Burgomaster Gulls and the Kittiwakes and the Puffins, who are always looking for a chance to be rude, took up the cry, and—so Limmershin told me—for nearly five minutes you could not have heard a gun fired on Walrus Islet. All the population was yelling and screaming: "Clam-eater! *Stareek* [old man]!" while Sea Vitch rolled from side to side grunting and coughing.

"*Now* will you tell?" said Kotick, all out of breath.

"Go and ask Sea Cow," said Sea Vitch. "If he is living still, he'll be able to tell you."

"How shall I know Sea Cow when I meet him?" said Kotick, sheering off.

"He's the only thing in the sea uglier than Sea Vitch," screamed a Burgomaster Gull, wheeling under Sea Vitch's nose. "Uglier, and with worse manners! *Stareek!*"

Kotick swam back to Novastoshnah, leaving the gulls to scream. There he found that no one sympathised with him in his little attempts to discover a quiet place for the seals They told him that men had always driven the holluschickie—it was part of the day's work—and that if he did not like to see ugly things he should not have gone to the killing-grounds. But none of the other seals had seen the killing, and that made the difference between him and his friends. Besides, Kotick was a white seal.

"What you must do," said old Sea Catch, after he had heard his son's adventures, "is to grow up and be a big seal like your father, and have a nursery on the beach, and then they will leave you alone. In another five years you ought to be able to fight for yourself." Even gentle Matkah, his mother, said: "You will never be able to stop the killing. Go and play in the sea, Kotick." And Kotick went off and danced the Fire-dance with a very heavy little heart.

That autumn he left the beach as soon as he could, and set off alone because of a notion in his bullet-head. He was going to find Sea Cow, if there was such a person in the sea, and he was going to find a quiet island with good firm beaches for seals to live on, where men could not get at them. So he explored and explored by himself from the North to the South Pacific, swimming as much as three hundred miles in a day and a night. He met with more adventures than can be told, and narrowly escaped being caught by the Basking Shark, and the Spotted Shark, and the Hammerhead, and he met all the untrustworthy ruffians that loaf up and down the seas, and the heavy polite fish, and the scarlet-spotted scallops that are moored in one place for hundreds of years, and grow very proud of it; but he never met Sea Cow, and he never found an island that he could fancy.

If the beach was good and hard, with a slope behind it for seals to play on, there was always the smoke of a whaler on the horizon, boiling down blubber, and Kotick knew what *that* meant. Or else he could see that seals had once visited the island and been killed off and Kotick knew that where men had come once they would come again.

He picked up with an old stumpy-tailed albatross, who told him that Kerguelen Island was the very place for peace and quiet, and when Kotick went down there he was all but smashed to pieces against some wicked black cliffs in a heavy sleet-storm with lightning and thunder. Yet as he pulled out against the gale he could see that even there had once been a seal-nursery. And so it was in all the other islands that he visited.

Limmershin gave a long list of them, for he said that Kotick spent five seasons exploring with a four months' rest each year at Novastoshnah, when the holluschickie used to make fun of him and his imaginary islands. He went to the Galápagos, a horrid dry place on the Equator, where he was nearly baked to death; he went to the Georgia Islands, the South Orkneys, Emerald Island, Little Nightingale Island, Gough's Island, Bouvet's Island, the Crossets, and even to a little speck of an island south of the Cape of Good Hope. But everywhere the People of the Sea told him the same things. Seals had come to those islands once upon a time, but men had killed them all off. Even when he swam thousands of miles out of the Pacific, and got to a place called Cape Corrientes (that was when he was coming back from Gough's Island), he found a few hundred mangy seals on a rock, and they told him that men came there too.

That nearly broke his heart, and he headed round the Horn back to his own beaches; and on his way north he hauled out on an island full of green trees, where he found an old, old seal who was dying, and Kotick caught fish for him, and told him all his sorrows. "Now," said Kotick, "I am going back to Novastoshnah, and if I am driven to the killing-pens with the holluschickie I shall not care."

The old seal said: "Try once more. I am the last of the Lost Rookery of Masafuera, and in the days when men killed us by the hundred thousand there was a story on the beaches that some day a white seal would come out of the north and lead the seal people to a quiet place. I am old and I shall never live to see that day, but others will. Try once more."

And Kotick curled up his moustache (it was a beauty), and said: "I am the only white seal that has ever been born on the beaches, and I am the only seal, black or white, who ever thought of looking for new islands."

That cheered him immensely; and when he came back to Novastoshnah that summer, Matkah, his mother, begged him to marry and settle down, for he was no longer a holluschick, but a full-grown sea catch, with a curly white mane on his shoulders, as heavy, as big, and as fierce as his father. "Give me another season," he said. "Remember, Mother, it is always the seventh wave that goes farthest up the beach."

Curiously enough, there was another seal who thought that she would put off marrying till the next year, and Kotick danced the Fire-dance with her all down Lukannon Beach the night before he set off on his last exploration.

This time he went westward, because he had fallen on the trail of a great shoal of halibut, and he needed at least one hundred pounds of fish a day to keep him in good condition. He chased them till he was tired, and then he curled himself up and went to sleep on the hollows of the ground-swell that sets in to Copper Island. He knew the coast perfectly well, so about midnight, when he felt himself gently bumped on a weed-bed, he said, "Hm, tide's running strong tonight," and turning over underwater opened his eyes slowly and stretched. Then he jumped like a cat, for he saw huge things nosing about in the shoal water and browsing on the heavy fringes of the weeds.

"By the Great Combers of Magellan!" he said, beneath his moustache. "Who in the Deep Sea are these people?"

They were like no walrus, seal-lion, seal, bear, whale, shark, fish, squid, or scallop that Kotick had ever seen before. They were between twenty and thirty feet long, and they had no hind-flippers, but a shovel-like tail that looked as if it had been whittled out of wet leather. Their heads were the most foolish-looking things you ever saw, and they balanced on the ends of their tails in deep water when they weren't grazing, bowing solemnly to one another and waving their front flippers as a fat man waves his arm.

"Ahem!" said Kotick. "Good sport, gentlemen?" The big things answered by bowing and waving their flippers like the Frog-Footman. When they began feeding again Kotick saw that their upper lip was split into two pieces that they could twitch apart about a foot and bring together again with a whole bushel of sea-weed between the splits. They tucked the stuff into their mouths and chumped solemnly.

"Messy style of feeding, that," said Kotick. They bowed again, and

Kotick began to lose his temper "Very good," he said. "If you do happen to have an extra joint in your front flipper you needn't show off so. I see you bow gracefully, but I should like to know your names." The split lips moved and twitched, and the glassy green eyes stared; but they did not speak.

"Well!" said Kotick, "you're the only people I've ever met uglier than Sea Vitch—and with worse manners."

Then he remembered in a flash what the Burgomaster Gull had screamed to him when he was a little yearling at Walrus Islet, and he tumbled backward in the water, for he knew that he had found Sea Cow at last.

The sea cows went on schlooping and grazing and chumping in the weeds, and Kotick asked them questions in every language that he had picked up in his travels: and the Sea People talk nearly as many languages as human beings. But the Sea Cow did not answer, because Sea Cow cannot talk. He has only six bones in his neck where he ought to have seven, and they say under the sea that that prevents him from speaking even to his companions; but, as you know, he has an extra joint in his fore-flipper, and by waving it up and down and about he makes a sort of clumsy telegraphic code.

By daylight Kotick's mane was standing on end and his temper was gone where the dead crabs go. Then the Sea Cow began to travel northward very slowly, stopping to hold absurd bowing councils from time to time, and Kotick followed them, saying to himself: "People who are such idiots as these are would have been killed long ago if they hadn't found out some safe island; and what is good enough for the Sea Cow is good enough for the Sea Catch. All the same, I wish they'd hurry."

It was weary work for Kotick. The herd never went more than forty or fifty miles a day, and stopped to feed at night, and kept close to the shore all the time; while Kotick swam round them, and over them, and under them, but he could not hurry them on one half-mile. As they went farther north they held a bowing council every few hours, and Kotick nearly bit off his moustache with impatience till he saw that they were following up a warm current of water, and then he respected them more.

One night they sank through the shiny water—sank like stones—and, for the first time since he had known them, began to swim quickly. Kotick followed, and the pace astonished him, for he never dreamed that Sea Cow was anything of a swimmer. They headed for a cliff by the shore—a cliff that ran down into deep water, and plunged into a dark hole at the foot of it, twenty fathoms under the sea. It was a long, long swim, and Kotick badly wanted fresh air before he was out of the dark tunnel that they led him through.

"My wig!" he said, when he rose, gasping and puffing, into open water at the farther end. "It was a long dive, but it was worth it."

The sea cows had separated, and were browsing lazily along the edges of the finest beaches that Kotick had ever seen. There were long stretches of smooth-worn rock running for miles, exactly fitted to make seal-nurseries, and there were playgrounds of hard sand sloping inland behind them, and there were rollers for seals to dance in, and long grass to roll in, and sand-dunes to climb up and down; and, best of all, Kotick knew by the feel of the water, which never deceives a true Sea Catch, that no men had ever come there.

The first thing he did was to assure himself that the fishing was good, and then he swam along the beaches and counted up the delightful low sandy islands half hidden in the beautiful rolling fog. Away to the north-ward out to sea ran a line of bars and shoals and rocks that would never let a ship come within six miles of the beach; and between the islands and the mainland was a stretch of deep water that ran up to the perpendicular cliffs, and somewhere below the cliffs was the mouth of the tunnel.

"It's Novastoshnah over again, but ten times better," said Kotick. "Sea Cow must be wiser than I thought. Men can't come down the cliffs, even if there were any men; and the shoals to seaward would knock a ship to splinters. If any place in the sea is safe, this is it."

He began to think of the seal he had left behind him, but though he was in a hurry to go back to Novastoshnah, he thoroughly explored the new country, so that he would be able to answer all questions.

Then he dived and made sure of the mouth of the tunnel, and raced through to the southward. No one but a sea cow or a seal would have dreamed of there being such a place, and when he looked back at the cliffs even Kotick could hardly believe that he had been under them.

He was six days going home, though he was not swimming slowly; and when he hauled out just above Sea-Lion's Neck the first person he met was the seal who had been waiting for him, and she saw by the look in his eyes that he had found his island at last.

But the holluschickie and Sea Catch, his father, and all the other seals, laughed at him when he told them what he had discovered, and a young seal about his own age said: "This is all very well, Kotick, but you can't come from no one knows where and order us off like this. Remember we've been fighting for our nurseries, and that's a thing you never did. You preferred prowling about in the sea."

The other seals laughed at this, and the young seal began twisting his head from side to side. He had just married that year, and was making a great fuss about it.

"I've no nursery to fight for," said Kotick. "I want only to show you all a place where you will be safe. What's the use of fighting?"

"Oh, if you're trying to back out, of course I've no more to say," said the young seal, with an ugly chuckle.

"Will you come with me if I win?" said Kotick; and a green light came into his eyes, for he was very angry at having to fight at all.

"Very good," said the young seal carelessly. "*If* you win, I'll come."

He had no time to change his mind, for Kotick's head darted out and his teeth sunk in the blubber of the young seal's neck. Then he threw himself back on his haunches and hauled his enemy down the beach, shook him, and knocked him over. Then Kotick roared to the seals: "I've done my best for you these five seasons past. I've found you the island where you'll be safe, but unless your heads are dragged off your silly necks you won't believe. I'm going to teach you now. Look out for yourselves!"

Limmershin told me that never in his life—and Limmershin sees ten thousand big seals fighting every year—never in all his little life did he see anything like Kotick's charge into the nurseries. He flung himself at the biggest sea catch he could find, caught him by the throat, choked him and bumped him and banged him till he grunted for mercy, and then threw him aside and attacked the next. You see, Kotick had never fasted for four months as the big seals did every year, and his deep-sea swimming-trips kept him in perfect condition, and, best of all, he had never fought before. His curly white mane stood up with rage, and his eyes flamed, and his big dog-teeth glistened, and he was splendid to look at.

Old Sea Catch, his father, saw him tearing past, hauling the grizzled old seals about as though they had been halibut, and upsetting the young bachelors in all directions; and Sea Catch gave one roar and shouted: "He may be a fool, but he is the best fighter on the beaches. Don't tackle your father, my son! He's with you!"

Kotick roared in answer, and old Sea Catch waddled in, his moustache on end, blowing like a locomotive, while Matkah and the seal that was going to marry Kotick cowered down and admired their men-folk. It was a gorgeous fight, for the two fought as long as there was a seal that dared lift up his head, and then they paraded grandly up and down the beach side by side, bellowing.

At night, just as the Northern Lights were winking and flashing through the fog, Kotick climbed a bare rock and looked down on the scattered nurseries and the torn and bleeding seals. "Now," he said, "I've taught you your lesson."

"My wig!" said old Sea Catch, boosting himself up stiffly, for he was fearfully mauled. "The Killer Whale himself could not have cut them up worse. Son, I'm proud of you, and what's more, *I'll* come with you to your island—if there is such a place."

"Here, you fat pigs of the sea! Who comes with me to the Sea Cow's tunnel? Answer, or I shall teach you again," roared Kotick.

There was a murmur like the ripple of the tide all up and down the beaches. "We will come," said thousands of tired voices. "We will follow Kotick, the White Seal."

Then Kotick dropped his head between his shoulders and shut his eyes proudly. He was not a white seal any more, but red from head to tail. All the same, he would have scorned to look at or touch one of his wounds.

A week later he and his army (nearly ten thousand holluschickie and old seals) went away north to the Sea Cow's tunnel, Kotick leading them, and the seals that stayed at Novastoshnah called them idiots. But next spring, when they all met off the fishing-banks of the Pacific, Kotick's seals told such tales of the new beaches beyond Sea Cow's tunnel that more and more seals left Novastoshnah.

Of course it was not all done at once, for the seals need a long time to turn things over in their minds, but year by year more seals went away from Novastoshnah, and Lukannon, and the other nurseries, to the quiet, sheltered beaches where Kotick sits all the summer through, getting bigger and fatter and stronger each year, while the holluschickie play round him, in that sea where no man comes.

Stickeen

J O H N   M U I R

*One of America's foremost naturalists and explorers, Scottish-born John Muir
(1838–1914) was a frequent visitor to Alaska. An indefatigable walker, Muir
traveled thousands of miles by foot in the United States, Canada, and Mexico.
He settled in California and worked to establish America's first forestlands
and national parks. His books include* The Mountains of California
(1894), Our National Parks *(1901),* The Yosemite *(1912),* Travels in
Alaska *(1914), and* Stickeen *(1909), excerpted here, which is a tribute to the
loyal dog who shared many of his Alaskan adventures.*

In the summer of 1880 I set out from Fort Wrangel in a canoe to continue the exploration of the icy region of southeastern Alaska, begun
in the fall of 1879. After the necessary provisions, blankets, etc., had
been collected and stowed away, and my Indian crew were in their
places ready to start, while a crowd of their relatives and friends on
the wharf were bidding them good-by and good-luck, my companion, the
Rev. S. H. Young, for whom we were waiting, at last came aboard, followed
by a little black dog, that immediately made himself at home by curling up
in a hollow among the baggage. I like dogs, but this one seemed so small
and worthless that I objected to his going, and asked the missionary why he
was taking him.

"Such a little helpless creature will only be in the way," I said; "you had
better pass him up to the Indian boys on the wharf, to be taken home to
play with the children. This trip is not likely to be good for toy-dogs. The
poor silly thing will be in rain and snow for weeks or months, and will
require care like a baby."

But his master assured me that he would be no trouble at all; that he was
a perfect wonder of a dog, could endure cold and hunger like a bear, swim
like a seal, and was wondrous wise and cunning, etc., making out a list of
virtues to show he might be the most interesting member of the party.

Nobody could hope to unravel the lines of his ancestry. In all the wonderfully mixed and varied dog-tribe I never saw any creature very much like him, though in some of his sly, soft, gliding motions and gestures he brought the fox to mind. He was short-legged and bunchy-bodied, and his hair, though smooth, was long and silky and slightly waved, so that when the wind was at his back it ruffled, making him look shaggy. At first sight his only noticeable feature was his fine tail, which was about as airy and shady as a squirrel's, and was carried curling forward almost to his nose. On closer inspection you might notice his thin sensitive ears, and sharp eyes with cunning tan-spots above them. Mr. Young told me that when the little fellow was a pup about the size of a woodrat he was presented to his wife by an Irish prospector at Sitka, and that on his arrival at Fort Wrangel he was adopted with enthusiasm by the Stickeen Indians as a sort of new good-luck totem, was named "Stickeen" for the tribe, and became a universal favorite; petted, protected, and admired wherever he went, and regarded as a mysterious fountain of wisdom.

On our trip he soon proved himself a queer character—odd, concealed, independent, keeping invincibly quiet, and doing many little puzzling things that piqued my curiosity. As we sailed week after week through the long intricate channels and inlets among the innumerable islands and mountains of the coast, he spent most of the dull days in sluggish ease, motionless, and apparently as unobserving as if in deep sleep. But I discovered that somehow he always knew what was going on. When the Indians were about to shoot at ducks or seals, or when anything along the shore was exciting our attention, he would rest his chin on the edge of the canoe and calmly look out like a dreamy-eyed tourist. And when he heard us talking about making a landing, he immediately roused himself to see what sort of a place we were coming to, and made ready to jump overboard and swim ashore as soon as the canoe neared the beach. Then, with a vigorous shake to get rid of the brine in his hair, he ran into the woods to hunt small game. But though always the first out of the canoe, he was always the last to get into it. When we were ready to start he could never be found, and refused to come to our call. We soon found out, however, that though we could not see him at such times, he saw us, and from the cover of the briers and huckleberry bushes in the fringe of the woods was watching the canoe with wary eye. For as soon as we were fairly off he came trotting down the beach, plunged into the surf, and swam after us, knowing well that we would cease rowing and take him in. When the contrary little vagabond came alongside, he was lifted by the neck, held at arm's length a moment to drip, and dropped aboard. We tried to cure him of this trick by compelling him to swim a long way, as if we had a mind to abandon him; but this did no good: the longer the swim the better he seemed to like it.

Though capable of great idleness, he never failed to be ready for all sorts of adventures and excursions. One pitch-dark rainy night we landed about ten o'clock at the mouth of a salmon stream when the water was phosphorescent. The salmon were running, and the myriad fins of the onrushing multitude were churning all the stream into a silvery glow, wonderfully beautiful and impressive in the ebon darkness. To get a good view of the show I set out with one of the Indians and sailed up through the midst of it to the foot of a rapid about half a mile from camp, where the swift current dashing over rocks made the luminous glow most glorious. Happening to look back down the stream, while the Indian was catching a few of the struggling fish, I saw a long spreading fan of light like the tail of a comet, which we thought must be made by some big strange animal that was pursuing us. On it came with its magnificent train, until we imagined we could see the monster's head and eyes; but it was only Stickeen, who, finding I had left the camp, came swimming after me to see what was up. When we camped early, the best hunter of the crew usually went to the woods for a deer, and Stickeen was sure to be at his heels, provided I had not gone out. For, strange to say, though I never carried a gun, he always followed me, forsaking the hunter and even his master to share my wanderings. The days that were too stormy for sailing I spent in the woods, or on the adjacent mountains, wherever my studies called me; and Stickeen always insisted on going with me, however wild the weather, gliding like a fox through dripping huckleberry bushes and thorny tangles of panax and rubus, scarce stirring their rain-laden leaves; wading and wallowing through snow, swimming icy streams, skipping over logs and rocks and the crevasses of glaciers with the patience and endurance of a determined mountaineer, never tiring or getting discouraged. Once he followed me over a glacier the surface of which was so crusty and rough that it cut his feet until every step was marked with blood; but he trotted on with Indian fortitude until I noticed his red track, and, taking pity on him, made him a set of moccasins out of a handkerchief. However great his troubles he never asked help or made any complaint, as if, like a philosopher, he had learned that without hard work and suffering there could be no pleasure worth having.

Yet none of us was able to make out what Stickeen was really good for. He seemed to meet danger and hardships without anything like reason, insisted on having his own way, never obeyed an order, and the hunter could never set him on anything, or make him fetch the birds he shot. His equanimity was so steady it seemed due to want of feeling; ordinary storms were pleasures to him, and as for mere rain, he flourished in it like a vegetable. No matter what advances you might make, scarce a glance or a tail-wag would you get for your pains. But though he was apparently as cold as a glacier and about as impervious to fun, I tried hard to make his acquaintance, guessing there must be something worthwhile hidden beneath so much courage, endurance, and love of wild-weathery adventure. No super-annuated mastiff or bulldog grown old in office surpassed this fluffy midget in stoic dignity. He sometimes reminded me of a small, squat, unshakable desert cactus. For he never displayed a single trace of the merry, tricksy, elfish fun of the terriers and collies that we all know, nor of their touching affection and devotion. Like children, most small dogs beg to be loved and allowed to love; but Stickeen seemed a very Diogenes, asking only to be let alone: a true child of the wilderness, holding the even tenor of his hidden life with the silence and serenity of nature. His strength of character lay in his eyes. They looked as old as the hills, and as young, and as wild. I never tired of looking into them: it was like looking into a landscape; but they were small and rather deep-set, and had no explaining lines around them to give out particulars. I was accustomed to look into the faces of plants and animals, and I watched the little sphinx more and more keenly as an interesting study. But there is no estimating the wit and wisdom concealed and latent in our lower fellow mortals until made manifest by profound experiences; for it is through suffering that dogs as well as saints are developed and made perfect.

After we had explored the Sundum and Takhoo fiords and their glaciers, we sailed through Stephen's Passage into Lynn Canal and thence through Icy Strait into Cross Sound, searching for unexplored inlets leading toward the great fountain ice-fields of the Fairweather Range. Here, while the tide was in our favor, we were accompanied by a fleet of icebergs drifting out to the ocean from Glacier Bay. Slowly we paddled around Vancouver's Point, Wimbleton, our frail canoe tossed like a feather on the massive heaving swells coming in past Cape Spenser. For miles the sound is bounded by precipitous mural cliffs, which, lashed with wave-spray and their heads hidden in clouds, looked terribly threatening and stern. Had our canoe been crushed or upset we could have made no landing here, for the cliffs, as high as those of Yosemite, sink sheer into deep water. Eagerly we scanned the wall on the north side for the first sign of an opening fiord or harbor, all of us anxious except Stickeen, who dozed in peace or gazed dreamily at the tremendous precipices when he heard us talking about them. At length we made the joyful discovery of the mouth of the inlet now called "Taylor Bay," and about five o'clock reached the head of it and encamped in a spruce grove near the front of a large glacier.

While camp was being made, Joe the hunter climbed the mountain wall on the east side of the fiord in pursuit of wild goats, while Mr. Young and I went to the glacier. We found that it is separated from the waters of the inlet by a tide-washed moraine, and extends, an abrupt barrier, all the way across from wall to wall of the inlet, a distance of about three miles. But our most interesting discovery was that it had recently advanced, though again slightly receding. A portion of the terminal moraine had been plowed up and shoved forward, uprooting and overwhelming the woods on the east side. Many of the trees were down and buried, or nearly so, others were leaning away from the ice-cliffs, ready to fall, and some stood erect, with the bottom of the ice-plow still beneath their roots and its lofty crystal spires towering high above their tops. The spectacle presented by these century-old trees standing close beside a spiry wall of ice, with their branches almost touching it, was most novel and striking. And when I climbed around the front, and a little way up the west side of the glacier, I found that it had swelled and increased in height and width in accordance with its advance, and carried away the outer ranks of trees on its bank.

On our way back to camp after these first observations I planned a far-and-wide excursion for the morrow. I awoke early, called not only by the glacier, which had been on my mind all night, but by a grand flood-storm. The wind was blowing a gale from the north and the rain was flying with the clouds in a wide passionate horizontal flood, as if it were all passing over the country instead of falling on it. The main perennial streams were booming high above their banks, and hundreds of new ones, roaring like the sea, almost covered the lofty gray walls of the inlet with white cascades and falls. I had intended making a cup of coffee and getting something like a breakfast before starting, but when I heard the storm and looked out I made haste to join it; for many of Nature's finest lessons are to be found in her storms, and if careful to keep in right relations with them, we may go safely abroad with them, rejoicing in the grandeur and beauty of their works and ways, and chanting with the old Norsemen, "The blast of the tempest aids our oars, the hurricane is our servant and drives us whither we wish to go." So, omitting breakfast, I put a piece of bread in my pocket and hurried away.

Mr. Young and the Indians were asleep, and so, I hoped, was Stickeen; but I had not gone a dozen rods before he left his bed in the tent and came boring through the blast after me. That a man should welcome storms for their exhilarating music and motion, and go forth to see God making land-scapes, is reasonable enough; but what fascination could there be in such tremendous weather for a dog? Surely nothing akin to human enthusiasm for scenery or geology. Anyhow, on he came, breakfastless, through the choking blast. I stopped and did my best to turn him back. "Now don't," I said, shouting to make myself heard in the storm, "now don't, Stickeen. What has got into your queer noddle now? You must be daft. This wild day has nothing for you. There is no game abroad, nothing but weather. Go back to camp and keep warm, get a good breakfast with your master, and be sensible for once. I can't carry you all day or feed you, and this storm will kill you."

But Nature, it seems, was at the bottom of the affair, and she gains her ends with dogs as well as with men, making us do as she likes, shoving and pulling us along her ways, however rough, all but killing us at times in get-ting her lessons driven hard home. After I had stopped again and again, shouting good warning advice, I saw that he was not to be shaken off; as well might the earth try to shake off the moon. I had once led his master into trouble, when he fell on one of the topmost jags of a mountain and dis-located his arm; now the turn of his humble companion was coming. The pitiful little wanderer just stood there in the wind, drenched and blinking, saying doggedly, "Where thou goest I will go." So at last I told him to come on if he must, and gave him a piece of the bread I had in my pocket; then we struggled on together, and thus began the most memorable of all my wild days.

The level flood, driving hard in our faces, thrashed and washed us wildly until we got into the shelter of a grove on the east side of the glacier near the front, where we stopped awhile for breath and to listen and look out. The exploration of the glacier was my main object, but the wind was too high to allow excursions over its open surface, where one might be dangerously

shoved while balancing for a jump on the brink of a crevasse. In the meantime the storm was a fine study. Here the end of the glacier, descending an
abrupt swell of resisting rock about five hundred feet high, leans forward
and falls in ice cascades. And as the storm came down the glacier from the
North, Stickeen and I were beneath the main current of the blast, while
favorably located to see and hear it. What a psalm the storm was singing,
and how fresh the smell of the washed earth and leaves, and how sweet the
still small voices of the storm! Detached wafts and swirls were coming
through the woods, with music from the leaves and branches and furrowed
boles, and even from the splintered rocks and ice-crags overhead, many of
the tones soft and low and flute-like, as if each leaf and tree, crag and spire
were a tuned reed. A broad torrent, draining the side of the glacier, now
swollen by scores of new streams from the mountains, was rolling boulders
along its rocky channel, with thudding, bumping, muffled sounds, rushing
towards the bay with tremendous energy, as if in haste to get out of the
mountains; the waters above and beneath calling to each other, and all to
the ocean, their home.

Looking southward from our shelter, we had this great torrent and the
forested mountain wall above it on our left, the spiry ice-crags on our right,
and smooth gray gloom ahead. I tried to draw the marvelous scene in my
note-book, but the rain blurred the page in spite of all my pains to shelter
it, and the sketch was almost worthless. When the wind began to abate, I
traced the east side of the glacier. All the trees standing on the edge of the
woods were barked and bruised, showing high-ice marks in a very telling
way, while tens of thousands of those that had stood for centuries on the
bank of the glacier farther out lay crushed and being crushed. In many
places I could see down fifty feet or so beneath the margin of the glacier-
mill, where trunks from one to two feet in diameter were being ground to
pulp against outstanding rock-ribs and bosses of the bank.

About three miles above the front of the glacier I climbed to the surface
of it by means of axe-steps made easy for Stickeen. As far as the eye could
reach, the level, or nearly level, glacier stretched away indefinitely beneath
the gray sky, a seemingly boundless prairie of ice. The rain continued, and
grew colder, which I did not mind, but a dim snowy look in the drooping
clouds made me hesitate about venturing far from land. No trace of the west
shore was visible, and in case the clouds should settle and give snow, or the
wind again become violent, I feared getting caught in a tangle of crevasses.

Snow-crystals, the flowers of the mountain clouds, are frail, beautiful things, but terrible when flying on storm-winds in darkening, benumbing swarms, or, when welded together into glaciers full of deadly crevasses. Watching the weather, I sauntered about on the crystal sea. For a mile or two out I found the ice remarkably safe. The marginal crevasses were mostly narrow, while the few wider ones were easily avoided by passing around them, and the clouds began to open there and there.

Thus encouraged, I at last pushed out for the other side; for Nature can make us do anything she likes. At first we made rapid progress, and the sky was not very threatening, while I took bearings occasionally with a pocket compass to enable me to find my way back more surely in case the storm should become blinding; but the structure lines of the glacier were my main guide. Toward the west side we came to a closely crevassed section in which we had to make long, narrow tacks and doublings, tracing the edges of tremendous transverse and longitudinal crevasses, many of which were from twenty to thirty feet wide, and perhaps a thousand feet deep—beautiful and awful. In working a way through them I was severely cautious, but Stickeen came on as unhesitating as the flying clouds. The widest crevasses that I could jump he would leap without so much as halting to take a look at it. The weather was now making quick changes, scattering bits of dazzling brightness through the wintry gloom; at rare intervals, when the sun broke forth wholly free, the glacier was seen from shore to shore with a bright array of encompassing mountains partly revealed, wearing the clouds as garments, while the prairie bloomed and sparkled with irised light from myriads of washed crystals. Then suddenly all the glorious show would be darkened and blotted out.

Stickeen seemed to care for none of these things, bright or dark, nor for the crevasses, wells, moulins, or swift flashing streams into which he might fall. The little adventurer was only about two years old, yet nothing seemed novel to him, nothing daunted him. He showed neither caution nor curiosity, wonder nor fear, but bravely trotted on as if glaciers were play-grounds. His stout, muffled body seemed all one skipping muscle, and it was truly wonderful to see how swiftly and to all appearance heedlessly he flashed across nerve-trying chasms six or eight feet wide. His courage was so unwavering that it seemed to be done to dullness of perception, as if he were only blindly bold; and I kept warning him to be careful. For we had been close companions on so many wilderness trips that I had formed the habit of talking to him as if he were a boy and understood every word.

We gained the west shore in about three hours; the width of the glacier here being about seven miles. Then I pushed northward in order to see as far back as possible into the fountains of the Fairweather Mountains, in case the clouds should rise. The walking was easy along the margin of the forest, which, of course, like that on the other side, had been invaded and crushed by the swollen, overflowing glacier. In an hour or so, after passing a massive headland, we came suddenly on a branch of the glacier, which, in the form of a magnificent ice-cascade two miles wide, was pouring over the rim of the main basin in a westerly direction, its surface broken into wave-shaped blades and shattered blocks, suggesting the wildest updashing, heaving, plunging motion of a great river cataract. Tracing it down three or four miles, I found that it discharged into a lake, filling it with icebergs.

I would gladly have followed the lake outlet to tide-water, but the day was already far spent, and the threatening sky called for haste on the return trip to get off the ice before dark. I decided therefore to go no farther, and, after taking a general view of the wonderful region, turned back, hoping to see it again under more favorable auspices. We made good speed up the cañon of the great ice-torrent, and out on the main glacier until we had left the west shore about two miles behind us. Here we got into a difficult network of crevasses, the gathering clouds began to drop misty fringes, and soon the dreaded snow came flying thick and fast. I now began to feel anxious about finding a way in the blurring storm. Stickeen showed no trace of fear. He was still the same silent, able little hero. I noticed, however, that after the storm-darkness came on he kept close up behind me. The snow urged us to make still greater haste, but at the same time hid our way. I pushed on as best I could, jumping innumerable crevasses, and for every hundred rods or so of direct advance traveling a mile in doubling up and down in the turmoil of chasms and dislocated ice-blocks. After an hour or two of this work we came to a series of longitudinal crevasses of appalling width, and almost straight and regular in trend, like immense furrows. These I traced with firm nerve, excited and strengthened by the danger, making wide jumps, poising cautiously on their dizzy edges after cutting hollows for my feet before making the spring, to avoid possible slipping or any uncertainty on the farther sides, where only one trial is granted—exercise at once frightful and inspiring. Stickeen followed seemingly without effort.

Many a mile we thus traveled, mostly up and down, making but little real headway in crossing, running instead of walking most of the time as the danger of being compelled to spend the night on the glacier became threatening. Stickeen seemed able for anything. Doubtless we could have weathered the storm for one night, dancing on a flat spot to keep from freezing, and I faced the threat without feeling anything like despair; but we were hungry and wet, and the wind from the mountains was still thick with snow and bitterly cold, so of course that night would have seemed a very long one. I could not see far enough through the burring snow to judge in which general direction the least dangerous route lay, while the few dim, momentary glimpses I caught of mountains through rifts in the flying clouds were far from encouraging either as weather signs or as guides. I had simply to grope my way from crevasses to crevasses, holding a general direction by the ice-structure, which was not to be seen everywhere, and partly by the wind. Again and again I was put to my mettle, but Stickeen followed easily, his nerve apparently growing more unflinching as the danger increased. So it always is with mountaineers when hard beset. Running hard and jumping, holding every minute of the remaining daylight, poor as it was, precious, we doggedly persevered and tried to hope that every difficult crevasse we overcame would prove to be the last of its kind. But on the contrary, as we advanced they became more deadly trying.

At length our way was barred by a very wide and straight crevasse, which I traced rapidly northward a mile or so without finding a crossing or hope of one; then down the glacier about as far, to where it united with another uncrossable crevasse. In all this distance of perhaps two miles there was only one place where I could possibly jump it, but the width of this jump was the utmost I dared attempt, while the danger of slipping on the farther side was so great that I was loath to try it. Furthermore, the side I was on was about a foot higher than the other, and even with this advantage the crevasse seemed dangerously wide. One is liable to underestimate the width of crevasses where the magnitudes in general are great. I therefore stared at this one mighty keenly, estimating its width and the shape of the edge on the farther side, until I thought that I could jump it if necessary, but that in case I should be compelled to jump back from the lower side I might fail. Now, a cautious mountaineer seldom takes a step on unknown ground which seems at all dangerous that he cannot retrace in case he should be stopped by unseen obstacles ahead. This is the rule of mountaineers who live long, and, though in haste, I compelled myself to sit down and calmly deliberate before I broke it.

Retracing my devious path in imagination as if it were drawn on a chart,
I saw that I was recrossing the glacier a mile or two farther upstream than
the course pursued in the morning, and that I was now entangled in a section I had not before seen. Should I risk this dangerous jump, or try to
regain the woods on the west shore, make a fire, and have only hunger to
endure while waiting for a new day? I had already crossed so broad a stretch
of dangerous ice that I saw it would be difficult to get back to the woods
through the storm, before dark, and the attempt would most likely result in
a dismal nightdance on the glacier; while just beyond the present barrier the
surface seemed more promising, and the east shore was now perhaps about
as near as the west. I was therefore eager to go on. But this wide jump was
a dreadful obstacle.

At length, because of the dangers already behind me, I determined to
venture against those that might be ahead, jumped and landed well, but
with so little to spare that I more than ever dreaded being compelled to take
that jump back from the lower side. Stickeen followed, making nothing of
it, and we ran eagerly forward, hoping we were leaving all our troubles
behind. But within the distance of a few hundred yards we were stopped by
the widest crevasse yet encountered. Of course I made haste to explore it,
hoping all might yet be remedied by finding a bridge or a way around either
end. About three-fourths of a mile upstream I found that it united with the
one we had just crossed, as I feared it would. Then, tracing it down, I found
it joined the same crevasse at the lower end also, maintaining throughout its
whole course a width of forty to fifty feet. Thus to my dismay I discovered
that we were on a narrow island about two miles long, with two barely possible ways of escape: one back by the way we came, the other ahead by an
almost inaccessible sliver-bridge that crossed the great crevasse from near the
middle of it!

After this nerve-trying discovery I ran back to the sliver-bridge and cautiously examined it. Crevasses, caused by strains from variations in the rate
of motion of different parts of the glacier and convexities in the channel, are
mere cracks when they first open, so narrow as hardly to admit the blade of
a pocket-knife, and gradually widen according to the extent of the strain
and the depth of the glacier. Now some of these cracks are interrupted, like
the cracks in wood, and in opening, the strip of ice between overlapping
ends is dragged out, and may maintain a continuous connection between
the sides, just as the two sides of a slivered crack in wood that is being split

are connected. Some crevasses remain open for months or even years, and by the melting of their sides continue to increase in width long after the opening strain has ceased; while the sliver-bridges, level on top at first and perfectly safe, are at length melted to thin, vertical, knife-edged blades, the upper portion being most exposed to the weather; and since the exposure is greatest in the middle, they at length curve downward like the cables of suspension bridges. This one was evidently very old, for it had been weathered and wasted until it was the most dangerous and inaccessible that ever lay in my way. The width of the crevasse was here about fifty feet, and the sliver crossing diagonally was about seventy feet long; its thin knife-edge near the middle was depressed twenty-five or thirty feet below the level of the glacier, and the upcurving ends were attached to the sides eight or ten feet below the brink. Getting down the nearly vertical wall to the end of the sliver and up the other side were the main difficulties, and they seemed all but insurmountable. Of the many perils encountered in my years of wandering on mountains and glaciers, none seemed so plain and stern and merciless as this. And it was presented when we were wet to the skin and hungry, the sky dark with quick driving snow, and the night near. But we were forced to face it. It was a tremendous necessity.

Beginning, not immediately above the sunken end of the bridge, but a little to one side, I cut a deep hollow on the brink for my knees to rest in. Then, leaning over, with my short-handled axe I cut a step sixteen or eighteen inches below, which on account of the sheerness of the wall was necessarily shallow. That step, however, was well made; its floor sloped slightly inward and formed a good hold for my heels. Then, slipping cautiously upon it, and crouching as low as possible, with my left side toward the wall, I steadied myself against the wind with my left hand in a slight notch, while with the right I cut other similar steps and notches in succession, guarding against losing balance by glinting of the axe, or by wind-gusts, for life and death were in every stroke and in the niceness of finish of every foothold.

After the end of the bridge was reached I chipped it down until I had made a level platform six or eight inches wide, and it was a trying thing to poise on this little slippery platform while bending over to get safely astride of the sliver. Crossing was then comparatively easy by chipping off the sharp edge with short, careful strokes, and hitching forward an inch or two at a time, keeping my balance with my knees pressed against the sides. The tremendous abyss on either hand I studiously ignored. To me the edge of that blue sliver was then all the world. But the most trying part of the adventure, after working my way across inch by inch and chipping another small platform, was to rise from the safe position astride and to cut a step-ladder in the nearly vertical face of the wall—chipping, climbing, holding on with feet and fingers in mere notches. At such times one's whole body is eye, and common skill and fortitude are replaced by power beyond our call or knowledge. Never before had I been so long under deadly strain. How I got up that cliff I could never tell. The thing seemed to have been done by somebody else. I never had held death in contempt, though in the course of my explorations I have oftentimes felt that to meet one's fate on a noble mountain, or in the heart of a glacier, would be blessed as compared with death from disease, or from some shabby lowland accident. But the best death, quick and crystal-pure, set so glaringly open before us, is hard enough to face, even though we feel gratefully sure that we have already had happiness enough for a dozen lives.

But poor Stickeen, the wee, hairy, sleekit beastie, think of him! When I had decided to dare the bridge, and while I was on my knees chipping a hollow on the rounded brow above it, he came behind me, pushed his head past my shoulder, looked down and across, scanned the sliver and its approaches with his mysterious eyes, then looked me in the face with a startled air of surprise and concern, and began to mutter and whine; saying as plainly as if speaking with words, "Surely, you are not going into that awful place." This was the first time I had seen him gaze deliberately into a crevasse, or into my face with an eager, speaking, troubled look. That he should have recognized and appreciated the danger at the first glance showed wonderful sagacity. Never before had the daring midget seemed to know that ice was slippery or that there was any such thing as danger anywhere. His looks and tones of voice when he began to complain and speak his fears were so human that I unconsciously talked to him in sympathy as I would to a frightened boy, and in trying to calm his fears perhaps in some measure moderated my own. "Hush your fears, my boy," I said, "we will get across safe, though it is not going to be easy. No right way is easy in this rough world. We must risk our lives to save them. At the worst we can only slip, and then how grand a grave we will have, and by and by our nice bones will do good in the terminal moraine."

But my sermon was far from reassuring him: he began to cry, and after taking another piercing look at the tremendous gulf, ran away in desperate excitement, seeking some other crossing. By the time he got back, baffled of course, I had made a step or two. I dared not look back, but he made himself heard; and when he saw that I was certainly bent on crossing he cried aloud in despair. The danger was enough to daunt anybody, but it seems wonderful that he should have been able to weigh and appreciate it so justly. No mountaineer could have seen it more quickly or judged it more wisely, discriminating between real and apparent peril.

When I gained the other side, he screamed louder than ever, and after running back and forth in vain search for a way of escape, he would return to the brink of the crevasse above the bridge, moaning and wailing as if in the bitterness of death. Could this be the silent, philosophic Stickeen? I shouted encouragement, telling him the bridge was not as bad as it looked, that I had left it flat and safe for his feet, and he could walk it easily. But he was afraid to try. Strange so small an animal should be capable of such big, wise fears. I called again and again in a reassuring tone to come on and fear nothing; that he could come if he would only try. He would hush for a moment, look down again at the bridge, and shout his unshakable conviction that he could never, never come that way; then lie back in despair, as if howling, "O-o-oh! what a place! No-o-o, I can never go-o-o down there!" His natural composure and courage had vanished utterly in a tumultuous storm of fear. Had the danger been less, his distress would have seemed ridiculous. but in this dismal, merciless abyss lay the shadow of death, and his heart-rending cries might well have called Heaven to his help. Perhaps they did. So hidden before, he was now transparent, and one could see the workings of his heart and mind like the movements of a clock out of its case. His voice and gestures, hopes and fears, were so perfectly human that none could mistake them; while he seemed to understand every word of mine. I was troubled at the thought of having to leave him out all night, and of the danger of not finding him in the morning. It seemed impossible to get him to venture. To compel him to try through fear of being abandoned, I started off as if leaving him to his fate, and disappeared back of a hummock; but this did no good; he only lay down and moaned in utter hopeless misery. So, after hiding a few minutes, I went back to the brink of the crevasse and in a severe tone of voice shouted across to him that now I must certainly leave him, I could wait no longer, and that, if he would not come, all I could promise was that I would return to seek him next day. I warned him that if he went back to the woods the wolves would kill him, and finished by urging him once more by words and gestures to come on, come on.

He knew very well what I meant, and at last, with the courage of despair, hushed and breathless, he crouched down on the brink in the hollow I made for my knees, pressed his body against the ice as if trying to get the advantage of the friction of every hair, gazed into the first step, put his little feet together and slid them slowly, slowly over the edge and down into it, bunching all four in it and almost standing on his head. Then, without lifting his feet, as well as I could see through the snow, he slowly worked them over the edge of the step and down into the next and the next in succession in the same way, and gained the end of the bridge. Then, lifting his feet with the regularity and slowness of the vibrations of a seconds pendulum, as if counting and measuring *one-two-three*, holding himself steady against the gusty wind, and giving separate attention to each little step, he gained the foot of the cliff, while I was on my knees leaning over to give him a lift should he succeed in getting within reach of my arm. Here he halted in dead silence, and it was here I feared he might fail, for dogs are poor climbers. I had no cord. If I had had one, I would have dropped a noose over his head and hauled him up. But while I was thinking whether an available cord might be made out of clothing, he was looking keenly into the series of notched steps and finger-holds I had made, as if counting them, and fixing the position of each one of them in his mind. Then suddenly up he came in a springy rush, hooking his paws in to the steps and notches so quickly that I could not see how it was done, and whizzed past my head, safe at last!

And now came a scene! "Well done, well done, little boy! Brave boy!" I cried, trying to catch and caress him; but he would not be caught. Never before or since have I seen anything like so passionate a revulsion from the depths of despair to exultant, triumphant, uncontrollable joy. He flashed and darted hither and thither as if fairly demented, screaming and shouting, swirling round and round in giddy loops and circles like a leaf in a whirlwind, lying down, and rolling over and over, sidewise and heels over head, pouring forth a tumultuous flood of hysterical cries and sobs and gasping mutterings. When I ran up to him to shake him, fearing he might die of joy, he flashed off two or three hundred yards, his feet in a mist of motion; then, turning suddenly, came back in a wild rush and launched himself at my face, almost knocking me down, all the time screeching and screaming and shouting as if saying, "Saved! saved! saved!" Then away again, dropping suddenly at times with his feet in the air, trembling and fairly sobbing. Such passionate emotion was enough to kill him. Moses' stately song of triumph after escaping the Egyptians and the Red Sea was nothing to it. Who could have guessed the capacity of the dull, enduring little fellow for all that most stirs this mortal frame? Nobody could have helped crying with him!

But there is nothing like work for toning down excessive fear or joy. So I ran ahead, calling him in as gruff a voice as I could command to come on and stop his nonsense, for we had far to go and it would soon be dark. Neither of us feared another trial like this. Heaven would surely count one enough for a lifetime. The ice ahead was gashed by thousands of crevasses, but they were common ones. The joy of deliverance burned in us like fire, and we ran without fatigue, every muscle with immense rebound glorying in its strength. Stickeen flew across everything in his way, and not till dark did he settle into his normal fox-like trot. At last the cloudy mountains came in sight, and we soon felt the solid rock beneath our feet, and were safe. Then came weakness. Danger had vanished, and so had our strength. We tottered down the lateral moraine in the dark, over boulders and tree trunks, through the bushes and devil-club thickets of the grove where we had sheltered ourselves in the morning, and across the level mud-slope of the terminal moraine. We reached camp about ten o'clock, and found a big fire and a big supper. A party of Hoona Indians had visited Mr. Young, bringing a gift of porpoise meat and wild strawberries, and Hunter Joe had brought in a wild goat. But we lay down, too tired to eat much, and soon fell into a troubled sleep. The man who said, "The harder the toil, the sweeter the rest," never was profoundly tired. Stickeen kept springing up and muttering in his sleep, no doubt dreaming that he was still on the brink of the crevasse; and so did I, that night and many others long afterward, when I was over-tired.

Thereafter Stickeen was a changed dog. During the rest of the trip, instead of holding aloof, he always lay by my side, tried to keep me constantly in sight, and would hardly accept a morsel of food, however tempting, from any hand but mine. At night, when all was quiet about the camp-fire, he would come to me and rest his head on my knee with a look of devotion as if I were his god. And often as he caught my eye he seemed to be trying to say, "Wasn't that an awful time we had together on the glacier?"

Nothing in after years has dimmed that Alaska storm-day. As I write it all comes rushing and roaring to mind as if I were again in the heart of it. Again I see the gray flying clouds with their rain-floods and snow, and ice-cliffs towering above the shrinking forest, the majestic ice-cascade, the vast glacier outspread before its white mountain fountains, and in the heart of it the tremendous crevasse—emblem of the valley of the shadow of death—low clouds trailing over it, the snow falling into it; and on its brink I see little Stickeen, and I hear his cries for help and his shouts of joy. I have known many dogs, and many a story I could tell of their wisdom and devotion; but to none do I owe so much as to Stickeen. At first the least promising and least known of my dog-friends, he suddenly became the best known of them all. Out storm-battle for life brought him to light, and through him as through a window I have ever since been looking with deeper sympathy into all my fellow mortals.

None of Stickeen's friends knows what finally became of him. After my work for the season was done I departed for California, and I never saw the dear little fellow again. In reply to anxious inquiries his master wrote me that in the summer of 1883 he was stolen by a tourist at Fort Wrangel and taken away on a steamer. His fate is wrapped in mystery. Doubtless he has left this world—crossed the last crevasse—and gone to another. But he will not be forgotten. To me Stickeen is immortal.

Jack London

WILLIAM STAFFORD

The late William Stafford is one of America's most recognized poets. Born and educated in Kansas, he received a doctorate from the State University of Iowa. From 1948 until his retirement, he taught as a professor of English at Lewis and Clark College in Portland, Oregon. In addition to receiving the 1963 National Book Award for poetry for TRAVELING THROUGH THE DARK *(1962), Stafford received a Guggenheim Fellowship, the Shelley Memorial Award, and the Award in Literature from the American Academy of Arts and Letters. He published 59 books of poetry. The poem "Jack London" is taken from his collection* THE RESCUED YEAR *(1966).*

Teeth meet on a jugular, pause, and bite:
all the world turns red but the falling snow,
and oh how quiet the river holds its flow
by one bank, then another—the vise of rock
and the force of summer fighting far below.

Another time, on an island, wedge birds
come, welcome to fly and exercise their song
on what divides all hope from land;
the sky holds where it is, but ready to move
when the forest answers softly after a storm:

He found such furs for the cold, called "Beauty,"
and "Courage" that fell through the ice, and a dog so wild
it howls the mountains higher, that howled
ages ago for us to come to the North
and exercise our song, from the island world.

The Gray Cub

FROM *White Fang*

JACK LONDON

*Jack London (1876–1916) was an American novelist, journalist, and
adventurer, known for his stories set in the Far North. His books include
THE CALL OF THE WILD (1903), WHITE FANG (1906), and THE CRUISE OF
THE SNARK (1911). This excerpt is from WHITE FANG, London's dramatic
story of a wild wolf-dog.*

He was different from his brothers and sisters. Their hair already
betrayed the reddish hue inherited from their mother, the she-
wolf; while he alone, in this particular, took after his father. He
was the one little gray cub of the litter. He had bred true to the
straight wolf-stock—in fact, he had bred true, physically, to old
One Eye himself, with but a single exception, and that was that he had two
eyes to his father's one.

The gray cub's eyes had not been open long, yet already he could see
with steady clearness. And while his eyes were still closed, he had felt, tasted,
and smelled. He knew his two brothers and two sisters very well. He had
begun to romp with them in a feeble, awkward way, and even to squabble,
his little throat vibrating with a queer rasping noise (the forerunner of the
growl), as he worked himself into a passion. And long before his eyes had
opened, he had learned by touch, taste, and smell to know his mother—a
fount of warmth and liquid food and tenderness. She possessed a gentle,
caressing tongue that soothed him when it passed over his soft little body,
and that impelled him to snuggle close against her and to doze off to sleep.

Most of the first month of his life had been passed thus in sleeping; but
now he could see quite well, and he stayed awake for longer periods of time,
and he was coming to learn his world quite well. His world was gloomy;
but he did not know that for he knew no other world. It was dim-lighted;

but his eyes had never had to adjust themselves to any other light. His world was very small. Its limits were the walls of the lair; but as he had no knowledge of the wide world outside, he was never oppressed by the narrow confines of his existence.

But he had early discovered that one wall of his world was different from the rest. This was the mouth of the cave and the source of light. He had discovered that it was different from the other walls long before he had any thoughts of his own, any conscious volitions. It had been an irresistible attraction before ever his eyes opened and looked upon it. The light from it had beat upon his sealed lids, and the eyes and the optic nerves had pulsated to little, sparklike flashes, warm-colored and strangely pleasing. The life of his body, and of every fibre of his body, the life that was the very substance of his body and that was apart from his own personal life, had yearned toward this light and urged his body toward it in the same way that the cunning chemistry of a plant urges it toward the sun.

Always, in the beginning, before his conscious life dawned, he had crawled toward the mouth of the cave. And in this his brothers and sisters were one with him. Never, in that period, did any of them crawl toward the dark corners of the back-wall. The light drew them as if they were plants; the chemistry of the life that composed them demanded the light as a necessity of being; and their little puppet-bodies crawled blindly and chemically, like the tendrils of a vine. Later on, when each developed individuality and became personally conscious of impulsions and desires, the attraction of the light increased. They were always crawling and sprawling toward it, and being driven back from it by their mother.

It was in this way that the gray cub learned other attributes of his mother than the soft, soothing tongue. In his insistent crawling toward the light, he discovered in her a nose that with a sharp nudge administered rebuke, and later, a paw, that crushed him down or rolled him over and over with swift, calculating stroke. Thus he learned hurt; and on top of it he learned to avoid hurt, first, by not incurring the risk of it; and second, when he had incurred the risk, by dodging and by retreating. These were conscious actions, and were the results of his first generalizations upon the world. Before that he had recoiled automatically from hurt, as he had crawled automatically toward the light. After that he recoiled from hurt because he *knew* that it was hurt.

He was a fierce little cub. So were his brothers and sisters. It was to be expected. He was a carnivorous animal. He came of a breed of meat-killers and meat-eaters. His father and mother lived wholly upon meat. The milk he had sucked with his first flickering life was milk transformed directly from meat, and now, at a month old, when his eyes had been open for but a week, he was beginning himself to eat meat—meat half-digested by the she-wolf and disgorged for the five growing cubs that already made too great demand upon her breast.

But he was, further, the fiercest of the litter. He could make a louder rasping growl than any of them. His tiny rages were much more terrible than theirs. It was he that first learned the trick of rolling a fellow-cub over with a cunning paw-stroke. And it was he that first gripped another cub by the ear and pulled and tugged and growled through jaws tight-clenched. And certainly it was he that caused the mother the most trouble in keeping her litter from the mouth of the cave.

The fascination of the light for the gray cub increased from day to day. He was perpetually departing on yard-long adventures toward the cave's entrance, and as perpetually being driven back. Only he did not know it for an entrance. He did not know anything about entrances—passages whereby one goes from one place to another place. He did not know any other place, much less a way to get there. So to him the entrance of the cave was a wall—a wall of light. As the sun was to the outside dweller, this wall was to him the sun of his world. It attracted him as a candle attracts a moth. He was always striving to attain it. The life that was so swiftly expanding within him, urged him continually toward the wall of light. The life that was within him knew that it was the one way out, the way he was predestined to tread. But he himself did not know anything about it. He did not know there was any outside at all.

There was one strange thing about this wall of light. His father (he had already come to recognize his father as the one other dweller in the world, a creature like his mother, who slept near the light and was a bringer of meat)—his father had a way of walking right into the white far wall and disappearing. The gray cub could not understand this. Though never permitted by his mother to approach that wall, he had approached the other walls, and encountered hard obstruction on the end of his tender nose. This hurt. And after several such adventures, he left the walls alone. Without thinking about it, he accepted this disappearing into the wall as a peculiarity of his father, as milk and half-digested meat were peculiarities of his mother.

In fact, the gray cub was not given to thinking—at least, to the kind of thinking customary of men. His brain worked in dim ways. Yet his conclusions were as sharp and distinct as those achieved by men. He had a method of accepting things, without questioning the why and wherefore. In reality, this was the act of classification. He was never disturbed over *why* a thing happened. *How* it happened was sufficient for him. Thus, when he had bumped his nose on the back-wall a few times he accepted that he would not disappear into walls. In the same way he accepted that his father could disappear into walls. But he was not in the least disturbed by desire to find out the reason for the difference between his father and himself. Logic and physics were no part of his mental make-up.

Like most creatures of the Wild, he early experienced famine. There came a time when not only did the meat-supply cease, but the milk no longer came from his mother's breast. At first, the cubs whimpered and cried, but for the most part they slept. It was not long before they were reduced to a coma of hunger. There were no more spats and squabbles, no more tiny rages nor attempts at growling; while the adventures toward the far white wall ceased altogether. The cubs slept, while the life that was in them flickered and died down.

One Eye was desperate. He ranged far and wide, and slept but little in the lair that had now become cheerless and miserable. The she-wolf, too, left her litter and went out in search of meat. In the first days after the birth of the cubs, One Eye had journeyed several times back to the Indian camp and robbed the rabbit snares; but, with the melting of the snow and the opening of the streams, the Indian camp had moved away, and that source of supply was closed to him.

When the gray cub came back to life and again took interest in the far white wall, he found that the population of his world had been reduced. Only one sister remained to him. The rest were gone. As he grew stronger, he found himself compelled to play alone, for the sister no longer lifted her head nor moved about. His little body rounded out with the meat he now ate; but the food had come too late for her. She slept continuously, a tiny skeleton flung round with skin in which the flame flickered lower and lower and at last went out.

Then there came a time when the gray cub no longer saw his father appearing and disappearing in the wall nor lying down asleep in the entrance. This had happened at the end of a second and less severe famine.

The she-wolf knew why One Eye never came back, but there was no way by which she could tell what she had seen to the gray cub. Hunting herself for meat, up the left fork of the stream where lived the lynx, she had followed a day-old trail of One Eye. And she had found him, or what remained of him, at the end of the trail. There were many signs of the battle that had been fought, and of the lynx's withdrawal to her lair after having won the victory. Before she went away, the she-wolf had found this lair, but the signs told her that the lynx was inside, and she had not dared to venture in.

After that, the she-wolf in her hunting avoided the left fork. For she knew that in the lynx's lair was a litter of kittens, and she knew the lynx for a fierce, bad-tempered creature and a terrible fighter. It was all very well for half a dozen wolves to drive a lynx, spitting and bristling, up a tree; but it was quite a different matter for a lone wolf to encounter a lynx—especially when the lynx was known to have a litter of hungry kittens at her back.

But the Wild is the Wild, and motherhood is motherhood, at all times fiercely protective whether in the Wild or out of it; and the time was to come when the she-wolf, for her gray cub's sake, would venture the left fork, and the lair in the rocks, and the lynx's wrath.

The Dark Song

FROM *Icebound Summer*

SALLY CARRIGHAR

Born in California, Sally Carrighar first tried a career in moviemaking, but eventually became a naturalist, writing eleven books including ONE DAY ON BEETLE ROCK *(1944),* ONE DAY AT TETON MARSH *(1947),* ICEBOUND SUMMER *(1953),* MOONLIGHT AT MIDDAY *(1958), and her haunting autobiography* HOME TO THE WILDERNESS *(1973). "Dark Song" is excerpted from* ICEBOUND SUMMER.

The bird's northward flight was like a reversal of time, for she had left the spring and was entering winter again. The green landscape disappeared where the trees did, soon after she reached the coast of the Bering Sea. Now the landward scene was an endless brown marsh with a wide river dividing it. The ice in the river had broken up and was tossing its way to the sea. The Eskimos thought that the moving ice sounded like a hoarse whisper, *kusko, kusko,* and therefore had named their *kwim,* their river, the Kuskokwim. The crunching noise reached the bird in the sky. But the speed at which she was flying soon took her beyond it, and then she heard only the quick *whuff, whuff, whuff* of her wings, which had been beating for most of each day since she left Victoria.

After she passed the Kuskokwim, the land was covered increasingly with white snow. At the Yukon Delta the beach showed a crust of ice, and northward the ice became wider, stretching above the shallow sea till it met the offshore field of loose broken floes. The bird turned out over it, for she must keep open leads in sight, inasmuch as she was a loon and could only alight and take off in water.

All the ice that was loose, not anchored to land, had begun its spring drift toward the polar sea. From the loon's height it looked smooth. Some of the ice was white; the snow had blown off the surface of other floes, and those were of many colors—pale green, blue, amber, and yellow, a mosaic of crystalline shapes fitted together and looking like marble, veined with the sapphire water of unfrozen channels. All the colors were visible to the bird.

The farther north she had traveled, the stronger the urge had become to push on. All this day she had been flying, and midnight approached. The horizontally coasting sun had slid close to the rim of the sea. Now in May it would dip out of sight briefly, but not long enough for true darkness to thicken. The light never lessened much, only became more delicate, with a shadowy shine in the air, so real that this bird flying through it must surely, it seemed, acquire a new gloss on her purple-black throat.

She tilted the rudder formed by the trailing webs of her feet and began to descend. Choosing a straight lead of water ahead, she dropped the clean arc of her body and soon was cleaving the surface, her breast a keel and her wings held aloft like black sails. When she came to a stop, she dived, her slender black bill turning down on her breast with a motion that seemed to draw her below. She darted about in the liquid tunnel between the deep masses of ice, pursuing a tomcod. When she had speared it, she came up and, tossing the fish in the air, caught it head-first in her throat. She took several more and then relaxed on the surface.

Other migrating birds had come down here to rest and to forage. A few satin-black cormorants floated and splashed on the water, a single eider duck stood on the edge of the ice, his webs curling over, and a flock of emperor geese sat in a close company on a near-by floe, their slate-gray bodies as quiet as granite boulders and all their white heads facing into the southwest breeze. The loon found a mated pair of her own kind, asleep with their long necks coiled over their backs and heads under their wings.

She stayed near them, although they were not of the flock familiar to her, the several dozen Pacific loons that were her neighbors at the Alaska breeding grounds in the summer and also down at Vancouver Island during the winter. The others had made their migration without this female, but she would find them again at the nesting marsh. She had had to come north alone, for she had lingered too long, one day, on a park pond in Victoria.

During the late months of winter she had been spending her days in the park. There, under the trimmed willows and along the brushed paths, walked human beings, and those who liked birds fed the waterfowl on the little lake. The loon was wary of most of them, but in one she felt confidence. The first time she saw him, a blue overcoat was buttoned snugly around his slight, aging figure, and he was wearing a gray felt hat and suede gloves—a human being as trim as a bird. It was the courteous way that he walked, however, that made the loon feel at ease with him. For there was no aggressiveness in his gait; no secret wish to strike betrayed itself in his motions. On that sunny morning the wind was brisk. Tired after a flight against it, the loon had come down on the pond, and among other, more restless humans, discovered this man, who had met her eye and who then sat down on a bench near the water's edge and continued to watch her.

She paddled nearer to see the silver knob on his walking stick, and his hands as he folded his gloves down off his fingers, turned the gloves right-side out and laid them beside him. He took a pipe and tobacco pouch from his pocket and unhurriedly lighted a smoke for himself, meanwhile observing the bird over his hand with the match. She was propelling herself back and forth, each time nearer the line of cemented rocks at the shore of the pond.

When the man had drawn a few puffs on his pipe he took a tin box from his pocket, opened the lid, and threw a dried shrimp to the loon. Other birds, ducks and gulls, came clamoring forward, and the loon swam farther away. The man waited until the others became discouraged and left. Then he tossed a second shrimp to the loon, dropping it at the edge of the water. Inconspicuously, without any apparent movement, she let herself sink and rose with the shrimp in her gullet. It became a small plot between the loon and the man that he would feed only her, and that both of them should so manage that the rest of the birds did not notice.

The loon preferred fish to shrimps, but she found a curious pleasure in being fed by that quiet human acquaintance. She formed the habit of coming each day to the park, and he always was there. Then one morning she did not find him. The next day she returned and for several hours paddled around on the pond. In the afternoon when she went back to her flock in the harbor bay, they were gone—they had set out on their spring migration without her. Several more days the loon went to the pond, and when her friend did not appear she gathered her strength, having no other luggage, and winging up from the placid water started north on a twenty-five-hundred-mile flight alone.

Although she was young, two years old, and had made the trip north only once before, she had not lost the way. Now her journey was nearly over. Just beyond the lead where she rested the shoreline turned east into Norton Sound. That was her route; before noon she would arrive at the head of the

Sound where the Unalakleet River entered it. On the surrounding marsh, spattered with ponds, soon her flock would be choosing their nesting sites. And she too would be rearing a brood—wouldn't she? This was the spring, the start of her third year, when she should find the male who would be her companion, perhaps for life. For most loons the migration was also the courting time; before they had reached the northern breeding grounds they were mated. This young female would still be single when she appeared there—but that could be true of some of the males too, surely. It was not an invariable rule that loons were paired before they had come to the end of their northward flight.

The loons' year was divided into an interlude in the alien country of docks and ships, where the sea was murky with oil, popcorn, and other refuse, and a shorter time of intense life in a wild birds' Eden. Here the sun's light came through air as pure as if no breath had ever been expelled into it. And this was the way things looked with no soot or smoke blurring them; every resting goose its precise, finely-outlined self, the brink of the ice floe showing each thread of its crystal lace, and the grass at the top of the sandy beach more than a band of vegetation—instead, a fringe of sharp, separate blades. Over everything, the blue sea, the brown and white earth, and the ice, was the nacreous tint of dawn, of the beginning, and so it would be all day.

The loon was ready to start the last lap of her journey. She turned into the Sound. Soon she had passed the rocks at Black Point, passed Tolstoy Point, where clouds of gulls were clamoring as they divided among themselves the pebbly nooks for the nests; and there at last was the swing of the shore where her river emerged between two long sandspits.

The river was frozen still, and the shelf-ice spread a few miles out over the sea—as far as the offshore bar. Many pools lay on the ice. They were silky blue-green when they were composed of sea water, an overflow through the tide-cracks, but were tea-color near the beach, where the water had drained from the land and was stained from the moss and lichens. Gulls, ducks, and geese floated around on the ponds, watching for fish, or stood on the ice digesting a meal. The fish would swim up through the cracks and out into the shallow water, where they were trapped in plain view of the birds. Arctic terns, preferring a gamier hunt, were flying along the cracks, suddenly making their sinuous downward turns as they dived. In the steamy debris on the beach, Northern phalaropes, snipes, and sandpipers ran about, catching insects as fast they hatched. And a loose flock of snow buntings tumbled aloft. They were females, the last of the spring, bound for the coastline nearest the Pole, where no vegetation was more than a few inches high, willows were vines that grew prostrate on the ground, and the cotton grass, which would reach to a man's knee at Unalakleet, on that most northern shore would but rise to his ankle.

Sandhill cranes, snow geese, and brandt were migrating over. The flocks made a web of shadow drawing across the softly glittering white expanse of the ice. Birds were everywhere. Most of those that had stopped at the marsh were known to the loon from last year, when as a juvenile she had come north, not to rear a brood, only to grow and mature. Late in the summer the birds had scattered to many parts of the hemisphere—the terns to the Antarctic, eleven thousand miles away—and now they were back at this small patch of coast, to which they had come by varying routes, but unerringly. And the loons?

Six were splashing out in the open water beyond the shelf-ice. As the female flew over, she could see tomcods milling along the lead, thousands of them, but the loons were not taking the fish. They were playing, in pairs, chasing, dipping their bills, flinging spray from their heads—three males and three females.

In the entire flock, however, were several times six. The loon turned upriver, first passing the sandspits. The channels that wound through the marsh grass were melting around the edges, and there loons were swimming, in couples. The female continued around the cliff, a good nesting ground; two loons had taken possession. She followed the river farther. Many sloughs were enclosed in its elaborate turns, and on some of them she saw loons, in the inevitable pairs.

The female was hungry. She swung around to return to the fishing grounds in the ocean. En route she passed over an arctic fox warming himself in the sun. He could be a reminder that predators would be here, foxes and wolves and the Eskimos with their guns.

Although the river appeared to be frozen, below its white, motionless surface a torrent was pouring seaward. For several weeks now the meltwater from higher creeks, entering the river, had licked out a channel within the softening ice in the stream. After this current passed out of the river's mouth, it divided and, unseen from above, flowed through some breaks in the underside of the shelf-ice. Finally cutting the sandbar, it escaped into the ocean. The loon swam along outside the sandbar until she came to the hidden flow. There she turned into the tunnels back in the ice.

A dim, blue-green light was suffused through the surface above. It showed the walls of the passageways polished smooth by the current, and it showed the harvest of last year's insects now being washed down by the melting snow on the distant mountainsides. Here many young trout were taking the insects, a feast for them. But nature, which gave generously to the fish with one hand, took away with the other hand. When the loon startled them and they swung away, their shiny sides, tilting, caught the light from above. A school of them thus became a stream of flashes, signals to any predator. Using both wings and webs, the loon overtook them easily. They were more firm and tasty than tomcods, but were not large enough to make the nourishing meal that the bird hoped to find.

She swam back to the open water beyond the ice, swung aside, and in doing so involuntarily solved her hunger problem. For the rows of white spots on her back caught the overhead light in a way that imitated the bright streaks from a school of small fish. A fat grayling, also foraging, shot up out of the gloom toward the bird. The loon seized it, rose to the surface and swallowed it. The grayling was almost too large for her throat, but the bird worked it down, throwing her head from side to side and arching her neck at the top to literally pinch the fish through her gullet.

It soon became evident that the tardy female was the only unmated loon in the Unalakleet population. She spent most of her time off the edge of the ice, apart from the others. Whereas they liked to float in the lee of a pressure ridge, the female took for her own the unsheltered water farther along. She had, of course, not started a search for a nesting site. She spent most of her time in preening her feathers—her white breast and black wings and her finely-striped throat—until now she was as sleek and handsome a bird as could have been seen anywhere on the shores of the Sound.

Before long she had one satisfaction the other loons did not share. A young Eskimo boy began coming out to the brink of the ice and befriending her. He had no particular wish to kill the bird, since the taste of loon flesh did not appeal to him. And not knowing that her natural fear of humans had broken down, he felt flattered because she had let him approach within reach the first time that he saw her. The next day he had brought her one of the tomcods he had caught through the ice for his father's dogs. Many times more he returned. She enjoyed the chance to receive food again from a human hand, and perhaps his companionship made her a little less lonely.

The rest of the loons were ignoring her. They had chosen their home-sites, but making the nests was not yet their main concern. The older birds would be using the nests of former years, and the younger ones would not start building until the ponds were completely thawed. Meanwhile they were absorbed in the yearly ritual of love.

They were high-strung birds, and one could believe that love was, for them, a very disturbing experience. During the night, in the lucent twilight, their cries spread without pause over the ice and the tundra. They were cries close to human tones, and sounding as if they expressed wild dismay. The musical cadence began with an introductory syllable, lifted to a long note, held as if waiting for an answer that never came, and then dropped to a brief, inconclusive finish. In the Eskimo village the people were kept awake—not so much by the volume of sound as by the emotion with which the cries saturated the air. The night seemed to pulse with grief, hopeless and inconsolable. Made restless, young Eskimo couples would wander out on the airstrip beyond the town, and even old women roused themselves from their reindeer-skin mattresses and went down on the sand to continue their work of gathering driftwood.

Or was the fulfillment the heartbreak? With some of the pairs of loons, now, the ritual was approaching its climax. One afternoon two of the mated birds paddled apart from the flock. For a while, with a trancelike stillness, they remained near each other. Then in perfect unison they began to swing back and forth, propelled by their webs to the left, a quick turn to the right, and back to the left. The female was low in the water, even the base of her throat was submerged, but the male was riding the ripples splendidly, with his graceful dark wings held high over his back. At the end of the dance the birds drew together, touched bills, let themselves drift apart, came near and touched bills again with an excited motion. The female of the pair suddenly dived then, in a flash of spray.

From the west a migrating loon was approaching. The spray caught his eye—or was it the single female that did? He came down in the water, a glide that furrowed the sea. When he stopped, he tilted his bill toward the sky and turned his head side to side to survey his surroundings. He must have liked what he saw, for after he caught and ate two or three fish, he idled along the edge of the ice, seeming to be in no hurry to go farther north.

His glance often fell on the unmated female. She watched him casually for a while, after which she swam back and forth with an arch in her throat and her head under the water, seeking a fish. She captured one, tossed it into the air and caught it prettily. Then she coiled her neck over her back and had a short nap. When she awoke, the new male was still there. The two of them paddled about in the water, appraising each other.

He became more daring. He began swimming past her, very near, with rapid, bold strokes. The female was agitated. She dashed away, kicking the water back with her webs, and was on the wing for a little flight over the ice.

Her young human acquaintance was there below, walking out toward the edge. Not fearing him, she did not change her course. He was carrying what seemed a bundle of strings in his hand. Actually it was a bola, a missile composed of six sinew thongs, knotted together at one end, with ivory balls attached to the other ends. The boy's father had used it in years past to snare birds, and the boy had been practicing with it.

When the loon flew above him, he whirled the balls and let go. They soared into the air and one of the thongs, touching the bird, swiftly encircled her wings. She fell to the ice, not injured but frantic to free herself. He picked her up and enclosed her body in one of his arms, with his hand firmly clasped on her throat to prevent her attacking him with her bill. When she still struggled, he gripped her head in his fingers. She fought, but he tightened his hold. Her heart was jumping. She could see nothing, but she could feel the swing of the boy's hip as he ran back to shore.

The boy took the loon into a cabin, where he wrapped a cloth tightly around her to keep her quiet, and laid her upon a table. An Eskimo woman and five or six children stood close about. They talked, in strong but relaxed voices. The small ones wanted to touch the bird, but her captor, whom the others called Isaac, kept pushing their hands away.

Isaac began to fashion a jess out of sealskin. After the jess was attached to the loon's leg, he tied the other end to a rope. Then all the humans left, and the loon on the table could hear a hammering.

Isaac returned for her. After he fastened the rope to a stake, he removed the cloth. His family stood in a circle around the bird. Nature had placed her legs, to be most efficient in swimming, so far back that she was almost unable to walk. But she flopped and hobbled out to the end of her tether and found that it gripped and held her like some unknown enemy. Panic-stricken, she threw herself over the sand while the children laughed, all except one girl about sixteen years old. When the loon tripped, the girl untangled the rope. "Naomi! Do not let her go!" Isaac cried, darting forward. But Naomi was not releasing the bird, only trying to make her comfortable. Many more children had gathered. Wherever she turned, all the loon could see was their brown-stockinged legs and bright calico parka-covers.

When it became quite certain that she could not escape, the loon settled upon the sand and pulled herself into her feathers. She was dazed with fear and exhaustion. Isaac brought her a dried tomcod and a pan of water, but the loon had no appetite for them. Except when she tried occasionally to flap away, she lay inert, all but unconscious.

She was not alone until evening. When she looked around then, she found that she was tied on the beach, near the last village cabin. Between her and the cabin were several dogs, each chained to a separate stake. Excited by the bird's presence, they had howled most of the day, increasing her terror. Now they had just been fed and were quiet. But dogs at the other cabins were baying. Occasionally they would all be silent, and then their clamoring sometimes started again in response to the cry of one of the loons in the water beyond the ice. The call, "Ark! Ark!" with which the loons often took flight, was picked up by the dogs. Northern huskies, the dogs themselves were unable to render a perfect bark, but the loons' voices set off their yapping.

A lane of water lay at the foot of the beach, above the ice. The loon tried to reach it, but the rope was not long enough. Her efforts attracted the children who came running to watch her. Later several adults came by. The people would stay up all night, it seemed. The sun had gone down and appeared again, and still the children were playing. But finally most of the humans were ready for sleep. Before Isaac left his new pet, he moved the fish and the pan of water in front of her.

The sun was gliding along the hilltops between the north and east. It was casting long shadows over the olive and wine-colored slopes, with their patches of snow, and the shelf-ice. The ponds on the ice mirrored the floating gulls and the ducks. An arctic owl foraged over the berry bushes and moss, its movements downy and hushed as it searched for lemmings. The loons' melancholy voices rose through the wide, soft, clear silence. Overhead was a dark loneliness, darkness diluted with tenuous sunlight, a distant ethereal dome pierced with stars.

Far up the beach appeared two human figures, Naomi, the Eskimo girl, and a white man taller than she. They came on at a slow pace, holding hands and sometimes in their conversation stopping to face each other. Naomi was going to show him the loon. When they drew near, she stepped ahead and took up the bird, tightly clasping her throat as Isaac had done. The man spread the toes of the loon's web with his fingers. The loon tried to draw back her bill to jab at his hand and he quickly let the foot go. Naomi put the bird back on the sand.

She and the man sat down on a driftwood log. Naomi was facing the ocean, her hands demure in her lap. Her companion straddled the log, with one foot on the top and an elbow cross his knee. He took the braid that hung over the girl's shoulder and tickled her cheek with the end. Naomi's smile had a shy delight in it; her lips did not part but her eyes were unable to hide their pleasure. The man's blue eyes sent her their flash at an oblique angle.

"Ahya-keenya—with a name like that, why do you let people call you Naomi?"

"You don't like Naomi?"

"Not as well as your Eskimo name. I'll never meet any other girl with a name a pretty as Ahya-keenya."

"Missionaries gave me Naomi."

"Ahya-keenya's the name I'll always remember you by."

Naomi's face did not change by so much as a flicker; she was as still as a wild creature, freezing at danger's approach.

"You go away?" she asked, after a moment.

"As a matter of fact, I do have to leave before long," he replied. "That was something I planned to tell you."

"Where you go?"

"I'm being transferred to Kodiak. It's a bigger station—an advance for me."

"Advance?"

"A better job, I mean. I'll be making more money."

Naomi was looking out over the ice now, absently drawing her fingers along the braid. Her voice was reticent, with the least possible chance of inspiring ridicule, as she said,

"We have big house. You could live with us."

"No—no, I have to go. I'm under contract to the Government. I signed a paper promising that I'd work up here for two years, and I have to go wherever they send me."

She risked a smile again:

"After that you come back?"

"I certainly will! We'll get a boat and a tent and you and I will go fishing for a long time. That's something I've always wanted to do."

"Maybe we go now? My family have fish camp up river. Plenty wood for fires. We could trap salmon-trout all winter."

"No—that wouldn't be right. I'm surprised at you. I told you I signed a paper. Would you want me to break a promise?"

"I want you to be here. How much longer you stay?"

"I don't know—whenever they send the plane. Maybe tomorrow, maybe next week." He swung both feet to her side of the log, and taking her hand in his, touched the knuckles, one by one, with his lips.

"I'm going to miss you, Ahya-keenya." He drew her close and they were quiet except for his roving hand, to which the girl stiffened.

"You send for me?"

"You wouldn't be happy in Kodiak. Lots of big brown bears down there. Bigger than polar bears. You're afraid of bears, you know—"

With her feet nimble in their skin *mukluks* Naomi jumped up and ran toward the cabin. He ran after her, but she dodged and eluded him, entered the door and closed it. He stood outside, tapping softly a few times. Finally he tried the latch, but the door had been locked. When he came to the beach again, the loon had an instant of fright. But the man had forgotten her; his foot kicked sand over her as he passed. He picked up a rock and hurled it at one of the gulls, and then walked away up the shore toward the distant white buildings beside the airstrip.

The single migrating loon was still here at the marsh. Soon after Naomi's companion had disappeared, the bird came in over the ice, crossed the beach, and continued on toward the mountains. The male gave no sign that he was aware of the captive, but soon he returned. He flew the course several times and perhaps he did know she was there, for the last time he passed the shore his harsh cry rang out. As she watched the strong beat of his wings and then saw the spray as he landed beyond the ice, she was roused momentarily.

After that he appeared every day. Once in the early morning when no human beings were out, he swung around and apparently paced off the strip of water between the ice and the shore. It was not long enough for a loon's landing and take-off, and he returned to the open sea. He and the captive had no real relationship; yet the frequent sight of him was a tie with her own kind—enough to keep her alive. One day she accepted a fish from Isaac, and occasionally after that others, but she was growing rapidly thinner and her plumage, once so silken, had become disheveled and dusty.

Everywhere else on this coast, the urgent delights of spring were approaching their peak. Barn swallows were cutting their arcs past the cabin roof, flying in threes, one leading, two in pursuit. Even a quick eye could hardly follow their turns, the breathless straightaway and the whiplash reversal, the darting, skimming, and flinging about of the scimitar bodies that never tired. Over the edge of the beach the arctic terns, soon to break up in pairs, engaged in an aerial race that brought their gregarious months to a brilliant climax. The entire flock would mount in the sky in a wheeling cloud. At one side of their circling the gray and white feathers were almost invisible; as the curve continued, the sun flashed on the white throats and lighted a whirl of sparkles; their swing progressed, and the scraps of gold flickered out—to be kindled again when the birds came around once more.

Insistent, and closer still to the consummation, was the courtship song of the Baird sandpipers. Many times a day one of the males would rise from the tundra. His white breast, as white as if it had pressed into snow, would flash as he zig-zagged upward until he had reached a certain point over a female below on the ground, where he would hover with vibrating wings a blur and his head tilting down. His vocal twirring was so long-sustained then, so commanding, and so intense that finally something must happen, the strain had to break. The little female would fly from her hiding place in the moss, and the triumphant male would come back to earth.

Pairs of longspurs were already building their nests, and the males often stopped to celebrate with aerial songs like an overflow of contentment. One would soar into the sky as lightly as if the melody carried him up. He would glide about, high for so small a bird, letting himself down a little way, climbing again and sailing, finally descending with wings quiet, slowly drifting down of his own weight, while his joyous song spilled from his throat, liquid and sunny. The savannah sparrows had laid their eggs. One with a nest near the tethered loon sang continuously from the top of a frost mound, a heaved plat of grass. At one edge of the mound, under a tussock, his mate was sitting upon the nest, and the male bird was keeping intruders away with the defiant earnestness of his *tsip, tsip, tseee, tseer*. There were battles too, the jaegers harassing the gulls, and the gulls competing with noisy cries, *mine, mine, mine*; but the sounds of the great festival drowned out the angry notes. From the small redpolls, the snipes, and plovers to the warbling cranes, snow geese and whistling swans passing across the sky, came an outpouring of inescapable poignant voices, making the very air quiver around the loon lying so nearly dead.

One other comfort beside the attentive male was helping to keep the breath of life fluttering in her. Naomi spent many hours on the beach, and she would talk to the bird:

"Ee-lahl-looak-bis suel-lik biak-dok. Beek-thruk kleu-ickbin adow-simik."

She was saying that herring would soon arrive. They would be caught in the nets; Naomi would bring one, large and fresh, for the loon. Naomi was sewing new *mukluks* for a young sister, but the work did not progress very fast, she so often sat with her hands in her lap and eyes turned across the ice. By now it was spongy and soft—too dangerous for the dog teams to go out on it. It was breaking up into blocks with wide crevasses between, and each day was wetter and looser, each day different. But Naomi was not observing the changes. Her eyes were vacant.

Naomi was most often there in the night, when the sun only shone as a burning gold line tracing the top of the headland farther along the shore. She would stay till the first wood-chopping was heard, before breakfast. There she had solitude; there she could weep and no one observe. It was surely no help to her that the offshore loons always sang, one would say, of joys never to be fulfilled. As their dark wailing lifted and dropped away, it seemed to speak for Naomi and, as well, for the captive bird.

She had been listening to the sound one night, when her glance fell on the motionless loon. She rose to her feet and picked up the loon impulsively.

"Maybe somebody out there wait for you! You are missing somebody?" She loosened the jess from the loon's foot, and with the bird in her arms started down to the ice.

She detoured around the water along the sand and set out on the slushy surface. The most precarious ice was that where the ponds of tidewater had lain. Twice she broke through and must throw herself forward upon a browner, grainier, firmer block. She could jump across some of the cracks but had to go to the end of others; all were now mushy-bordered. In places the ice was heaved, and there it was porous; Naomi circled aside.

Finally she reached the ridge of tumbled slabs out at the edge. She walked to its end, where the ice simply disintegrated into the sea. She laid the loon on the watery surface. The loon skittered along to the sea's open depths, where she dived at once, taking her torn, dirty plumage, and her hunger, down into the haunts of fish.

Immediately she caught a trout and a few tomcods; in her present state she was not waiting for delicacies. With her hunger appeased, then, she floated and preened. She dived and splashed, dipped her head, and ran her bill down her feathers to smooth them. The food and the cold sea had already begun to revive her.

Approaching from under the water where he had seen her white breast, the single male rose at her side. With possessive and arrogant eyes he began to swim past. Each time he was nearer; now his wake washed against her throat.

Naomi had stood near the edge of the ice, watching the loon rediscover her freedom. When the male appeared Naomi smiled; when he started his courtship the smile faded, although her eyes were no less sympathetic. She turned to go. At the loon's last glimpse of her, she was making her cautious way over the ice. She was not hurrying. The beach would be lonelier now, without the bird.

On the pearly gloss of the water the male continued his sweeping march, back and forth. The movement itself was a call. The female loon felt an answering impulse beginning to stir. The next time he went by, she swung into his wake and followed him, and her motions became as one with the male bird's.

Gentle Ben

WALT MOREY

Walt Morey is the author of many adventure stories for young readers, including HOME IS THE NORTH *and the popular* GENTLE BEN *(1965).* GENTLE BEN, *excerpted here, is the story of a lonely boy's love for an Alaskan brown bear suffering in captivity. Morey's Orca City is a fictitious Alaskan fishing village.*

Each day Mark Andersen told himself he would not stop that night. He would walk right by the shed and not even glance inside. But about two o'clock every afternoon he'd begin thinking of stopping, and the next thing he realized, there he was, his schoolbooks in one hand, a paper bag in the other, staring into the yawning black mouth of the doorway. He knew what would happen if his father learned of it. He feared his father's anger more than anything else. But his desire to enter the shed was so great it drove his fear into the back of his mind, where it gnawed at him like a mouse in a wall.

He squinted his eyes, concentrating on the house several hundred yards down the trail. His mother was not in the yard or in the kitchen window that faced in his direction. She had not waved to him on his way home from school for several weeks now. He had a vague feeling that somehow this fact was important. He worried about it for a moment. Then he turned toward the black interior of the shed, and forgot all else.

"Just once more," he told himself. "This is the last time."

He stepped into the cool, musty dimness, and was momentarily blinded. He stood perfectly still, waiting, listening. He heard the soft pad of feet, the dry rustle of straw, the rattle of a chain. A heavy body brushed against him, almost upsetting him. The next moment the paper bag was almost ripped from his hand.

His exploring hand touched coarse fur, a broad head, a pair of stubby tulip-shaped ears. When his eyes became accustomed to the gloom, he made out the great blocky shape of the bear. He put both arms about its huge neck, and murmured, "I almost didn't come today. I sure am glad to see you, Ben." Ben twisted his big head, trying to reach the sack. Mark said, "All right, but wait a minute."

Ben was fastened with a chain about his neck; the other end was tied to a post in the center of the building. Because the chain was so short that he could not reach the door or the sunlight, most of his five years had been spent in the building's inner gloom.

Mark went to the post, untied the chain, and transferred it to another supporting post nearer the door so that Ben could get some sunlight while he was there. Before Mark left, he always retied the chain to the center post, just as it had been, so Fog Benson would never guess anyone had been there.

Mark disliked Fog Benson. He always looked dirty. He spent most of his time in the bars, where he talked loud, bragged, and was quarrelsome. Mark's father had said he was sure that Benson was a fish pirate. Mark knew he was mean to Ben. He always kept the bear chained, and sometimes he didn't feed him for days. Then maybe he'd just throw a loaf of stale bread onto the floor.

Mark never worried about Benson finding him in the shed. Fog, like every other man who owned a seine boat, was busy getting it ready for the approaching salmon season.

Ben padded to the end of the chain and stood in the open doorway. It was a warm day, and sky and land were as bright as a new belt buckle. Ben blinked his little eyes at the bright sunlight. He swung his big head right and left as his delicate nostrils eagerly sampled the fresh spring air. Ben was not yet a full-grown brown bear, and he was painfully thin and bony from lack of enough food for his huge frame. Even so, he was a tremendous animal, with great ropes of muscles rippling continuously under his light taffy-gold coat.

Mark sat down in the sun-drenched doorway and began opening the paper bag. "I saved one of my sandwiches for you, and a couple of the kids didn't eat all theirs so I brought them along, too."

Ben tried to get his big black nose into the sack, and Mark pushed it away. He hit the back of Ben's front legs just above his feet and said, "Down! Sit down, Ben." He patted the floor beside him. Ben stretched out, big forepaws extended. Mark didn't know how he had taught Ben that, or even if he had. But Ben always lay down where Mark did it.

Mark tore the sandwiches into chunks and held them in his palm. Ben lifted the pieces so deftly Mark scarcely felt his tongue. The bear ate them with a great smacking of lips. When it was all gone, Ben pushed at his hand, looking for more. Mark gave him the empty sack, and Ben ripped it apart, snorting and huffing at the aroma that remained. When he was satisfied there was no more, he dropped his big head on his forepaws and lay looking out at the bright spring day.

Mark wished suddenly that Jamie was here so he could share Ben. Jamie had been almost two years older, and much bigger and stronger. It had always been Jamie who thought of the things they should do and the places to go. He still missed Jamie. He guessed he always would. "Jamie would have liked you, too," he said to Ben, and rubbed the fur under his chin.

Ben stretched his neck, closed his eyes, and grunted like a pig, in pure ecstasy. Mark leaned back against Ben's solid side, one arm lying along his neck. His fingers scratched idly at the base of Ben's tulip-shaped ears. Ben twisted his head so Mark could scratch first one ear, then the other.

"I bet you wish you were out there where you could get some of that long green grass and roots and skunk cabbage," Mark said. "This is spring, and bears need that kind of food to prepare their stomachs for summer. I guess you've never had those things." Of course, he knew Ben hadn't. Fog Benson had captured him when the cub was six months old. He had killed Ben's mother and brought the young bear to town to show him off. And because Ben had cried for hours for his lost mother, Fog had laughingly named him "Squeaky Ben," after a local character with a querulous voice. As the cub grew and it became apparent his size would be tremendous, the "Squeaky" part was dropped.

"If you were mine," Mark reflected, "I'd take you down to that stream just beyond the flat. The grass is half as high as I am, and there's lots of roots and things. There's rocks, too. And we'd turn some over and you could eat the grubs and mice under them. If you were mine—"

Mark had been saying this to himself since the first night he had stopped to see Ben. He often lay in bed thinking of it before going to sleep. And he thought of it in school, too. He had got a poor grade in spelling the other day just because he'd been planning his visit to Ben.

After school Miss Taylor had talked to him about the spelling. She had his paper on her desk and was looking at it, shaking her head. "Mark," she said, "you didn't even write down half those spelling words. I'm sure you knew them, so that's not the reason. You were daydreaming again, Mark. You've been doing a lot of that lately. Is there something wrong?"

"Oh, no," he said hastily, "I was just—just thinking."

She said gently, "I know it's spring and there are only two weeks of school left; but try to pay closer attention, Mark."

Several times Mark had thought briefly of suggesting to his father that he buy Ben. Fog Benson would probably be glad to get rid of the bear, judging by the way he neglected him. But if Mark hinted at such a thing, he would have to admit he had been stopping to see Ben, and his father's anger was a thing Mark did not want to face.

He wanted to be friends with his father and feel that same closeness there had been between his father and Jamie. Jamie would have been a big man. He had gone on the boat that last summer, and Mark had listened enviously as Jamie and his father discussed fishing and boating problems in man-to-man fashion. But he could never do that. He was not going to be big. And he was afraid of his father's temper, the harshness of his voice. The look from his father's blue eyes when he was displeased could freeze you inside. Mark was sure he would never know such warm companionship with his father. Jamie had got it all. He wondered what would have happened if Jamie had asked for Ben.

Mark rubbed his cheek against Ben's broad forehead, hard as rock covered with fur, and said: "If you were mine I'd feed you up until you were as round as a seal. You'd grow and grow until you were the biggest bear in the whole world, I bet. And I'd train you to walk right behind me all the time. In the summer we could go down to the dock and watch the cruise ships come in, and people would 'Oh' and 'Ah!' at us and take pictures. And you'd follow me around like a dog—" At this, Mark paused, struck to his very heart with joy at the thought of arousing such love and devotion in what would be the biggest bear in the whole world. Wouldn't that be something! he thought blissfully. I bet I'd be the only kid in the whole world who had a bear for a pet. Gee!

He snuggled his thin shoulders tighter against Ben's broad, solid side. He was tired. It seemed like he was always tired. And the warm sun soaking into him made him a little drowsy. He watched the sun through half-closed lids as it dropped toward a white peak. It was going to land right on top like a marble on a mountain. He'd have to go soon. He had to get home before his father. Mother had never asked what made him late, but Dad would.

Off to his left the green and yellow tundra stretched away in gentle rolls and hollows that were broken here and there by the darker green of patches of brush and a ragged line where the creek cut through to the sea. The tundra looked dewy fresh and clean from its long winter under the snow. In the distance the Aleutian Range reared a row of white heads into the blue. Already the snow had melted from the beaches and surrounding lowlands. As the hours of daylight lengthened, the snow line crept farther away. It crept up valleys and canyons, across slopes and razor-sharp ridges until, by the time summer arrived, it would have retreated to that range of white heads, where it would stop.

Below, on his right, lay the uneven roofs of homes and stores of the fishing village of Orca City. Its one mud street, black and drying under the warm sun, slashed straight through the center of town to the bay and the sea, which stretched away, flat and endless, to the distant horizon.

A dozen boats lay at the dock, but the outreaching sea was empty. Soon it would not be. The opening of the Alaskan salmon run was but two weeks away, and excitement was beginning to grip the town like a fever. Mark knew about that; his father was a seiner, and his boat, the *Far North,* was one of the finest seiners in Alaska.

Everyone in Orca City made his living from the salmon run in one form or another. "Take the salmon run away," his father once said, "and Orca City would be a ghost town in a month." Naturally, everyone became more excited as opening day drew nearer. Fishing boats would begin to arrive any day now, and Orca City would fill with strange men who had come north to work in the seven canneries along the coast and aboard the fish traps. Soon, more than a thousand seiners from as far south as California and even Mexico would be moored in the bay. Orca City's three or four hundred people would swell to several thousand.

Even now repair crews were making the canneries ready. Aboard boats men were working feverishly, overhauling fishing gear, repairing motors, getting their boats seaworthy. Huge floating fish traps, made of logs and chicken wire, that would catch hundreds of thousands of salmon in a few weeks were being towed to locations at sea where they would be held in place with great anchors. Other traps, made of pilings and wire, were being built right on the trap sites at sea. All day and night the whoosh-stomp of pile drivers would be heard up and down the cost as they sank hundred-foot pilings deep into the bottom of the sea to form the shape of a trap.

Like a sprinter crouched in the starting blocks and awaiting the gun, Mark thought, everyone was getting set for the morning the Bureau of Fisheries would announce the opening of the season. Then boats would begin scouring the sea, hunting schools of salmon. The canneries' doors would swing wide. Aboard the traps watchmen would close the "Sunday apron," the wire door that let the salmon escape from the trap back to sea before the season opened. The Alaskan salmon run would be officially on.

The brown bears, lean-flanked and rough-coated from their long winter's sleep, would amble down off the high snow fields and congregate along the spawning streams. There would be colossal battles for choice fishing sites; but once those were decided, the animals would all settle down to eating their fill every day as the returning salmon fought their way upstream to spawn. Herds of seals and sea lions would mass on jutting points of land and along rocky shores of islands to dip into the run for their annual feast. They would charge into the nets of seiners, ripping them to shreds, and spend hours searching for the opening to a fish trap, trying to get at the thousands of salmon inside. Eagles, hawks, crows, and foxes would vie with the brown bears, seals, and sea lions at every stream and sandbar. Over all would circle hordes of screaming gulls scouring land, sea, and the beaches, cleaning up, to the last morsel, every crumb left by previous feeders.

Fish pirates in dark-painted boats, running without lights, their names and windows blacked out, would creep in under a blanket of fog or the protective covering of a dark night to steal salmon from the fish traps. More than once the sound of gunfire would lace the stillness as some hardy trap watchman fought to protect his silver harvest.

Other pirates, called creek robbers, would slip into the forbidden spawning streams and seine salmon in the act of spawning. Every living thing would get its share of the huge harvest from the sea, and there would still be ample left for spawning.

During the feverish month or six weeks of fishing the canneries and the hundreds of fishermen must make their year's wages. Then, as quickly as it had begun, the season would end.

The traps would be taken from the sea; the canneries' doors would close. One morning all the people and fishing boats that had come north would be gone. Orca City would again be a quiet Alaskan village, its streets empty of all but its regular inhabitants. The bay would have only a few dozen boats left. The brown bears, rolling in fat now, would begin preparing for their winter sleep.

Only Ben would have had none of this harvest. He would have spent all summer chained in the dark interior of the shed, living on an occasional loaf of old stale bread. Ben would not be fat for his winter's sleep.

It was not really warm except directly in the sun. Finally the shadow cast by the eaves of the buildings reached Mark and Ben. A chill breeze came up off the sea and stirred the boy's fine hair. It was neither blond, like his father's, nor black, like his mother's. It was an indefinite in-between brown. His frame was not heavy-boned for thirteen, and there was a delicate look about him. His cheeks were too thin, too white, and his brown eyes were dreamily wistful. They looked too large for his small face.

The bite of the wind finally roused Mark. He started up guiltily. He had to get home. He untied the chain, and said, "Come on, Ben." At the first tug Ben rose and dutifully followed the boy into the dark interior of the shed. Mark retied the chain to the center post exactly as he had found it. Then Ben sniffed at the boy's hands, where the faint aroma of sandwiches still lingered, and his red tongue licked Mark's fingers experimentally.

"I guess you're still hungry," Mark said. He patted Ben's broad head. "I wouldn't have to leave you like this if you were mine. I've got to go now. I'll come again as soon as I can."

Mark gathered up his books and sweater and hurried down the trail toward home. The wind had ruffled the flat surface of the distant bay, and a big fat cloud was bulging into the sky behind the Aleutian Range. It must be a little later than usual, he thought. The sun was poised on top of the mountain.

The Field of the Caribou

JOHN HAINES

Distinguished American poet and essayist John Haines was born in Norfolk, Virginia, in 1924. For more than two decades, beginning in 1947, Haines homesteaded seventy miles south of Fairbanks. A prolific writer and winner of many awards, Haines is a former poet laureate of Alaska. "The Field of the Caribou" is taken from his poetry collection WINTER NEWS *(1966). "Wolves" was published in* THE STONE HARP *(1971).*

Moving in a restless exhaustion,
humps of earth that rise
covered with dead hair.

There is no sound from the wind
blowing the tattered velvet
of their antlers.

The grey shepherds of the tundra
pass like islands of smoke,
and I hear only a heavy thumping
as though far in the west
some tired bodies
were falling from a cliff.

Wolves

JOHN HAINES

Last night I heard wolves howling,
their voices coming from afar
over the wind-polished ice—so much
brave solitude in that sound.

They are death's snowbound sailors;
they know only a continual
drifting between moonlit islands,
their tongues licking the stars.

But they sing as good seamen should,
and tomorrow the sun will find them,
yawning and blinking
the snow from their eyelashes.

Their voices rang through the frozen
water of my human sleep,
blown by the night wind
with the moon for an icy sail.

Wolves, for John Haines

TOM SEXTON

Tom Sexton is a retired university professor, editor, and poet who writes many of his poems at his remote cabin in the wilderness near Talkeetna, Alaska. He founded and edited Raven, *an Alaska literary magazine, organized some of the first writers' conferences at the University of Alaska Anchorage in the 1970s, and is the author of several collections of poems, including* LATE AUGUST ON THE KENAI, THE BEND TOWARD ASIA *(1993), and* A BLOSSOM OF SNOW *(1995). Sexton has dedicated his poem "Wolves" to fellow poet and friend, John Haines. "Wolves" is taken from* THE BEND TOWARD ASIA.

While his friends drag
a stringer of bright fish
up the trail,

a fisherman throws
dark salmon into
a slough from

his skiff.
They float belly-
up in opaque

silt. Overhead
small planes carry
hunters who are

dreaming of wolves
they will run
to ground from the air

before the kill.
I imagine you bent over
the last sliver

of open water. You're
looking for dog-salmon
to gaff before ice

and hunger set your table.
In dreams, wolves call
from their snow-

bound island, and you wake
and walk to the river
the moon's splayed paw on
your shoulder.

The Red Snow

JAMES GREINER

James Greiner (1933–1992), bush pilot, wilderness guide, and naturalist, worked for many years as the curator of the University of Alaska Museum in Fairbanks. His books include WAGER WITH THE WIND: THE DON SHELDON STORY *(1982) and* THE RED SNOW: A STORY OF THE ALASKAN GRAY WOLF *(1980). In this excerpt from* THE RED SNOW, *Greiner offers insights into the life of a Tanana River Valley wolf pack.*

A solitary raven spiraled slowly against the window of sky framed by the ravine's upper walls, its wings luffing softly in the cold afternoon stillness. Missing flight feathers formed clearly visible slots as the bird hung motionless on the waning updrafts, then disappeared as it swung away from the ledge rocks on folded wings only to return once more. Nothing moved in the gloom below, yet it was as if the black carrion eater were reluctant to leave its vantage point above the drainage.

Blue slabs of rotting glacier ice still clung to the winter-wet rocks above the bed of St. George Creek, and the flow of black water was shriveling visibly with the quickly dropping evening temperature. During midday the canyon had boomed with the sound of tumbling water, its volume fed by a feeble early May sun from the vast snowfields above. Now only the metallic trickling remained, and even this would be frozen to silence with the coming of the spring twilight, leaving thin lacelike shells of rime ice capping the slate-colored rocks.

The creek, like hundreds of others, flowed insignificantly from its origins in the ponderous north wall of the rugged Alaska Mountain Range. Totally dependent upon annual snowfall, it was fattened by glacial melt and the liquification of countless tons of decaying snow during the brief Arctic spring. By midsummer it would not be a creek at all, only a dry bed of bleached pebbles and rusted rock brought to intermittent life by infrequent rainsqualls as they pelted the barren slopes above.

Farther down the drainage, and out of sight around its final bend above the valley floor, a broad shale field received the sporadic contributions of St. George Creek, splitting and further subdividing them among the ice-scarred dwarf willows along its lower edge. Then lower still, and after being absorbed by the loose rock, the creek emerged from its brief underground ramblings saturated with silt and buckskin brown in color. Finally, after reforming in a common bed, it flowed haltingly onto the flats toward its confluence with the bigger Wood River.

The Wood, one of several large streams which bisected the lowlands, flowed in a northwesterly direction to eventually merge with the broad and sluggish Tanana as it meandered toward its own union with the mighty Yukon. Then still later, and more than eight hundred miles from its birthplace in the rocks of the Alaska Range, St. George Creek became an unnoticeable part of the Bering Sea.

This day in May had been little different from those which preceded it. Beneath a sour-bisquit-dough sky, only the damp wind from the flats had served as an almost unnoticed reminder that sixty-below-zero temperatures were once more a thing of the recent past. Spring had been slow in coming, even by Alaskan standards, and the weak, infrequent sun had served only to send scurrying spots of brilliance across the mountain slopes, bringing the siksiks, or parka squirrels, from their burrows for brief periods during midday. Patches of granular snow still lingered beneath shadowed ledges in the bottom of gullies and beneath the stands of black spruce at the foot of the slopes.

To both the eye and ear, the ravine which carried St. George Creek seemed devoid of all life, as though stunned by the returning cold of late afternoon. Only the occasional glassy tinkle of frost-dislodged shale broke the silence which hung like a mantle over the drainage, a silence made even more complete by thin tendrils of fog which condensed beneath the last vestige of warm air as it slid over the cold of the creekbed itself. Even the orange and red smears of lichen that added meager color to a world of rock had faded to drabness, bespectacled by water droplets which glazed to hardness even as they formed.

The wolf was a drifting blot of gray as she ascended the ravine, her winter-long claws rasping faintly as she slipped on the ice-sheathed rocks.

Not trotting as wolves usually do, she seemed to move in a leisurely manner, but her panting and sagging belly betrayed the illusion. Pregnant with what would likely be her last litter of pups, she stopped frequently to sniff the invisible trail she followed among the rocks and broken tapestries of blue ice. Then, after slipping badly, she paused to lick her pendulous udders, which were tender with the traveling she had done during the long afternoon.

The bitch was small by the standards of her kind. Even given the fluids and life that bloated her, along with the bellyful of rotting caribou flesh she had consumed, her weight was less than sixty-five pounds. Had it not been for her advanced pregnancy, she would have preferred to feed at night, but hunger dictated otherwise.

There were six adult wolves in the St. George Creek pack, including the little gray bitch. A huge black male, her conjugal mate since her first period of annual heat, was as much an exception to standard size as was the small female. During times of seasonal prime, he weighed almost 130 pounds and stood three feet high at his roached shoulder. There was little doubt that his physical size and age were factors which established him as leader of the pack, yet his position of dominance was not absolute. Though he bore undisputed authority over most of the others, his mate, the small gray bitch, was also an influential member of the St. George Creek pack. Though she respected and followed him, her reaction to his dominance within the group was less rigid, and was probably a normal result of both her sex and the fact that he was her full brother.

Two buff-tan males, both two-year-old sons of the black leader and the gray bitch, formed the hunting nucleus of the pack in company with their sire. With the passage of their second winter of life and recent sexual maturity, they had attained true adulthood.

The remaining members of the St. George Creek pack were adult females. Each bore the white coloration of their common father, and were the only members of the pack that did not claim the bloodlines of the black leader.

Whelped during a heavy rainstorm which flooded the den occupied by their mother before she had licked them dry, they were the only survivors in a litter of seven pups. Then, during their second winter, both of their parents fell victim to an experienced trapper, and the pair had left their home range on the bleak MacCombe Plateau more than eighty straight-line miles to the east of St. George Creek. They had traveled alone during the balance of a severe winter, and during the following spring joined with a small group led by the black.

The merger was a rarity, for seldom do wolves join the packs of other leaders, or, more properly, are they allowed to join by the strange pack. Sheer coincidence may have been the catalyst for acceptance, as one of the white bitches was in estrus when the wolves met, while the other had just finished with her own heat period.

The small size of the black's pack may also have been responsible for his giving reluctant permission to the white wolves to first follow at a respectable distance and then finally be accepted as regular members of the St. George Creek pack. Had either or both these circumstances been absent, it is more than likely that the big wolf and his adult sons would have routed the strangers or even killed them.

Both were, as a result of the absence of parents during their second year, more inexperienced where hunting was concerned than they would have been after a more normal adolescence. As resident members of the pack, they occupied the lower end of the social order headed by the huge black but more rigidly enforced by his mate, the gray bitch.

Two days earlier the black wolf had led the others away from the remnants of the caribou carcass in search of better meat, and upon his return he would continue to aid his two adult sons in the care of his pregnant mate. Since the pack's departure, the gray bitch had made several of the five-mile journeys to the carcass, seemingly content with the nearness of her solitary meals.

Several foxes, a dozen or more of the ubiquitous ravens, and a wolverine competed with her for what was left of the more than two hundred pounds of meat that the caribou had once represented. The foxes required and ate little, while the ravens consumed surprising quantities of the softening flesh, and the bearlike wolverine seemed obsessed only with the stolid ambition to carry away every last scrap, eating only occasionally while present at the kill.

The wolverine had left scuffling trails which led to all points of the compass away from the kill, and while dragging each chunk of meat and hide, he had paused only long enough to hastily chew away those parts of his booty that became tangled in the stunted willows. His efforts that afternoon resulted in the disappearance of the entire antlered head as he resolutely dragged the twenty-pound burden to a point more than half a mile from the carcass. Each cache of meat he established was doused with his sour musky urine, then buried beneath patchy loose snow and thawing earth, to be exhumed at some later date. That the wolverine would forget the location of virtually all these morsels was of little concern to him, and his short-sightedness was surpassed only by his exceedingly foul disposition.

During the two days just past, the forty-pound animal had visited the carcass while the gray bitch dozed nearby, and she had tolerated his presence. The short-legged, chocolate-brown animal moved constantly as he fed, the yoke-shaped mantle of long yellowish guard hairs over his hips and flanks rippling as he worked at the carcass. Reluctant to feed while the pack was in attendance, he watched the sleeping bitch with small hazel-colored eyes while grunting shallowly with the effort required to work chunks of frost-marbled flesh from the rotting carcass. The foxes possessed far less courage than did the wolverine and a mere fraction of his ambition. They vacated the kill when the gray bitch approached and returned only after she departed.

Eleven years of life had been an eternity for the small gray bitch, a span punctuated regularly by events which had taught habit patterns rooted in momentary incidents of panic sometimes coupled with physical pain. As she continued her slow climb of the darkening creekbed, her slight limp became obvious and she flinched involuntarily at some imagined threat.

Once clear of the drainage's steepest part, and following a vague sheep trail which snaked among the dead, snow-matted grass and dwarf willows, she began to trot steadily. Then, higher on the clearing, tendrils of vapor obscured her as she covered the final quarter mile to the domelike promontory which housed the den. Located well away from the rocky bed of St. George Creek in a hanging treeless meadow, its mouth was made visible only as she paused to enter it.

Dug by foxes during some long-past time, the den was set twelve feet deep beneath the meadow's skin of powdery, acid soil. Slanting downward for almost eight feet through glacial debris, it turned at right angles to the main passageway before ending abruptly in a cul-de-sac only slightly larger than the small wolf. The den had no other entrances or exits. The soil surrounding the den chamber itself consisted of powdered rock fines, and because of its elevation and origin, was free of permafrost. As such, it was dry, a fact which long ago made the site acceptable to those who used it.

The floor of the den was littered with use-worn pebbles and small sticks, but was devoid of bones and other debris. It was a place of total darkness, to be used by scent and feel alone. The gray bitch knew it well, for she had whelped here during all but two of the nine springs that had passed since her first heat period.

Above ground, the den's mouth was hidden among the nodding tufts of wiry sedges and porous slab rock that covered the entire dome, and was nearly invisible. Even the shelf of loose soil kicked out by the early generations of red and cross foxes that created the excavation in the beginning had begrudgingly accepted the infinitely slow growth of moss, lichens, and saw grass, so that only the deep-cut and narrow trail which vanished into the mouth of the den set the place apart from the rest of the hillside. On this day in mid-May it was the only one of four others above the creek that was occupied for the purpose of birth, for the St. George Creek pack boasted only one pregnancy this year.

Though she had never brought food here, the interior of the den reeked with the scent of the caribou carcass that saturated her coat, for it was beginning to decompose in the scant warmth of the lengthening days. Due to her advanced pregnancy, the gray bitch had rested frequently while feeding among the slatted rib bones and other debris which protruded through the snow. At other times she moved away, sometimes several hundred feet distant, to lay up in a more preferable position, one usually open to the sun's warmth and at an elevation higher than the kill.

With use, the site of the kill had become hard-packed, the snow stained brown with blood and yellowed by the scattered oily contents of the caribou's paunch. If seen from above, the place would have resembled a huge wagon wheel, the carcass itself forming the hub, and trails made by the gray bitch and other visitors to the kill, the spokes, which radiated outward in numerous directions.

The St. George Creek pack had merely been the final mechanism which brought death to the caribou, and its carcass had represented a gratuity not to be passed by. The barren, spindle-antlered cow had, in fact, already been dead on its feet of simple old age coupled with the long-term inroads of stomach parasites as she stumbled out onto the remnant snow pan that fanned away from the tiny creek. Open-mouthed and panting, she sought escape from the heat of the spring sun, heat made oppressive by her thick, dull, and as yet unshed winter coat of hollow hair. Each spring during her long lifetime had held similar periods of suffering the sudden need to adapt physiologically to a brief world of heat after seven months of absolute cold. Lying on the slushy snow seemed to reduce the added torture perpetrated by the already present clouds of tiny gnats, and it is likely that she would not have fled even had she been able to regain her feet fast enough to avoid the wolves that smothered her.

For the pack, the cow had represented an easily attained supply of fresh meat, and the short five-mile distance that separated it from the den made it more than accessible to the gray bitch. Had the winter just past been more severe, the entire pack would easily have consumed the carcass during the first day of the kill, but travel was easy and game becoming plentiful. The black had fed lightly, as did the others, after which they struck out across the pans of granular snow and thaw-drenched reaches of open tundra to hunt elsewhere. The gray bitch had not accompanied the pack.

Because of her advanced pregnancy, the old female continued to placate her insatiable hunger here. For her the carcass was a bounty in a land that offered few, while for the solitary wolverine it was merely a luxury to be gloated over and hoarded in well-fed greed, then ultimately wasted through simple forgetfulness.

Were the small gray bitch of fewer years and shorter experience, it is likely that she would, by now, be well on her way to a slow, almost imperceptible death by starvation. Her gimped hind leg, her small size, and badly worn teeth, coupled with the pregnancy, which, because of her age, should not have occurred, would have tipped the delicate scales long before. Only her inclusion in the black male's young constituency had made this, her eleventh summer, possible.

Yawning in the darkness of the den, she nipped at her tufted flanks in an idle effort to still the kicking pups, then shifted her position among the smooth, hair-matted irregularities of the den floor. Though she had visited the caribou carcass daily, her meals there had become hurried, almost urgent, and as a result she had spent increasing periods of time in the den. Each day during the past week, the trip back had become more burdensome, and today her labored panting persisted long after she had regained her wind.

Above and beyond her sight, the den opening had winked out, and her ears flicked as a small bridge of ice collapsed somewhere in the darkness of rocks above the meadow. Then, after turning several times and finding no comfort in the doing, she stood bent-legged in the total darkness before scratching at the unyielding floor of the den.

....

Bright midmorning sunshine flooded the steep hillside in the spruce where the pack lay scattered among a jungle of deadfall timber and upturned root snags. The two white bitches were absent, and the black raised his head slowly to test the almost nonexistent breeze that washed the place. Only the faintest odors of spruce pitch and bark along with the slatelike scent of old snow were evident, and after several long minutes the big wolf tucked his long muzzle beneath his tail once more and closed his eyes.

The wolves had returned often to the tiny clearing since their last arrival in the valley of the Tatlanika. Well away from the river and almost four miles from the cabin of Jake Tatum, it was a place of natural concealment. The old man's travels took him well away from the pack's loafing place rather than nearer to it, and, as a result, his trails were concentrated on the valley floor to the west of the cabin.

With the slow passage of March and its final surrender to early April, the first real promises of warm weather became more frequent and genuine. The warming air produced white hoarfrost on the still-frozen and snow-free earth beneath undercut banks.

Close by the three sleeping wolves, translucent curls of bark were bright highlights along the trunks of birch as they picked up the sun glare behind them, and the spruces and dense alder thickets were alive with small birds, most of them winter residents. Chickadees, with their jaunty, jet-black caps, buzzed while nervously exchanging places on needle-dense limbs while slate-colored juncos flashed their stark-white tail feathers in swooping flight. Canada jays added their solemn calls as, in pairs, they too investigated the secret shadows beneath the brooding trees. Flights of Bohemian waxwings paused among the tops of leafless aspens and, higher along the crests of the sunlit hills, groups of the ever-present ravens tumbled and swooped, at play in the warming air.

The wolves had, in an almost unnoticeable manner, also changed their daily habit patterns. The tight-knit closeness that marked the interminable winter months had given way to more casual movements, as witnessed by the early departure of the resident bitches earlier that morning.

The old bitch had watched them take their leave from her resting place in a sun patch along the rotting spruce trunk where she lay even before the sun had truly begun to warm. They had stood, shaken the snow from their coats, urinated in turn, and then glided slowly downslope to disappear into the cobalt shadows at the clearing's edge.

The pack's renewed desire to sleep away the daylight hours was, in all probability, triggered by the returning sunlight. Diurnal periods were now more than twelve hours long, and with their rapidly burgeoning duration, the land's exposure to the higher sun brought a more permanent warmth that made long periods of idle dozing not only an enjoyable but profitable venture. Such idleness during the warm hours propagated conservation of the meager energy stores of winter.

To all outward appearances, survival for the black wolf and his followers seemed guaranteed now, but their still-cramped guts caused the dozing wolves to whimper and intermittently stretch their forelegs before once more slipping into an almost lethargic half-sleep. It was this forced wakefulness that had caused the two white females to leave the clearing that day, and this was the factor which brought them ultimately to the bank of the Tatlanika where they sat on the brilliance of open snow to watch the silent cabin of Jake Tatum.

Both wolves had gone there by choice rather than mere chance. While still a mile upriver, they had scented the thin haze of spruce smoke that scurled among the trees and washed the open snow of the river. At first the scent had been almost nonexistent, yet enough of it had been present to cause the pair to swing downriver toward its source. Then, as it strengthened, it built the strange warmth of attraction, and casual interest gave way to open curiosity.

The white wolves had closed to a point less than three hundred yards from the cabin, which was now clearly visible from their vantage point on the open snow of the river's opposite bank. As they watched, only the thin wisps of white smoke that issued from the rusted tin pipe chimney gave movement to the place, yet it was enough to hold their attention closely.

The distant belling of a raven intruded upon the silence and caused both wolves to pitch their ears forward while they continued to watch the smoke, which thinned visibly as the minutes passed. With the sun strengthening, several gray jays began to make patient sorties to the pile of frozen carcasses, flickering across a patchwork of sunny places on unmoving wings.

The minutes continued to slip away, and after retreating a short distance along their back trail, both wolves made a brief excursion onto the open ice of the river before once more returning to their watching place. Their initial apprehension slowly gave way to familiarity, and the pair finally crossed the open river to slip into the dense fringe of willow brush on the other side. It was here that they inadvertently discovered the airplane.

Approaching cautiously, they quietly sniffed the base of the drum that anchored one of the craft's wings, then shied away from some insignificant sound before slipping into the willows once more. The faint scents of engine oil and high-octane gasoline that had been brought to life in the warming air tingled in the noses of both wolves as they returned hesitantly to sample more of the scent.

Another half hour passed during which the white wolves lingered in and behind the security of the dense willow. Finally they began a cautious approach toward the cabin itself, but not before circling to its downwind side. As they slowly negotiated the clearing's edge, they encountered the abrupt curtain of heavy feral scent that drifted from the carcass pile, and they paused to fill their noses with the vaguely familiar but unidentifiable mix. Moving once more, and just beyond the snow-covered heap of the slowly decaying remains of the old man's efforts, they encountered the warmer scent of the old husky dog as she lay curled in late sleep in the shelter box.

Examining the new scent, both of the wolves, with slowly wagging tails, sat upright on the snow and faced the direction from which it came. Its density and warmth told them that its maker was nearby, and as if to offer proof, the dog shook herself, the chain which held her in the old man's absence tunking hollowly on the boards.

With the unexpected sound, both wolves stood and advanced slowly, their earlier caution diluted now by the increased scent and the sounds which accompanied it. Ten feet from the entrance to the husky's makeshift bed, they stopped and once more sat on the packed snow, their tails still wagging and their lolling tongues hidden behind the vapor plumes their breathing made.

Tatum's husky was an old dog, her pale blue eyes already clouding with the milky blindness of senility. As she rose to stretch and shake, there was nothing to warn her of needed caution, and after yawning deeply, she stepped out into the bright sun, which momentarily blinded her.

The dog's appearance merely hastened the inevitable, and her failing eyes caught only blurred movement before she was knocked from her feet and quickly pinned by her throat on the snow. She died without sound beneath the weight of the white wolves, each of which outstripped her by more than thirty pounds. Then, as they attempted to drag her carcass away from the cabin, the chain which tethered it came tight, and the wolves fed on the spot. By midafternoon only the husky's head and half of its attached spinal column remained, made macabre by the still-attached collar and chain.

Long shadows lanced across the river snow as the late afternoon sun dropped lower behind the dense spruce near the cabin, and the air cooled quickly. After dozing several hundred yards away, both wolves stood and stretched their legs before returning to sniff the dog's pathetic remains. Then, turning, they walked slowly toward the river.

....

The old man had worried about the husky when he set the double-springed number-three traps near the base of the carcass pile. A wolverine had visited the place on several occasions while he was away, however, and at the time this seemed to justify a decision to set them. The traps had then lain beneath the building snow, and after several weeks the old man had forgotten them.

One of the white wolves paused to urinate as she passed the carcass pile, after which she swung toward it. As she reached for the intoxicating scent with her nose, the small trap closed upon her right forepaw. She made no outcry, but leaped straight into the air to be jerked rudely back to earth by the drag chain, which was firmly frozen where it was attached to the rock-hard trunk of a long-buried carcass.

The trap that imprisoned the white bitch was not a large one. It gripped less firmly than a bigger trap, and produced less of the numbing shock upon closure. Thus, with the passage of only a few minutes, excruciating pain quickly coursed upward into the white wolf's leg, making her whine and pant deeply. Each small movement she made against the hold and pull of the trap caused a cramping agony, which soon spread into her chest and forequarters. Instead of causing her to increase her efforts to break free, the pain rather than the mere mechanical holding strength of the trap caused her to crouch protectively over her crushed paw. She continued to whine raggedly as her sister watched from the deepening shadows.

Darkness was almost complete when the distant, popping drone of Tatum's snowmobile drifted into the trapped wolf's consciousness, and she paused in the licking of her forefoot to listen. Minutes later she sat upright to watch the approach of the machine's headlight as, seemingly disembodied, it cut a jerking, erratic path through the darkness.

The old man swung the machine across the riverbed, and as he topped the gentle slope on the cabin side of the river, the snowmobile's brilliant light caught the red glow of the white bitch's eyes.

Stopping, and with the machine at idle, Tatum slipped the heavy mitten from his right hand and reached slowly for the rifle that rode in a crude scabbard beneath his leg. Momentarily confused by the wolf's reluctance to flee, he remembered the traps moments before the rifle's pop extinguished the glowing eyes in the snow beyond. After dragging the body of the white bitch to the area of hard-packed snow near the entrance to the cabin, the old man lit a lantern and quickly built a fire in the Yukon stove. As his eyes became accustomed to the light, he cursed a small leak in the roof that had, during the day, created a small stalagmite of clear ice on the table's worn oil-cloth surface. Later, perhaps tomorrow, he would scrape the thawing snow from the roof and somehow repair it.

Sipping the scalding coffee and listening to the mind-warming sounds made by the crackling spruce pitch in the stove, he reflected upon his unexpected good fortune that the white wolf had ventured so close to the cabin. Hunger had obviously been the reason, and the carcass heap seemed a reasonable goal for such needs. As the first warmth of the stove pushed the wall of cold air ahead of it, the old man spoke to the husky, and the unnatural quiet that followed intruded slowly upon his wandering thoughts.

In the hissing pressure lantern's sterile light, the grim and pathetic remains of the dog seemed to leap upward from the snow at the old man's feet. He cursed bitterly before turning back to the cabin. As he passed the stiffening carcass of the white wolf, its well-distended belly seem to mock the hunger that brought it here, and seemed repulsive.

Despite his exhaustion, the old man sat in the circle of the lantern light long after the strips of moose he had hastily thawed and fried had been eaten. The meat had tasted flat, as did the whiskey he drank from the bottle before him, and as he sat, the trapping of wolves took on a new aspect, one of revenge. A plan drifted into the old man's numbed mind, a plan which focused upon the red airplane that stood encased in the snow outside.

Woodsman

FROM *Make Prayers to the Raven*

RICHARD K. NELSON

A cultural anthropologist and Sitka resident, prolific writer Richard K. Nelson
was awarded the John Burroughs Nature Writing Medal for his book
THE ISLAND WITHIN *(1989). "Woodsman" is excerpted from* MAKE PRAYERS
TO THE RAVEN: A KOYUKON VIEW OF THE NORTHERN FOREST *(1986).*

I t is as real as any other creature in the vast Koyukon wildland, but far
more mysterious. It is always there, somewhere, but almost never seen.
It is an incongruous sound in the distance, a movement just beyond
the thicket, a diabolical laugh in the darkness. It is something unac-
countably thrown toward a lonely hunter, meat that vanishes in the
night from drying racks, something stolen from an unattended camp, a
child gone without a trace. It is called *nuhu'anh* (also *nik'inla'eena* or *nik'il'-
eena*), "it sneaks here and there." And in English it is named woodsman.

Long ago, before the security of modern times, Koyukon people occasionally ran perilously short of food in their remote camps. Sinking toward
death from starvation, people would sometimes resort to the almost
unthinkable desperation of cannibalism. But the price was very great
indeed. Anyone driven to the point of surviving on human flesh (or sometimes a person who committed murder) would vanish into the forest. There
the culprits became wild, suddenly lost fundamental aspects of their
humanity, and never again returned to the society they had left. Although
it has been many decades since anyone fled this way, woodsmen still stalk
the wilds, hiding themselves almost completely from human contact, living
more like animals than humans.

To some degree, in fact, they have become animals. Although they
remain human in appearance, their bodies are covered with short fur.

According to Jetté (1911:105), they have long arms and clawlike nails. They are both male and female, but they live a solitary existence. People speculate that they must get together sometimes to produce offspring, but this is not known from Koyukon tradition. Woodsmen are in many respects super-human, in both physical and spiritual ways. Their life span must be very long, far beyond that of ordinary people—otherwise they would likely have died off by now. They run so swiftly that even in the open they are difficult to see. Three men who saw a woodsman run across a meadow said that only the dust settling behind it was visible. And they have other powers as well, because woodsmen can vanish at will. Their spirit is so potent that they seem almost to be spirits themselves.

In the winter woodsmen retire to dens much as bears do. This, and their power to leave no trace, explains why their tracks are so rarely found. The few people who have seen footprints say they are humanlike, but longer, quite narrow, and with the big toe set apart from the rest. Perhaps the most tangible contact people have with them is when someone stumbles across a den:

In 1953 my brother and I were trapping beaver up there. My old man and other people used to say there's a hill up there called Nuhu'anh Kkuno. *That means "woodsman's house." They always tell us, don't walk around on that hill, so we always kept off of it. But my brother didn't know. He was trapping beaver right in that area. He checked his set, and beaver had cleaned up the bait.*

So he started to climb that hill, and the higher he got it looks like it's better for bait up above; and finally he got right up on top. There's a big hump over there, like a bear den. So he forgot about his bait and he started to walk over there. He said you could just kneel down in the opening; it's kind of oblong. He cut a stick and he shoved it inside, to see if there's a bear inside it. But the stick he cut was too short. Pretty soon he cut one off that's twenty-some feet long, I think he said. He shoved it in there, but no end yet.

Pretty soon he went back to his dogs and got his .30-30. Went back up there and got birchbark, dry birchbark, and he burned it. He started to crawl back in there with it. He wanted to see what's back there, I guess. And he shoved that stick in, so it's going in ahead of him. And the farther back he got in there, he said it was so much stink. *Whatever was in there—probably woodsman breath or something—it was so much stink he said he had to get out. And he barely got out. Something like gas fumes. Boy, he said, it was just terrible! He just left it right there.*

He came home that evening. When he came in, boy was he sick! He started throwing up. Then he came out of it. I told him that's a woodsman's house, and first thing he started talking about is we should get people—capture it. I told him if you did that you'll always have tough luck and all that, so finally he gave up on it. Quite a few years later, when I worked on the river, I'd tell that story. They'd try to talk me into taking them there, but I wouldn't do it. Even if we did go there, you know, probably it wouldn't be there; probably nothing at all, not even a sign of the den. If you did catch one, your family would suffer for it.

Certain places scattered around the country are known as woodsman haunts, inhabited by these creatures for many years. People usually try to avoid these spots when they set up camps, although some are much less frightened than others. Woodsmen are mainly regarded as a nuisance rather than a serious threat. They often steal meat, fish, and other things from summer camps; and they harass people by whistling, throwing sticks, or making evil-sounding laughter nearby. I was told that "a woodsman will play tricks on people too, if it's a playful one—like stretching somebody's fishnet out in the trees." Probably all adults in the Koyukuk villages have experienced these things many times, though to my knowledge none has ever had a clear look at the creature itself.

The sound of shots somewhere out in the wilds, when no one should be around, also reveals the presence of woodsmen. Over the years they have managed to steal rifles and ammunition from camps. A man said that once he heard shots and went to investigate. Alongside a beaver pond he found the moss tracked and pressed down, and so he concluded that a woodsman had been shooting at beavers.

The greatest threat from woodsmen is their desire to steal children and raise them as their own. This is one way, people speculate, that they keep from dying out. I heard stories of children vanishing without a trace, including some within the lifetime of today's adults, and each case was attributed to a woodsman. Once, for example, a woodsman took a baby from between its sleeping parents. The father, who was a medicine man, awoke and gave chase. Seeing that the creature was a female, he shouted that he would "make her his wife," so she finally slowed down and he managed to catch her. Then he hit her with a killing blow and got the child back. When the baby grew up, his eyes had a mongoloid shape, as people often say the woodsman's eyes do. And he was an incredibly fast runner, "so fast you could hardly see him."

Jetté (1911:105) learned at Nulato that if a woodsman pats a sleeping child's head, the child will grow up to become a shaman; and an adult who even sees one may become insane. To avoid this, a person must either be gentle toward the creature, stroking and caressing it, or must kill it and then eat its liver (to avoid retribution from its spirit). My Koyukon teachers advised leaving woodsmen alone, trying to avoid them as much as possible. They are not really threatening to adults, as long as people tolerate their malicious theft and prowling. They are only unfortunate recluses, after all, and it is best to pity them for the life they have led. The old-timers also advise that people who see a woodsman should refuse to be afraid; otherwise the fear will make them temporarily sick.

> South Fork people went bear hunting one fall, this was long ago. Pretty soon somebody hollered, thought he found a bear den. So they all gathered up there. But then they heard something crying in there, just like a person. Well, the old-timers found out right away when they heard that, so they talked to the woodsman. They told him, "We only made a mistake, that's all. We'll just walk away, and you just mind your own business too." They could capture it that time, but they didn't want to bother it.

A Huslia man told of an experience he had one spring while hunting muskrats with a young companion. When he suggested they camp for the night at a certain spot, his partner said no—his grandmother had warned him it was a woodsman's haunt. "I don't know what got into me," he said. "I told him there used to be woodsmen long ago, but they all got old and died. You know, that's really what some people say."

The two men finally bedded down; but sometime during the night the one who told the story began to hear something. It was coming toward him, but he was unable to wake up, as if he was "hypnotized." All at once his blanket was torn off him, landing about twenty feet away. He jumped to his feet but saw nothing except a wiggling branch that the woodsman had brushed as it fled. "That woodsman probably bothered me because I said those things, acted tough. He probably wanted to show what he could do to me. I never talked like that again afterward."

One of my Koyukon instructors said that when he was young he thought he would try to kill any woodsman he saw, but now he would leave it alone. Anyone who did manage to kill one of these creatures should tell no one, because doing so would bring illness and every kind of bad luck to that person's family. Traditionally, a Koyukon person nearing death would tell someone the bad things he or she had done. Killing a woodsman was among these. But only one person has ever made such a revelation; many years ago a man said he had killed three during his life. All of them were in the general region of Hughes and Huslia, all were females, and all harassed him beyond his tolerance before he killed them.

The first happened during fall, when he was hunting alone. He had killed too much game to carry in his canoe, so he made a little smokehouse and camped there while the meat dried. But each night some of the best meat would disappear, and he suspected that the thief was a woodsman. Then one night he saw the woodsman enter his smokehouse, check the meat in the moonlight to find the best pieces, and make off with an excellent fat goose. This was too much for his patience, and as the woodsman began slipping away he shot it with his rifle. "It yelled just like a dog . . . just like you whipped a dog. And he heard it fall down over there." He never moved and never slept for the rest of the night, and when daylight came he looked to see what he had killed. Not far from the smokehouse he found it, a young female covered with short fur. Strangely, it wore high-laced shoes and a small black hat and carried a fancy brass-handled knife. He took it to a nearby creek, where he cut its remains into pieces and put them in the water.

The other two he also encountered while hunting alone, and each time the woodsman followed him as he tried to get away from it. One stayed near him for several days, sometimes laughing diabolically; finally, as it came closer, he shot it. The other pursued him as he paddled across lakes and portaged between, gradually catching up to him. In the end it grabbed hold of him; "I don't know, probably it wanted to hug him, make love to him, I guess." He killed this one with his knife. Both of these he cut up and disposed of as he had the first.

Sometimes after the last incident his wife had a child, and he gave it a name meaning, "I got scared suddenly." Koyukon names often tell something as a "riddle," and from this people were able to surmise what had happened. So the stories he told before his death only confirmed what everyone already suspected. "I guess there's lots of other people that killed woodsmen too, but they never said anything about it."

Koyukon people often speculate on the ultimate fate of the woodsmen, whether these obscure and enigmatic creatures are disappearing forever from the wildlands. For a period of years there seemed to be fewer and fewer encounters. Perhaps, people thought, they were dying off because starvation was a thing of the past and no one occurred again around the camps, and each summer there are reports of woodsmen heard near their old haunts.

Some elders suggest that they had retreated, for reasons unknown, to the region of the Alaska oil pipeline. Then, disturbed by the activity and intrusion there, they were driven back to their home country. But others feel that there are more encounters now simply because village people are spending the summer in camps again. For a while woodsmen had the forest to themselves; but now people have returned. And the night sounds of the sneaker are heard once more.

All spring this woodsman was bothering us. It even took our matches, or we missed rifle shells, you know. We knew there was nobody around, and yet we'd hear shooting, in different areas, about every night or every other night. We knew there was a woodsman around.

Every once in a while we'd hear somebody whistle at us. Another time it threw a stick at us too—that's when I really saw that stick. Not a stick you just picked up now; he carried that a long time, you could see it. It wore out. It landed right by us. My old man went over, picked it up, threw it back where it came from. He was not scared . . . no. Sometimes they tell a woodsman, "I'm going to cook your liver!" That's the way you scare him away. But my old man didn't. I figured any chance I get I'm going to kill him, not tell my old man about it.

One time I heard it real close. I was sitting down below the bank, watching beaver way out in the lake, and pretty soon I thought I heard my old man coming back. He came just above me, then he just let out a sharp whistle. I should have known right there, that's not my old man. So I whistled and I was coming out. Whatever it was, it just took into the brush right there! Then I knew. I knew right there, that's not the old man. I was scared. I was really scared.

Only place I felt safe was right there under the bank, so nothing could get me from behind my back. So I loaded up my .30-30, all ready to shoot. Pretty soon I hear something coming back. I figured before he gets any chance at me I'm going to shoot him. Then all of a sudden I saw it was my old man, carrying two big beaver! But he never saw I had my gun pointed at him. Right away I told him a woodsman was there, but he never said anything.

After we got home he told Mom he heard a woodsman real close; first time. He was packing those two beaver, and right there in the big trees a woodsman just let out a sharp whistle. But he knew better, not to face that way. He didn't even look . . . just kept on walking. That's what I always say about my father, you couldn't scare him. Old man used to tell us it's not going to bother you; it's only teasing you. So when you hear him, just don't mind him, just let him go. He'll mind his own business.

Lives of Animals

LINDA SCHANDELMEIER

Poet Linda Schandelmeier grew up near Anchorage on a 160-acre homestead, but she has lived in Fairbanks since 1967. She works as an elementary schoolteacher in Fairbanks, and also teaches creative writing. Her writing has appeared in many magazines, books, and literary journals, including permafrost, Inroads, Alaska Quarterly Review, Red Cedar Review, The Northern Review, *and* THE SKY'S OWN LIGHT. *"Lives of Animals" and "Winter" first appeared in* permafrost *(1981).*

In snowy months
when light is rare
and filters down like powder
I notice the lives of animals.

Voles, hares, others whose shapes
escape me, their tracks
slim tongues of selves, everywhere
inhabiting the darkness.

From the stove
I suck in warmth
and look out.

The moon,
treacherous and icy,
beckons like a camellia opening.

Small shadows
move over the snow.
There also waits
the blue fox cold.

Winter

LINDA SCHANDELMEIER

Everywhere, ravens
as if winter is a shield with raven shapes.
Today the call of ravens,
insistent, overhead,
and the stillness of a raven in a spruce tree.
Their bodies keep a dark heat,
behind them even the sun is brittle.

Guardians of winter,
collecting nightfall in feathers,
the sun is their halo
and the crescent moon rides on black wings.

If I could speak to them
winter would not tangle in my chest.
I would not be afraid of turning into stone.

At the Tetlin River

CAROLYN KREMERS

*Carolyn Kremers is a musician, teacher, poet, and nonfiction writer who lives
in Fairbanks. Her poems have appeared in* Alaska Quarterly Review, Denali
Alpenglow, permafrost, The Prose Poem, Runner's World, Steam Ticket,
and elsewhere. Her first book of nonfiction, PLACE OF THE PRETEND PEOPLE:
GIFTS FROM A YUP'IK ESKIMO VILLAGE (*1996*), *describes her experiences
teaching in a remote Yup'ik Eskimo village, as well as her love of flute playing
and her strong attachment to the Alaskan wilderness. "At the Tetlin River" was
first published in* Tundra Drum *in 1993.*

She moans at your approach,
white breath crowding
around her like a coat

and I follow, needing
her rufous beauty,
not wanted it captured but wanting

to witness your ability
to feel and not feel. Your blue strength. Free
in this forest, you press her neck firmly

under your arm and I see
your face, not cold, hear all her air
forced out in a wheeze, released

with the pain in her paw, out the ends of her long black-tipped hair.
When she is still you hand me the body,
knowing I must touch it to share

the warmth slipping oddly
from her fur into you, like a pact.
I lay the red fox gently

on the snow where she'll soon freeze whole
and you reset the trap
she stumbled into, meant for wolves.

Grizzly Habitat

FROM *No Room for Bears*

FRANK DUFRESNE

*Frank Dufresne (1895–1966) was a naturalist, editor, and writer. A longtime
director of the Alaska Game Commission, he also was associate editor of*
Field and Stream *magazine and a frequent contributor to numerous other
popular periodicals. His books include* MY WAY WAS NORTH *(1966),* ANIMALS
AND FISHES OF ALASKA, THE GREAT OUTDOORS, *and* NO ROOM FOR BEARS
*(1965), which addresses the poignant issue of loss of habitat for bear species in
a developing world. "Grizzly Habitat" is taken from* NO ROOM FOR BEARS.

T he fire had burned low that night the grizzly came into camp. Hosea
had fallen asleep and I, who should have been on guard, had done
the same. In the darkness a smoldering spruce log burned in two
and collapsed with a crash. Showers of sparks flew like fireflies into
the treetops and a tongue of flame licked at the misty forest. I came
awake with a start. No more than a pebble's toss away stood one of the
biggest grizzly bears I had ever seen.

As I groped for my gun I could feel my throat pounding. Maybe I
should call out to Hosea, I thought, and then there wasn't any need. The
guide was already awake. Silently, he rolled to a sitting posture, his hands
gripping his .375 rifle ready for action.

"Heave some more wood on the fire," he said quietly, not taking his eyes
off the bear. "Stir it up real good."

He didn't have to tell me that trouble had arrived, and that what happened next could be very important to a couple of deer hunters. Whatever
it might be, we'd asked for it. We'd started down from one of Admiralty
Island's snow peaks in late afternoon, following a deeply rutted bear trail
used by the brown giants for centuries. The sun went down and its after-
glow, which we'd been relying on to light us down the final three miles to
our anchored gas boat, was suddenly blotted out by a rolling fog bank that
hung like drapes from the low limbs of the evergreens. It had blinded us in

a moment. With visibility reduced to arm's length we were bogged down for the night amidst the heaviest concentration of brown and grizzly bears in all Alaska. We'd made it even worse. We'd baited ourselves with prime grizzly food. Dripping blood-scent all the way down from the high meadows and now spread-eagled across a downed log between us were two freshly killed Sitka bucks.

Hosea had accepted the situation calmly. While we could still see enough to grope our way among the massive tree trunks, he led the way to a wind-fallen spruce. He pried off some bark slabs, reached underneath for a hand-ful of dry splinters, and touched off a fire. In its growing light we gathered heaps of fallen branches to last us through the dark hours. We knew that during the night several grizzlies would be using their trail to visit the salmon spawning streams down in the valley. They'd smell the venison and they'd want it. How far would they go to take it away from us? We'd soon find out.

The big grizzly had reared to full height to peer down at us across the firelight, its massive head swaying from side to side as it studied us carefully. Its eyes, shining like red lights as they reflected the flame, showed neither anger nor fear, only intense curiosity, as the huge beast tried to figure out what two humans were doing in its woods after dark. It had never encoun-tered a man at such close range, and certainly not in the nighttime when the advantage was on its side. It was making up its mind. I remembered some-thing Hosea had once told me: that a wild grizzly is not only one of the most intelligent of all beasts, but it recognizes man as its sole challenger for supremacy.

"Give a grizzly a chance to look you over, to catch a snootful of human scent; give it the time and opportunity to make a dignified retreat," Hosea had counseled, adding, "It might go away, or it might attack." But the guide wasn't talking now. The bear was too close. It could be on us in a split second, and our chances for stopping it cold were none too good in the flickering firelight.

Like some other bear men, Hosea often talked to the grizzlies when he was trying to gauge their moods, not loud but in the moderate tones one might use to placate a barking dog. "Take it easy, big boy," he called out now. "You better mosey on down to the creek and fill up on salmon. You can't have our deer." In an aside to me he added, "While he's standing still I could take him through the brains and end all this, but maybe we won't have to. Maybe he'll listen to reason."

The bear was, indeed, listening. Its ears were cocked. Its black, rubbery nose was thrust forward as its flaring nostrils sniffed the air. The tantalizing aroma of deer flesh told it to charge. The curtain of fire told it to go away. The sight and sound of man confused it. Dropping to all fours the grizzly padded into the eerie shadows and started circling around the burning limbs. So far it had uttered no sound, but in the damp gloom of the big trees I could hear the click of teeth as it champed its jaws nervously.

"That's not a good sign," observed Hosea. "Better stoke up that fire again." I did, and the grizzly's hairy rump looked like a haystack as it faded away in the fog-filled night.

A half hour passed. A yearling weighing 300 or 400 pounds came shambling down the trail, stopped to look us over, then moved gingerly on its way. Not far behind came a female with two small cubs. The cubs sat up like a pair of coons, fascinated by the campfire, all eyes and ears and questing noses toward the first human beings they had ever seen. They started forward to do a better job of it and were cuffed soundly on their backsides by the mother. Squalling loudly, the cubs fled down the trail. We could hear the female scolding long after they'd vanished into the inky forest.

There was no sign of the giant grizzly; only the slow drip-drip of moisture falling off the trees and the hiss of a drop hitting the embers. The rhythm of it made me sleepy again. Following a long day of climbing and backpacking my eyelids were heavy, and I told Hosea now was as good time as any for me to take a nap. Hosea said to go ahead and he'd try to keep a watch on things. "You know," he added casually, "that grizzly is still out there looking at us."

I decided to stay awake. Hosea's remark had refilled the night with danger. Hopefully, I suggested that the bear had gone on down the trail to join the others at the salmon riffles. Hosea didn't answer for twenty minutes, then all he said was "Look!" My eyes followed his pointing figure to a pair of red-hot coals glowing in the dark.

Though the guide held his rifle at ready and cautioned me to do the same—but not to fire unless he did—Hosea said he didn't think this was an attack situation. He reasoned that if the grizzly already had the deer in possession it would fight to death to keep it. Now the bear was in the position of being the aggressor so it might be different. "There's a code of behavior among these hairy brutes." Under his week-old stubble Hosea managed a wry grin. "I wish I knew it better."

The two live coals floated several feet higher in the velvety blackness, and I knew the grizzly had reared on its hind feet to examine us again. Then, suddenly, the lights dropped and blinked out.

"Now what?" I whispered.

Looking back on it now, I don't really think Hosea was surprised at what happened next. I think he'd been expecting something like it all that night. Suddenly, the ebony stillness was shattered by horrendous roars. The awful bawls echoed ventriloquially through the fog and seemed to shake the very ground where we stood. Again and again came the frightful outbursts, the more alarming because I was finally able to pinpoint the source. The grizzly had moved and now it was directly behind us.

I don't know what the bear expected us to do—possibly bolt into the forest and leave it in charge of the two dead bucks. That's what another lesser bear might have done at the bellowed commands. I, too, felt like running but knew better than to leave the campfire. Hastily, I joined Hosea on the other side, and with a wall of flame between us and the grizzly once more, we waited with thumbs pushing against the safeties on our rifles, ready as we possibly could be for a charge.

In the hair trigger silence every flickering shadow took on the shape of a bear. Minutes passed, then hours, with nothing to break the tension. At daybreak each of us shouldered his deer siwash-fashion, with the front legs toggled through the hamstrings and with rifles resting across the racks made by the outthrust hind legs. The deep pad prints led down along a steep hogback. Hosea, showing the way, halted and pointed below to a salmon spawning river rippling under the hemlocks and devil's-club. A female bear and two smallish cubs were sharing a fish on a gravel bar, and a fair-size yearling was romping in the spray of a waterfall, more playful than hungry. Hosea kept waiting for something else to show and finally it did. A giant male came swaggering out of a tunnel through some salmonberry brush into the river and picked up a humpbacked salmon in its teeth. He shook it viciously.

"Well, the bears are all down there," observed the guide. "Want to go down for a closer look?"

"Some other time," I said.

"Some other time" turned out to be the next day. With our fat Sitka bucks safely hung in the rigging, and fortified by a restful sleep on the gently rocking gas boat, Hosea and I rowed ashore in the dark moments before dawn.

Together, we dragged the light skiff atop squishy kelp bulbs and over squirting clams to the high-tide line, made the painter fast to a barnacled rock and started trudging across an open meadow shoulder-deep in wild ryegrass. Because our man-scent would carry upstream, we made a wide detour before cutting straight into the river to hit a spot several yards above the steep falls beyond which no salmon could migrate.

We moved cautiously down in our rubber-bottomed pacs to a huge fallen tree overlooking the cataract and settled ourselves behind it for an all-day vigil. Though Hosea carried his heavy rifle—he seldom went ashore on Admiralty Island without it—he would not use it unless we were charged. We'd try for a few camera shots, but mostly we were here on this primitively beautiful Southeastern Alaska stream to observe the ways of a grizzly with a salmon. We didn't have long to wait.

Across the river and up the hogback on the old bear trail a rust-colored sow bear with twin cubs stood looking down. Had they seen us? The bears answered our question. One cub after another came sliding and tumbling eagerly down the steep incline, followed at a more sedate pace by the mother. They whisked out of sight in a thicket and a moment later we saw them splashing water in front of us within a hundred feet. Like a doting parent, the female watched her whining youngsters wade up to their necks in the river, grabbing at passing fish. When they turned to mother pleading for help, the female strode out into the water, lowered her head completely out of sight in the current and came up with a salmon dangling from her jaws. Followed by the squealing cubs, she bore her catch out on a gravel bar, laid a paw on its head, and with one slash of her teeth ripped the skin completely off one side. Bickering like little demons, the furry balls sunk their baby teeth into the soft pink flesh. When they had stripped one side bare the mother yanked the remaining hide off and joined her children for breakfast.

In the early sunlight a flock of short-billed gulls came flying upriver from the tide flats, screaming and hovering over the bear family, swooping daintily to snatch bits of salmon out of the very jaws of death. A swish of wings brought a black raven to the scene. It danced a lively jig on its feet as it hopped in and out, narrowly missing angry paw swipes and gnashing teeth, feinting here and grabbing there for tidbits. More bird trouble continued to arrive. With full daylight came more gulls, bold glaucous-winged varieties strong enough to make off with the entire skeleton of the salmon.

The mother fought off the winged pests for a while, then planted herself squarely over the picked bones, head waving from side to side as if in deep thought. A solution came to mind. Without a further glance at the haggling birds she sloshed out into the river and fished out another salmon. She was holding it in her jaws when she suddenly grew tense. She'd sensed danger.

Squatting in the water the she-bear swung her eyes from the waterfall across the log in front of Hosea and me, then continued to scan the river bank before leading her cubs out of sight into a low jungle of giant helle-bore and alders. For a while the gravel bar was deserted save for the birds. We had the feeling that other grizzlies, hidden as we were, were surveying the river cautiously before venturing out into the open. Whether they had sensed human presence, or were maintaining a wary respect toward their own kind, we couldn't tell. In the end it was the yearling who broke the spell.

With utter disregard for proper bear behavior, the youngster came galloping down the hillside with all the grace of a boy in a potato-sack race, ripped through the underbrush, and somewhat dazed by the buffeting, splash-landed in the middle of the pool. In frantic alarm at the watery explosion a flurry of salmon tried to jump straight up the waterfall, fell back, and when one of them drifted downstream, the yearling recovered enough to clap its jaws over the spent fish. Surprised at its own smartness, the yearling looked around as though expecting applause. But what it got was an angry *whuff!*

The half-ton giant behind it had slipped through the timber without a sound. Now, with one peremptory snort it took charge of the fishing hole. The chastened yearling slunk away with its salmon, and the female kept her cubs out of sight while the big boar proceeded to catch and eat two salmon before stretching itself on the sand to rest. In a few moments yearling, mother, and cubs came out of hiding, though careful to keep their distance from his majesty. I could see now what Hosea meant by the grizzly's code. Pretending not to notice one another, the great carnivores shared the pool and took their turns fishing. I held up a hand with fingers spread to denote five bears in this one spot. Silently, Hosea did the same, then extended the index finger on his other hand. Six bears! With this thumb the guide motioned toward the base of the falls. It was behind my right shoulder, and the distance couldn't possibly be more than fifteen feet away!

With infinite care I turned my head and rose high enough to peer over the waterfall. Below me was the oldest living bear I have ever seen, a Methuselah among grizzlies. Its long muzzle was hoary with age, and its matted coat was like a heap of rags. It was deeply swaybacked; its head hung low. It stood close enough to the falls for the water to keep it drenched. The massive front paws rested in a shallow basin filled to the brim with wriggling salmon that had failed to clear the waterfall and fallen into a natural trap among the rocks. Though it was surely the choicest stand on the river, not one of the other bears had come near it all day. It was grandpa's private fishing hole.

The odds against this grizzly patriarch surviving the heavy snowfall of the Admiralty Island winter must have been great. Yet, like the other bears, it had come pushing out of its den in the high crags in April or May to plod downward across melting drifts in search of a strong cathartic to loosen the resinous plug that had sealed its intestines shut for almost half a year. The remedy had been the violently pungent root of the skunk cabbage, snow lily bulbs, and hellebore stalks. Like the other grizzlies, Methuselah had doubtless snuffled and pawed along the bottom of snowslides for the carrion of winter-killed deer and lesser creatures, and even the carcasses of less fortunate bears. Down on the Admiralty beaches it had eaten enormous quantities of tender spring grass seasoned with crabs, clams, and beetles secured by turning over boulders along the bared flats at low tide. All this to still the hunger rumblings in its pendulous belly until nature's bounty filled the rivers with the annual coming of the silver hordes, five kinds of salmon homing to their spawning streams from thousands of miles at sea to perform a miracle of migration. More than any other factor the salmon had given Admiralty Island a grizzly and brown bear population density unequaled anywhere else on earth. One bear to each square mile! Five times more bears than people!

Toward the noon hours grizzly activity slowed along the river. I was dozing in the warm sun when Hosea nudged me. The big male bear had lifted its head and was looking directly at the log behind which we were hidden. I didn't think it had seen us because we were completely screened by the lacy foliage of a hemlock branch. Nor had we uttered so much as a whisper to one another. What we feared most was a tiny whiff of our hated man-scent eddying back against the breeze. Was this what had happened? After a long stare, the big grizzly rolled to its feet and came swaggering out of the shadows toward us. At the water's edge it reared up on its giant frame, looking ten feet tall as it peered across the river. Then it dropped heavily down on its forefeet, swung about, and paddled into the dark shadows. When it failed to show up again I glanced behind our lookout with some apprehension, wondering if we were about to witness another flanking maneuver like this same bear had tried two nights before on the mountainside.

Hosea's finger touched me on the shoulder to turn me around. The big male was back again at the same spot. This time it came wading halfway across the river, and with water running off its hooked claws lifted up and gave us another hard look. Out of the corner of my eyes I saw the guide's fingers tighten once more on his rifle. Then, suddenly, the heat was off for a moment at least. A salmon drifted past and the bear couldn't resist picking it up.

But we knew something was wrong when the beast bit a chunk out of the salmon's back and then dropped the limp carcass on the gravel bar. It paid no attention when a bald eagle flopped heavily from a low snag to claim the spoils. Screaming gulls and croaking ravens gathered to harass the king of birds at its feast.

There was no sign of the mother and cubs and the yearling. Something had caused them to vacate. As the big male followed them into the forest gloom the hackles along its shoulders stood stiffly erect. For the first time that day the guide spoke. "We'd better keep our eyes peeled. The time to worry is when you can't see 'em."

I raised up to look over the log again and it was reassuring to see Methuselah at the same old stand under the falls. His sagging back was damp with spray. Salmon slithered over his paws and under his gray nose, waiting to be picked up. But there was no evidence that the aged grizzly had eaten, and the thought came to me that maybe, like the other bears, he was beginning to tire of a straight diet of salmon. The same thing happened every summer. After a spell of fish, the bears commenced mixing the pink flesh with blueberries, gathering the berries first along the beach where they ripened earliest, then working their way into the mountains for the late harvest that lasted until denning time.

Although Hosea and I now began conversing aloud there was no indication that the hoary old timer heard us, or at least not well enough to identify it as a human sound. Undoubtedly, he was deaf and when he swung his head downstream for a moment his eyes seemed to be glazed with a bluish film. It had taken Methuselah five years to attain adult size. Had this now been multiplied by the factor of seven to produce the bear life span of thirty-five? Was the old giant living his last summer?

Paying the aged grizzly no more attention than if he were a moss-grown boulder, an otter came sliding over the brink of the falls and plunged into the bubbling water twenty feet below. I watched the glistening streak of its long body along the bottom, fluid as mercury, before belly-whumping over the shallow riffles around the bend of the river. Soon another otter came along to follow the exact procedure. The salmon, which had parted to let the exuberant pair through, resumed their spawning. With furious energy the females used their tails to thrash out redds in the gravel, then squeezed out a string of pink, pea-sized eggs to be fertilized with whitish clouds of milt from the quivering males. Handsome Dolly Varden trout darted around each spawning pair to snap up the free-floating waste eggs. As each salmon exhausted its roe sac, it drifted dying in the current, easy prey for the bears when they came back to feed again at dusk.

When they did, Hosea and I would be back aboard the gas boat bucking the tide for home. Before we left I took a long look at one of the most perfect grizzly habitats left in the world. I wondered how much longer it would last.

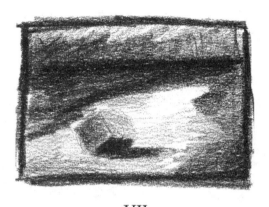

VII
....

Into the Now

The Changing Times

FROM *Kahtahah*

FRANCES LACKEY PAUL

Frances Lackey Paul (1889–1970) was a teacher in a federal school in Juneau. She wrote KAHTAHAH *in 1938 for her Tlingit students, who had no textbooks that reflected their Native heritage.* KAHTAHAH *was the first children's book with a Tlingit heroine—and the first based on a real Tlingit person of the late 1800s. Frances Paul's husband was Tlingit, and through his family connections she was able to gather oral history and access material about Tlingit customs, legends, and folklore that was then available to few ethnologists. "The Changing Times" is a chapter from* KAHTAHAH, *which was published in 1976.*

That winter there was trouble in the village of the Stikheenquan. Before the ice had formed some white men with gold in their pouches came down the Stikine River and built cabins at the edge of the Indian village. They took some Indian girls to live in their cabins, but did not ask for them in an honorable manner. When one man tried to talk to Kahtahah, Snook was very angry. He wanted to kill the white man, but he felt the power of the changing times.

The head chiefs of the 10 Great Houses of the village held many solemn councils around the center fires, but they could do nothing but talk. Over on the edge of the ocean, at Sitka, where the Russians had built their stockade, the "Boston men" now had gunboats and soldiers. No one knew when a gunboat might come to the Stikine village, and whenever the gunboat sailed up, soldiers with guns came ashore.

The captain of the gunboat called the chiefs together and said that wrongdoers had to be turned over to him for punishment. He said that the Boston men had now bought the country from the Russians, and that the chiefs of the Great Houses should no longer determine the punishment for their own households. The Indians no longer dared to demand a life for a life from those who had insulted them. Only the captain of the gunboat had the power to punish, and all the people had to obey the white man's laws, or they would be punished. Whenever the captain sailed away he had one of his big guns fired "in their honor," he said, but they knew it was a warning for them to obey.

Snook did not know what to do. He respected the captain of the gunboat and feared the power of his soldiers, but the white men living at the edge of the village were not like the captain of the gunboat. Snook wished that he still had the strength and fire of his youthful days.

One afternoon in December, just before the early dark, Kahtahah and Tsoonkla were playing across the bay outside the Teehitton house. On the ground snow lay about a foot deep with a hard crust on top. The girls were amusing themselves by stamping through the hard crust in a sort of follow-the-leader game.

Through the gray dusk they saw a small canoe draw up to the beach, and a man and a woman came to them over the white snow.

"Which house is the Great Raven House?" the man asked.

"Where the tall Raven pole is," Tsoonkla answered. "This is also a Raven house where the Teehitton live, and over there is the Kiksuddi house. You will be welcome there also."

Both the man and woman seemed very cold and tired. They looked longingly at the nearby Teehitton house, but turned and trudged through the snow to the Great Raven House.

"They have come on a long journey," Kahtahah said. "It is hard to travel in bad weather. See how tired the woman is! She can hardly walk." They watched the strangers until they reached the Great Raven House, and then went on with their game.

Later in the evening the chief of one of the smaller Raven houses came to see Snook. The two old men talked together in low tones for a long time. Kahtahah could see that they were troubled. After the visitor left she went over to Snook and sat down beside him.

"What is troubling you, Father?" she asked. "Has it anything to do with the strangers who came to the Great Raven House this afternoon?"

Snook called his household together.

"The strangers who came to the Raven house are kinsmen of the chief. The young man and woman both belong to the Raven clan and yet they have married each other. They have fled from their own village and are asking refuge among the Stikheenquan."

Everyone sat as though carved in stone. The strongest law of the Tlingit people! A member of the Raven clan MUST NOT marry another Raven. A

Wolf MUST NOT marry a Wolf. It was as though a brother had married his sister.

No one spoke for a long time. A young man from the Great Raven House came to the door. "Our chief is calling a council at his house, and wishes the help of your advice."

Snook stood up and shook his head grimly. "Tell your chief I have no advice to give to the Raven clan. He knows how a chief of the Wolf clan punishes one who breaks the law."

Kahtahah shivered. She looked at Snook in wonder. Where was the kind father she had always known? This man who looked so grim and fierce filled her with fear. She remembered an old story that her foster mother had whispered to her. Long before she was born, when Snook was still a young and vigorous man, his niece had left his house to run away with one of her own clan. Snook had followed them and had brought back his niece. In the presence of his whole household he had condemned her to death for having broken the Tlingit law. He took her out with him in a canoe but returned alone. No one ever mentioned her name in his presence again.

Kahtahah shivered. This was the first time the story had seemed real to her.

Late that night the chief of the Great Raven House himself came to Snook's fireside. All evening while the council met to determine the fate of the young people, Snook had sat alone, silent and grim. The women of his household had not even dared to offer him food. The Raven chief sat down beside Snook, took out his box of leaf tobacco and offered it to him. The two old men smoked in silence for some time. Then the Raven chief spoke: "My kahnee (brother-in-law), my head is low. My grandchildren have broken the law. I have grown old and weak. The power of the white man is strong. I cannot fight the white man."

"So, the guilty ones will be protected in your house because the law of the white man is stronger than the law of the Tlingit," answered Snook. "What does the white man care about Tlingit law or Tlingit honor? It has always been the Tlingit law that a brother may not marry his sister."

"It is true that the law is an old one," the Raven chief said. "It's so old that we do not know the beginning. We Tlingits have many customs whose meaning we do not understand, and this law of the clans is such a one."

"We understand that a brother may not marry a sister," protested Snook.

"But there is no blood relationship between the young people," countered the Raven chief.

"It is still the law that they may not marry," Snook stubbornly maintained.

The old Raven chief stood up and drew his blanket tightly about him as he prepared to leave. "We have held our council, and we have decided. The times are changing. The white people are among us to stay, and if we break the law of the white people the captain of the gunboat will turn his guns on our village. Then the blood of our children and our grandchildren will be on our heads. How can the Tlingit fight the gunboat? We do not know, but perhaps the law of the white man is better than our law. We are willing to try the white man's way. The young people will have a home in my house. That is all."

Snook smoked another pipeful in silence after the Raven chief had gone. Then he spoke to his family. "If these young people had not been willful, this trouble would not have come to our people. Let all within the household beware of bringing disgrace to our name in this manner."

Kahtahah knew that Snook would never forgive one of his young people who had disobeyed the law of the clans and brought terrible disgrace to his name.

Ice Palace

E D N A   F E R B E R

*Novelist, short-story writer, and playwright Edna Ferber (1887–1968) was
the best-selling author of many American classics, including* So Big *(which
won the Pulitzer Prize in 1924),* Show Boat *(the basis for the Broadway
musical), and* Giant. *Her last novel,* Ice Palace *(1958), excerpted here, was
written after Ferber visited Alaska. Ferber's fictitious Alaskan city, Baranof, is
not unlike Fairbanks or Anchorage in the 1950s.*

Every third woman you passed on Gold Street in Baranof was
young, pretty, and pregnant. The men, too, were young, virile, and
pregnant with purpose. Each, making his or her way along the
bustling business street, seemed actually to bounce with youth and
vitality. Only an occasional old sourdough, relic dating back to the
gold-rush days of fifty years ago, wattled and wary as a turkey cock, weaving his precarious pedestrian way in and out of the frisky motor traffic, gave
the humming town a piquant touch of anachronism.

An exhilarating street, Gold, though the stores and office buildings that
lined it—one- or two-story cement or wooden structures—were common-
place and even shabby. The enlivening quality was inexplicable, but ardent
Alaskans sometimes attributed it to the piercing quality of the Arctic light
and the dryness of the atmosphere. Middle-aged tourists, weary after thousands of miles of travel over this seemingly boundless territory—whether by
plane or by a combination of plane, train, ship and automobile—were puzzled
and plaintive as they viewed the haphazard town of Baranof for the first time.

"Everybody walks as if they had springs in their shoes. Or maybe it's
because you're all so young."

If the visitor's guide happened to be Ott Decker, Secretary of the Baranof Chamber of Commerce, he would reject this with the mysterious light-
heartedness that seemed to suffuse most near-Arctic citizens.

"Young's got nothing to do with it. Around here you can live to be a hundred, easy, unless you're shot, or your plane cracks up on you, or a bear sees you first."

"Well, it's something. A kind of a crazy something. No offense. I just mean, what makes them bounce?"

"My opinion, it's the violet rays or the magnetic pole—we're not so far from the North Pole, you know, when it comes right down to geography—or it's the radiant northern, uh, isotopes or something."

"Now wait a minute. Just a minute. Radiant. I always understood you had winter about eight months in the year, and no sun to speak of."

"That's right. But you feel great. And summers! Say—summers! Like today. Daylight round the clock twenty-four hours. And you know what? You don't need sleep. You feel hopped up all the time. Take the Eskimos up here in Kotzebue and Oogruk and Barrow and around where it's really tough going. Always laughing their heads off. For what! They got nothing to laugh at. They just feel good. Everybody feels good. I don't know. It's a kind of a balloon feeling."

It was true that everything in Baranof seemed exaggerated. Edges sharper. Skies bluer. Mountains higher, snow deeper, temperature lower, daylight longer, sunlight briefer, depending on the season. The very air sometimes seemed more utterly still than anywhere else in the world, yet it pulsed almost palpably with life. When the wind blew it blew harder. Down in southeast Alaska—the region facetiously called the Banana Belt—the Taku screeched and whistled about your ears in season. In the remote north villages on the Bering Sea or the Arctic Ocean the polar blasts in February could strangle the breath in your throat and force it back into the reluctant lungs. Deceived by the dry air, you could freeze your face and walk about, unknowing. Baranof wore parkas, fur-hooded, through the winter. This gave pedestrians the anonymity of dominoes at a masquerade. There was a favorite joke, often quoted. "Winters in Baranof, speak to anything that moves. If it's standing still, call the ambulance."

Off to school on the bitter black winter mornings the children were round bundles of wool and fur, their eyes peering out like those of small woodland creatures in a nest. Mothers, standing briefly in the doorway, would call, "Now remember, don't run! Even if you're late—don't run." They knew the danger of the quick intake of breath like icy knives into the warm scarlet lung tissue.

Across the winter night sky swept the northern lights, eerie dazzling curtains of swaying green and blue and orange. Then, miraculously, June came, it was summer, it was daylight round the clock. The thermometer that had registered sixty below zero in January now might show ninety above. Yet there was Baranof and much more of Alaska besides, dry and cool, energetic and somewhat crazily high-keyed in an agreeable way under the constant compulsion of the weird Arctic sun. Up, up far north in Barrow on the shore of the frozen Arctic Ocean the United States flag whipped aloft in the wind for eighty days and eighty nights, for there was during that period no sunset hour in which to lower it. If you happened to be soaring in a comfortably cosy plane above Bering's ice-locked coast, nibbling a ham sandwich and sipping hot strong coffee, you could see just over there, beyond the two island dots that were the Big Diomede and the Little Diomede, the black strangely menacing line that was the coast of Siberia.

But here in mid-Alaska a kind of carefree mood took hold. Baranof stayed out of doors every possible minute. You played baseball at midnight. Your wife tended her garden at eleven P.M. Your children frisked like leprechauns far into the night. Perhaps you slept from midnight through the hour or two of rosy twilight until, like a blindingly dazzling scimitar thrust through a scarlet velvet curtain, the sun rose again at one or two o'clock in the morning. This brief interlude of repose seemed, magically, to suffice, both for the sun and you.

If you were young and in love you might stroll hand in hand down to the water's edge to delight romantically in the glorious color above and the pastel reflection below. Mount McKinley, king of all the peaks on the North American continent, white-crowned in the summer, white-robed in the winter, looked in this midsummer midnight light like the gods' Valhalla—or a gigantic scoop of raspberry and orange sherbet. Baranof citizens adjusted to this summer-winter variant of one hundred and fifty degrees as nonchalantly as they digested the local moose steaks in January or the monster home-grown strawberries in August.

As for grubby Gold Street—it compensated in scenery for what it lacked in architectural grace. At one end the shabby thoroughfare met the mountains that reared their incredible height, peak on peak, a screaming white. At the other end the water curved to hold the town in its icy arms. It was a setting of diamonds and pearls surrounding a blob of agate.

If you were an Important Person arriving by air to visit Baranof you were officially met at the smart little airport by Bridie Ballantyne or Ott Decker or both. If you were a Very Important Person you were met by Chris Storm. Christine Storm. Only her grandfather Czar Kennedy and her grandfather Thor Storm called her Christine. As First Assistant to the General Manager of Alaska Public Relations, Christine Storm's appearance was likely to mislead the average tourist; but then, she never was assigned to small fry. She was reserved for any visiting President of the United States who condescended to the Territory (none in her day); Senators and Congressmen (National); Big Business Types (with Wife); Big Game Hunters (minus Wife) with guides flying small maneuverable planes in search of polar white or mammoth brown bears.

Born in Alaska, the daughter of a father and mother born in Alaska, the granddaughter of two grandfathers who were considered Alaska history, Chris Storm was almost as outstanding as Mount McKinley. Certainly in the wintertime, if assigned to a Very Distinguished Visitor, Chris was a striking figure there at the airport gateway as the big four-engine plane from Seattle drummed down out of the heights to the runway that now stretched its impressive length in what had been, less than a half century ago, literally a howling wilderness.

Dramatically, she dressed the part of native daughter. Her official winter greeting costume was a pure white fox parka intricately bordered with a delicate frieze of Eskimo symbols in black sealskin. Her grandfather Thor Storm had told her that some of these symbols were phallic or otherwise sexual, which interested her, as did all Eskimo lore, and sometimes, quite matter-of-factly, she would obligingly explain these to inquiring visitors.

"My, that's a lovely coat!" the wife of a V.I.P. from Outside would exclaim.

"It's called a parka, and we pronounce it parky, no one knows why."

"All those little figures and things in the border. Now that one—it looks like two little hills with a valley between. Do the signs have any significance, do they mean anything, sort of like the writing on caves and tombs in the Orient? Mr. Rauschenbusch and I took a trip around the world last year."

"Oh, that. That's part of a legend in which an Eskimo sees the back of his wife as she bends over the cooking pot, he dreams he must find his way through the two hills to the valley."

"What! Sh! The men will hear you. What's this one?"

The white fox parka, with its hood of white wolf, was a fitting frame for the girl's brilliant face. Slim white fur mukluks and gloves completed the dazzling effect—too dazzling, her enemies said. In the rather rueful way she sometimes had when speaking of herself Chris agreed with them. "In this outfit I look like that girl in the beer ads. But it's good Alaska publicity."

Then, in summer, hot or cold from June to September, Chris's costume as Greeter and Guide was the most feminine of cottons or silks, her golden arms bare, the bodice fashionably low cut, as proof that Alaska was a summer resort.

Visitors often mistook her for something purely ornamental, like the scenery. They were completely wrong. They were wrong about the scenery too. Hidden in those fabulous peaks and creeks and torrents were copper and gold and uranium and platinum and cobalt and tin and tungsten and nickel and lead; in the tundra and flatlands coal and oil; in the vast streams and inlets and seas millions of finned and furred creatures from salmon to seals to whales. But they were not for the casual passer-by. Beneath Chris Storm's shining surface, too, there were hidden treasures and wonders of mind and heart and spirit.

The three Baranof Professional Public Relations stars used three quite different weapons with which to do battle with the world known as Outside. Christine, deceptively blithe and débonnaire, tickled you with a poniard of gaiety, but you never felt sure that she might not drive it suddenly into your ribs. Bridie Ballantyne used a verbal shillelagh wrapped in cotton velvet. Ott Decker, good Chamber of Commerce Secretary that he was, just laid on with a shovel.

For example, though her laugh was merry, her way lighthearted, Chris's statements were sometimes dramatic. Listeners were likely to recall them, thoughtfully, following the more spectacular moments of their trip.

"Yes," she would agree, apparently in charming deference to the stranger's comment. "Yes, this is a gigantic wilderness. With neon lights, of course; and hydrogen bombs and dog sleds and radar and Eskimos and crab meat *au gratin* and skin boats and juke boxes and art exhibits and symphony concerts; and moose sometimes ambling down Gold Street in a real tough winter."

The Visitor from Outside, puzzled and vaguely resentful, would wave an arm with a gesture that embraced the incredible landscape.

"Some country you got here, that's for sure. I thought it would be different. Of course, it's different, all right, but other ways it's more like back home than I thought. Not like it, exactly, but—"

"We're people—all kinds of people—just like you in the States. We're white and black and brown and young and old and smart and dumb. But we're absolutely different in one way."

"How's that?"

"Would you like to pay government taxes if you couldn't have a voice in the state you live in, and couldn't vote for President of the United States? Would you like taxation without representation?"

This challenge they found disconcerting in a girl as attractive as Chris. "I'll say I wouldn't like it. I wouldn't stand for it. Why don't you write your Congressman and Senator in Washington, tell 'em to get on the job, or out?"

"Don't you know that Alaska has no Congressman or Senator in Washington! We're a Territory. Everything we do, and everything the Territory yields, goes out. Outside. Everything goes out and nothing stays in. Gold. Copper. Timber. Fish. Millions and millions and millions a year. Outside. We're slaves."

"Oh, now, say!" After all, the Visitor had not come all this long distance to listen to soapbox speeches, even though delivered by a pretty girl. "What's a girl like you bothering her head about whether you vote for President? Let him worry. I know what I'd do if I was President. I'd appoint you a Cabinet Member. Secretary of Beauty. You'd send bunches of beauty delegates over to Russia, they'd send bunches over here. No more war. The Russians keep sending over those bullet-headed fellows with eyes like mean oysters. Who loves them! Nobody."

Perhaps, casually, an Outsider undergoing the Visitor's Treatment might say, "Where's your home, Miss Storm? You certainly don't look like an Alaskan."

They did not know that Christine Storm had been known to Alaskans since the day of her fantastic birth. She had become a legend.

"I don't know how you think Alaskans should look. But I'm an Alaskan."

"That right! Born right here in Baranof?"

"I was born in a caribou in a blizzard up in the Wood River country."

Baffled, smiling uncertainly, the visitor might catch the word caribou and cling to it. "Caribou? Let's see now, there's a town called Caribou, I think it's in North Dakota though. Or was it Canada I saw it? But I understood you to say you were Alaska-born."

"I didn't mean a town called Caribou. I meant a caribou."

"I don't get it. I must be dumb."

"A caribou is a huge sort of reindeer and I was born inside of one that my father shot when he and my mother were caught in a blizzard on a hunting trip. I wasn't due for another three months but they say my mother was one of those dauntless girls—a kind of Alaska version of the Scott Fitzgerald type that was the fashion then. Grandpa Kennedy—her father— had sent her to Vassar, she knew Edna St. Vincent Millay. Anyway, what with the blinding blizzard and the stumbling around, and no shelter, and only the dog sled, I started ahead of time. Even if my father had had a chance to build a snow-block shelter, there wasn't time. By some miracle he shot a caribou. He slit the caribou's belly and gutted it and put my mother inside on the furs from the sled, it was blood-warm for a little while, and sheltered, and it kept her from freezing and me, too. And that's where I was born."

The listener would appear somewhat hurt. "Who you trying to kid?"

"But I'm not. It's true. Ask anybody."

"Now let me get this. There was a caribou handy, and he shot it and slit it and gutted it, you said, and then your mother—"

"My mother died. I don't know why *I* didn't, but I didn't."

"Now look here, Miss Storm, I may be what you Alaskans call a—what's that word?—uh—che——"

"Cheechako. We here in Alaska pronounce it cheechawker, it comes from a word in the Chinook language, it means——"

"I know what it means. Same as tenderfoot in the West. But I don't buy that story of yours, Miss Storm, cheechawker or no cheechawker."

But then, even the girl's appearance had a tinge of incredibility. Her eyes were black, her hair golden. Baffled by the unusual combination, strangers assumed that the yellow hair was tinted. The eyes were long, narrow, and ever so slightly pinched at the outer corners. The skin warmly golden, but this, too, was complicated by a faintly pink touch on the rather high cheek-bones like the flush on the cheek of a good English peach espaliered against a sunny brick wall in, say, Kent. Most people considered her quite a beauty, but the cynical said, not with that jaw line, you could break your knuckles against that, and your heart, too. A lot have. Heart, I mean. Ott Decker, and they say that son of Dave Husack in Seattle, and practically every young guy in the Territory. But a lot of them think she's too bossy and independent. I'll say this for her; anybody who knows her will say she isn't stuck up. I guess Bridie Ballantyne saw to that. And Thor Storm. Maybe

Czar Kennedy, but I've got a hunch he isn't as democratic as he pretends. But Bridie! She'd get my vote for President.

Bridie Ballantyne, in her own way, and within a more limited geographical area, was perhaps as well known as Chris. In Bridie as guide and hostess the tourist was treated to an exhibition of local pride unexcelled since Chauvin himself. Though no one knew her exact age it was roughly estimated at between sixty-five and seventy. She lied about it or ignored it.

In a region of almost fanatic joiners Bridie Ballantyne was a member in good standing of practically every group banded together in gregarious Baranof. With five hundred or even a thousand miles between you and the next town, Baranof—and all Alaska—had to manufacture its own fun. A lonely people in a far-off wilderness long before the airplane began to weave its gossamer web from the Atlantic, from the Pacific, across land and water to the Arctic, they had perforce contrived their own social life as pioneers have since the wandering tribes of Israel.

Bridie was President of the Pole Star Chapter of Women of the Moose; luck-struck player in the Ice Palace Canasta Club; Charter Member of the Far North Poker Poke; the Pioneers of Alaska, the Sourdoughs, the Daughters of the Midnight Sun, the Eaglets Eyrie, the Chamber of Commerce, the Hostess Dinner Club, the North Stars, the Garden Club, the Optimists, the Art Guild, the Music Circle (she couldn't carry the simplest tune), the Dinner Speakers. She appeared weekly on the local television program. She knew the town from the spanking new airport at one end to the primeval tundra at the other; from the latest rookie's frightened bride arriving at Kinkaid Air Force Base to the most desiccated sourdough in his leaky log cabin in the weeds at the edge of town. She belonged to the Baranof City Council and there was talk of her running for Territorial Congresswoman against Shaw Gavin, a hard-core politician of twenty-five years' standing and a minion of the Big Boys in Seattle and Washington.

Though Bridie's interests were myriad her chief delight was the job of piloting visitors around town. She invited them for a cup of tea or a mouthful of sherry in her cluttered one-room apartment at the Ice Palace. She loved company, she loved Baranof, she loved life. Ott Decker said that to hear her carry on you'd think Alaska was the Promised Land with built-in refrigeration. She talked. She talked incessantly with an enthusiasm that was contagious. In fifty years of Alaska she had seen the worst and the best of it. She held forth to strangers, to friends of half a century. As she talked, her elaborately coiffed steel-gray hair and her blue eyes and her good clear skin seemed to give off sparks. She always spoke of Alaska as We.

"We're one fifth the size of the whole United States, did you know that, now? And two times the size of that little bitty Texas they're always yawping about. And bigger than a whole parcel of European countries put together. Folks don't know. Folks Outside just don't know a thing. Ignorant as moose. Here in Baranof and Anchorage and Fairbanks and Nome and even towns more north it's no colder than towns in Finland and Norway and Sweden and Denmark—let alone that Russia. But all those millions of American tourists traveling over there, you don't hear them complaining about those places being cold or uncomfortable. Oh, my, no! They're quaint and novel and so different, and the scenery! And here we are, a mass of beauty, can you picture now what any of those countries in Europe would give for a grand big lovely rich place like Alaska! The highest mountain, old Mount McKinley. And Matanuska Valley can grow you the biggest cabbages in the world, let alone strawberries and potatoes and greens and grains. And you could graze cattle by the million but those witless ones in Washington won't let us own the land, let alone work it. Look at it! Sun all day and all night, summertime, and you feel as if you'd had two glasses of good dry champagne."

"Mosquitoes?" her listener might venture, timidly.

"Who minds a mosquito now and then! It's exercise. Winters you relax and enjoy your home and your friends and read, and just when you're beginning to be tired of all that comfort, why, next thing you know the ice goes out with a bang—and it's spring. But who owns us! They do. Outside. They get the good of it all. And what did it cost back there in '67 when that Seward pulled a fast one on Russia? Seven million dollars, can you fancy that! For the most wonderful darlingest richest chunk of land in the world. Seven million dollars! I could die laughing. Why, they lay that down as first payment on a fifty-foot corner lot in New York City."

Her hearers, now taking a bedazzled glance around the unkempt little town, would wag their heads feebly, whether in exhaustion or admiration or conviction. "Sure is. Sure do. Well, that's mighty interesting. Whew!"

Ott Decker's approach was more in the Chamber of Commerce tradition. Hailing originally from California he had miraculously transferred his fealty to the Far North. His enthusiasm for this wild and remote territory was as strong, in its way, as Chris Storm's somewhat neurotic emotion or Bridie Ballantyne's hearty trumpeting. There were even those who thought he overdid it. Ott, shrewd operator that he was in the devious world of public relations, knew that the summer tourist from Kansas or Ohio or Nebraska was not interested in Alaska frustrations, resentments or politics. Personal resentment was, indeed, more likely to figure in the visitor's own comment. Standing in the midst of Gold Street he viewed its supermarket, its cafés, its dress shops, drugstores, banks, airplane travel bureaus, florist shops and bars bars bars. As he dodged its pale blue Buicks and rose-pink Fords his tone took on a peevish edge.

"It doesn't look any different from Powell Street back home."

Ott would quirk a derisive eyebrow, though his manner was hearty. "You figured Alaska would be saloons and dance halls and shooting and girls in spangled tights like in the movies?"

"Well, maybe not altogether, but when our plane stopped in Juneau, our first stop on the way up here, why, there was a place, we had a drink there, sawdust on the floor and a fella at the piano in shirt sleeves, and rough-looking characters at the bar, and you got your change in silver dollars."

"Oh, that. Sure." Ott was amiable and tolerant. "That's the new Fish and Gold saloon. It's rigged for hicks from Outside. Chicago and New York and Detroit and so on."

"You mean nobody pans gold any more, or hunts bears or lives in igloos? Or shoots up saloons?"

"Course we do. There's gold, lots of it. Like to pan some? That's part of our tourist-entertainment program. I'll drive you out to the dredge right outside of town at Moose Lake, it's the biggest gold dredge in the world. Glad to show you. And polar bears, well, depends where you are. They don't go walking down Gold Street, that's for sure. And Alaska brown bear—well, you'd have to go down to Admiralty or to Kodiak and you better be quick on your feet because they sometimes weigh two thousand pounds and stand thirteen feet high. Let's see now—shooting up saloons—well, most of 'em are cocktail bars now with that music piped in, all the hit numbers from the new Broadway musical shows. It's got so you have to elbow your way past the bobby-soxers to get to the bar. Let's see now, you said igloos. Some of the boys from Kinkaid Air Base built us a dandy snow-block igloo right there on the corner of Gold and Polaris in front of the USO Building for our annual Winter Festival. It was one of the attractions. Course it all melted down months ago."

Disillusionment on the face of the Outsider roused Ott to fresh effort.

With a spacious gesture he would point toward a structure that, somehow unbelievably, rose fourteen stories high against the background of mountain and water and sky.

"How about that! Speaking of igloos—how about that! That's the Ice Palace. We call it."

Where the People Are

RUBEN GAINES

*Ruben Gaines (1913–1994) was a storyteller and pioneer broadcaster who
delighted listeners with his characters like "Pop" and "Chilkoot Charlie," and
illustrated some of Alaska's first television weather maps with original animal
cartoons. His poetry collections include* ON DISTANCE AND RECALL *(1980),*
A CHUGACH ALBUM/ON YOUTH, *and* MOUNTAIN LYRIC *(1990). Typical of his
poems are unrhymed, periodic sentences. "Where the People Are," from*
ON DISTANCE AND RECALL, *is a poignant description of the plight of a
displaced Alaska Native on his first visit to the city.*

old Isaac Bendo,
  leaning backward on
  the curb, heels
  hanging over, arms
  outstretched and
  pumping like he's
  flying, mumbling
  incantations no one
  listens to, is
  imitating Raven,
  God no one
  remembers, and he
  herds the salmon
  toward the fish
  camp out in Coho,
  where his mother,
  brothers, sisters,
  neighbors wait with
  set nets: plenty
  fish this year
  for dogs and people

his ancestral
  sense of balance
  keeping him from
  falling in the
  gutter, he's a
  hunter, a provider:
  gonna keep them
  Coho Village
  people goin'
  through the winter,
  Isaac mutters,
  gonna go for
  black bear
  pretty quick

ole Isaac,
  swaying on the
  icy sidewalk by
  the Polar Bear,
  has never left
  his home; his
  eyes are sighted . . .
  keenly, as along
  the barrel of a
  magnum
  rifle,
  not slit
  almost shut,
  like when
  he shields
  them from
  the bold
  Caucasian
  stare . . .
  on Coho Village,
  where the people
  are, when they
  are waitin' for
  the hunter.

Ballet in Bethel

FRED BIGJIM

Fred Bigjim is an Inupiat Eskimo from Nome and Sinrock, Alaska. Educated at Harvard University, he is the author of several poetry collections that combine memoir and cultural anthropology, including SINROCK *and* WALK THE WIND. *Bigjim's poems have appeared in* Wicazo Sa Review, We Make a Fire, *and the* Alaska Quarterly Review. *With James Ito-Adler, Bigjim co-authored* LETTERS TO HOWARD: AN INTERPRETATION OF THE ALASKA NATIVE LAND CLAIMS *(1974), which presented Native views of the 1971 Alaska Native Claims Settlement Act. "Ballet in Bethel" first appeared in the* Alaska Quarterly Review *in 1986.*

Ballet in Bethel.
Skintight dancers spinning across a stage,
Displaying only fantasies of a foreign world.

Opera in Shishmaref.
Piercing and screaming, the words unknown to all,
The sound shatters the stillness of the night.

Mime in Elim.
Stark faces of fools
Saying nothing.

Repertory Theater in Barrow.
Actors waiting for Godot
In a play that never reaches our world.

Symphony in Wales.
Instruments of time
Being blown by history
Of one world overpowering another.

Impact disguised as cultural creativity.
Upheaval replacing the entertainment
Of the ceremonial dances,
The blanket tosses, folklore,
And games of strength.

No more cultural gatherings,
Only a ballet in Bethel.

The War Canoe

JAMIE S. BRYSON

Jamie S. Bryson is a fiction writer, journalist, and bush pilot originally from San Diego, California. In 1970 he moved to Southeast Alaska to run the Wrangell *Sentinel. He later founded the Petersburg* Pilot. *Beginning in 1983, Bryson and his wife spent five years sailing around the world in their thirty-foot bluewater sailing vessel* Ave del Mar. *Today they live aboard the* Ave del Mar *in Harris Harbor, Juneau. Bryson's love for Southeast Alaska and its people crystalized in* THE WAR CANOE *(1990), a work of fiction for teen readers, set in Wrangell.*

It was the first time anyone could recall Mickey Church as anything but trouble in school. It was the first time anyone could recall Mickey Church studying. But Dr. Bernet was having a strange effect on Mickey and it brought about both those turnarounds in the boy.

In fact, Dr. Bernet was having that effect on a number of students. Strange as the teacher appeared with his intense and direct way and his outlandishly—for Wrangell—formal dress, he was becoming popular. The man knew each of his students by name and addressed them in the hallways with great energy and with an affection that they sensed accurately as genuine. He called out loud and squeaky greetings to them on the street and they responded cheerfully. It was going very well for Dr. Bernet.

The students were deep into the study of Tlingit culture. It was a revelation to most of them that they lived in a town so rich in history, the very town they always had thought of as plain, dull and ill-begotten.

Dr. Bernet traced the Ice Age and how it had fashioned the land and seaways between. He spoke of the Tlingits with such feeling and intensity and from such an obvious depth of knowledge that Mickey found himself electrified. So much so that in search of more about his past he stepped for the first time across the threshold of the city library.

When Mickey shyly approached the desk and addressed Mrs. Preston, saying almost in a whisper, "I want a book on Tlingits," the librarian, a loving, gray-haired old soul and a keen observer of Wrangell's young people, knew exactly how to handle the situation.

As if Mickey were a regular, she said in a friendly but professional tone: "Good afternoon, Mickey. You've timed it just right, you know. We have a new book in." The librarian took Mickey to the shelf, talking softly to herself along the way as she gave the boy a subtle lesson in book-finding. She read off the authors. Said, "Let's see—A, B, C, D,—ahhh! We've found it," and pulled out the book. At the desk she quickly typed up a library card for the boy, handed it to him, stamped his book and handed him that and turned to another patron.

Mickey proudly carried his volume to a table and began to read. Later, with the book tucked securely under his arm, he left the building, but soon had it open again, reading as he walked along Main Street, where he collided with Tim Sipe. And that meant trouble.

"Say there, Indian," said Tim, the mill foreman's son, a bully of sparse and cruel intellect, "watch where you're walking, you jerk." And with that pronouncement, he shoved Mickey off the sidewalk into the water-filled gutter. The library book slipped to the wet walkway, its binding plastered to the concrete and its pages fluttering. The bully walked on, giving the book a vicious kick, which sent it skittering.

Mickey felt red rage. He lunged after Tim, caught the bigger boy, and unleashed a heavy clout to Tim's shoulder, spinning him around. Astonished, Tim grasped Mickey by his jacket lapels and hurled him against the door of the hardware store, then hunched to punch. The hardware store door opened at that moment and Andy Grimsby, all three hundred pounds of him, filled it. Grimsby raised an index finger high and waved it meaningfully at Tim. The boy spat out a curse, lowered his threatening right fist from under Mickey's nose, and stalked away down the street.

"Thank you, Mr. Grimsby," said Mickey.

"For nothing," chuckled the big man. "I was only trying to protect Tim." The hardware-store man laughed again from deep down inside his ample frame and backed inside, pushing the heavy door shut after him. A shaken Mickey picked up his book, carefully brushed the water and dirt from it, and continued on course.

As he neared the shore where a coarse gravel beach backed by high grass and timber awaited, Mickey closed the gas valve and the big outboard motor

choked and died. The rooster tail behind his aluminum scow collapsed, fell
upon itself, and humped into a wave that chased the scow down, lifted the
stern gently, and passed underneath to break in a foam on the beach.

It was a misty morning but the skies above were clear, promising that the
sun ascending over the mountains of the island would bring at least a measure of warmth soon. The surface of the strait was leaden and flat and seabirds circled and dived there. Crows and ravens called from the land. The
water beneath the flat-bottomed scow chuckled as the boat coasted in. The
rough beach led to a grass-covered stretch between gravel and the timber.
This was Old Town. Here Mickey's ancestors had once lived.

Mickey thrust an oar over the scow's stern and guided the craft in
between rows of heavy stones arranged like shoreline ferry landings. There
were other such rows. These and a few stumps, which had been totem poles,
and some mounds of earth where buildings or fires might have been, were
all that remained to show that once this was a busy place. The hand-hewn
Tlingit canoes made of massive cedar and spruce logs had once lain in
grandeur between the rows of rocks.

Mickey felt at ease running his own boat into this spot and securing
it between these ancient and revered stones carried here by Tlingits like
himself.

The boy toured the little village site, moving slowly, thoughtfully. He felt
detached and strange. He felt secure. Here the incident with Tim Sipe was
all but forgotten; it paled in this ancient, important place.

Mickey removed his wool jacket and shirt, ignoring the sharp chill of the
morning. He pulled off his boots, rolled his trouser cuffs and walked into
the ice-cold sea. His legs hurt at once, the water sending up waves of pain.
He reached down and took hand-cups of seawater and threw it onto his
head and back, making himself smile through it. Youths in past years came
to the sea to toughen themselves for battle and for the hunt. They would
plunge into the straits and when they could no longer stand the numbing
cold, they would stand on the rock and gravel beaches naked and beat one
another with sticks.

Mickey retreated finally to the grass and sat shivering there, seeing in his
mind's eye a dozen boys like himself, naked and plunging into the sea. It
had obviously happened like that, and right here at this place.

He leaned against a log, beginning to warm up. The presence of all who
had lived and labored and died here was a fact to Mickey. They were here.

Their spirits were around him, but he did not feel frightened or threatened. Quite the opposite, he felt welcome; the ghosts were at ease with their reposing young visitor. The sun climbed at last from behind the peaks and its pale light spread over the ancient land. Mickey's eyelids fluttered and he dozed.

He opened his eyes sleepily, squinted along the shore and saw movement—a dim, dark something was against the beach. He stared hard as the shape grew in size. When it finally came into focus, Mickey gasped.

A dark Tlingit war canoe sped silently along the shore. Its more than twenty paddlers stroked in a strong, easy rhythm. The craft had a haughty thrust-out bow and was elaborately decorated with carved, bold white swirls along its sides. Enormous painted-on eyes glowered just back of the sharp, high stem.

It came on, close against the beach, moving very fast and growing quickly ever larger. Mickey could see now that one occupant of the craft was not paddling. He was a swart, flat-faced individual wearing a funnel-shaped hat, a blanket robe, highly decorated, thrown regally across his broad shoulders. He occupied the high bow of the canoe, sitting well above his companions. He stared straight ahead. The paddlers bent to their work, each making a silvery swirl to mark the place where his paddle punched the cold morning sea. Here was a breathtakingly beautiful, haunting sight.

The canoe closed the point where the boy sat wide-eyed and barely breathing. The man in the bow barked something in a guttural sing-song voice and his companions briskly shipped their paddles. The canoe glided soundlessly in the morning stillness, losing weigh, and stopped, rolling gently opposite Mickey. The canoe's paddlers, their naked torsos and muscular arms glistening, sat rigid, staring ahead.

The man in the bow did the same, but finally swung slowly and stared at the boy across the water. Mickey gazed back unafraid. The boy felt a great pride in his past and in these men who reigned supreme in this land once and whose spirits reigned supreme still—forever.

That was all. The paddlers took up the rhythm once more and the canoe moved off, picking up speed quickly. It finally disappeared around a rocky point and did not reappear.

It was a dream. Mickey assured himself that it was a dream as he pushed his scow into the strait and shakily started the motor.

But it seemed real, and the impact was real enough. Mickey saw the canoe in his mind still and he saw the men. And the germ of an idea was planted that day. It grew and gripped the boy Mickey Church so firmly that it changed his life and assured his future, and through the years touched many and made their lives richer, too.

"Weel," drawled Blackie, tugging with grease-blackened fingers at the bill of his cap. "I reckon it could be done, Mickey. Sure it could, but it would take some doin'."

Mickey reposed in a checker-playing chair, his heels resting on the edge of the stove. His library book was propped in his lap, open to a picture of a Tlingit canoe in full race along a misty, timbered shore.

"Where do you reckon you could build it?" asked Blackie.

Mickey looked innocently at Blackie and gestured with a wave at the crookedly hanging door that separated the office from the dank, cavernous shop beyond. "Actually," he said, "I was sort of thinking . . ."

Blackie stroked his bristled chin. He peered at Mickey with his close-set eyes from under dark brows. Blackie was in deep thought and when Blackie thought—it could be awesome.

Blackie came out of his reverie. "I know where we can git the log," he said. "It's a-gonna have to be a big 'un."

"Yipes," Mickey cried, jumping up and running past Blackie into the shop. Mickey measured off the length of the old building's interior with careful steps along the damp, sagging, timeworn planking. He found there was forty-five feet of work space, provided Blackie was willing to remove a ton of rusty, greasy junk and an old Ford station wagon—and if a falling-down, roofless rear porch might somehow be used.

Blackie snorted at the idea of removing the car, which rested on tireless wheels and was piled high with old parts and other miscellaneous junk.

"I was gonna fix that car up," Blackie said, pulling a face. "It's a good one."

"Yeah," said Mickey, peering through a broken window at the torn and junk-jammed interior. "Sure."

"May as well haul her out of here, if you say so," Blackie conceded, giving the boy a wink. "Probably be ten years 'fore I get to her anyway."

Blackie finally led the way back to the office. "Now, let's look at that-there picture in the book," he said, and they opened up the volume again. "My, myeeee—ain't that a purty boat. Lookie at that thingamajigger on the front-end. Now, that's a-gonna take some doin' to carve that out."

....

Bill the Blowdown King was a tree-faller-turned-boss. That meant he had his own logging show. But it was a gypo outfit. That is, it wasn't much of one.

Bill was a tough little man whose people some time back came from Ireland to America and built railroads. Bill's grandfather drifted to Oregon and Bill's father drifted to Alaska and Bill hadn't drifted anywhere. He was part of the land. A small, sinewy, dark, crinkly-faced, bright-eyed man, Bill had left the surety of working for someone else felling trees to become a blowdown logger. Bill was sort of a logging clean-up man, taking on the always chancy and always frustrating and dangerous work of cleaning out areas of timber flattened by high winter winds. He like his work, though. Currently, he and his partner, a bearded, silent giant gargoyle named Simon, were laboring on an unlikely lee shore twenty miles from Wrangell on Clarence Strait, getting together a log raft of blown-down hemlock and spruce. The work was done with a worn-out tractor of uncertain vintage, muscle-power, and just plain meanness. The logs were high in the hills that rose wet and swampy from a windblown, rocky beach on whose shore clung Bill's one-trailer (sleeping), one-shack (cooking and tool-storage) camp.

"We get this raft in the water," he told Simon cheerfully as the two stood in their tin hats, soaked with rain, on the beach beside their smoking, complaining Caterpillar, "and we'll go to town and have a party."

Bill figured the raft would fetch ten thousand dollars, enough to pay off all his bills for the season, repair the tractor for next year and finance at least part of a winter of revelry. He calculated that according to the regular routine of his life he would party for half the winter and spend the other half in jail.

"We get this raft behind the tug in, say, a week," he told Simon, "then we close this place up for the winter before the first snow gets here. We collect our money, we pay the bills, and we spend the rest on you-know-what—fun."

Simon smiled a slow smile, his lips bright red and moist behind his jet-black beard. His eyes twinkled.

Suddenly a blue Cessna 185 floatplane roared over the beach. It was Elwood Waters, Wrangell's number-one bush pilot, with the regular weekly grocery delivery. Bill and Simon rushed to the shore and pushed their rust-bucket of an iron workboat into the chilly sea. Bill jerked the outboard motor into wheezing, then roaring life and the boat began to make its way through outlying rocks and reefs toward the airplane, which had alighted on the water and was bobbing quietly half a mile from shore.

The little pilot had strict orders never to venture with an airplane anywhere near Bill's beach, no matter how much the logger tried to talk him into doing it. No one—not even Bill—knew where all the rocks were.

"And rocks," Elwood's boss had said with great seriousness, "sink airplanes, Elwood."

The boss had wrinkled his face into a terrible pucker and placed it very close to Elwood's face and added: "Bill will always try to get you to taxi the airplane to the beach. He will not try to get you to do that sometimes, Elwood. He will try to get you to do that every time. Don't do it, or you're fired!"

The warning had the ring of steel to it. Elwood figured his boss meant it. It had, however, come too late by several weeks. Elwood had been enticed toward the beach by the tough little Irish logger and by some miracle Elwood and the boss's airplane escaped unscathed.

Bill had arrived beside the bobbing Cessna without Simon. "He's up in the woods, can't come." The logger had shaken his head sadly and looked at the boxes and bags filling the Cessna's little cabin. "We'll have to get these supplies into the boat ourselves, Elwood. Lot of work. Unless," added the gypo-logger, "you wanna come to the beach. I'll guide ya. Know these waters like the back of my own hand. Besides, breakfast's on. Got fresh eggs, grits, steaks, hot coffee. *Doughnuts.*"

With Bill driving the outrageous iron boat and Elwood following in the Cessna, they made their way shoreward.

The iron boat was making speed, pushing a creamy wave before its blunt and rusty bow and trailing a nice little rooster tail. Elwood, his hand on the throttle, toes perched on the rudder pedals gingerly, and his heart in his mouth, followed along at about fifty yards, also cutting a rooster tail. Just as it seemed they would make it nicely, the iron boat reared like a harpooned whale, jerked violently around, and stopped short. Bill, who had been standing grandly at the tiller, was levitated. He sailed majestically out of the boat in a perfect arm-and-leg-waving arc and crashed in a frothy splash into the sea.

Elwood's eyes widened, an "Oh gosh!" exploded from him, and a booted left toe mashed a rudder pedal to the cockpit firewall, while the throttle went in in short bursts. The Cessna responded, turning sluggishly at first for the open sea. How close to the rocks he came Elwood couldn't tell, but it was close. Finally, the airplane was pointed seaward and Elwood jammed the throttle in to the stop. The engine roared, the prop bit the air viciously with a loud wail and the plane, skittering from wave to wave, made for safety offshore.

Half a mile away Elwood finally killed the engine and the airplane came to a bobbing, dripping stop. The little pilot, breathing heavily, opened the cockpit door so the cool air bathed him. He lay back in the seat, eyes closed, saying over and over again: "Thank you, Lord, thank you, Lord."

Eventually a sopping, grinning, thoroughly unperturbed Bill arrived. "That's one I didn't know about," he called from the iron boat. "I reckon I know 'em all now—every last one. So let's get going." He waved for Elwood to follow and turned the boat for the beach again, opening the throttle.

Elwood made no effort to move from his position. He just turned his head and stared after the boat until Bill eventually turned around and motored back. The two silently unloaded the groceries while the airplane and the rusted boat bumped and banged together in the swell.

The last box of groceries went into the battered boat and Elwood climbed into his seat, preparing to leave.

"Oh," he said, pulling an envelope from his pocket and handing it down. "Blackie gave me this; said be sure you got it."

Bill took the grease-stained envelope and ripped it open, read the terse note it contained:

Bill, I'll take my favor now. One good—and I mean good—red cedar log. Length 40 feet minimum. Girth 16 feet. Delivered. Keep quiet about this, and don't tell me you can't find one neither.
                    Blackie

Meanwhile, in town, pounding and sawing sounds were emerging from Blackie's garage. The noise raised no eyebrows on Main Street. Blackie always had projects going in the old building at all hours of the day and night—or his friends did.

This time the noise heralded an expansion. Blackie was building a partition out of rough lumber and canvas, dividing the shop. He left space in front for the occasional car repair job. In the partition he put an old wooden door and on it he hung a sign that said PRIVATE—NO ENTRY.

Later, when anyone asked him what was behind the door, Blackie said he was going to build a boat in there to go back to fishing, but that for the meantime it was just a junkhole.

Blackie expanded the working space of the new shop by building a tent on wooden frames over the old loading dock at the rear. The dock was connected to the shop with double doors, which Blackie and Mickey dismantled. From the harbor side Blackie's place looked like a gypsy camp, but nobody gave it a second thought. After all, it *was* Blackie's.

On a rainy night ten days after he received the note, Bill stomped up the stairs to Blackie's apartment and pounded on the door. Blackie opened up and peered outside.

"Got your log," Bill said. "Where do you want her?"

Two hours later, on the high tide, Blackie and Bill jerked the big log from the bay up into the building, using Blackie's old tow truck.

Next day, Mickey hurried down after school. He and Blackie looked at the tree on the floor. It took up the length of the room and stuck out into the tent. It was always chilly in the building except sometimes in midsummer, but the massive log, fresh from the woods and from a twenty-mile trip behind Bill's iron boat, made it seem forebodingly damp and cold.

Blackie ducked into the office and returned with a cylinder of drafting paper. He unrolled the paper onto the workbench, weighted it down, and showed Mickey a working sketch of the canoe. It looked for all the world like the one Mickey had seen in his dream, right down to the carved decorations and the graceful bird-neck of a reaching bow. It startled him.

"Me and the wife drew it up last night," Blackie said. "The wife, she knows a thing or two about canoes."

Mickey took the paper reverently and tacked it to the wall where the filtered light from the dirty windows struck it and made it look ancient and weathered. Then he took a hatchet from the workbench and walked to the log. He struck a chip from it.

"First lick," he said to Blackie.

"First one, replied Blackie. "But you gonna need more than that-there hatchet, chile."

Blackie reached under the workbench, pulled out a huge chain saw, started it and, humming to the high wail of the saw, began on the log.

The Scene and the People

FROM *Out of the North*

RONALD JOHNSON

World War II veteran Ronald Johnson came to Alaska in 1951 during the rough-and-tumble growth of Alaska's biggest city, Anchorage. He writes about his experiences in OUT OF THE NORTH *(1991). Johnson lived for several years in Wasilla, Alaska, and now makes his home in Hawaii, where he is a professor of psychology at the University of Hawaii.*

The strongest and most vivid visual image of Anchorage that I have is this: it is dark, 5:30 A.M. on a cold March day. I am walking down C Street. Street lights on, it is spitting snow, and I'm on my way to meet my work partners and go to work. No one on the street except for one small bunch of folk huddled together under a street light between 4th and 5th on C Street. Walk up. See the guys inside a circle drawn with chalk on the sidewalk. (Who is the thoughtful one who is the keeper of the chalk?) Inside the chalk circle, small change on the sidewalk. The guys—the most learned losers in the world—were gathered. As each one joined the circle, he would throw whatever change he had into the circle: 13 cents here, 11 cents there, it adds up. There is 86 cents; 13 cents more and you can buy a bottle of cheap muscatel—muskadoodle—at the all-night liquor store. I come along, lordly in my largesse; I am working. I throw in a quarter. Enough for the bottle and a little seed money for the next. Some trusted old-timer takes the money, goes and gets the bottle, brings it back, opens it up, slugs it down, coughs, snorts, and spits, and passes it on. It comes to me. I take my drink and head on down C Street to meet my work partners. Or else stay in the circle for one more bottle's worth, to hear about Alaska and about life from the guys that know all about both Alaska and life but haven't mastered either.

....

The idea of civil rights had not reached Anchorage in the '40s or '50s. Everyone had lots of rights, but didn't expect the government to do anything about it. You had exactly as many rights as you were willing to fight for. You could, to a fair degree, do whatever you wanted to. But if what you did got in the way of someone else's rights, then that someone else might kill you. Sensible people didn't push their luck by tramping on the rights of other people.

This was way before any anti-discrimination laws, and black people had it hard. Not that they weren't ready to fight for their rights, but most of them had come from places a lot more prejudiced than Anchorage and, besides, they were making money, so they didn't fight as hard as they might. The whole system was against them then, and they knew it, and also knew it was almost straight suicide to fight the system. Every now and then one of them would do it—almost like a Malay running amok—seeking death with honor. He'd kill a few people, the cops would shoot him down, and one more badass would bite the dust.

Now there are laws that are enforced aimed at ending discrimination. Good. But the bad thing that has changed across time is that despite legal equality it has gotten to be more difficult and uncommon for blacks and whites to be friends. Louis Rodrigues and I were good friends. We met in a white "patron"-black "client" kind of way, but we became real friends, working on the same jobs, talking, eating, drinking, hitting the bars together.

The way we met was like this. I was working at Indian Creek on a blacktopping job and had to get the hot plant cracked off by about 4:30 in the morning if we were going to start blacktopping at 7:00 A.M. Turner and Henry worked on the blacktopping crew. They both were big and black. They'd been with the company a long time. So they got overtime for going down to Indian Creek and oiling down/cleaning up the Barber Green laydown machine (a truck dumps the asphalt into a bit at the front of the Barber Green, the Barber Green lays it down on the road) and busting in the tops of the barrels of asphalt as needed, along with sand and gravel, to make blacktopping. I fired the boiler off and started heating asphalt and mixing it to make blacktop. We were the only three people leaving Anchorage for Indian Creek before 4:00 A.M., so Turner and Henry rode with me in my pickup. I picked them up every morning and took them home every night. They paid for the gas. Many a morning, driving together, talking all the way. They'd forget that I was white and I heard some interesting tales. But back to Louie.

Turner was at least six feet tall and Henry was a real giant—broad and about 6 feet 4 inches or so. Both hard and self-sufficient men. They both were deeply religious. Since they both were so religious it surprised me when Turner started talking to me one morning. He and Henry obviously had discussed the matter a good deal before they decided that Turner should talk to me. Turner wanted me to use whatever pull I had with construction companies to get Louie Rodrigues a job and get out of jail.

The vagrancy charge was a very handy thing for the police. If you had a real badass around, but couldn't catch him at anything, you could arrest him for vagrancy—basically for being alive and not having visible means of support—that is, no job. Obviously, a law that was enforced quite selectively and, according to Turner, was now being used on Louie. Louie was a pimp, which is why I was surprised at Turner's and Henry's concern. Couldn't be caught at anything, so the cops had vagged him. 15 days for vagrancy, then out the jail door, re-arrested, then 15 more days for vagrancy. He'd done two gigs and was going to be out after his third one pretty soon. He needed a job. I don't know why Turner and Henry were concerned; they were religious, they worked hard, and had no high regard for the black sporting set. Maybe all that mattered to them was that a black man, smart enough to beat whites, was being shit on. Anyway, they wanted me to find Louie a job and I had only about a week to do it in.

Anchorage was a union town, at least in construction, and that's all I know. Times weren't bad but they weren't that good either. So it would be hard to get him into the union and get him a job—since he had to be in the union to get a job and had to have a job to get into the union—especially with him in jail.

I said I'd try. That night, after work, I drove around (not many people had phones) to see construction foremen and superintendents I knew. I saw quite a few people and had quite a few beers before I got a lead. I saw Don Clark and he told me that his brother Ken was pour superintendent on some barracks being built by MK-PK, and they needed buggy men. (The concrete would be delivered in trucks, pumped up to the level of the pour, but then dumped into buggies sort of like two-wheeled wheelbarrows; the buggies then were pushed to where the concrete went into the forms that made the wall. Buggy men did the pushing and buggy men were black.) I saw Don's brother and told him that Don had sent me. I told him that I wanted a job pushing buggy for a black guy I knew. Don't brother said, "Fine, I'll call the hall and call for your guy—what's his name?" I told him, "Louis Rodrigues." The next day after work, I stopped in at the laborer's union and talked to the business agent. I told him about this deserving black guy with a wife and kids and no job. I told him that MK-PK were going to put in a call for this black guy but that he wasn't a member of the union. I said I'd pay the initiation fee in cash (giving the business agent a chance to pocket it if he wanted to do so) and told the agent he'd be doing a very good deed. He took the money, typed out the union card, and gave it to me.

I hadn't seen Louis Rodrigues yet. I walked over to the jail and asked to see him. I gave him the card and told him I'd bring the job slip to him as soon as he told me when he'd get out. If I remember right, I saw Louie on a Thursday and he got out on Monday. So, I got Don's brother to make out the job request for Monday, and delivered that to Louie on Friday night. I knew that he wouldn't get out of jail till midmorning on Monday, but told him to take a cab to the jobsite and plan on working Monday afternoon. The next morning on the way to work I told Turner and Henry that I thought everything was going to work.

Louie was being visited by delegations of his whores, bringing him food, commiserating, taking orders, etc. So he ordered some work clothes. On Monday morning, the police turned him loose and let him walk about 10 feet before they arrested him for vagrancy again. He showed them his union card and his job slip from the union hall so they had to let him go. He went home, put on his work clothes, caught a cab, and was out on the jobsite by 11:00.

The next morning, I started asking questions while Turner and Henry and I were going to work. It turned out that Louie was Cuban by birth (later, he told me, "I'm really a Cuban but everyone up here says I'm a nigger so I guess I am"), was a slick and heavy gambler, had about as big a string of whores as any in Alaska, and kept them well in line.

Louie stuck with the buggyman job. It was hard work and he'd been years away from hard work so he must have been very tired by the end of the day—usually 10-11 hours of hard work. But he kept at it, as he promised he would. He still had to be up half the night running his string of whores, paying off cops, collecting his take, gambling whenever he had a chance, being hard toward guys who'd like to take over his girls, etc. I regarded him as old—he probably was about 35 or 40—and was amazed at his vigor. I had to get up at about 3:30 or 4:00 to go to work, while he didn't have to get up until maybe 5:30, but even so, I was amazed at his late night stamina. I used to see this stamina because by this time I'd spent evenings with him. I'd told him he didn't owe me anything, but every once in a while he'd tell Turner or Henry to tell me that he'd be over to see me. He'd drive over and pick me up and we'd hit *his* Anchorage. I'd go with him, but have him drive me home by about 11:00, unless it was a Saturday night and I wasn't working on Sunday. Then I'd make a night of it.

My Anchorage was downtown in places like the Scandinavian Club, if I wasn't with a woman, the 515 and such like if I had one. His Anchorage was Eastchester Flats. Eastchester Flats was a valley in which nearly all the blacks then lived. Some naughty soul, obviously a lineman or a logger used to using climbing gear, had climbed an electric pole to put, very high up, a big plywood sign that said "Valley of 10,000 Smokes" after the name of the national park. With thousands of blacks in Eastchester Flats, the name stuck. Louie's favorite spot was the Kit-Kat Club. He'd haul me down there and he'd have Johnny on the rocks and I'd have beer and then we'd talk.

He'd been a pimp most of his life and had become resigned to the feck-lessness of whores and to their need for direction, even with regard to the most minor of decisions. Now he'd been loose in a world of men—good, hard men who made decisions (often bad ones) in seconds, acted on them, and then took the consequences of them without any whimpering. He was a winning person, he was bright, he worked hard, he enjoyed construction, so it wasn't too long till he was buggy crew foreman. Then he had to direct the work of others. Back in the executive role, but directing a bunch of buggymen during a concrete pour is a lot different from directing a bunch of hookers. The problems are different and solving the problems is more constructive. Ken Clark still was pour super and was most pleased with Louie, so he taught him how to estimate the size of the pour, spacing of time between concrete trucks, and all the rest one needs to know to be a good pour superintendent. This didn't happen overnight, but Louie did learn well. Louie's unfavorite topic was his string of whores. He was sick of their silly problems, their larcenous ways, their squabbles with one another, having to pay off cops. He took the money, of course, but didn't really need it. He did enjoy being the big black boss pimp, it gave him status. He was in conflict. He liked construction and was doing well at it. He didn't like pimping, but got a lot of rewards out of it. He was out in a world of free men, speaking his mind, and at the same time had to be affectionate, every once in a while, to each of the 20 or 30 hookers whom he despised. All pimps despise women, but Louie had reached the point that he knew that he didn't need them.

Why did he keep on pimping then? One incident is enough to explain it. We were sitting at the Kit-Kat having a few drinks about 10:30 one summer night, enjoying ourselves, talking, and eating soul food. In comes one of his girls, interrupting us. "Louie, see what I got you." She hands him a nicely wrapped gift. He opens it and takes out a Parker 64 pen and pencil set. Gold, expensive, *the* gift of that particular year. Louie looked at it, looked at her, she smiled at him and stepped closer to him, maybe expecting a kiss. He gave her a very hard open-handed slap across the face. She staggered backwards on her high heeled shoes for about six steps and fell on her ass. She sat there on the barroom floor, legs spread, crying. He gave her a hard look and crooked his finger. "Come here, bitch." She got up, whimpering, came toward him warily, stopping a few steps away. He crooked his finger again. She came closer. "Where'd you get this?" he demanded. "J. Vic Brown's? You go back there as soon as they open on Monday morning, tell them you don't want it, get the money back and then *give me the money*, bitch." Still crying, she said, "Yes, Louie." He said, "OK. Now go out and make some money and bring it to me and don't you ever spend any of my money on shit like that again or I'll kill you." She headed out to make some money.

Louie turned around to me and said, "I suppose you thought that was a bit harsh." I said, "Yes, I did." He said, "Well, maybe I was a bit harsh, but you really don't know these girls. They are so damned dumb and if you let them make decisions about something like a pen and pencil set, pretty soon they'll be making decisions about important things. They'll screw up, and then I'll have to deal with cops and lawyers. So it's better for me and for them if I make the decisions. You know, they really are a pain. Would you want to take over half of them? It would help me; you'd make a lot of money and I'd show you how to do it." But I said, "No." Before starting to hang around with Louie, I'd had a prejudice against pimps, but any man who manages the lives of 20 or 30 good looking, trouble making, not very bright women, deserves sympathy. Most guys who want to take on the job don't know the problems involved. Not me; I didn't want any part of it; a simple and untroubled life is best.

Louie finally got to be pour superintendent. He cut his string down to four—all good looking, all of them bright enough so that they didn't get into too much trouble. Enough to give him some variety in his sex life, a fair amount of money and status, but none of the headaches of keeping a big string going. The best of both worlds.

I was only one of many people who had adventures in the Scandinavian Club. It was not unusual that people had more exciting adventures than they set out to find while they were in the Scandinavian Club. I had a few adventures, but they all were pleasant ones. The experience I remember best wasn't an adventure at all. All it involved was standing around and watching.

Bud and I had put in a hard week on construction and had Sunday off for a change. We were going to hit it hard that Saturday night. We started out by having steaks at the Buckaroo and then went over to the Scandinavian Club to have a few beers before heading out to Fort Starnes and the 1042 Club.

The Scandinavian Club was on the corner of 5th and C. The entrance was on the corner, so that you walked up three or four steps from either 5th or C and then you were in the bar. The barfront faced onto 5th and there was room for a few people to sit at the bar on the C Street side, so that you could look out the window and the doors onto either 5th or C. That is where we sat. Along the barroom there was a dance hall area further down toward C Street, with a partition between the bar and the dance hall. The place wasn't going to get any of the Anchorage carriage trade (and I suspect that such existed, though I never met any of those folk) so the bar and backbar were heavy, old-fashioned, and excellently done. There were no pictures or works of art, the tables and booths were pretty beat up, and it all needed painting.

The owner had always been a friend. Fellow Scandinavians, we had a similar world view. I'd usually stop in to scoff a few beers with him before going on to more serious drinking, or to gambling or the pursuit of women. That is why Bud and I stopped in, but the owner wasn't there. It still was early—about 8:30 at night—and the only people in the bar were a few drinkers, the bartenders, and an old Finnish woman who played songs on the accordion if you paid her.

The Scandinavian Club was a fairly tough bar and it got tougher as the night wore on. The clientele consisted of rugged people who, apart from general orneriness, hated to wait when they wanted a drink. This made it necessary to have a lot of bartenders. They looked as though they were identical twins except that there were seven of them. Each one of them had sort of sandy red hair, half balding. Each of them was small—about 5'4"-5'5". Each one of them carried a big blackjack in his right back pocket, and each of them was quick and skillful in using it. The old Finn woman sat on a kitchen chair on the barroom side. Dumpy, gray, and a bit too lippy. She had a good accordion strapped on and a tin cup beside her for collecting her donations.

Construction stiffs talk about women once in a while, but their main obsession is construction. Bud and I sat there, drinking our beers and talking about dirt moving. A quiet time, good food in the belly, good beer going down to join the food. At peace with the world—just like that glorious summer of 1946, when the war was over and we'd won, we all had money, and weren't working yet. A couple of beers worth of peaceful discussion and then the logger from Shotgun Cove came in.

Shotgun Cove is on Prince William Sound, a long way from anywhere. People from Shotgun Cove didn't get to town often, so they made the most of it when they got there. This one was a big, burly, Squarehead type, all dressed up for the big city. Pendleton shirt, open about halfway down to show off the handsome dark gray long-handled underwear fancied by real timber beasts, "Can't Bust Em" black jeans, and boots. Probably just out of the Finn bath—clean, and hair slicked down. He walked up to the bar and got a beer. Down it went and he started on another. Then he noticed the old Finn woman.

Beer in hand he walked over and said, "Will you play the Swedish Waltz?" She gave him a smirky kind of a sneer. Swedes ran Finland for a long time and the Finns haven't forgotten it. She said, "No, I can't, but I can play 'Life in the Finnish Woods.' " Now the music is exactly the same for the two songs—they just have different names—and, I suppose, different words to go with the music—in Sweden and Finland. So she was insulting to the logger from Shotgun Cove. He responded straightforwardly enough. He swung his arm aback and then gave her an open-handed slap across the face that knocked her and her accordion off the chair and sent her, the accordion, and the chair straight along the floor till they fetched up against the wall.

The bartenders may not have seen an old Finn woman hooked up to her accordion flying across the barroom before, but they sure had had their share of drunks and of fights. All of them came out from behind the bar, blackjacks in hand, to handle the big Squarehead.

Seven to one is good odds, but he was big and quick. Even with black-jacks they had a hard time pressing him out of the doors, down the steps, and onto the sidewalk. They might have stopped there—they'd thrown him out—but he'd blacked some eyes, bloodied some noses, and also done some kicking before they got him out, so the bartenders followed him out onto the street and kept at him.

Bud and I were still sitting at the same bar stools. We had almost full beers and a good view of the street. We watched the show. It was like a bull being attacked by dogs. The bartenders circled him, jumped on his back, bashed him with their blackjacks whenever they got a chance, hit him with their fists, made jumping kicks. He was like an old bull. Three or four bartenders would be grabbing him and then he'd roar a little and start picking up bartenders and throwing them.

By now it was about 9:30 at night on a fine summer Saturday night in the middle of construction season. Everyone had money, everyone was out, and pretty soon there was a big circle of people all around the fight. By this time, Bud and I had taken our beers out onto the steps to watch the fight. It would move up onto 5th Avenue and then the battle would move toward 4th. As the fight moved, the crowded circle watching it would move, too. Whenever the fight would move down about 50 feet toward 4th Avenue, the crowd would be standing next to an alley. And in the alley were a bunch of GIs. We watched them as well as the fight. Whenever the fight swayed far enough toward 4th Avenue, the crowd of watchers would be right outside the alley. Then a couple of GIs would grab someone and haul him into the alley. We could see this much but couldn't see what happened in the alley. It was pretty clear what did happen, though. Someone would be yanked in. A minute or two later, he'd come wobbling out with blood running down off the top of his head into his eyes. Blackjacked and rolled. The fight continued and very excitingly at that. By now over a dozen watchers had been grabbed, blackjacked, rolled, and pushed back into the crowd, stumbling about and dripping blood. The bartenders kept banging away, but the logger was one hard guy. He'd knocked five of the seven bartenders out of the fight. Some of them still could stand up and walk around, but they declared individual truces. They weren't in it any more. By this time the logger was well battered. His shirt was gone and so was the top half of his long-handled underwear. Two bartenders still active. Then they all stopped. The crowd began to move away. The GIs quit rolling people. Bud and I went into the bar and stood there at the bar. One bartender came in and went behind the bar. The logger said, "Give me an Oly," the bartender cracked out the beer, the logger paid for it and took a big long drink. By this time, the Finn woman was back on her chair with accordion in hand. The logger went over to her and said, "Will you play the Swedish Waltz?" She said, "Yah, I can do that." He put the obligatory quarter into her cup and then some more silver money as well. She played the Swedish Waltz.

Shattered Dreams

FROM *Johnny's Girl*

KIM RICH

Anchorage writer Kim Rich is a former journalist for the Anchorage Daily News *whose work has appeared in* Alaska *magazine and* Mirabella. *She teaches at the University of Alaska Anchorage and Alaska Pacific University. "Shattered Dreams" is excerpted from her book* JOHNNY'S GIRL *(1993), a memoir of her childhood as the daughter of Johnny Rich, a prominent member of the Anchorage underworld in the 1960s.*

For most who were in Anchorage in the early 1960s, few things in their lives compared with events of Good Friday, March 27, 1964. There was life before The Earthquake and life after The Earthquake. But for me, the earthquake had virtually no emotional impact. By the time the quake occurred, my life had already fallen apart.

The quake began at 5:36 P.M. and was a monster, measuring 8.4 to 8.7 on the Richter scale—the worst ever in North America. The epicenter was near the headwaters of Prince William Sound, only eighty miles east of Anchorage, striking at the heart of Alaska's population center.

A terrible rumbling was felt throughout an area of half a million square miles. In Anchorage, the earth rippled and pitched like giant ocean waves. Telephone poles slammed from one side of the ground to the other; parked cars bounced as if they'd been placed on trampolines, and tall buildings swayed violently, like palm trees caught in a hurricane-force wind.

Throughout south central Alaska, many people watched horrified and helplessly as their loved ones and coworkers were swallowed by shifting slabs of earth or buried in cascading waterfalls of rubble. Throughout the ordeal, the sound of glass breaking and groaning timber filled the air. Some thought it was the end of the world. Others were convinced that the Russians had dropped a nuclear bomb on Fort Richardson.

I was at my mother's friend Midge's house sitting on Terry the baby-sitter's lap, alternating between moments of watching *Fireball XL5,* a silly black-and-white show about puppet space travelers, and breaking into sob-bing fits. Terry was the babysitter for me and Midge's two sons, Tony and Bobby. I was miserably unhappy because Midge was taking Tony for a hair-cut and I wanted to go with them, but instead I was made to stay home with Terry, along with Bob and Vern, a couple of Midge's friends who'd stopped by with a bucket of chicken.

I'd worked myself into a raging fury, kicking, yelling, screaming. Terry did her best to calm me.

We were in the chair that faced the television set. Behind the TV was a small dining area where a picture window looked out onto the parking lot at the front of the duplex. As Midge was sliding behind the steering wheel of her car, it suddenly began rocking in slow motion, looking as if it was going to come through the window. I thought, *Why is Midge trying to drive the car into the house?*

Simultaneously, the whole apartment began rocking in the same slow, sick way. Terry tried to stand, but the floor buckled under her feet and threw her sideways and we fell back into the overstuffed rocker.

While still looking out the window, I saw Bobby ride up from his newspaper route on his bicycle. He threw the bike down and grabbed the car's passenger door. Midge was now standing at the driver's side as they both strained to keep it from bounding into the building. Tony was inside, caroming around like a human tennis ball. Terry jumped up a second time, this time pushing me out of her lap.

"Earthquake!" she screamed.

Everything kept moving. *Fireball XL5* was still on the television—until the set tipped backward and crashed to the floor. Pictures rattled and banged on the walls, swinging like crazed pendulums. The kitchen cup-boards flew open, sending their contents crashing to the floor.

Terry dragged me to the front door, staggering like a drunk. Then she handed me over to Bob. Another tremor hit and my head was slammed against the doorframe as we passed under it. He let out a loud laugh when I cried out, "I wish I was in California."

"Yeah, me too, baby," Bob said as he rushed out to the street where the shaking continued.

By the time we'd reached the middle of the road, there was already a wide, deep fissure that disappeared beneath Midge's duplex. Once outside, I heard a terrible snapping noise, like a dozen firecrackers exploding. It was the windows breaking in the McKinley building, only a few blocks directly south of the duplex.

After five minutes, the shaking finally stopped. The first thing I noticed was the McKinley building seemed to be leaning our way, giving me the feeling it could fall on us. We huddled in the street only a few moments before my father came running toward us, looking disheveled and haggard.

My father had been at the Safari, in the middle of taking a shower, when the quake started. He jumped out, grabbed some slacks, and ran into the hallway, where he met half a dozen guests headed for the stairs. He ran past them, checking the rooms to make sure everybody was out. As he turned to head back toward the stairs, the floor tilted downward. He began yelling for Yukon. The dog had run out of the room with him, but was nowhere in sight. My father grabbed the stair railing but the stairway walls began to cave in, so he ran back toward his room, where Yukon stood on the bed. He kicked out the window overlooking the back alley, grabbed the dog and heaved him outside, then jumped behind him. By the time he landed on the ground the two-story Safari had become a one-story building, its first floor sinking into the ground. When the earth had stopped shaking, 115 Alaskans were dead, nine in Anchorage.

Fourth Avenue was a wreck, and none of it was more devastated than the district around the Safari. The ground had sunk twenty feet, swallowing whole buildings and leaving bars, pawnshops, stores, restaurants, and other structures in heaps of cracked glass, smashed timbers, and shattered signs. The Safari was gone, along with the Scandinavian Club, the Frisco Bar, Koslosky's Men's Store, Northern Jewelers, and dozens of other businesses.

The stores that were left leaned against one another like staggering winos. Some had been ripped from their foundations, others looked untouched until you realized that what looked like the first floor was the second, squashed down as if under the palm of an angry giant. The Denali Theater had sunk below street level, its huge neon sign inches from the ground.

The streets were strewn with vehicles that the earthquake had tossed like jackstraws. Ironically, the destruction spared a banner strung across 4th Avenue to promote a play running at Alaska Methodist University. In big white letters, the words OUR TOWN flapped quietly above the wreckage.

Anchorage's death toll could have been much worse: Most of the town's

small, sturdy buildings were located far away from the slide areas; the earthquake occurred late in the afternoon at a time when most people had
already left work and were at home, and whatever fires broke out were easily
contained, and because it was a holiday, school was out of session.

As darkness fell, teams of civilian and military search and rescue squads,
aided by flashlights, began sifting through the rubble on 4th Avenue and in
neighborhoods where the homes had been destroyed, looking for survivors
and trying to retrieve bodies. Servicemen on the bases began cutting fifty-
five-gallon barrels in half and fitting them with plywood tops for makeshift
outhouses to be distributed to the badly damaged areas. It was announced
on the radio that within a few days, typhoid immunization centers would
be set up around town. Everyone was advised to get the shots.

   That night, families camped in what was left of their homes or bunked
with friends whose houses survived intact. Countless aftershocks shook
Anchorage, rattling what was left of everybody's nerves. In between momentary dashes out the front door (in case the roof was going to cave in), families sat close to their radios listening to disc jockeys pass along emergency
messages. With most of the phone lines down and those that were up
reserved for emergency use only, radio became the only communication link
between residents who didn't know if their friends or family members across
town were still alive.

   In addition to emergency messages and the latest Richter scale reading
on the last tremor (there were several that night) came the tidal wave warn-
ings. At one point, the neighborhoods of Bootlegger's Cove, South Addition,
and Turnagain were evacuated by a false alarm. The wave rolled in, measuring only three feet. But who wanted to take any chances?

   Midge, my father, Tony, Bobby, several others, and I stayed at the home
of a friend. There was no electricity, running water, or heat. For us, like
many others, it was a cold night's rest as the outside temperature dipped to
20 degrees.

   As my father tucked me into bed that night I wondered if the Easter
bunny would still come. My father had other worries. The Safari was gone,
and although the house on Fireweed Lane had sustained only minor
damage, the rest of his life was a ruin. His livelihood—at least, the one he
claimed when paying taxes—was gone. My mother, who'd been hospitalized
since January, had been diagnosed as hopelessly schizophrenic.

Winter Ferry: Haines to Juneau

FROM *Glacier Bay Concerto*

RICHARD DAUENHAUER

*Richard Dauenhauer was born in New York State in 1942, and has lived in
Alaska since 1969. A well-known language researcher, teacher of comparative
literature, and poet, he was Alaska's poet laureate from 1981 to 1988. He
has received numerous prestigious awards, including a Woodrow Wilson
Fellowship, a Fulbright Fellowship, an Alaska Governor's Award for the Arts,
and an American Book Award. He is Director of Language and Cultural
Studies at Sealaska Heritage Foundation, Juneau.*

> Glacier Bay National Monument
> 1780
> glaciers
> as far as Icy Strait
> retreat by 1860
> to Tlingit Point
> uncovering the homeland
> abandoned in advance
> of pressing ice.
> 1925
> Glacier Bay withdrawn;
> 1936
> FDR
> opens it to mining.
> "Any scars
> on the face of nature
> would be infinitesimal in comparison
> with the magnitude and grandeur
> of the National Monument,
> and, in any event,
> nature would obliterate

mining scars up there
in half a generation.
Let us cut
red tape
and get the thing
started."

"All laws
of the United States
which apply to public lands
and which relate
to entry upon
and use and approbation
of such lands
for mining purposes
shall apply within
Glacier Bay National Monument,
Alaska, notwithstanding
the reservation contained
in the proclamation of the President
dated February 25,
1925."

1955
homestead lands
exempt
by presidential order.

"Glacier Bay
was like an ice box
full of food
for Hoonah.
They closed it off.
They bring up
thirty thousand tourists,
jets coming, jets going,
but we can't land.

Got stormbound there
four days once,
went for ribbon seaweed,
got stormbound,
the hotel cost us
two hundred dollars.
Glacier Bay:
Fish and Wildlife
closed it down.
We can't set foot
on shore,
we can't get off the skiff.
Thirty thousand tourists
every year."

Mining claims still valid,
claims still being worked
in National Parks and Monuments:
Grandfather Rights, they call it,
Grandfather Rights.

And so the agents
boarded Tlingit boats,
confiscated
subsistence hunters' guns,
threw the game
overboard,
and levied fines.
Hunting on the homeland
is against the law.

The Woman Who Married a Bear

JOHN STRALEY

John Straley, a mystery writer from Sitka, has worked as a blacksmith,
a wilderness ranger, an oral historian, and an investigator for the
Public Defender of the State of Alaska. He has written three novels about
hard-drinking private-eye Cecil Younger—THE WOMAN WHO MARRIED
A BEAR *(1992),* THE CURIOUS EAT THEMSELVES *(1993), and* THE MUSIC OF
WHAT HAPPENS *(1996). In this excerpt from* THE WOMAN WHO MARRIED A
BEAR, *Younger, en route to an investigation in Steller, Alaska, passes through*
Anchorage.

There are some questions so graceful that they should only be asked,
because at some point it becomes interruptive to try and answer
them.

One of the most time-consuming questions asked in this part
of the country involves where the "real Alaska" is. Most of the
people living north of Haines consider southeastern Alaska to be a suburb
of San Francisco, inhabited by drug-addled phoneys and bureaucrats, with
a few loggers and fishermen holding on against all odds. The phoneys and
the bureaucrats have an image of the modern white resident of the north as
a 400-pound Oklahoma building contractor with a 50-pound gold-nugget
watchband and an antebellum attitude toward the darker races. Anchorage
falls in the middle of this mess.

Anchorage grew up too fast to keep pace with its ability to dress itself.
Today its buildings mostly resemble monumental subarctic toasters, all
reflective surfaces to steal the beauty of the surrounding landscape.

Anchorage is hip deep in the twentieth century. In a downtown bar you
can find a deranged redneck watching a Rams game on the wide-screen TV
alongside an arts administrator who is working on a production of *Waiting*
for Godot to tour the arctic villages. Both of them will walk around the
Eskimo man bundled up asleep on the sidewalk, but the arts administrator
will feel an ironic sense of history.

During a heated discussion on the "real Alaska" issue, I heard a woman from Eagle River say to a man from Tenakee, "Okay, smart-ass, if Anchorage isn't an Alaskan city, what is it?" This might be one of those graceful questions. As my plane was flying over the city in preparation for the landing, it ran through my mind many times, like the mantra of an urban planner: "What is it?"

There were several people I would have liked to see but I wouldn't have time. There was the painter who took a knock on the head and could then speak Polish; there was one of the best mandolin players on the West Coast who lived in a trailer in the spectacular neighborhood of Spenard; and there was the sewage system engineer who could bench press 460 pounds. But I only had half an hour between planes.

On the trip to Anchorage I had read the information from the airline's file. None of the principals in the case had flown in or out of Sitka right before or after Todd was shot. Neither Walt Robbins nor any of the Victors were on the lists. Nor were there any R. Walters or Victor Lances or the like. I'd thought of that.

I read through Alvin Hawkes's medical file while I waited for my Stellar-bound jet to take off. The sun was setting and the temperature outside was near freezing. I glanced up and saw the baggage handlers packing cases of beer onto the conveyor belt. These cases were being checked through as excess baggage. Stellar is a damp community as far as alcohol goes. It's illegal to sell liquor but not to possess it. So any trip to Anchorage, whether business or pleasure, requires excess baggage.

If you live in southeastern Alaska and are used to being stared down at by the mountains with your back against the ocean, the country around Anchorage is a reprieve. The horizons are broad and open. The mountains slope up from the tidal flat, cupping Anchorage but not crowding it against the shallow waters of Cook Inlet. There is a much safer feel to landing or taking off in Anchorage than there is in Juneau, where the mountains stick up like granite nets that will catch you if you overrun the runway.

Anchorage

T O M   S E X T O N

*Tom Sexton, appointed Alaska's poet laureate in 1995, is a retired
university professor and author of four collections of poetry. Born in Lowell,
Massachusetts, Sexton moved to Alaska to teach writing, founded the creative
writing program at the University of Alaska Anchorage in 1970, and served
for many years as the poetry editor for* Alaska Quarterly Review. *The poem
"Anchorage" first appeared in* THE BEND TOWARD ASIA *(1993).*

> *"A woman without a lamp" is an expression which betokens,
> of all beings, that most wretched among the Eskimo.*
> —Walter Hough

While I pour my cup of morning tea,
a dark bird tears at something in the gutter
beneath a streetlight hissing in the sleet.
Hotels send out signals from their ridge.
Once again, I see that homeless woman,
her bruised face holding water like a font,
the police lifted from a plastic tent
hidden in the woods below our subdivision.
Their searchlights sweeping through the underbrush
found the hut of those who fled the sirens.
Not far from here, her ancestors would gather
to net quicksilver smelt, candle fish, that old
women burned in soapstone lamps on winter nights,
their voices coiled in endless shoals of light.

Progress

KAREN RANDLEV

*Karen Randlev lived in Alaska for six years, where she traveled for the
poets-in-the-schools program and won a Merit Award for her poem
"Old Woman and the Ice Cave" from the Alaska State Council on the Arts.
She was born in Evanston, Illinois, and is a graduate of Cornell University
and of the Writing Seminars of Johns Hopkins University. Several of her poems
about Alaska appear in the anthology of Alaskan women's writing,* HUNGER
AND DREAMS *(1983). Randlev's first book of poetry was* LIGHT RUNNER *(1987).
Her poem "Progress" was included in the anthology* A NEW GEOGRAPHY OF
POETS *(1992).*

I first went to Fairbanks in '76,
it was the height of the pipeline,
but it didn't hit me until this cute guy
offered me some Juicy Fruit in the Coop Drugstore
on Two Street. Those were the days.
I'd never seen a summer so long;
The sky came right down to the land;
it was hot as hell. For all that
I put my house on the Market, packed
up the dog and my kid, and drove up the Alcan
from Seattle to Tok.
I lasted six years.
When I went back to Fairbanks,
catching food poisoning from potato salad
on the way—throwing up in the john
of the Budget Rent-a-Car on Airport Road,
things weren't the same.
Those sweet Juicy Fruit guys were gone,
Two Street was trying for respectable,
and every corner had a shopping mall
selling pistachio nuts and gourmet-delites

from the lower '48.
I couldn't stay as long this time;
I turned in my cheap Super Saver
for a regular tourist fare and fled.
The fireweed was still there, but even the hippies
on Chena Pump looked like Berkeley.
It was time to go home.

Burying the Tongue Bone

SETH KANTNER

Seth Kantner is a writer, photographer, and commercial fisherman who attended the journalism program of the University of Montana. He grew up in the bush of northwestern Alaska and currently lives beside a river in the Brooks Range. His work has appeared in Outside *magazine. His short prose piece "Burying the Tongue Bone" was first published in* FROM THE ISLAND'S EDGE: A SITKA READER *(1995), edited by Carolyn Servid, a collection of work from participants and presenters at The Island Institute's annual summer writers' conference. This memoir deals with the values of the place where he grew up in the western Brooks Range.*

In the stories I grew up on there were no spelling-bee winners, no inventors or rich men. Those would have been pale unheroes. The stories were the old Eskimo ones of hardships and hunts, lost dog-teams and snowed-in trails, told by travelers spending stormy nights around our stove.

"Yep. Lotta barking and my dogs run away in the night. I had nuthin'. Not even rifle." Old Stoney Williams would laugh as if it were the funniest thing that could have happened to him. I'd bend close to the kerosene lamp, waiting for more, picturing him on the wide dark tundra and wondering if I'd ever be old enough to have those stories to tell, dreaming of being tough and able to laugh into storms like the old-timers. Stoney called me by my Inupiaq name and talked slow as if it were important that I understand.

But on rare trips to the village thirty miles upriver, ready fists reminded me that I was a white kid, an uncommon sight, not a native species of the Arctic. I couldn't claim the oldest stories, the mystical ones cloaked in nativeness and the past that I longed to be linked to, the ones about caribou with long teeth and the pike head out there in some lake swimming with only its guts trailing behind, the little strong-armed *inukuns* trying to strangle sleeping hunters. Those stories, I learned, could not be my own, even though they were hung before me like wonderful tempting objects in a native store where white people weren't allowed credit.

In the village I heard from Outside schoolteachers that money was very important, and I learned from their pupils that no amount of dirt on my face and in my hair would make me Eskimo. And that a thirty-word English vocabulary was more admirable than a hundred-word one that evoked responses of "Sure always try to be smart," and "Whachew try to prove, honky?"

Classics like *The Scarlet Letter,* about Pilgrims, meant nothing to me. Those weren't my grandparents, not my ancestors. I never learned "The National Anthem." It belonged to the country of America.

Now for years high-top tennis shoes, basketballs, and TV have been covering over the old stories, the old reasons for hunting, the reasons for making heroes out of hunters who laughed at the cold. I searched for new stories to own in the alleys of wet concrete, between the tall close skyscrapers that squeeze you in a city. I learned to drive cars and talk about them. "Year, '65 Mustang. Cool ragtop." And to call random 800-numbers from pay-phones when I was lonely to hear a woman's voice that wasn't frightened of me. The world of malls and movies and Kmart was sometimes fun, but always like a science fiction movie, never real. So it was easy to laugh at the hard city-times like a bad storm. But cement is harder and colder than any ice, to me, anyway.

I went home. To the tundra; that is still the same. I'm lucky it hasn't changed. And in the village I returned to the people who were often hard on me for being white, but they were the same elders who told me the old stories, showed me how to bury a bear's tongue bone to let the spirit come back. And the same kids that once pounded me for being white were the ones who had also laughed and showed me how to open easily the tough plastic on a bag of potato chips. "Come on Apikiilik, you don't need knife. Been in camp too long?"

Now enough years have finally passed, or maybe just change has left us all stunned, like a gun going off too close to your ear. But we share stories now. Not all of them. Not way back where we're from. We share what we know of our own past and this strange present, maybe because we see we're going to share the future now. *Aarigaa,* it's better now.

Salmon Egg Puller—$2.15 an Hour

NORA MARKS DAUENHAUER

Born in Southeast Alaska, Nora Marks Dauenhauer, a Tlingit, is a poet with a degree in anthropology. Dauenhauer and her husband, Richard, live in Juneau and are the editors and principal researchers of the series "Classics of Tlingit Oral Literature." She is the author, with her husband, of BEGINNING TLINGIT *(1976),* TLINGIT SPELLING BOOK *(Third Edition, 1984), and several other works, which are among the first published Tlingit grammars. Her first collection of poetry was* THE DRONING SHAMAN *(1988). "Salmon Egg Puller— $2.15 an Hour" is excerpted from* RAVEN TELLS STORIES: AN ANTHOLOGY OF ALASKAN NATIVE WRITING *(1991), edited by Joseph Bruchac.*

You learn to dance with machines,
keep time with the header.

Swing your arms,
reach inside the salmon cavity
with your left hand,
where the head was.

Grab lightly
top of egg sack
with fingers,
pull gently, but quick.
Reach in immediately with right hand
for the lower egg sack.
Pull this gently.

Slide them into a chute to catch the eggs.
Reach into the next salmon.
Do this four hours in the morning
with a fifteen minute coffee break.

Go home for lunch.
Attend to the kids, and feed them.
Work four hours in the afternoon
with a fifteen minute coffee break.
Go home for dinner.
Attend to kids, and feed them.

Go back for two more hours,
four more hours.
Reach,
pull gently.

When your fingers start swelling up,
soak them in epsom salts.
If you didn't have time,
stand under the shower
with your hands up under the spray.
Get to bed early if you can.
Next day, if your fingers are sore,
start dancing immediately.
The pain will go away
after icy fish with eggs.

The Men and the Work and the Northern Mystique

FROM *Inside the Alaska Pipeline*

ED MCGRATH

Ed McGrath moved to Alaska in the 1970s to work on the trans-Alaska pipeline. He spent most of his time at Prudhoe Bay on the arctic coast of the Beaufort Sea. "The Men and the Work and the Northern Mystique" is excerpted from his memoir INSIDE THE ALASKAN PIPELINE *(1977).*

T he North Slope in winter is like nothing so much as the moon. It has a few essentials that the moon is missing—air, water, a slightly more agreeable climate—but for the most part you have to bring your own life-support system with you. Eskimos, of course, have lived here for centuries, but they had knowledge that it took them centuries to acquire, and ways of doing things that are perfectly adapted to their specific environment. Even with their great knowledge, they lived hard lives and the threat of death by starvation was ever present. If you're a white man you might as well be on the moon.

In the wintertime it is unendingly white, the whole country covered with snow ranging from a few inches to several feet deep, depending on the drifts. There are almost no landmarks. Pingoes, little hills of ice thrust up by the heaving of the ground as it freezes and thaws, can be seen if you're no more than a few miles away. On a clear day the Brooks Range, eighty miles to the south, is visible. Other than that there is nothing distinctive to be seen, save the oil wells, buildings, and roads of the pipeline.

The land is amazingly empty in the winter. A few misguided caribou will spend the dark days there, for some reason not having migrated south with the herd. They paw through the snow and eat the moss that insulates the ground and keeps it frozen year round. Occasionally you see a raven, the hardy bird that shows up wherever there is garbage. There are foxes with gleaming fur, Arctic foxes that like to hang around the camps for the free food; sometimes you see a fox, more often you see their tracks. There are wolves too, but wolves are shy and seldom show themselves. These animals are spread out widely across the country; the land won't support dense populations.

In the winter it gets cold, though the extremes are no colder than in the interior of Alaska. But there is the wind and the dark. Prudhoe Bay sits near the 72nd parallel, five degrees inside the Arctic Circle, and the sun does not shine there for over two months. In the summer, of course, the sun stays above the horizon continuously for over two months. The land of the midnight sun is the land of the noonday moon. Although the sun doesn't come up, there is a bit of ghostly light each day, even on the twenty-first of December. A short pre-dawn is followed by a short twilight and then it's dark for another twenty-one hours.

The wind blows incessantly. There are no mountain ranges to channel it, so it blows east-west, sometimes clipping along at forty knots or more, very infrequently dropping off to calm. In the summer you want the wind to blow—it keeps the mosquitoes down. There is nothing in the natural environment to stop the wind, so the unnatural obstacles, the raised roads and buildings, bear the brunt of the drifting snow.

The Arctic is a desert, or very close to one. If it weren't for the permafrost (the perpetually frozen ground that holds the water on the surface) the Arctic would look like parts of Arizona or New Mexico. It gets only about three inches of precipitation per year. As it is, these three inches stay near the surface, so that there are large rivers, hundreds of creeks, and, in the state as a whole, 3 million lakes that are larger than twenty acres. In the winter, of course, everything in the Arctic is frozen and covered with snow, so the water can't be distinguished from the land. Not even the Beaufort Sea is discernible under the drifted snow, looking only like more of the same. From any of the camps at Prudhoe Bay you can look out on the bay, but in wintertime it looks no different than the land.

I was in Prudhoe Bay for weeks before I learned to feel in any way comfortable with this setting. It is utterly alien, much more so than an expanse of desert or prairie. When I first arrived there in January the sun was hidden behind the curve of the earth, and to make it even worse I hit a cloudy period.

Even when daylight comes it doesn't clearly mark the southeast, where the sun begins to rise once again toward the end of January. With clouds diffracting the light it is hard to tell which side of the sky is brighter. I never could get my directions straight.

When the sun first begins to peek out after its two-month rest, it appears as the glass globe of an old-fashioned floor lamp, hugging the horizon. Even then directions are difficult to determine. The sun swings in a short arc and then it is dark again. But day by day it rises higher in the sky, and although there are sure to be dark days, the daylight is ever increasing. About the middle of March you can even begin to feel optimistic about spring.

If the oil is to be gotten out of the ground and shipped south, that job has to be done by men (and a few women) and it unfortunately has to be done in Prudhoe Bay. What kind of man is it who will enter this alien place and begin to do the job that he is experienced in doing in Louisiana or Texas?

A partial answer to this question can be given by listing the various sorts of work that have to be done, and the union that handles each line of work.

The Teamsters are known as truck drivers, but in reality they do a good deal more than that. One out of every ten members of the Alaska work force is a Teamster, and they are unquestionably the most powerful union in Alaska. Among the Teamsters are included not only truck drivers, but bus drivers, warehousemen, forklift drivers, clerical workers, and surveyors. The Teamsters have simply been there to organize anyone that wanted to be organized, and probably more than any other group, they have profited from the pipeline.

The building construction people also figure heavily in the work force. Carpenters, electricians, plumbers, iron workers, sheet metal workers, and laborers are all needed to build and maintain the camps. To cook the food in the camps and keep them clean, the Culinary Union provides cooks, helpers, and bullcooks (the camp version of a maid). All rooms are cleaned daily, the only item that a worker has to attend to being his laundry.

When it comes to construction of roads and the pipeline right-of-way, it is the Operating Engineers who handle the equipment. Except for forklifts in warehouses and certain small drills, which are run by laborers, the operators run all the equipment—drills, backhoes, draglines, front-end loaders, Cats, sidebooms, cranes, etc. The laborers supply powdermen, or blasters, as well as the usual toters and diggers.

But the group most essential to pipeline building is the pipeliners, coming from the Pipewelders and Fitters Union, which has its only local, #798, in Tulsa, Oklahoma. The pipeliners work with the pipe—they position it, weld it, X-ray the welds, test it, and have a hand in installing the supports beneath it.

The 798ers, as they are called, are a living myth. They are known as the roughest, toughest, least-willing-to-take-any-shit-from-anyone, meanest, drinkingest, fightingest union that you'd ever hope to lay eyes on. The Teamsters may have power, the ironworkers may have high wages, but the 798ers have it made. There are only about 5,000 men in the pipeliners' union, and they have a virtual monopoly on the business, or at least they act like they do.

798ers are to a man southerners. They grew up in the south, they do most of their work there, and they like to think that wherever they go they bring home right along with them.

You can spot a 798er from a mile off. Whether they weld or not, and many of their jobs have nothing to do with welding, they wear multicolored cloth caps with short bills that can be put on backwards in case the wearer wants to slip a welder's helmet over his head. They wear cowboy boots and jeans. They have short hair. They are almost all country boys, most have not gotten very far in school, and speak strictly Southern English.

And so far as I know they are all white. I have heard rumors that there are black pipewelders, or at least black apprentices, but I never saw one—there for damn sure aren't very many. As a Mississippi welder once told me, "I don't know whether there are any niggers in the union right now, but up till a few years ago there sure wasn't. And you have to give the Klan a lot of credit for that." The pipeliners are dinosaurs, a tiny group of men that survives by having as its specialty a minuscule bit of technological expertise. But, son, them boys can flat weld pipe!

Even with the Alaska-hire policy, which for at least the first two years of the pipeline was not very stringently enforced, the workers who are from the lower 48 (as the rest of the United States is known in Alaska) are probably in the majority. As I have said before, the laborers are solidly Alaskan. The Teamsters have a good number of Alaskans in their ranks, but also huge numbers of truck drivers from the northwestern and central United States. There were a lot of Alaskans already in the building trades, and so, many of the plumbers, electricians, and carpenters are from Alaska. But the hard core pipeline builders—the 798ers to be sure, and the specialty equipment men, such as sideboom operators—are southerners. A major pipeline had never been built in Alaska before, and so Alaskans did not have the requisite skills; nor did anyone seem interested in teaching them.

The way that the various groups relate to each other cannot be described as outright war, although it has sometimes come to that, nor as friendly and peaceful, though strong friendships are often made and sometimes continued. There is a certain amount of clannishness—the pipeliners stick together because that's the way they do things, and the pipelining hippies stick together because they haven't got any other choice.

The first tenuous communications between these two groups take place in the warm-up shack. Pete the welder winks at Jack the sideboom operator: "You know, I reckon the reason these fucking hippies never get any work done is because they're stoned all the time on that there marijuana."

"I reckon that might be true," allows Jack.

And there might be one especially adventurous laborer or Teamster who'll say, "Well, at least we don't come to work with a hangover."

And then the argument begins. Sometimes it takes place as friendly banter, and sometimes it can get downright nasty. There are a multitude of issues to be wrangled over. Two diametrically opposed lifestyles collide. There is the question of race. Southern pipelayers are divided evenly between simple racism, which is so common that you get used to it, and good old down home pickhandle swinging bigotry. On the other side are those who just generally believe that blacks or chicanos are the same as anybody else and find the constant racist statements intolerable. It can get vicious.

In 1975, down at Tonsina on the southern half of the line, a bus driver was beaten and left unconscious in a ditch when he defended the right of a black laborer to sit wherever he wanted on the bus. The pipeliners were insisting that he go to the back of the bus. The Teamsters walked out for three days and several men were arrested.

In another incident two laborers took on half a busload of pipeliners, lashing out with two-by-fours as the men one by one exited from the bus. Individual fights are common, and would be much more so if there weren't a strong prohibition against fighting on the job. Anyone who gets into a fight is automatically fired, so the workers at least think twice before throwing any punches. That's official policy, at any rate.

But violence abounds. A friend of mine reported that on a crew working between Fairbanks and Livengood, it was the practice of the 798ers, as a sort of initiation rite, to pull down the pants and grease the balls of laborers who happened to invade their territory. The 798ers had a warm-up shack with a sign on the door permitting entry only to workers belonging to their union. Anybody who went near this shack was subject to retaliation. My friend, a six-foot-four-inch mountain man who stays in top physical condition and is absolutely fearless, was the only none-pipeliner member of the crew who escaped routine harassment. He was known as "Bearclaw" because of the necklace of grizzly bear claws that he wore. He would explain, fingering the two and a half inch long claws, "I don't like to kill, but this bear came after me and it was either me or him. I take care of myself." They left Bearclaw strictly alone. I experienced the end of harassment after I took to carrying around a number two sand and gravel shovel and letting it be known that I considered the tool of my trade a dangerous weapon.

The Man All Covered with Mouths

FROM *Stalking the Ice Dragon:*
An Alaskan Journey

SUSAN ZWINGER

Writer and adventurer Susan Zwinger is the author of STALKING THE ICE
DRAGON: AN ALASKAN JOURNEY *(1991), an account of her solo travels in the
Alaskan wilderness, from which this selection is excerpted. Zwinger, an
environmental educator, has worked for the National Park Service in Alaska.
She currently lives on Whidbey Island in Washington state.*

A ugust 22: Coldfoot, Alaska
Population between 18 and 70, depending upon season.
Around 1899, a town sprang up at the mouth of Slate Creek
and bore its name. In 1902, it was just a gambling den, a
couple of roadhouses, two stores, and seven saloons. About a
decade later, the miners moved on up to Nolan and Wiseman, villages just
north of here, and Coldfoot belonged to the ghosts.

Coldfoot is the site of the 1900 gold stampede at Slate Creek and home
of the 350-mile Coldfoot Classic Dog Sled Race. The gold dreamers, it is
said, would get up as far as the Koyukuk River, get cold feet, and retreat.

It is late morning. I tell the burly gas attendant that he lives in a grand
spot on the planet.

"Yes," he snarls, "*if* they would quit regulating us and let us live! There
is all this big beautiful land out there and they don't let us work it. The
regulations-makers down there in Washington don't understand that we
have to make an existence on it. I have this job but nowhere to live. There
is no land available for us to buy just to put a cabin on. We all live in trailers like gypsies. The goddamned senators don't understand . . . goddamned
federal government . . . goddamned Juneau. . . ." I am backing out as
sweetly and subtly as possible.

Richard Mackey, owner of the Coldfoot Gas Station Kingdom, asks me if I am having a good time. "Yes!" I gush, "I love Alaska." He is pleased with my answer; he advises me on places to see and camp, and suggests a ride over the Brooks Range.

"Or you can drive on up Slate Creek quite a ways when it isn't raining, and hike out in endless wilderness from there. You are also welcome to sleep anywhere on this property—probably over there with the trailers." His eyes are intense blue, as if he alone carried enough life for several men. Later, I was to learn that he, and later his son, had won the Iditarod, the famous dog sled race across Alaska, and was quite well thought of across the state. For such a man graciously to stop and give information to a stranger gave me a clue to the Richard Mackey legend. According to one story, Mackey was awarded the Coldfoot lease when a state official demanded to know where he could get gas services around the middle of the Haul Road. Mackey laughed uproariously and pointed to a large mudhole, saying, "Right over there. At least that's where the government promised to build us a village-supply post, but it's never quite gotten to it."

At that time, a rig had to make it 340 miles from the Yukon River up to Prudhoe Bay with no gas stops, no place for a good hot meal. Mackey opened his all-in-one service island, but because it was not federal the government supplied no housing or land for housing. The airport, the motel, a friendly restaurant, the bucket and sponge available to anyone desiring to know what color his rig once was, make quite a kingdom, indeed. Everything one could want on the road. Well, almost everything.

I have that delicious anticipation of going where few people get to go, farther north than I've ever gone, and over rough and dangerous road. Gassed, washed (the truck is black, it turns out), fed, talked with, informed, I turn up that long dusty ribbon to the northernmost realms. It is good, and all's right with the world. Seventy miles up the Haul Road to Atigun Pass a blonde wolf is carrying the leg of something. She flees when I stop, used to truckers with guns. A red fox flows across the road in front of me. To either side are copious *Coprinus comatus*: shaggy-maned mushrooms, white missiles rising from subterrestrial silos. Slowly the Brooks Range builds before me, lofty angular sediments earlier deposited as sea on the Alaskan continent. Pushed inland by a convergence with another mysterious continent, this lower Brooks Range rock rises perpendicular to the earth.

The checkbooth man asks me to stay and chat. He introduces me to Wayne. Wayne is an engineer with "The Company." "What company?" I ask. Wayne doesn't know. He signed up in Houston, Texas. Really good money, though. "Don't know my employers," he says animatedly. "They just pay me. Wizard of Oz at the Gates of the North hiring company." Gate man checks me out: Yes, I can change a tire (been practicing). Yes, I can survive to minus 30 degrees. Yes, I have water. No, I am not insane (one tiny lie).

Sunset. The steep shadow of the Brooks Range peaks. Out east over the Chandalar Basin, a spacious basin 20 miles wide at the top of the world, an immense rainbow's end is immersed in the valley and vaults twenty miles into the sky. Then a second, and a third, each reversing the order of color, expand exponentially until an eerie glow buzzes through the immense space. Lavender and orange permeate the entire atmosphere; each mist droplet is charged and incandescent.

The Gatekeeper of Oz officially warns me to turn around. He cannot legally prevent me because I, representing the People of the United States, own this land. He does not let me through officially, but knows I am going. "Only one other woman has come up here solo," he says, "but she was driving a fancy sports car as a publicity stunt from the tip of South America."

My windshield had just been broken by the first eighteen-wheeler whose driver smiled at me. One inch higher and I would have had to alter my bra; one foot higher and I should have had to learn braille.

Tomorrow: Pingos! Salt playas. Other wonderful and weird forms water takes up here! All await me over Atigun Pass and beyond, on through the lake-spotted plain of the North Slope—essential nesting grounds for all the Americas—on toward the North Sea. Rhythmic ice-filled mounds rising to announce a change of vegetation. My eyes wallow ecstatically in an unknown land.

August 23: Atigun Pass Camp

My camp is of glorious dimension. High enough to see great distance in all directions. Due west it plunges down to a stream. To the north, a high promontory bright red with bearberry. Northwest, a vertical gray wall dotted with Dall sheep. I will live here for five days and must conserve drinking water (use melted fridge water for dishwashing). Stream water, one-half-hour down and longer up, and must be boiled for five minutes, compliments of giardia.

Giardia, so legend goes, began in the '60s in my home state of Colorado when backpackers came back from Russia and deposited the critters near

Aspen. Even at 10,000 feet, the giardia cysts can live in the ice. Moving through a fecal-oral route that can come in a high mountain trickle from marmot, it survives in a cyst stage up to two months at 17 degrees F., and for one month at 70 degrees F. Exposed to boiling water, it survives two minutes or more, depending on the altitude (atmospheric pressure).

Since it came over from Russia, it has followed aspiring skiers back to New Hampshire, New York, Pennsylvania, Utah, Oregon, Montana, Washington, and California. I am always surprised by longtime campers who blithely say, "I've always drunk water right from the stream and will continue to do so," as if change in nature was not possible. The consequences are serious.

This pathway north is an icy test tube for viewing the clash of man and nature. Humanity's instinct not just to survive but to increase is as strong as a spruce's roots penetrating basalt. Human instincts produce self-perpetuating habits, in and of themselves rewarding: for instance, what might originally be practical turns perpetual: the pain of martyrs, the pleasure of aesthetics, the arguments of philosophers, the unrestrained growth of religions or monarchs. Growing for their own sake, detached from the original need.

Third day out, too much health food grains and soups, I hear voices. Overriding Consciousness is saying:

"Ah, we came *so* close this time with mammals."

"You mean because of brain volume in *Homo sapiens*?" snaps E., testily.

"Okay, okay," says O. C., "so we forgot to give them wisdom."

"Nor any overall awareness of the entire system and the complexity of Ourself as one Organism," says Big E.

"But we gave them a highly organized system of government for that: democracy, Rockbrain," whines O. C.

"Didn't even organize them as well as ants."

"All right, we screwed up again. Let them blow it up, ruin it all—we'll begin again right away."

"But what about the radioactive lithosphere? Or the indestructible polyurethanes? And where do we dump the chlorofluorocarbons?"

"Some volcanoes will exchange the surface with the interior, then an ice age or two. . . ."

"But how will we ever develop wisdom?"

"Got me!" says O. C.

....

The pipeline snaps along beside the road, silver, thin, and fascinating, sag bends dipping first below ground and then above, a reptilian Slinky. The technology is rather elegant: picking up the colors of nature, it sings in pizzicato counterpoint to the mountains.

Pipeline personnel in their bright red trucks are relaxed and friendly. This is a jubilant example of environmentalists having done their job well and of engineers responding brilliantly: The pipe of the underworld, it disappears under the caribou, then flies with the sky deities some twenty feet in the air. American ingenuity at its best, a technology to be copied by other nations.

But Alyeska has big plans, technology gone mad with its monarchy. An English king once described himself as the phallus of his people; here, there is 700 miles of it down to the sea. Technology begetting technology. Some fanciful technological mythologies have been created by the oil industry and evolved to self-perpetuation up on the Beaufort Sea. Allow me to tell a few:

Once upon a time—in 1979, to be exact—there was thought to be 320 trillion cubic feet of gas and 40 billion barrels of oil under the Beaufort Sea. Global Marine Development was busy growing a mythical beast: the hovering barge. These football-field-sized barges would hover seven feet above the sea ice or the tundra. Self-propelled on an air-cushion system, they would weigh 3,000 tons and support 250-ton cargo, or 10,000 barrels of oil. They would move along the ground by winches, wheels and paddles, drilling holes down into the sea and the tundra. And the Canadian government plans an entire fleet of icebreakers with 150,000-horsepower engines which would require 17,000 tons of fuel a month to drive a conventional steam turbine. At a cost of 300 million 1977 dollars, these air cushion icebreakers would crumple the sea ice under their weight.

Yet another fantasy technology was reported by the Smithsonian (Boslough 1981): a 15.2-million-dollar rig to float over land and sea, capable of probing 4 miles down. It would cost $100,000 a day to run. Men would sleep, eat, play, and work on board, earning $70,000 a year. It was to probe the oil-rich area in the Beaufort Sea just east of Prudhoe Bay, prime wildlife calving and nesting grounds. The Anglo Energy Company built one such drilling unit in Edmonton, Washington. It rose fourteen stories high. Broken down, it would be hauled thousands of miles by 125 trucks.

On the steep slope up Atigun Pass I climb, gathering shaggy mane mushrooms, and find strong evidence of a moose orgy. The blue Kentucky-type grasses look silly, out of place, but they were sensible to plant on the upheaved turf: one could not make this back into tundra, could not return it to fragile heaps of rock and moss and grass hummocks. Instead, pipeline botanists began with the second skin that forms on solid ground. The caribou love it. They dig in the pipeline soil cover with flexible hooves designed to dig through snow for their winter food, lichen.

I have entered a land of magnitudes, not only in size but in quality of light and staging of stone: the Brooks Range.

THE BROOKS RANGE: EARTHWARP EXTRAORDINAIRE

Each mountain range penetrates one's consciousness in a distinct manner when first encountered. I, to this day, remember vividly my first view of real mountains. Near my thirteenth birthday we drove westward in a covered (station) wagon named Moby Dick, the Great White Chrysler. I had seen picture postcards, but did not believe that such an artificial landscape could exist: Who would believe such an absurdity of vertical blue zigzags? It was early morning. We had slept fitfully in a bad motel in Kansas. When we began, there was nothing at all on the western horizon.

Then suddenly, bam. On the horizon. That low purple zig-zag, just like in the postcards. And slowly, slowly they rose. I sat in the back-back of the station wagon with my eyes glued to the front windshield. The mountains continued to grow, swallowing more and more of the blankness that Kansans call sky.

The zig-zag swallowed more and more, took on detail, but mostly remained a deep purplish blue, which I could not believe. After all, those cards had been doctored in the darkroom: thousands of lies sent home from the glorious West. No, this did not, could not exist. In postcards I could see the edge of the blue where it did not match up to the form below. But these! These "Rockies" were BLUE! A deep royal blue, a blue of deep ocean in sun, a blue as in a Night Watch plaid. And so they rose upward to fill a third of the sky, and to fill the next two-thirds of my life with a richness, a texture, and a *raison d'etre* I cannot imagine having developed anywhere else.

The Brooks Range is a thick gruel of mountains from 4,000 to 9,000 feet high, interlaced with glacial valleys that demarcate the North Slope from the Yukon drainage below. Named for Alfred Hulse Brooks of the Alaska Geological Survey, they were the Rocky Mountains until 1826. The name was a misnomer, as they are entirely distinct from the Rockies of Canada and the Lower Forty-eight. Mighty rivers dip southward through Paleozoic rock, the gray shale of deep seas, and through river gravels and shallow carbonates of organic material.

ATIGUN PASS

AVALANCHE AREA
DO NOT STOP NEXT 44 MILES.

Dark soup again, so dark I cannot see past the black hood of Die Fledermazda. Beside me, the song of a braided stream, which starts an inch below the top of the pass. The fog is rolling over, constantly revealing and covering steep unstable shoulders of talus. Hard driving, socked-in fog and steep drop-offs, a thin coat of slip-mud underneath the tires. There is a golden glow from the groundcover as if lit from underneath. At the top of Atigun Pass, the Continental Divide, I watch the water go in two opposite directions. Below, tiny men moving slowly as if on Pluto, reinstalling a section of flawed pipe.

This area is extremely dangerous for the pipeline men. Buried in insulated concrete cribbing, the pipe penetrates part of the mountain on the steep slope. Many peaks in the immediate area exceed 7,000 feet, only 130 miles from sea level.

PURE ARCTIC TUNDRA

Since visibility is zero over Atigun Pass, I retreat and plan a hike just south of there up Table Mountain: a moody elemental walk straight up its steep slope, hopping from one mud boil to the next. Four miles up, made it to the first shoulder, which I perceived to be most of the way up. Later, from Atigun Pass, I was to learn it was barely a quarter of the way.

From it: such a thunderstorm display! Not just one, but many of them at a great distance, roiling themselves over peaks from far west, Gates of the Arctic National Park and Preserve, crashing like surf in the north, threatening from the east. Yet none approach the wide Chandalar Shelf. Thunderstorms, like Dall sheep, prefer not to leave their steep mountain slopes for the open. Rain squalls hit on and off.

I love potent storms as much as any beautiful natural phenomenon. It is seeing diagrams of Earth's patterns of energy release, from oceans, sun, mountains, and atmosphere. Thunderstorms restore the center of the continents with water requisitioned from the oceans. They return to earth a negative charge that has slowly dissipated into the atmosphere. This is why the air around waterfalls and after big storms smells so refreshing: negatively charged ions. I seek telltale paths of immense storms, those that leave scars across people and landscape, not for the love of destruction, but to be reminded, ultimately, of what is in charge.

Cumulonimbi here are magnificent, towering giants that reduce mountains to small muttering tooths. They extend eight miles straight up into the troposphere, that part of Earth's atmosphere between the ground and the stratosphere. Alaska is particularly good at overloading air with great amounts of water, powering it up steep slopes, so that these cloud beasts develop in time-lapse motion. Today was terrifying and thrilling at once; like prey, I had to keep a sharp eye on the circling storms.

Growing up the daughter of a pilot, one learns about the turbulent interiors of these clouds full of strong electrical fields. Each thunderstorm becomes an entity of its own, developing its own charge, a negative one at its base, which we feel in our scars and bones. In the high puff pastry and anvil tops there is a positive charge. The land and the atmospheric beasts become so charged that they create nasty exchanges between heaven and earth that terrify humans.

Metaphorical spears shoot out of God-fingers with awesome randomness, killing one, leaving the next unharmed. Their paths can carry 200,000 amperes, instantly heating to millions of degrees the object of their affection, which expands, then explodes (Schaefer and Day 1981).

Lightning shoots across cultures as spiritual illumination, the descent of power from heaven to earth. Krishna holds the *varja,* the thunderbolt that holds both destruction and refertilization: their balance means eternal transcendence. Our national symbol holds lightning in one talon and peace in its other, the Seal of the United States. Apollo's arrows are lightning as well as rays, and symbolize piercing masculinity, the benefit of mankind and also the scourge of war.

In a balance that provides scientists of the U.S. Forest Service with an ideal metaphor for lightning-produced forest fire, the Tibetan God Dorje's sceptre (thunder) symbolizes virility/power (method) in balance with the feminine (wisdom). The result of a good balance is paradox, the act of compassion, power in passivity. Translation: natural burns are good if they are allowed periodically, not suddenly after many years without a fire.

Thunder mumbles low in the distance. It could easily be the voice of divine anger or the fecundity of the sky god made audible. Humankind has so long attempted to repeat that sound and to channel its dangerous power: bull-roarer, the dragon, the hammer, the drum. After one of those god-awful job aptitude tests in college, in which one's life's work is determined by entering little blackened dots into numerical slots (Would you rather go to a movie with good friends or clean doorknobs?), I decided it would be best for me to become a Siberian tribal shaman. I could have danced to a drum made of sacred skins and forest bones, translating, through rhythm, man's tongue to summon the spirits. Instead, I just sit in the cab watching the rain pelt.

Exhausted after the tundra haul, I shall never move again. Until, against the dark gray stone wall, white dots are moving! Dall dots! One-half-mile along a precarious edge I move until they develop legs. Sheep legs! A little closer and they have heads and are grazing pastorally on a green shoulder of mountain. One up on the ridge has run down and appears to be "playing" frantically with the others, butting them into a knot. How odd: this play among adults who should conserve precious energy for winter.

Closer. Look again. Can't believe my eyes: a dark figure lumbers after them. A wolf? No, too large.

Bear! Huge white slash down its side and a muscular hump on its back. Grizzly! My hands shake.

Bear! My circulation stops, adrenaline zings out to my fingertips and toes. Not out of fear, but out of respect. The white slash and the muscular hump chant grizzly. The magnificence of the beast at the top of the food chain, Elder Bear to Native Americans. There is, they tell us, a human inside of each bear, who is here to share his wisdom and power with us. This is true, absolutely. Only now it is through scientific terms.

The largest land mammal on our half of things, 9 feet high and weighing more than 1,000 pounds inland (1,500 pounds where they are able to eat salmon), they are the smartest predators on land, smarter than foxes, wolves, or coyotes. They also are powerfully fast, fifty yards in three seconds. Their moods are powerful and change from aggression to whimsy in a matter of moments.

The bear galumphs after the sheep clumsily; his feet sink into the mire between tufts. The bear circles around, unseen by the sheep. The chase is on! Sheep and bear do not see one another. The leader on the rise walks cautiously to the depression where the other three are. The bear galumphs across more tundra above them slowly. The guard sheep spots him and there is instant movement of all toward the rock precipice, walking steadily to conserve as much energy as possible, yet fleeing. The entire chase seems to take place in slow motion, each animal carrying out a role vital to survival while conserving as many calories as possible. They step over sheer cliffs, cliffs too steep even for my rock-climbing buddies. An older one now places herself behind the youngest of the seven, to encourage it to keep up and to keep an eye on it. How intelligent they seem compared to humans, who leave kids alone in cars.

As they traverse, I look for a sight of the bear. Finally, just on the horizon, a tiny speck, the arch of leg and body as he takes one long last longing glance and disappears over the knife edge of the ridge.

As in most of this journey, I feel elation and heightened awareness, not fear. I restlessly look around me constantly. Literature warns that people who have high-range hearing loss are most vulnerable: they do not hear the twig snap that is the difference between life and death.

For centuries, human fear has shot grizzlies for the hell of it. There are only 900 left in the Lower Forty-eight: the last one in California was shot in 1916; in Arizona, 1935; in northern Mexico, 1957. In 1968, many died at the hands of Yellowstone Park rangers after the deaths of two young women in their tent. At the same time that year I was a camp counselor in the Sangre de Cristos, New Mexico, seven miles out in the wilderness camp with twenty-nine eleven- to thirteen-year-olds. A crazed black bear carried off our food locker. My fellow counselor lay in the dark, clutching a five-inch hunter's knife to protect the children. We watched as the bear picked up the heavy metal locker like a toy and reduced it to splinters with singular blows of his two arms. The trigger in Yellowstone was a sudden change in policy: closing the garbage dumps to the garbage-dependent grizzlies. Forgetting how to eat berries, bears found campers were faster—and fatter.

The sheer cirques and valley walls come alive with white dots moving, always moving. By the time my eye learns how to see them, I have spotted more than eighty. I try to imagine how frightened those four must feel: the loss of precious feeding ground and time; to stand now on a steep scree, balancing, watching, always wary.

Legend says the grizzly taught humankind everything we know; he was Brother Bear. Just as it came time to disclose the secret of hibernation, we grew impatient and killed the bear. Now we must remain awake throughout the long, cold, dark winter in dank houses (Thomas 1988). Humans have only a weak second-best: marijuana, a type of hibernation. Athapascans speak of Winter Bear who, forced out of his sleep in early spring by hunger, is a very ill-tempered beast, indeed.

Alaska, Siberia, and Canada are the last land of grizzlies on Earth. They need more than a thousand square miles of wilderness to exist, fifty square miles a day to feed. At night they may travel eight miles to new territory for food. Unlike the black bear, who is more of a vegetarian and whose flesh tastes sweet and rich, grizzlies are omnivorous. John Muir said that to grizzlies the whole world is food—except granite.

As a young girl I had a fantasy that a bear husband would drag me to his cave and I would become his She Bear, reverting to the wild. Unlike the adversarial approach of my young "mountain men" friends, I saw the Great Ursa as lover, not as adversary. John Donne once descried woman's reaction to Death as Lover as her longing for the ultimate lengthy embrace. My fear in the wilderness is substantially different from that of men I have known. I feel part of the long continuum of life and death. I mostly fear to be disconnected—no husband, no children, no family.

I think as the hunter, too, crawling into his bear skin and wandering in his bear mind and bear body, crossing steep scree, the pads of my feet sore on the volcanic stone. There is nausea in the pit of my stomach; muscles ache with it. I will sleep deeply (not really hibernate) without urinating or eating beginning the end of September, a month away. Just one fat-sheathed sheep could make all the difference. Now I must come out of my hibernation prematurely and scavenge the steep winter snows. I hurdle through tundra in the dusk, seeing in my brain's eye the blood-twitching red meat, the delicious fat hanging in drapes from the inside of the skin. I feel my powerful jaws crushing down on the skull with delight, the brain squirting out, protein rich caviar, that greasy thick wool in my mouth.

It is not just the meat I enjoy; it is the chase, the exhilaration of moving over the land. That metallic sting of fear again and again.

The temperature drops from 48 to 38 while I watch. It begins to rain steadily, filling depressions. Bear! Symbol of resurrection, from his cave in spring. Symbol of Russia. Tied in with initiation rituals of young girls, with the Dianic Hunt of the Night (Greek), and in Japan with benevolence and wisdom. Life at its finest: meeting the Magnificent Bear.

I will come back greatly changed, looking to predators for my answers.

To the bald eagle, with seven-foot wingspread and eye seven times keener than the eye of man. To the peregrine falcon, who flies at 180 mph. To the osprey, who hunts by diving headfirst into the sea. Even to the tiny territorial shrew, whose heart beats a thousand times a minute, and to the water shrew, who eats constantly or will die.

The attitude of humankind toward predators is still in the Dark Ages. According to the Alaska Department of Fish and Game, even with no legal aerial shooting last year 1,064 wolves were killed, an increase of 39 percent over the year before, the highest kill in the last ten years. Still, there is not enough focus on and money for enforcement and prosecution; illegal killing is regarded by some with a twinkle. The killing of wild predators is tacitly admired. Fall 1987: 6,000 wolves in Alaska, down from 15,000 less than a decade ago.

NIGHT

By lantern light, I reawaken the stream pebbles I gathered at the top of Atigun Pass:

1. One conglomerate with uneven chunks of jasper, rose quartz, obsidian. The matrix is gray.

2. Two metamorphic river pebbles with white streaks all the way through: quartz intrusions going at all angles to themselves.

3. Dark gray slate, thinly layered and partially metamorphosed. Some hard nephrite mixed in with sedimentary rock, cracked with the uplifted dome of Brooks Range, like a dried mud cake punched up from underneath. Through every hairline crack squeezes quartz. Gypsum veins cross the quartz, perpendicular: one thousand feet of seawater condensed to two inches of gypsum.

The keys to continents right here in my hands! Each pebble has gone through many changes, moving here from other continents, going down inside the earth and coming back again.

Parts of these pebbles moved about as animals in the sea, then were molten myth-globs inside the earth bearing the weight of high mountains.

Walking on the top of the tundra is walking on the back of a bear. Its muscles ripple. One sinks in. There is no question in my mind that it is entirely alive: sucking, swirling, unpredictably certain. Covered with silver fuzz in tiny lobes all over, like lace, it glows lighter than the sky. When walking the tundra, silver moss means "a dry place to put one's foot." A brilliant crimson moss cradles streams and means a place to get one's knees wet.

The Native Villages

FROM *In the Wake of the EXXON VALDEZ*

ART DAVIDSON

Art Davidson is an Alaskan mountaineer, businessman, and nonfiction writer. His books include MINUS 148°: THE WINTER ASCENT OF MT. MCKINLEY *(1969) and* ALAKSHAK: THE GREAT COUNTRY *(1988). On March 24, 1989, the oil tanker* Exxon Valdez *went aground on Bligh Reef, spilling more than ten million gallons of crude oil into the pristine waters of Alaska's Prince William Sound. In this excerpt from* IN THE WAKE OF THE *EXXON VALDEZ (1990), the first comprehensive treatment of the oil spill, Art Davidson examines how the devastation affected Native life in one small village.*

The village of Chenega Bay lies 30 miles to the southwest of Bligh Reef. Chenega Bay had experienced an unexpected catastrophe before. Twenty-five years earlier to the day, the Good Friday earthquake set off a tidal wave that swept away the old village of Chenega. When the tsunami crashed ashore, children were literally swept from the arms of their parents. Swirling water crushed village homes—one house was swept away as a woman stood in the doorway calling to her children. The survivors had to leave Prince William Sound, and for twenty years they drifted between various jobs and welfare, always yearning to return. In 1980, village leaders finally found a way to rebuild Chenega, renaming it Chenega Bay. Homes went up. Families returned. People reestablished their bond with the sea. Then the oil spill hit.

The villagers' first reaction to the spill was to call for their priest. The region's minister flew in to offer consolation and support. He was soon followed by helicopters and float planes full of Exxon and state officials and reporters from as far away as London and Australia. With currents sweeping the oil toward Chenega Bay, boats of the Mosquito Fleet soon swarmed offshore, as fishermen tried to save the nearby San Juan hatchery. By April 10, the oil had reached Chenega Bay, and the quiet village had swollen from 80 people to more than 250.

"We've been inundated by anyone and everyone," said Darrell Totemoff of Chenega Bay. "We're all too busy to be depressed right now. Everyone is in shock and confused by all the activity in the village. Seems like Good Friday brought us another disaster."

With so many people combing the beaches for oil, villagers feared that artifacts from ancient village sites and burial caves would be disturbed. These ties to their ancestors have a personal and often sacred value to Native villagers. The artifacts also have such tremendous commercial value that old village middens and graves are often vandalized. As protective measures, Exxon hired archaeologists to survey beaches in advance of the cleanup crews and instructed workers not to venture above the high-tide line or into caves. Nevertheless, problems arose.

"The less that's known about these places the better," said Michael Smith, who spent much of the summer trying to help protect cultural sites within the sound. "The spill blew the cover on an awful lot of these places. One tragedy involved a burial cave on one of the islands. It was found by beach workers who went into the cave and built a warming fire. As light from their fire lit the cave, a skeleton became visible in the shadows. They called a state trooper, who collected the remains and sent them in for forensic analysis."

The people of Chenega Bay were incensed that the bones of one of their ancestors, a young man, had been shipped off in a bag to be weighed and measured. The remains in this burial cave were so sacred that even the region's cultural heritage program, which had surveyed the sound for ten years, did not know the location of the cave; the secret had been kept by a handful of elders. The bones, which were eventually reburied by the village people, predated Captain Cook's voyages and the arrival of Russians in Alaska.

As the oil continued to wash ashore around Chenega Bay, wildlife died and people were physically affected. "There have been fumes in the air, and my face has felt as if it were burning," said Paul Kompkoff, Sr., sixty-six, who raised six children with his wife, Minnie. Normally, they would have been busy gathering subsistence foods and working at commercial fishing during the summer, but this year most of the family cleaned beaches. "We found three deer lying together on Knight Island," Kompkoff said. "People walked right up to them, thinking they were asleep, but they were dead. They had oily kelp in their mouths. On Seal Island, six seals were lying on the beach between the work crews. They were too sick to move."

Kompkoff recalled how in past years he watched whales, porpoises, and sea lions playing in Chenega Bay. This year, only the sea gulls were there as usual. "In some ways the village is doing fairly well," he said. "Free food is being brought in by Exxon, and most people are being paid for financial losses. But what's going to happen in two or three months? Exxon officials don't understand why the oil spill is so bad for the Native way of life."

Chugach Alaska, an organization representing Natives of the region, has filed a lawsuit to recover damages for Chenega Bay and other Native villages. "What good will that do?" Kompkoff asked. "This spill has taken our lifestyle away and our livelihood. I keep thinking of moving, but where would I move to? The best anyone can do is starting cleaning. The oil will be here for many, many years."

English Bay and Port Graham are two Native villages approximately 150 miles southwest of Bligh Reef. When sheets of oil came ashore in early May, the Native villagers faced things they thought would never happen. Salmon had always been their main source of food, but in 1989 the smokehouses and drying racks were empty. The pink salmon returned to the area, swimming and leaping through the clear pools and falls of the river near the villages. However, no one bothered to catch them after a villager caught one whose guts were oily and whose eggs were shriveled and blackened.

Offshore, a reef appears at low tide. Crabs scurry along the crevices, and clams, chitons, and mussels cling to the dark rocks. This year, for the first time anyone could remember, no villagers went out to the reef to gather food. Irene Ukatish went out to check the chitons, or *birdarkies,* as her people call this relative of the abalone. When healthy, *birdarkies* grip the rocks so tenaciously they have to be pried loose with a strong knife, but now they were falling from the rocks with the slightest touch. "I don't trust food from the sea anymore," she said. "We're not getting any kind of seafood."

Biologists began studies of English Bay and Port Graham seafood in April, but three and a half months later the results were still inconclusive. Some shellfish showed contamination; some didn't. Procedures to detect oil in seafood were difficult to develop. Dr. Thomas Nighswander, with the Indian Health Service, reported that samples of seal meat—another staple of the Native diet—were locked in freezers while attorneys debated legal issues connected with the *Exxon Valdez.*

Several times, Exxon representatives told villagers to go ahead and gather their traditional food and store it until test results were in. "But the beaches were stained and splattered with oil," Roberta Ukatish said. "Who wants to pick mussels, *birdarkies*, or snails where you can see that oil?"

At the end of August, Roberta's father, Vincent Kvasnikoff, said, "Every day we see that sheen out there. Tar balls are still washing up on the beaches. I asked Exxon's people, 'What about a year from now, when the oil has sunk to the bottom? What about the halibut, the cod, and other bottom fish?' They couldn't answer."

Large Exxon and VECO paychecks from beach cleanup work provided some villagers with enough money to ship in commercial brands of food. However, not everyone made money, and, in any event, buying food from a store isn't the same as getting it from the sea yourself. "The money is great to have, but it doesn't replace the sense of community people normally have from catching and preparing their own food," Wally Kvasnikoff said. "Every one of these houses put up at least 200 fish last year. We've been doing that for ages. Without that, we walk around like zombies. Exxon's money can't replace that part of our lives."

Port Graham Chief Meganack tried to describe why this subsistence way of life—the gathering of food from the land and sea—means so much to his people. "When the days get longer, we get ready. Boots and boats and nets and gear are prepared for the fishing time," he said. "The winter beaches are not lonely anymore, because our children and grownups visit the beaches in the springtime and gather the abundance of the sea: the shellfish, the snails, the chitons. When the first salmon is caught, our whole village is excited. It's an annual ritual of mouth-watering delight. When our bellies are filled with the fresh new life, then we put up the food for the winter. We dry and smoke and can hundreds of fish to feed each family.

"It was in the early springtime," Meganack said. "No fish yet. No snails yet. But the signs were with us. The green was starting. Some birds were flying and singing. The excitement of the season had just begun. And then we heard the news. Oil in the water—lots of oil, killing lots of water. It's too shocking to understand. Never have we thought it possible for the water to die. But it is true. We walk our beaches. And the snails and the barnacles and the chitons are falling off the rocks. Dead. Dead water.

"We caught our first fish—the annual first fish, the traditional delight of all—but it got sent to the state to be tested for oil. No first fish this year. We walk our beaches, but instead of gathering life, we gather death. Dead birds. Dead otters. Dead seaweed.

"Before we have a chance to hold each other and share our sorrow and loss, we suffer yet another devastation. We are invaded by the oil company offering jobs, high pay, lots of money. We are in shock. We need to clean the oil, get it out of our water, bring death back to life. We are intoxicated with desperation. We don't have a choice but to take what is offered. So we take the jobs, we take the orders, we take the disruption."

Chief Meganack saw his people losing their trust in each other and fighting. After being bossed around on the cleanup crews, some villagers showed signs of agitation. "Our people get sick," he said. "Elders and children in the village. Everybody is touchy. People are angry. And afraid, afraid and confused. Our elders feel helpless. They cannot work on cleanup. They cannot do all the activities of gathering food and preparing for winter. And most of all, they cannot teach the young ones the Native way. How will the children learn the values and the ways if the water is dead?

"The oil companies lied about preventing a spill. Now they lie about the cleanup. Our people know what happens on the beaches. Spend all day cleaning one big rock, and the tide comes in and covers it with oil again. Spend a week wiping and spraying the surface, but pick up a rock and there's 4 inches of oil underneath.

"We fight a rich and powerful giant, the oil industry, while at the same time we take orders and a paycheck from it. We are torn in half. . . ."

Skin

FROM *In Extremis and Other Alaskan Stories*

JEAN ANDERSON

Jean Anderson is a fiction writer, freelance editor, reviewer, and college lecturer who has lived in Fairbanks since 1966. Anderson was a founding staff member and an early editor of the University of Alaska Fairbanks literary journal permafrost. *Her fiction and poetry have appeared in* Stories *magazine,* Harper's, Orca, *and* Chariton Review. *"Skin" was first published in the Alaska women's anthology* HUNGER & DREAMS, *and then appeared in her collection* IN EXTREMIS AND OTHER ALASKAN STORIES *(1989).*

On the sidewalk outside Co-Op Drug, and in the street, drunks shimmered like mirages. Lucy watched them from Co-Op's entryway, their slow steps twisted by the door glass to a dance that swayed and wavered, ugly, catching the noon heat. The sight made her think, miserably, of her girlhood, these Second Avenue drunks in Fairbanks so like all the ones she remembered from home, from Rampart, drunken Indians. One of those Rampart drunks had been her youngest uncle, and she could still—even after the sliding away of forty-five years—not think of Uncle Ralph without seeing saliva—Or a thick string of drool, maybe—Saliva, which hung always, it seemed in her memory, from Uncle Ralph's lips—

He'd died of drink. At twenty-seven. There at home, dragged in from the riverbank to die quietly in her parents' bed, not of TB as they said in Rampart, but of drink. She'd been eleven, her face hidden (for days after, it seemed—) for days (and before—) in the dusty, warm peace of the dog's coat, there on the porch. The old dog, Scout he had been, panting, panting, so warm. And her whole face and body pressed down on the porch floor into deepest dog—

Now she opened one glass door slowly and stepped out, dry heat rising from the cement like old wind. She stopped there where she stood, her white slacks glowing as cloud above the yellow plastic luster of her sandals.

And the door's swish and thud behind her was a sound, erasing all her careful intent—which had been to stride, purposefully, through these clusters of wavering, shabby men (and some women, too) who were "visiting"—"Visiting" here on the sidewalk in Fairbanks—Drunks. To walk among these drunks without looking to left or to right, until she reached the parking lot and the cool, dark safety of the Lincoln—

Instead she stood still, her heart thumping as she pulled sunglasses from the flowery pouch that was the front of her *kuspuk* blouse and adjusted the silvery ear hooks. With two fingers (fingers which shook stupidly) she pushed against the nosepiece, its sheen of glass stars rough to her fingertips even when she was sure the glasses rode squarely upon the short bridge of her nose, and—yes, all the world was green. She straightened her spine then and stepped forward again, the hot air surging, catching up her face and her body in thickened heat as she left the pale shade of Co-Op's marquee—

Maybe Howard had been right. He had not wanted her to come. She had, Howard said, her reputation to consider. "Watch and see, Lucy," he'd said. "You'll be sorry. You'll dirty those new sandals in sidewalk beer. Or vomit—" And he'd frowned with the face of his own joke, those last words of Howard's still following her when she backed the perfect, ten-year-old Lincoln down the driveway at eleven. Its air conditioner beginning to hum and her eyes seeing only the dishes stacked neatly in the dish drainer, Howard's pipe in his one hand and the striped dish towel draped over his shoulder in just that way she always told him not—

And she'd driven downtown so slowly, careful, those words humming: "You'll be sorry—" And herself walking so slowly then, half dazed, and trying, trying to feel—casual. Walking at first (like practice) through Penney's bright aisles, dazed—Because in Penney's you never saw drunks.

But Co-Op was doing July inventory, had advertised rabbit skins. White and cross rabbits too, as it turned out. More fine than the newspaper sketch she had smoothed with her fingers on the kitchen table, for Howard. Two thick and beautiful stacks of them, so soft and silky and luxurious, though of course only rabbits—For 79¢ each. It was a bargain. She could not remember seeing such a bargain. And Roxanne, her own only grandchild, and Rita's only daughter, was pregnant for the first time. Only—? As Rita was Lucy's (and Howard's) own only daughter, only—? Their only child—For Howard had not been—And she herself, no—

But surely Roxanne would produce a female child. Another beauty. The fourth, in generations, she would be—And these rabbit skins would become a new baby bunting for her. Booties too, yes—Beautiful and white, with those soft, soft red-brown spots like patches of time caught up—And—Beautiful.

Lucy pulled the crackly pinkness of the plastic Co-Op sack (filled up with the sixteen cross-rabbit skins) tight against her breasts and began to step off the curb. Second Avenue was a smell like beer and sweat, the hot breath of cars—And noise that swelled in your ears—But those rabbit skins had all been gentle and clean, pure to your fingers, there in Co-Op, and she would begin the bunting today. This afternoon—

Because skin sewing was something you could love safely. An Indian thing, for she remembered her aunts and her grandma and sometimes even Mama, too, sewing skins, in Rampart. And Howard could tease her about it, though he rarely did anymore. Because people were beginning to call her "an Athabaskan artist" now. A skin sewer. "Preserving a traditional art form." That was what that last woman, from the Arts Association, had said. In the school, in May—

But once, that one time only, Howard calling her "my skinny squaw"— That time when Roxanne (a little girl then) had braided the long neck-curls—(Herself Roxanne's own "Mem-mem" then—) Roxanne braiding Mem-mem's "little Orphan Annie perm," which was what Howard still always called this hairstyle—(Because he'd chosen it: "One of the first ones in Fairbanks too, Lucy!" His face proud, beaming—) Those neckcurls twisted into a single short cluster of braid: "My skinny squaw—"

But Howard had always been more a father. Twelve years old—She, always, "the baby," the prettiest and youngest, at home too, back in Rampart. And—

And it was no lie to live now in their own suburban house. A clean and beautiful home. Her neatly-boxed skins all kept in the pantry beside the dishwasher. No lie to love—Because, yes, she did love the skins—Sewing them. Touching—

And Howard was an Indian too, of course.

And she felt only sometimes that small twinge of something (like shame it seemed, though that was ridiculous—) when she and Howard went (as they so often did now) to address the grade school children in Fairbanks. Telling those children—Telling them, now that Howard had sold his optical shop and retired completely—(Two years ago that was—) Telling all those sweet gardens of child faces what it was to be an Indian— (The soles of the yellow sandals sticking—In beer, maybe—? Not—? But almost across now, to the parking lot, yes, there soon—)

And, yes, you could love skin sewing—

"The skins were always clean that's what I remember," she'd said last May, her mind—and her soul too—pulling away from her so strangely there as she stood on that cool, foreign little stage— (For the stages, in the gyms they were always, never really became—) There, during the most recent grade school visit. In May, it was—And Howard staring so strangely across the stage into her face, shaking his head slightly, frowning that small, small frown—

"The skins were always clean—" Her own voice. "The fur was warmer that way, warm and clean. And the Indian people, back home, the old people, they shook them carefully. Before and after using them, they shook them to keep them clean. And there was a fine, pure scent too—" Shaking her own head—"I don't know—They cared for them, though, it's true. Hung them from moose or caribou horns on the walls of the cabins inside, yes, sometimes. And they were beautiful. So beautiful—Some made into parkas and hats and the small baby things—Or blankets crocheted from strips of rabbit skin—So soft and always clean—Always—" Howard's small frown—

Oh, it frightened you, to feel your own mind dance away from you like that, carrying something—your soul or your spirit—Carrying your whole self dancing away into some past that seemed almost a future, and seemed right—Yes, right.

And now someone was saying, a voice behind her saying: "Lucy. Goddamn, Lucy, that's you—"

And she was turning to meet the voice. And yes, yes—No.

It was George. For thirty-five years, maybe, she had not seen him once. George. And he still stood like a skinny boy there, slim and wiry as any boy—but balder, a little—His body wavering before her eyes. George.

And he was hugging her then and the rabbit skins, hugging—That plastic sack crackling between them there, in the street in front of—While cars moved around them and someone laughed—

"Oh, George," she said, her own voice saying it. "George— George—"

"Goddamn if it isn't you," he said. "Goddamn if it isn't you, Lucy." No drool from his lips and he smelled only of cigarettes, but his body still—Yes. It wavered away from her and then close again—And tears, yes, tears. She was weeping against his chest. Cigarette smoke—

"Don't cry, Lucy," George said. "Come have a beer." And he was holding a sack, the pink crackly sack of rabbit skins under his right arm, pushed way up under his armpit, her shoulders held tight with his left arm—Weeping, she—He taking the sunglasses from her face and leading her across the street and in—Yes—Into the worst bar of them all. The worst Native bar where Lucy had never, ever been before—

"You look—" she said, trying not to cry—

"Firefighting," George said. "I've been firefighting. At Nenana—" And he was grinning, hugging her again, his body smoky but with cigarettes only—And she—yes, crying, hugging—

"Thirty-five years," George said. "Thirty-five. Yes, Lucy, it's you." And he was hugging her again.

"Two beers," George said. "Two," holding up two fingers toward the back of—And people were looking—A laugh—And a chair, yes, a chair—George was fitting her body to that dirty-looking kitchen chair.

"A beer," George said, pushing the glass into her fingers. "You look fine," he said, "not like an old lady, Lucy—"

"And you—" Only crying a little— "George. Oh, George—"

"Well, we should have," he said, putting his own glass on the table with both hands. "When we were eighteen in Rampart, Lucy, we should have got married and be damned if—"

And her whole life—No, no. He could not take her whole life from her like that. Catch up her whole life and take it back. No. "Oh, George," she said, "but we—"

"I know," he said. "I know, Lucy. I was too damned rough for you." And he was crying too, almost, then laughing—A drunk's laugh. Uncle— Then grinning, grinning, holding her right hand— The pink sack on his knees now—Grinning. "Not an old man yet, huh? Firefighting," he said, thumping his chest. "In Nenana." Grinning—

Still crying, she—"At fifty-six? Firefighting, George?" He, too, fifty-six—firefighting. "Oh, George," she said, "you—"

"No, no," he said. "We, Lucy. We. We still have it." Then: "Drink your beer, Lucy." And he, curling her fingers around the cold wet— With his fingers—

"I don't want any beer, George—" Her glass on the table. There. And the skins, yes— Back on her lap, yes. Safe. The plastic crackle— He patting her both hands—Holding them, holding— "George, I—"

"Yes," he said. "Yes, Lucy, we still—"

"No," she said. "No, George, I've got to—"

Grinning, grinning—"Yes—"

"I'm married, George, and my life has been—"

"Yes," he said. "I know. I can see that, Lucy." That laugh again, then grinning, grinning, holding her both hands. "I can see—" Then, suddenly: "By Christ, you're a white woman, Lucy!" Like a shaman speaking, in him, George— But no shaman, George. Him laughing again, that laugh like a cough— Uncle—

"No, George, I—" But that laugh again—

"Yes, Lucy, a white woman! And still my Lucy," more softly now, patting her both hands with his. "Still prissy—" And that laugh—"You're a prissy white woman now, Lucy."

And: "George!" She, yes—That slap. The sound. Her own fingers tingling, and—Even in the darkness, the beery half-light of that ugly bar—Yes, red. Her own hand's mark there bright against his cheek. Red, red, her own hand's mark—

All the way to the parking lot, through her tears, Lucy could still see it. Even when she leaned, hot, with both hands and her forehead pressed against the searing white metal of the Lincoln's perfect paint. That ache in her throat now and sobbing. Yes—She could still see that spot, bright against his cheek like a scrap of red fox skin.

Alex Marks, Tlingit Carver

RICHARD SPEAKES

As a young man, poet Richard Speakes worked as a cab driver in Juneau, Alaska. His poem "Alex Marks, Tlingit Carver" is taken from his book of poems entitled NECESSITIES *(1979). Individual poems by Speakes have appeared in* Poetry, Poetry East, Iowa Review, Seattle Review, *and many other magazines and journals, and he published a later book of poems,* HANNAH'S TRAVEL *(1982). For the past ten years, he has been on the English faculty at Santa Rosa Junior College in California.*

The dead man stares through years
like a totem he'd carved, wide-eyed
in any light, the legendary struggle
put to rest in wood.

He told it to me, the raven on top
diving into the sprawl of frog below.
The tale was a haven he could live in
as if it were a pond ten thousand generations
taught him to leap in bellowing
in the sun, snagging dragonflies,
bulging his throat at the moon.
It didn't matter where he was in the story,
but to be in it, that was warmer than whiskey,
the foul house he slept in alone.

Maybe he went out empty in the night,
flopping about beneath the moon, and
saw what had never been told diving
out of the sky, something that made drinking
anti-freeze so much like sprawling
plop in the water his totem could stare on,
the tale unchanged in its wide eyes.

A Cold-Blooded Business

DANA STABENOW

Anchorage writer Dana Stabenow draws on her experiences aboard commercial fishing boats and working on the trans-Alaska pipeline for her popular, distinctive mystery series featuring Kate Shugak, an Aleut private investigator. Included in the series are A COLD DAY FOR MURDER *(1991),* DEAD IN THE WATER *(1993),* A FATAL THAW *(1993), and* PLAY WITH FIRE *(1995).* A COLD-BLOODED BUSINESS *(1994) is excerpted here.*

The spring breeze ruffled Mutt's coat with a gentle hand and was soft on Kate's cheek, and stayed that way up the curve of the trail to Second Avenue, where the Coastal Trail ended and the city streets began. Beyond the alder-infested slope to their left was the Alaska Railroad station depot, the railroad yards and Anchorage's waterfront, a stretch of mud flats constantly renewed by glacial silt washed down the Matanuska River into Knik Arm. Kate turned right on E Street and walked up to Fourth Avenue. Half the galleries she remembered had been replaced by stores selling T-shirts appliqued with pictures of eagles on the wing against a setting sun and "Alaska—The Great Land" printed beneath. She found one with a dog sled team and musher on it and an inscription which read, "Alaska—Where Men are Men and Women Win the Iditarod." Kate, who bought her plain white T-shirts by the dozen from Hane's discount catalogue for six bucks each, bought one of these for sixteen dollars that she told herself was for Mandy.

A block down Fourth, in the window of a gift shop with the straightforward name of Alaska Native Arts & Crafts, an ivory otter caught her eye. Up on his hind legs in the midst of a menagerie sculpted from soapstone, antler, jade and wood, tiny paws held just so, thick tail disposed in a graceful curve, whiskers immaculately groomed, he stood just three inches high, black eyes bright with curiosity, every detail faithfully and exquisitely rendered. He was irresistible. He also looked familiar. Kate went inside, Mutt padding next to her.

The clerk, a woman of character, included both woman and wolf in a friendly, unruffled smile. "Hello. May I help you?"

Kate nodded toward the window. "The ivory otter. The one next to the soapstone bear. Is that Wilson Oozeva of Gambell?"

The woman's smile widened. "You have a good eye." She went to the window and brought back the carving. "He's good, isn't he?"

The little otter sat on the glass-topped counter between them, a soft gleam of ivory perfection. Touching one forefinger to the otter's perfectly groomed fur, running it down the thick curve of the tail, Kate said, "Yes. On his good days, one of the best."

"Do you carve yourself?"

"No."

"Ah. A collector, then."

Kate shook her head. "No."

Her scarf dragged her collar open, exposing her scar, but all the woman said was, "Were you interested in buying this piece?" She smiled again. "To begin a collection, perhaps?"

Kate's first, instinctive response was refusal. She had no use for knick-knacks which existed solely to be dusted. But when she started to shake her head the otter caught her eye, his bright, black gaze fixed on her face, his head cocked at an inquisitive angle, and suddenly she heard John King's voice saying, *Plus expenses, of course. Should run you, oh, say, around $250 a day.* She reached out and picked him up. He looked up at her from the palm of her hand, vital, expectant, fairly quivering with life. Any minute now he was going to drop to his forepaws and scamper up her arm. "How much is he?"

"Two hundred dollars."

"Okay," Kate said. She wondered what Jack would say. Well, he was the one who had told her to find something to justify her expense account with. "And after all, we have to support the home team," she told Mutt when they were in the street again. Mutt raised a skeptical eyebrow. Kate ignored her and tucked the tiny box carefully away in the inside pocket of her jacket.

She found a Book Cache and, physically incapable of passing a book store, any book store, entered and emerged thirty minutes later with a hundred dollars' worth of books, one of them actually in hardcover. She felt a little dizzy. She'd never been in Anchorage before with this sense of having money to burn. It was unnerving to realize how easily she could seduce herself into spending it.

She wandered back up the street, determined to avoid further temptation at all costs, when through another window she caught sight of a painting so stunningly bad the vacuum it left behind in the artistic firmament sucked her in the door. It proved to be only one of an entire glorious exhibit by a single artist, presided over by a woman wearing a square-shouldered smile featuring her dentist's best and most lucrative work. The smile faded as she took in Kate's worn jeans, shabby windbreaker and brown skin. Her assistant, a young edition dressed for success in the same dark suit and the same perfect, porcelain smile, came forward in response to some signal Kate missed. "I'm certainly sorry, but we don't allow dogs in the gallery."

"Okay," Kate said agreeably, and nodded to Mutt, who, after a long, considering look that caused the younger woman to back up a step, shouldered through the swinging glass door and took up a position directly outside. Kate smiled. "Okay?"

The young woman's gaze moved from Mutt to Kate, falling to the open collar of her shirt. At the sight of the scar her face lost color. "Uh, certainly." A significant harrUMPH came from behind the counter. "Certainly," she said in a stronger voice, shocked gaze unable to lift itself from the scar. "My name is Yvonne. Was there something I could help you with?"

"No, thanks, Yvonne, I just saw the picture in the window and wanted to take a closer look." She looked over Yvonne's shoulder and her eyes widened. "Oh," she breathed. "That would be by the same hand, wouldn't it?"

"Yes." Yvonne followed Kate to a red and purple monstrosity that covered most of one wall. Kate stared, enraptured. It was a sunset. She looked closer. Something resembling medical gauze and mirrored chips of glass and what might have been a razor blade had been incorporated into the globs of paint. In another corner a syringe with a broken needle had been glued to the canvas. Not a sunset, after all, Kate decided, but the residue of a run-in with Jerry McIsaac. She couldn't quite reconcile that theory with the peony in the third corner, though. A lily she could have understood, but not a peony. An obvious lack in her critical facilities, but oh well.

"Quiet an interesting technique, wouldn't you say?" Yvonne said brightly, next to her. "Carroll is one of our most promising young artists. Notice how the effrontery of line clashes with the insolence of color, and how his choice of supplementary media connect the two to make a statement."

Kate hung on every word "I hadn't quite seen it that way," she said, adding earnestly, "And what statement would that be, exactly?"

Yvonne started to tell her and was stopped by another meaningful harrUMPH. Kate repressed a grin and stepped back, immensely relieved that she'd already justified her expense account. There were some things even RPetCo's money did not deserve to be spent on.

The door opened behind them, and Kate turned, curious to see who else had been suckered inside by the putative picture in the window.

He was an old man, dressed in dirty jeans and a red wool shirt frayed at the elbows. He had no coat. His face was dark and seamed, his black hair lank, his eyes rheumy and he needed a shave. A battered cardboard box under one arm, he stopped just inside the door, converged upon by both dress-for-success suits in the same moment. "Yes, sir, may I help you?" the older woman said. Her tone was sure she couldn't.

He held out the box. His movements were slow, made so by age or alcohol or both. "This is my work."

"We don't buy art," the older woman said.

"This is my work," the old man repeated, his voice rising.

The woman's voice rose to match his. "We don't buy art. Go down to Taheta or one of the other shops. We don't buy art."

The old man seemed bewildered by the force of her reply. "This is my work. All I want is $200 to get home."

The woman's voice rose to a shout. "We have no money to buy art! Go to Taheta!"

"All I want is to get home!"

Kate pushed between the two women. "Let me see, uncle," she said to the old man, her voice gentle.

She could smell the alcohol coming off him from where she stood, but he held himself erect. When he saw Kate, his bleary eyes widened. He spoke a phrase and she shook her head. "I'm sorry, uncle, I have no Yupik. Please, show me your work." To Yvonne's boss, she said, "Mind if we sit here for a moment?"

She did, but something in Kate's cool gave her pause. "Of course not," she said finally, forcing an insincere smile. She glanced through the glass door, obviously nervous that another, legitimate customer might be discouraged from entering her gallery when they saw the customers she was currently entertaining. There was only Mutt, who yawned at her through the glass door, displaying her fangs to advantage, and she retreated hurriedly behind the counter.

Kate slipped a hand beneath the old man's elbow and guided him to one of the chairs against the wall. "Sit, uncle."

"I just want to go home," he said, his voice exhausted of energy.

"I know," she said. "I know. Please, show me what you have."

The cardboard box was filled with pieces of ivory carved into animal figures. There were walruses and caribou and bears and salmon and otters. The best piece was a sleek, fat seal, with a impish, grinning human face peeking out of the fur on his back. All were old, very old, yellow in color and cracked, their edges worn smooth.

Kate replaced the little seal with a reverent hand. "Uncle," she said, looking up at him, "where did you get these?"

"They are my work." He refused to meet her eyes, but a tinge of red crept up into his cheeks, and she knew. She folded the lid of the box down and reached for her wallet. The little otter and the books had dug a big hole in her reserve of cash. She debated whether to take him over to the other gallery, and rejected the notion at once. If she could keep him from selling them, she would. "Here's forty dollars. No, uncle, keep your work. It is too good to sell. Take it home."

"I can't get home," he muttered, shoving the box back at her. "I don't have any money."

She folded his hands around the bills, and spoke slowly, holding his rheumy eyes with hers. "This is all I have right now. I'll get more, and meet you in front of the Army-Navy Surplus store tomorrow morning. I'll give you a ride to the airport and put you on a plane. Where do you live, uncle? What is your village?"

He looked at her, dazed. "Savoonga. I just want to go home."

Savoonga, on St. Lawrence Island, at the southern entrance to the Bering Strait and closer to the Chukotsk Peninsula of Siberia than to the Seward Peninsula of Alaska. Gambell was on St. Lawrence Island, too. Instinctively she reached inside her jacket and touched the box holding the little otter.

There were restive movements from behind the counter. In a calming voice Kate repeated her words, and hoped they got through. Again, he pressed the box on her, and this time she took it. She was afraid of what he'd do with it if she didn't.

They went outside together. He smiled when he saw Mutt and said something to her in Yupik. Mutt ducked her head, flattened her ears, gave her tail an ingratiating wag and even went so far as to give a small yip in salute. The old man smiled kindly at both of them in farewell. "Don't forget, uncle, tomorrow morning," Kate called. "In front of Army-Navy, about ten o'clock. All right?"

He raised a hand and shuffled off. To Mutt Kate said, "And when did you learn to speak Yupik? I thought you only spoke Aleut."

Mutt raised a superior eyebrow and didn't reply in either tongue.

Kate spent her last two dollars on a caffe mocha double tall and walked the two and a half blocks to the Downtown Deli, juggling bag, box and coffee cup and trying hard not to feel depressed.

Perspectives

FROM *Edges of the Earth*

RICHARD LEO

*Richard Leo moved to Alaska from New York City in 1981. His experiences
as a homesteader, first-time cabin builder, and parent in the bush outside
Talkeetna furnished the material for his acclaimed memoir* EDGES OF THE
EARTH *(1991). His second book continues the saga of his Alaska experiences,*
WAY OUT HERE: MODERN LIFE IN ICE-AGE ALASKA *(1995). "Perspectives" is
excerpted from* EDGES OF THE EARTH.

On a late-February day when the sun rose far enough above the
horizon to provide the first radiant heat since October, I
explained to Janus that the traveling season was coming. I told
him that I was going to the Brooks Range for a month but that
he could play with his friends in Talkeetna.

He wanted to go with me.

We had gone on dogsled trips together twice that winter.

He didn't understand why I would now go into the mountains for so
long without him. I tried to make him understand how remote the Brooks
Range was. "Look on this map. Four *hundred* miles from where we live is
the Brooks. It's the only mountain range on earth that's completely above
the Arctic Circle. Remember that giant map covering the whole wall of the
library in Anchorage? It has empty white spots on it. That's *unmapped* land,
never seen by—"

"Yeah, yeah," said Janus, pouting.

The Loussac Public Library in Anchorage, a new glass-and-chrome
edifice stocked with an impressive number of oil-revenue-funded volumes,
listed in its state-of-the-art, computerized inventory one hundred thirty
books on "Antarctica," forty-one on the "Amazon," but just six on the
"Brooks Range." Three of those six were fifty years old.

Where else on earth was there such unexplored, unimaginable wilderness?

I'd seen the Ice Age landscape of the upper Susitna Valley. It was the same environment—cave bears and glaciers!—that had shaped human evolution across fifty thousand years of blinding winters and brief riotous summers. Our now-instinctive dispositions toward herding and aggressive dominance and awe had been sorted and codified amidst such wilderness as still existed only marginally. Even now people were intruding on the Susitna Valley—here I was!—signaling the end of the last great perspective we'd ever have on our origins. We wouldn't find it in satellite transmissions from the moon. Nor from the three-thousand-year-old *Tao Tê Ching.* Nor from anything *we* had recorded.

I wanted, I needed, to see the seven-hundred-mile-long Brooks Range.

My partner, Murphy, with whom I agreed to travel because it seemed less irresponsible than going alone, was a photographer recently arrived in Alaska. He had settled north not for big bucks or for job offers better than other offers (he was good) but for the Alaska that few eyes had seen. He, too, even after a sea kayak trip down the southern coast of Chile, held no preconceptions but only fantasies about what we might discover on the slopes of the high arctic within an ocean-mirage sighting of the North Pole.

Over beers on Fourth Avenue in Anchorage (Yupik Eskimos dancing traditional dances to the beat of the sallow-faced country-western house band; eighteen-year-old U.S. Navy sailors on leave in one of their recruiting-advertised "exotic" ports chatting with giggling aboriginal village girls), we had decided to go in winter. The Gates of the Arctic National Park, through which we'd travel, was visited by Sierra Club types and journalists only in summer, and then but rarely.

In early March, at thirty-five below zero Fahrenheit, we started from the place where we parked our cars. We'd had only a vague idea of where we might jump off from the North Slope Haul Road, a narrow gravel conduit from the Fairbanks end of Alaska's truncated road system that then cut through the central Brooks Range to Prudhoe Bay, where huge trucks in convoys continued to bring shipments to the oil development on the Arctic Ocean. The road was owned by the oil companies and restricted to their private vehicles.

We drove to the foothills of the range without seeing any warning—no armed sentries or checkpoints—except for a sign half buried in drifted snow reading PRIVATE ROAD.

Plainly, the 412-mile-long winding rock road with only two gas stations and the most severe shifting weather on the Triple A's maps held its own intractable restraints.

We parked outside a trapper's cabin in Wiseman. The current 250-page, nationally distributed, Alaskan-produced authoritative guide to Alaska's road system listed Wiseman as a "ghost town." In all the reading (six volumes) and talking (every professional guide I knew in Talkeetna) that I'd done, I learned that only two communities had ever existed in the length of the Brooks. One was a tiny Eskimo village across the Arctic Divide on the Anaktuvuk River. The other—Wiseman—had been abandoned at the end of the Alaskan gold rush.

Behind the trapper's house was a bigger cabin with a satellite TV dish near its front door.

Forty or fifty people, it turned out, lived in Wiseman: two trappers, a dogsled racer, hunting guides, and aging miners who still worked their claims.

Such was the knowledge about remote Alaska even in the 1980s, even within Alaska.

The trapper, who had immediately come out of his house to introduce himself ("They call me Mad Joseph"), was shy and cordial. He invited us inside to meet his wife and six-month-old baby girl. He pointed out the start of his trail that would take us through one pass into the heart of the mountains, where we'd then be on our own.

When Murphy and I went outside we untied the sled from the roof of the car. As we harnessed my dogs, Mad Joseph reminded us that at 1:00 P.M., the heat of the day, it was still thirty-five below. Then he wished us luck.

Murphy, on skis, took off ahead of me. Five minutes after my dogs and I streaked past him he was lost to my sight within the thin spruce cover of the lower hill slopes. While I waited for him to catch up, I took a spare sled line from the top of my pack, fixed it to the back of the sled, and stretched it out ten or fifteen feet along the tracks of the runners. When he reached me, Murphy, an excellent skier but no match for a dog team, fastened the line to the middle of his poles. Holding the poles horizontal to the ground, he gripped them with one hand on either side of the line.

"Who knows?" he called, to say that he was ready.

I towed him like a water-skier. He lunged and wobbled and then found his balance. He grinned. That was how we discovered how best to travel.

During the next few days, I put into the top compartment of my pack a white ptarmigan wing with bloodstains on it, the silken tuft of arctic fox fur from the trampled ground beside the wing, a fragment of a caribou antler, a chunk of lichen-red shale, and a swath of wool sliced from the hide of a Dall sheep that was, as we could see from the fresh wolf prints twice the size of those made by my large dogs, still in the process of being eaten.

They were for Janus. For Melissa, I didn't know what to bring, though it seemed important that I carry something back for her, too. On this wilderness trip I had, as always, regrets. I waited for the revelations.

We passed beneath the Frigid Crags, past Boreal Mountain, into the Valley of the Precipices. We careened up miles of glare-ice overflow. Caribou tracks covered the ground in places like birch leaves in the autumn forest. The temperature remained a constant twenty-five to thirty-five below.

With each succeeding river canyon that we crossed, the peaks angled in wildly different directions like storm-whipped waves frozen at the End of the World, the signature of the geologically complex Brooks. While Murphy took pictures and I took mental snapshots, we repeated, independently of each other, "Yes."

It looked to be about as far into true wilderness as we'd get in our lives, as it was *possible* to get.

When we crossed the Arctic Divide in high-pass winds so violent the dogs' noses bled, the spruce that had lined the southern slopes vanished. There was nothing on the northern slopes but rock and wind-sculpted snow extending as far as we could see. But we were running downhill now, following a drainage toward the Arctic Ocean. Setting up camp that night was grim work. Murphy frostbit a finger or two. I was hypothermic. But when we collapsed into our bags we both exploded with the laughter of children.

Then we reached Anaktuvuk Pass, pop. 200.

When we came over the final ridge, where dozens of caribou antlers stuck up through the snow, the village was so tiny below the surrounding unvegetated peaks that I thought at once of the remote Himalayas. As we got closer in the wind that blew the sled from side to side, I saw that the village was not built of moss-chinked rock and stretched hides, but of plywood and sheet metal, with typical American telephone poles carrying wavering power lines in a grid above the town.

We cascaded down the slope to the edge of the settlement and came to a stop beside a huge diesel truck. There were two Native guys inside. The driver rolled down his window and said casually, "Hey. Pretty wild," meaning me and Murphy.

The truck carried the chemical waste of flushless toilets—"honey buckets"—to a dump site outside of town, as the driver explained in answer to my first blurted question: "What *is* this?" A decal on the side of the door said SANITATION DEPARTMENT, NORTH SLOPE BOROUGH, ALASKA.

I was disoriented by the imposing truck a hundred miles from any other road, but the sanitation workers didn't seem at all startled by a dogsled coming out of the mountains. We chatted for a few minutes—"Pretty cold, huh?"—and then a snowmachine streaked between houses up the wind-scoured gravel main street at the far end of which we stood.

It was one of the village elders, the man who welded broken snow-machines and kept the only working dog team in the village, who prepared income taxes and presided over the crucial school board in a community where more than a third of the residents were school-age, and who never, never, unlike the younger mayor, unlike the much younger bucks, flew to Fairbanks or Barrow to "party."

He stopped at our side, cut the engine, and grinned. Even beneath his wolf-ruffed parka hood his eyes sparkled. He was a mensch, a magus, the sachem figure of the village.

He escorted us to his home. Inside, the walls were covered with the world's largest collection of ritual Eskimo masks—the faces fashioned from caribou skin and wolf fur.

His name was Orv and he was a pure-blood Norwegian from Minnesota.

For ten years, with his lovely, twenty-year-younger wife (just as white as he was), he had lived in Anaktuvuk, teaching school, fixing broken plumbing, arbitrating disputes, giving dogs to residents determined to return to the "old ways" who then gave the dogs back to him in favor of 500-cc Ski-doos.

Orv took us on a tour of Potala Disneyland. We saw the electric sauna and Olympic-size swimming pool in the new kindergarten-through-twelfth-grade school (computers, full-court gym, complete wood- and metalworking shops). We saw the twenty-machine laundromat. We saw the $250,000 garbage collection truck with 000006 miles on its odometer—its cab filled with drifted snow—that was supposed to but didn't work in the high arctic. We saw caribou hides and wolf skins draped over the porches of oil-heated houses inside which, by satellite, twenty-two channels came in loud and clear while the aboriginal residents, fans all, tuned in Super Station WGN to pick up a Cubs game.

Murphy took no pictures. "This is all too bizarre," he explained.

Orv, better able to explain, told us that the oil tax revenue accumulated to the North Slope Borough—six villages, five thousand people in an area not much smaller than Wyoming—in less than a generation had converted a hunter-gatherer people to the American dream, where money was easy and All-Star second baseman Ryne Sandberg was a hero. Cargo planes brought in goods—VCRs, sirloin beef, full-sized yellow school buses, Tupperware. Inupiaq was spoken in every Native home.

At an early-April Easter Sunday gathering of all the white schoolteachers in the village—which was all the teachers, which revealed as much as anything—Orv and his wife, Anne, introduced Murphy and me to the dozen assembled people and then disappeared. We met an almost three-hundred-pound man who raised Pekinese dogs for show, which he kept in paper-lined cages inside the house. "Come to Papa," cooed the fat man, holding out a piece of ham, calling one precious dog that had a satin bow in its neck fur. We met an English teacher who broke into a beaded sweat visible on his forehead when I asked him what he planned to do after retiring from teaching in Anaktuvuk. "Oh," he said, eyes becoming glassy. "Oh. Well. I make forty-five thousand a year teaching in the bush, you see, and retirement from twenty years' service gives me twenty thousand a year, you know. And I, well I . . . I really don't know for sure just *what* I'll do. But I'm going to hang on! I *am!* I've only got two years to go! Just two more years! I'm going to make it!" We met the school principal, who in answer to my innocently social query replied, "What do *I* do? Hmm. Ahh. I run things. Yessss. I'm in charge. Heh-heh. I am in charge. Ha-ha!" He seemed so precariously sane that I turned my attention to the baked turkey.

When Murphy and I had finished stuffing ourselves, we retired from our generally ignored status as visiting guests. We raced through the unabated wind and cold back to Orv and Anne's.

"That was the most incredible, Felliniesque, culture-shock nightmare I've ever seen in any travel I've ever taken," I announced.

Orv blanched. He looked down. "They *are* a little different from the rest of the village," he said.

"This is how the Eskimo kids learn about the wider world?" I cried. "From those loonies?"

"Twenty-five years ago Anaktuvuk didn't exist because the people were nomads," Orv said. "But now every Native village in the state has telephone and television links, and enough oil money to bring us all into the twenty-*first* century."

"And yet they still make masks and wear wolf," said Murphy.

"Oh, they haven't forgotten everything," said Orv. "Yet."

Grandma and the Eskimos

RICHARD ALLEN BLESSING

*Born and reared in Bradford, Pennsylvania, Richard Blessing earned his
undergraduate degree at Hamilton College in upstate New York and his Ph.D.
from Tulane University in New Orleans, where he also taught and served as
the football coach for the University of Louisiana at New Orleans. His awards
include a Guggenheim Fellowship and a National Endowment for the Arts
Fellowship. He was a professor of English at the University of Washington in
Seattle. His many publications include* WINTER CONSTELLATIONS *(1977) and*
A CLOSED BOOK *(1981). Blessing's short story "Grandma and the Eskimos"
was published in a posthumous collection of his work entitled* POEMS AND
STORIES *(1983).*

Y our Eskimos, now," says my uncle. "In Alaska the Eskimos
would handle this thing right."

From another room the voices of women rise and fall like
sirens that are far away.

My uncle lifts the lid on the kitchen stove. Flames make
shadows play over his angular face. He reaches in the woodbox, lifts out
three small birch logs and drops them in the fire. He tosses in the stub of
his cigarette, then replaces the lid.

"Yessir," he says, "your Eskimos, they'd handle it right."

My father puffs his pipe and says nothing. He can do this. It's his trick,
like weather so nice nobody notices.

"Somebody gets old like that, can't go it, you know," my uncle says,
"Eskimos just set her out on the ice. Say good-bye. Go off and don't think
about it no more."

A snowy wind drives across my uncle's wide winter fields, rattles the
steamy windows of the old farmhouse. It is cozy to be in the dark warm
kitchen with the two men, cozy to smell the home-baked bread, the tobacco
and beer. The flames rise and fall behind the stove grate.

"What happens then?" I ask.

"Why, there doesn't anything happen," says my uncle. "They just go off
is all."

"I sent you to bed an hour ago," says my father, setting down his can of beer. He is not so nice now.

"No," I say. "What happens to the one on the ice?"

"All right," says my father. "No more of that now. Up to bed."

"All right," I say. I get up, and the woman sound is loud, more shrill than wind.

"What's the matter with Grandma?"

"Ain't nothing the matter," my uncle says. "Just women is all."

"Is she crying?"

"Skowhegan," says my father. "That old folks' home. She doesn't want to go."

"Why does she then?"

My uncle goes to the window and looks out at the dark and at the snow coming on and on. He takes down his wool jacket from its peg, the checkerboard one, only green where the red should be, the one with the shoulder patch saying MAINE STATE GUIDE. He pulls it around his shoulders.

"Why does she then?" I say again.

"What can you do?" my father says.

"That's it," says my uncle. "What can a man do?"

"We have to get home to Pennsylvania," says my father. "I have work. Your mother has work. Your Aunt Pauline, she's got the post office."

"I can't be here day 'n night," says my uncle. "What can you do? She can't do nothing for herself."

"Come on," says my father. "I'll get you in bed."

We go out of the warm kitchen into the drafty dining room. The linoleum is cold on my stocking feet. We pass between the mangle and the round oak table and through the parlor where no one ever sits and where I am not allowed to play.

Grandma's room is off the parlor, but the door is closed.

"Come on," says my father. "That's no place for us."

We come to the dark stairs and my father pulls the long string that hangs down from the light at the landing.

A voice behind the closed door, my mother's or my Aunt Pauline's, I can't tell which, says, "Don't say things like that, now, Mama. I can't stand it when you say things like that."

"Things like what?" I ask my father, but he puts a firm hand on my back and starts me up the stairs.

"It's nothing for us," he says.

At the landing we look together out the high window at the white barn and at the snow drifting across the stubbled fields all the way to Chadbin's.

"I bet it's cold," I say. "Carl and Clair, did you know, when they have to go to the bathroom, they have to walk outside?"

"Sure," says my father. "What did you think?"

"I'm glad we don't."

"Indoor plumbing," my father says. "Noblest advance of civilized man."

I like the old high-ceilinged bedroom with the big white bed, wide enough for two grownups, where I sleep by myself. I like the picture of my aunt and my mother in the wooden oval frame where they stare out all night like two serious dolls.

Wind shakes the house. I pull the quilted comforter up to my nose and pretend there are wolves. I am sinking down into the feathery mattress. My father sits beside me on the bed.

"Is Mama crying?"

"Hush," says my father. "Maybe a little. Go to sleep."

"I can't. Tell me a story."

"No. Tomorrow's a long, long day."

"Tell me about the Eskimos."

"Eskimos? I don't know that. That's Alaska."

"What about the one on the ice? Uncle Maurice says they go off and don't think about it again."

"I don't know."

"He wouldn't lie."

"No."

"Does the one on the ice just get a cold and die?"

My father, who almost never touches me, brushes back my hair.

"It's going to sleep, is all," says my father. "And then dreams."

"What does he dream, the one on the ice?"

"I don't know. An Eskimo dream."

"What?"

"Lots of things. Maybe about killing his first seal or a white bear he saw once on an ice cake. Maybe how the snow was the morning his little boy was born."

"Good dreams?"

"Sure," says my father, getting up to go downstairs. He is tall in the doorway, and strong-looking.

"That's good."

"Sure."

From downstairs the sound of the women rises up and I think again about wolves circling in the dark fields outside.

"Daddy," I say, "I never want to be old."

"Hush," says my father. "It's all right. Really, it's all right."

"I'm never going to be," I say.

"Kid," says my father, "it's the best there is."

Beat the Qaaviks

FROM *The Last Light Breaking*

NICK JANS

Nick Jans is a teacher and writer in Ambler, Alaska. In the past seventeen years, he's also managed a trading post, worked for a big-game guide, and traveled over fifty thousand wilderness miles. Jan's nonfiction and poetry have appeared in Alaska *magazine,* National Fisherman, Christian Science Monitor, *and* Rolling Stone. *His work has won several awards, including the 1987 James Hall Prize for fiction from the University of Washington. He has written two books:* THE LAST LIGHT BREAKING: LIVING AMONG ALASKA'S INUPIAT ESKIMOS *(1993) and* A PLACE BEYOND: FINDING HOME IN ARCTIC ALASKA *(1996). "Beat the Qaaviks" is taken from* THE LAST LIGHT BREAKING.

The Noatak Lynx are playing their archrivals from the coast, the Kivalina Qaaviks (Wolverines). The green-clad Lynx are up by seven points late in the fourth quarter, but the Qaaviks, like their namesake, are going down fighting. The Noatak middle school students, thirty strong, chant and clap in deafening unison with the three cheerleaders.

"BEAT 'EM, BUST 'EM, THAT'S OUR CUSTOM . . ."

From the coaches' seat on the Noatak bench I hold up two fingers, and the Lynx set up a half court offense, passing, feinting, using the clock as we've practiced a dozen times. But Steven Koenig, the Qaavik star forward, anticipates a pass and steps up for the steal. He drives the length of the court and swoops past a defender, flipping in a reverse layup and collecting a foul. A roar of dissent goes up from the partisan crowd, while the thirty Kivalina fans, windburned and frostbitten after their sixty-mile snow machine ride, shout their approval.

"He sure foul!"

"Man, ref, so cheap!"

"Just like you can't see!"

"Don't listen to them, they don't know nothing!"

The two local officials, one a white high school teacher, the other a young village man, a former Lynx, try to ignore the abuse. After he's ridiculed by name, though, the young man turns to the offender and offers his whistle and shirt.

"Want to ref, *kumaq?*" Kumaq is Inupiaq for head louse. The older women, bundled in their bright flowered calico parkas even in the gym heat, cackle; others join in the laughter, and the game goes on.

Koenig, whose father captains a traditional whaling crew, sinks the free throw, and the lead is down to five. Rattled, my sophomore point guard dribbles the ball off his foot as he tries to break Kivalina's press. Koenig has his radar switched on now; he sinks an impossible eighteen-foot jumper off the inbound pass, and the Lynx lead by two with thirty seconds on the clock. I call time, and my team gathers in a tight huddle as an earsplitting female voice launches into a singing call and response, a third of the crowd, child and adult alike, joining in. The heating ducts rattle and the walls of the tiny gym boom with a hundred screaming voices:

"Beat the Qaaviks . . ."

"BEAT THE QAAVIKS . . ."

"Somebody oughta . . ."

"SOMEBODY OUGHTA . . ."

"Somebody gonna . . ."

"SOMEBODY GONNA . . ."

"Beat 'em . . ."

"BEAT 'EM . . ."

The Lynx inbound the ball, beat the press, and manage to ice the ball for the win. Kids pile out of the stands, mobbing the home team, high-fiving and joining in a hand-linked jumping mass at center court. Parents beam their satisfaction, and old men hobble up to me, showing the gaps in their teeth.

"We sure win them, ah?"

"Real good our boys this time!"

"Sure glad we never lose to them Kivalinas!"

I shake hands and smile back, equally relieved. The Lynx are in the chase for the regional championship, and everyone expects great things of us. After four years of coaching, I know how much winning means to the village, and how quickly I'll be blamed if we lose.

The crowd disperses slowly. Tomorrow is the second game, and then, weather permitting (Kivalina is notorious for the worst winds in the region), the Qaaviks will fly in chartered Cessna 207s back to their home village; the

Noatak girls, who have been playing there, will return on the backhaul. The total cost for transportation is over $400, and this is an inexpensive weekend, since the two villages are relatively close to each other and to Kotzebue, the home base of the charter company. When you figure that there are eight small villages in the Northwest Arctic Borough School District with basketball teams, and that each school plays between ten and twenty regular season games, two per trip, you get an idea of the expense—and that's just travel. Not counting the buildings, the yearly cost for the school district's basketball program—coaches, uniforms, equipment, travel—is well over a hundred thousand dollars. The People want basketball that badly. The residents of Ambler, when asked for input on the design of their new school, specified that a gym was first on the list, and they got what they asked for: a basketball floor with cramped classrooms tacked on as an apparent afterthought.

The whole phenomenon is astounding when you consider that fifteen years ago, only three of the ten villages in the NANA (Northwest Arctic Native Association) region had gymnasiums; twenty years ago, only Kotzebue, the hub of the region, had one. Noatak has had its gym for less than ten years. Each village was guaranteed its own high school (and by extension, its own basketball court) by the state supreme court decision known as the Molly Hootch consent decree, which was implemented in the mid-1970s. The suit argued that every child had a right to a complete education in the home village, instead of being sent to large regional schools. The state of Alaska was obliged to build a high school in each village that requested one—close to a hundred buildings, and the teachers to staff them.

Luckily for the state, implementation of the Hootch decree coincided almost exactly with the completion of the oil pipeline. In Noatak, the last village in the region to get their school (completed in fall of 1981), construction costs ran well over a million dollars, and the tab for a new elementary was nearly two million.

Apart from education, the state's lavish expenditure altered village life forever. Noatak is a typical case: in just a few years the new gym with its basketball court has become the center for the young of the village, just as the church is for the elders. Many students arrive at school a half hour early so they can shoot baskets, and they'd play ball every day in physical education class if they could hound me into it. After school there is an hour and a half of basketball practice. All but two of fifteen high school boys are on the Lynx team, and the percentage is nearly as high for the girls on the—dare I say it—Lynkettes. After practice the kids walk home, eat supper, do some chores or a little homework, and head back for their scheduled hour in the gym, which they get six nights a week. While they're waiting for the elementary school and junior high students to have their turn (toddlers are out there dribbling rubber play balls, seven-year-olds heaving shots over and over at the hopelessly high rims), they socialize and do homework. At precisely 8:00 P.M. they're on the floor, shooting around and choosing sides. After their time is up, they watch the young men of the village play city league pickup games. There's a ten o'clock weeknight curfew for students; at the constable's siren they head home to watch television or finish their homework. At 7:30 the next morning, a handful of the faithful are out there again, shooting layups.

You won't find many tall players this far north; pureblooded Inupiat reach six feet only rarely, while the largest half-breeds clear six two. The big man for most teams is around this height, while occasionally a true monster of six four might emerge, forcing coaches to devise defensive strategies to neutralize this Eskimo Abdul-Jabbar. Lack of height prevents most otherwise talented players from ever going on to college ball, where the average guard is taller than most village centers. If the local sport of choice were hockey or baseball, the ranks of college and even professional teams might well be sprinkled with wiry, explosive defensemen and shortstops with names like Ontogook, Foxglove, and Cleveland.

But basketball is one of the few sports that could have caught on in the Alaskan bush. Field sports are out of the question; in the northwest arctic, the first snow flies in September, and is still melting when school lets out. It's too cold outside for hockey most of the year.

Individual sports—cross-country running, skiing, and wrestling—would seem perfect for small schools, since they require little equipment or indoor space, and even schools like Deering, with its nine high school students, could field athletes on an equal basis. A few years back, cross-country skiing was a varsity sport in the northwest arctic; Noatak, in fact, produced some of the finest skiers in the district, until basketball came along. Now skiing is officially dead as an interscholastic sport. Wrestling and cross-country running have yet to gain regional acceptance, though in 1982, Eliot Sampson, a pureblooded Inupiat from Noorvik, shattered the course record on his way to winning the state cross-country title. Eliot, nicknamed "caribou legs" in his home village, ran away from everybody—the big-school

Alaskan urban kids with their high-tech shoes and expert coaches—smiled shyly, and returned home to lead Noorvik to the state finals in basketball.

When you see how the northwest arctic villages have dominated the state in basketball, you can better understand the lack of interest in other sports. The best local teams, some from schools with fewer than thirty students, sometimes beat schools six or eight times larger—Kotzebue, Dillingham, and Nome. Since then, northwest arctic teams have won eight state titles and finished with Caucasian players five inches taller and twenty-five pounds heavier than their Eskimo opponents. In 1985, for example, my Noatak boys' team, with our tallest player at five feet ten inches, faced Klawock, which had two players at six feet four—and almost won. In other years, Kiana, Ambler, and Noorvik have won the title against far larger opponents.

There are different ways of interpreting the impact of all this time spent at the gym. Even though parents turn out for all the games, many also complain that basketball takes up too much of their children's lives. Few boys are out hunting ptarmigan or rabbits after school, or following their fathers on their traplines. Most girls have never learned the traditional skills of cutting fish or preparing caribou sinew for thread, though their mothers do these things and much more in everyday life. A common complaint among parents is, "*Adii,* just like my kids are never home. Always school."

Much of that school time is pure basketball. Parents could certainly stop or slow this trend if they wished, but exerting such control seems a strange notion to most Inupiat; children have always been free to choose. Besides, school is recognized as a good thing, as it has been since the first missionaries established schools around the turn of the century, drawing scattered camps together into villages. From that time on, the Inupiat were moving inexorably toward a future of orange balls and fast breaks, toward a time when the warm, communal atmosphere of the gym would seem a natural extension of their culture.

Clarence Wood takes a darker view. Though his two boys have both played ball for the Ambler Grizzlies, he's never seen a game. Even the year that the boys won a state title, he refused to watch. "I tell you what," he grumbles, pointing at the gym across from his house. "That's a bullshit in there. One big bullshit." Disgusted, he loads his sled to go caribou hunting alone.

Basketball is more than a childish preoccupation. There are no less than six men's city league teams in Noatak, each with a roster of at least eight, plus three women's teams. Nearly everybody between ages 18 and 35 plays on one of these; there are two hours per weeknight allotted to city league, and on weekends when the gym is free of school-sponsored games or activities, the games start at six and go to eleven, sometimes on both Friday and Saturday nights: the Renegades versus the Bullets, the Napaaqtugmiut against the Warriors, the Cousins versus the Women's City League, and so on. No one remembers the scores, and few remember who won from week to week, though some games are hotly contested, sometimes degenerating into shouted obscenities and shoving matches. Players jump from one roster to another, and the style of play is freewheeling, more reminiscent of in-your-face street ball than the organized play of the high school teams.

Perhaps the saddest vision in village basketball is that of a former high school hero, a former regional all-star, who now lives to play city league. Maybe he was a great high school athlete, but he was also only five feet seven inches, and had no desire to leave the village for college in the first place. He stayed in school mostly for basketball, kept up his grades so he could travel with the team. Now, five years after graduation, he is still living at home, sleeping most of the day, waiting for the gym to open at 10:00 P.M. so he can relive a time when people cheered him and the games mattered. There are more of these city league heroes than you'd wish. Some actually consider themselves professionals because local sponsors buy them uniforms and fly them to tournaments. One former player of mine smiled as he described city league as his "career." Some go away to college or technical school and come back six months later; a few enlist in the Army. I can't help wondering what their lives would have become without basketball—better, worse, or the same?

You could consider all this basketball a travesty, Outside influence run amok, all these thousands of man-hours wasted. True, many of the young have become much less active in traditional ways, but others do run traplines and hunt caribou and keep their extended families in firewood in addition to playing ball; food does get cooked, new mukluks are sewn, and babies are raised. Many villagers will say there is less drinking because of the gym, and certainly most of the young men in town and many of the women are in fine shape from their nights of running up and down the floor. Serious violence—fights and gun play—seem to be on a decline regionwide, and maybe this decrease is partly due to a healthy release of aggression on the court.

Also, basketball, especially at the high school level, is a tremendous source of village pride. When Kiana swept to both the boys' and girls' state titles in 1984, the village and the region exploded in a frenzy of Eskimo patriotism. In a time when the Inupiat find themselves increasingly dominated by outside forces, basketball is, paradoxically, a source of assurance and identity.

Basketball also provides a community focus, taking over the function of traditional Eskimo games. In the past, a community would divide into teams or a neighboring village would visit for the purpose of friendly competition, and there would be an evening or even days of games, resembling a modern track and field meet in organization and aspect. The individual events were, for the most part, ones that could be held in the more limited space afforded by a community building or even a large home during the long, dark winter. Feasting, exchanging of gifts, trading, wooing, and simple socializing were as important as the actual competition. Some games focused on brute strength. Consider the head pull, a woman's game where two competitors faced off in pushup position with a wide strap or belt hooked over their necks. The idea was to pull the opponent over a line or yank the belt free of her arched neck. Other games, like the one-foot high kick, were a test of both agility and explosive power; here, a small hide ball was suspended on a string, and the competitor had to take off from one foot, strike the ball with the other foot, and then land balanced on the striking foot. The event was held like a modern high jump, with competitors eliminated as they missed, the mark growing higher until only one remained.

Some events, like the seal hop and the ear pull, were simple tests of pain and endurance. In the seal hop, contestants were in a lowered pushup position on toes and knuckles; the idea was to hop the longest distance without allowing any other part of the body to touch the ground. The hopping surface was often hard or irregular, and skin, even flesh, was abraded from the knuckles as the contestants hopped along the floor, muscles straining.

There were other games: the two-footed high kick, leg wrestling, finger pull, and stick jump. People still play these games, but less and less frequently at the village level.

It's basketball they want. On winter nights the cry echoes across the expanse of bush Alaska:

BEAT 'EM, BUST 'EM . . .

In just a few years, it's become their custom.

c. 28,000 B.C. People from the Asian continent migrate across the Bering Land Bridge into Alaska. Their descendants will become the three Native groups of Alaska: Aleuts, Eskimos, and Indians; their legends are the first known stories of Alaska.

1741 The Russians, led by Vitus Bering, land in Alaska and claim it for Russia. German naturalist Georg Steller, an expedition member, documents many Alaskan animal and plant species for the first time.

1741 *Journal of a Voyage With Bering, 1741–42* by Georg Wilhelm Steller.

1742 Russian *promyshlenniki* (fur traders) begin concentrated hunting of sea otters for trade in Russia and China.

1768 The Steller sea cow becomes extinct as a result of overhunting for food.

1778 British explorer Captain James Cook maps the Alaskan coast.

1780 *The Journals of Captain James Cook.*

1784 The first Russian settlement is established on Kodiak Island.

1791–1795 British explorer George Vancouver sights Mount McKinley from Cook Inlet.

1799 Sitka is established as the capital of Russian America.

1821 Father Ivan Veniaminov, a twenty-four-year-old Russian Orthodox priest, arrives in the Aleutians to work among the Native peoples of southern Alaska.

1825 The sea otter is hunted almost to extinction in Alaska and down the Pacific coast to California.

1835 American and French whaling vessels begin to hunt in Alaskan waters.

1839 *Notes on the Islands of Unalaska District* by Father Ivan Veniaminov, the first in-depth study of Alaska's Aleut and Tlingit people.

1854 *The Discovery of the North-West Passage* by Captain R. McClure.

1861 *A Voyage to the North Pacific* by John D'Wolf.

1867 The United States purchases Alaska from Russia for $7.2 million.

1869 The first stern-wheeler steamboat navigates the Yukon River. The first newspaper in the Territory, *The Sitka Times,* is published.

1878 The first salmon canneries are established at Klawock and Old Sitka in Southeast Alaska.

1879 John Muir visits Alaska for the first time.

1880	Gold is discovered at Juneau.
1886	*The History of Alaska, 1730–1885* by Hubert Howe Bancroft, the first full-fledged history of the Territory.
1891	The first oil claims are staked in the Cook Inlet area.
1893	Gold is discovered on Birch Creek; Circle City is founded.
1896	George Carmack strikes it rich on the Klondike River; Dawson City is founded.
1897	Steamships carrying "tons" of gold arrive in San Francisco and Seattle, starting the Klondike gold rush in Yukon Territory. Jack London arrives in the North.
1898	Nome is founded after a gold strike on Anvil Creek. Rex Beach, Hamlin Garland, Wyatt Earp, and Joaquin Miller come North.
1899	The Harriman Alaska Expedition explores Alaska; naturalist William Dall is included in the party.
1900	The White Pass & Yukon Route railroad (Alaska's first railroad) is opened between Skagway and Whitehorse. Federal Judge James Wickersham arrives in Alaska. The Kennecott Copper Mine is discovered. *The Spoilers* by Rex Beach.
1901	*Alaska, the Harriman Expedition 1899* by John Burroughs, John Muir, et al.
1902	Fairbanks is founded by E. T. Barnette. *To Build a Fire* and *A Daughter of the Snows* by Jack London.
1903	The U.S.–Canada boundary is finalized. *The Call of the Wild* by Jack London.
1904	Landscape painter Sydney Laurence arrives in Alaska. Robert Service comes to Whitehorse, Yukon Territory. Baedeker's U.S. guidebook includes several pages on Alaska, the beginning of the tourism industry in the Far North. *The Sea Wolf* by Jack London.
1905	$6 million in gold dust is taken out of the mines north of Fairbanks; the population of Fairbanks reaches 2,500.
1906	Juneau becomes the capital of Alaska Territory. The Great Fairbanks Fire in May destroys the center of the city. *White Fang* by Jack London.
1907	*Songs of a Sourdough* and *The Spell of the Yukon and Other Verses* by Robert Service.
1908	The first automobile arrives in Fairbanks. *The White Trail* by Alexander MacDonald.
1909	*Ballad of a Cheechako* by Robert Service. *Stickeen* by John Muir. *The Silver Horde* by Rex Beach.

1910   The Sourdough Expedition climbs Mount McKinley's North Peak. *Lost Face* by Jack London. *Harriman Alaska Series: History, Geography, and Resources* by William H. Dall, et al. *Hunting with the Eskimos* and *An Athabascan Princess* by George Fenwick.

1911   Margaret Murie, age nine, arrives in Alaska, and later becomes the first woman graduate of the University of Alaska. Copper mining begins in Alaska and eventually exceeds the production of gold. *The Young Alaskans on the Trail* by Emerson Hough.

1912   Mount Katmai erupts on June 6, in one of the largest volcanic explosions in recorded history, creating the famed Valley of Ten Thousand Smokes. *The Iron Trail* by Rex Beach. *Smoke Bellew* by Jack London.

1913   The first airplane flight in Alaska takes place, at Fairbanks. The first automobile trip is made from Fairbanks to Valdez. Hudson Stuck and team make the first successful ascent of Mount McKinley.

1914   President Woodrow Wilson authorizes construction of the Alaska Railroad, America's only government railway, to run 470 miles from Seward to Fairbanks. *The Ascent of Denali* and *Ten Thousand Miles with a Dog Sled* by Hudson Stuck. *Kazan the Wolf Dog* by James Oliver Curwood. *The Rover Boys in Alaska* by Arthur M. Winfield.

1915   A wilderness railroad construction camp is established at Knik Anchorage on Cook Inlet, which will become the city of Anchorage. *Travels in Alaska* by John Muir. *Alaska Days with John Muir* by S. Hall Young. *Five Little Starrs in Alaska* by Lillian Elizabeth Roy.

1916   *The Quest of the Golden Valley* by Belmore Brown.

1917   U.S. Congress establishes Mount McKinley National Park. *The White Blanket* by Belmore Brown. *Baree, Son of Kazan* by James Oliver Curwood.

1918–1919   A spanish flu epidemic kills about half of Alaska's Native population.

1919   *Nomads of the North* by James Oliver Curwood.

1922   Roy Jones makes the first airplane flight up the Inside Passage, from Seattle to Ketchikan. The University of Alaska opens in Fairbanks. *The Radio Boys Rescue the Lost Alaska Expedition* by Gerald Breckenridge. *The Alaskan* by James Oliver Curwood. *The Eskimo Twins* by Lucy Fitch Perkins.

1923   The Alaska Railroad is completed from Seward to Fairbanks.

1924   Pioneer aviator Noel Wien makes the first flight from Anchorage to Fairbanks, and establishes Wien Airways.

1925   Diphtheria epidemic hits Nome; Scotty Allen, with his lead dog Balto, and Leonhard Seppala rush serum by dogsled from Anchorage to Nome. *Child of the Wild* by Edison Marshall. *Rocking Moon* by Barrett Willoughby.

1926   *Nanook of the North* by Julian W. Bilby.

1927   *A Bibliography of Alaskan Literature, 1724–1924* by James Wickersham.

1930   *The Wilderness of Denali* by Charles Sheldon. *Navarre of the North* by Esther Birdsall Darling.

1931   Charles Lindbergh and his wife, Anne Morrow Lindberg, land at Barrow during their pioneering flight from New York to Tokyo. *Eskimo* by Peter Freuchen.

1932   Joe Cronson makes the first glacier landing in an airplane on Mount McKinley.

1933   *Arctic Village* by Robert Marshall. *Alaskans All* by Barrett Willoughby. *Luck of the Trail* by Esther Birdsall Darling. *Argonaut* by Honore Morrow. *Silver Chief, Dog of the North* by Jack O'Brien.

1934   *The Archaeology of Cook Inlet, Alaska* by Frederica De Laguna.

1935   The Matanuska Valley farming community is established by the U.S. government. *North to the Orient* by Anne Morrow Lindbergh.

1937   *Flora of the Aleutian Islands* by Eric Hultén. *Lost Empire* by Hector Chevigny. *Silver Chief to the Rescue* by Jack O'Brien.

1938   Construction begins on Ladd Air Force Base near Barrow (later Fort Wainwright), a cold-weather testing site. *Fog on the Mountain* by Frederica De Laguna. *Susannah of the Yukon* by Muriel Denison. *Kahtahah* by Frances Lackey Paul.

1940   *Alaska Holiday* by Barrett Willoughby.

1941   *Son of the Smoky Sea* by Simeon Oliver, one of the first books written by an Alaska Native. *Flora of Alaska and the Yukon* by Eric Hultén.

1942   The Japanese occupy the islands of Attu and Kiska in the Aleutian chain. The "Alcan" (Alaska–Canada) Highway is completed, the overland route from the Lower 48 through Canada to Alaska. *Fifty Years Below Zero* by Charles Brower.

1943   Attu and Kiska regained by U.S. forces.

1944   *The Wolves of Mt. McKinley* by Adolph Murie. *Heaven Is Too High* by Mildred McNielly.

1945   *The Flying North* by Jean Potter. *Alaskan Igloo Tales* by Edward Keithahn and George Ahgupuk.

1947   *Home Country* by Ernie Pyle. *We Live in Alaska* by Constance and Harmon Helmericks.

1948   Wartime travel restrictions are lifted and tourists begin to drive the Alaska Highway. *Watch for a Tall Sail* by Margaret E. Bell. *Snow Dog* by Jim Kjelgaard.

1949   *The Totem Casts a Shadow* by Margaret E. Bell.

1953   *Icebound Summer* by Sally Carrighar.

1955   Construction begins on the Distant Early Warning (DEW) Line 3,000 miles across Alaska and Canada. *Born on Snowshoes* by Evelyn Shore.

1956   The Alaska Constitution is signed at the University of Alaska Fairbanks to gain support for the statehood movement.

1957   Oil is discovered on the Kenai Peninsula. *Sitka* by Louis L'Amour. *Two in the Far North* by Margaret E. Murie.

1958   *Arctic Wild* by Lois Crisler. *Ice Palace* by Edna Ferber.

1959   Alaska becomes the forty-ninth state of the United States. *I Am Eskimo, Aknik My Name* by Paul Green.

1960   *Look to the Wilderness* by W. Douglas Burden.

1962   *A River Ran out of Eden* by James Vance Marshall.

1963   Alaska State Ferry service begins between Southeast Alaska towns and Seattle.

1964   The Good Friday earthquake and tsunami kill 115 people in the worst recorded quake in North America.

1965   *Russian America: The Great Alaskan Venture, 1741–1867* by Hector Chevigny. *No Room for Bears* by Frank Dufresne.

1966   *My Way Was North* by Frank Dufresne. *Winter News* by John Haines. *An Alaskan Reader, 1867–1967*, edited by Ernest Gruening.

1967   The first Iditarod Race is staged over a twenty-five-mile course. *Dictionary of Alaska Place Names* by Donald J. Orth.

1968   Oil is discovered on the North Slope.

1969   The first successful winter ascent of Mount McKinley is completed by Art Davidson and team. *Minus 148°* by Art Davidson. *Monarch of Deadman Bay* by Roger Caras.

1970   First successful solo ascent of Mount McKinley is completed by Naomi Uemura. *The Last of the Bush Pilots* by Harmon (Bud) Helmericks.

1971 U.S. Congress passes the Alaska Native Claims Settlement Act. *The Stone Harp* by John Haines.

1972 *Julie of the Wolves* by Jean Craighead George.

1973 The annual Iditarod Trail Sled Dog Race is established (1,049 miles from Anchorage to Nome). Construction begins on the Trans-Alaska oil pipeline. *One Man's Wilderness* by Richard Proenneke and Sam Keith.

1974 *Wager with the Wind* by James Greiner.

1975 *The Year of the Polar Bear* by Thomas J. Koch. *An Alaskan Memoir of a Vanishing Frontier* by Denton H. Moore.

1976 *Tisha* by Robert Specht. *Change and Other Short Stories* by Charles J. Keim.

1977 The Trans-Alaska oil pipeline is completed. *Coming into the Country* by John McPhee. *Island Between* by Margaret E. Murie. *Alaska Blues* by Joe Upton. *Haida Dictionary* compiled by Erma Lawrence.

1979 *Highliners* by William McCloskey.

1980 Census shows that Alaska's population increased 30 percent during the 1970s. Alaska National Interest Lands and Conservation Act (ANILCA) is passed, affecting 131 million acres, many of which are set aside as wildlife refuges, national parks, and wilderness areas. *Shadow of the Hunter* by Richard K. Nelson. *The Red Snow* by James Greiner.

1981 *Slade's Glacier* by Robert F. Jones. *Winging It!* by Jack Jefford.

1982 *News from the Glacier* by John Haines.

1983 *Make Prayers to the Raven* by Richard K. Nelson. *Sinrock* by Fred Bigjim.

1985 Chevron Oil drills an exploratory well in the Arctic National Wildlife Refuge, sparking debate about the opening of the North Slope. *Dogsong* by Gary Paulsen.

1986 *Arctic Dreams* by Barry Lopez.

1987 *Tales of Ticasuk* by Emily Ivanoff Brown. *Once Upon an Eskimo Time* by Edna Wilder. *Libby* by Betty John.

1988 Vernon Tejas completes the first successful solo winter ascent of Mount McKinley. *Alaska* by James A. Michener.

1989 The tanker *Exxon Valdez* runs aground, dumping 35,000 tons of crude oil into Prince William Sound, the worst oil spill in U.S. history. *In Extremis and Other Alaskan Stories* by Jean Anderson. *The Stars, The Snow, The Fire* by John Haines. *Chills and Fever:*

Health and Disease in the Early History of Alaska by Robert Fortuine.

1990   *Road Song* by Natalie Kusz. *Mother Earth Father Sky* by Sue Harrison. *Ashana* by E. P. Roesch. *In the Wake of the* EXXON VALDEZ by Art Davidson. *For Healing Our Spirits: Tlingit Oratory* by Richard and Nora Dauenhauer.

1991   *Survival* by Nancy Lord. *Murder on the Iditarod Trail* by Sue Henry. *A Dena'ina Legacy* by Peter Kalifornsky. *Heroes of the Horizon* by Gerry Bruder. *Working on the Edge* by Spike Walker. *The Island Within* by Richard Nelson.

1992   *A Cold Day for Murder* by Dana Stabenow. *The Raven and the Totem* by John Smelcer. *Favorite Eskimo Tales Retold* by Ethel Ross Oliver. *In the Shadow of Eagles* by Rudy Billberg as told to Jim Rearden. *The Woman Who Married a Bear* by John Straley. *A Republic of Rivers: Three Centuries of Nature Writing from Alaska and the Yukon* edited by John A. Murray. *The Wake of the Unseen Object: Among the Native Cultures of Bush Alaska* by Tom Kizzia. *Raven's Children: An Alaskan Culture at Twilight* by Richard Adams Carey.

1993   Alaska Department of Fish and Game announces a plan to revive aerial hunting of wolves. *Shadows on the Koyukuk* by Sidney Huntington as told to Jim Rearden. *Two Old Women* by Velma Wallis. *The Owl in the Mask of the Dreamer* by John Haines. *The Bend Toward Asia* by Tom Sexton. *Johnny's Girl* by Kim Rich. *The Last Light Breaking* by Nick Jans.

1994   Population of Anchorage reaches 250,000 (population of entire state is about 608,000). *Degrees of Disaster* by Jeff Wheelwright.

1995   *Summer Light* by Elyse Guttenberg.

1996   *Disappearances: A Map: A Meditation on Death and Loss in the High Latitudes* by Sheila Nickerson. *A Place Beyond: Finding Home in Arctic Alaska* by Nick Jans. *Into the Wild* by Jon Krakauer. *Place of the Pretend People: Gifts from a Yup'ik Eskimo Village* by Carolyn Kremers.

ALASKAN NATIVE LEGENDS AND FOLKLORE

Beck, Mary L. *Potlatch: Native Ceremony and Myth on the Northwest Coast.* Seattle: Alaska Northwest Books, 1993.

———. *Shamans and Kushtakas: North Coast Tales of the Supernatural.* Seattle: Alaska Northwest Books, 1991.

Brown, Emily Ivanoff. *The Longest Story Ever Told: Qayaq, the Magical Man.* Anchorage: Alaska Pacific University Press, 1981.

Bruchac, Joseph, ed. *Raven Tells Stories: An Anthology of Alaskan Native Writing.* Greenfield Center, N.Y.: Greenfield Review Press, 1991.

Dauenhauer, Richard, and Nora Dauenhauer. *Haaa Tuwunaagu Yis, for Healing Our Spirits: Tlingit Oratory.* Seattle: University of Washington Press, 1990.

De Laguna, Frederica. *Tales from the Dena: Indian Stories from the Tanana, Koyukuk and Yukon Rivers.* Seattle: University of Washington Press, 1995.

Erdoes, Richard, and Alfonso Ortiz. *American Indian Myths and Legends.* New York: Pantheon, 1984.

Frost, O. W., Marianna Bunger, and Margritt Engel, eds. *Tales of Eskimo Alaska.* Anchorage: Alaska Methodist University Press, 1971.

Kalifornsky, Peter. *A Dena'ina Legacy.* Fairbanks: Alaska Native Language Center, 1991.

Keithahn, Edward. *Alaskan Igloo Tales.* Seattle: Alaska Northwest Books, 1974.

Norman, Howard. *Northern Tales: Traditional Stories of Eskimo and Indian Peoples.* New York: Pantheon, 1990.

Smelcer, John. *A Cycle of Myths.* Anchorage: Salmon Run Press, 1993.

Tenenbaum, Joan M., compiler. *Dena'ina Sukdu'a: Traditional Stories of the Tanaina Athabascans.* Fairbanks: Alaska Native Language Center, 1984.

FICTION

Arnout, Susan. *The Frozen Lady.* New York: Arbor House, 1983.

De Laguna, Frederica. *Fog on the Mountain.* New York: Doubleday, 1938.

Doig, Ivan. *The Sea Runners.* New York: Atheneum, 1982.

Harris, Jana. *Alaska.* New York: Harper & Row, 1980.

Hawkes, John. *Adventures in the Alaskan Skin Trade.* New York: Simon & Schuster, 1985.

Johnson, Ronald. *Out of the North.* Kaneohe, Hawaii: Plover Press, 1991.

Kesey, Ken. *Sailor Song.* New York: Viking Press, 1992.

Lund, Robert. *The Alaskan.* New York: Bantam, 1953.

Marshall, Edison. *Princess Sophia.* New York: Doubleday, 1958.

Marshall, James Vance. *A River Ran out of Eden.* New York: Morrow, 1962.

McCloskey, William. *Highliners.* New York: McGraw Hill, 1979.

Shaine, Benjamin A. *Alaska Dragon.* Fairbanks: Fireweed Press, 1991.

Vidal, Gore. *Williwaw.* New York: Dutton, 1946.

Willoughby, Barrett. *Rocking Moon.* New York: Putnam, 1925.

NONFICTION

Barker, James H. *Always Getting Ready, Upterrlainarluta: Yup'ik Eskimo Subsistence in Southeast Alaska.* Seattle: University of Washington Press, 1993.

Blackman, Margaret B. *Sadie Brower Neakok, an Inupiaq Woman.* Seattle: University of Washington Press, 1989.

Cantwell, Sister Margaret. *North to Share.* Victoria, B.C.: Sisters of Saint Ann, 1992.

Carey, Richard Adams. *Raven's Children: An Alaskan Culture at Twilight.* New York: Houghton Mifflin, 1992.

Chandonnet, Fernand. *Alaska at War.* Anchorage: Alaska at War Committee, 1995.

Collins, Julie and Miki. *Trapline Twins.* Seattle: Alaska Northwest Books, 1989.

Crisler, Lois. *Arctic Wild.* New York: Harper & Row, 1968.

Fitzhugh, William W., and Susan A. Kaplan, eds. *Inua: Spirit World of the Bering Sea Eskimo.* Washington, D.C.: Smithsonian Institution Press, 1982.

Ford, Corey. *Where the Sea Breaks Its Back: The Epic Story of Early Naturalist Georg Steller and the Russian Exploration of Alaska.* Seattle: Alaska Northwest Books, 1992.

Garfield, Brian. *The Thousand-Mile War.* New York: Nelson Doubleday, 1983; Fairbanks: University of Alaska Press, 1996.

Hildebrand, John. *Reading the River: A Voyage Down the Yukon.* Boston: Houghton Mifflin, 1988.

Hirschmann, Fred (photography), and Kim Heacox (text). *Bush Pilots of Alaska*. Portland, Ore.: Graphic Arts Center Publishing, 1989.

Jacobs, Jane. *A Schoolteacher in Old Alaska*. New York: Random House, 1995.

Kizzia, Tom. *In the Wake of the Unseen Object: Among the Native Cultures of Bush Alaska*. New York: Henry Holt, 1991.

Krakauer, Jon. *Into the Wild*. New York: Villard Books, 1996.

Kremers, Carolyn. *Place of the Pretend People: Gifts from a Yup'ik Eskimo Village*. Seattle: Alaska Northwest Books, 1996.

Langdon, Steve. *The Native People of Alaska*. Anchorage: Greatland Graphics, 1992.

Lindbergh, Anne Morrow. *North to the Orient*. New York: Harcourt, Brace, Jovanovich, 1935.

Marshall, Robert. *Arctic Village*. New York: Smith & Haas, 1933.

McPhee, John A. *Coming into the Country*. New York: Farrar, Straus & Giroux, 1977.

Muir, John. *Travels in Alaska*. Boston: Houghton Mifflin, 1914.

Murie, Adolph. *The Wolves of Mt. McKinley*. Seattle: University of Washington Press. 1944.

Murray, John A., ed. *A Republic of Rivers*. New York: Oxford University Press, 1990.

Nelson, Richard K. *The Island Within*. San Francisco: North Point Press, 1989.

Nickerson, Sheila. *Disappearances: A Map: A Meditation on Death and Loss in the High Latitudes*. New York: Doubleday, 1996.

Oliver, Ethel Ross. *Journal of an Aleutian Year*. Seattle: University of Washington Press, 1988.

Oliver, Simeon. *Son of the Smoky Sea*. New York: J. Messner, 1941.

Potter, Jean. *The Flying North*. New York: Macmillan, 1947.

Ray, Dorothy Jean. *The Eskimos of Bering Strait, 1650–1898*. Seattle: University of Washington Press, 1991.

Shore, Evelyn Berglund. *Born on Snowshoes*. Boston: Houghton Mifflin, 1954.

Strohmeyer, John. *Extreme Conditions*. New York: Simon & Schuster, 1993.

Stuck, Hudson. *The Ascent of Denali*. New York: Scribner's, 1914.

Weeden, Robert B. *Alaska, Promises to Keep*. Boston: Houghton Mifflin, 1978.

CHILDREN'S BOOKS

Chandonnet, Ann. *Chief Stephen's Parky.* Niwot, Colo.: Roberts Rinehart, 1993.

Curwood, James Oliver. *Kazan the Wolf Dog.* New York: Grosset & Dunlap, 1914.

George, Jean Craighead. *Julie of the Wolves.* New York: Harper & Row, 1972.

Morey, Walt. *Home Is the North.* Hillsboro, Ore.: Blue Heron Publishing, 1989.

O'Brien, Jack. *Silver Chief: Dog of the North.* Philadelphia: Winston, 1933.

Paulson, Gary. *Dogsong.* New York: Bradbury Press, 1985.

Pedersen, Elsa. *House upon a Rock.* New York: Atheneum, 1968.

POETRY

Alaskan Embers: Stories, Tales, Anecdotes, Vignettes, Poems. Anchorage: MMUKC Publishers, quarterly.

Alaska Quarterly Review. Anchorage: University of Alaska Anchorage, College of Arts and Sciences.

Alaska Women Speak. Anchorage: Alaska Women Speak, quarterly.

Dauenhauer, Nora Marks. *The Droning Shaman.* Haines: The Black Current Press, 1988.

Hedin, Robert, and David Stark, eds. *In the Dreamlight: 21 Alaskan Writers.* Port Townsend, Wash.: Copper Canyon Press, 1984.

Hutton, Brian, with Mark Muro, Linda Kay Davis, and M. Otis Beard, eds. *North of Eden: An Anthology of Alaskan Writings.* Anchorage: Loose Affiliation Press, 1995.

McCarriston, Linda. *Eva-Mary.* Evanston, Ill.: TriQuarterly, 1991.

Smelcer, John E., and D. L. Birchfield, eds. *Durable Breath: Contemporary Native American Poetry.* Anchorage: Salmon Run Press, 1994.

ABOUT THE ANTHOLOGY EDITOR

Wayne Mergler was born in Lynchburg, Virginia, in 1944, and grew up in Ohio, Georgia, and Europe. He came to Alaska in 1968 and has lived there ever since, reading and collecting Alaskan literature. After teaching literature, writing, and drama in the Anchorage public schools for twenty-five years before retiring, he devoted himself to writing. For several years he has contributed a column about books to the *Anchorage Daily News*. His fiction has appeared in *North of Eden: An Anthology of Alaskan Writings* (1995), and he is currently at work on a novel. He and his wife live in Anchorage. They have three children and three grandchildren, all Alaskans.

ABOUT THE FOREWORD WRITER

Poet and essayist John Haines is one of America's most distinguished men of letters. Born in Norfolk, Virginia, in 1924, he came to Alaska in 1947 and homesteaded in the wilderness for nearly two decades. He is the author of several major collections of poetry, a memoir, and, most recently, *Fables and Distances,* a collection of essays, reviews, and letters. Among his many awards are two Guggenheim Fellowships, a National Endowment for the Arts Fellowship, an Alaska Governor's Award for excellence in the arts, and a Lenore Marshall/*Nation* prize for poetry. John Haines lives with his wife in Anchorage.